LAWYERS AND STATECRAFT IN

*Renaissance Florence*

# LAWYERS AND STATECRAFT IN

# *Renaissance Florence*

### BY LAURO MARTINES

PRINCETON, NEW JERSEY

PRINCETON UNIVERSITY PRESS

*1968*

*for them, wheresoever*

*my father and mother*

# Acknowledgments

Although I began taking notes for this study in 1956, it was not until 1962 that I was able, during four years spent in Florence, to devote myself to it. For the freedom to do this I owe a debt of gratitude to the American Council of Learned Societies, to the John Simon Guggenheim Memorial Foundation, and to the American Philosophical Society of Philadelphia.

Study and library facilities, a most attractive setting, and some memorable lunches were provided by the Harvard University Center for Italian Renaissance Studies at I Tatti, the villa left to the University by the generosity of the late Mr. Bernard Berenson.

I shall always be grateful to the historians, European and American, who gave their backing to this enterprise.

When the need arose, an old friend, Professor Gino Corti, came to my aid with his paleographic skills. Signor Ivaldo Baglioni, of the National Library of Florence, has for years been uncommonly helpful and I thank him. My warm thanks go also to Miss Gloria Ramakus, who gave up countless Sundays and holidays to type and retype the manuscript.

The gray routine of scholarship was dispelled by Julia Martines, *moglie arguta,* and the companionship in Florence of the Teissiers, Lucien and Maura.

# Contents

Acknowledgments     vii

Abbreviations     xii

I. An Approach     3

## *The Profession*

II. The Guild     11
    1. The Function of the Guild     11
    2. Policies and Organization     16
    3. Lawyers and Notaries     26
    4. Political Vicissitudes and Parallels     40
    5. The Course of Change     54
    Sources     57

III. Backgrounds and Foregrounds     62
    1. Society     62
    2. School     78
    3. Cases and Fees     91
    4. Careers     106
    Sources     112

## *Government and Statecraft*

IV. Legal Aspects of Sovereignty and Magistracy in Florence     119
    Sources     129

V. Problems of Internal Government     130
    1. The Judiciary     130
    2. Jurisdictional Problems     145
    3. Administrative Problems     169
    4. Legislation and Constitutional Affairs     183
    5. The Political Struggle     204
    Sources     215

VI. Aspects of Territorial Government 220
    1. Justice and Judicial Office 220
    2. Controversy Reserved for Executive Action 225
    3. Rebellion 232
    4. Administrative Questions 237
    Sources 244

VII. Florentine Relations with the Church 246
    1. Introduction 246
    2. Taxing the Clergy 251
    3. Rotal and Cameral Lawsuits 270
    4. Church Councils 286
    5. A Note on Papal Power 301
    Sources 307

VIII. Problems of Diplomacy 311
    1. Outlines of a Tradition 311
    2. The Negotiation of Treaties 316
    3. The Interpretation of Treaties 330
    4. Arbitration 347
    5. Reprisals and Trade Agreements 359
    6. Open Questions of International Law 374
    Sources 382

## The State

IX. The Florentine State 387
    1. Lawyers and Oligarchy 387
    2. The Executive Power 397
    Sources 404

X. Lawyers Look at the State 405
    Sources 448

XI. Florence and Milan: Toward the Modern State? 456
    1. Milan 457
    2. The Course of Change 464
    Sources 476

## CONTENTS

# *Appendix*

Lawyers in Florence: 1380-1530     481

   1. Lawyers from Old Families     482

   2. New Men     491

   3. Outsiders     498

   4. A Miscellany     505

     Sources     508

Index     511

# Abbreviations

*ACP*: *Atti del Capitano del Popolo*

*AEOJ*: *Atti del Esecutore degli Ordinamenti di Giustizia*

*AGN*: *Arte dei Giudici e Notai*

*AP*: *Atti del Podestà*

ASF: Archivio di Stato di Firenze

*ASI*: *Archivio storico italiano*

BNF: Biblioteca Nazionale di Firenze

*C*: *Code (Corpus Iuris Civilis)*

*Cod. Vat. Lat.*: *Codici Vaticani Latini*

*CP*: *Consulte e Pratiche*

*CRS*: *Corporazioni Religiose Soppresse*

*D*: *Digest (Corpus Iuris Civilis)*

*DBCMLC*: *Dieci di Balìa, Carteggi, Missive: Legazioni e Commissarie*

*DBCR*: *Dieci di Balìa, Carteggi, Responsive*

*DBLC*: *Dieci di Balìa, Legazioni e Commissarie*

*DBRA*: *Dieci di Balìa, Relazioni di Ambasciatori*

*DSCOA*: *Deliberazioni dei Signori e Collegi, Ordinaria Autorità*

*DSCSA*: *Deliberazioni dei Signori e Collegi, Speciale Autorità*

*Inst.*: *Institutes (Corpus Iuris Civilis)*

*LF*: *Libri Fabarum*

*Magl.*: *Magliabechiana*

*MAP*: *Mediceo avanti il Principato*

*NA*: *Notarile Antecosimiano*

*Nov.*: *Novels (Corpus Iuris Civilis)*

*OCMLI*: *Otto di Pratica, Carteggi, Missive, Lettere e Istruzioni*

*OCR*: *Otto di Pratica, Carteggi, Responsive*

*Prov.*: *Provvisioni*

*SCF*: *Statuti del Comune di Firenze*

*SCMC-I*: *Signori, Carteggi, Missive, I Cancelleria*

*SCMLC*: *Signori, Carteggi, Missive, Legazioni e Commissarie*

*SCRO*: *Signori, Carteggi, Responsive Originali*

*SCS*: *Statuti dei Comuni Soggetti*

*SDO*: *Signori, Dieci, Otto di Pratica, Legazioni e Commissarie*

*SRRO*: *Signori, Carteggi, Rapporti e Relazioni di Oratori*

*Statuta*: *Statuta Populi et Communis Florentiae*, 3 vols., Freiburg, 1778-1783

*Strozz.*: *Carte Strozziane*

*UDS*: *Ufficiali dello Studio*

LAWYERS AND STATECRAFT IN

*Renaissance Florence*

## Chapter One

# An Approach

I offer here a study of the place and achievement of lawyers in Florentine statecraft. This may seem a narrow interest, but in fact, owing to the critical public functions and prominence of lawyers, it has the interest and breadth of Florentine political institutions. And these in turn—more than is often suspected—conformed to types found all over central and northern Italy from the fourteenth to the sixteenth centuries. The last chapter, centering on a comparison with Milan, seeks to catch the similarities.

With few exceptions, notably in Chapter II, where some space is given to events before 1380, the period spanned by this inquiry is the 150 years from about 1380 to 1530. Statecraft is defined by dictionaries as the art of government or skill in the management of state affairs. The word entails a stress on technique, on the *way* matters of state are handled; it thus seemed to belong in the title of this inquiry. To study the distinctive place of lawyers in the conduct of public affairs is to focus attention on the expert and his skills. Moreover, the organization of politics in Florence was such that the lawyers whose activity we shall be studying were nearly always politicians and statesmen in their own right. All the more is the word "statecraft" justified in the title.

Wherever we look in Florentine public affairs, we find lawyers at work: in diplomacy, in relations with the Church, in territorial government, in the formulation of policy, in administration and adjudication, and in the political struggle proper. Why was this? What explains the omnipresence of lawyers? What functions were they performing? How did their prominence reflect on the nature of the Florentine state? On the practice of politics in Florence? What was their view of the state and what did they say about it?

These questions run through the present inquiry. My concern has been to understand the nature and exercise of political power in Renaissance Florence. But so comprehensive an interest required a focus. This was the value of putting lawyers at the center of things: they provide the distinctive feature of the approach in this study.

The method of getting at historical events through the study of groups gives a unique advantage. On the one hand—unless his sample be unwieldy—it allows the historian to observe individuals, to get away from impersonal factors to the men who made decisions. On the other hand, the method takes him beyond individuals to groups, and from here he may look on to power blocs or social classes. These legitimize the historian's concern with forces which no analysis of individuals can satisfactorily explain. The study of groups thus looks two ways, and each may be used as a check on the other. We cannot do without individuals in history, but neither can we do without impersonal forces. The face in the crowd is not more real than the crowd.

Generally speaking, lawyers in Italy began to enter the upper spheres of government and politics in the course of the twelfth century. Connected with this rise, and in part promoting it, were the demands of popes and emperors, the pressing needs of the new city-states, and the revival of scientific jurisprudence in the study of Roman law. The Renaissance had no monopoly of the use and pre-eminence of lawyers in government and statecraft. This was already true in the twelfth century.[1] And yet a study of the Middle Ages, executed along the lines of this inquiry, could not be done. It is only for the period after 1300 that the riches in Italian archives permit the historian to follow in detail the careers of many lawyers and to pinpoint public-law cases in continuous series and large numbers.

The early stages of this study swiftly revealed that every generation of Florentines produced some five or six lawyers of great public distinction. But the fact that they were also key figures in statecraft, that they provided critical skills, did not become apparent for a long time. There is a difference between being prominent and being indispensable. Constantly found in all branches and phases of government, lawyers were apparently doing things that could not be done by others. This may seem obvious, but what it signified was complex and obscure. To get at the underlying

[1] E. H. Kantorowicz, "Kingship under the Impact of Scientific Jurisprudence," *Selected Studies* (Locust Valley, New York, 1965), pp. 151ff.

significance it was necessary to go to the point of contact: to see precisely where lawyers were being deployed and to learn how and why. Examining their public functions, I found that their critical prominence was the necessary feature of a given polity, of a particular type of political and social organization. Lawyers may also of course enjoy exalted place under other polities. Most modern states employ teams of lawyers. These men tend, however, to remain in the background—faceless figures. Who can name the lawyers of the British Foreign Office or of the American State Department? But at Florence, and in Renaissance Italy generally, lawyers were key men in politics, while being equally well known as men of the law. A major task was to account for this fact. Part of the explanation has to do with the organization of the executive sector of Florentine government, but part also concerns the fact that the Republic was an oligarchy.

Government in Florence was of and by the few. At no point in the period from about 1390 to 1530 were there more than 4,000 Florentines who could boast of having full-fledged political rights, and during all but twenty years of this time-span the total stood much nearer 2,000 or 2,500. Here was the ruling class in its entirety.[2] Within this class there was a group which I shall often refer to as the "inner oligarchy." Depending upon the period, this group included some 400 to 700 men from the leading families. They constituted the effective ruling class. Most of the lawyers whose names will dominate the present study were of this class. The choice was not mine. I sought to collect information on *all* lawyers active or even temporarily resident in Florence between about 1380 and 1530. Owing to gaps in the documents, I may have missed a few men but none who was active in public life. All qualified lawyers who came to my attention have been entered in the Appendix, which lists nearly 200 civilians and canonists.[3] Of these, more than 100 actively participated in Florentine public affairs (i.e., held office); and of these, again, public prominence was attained by about seventy-five, some fifty of whom were men of the first political importance. I produce these figures to show that the inquiry seeks to be complete.

[2] References on pp. 206, 388-89.
[3] Notaries, who differed from lawyers both in their preparation and functions, are not included. Scholarship often confuses the two. See Ch. II, 3.

The political study of Florentine lawyers is in some respects a study of oligarchy. Often active in the inner circle of the oligarchy, pre-eminent in public life, born in most cases to typical families of the ruling class, the lawyers in the forefront of this study were representative figures. But there was also their unrepresentative feature—the fact that they were professional men. This disinguished them from bankers, merchants, rich tradesmen, *rentiers*, and others,[4] and was still another reason to study them. Their representative side, perceived in much of their political behavior, grouped them with the other members of the oligarchy. The effects of this will be evident in the succeeding chapters. But their distinguishing feature—the possession of legal skills put at the service of the state—served to draw the inquiry away from more commonplace matters, fixing it instead on the more technical and specialized functions associated with affairs of state. This provided a means of obtaining a clearer and finer understanding of the Florentine state. No other social or professional group, not even the notaries,[5] offered as excellent a standpoint from which to study political processes. Lawyers alone were deeply involved in the technical questions—constitutional, diplomatic, territorial —the raising of which served to expose the inner workings, the distinctive nature, of the state and statecraft.

Before indicating the plan of this book, I should say that I considered dividing the most difficult section (Chs. IV-VIII) into two parts: one on the lawyer as functionary, the other on the lawyer as policy maker. Though such an arrangement would have made for a more rational narrative, I rejected it on grounds of its false assumption. In the political world of Renaissance Florence, there was no sure distinction between the lawyer's ordinary and his more exalted functions. He often operated in a vast gray area. As an ordinary functionary, he could take action which might well have a determining effect on policy. As an alleged policy maker, when holding forth on a particular question, he might have no influence whatsoever. The form of the modern state, already adumbrated in Renaissance Florence, calls for a clean distinction between decision

---

[4] Lawyers, however, often engaged in business activity or had notable income from land and government securities.

[5] They composed much too large and unwieldy a group.

makers and functionaries; but if our concern be lawyers rather than notaries or other lesser men, the distinction has little bearing on our problem, owing to the nature of the Florentine oligarchy and the place of lawyers in it.

I begin in Chapter II by analyzing the guild of lawyers. Chapter III goes on to a treatment of the legal profession itself and explores the background, social and economic, of lawyers. The five succeeding chapters[6] review and analyze the performance of lawyers in all aspects of Florentine public life. In the course of these chapters the outlines of a particular system of state begin to emerge, and are fully elaborated in the last three chapters, which dwell on the nature of the Florentine state and draw on a comparison with Milan. There again the figure of the lawyer provides the approaches or holds the focus of study.

Readers who see historical study as a search for typological models, or who believe that history is first and foremost the history of ideas, may wish to read this book backwards. The last chapter tries to establish the identity of "the Renaissance state." The preoccupation of the penultimate chapter is with *ideas* as such—legal ideas of the state. I have approached these ideas from the world of affairs—from a concern with politics, with oligarchical government, and with society. If some legal historians find an element of politico-social determinism in this study, it is because they approach affairs from the world of ideas. The perspectives of a study condition it, and no man can command all perspectives. History has more imagination than historians.

[6] Ch. IV serves to introduce the major themes.

*The Profession*

## Chapter Two

# The Guild

## *1. The Function of the Guild*

There is an element of irony in studying the Florentine guild of lawyers and notaries (Arte dei Giudici e Notai). If ever in Florence a guild stood as patron and tutor over the practice of recording and preserving the important transactions of everyday life, it was this one, yet its archives are among the poorest of those that come down to us from the twenty-one guilds of republican Florence. Two floods (in 1333 and 1557) carried away or destroyed hundreds and probably thousands of registers which had been stored in the old palace of this corporate body. With those registers went account books, collections of statutes, consular deliberations, lists of members, legal *consilia*, and, one may as well say, most of the detailed history of the guild. For this reason both Robert Davidsohn and Alfred Doren, when they came to discuss the guilds of Florence, were not as informative about this one.

The earliest surviving statutes of the guild date from circa 1344 and, although many of the vellum folios have been damaged, most of the rubrics are legible.[1] Apparently complete, these statutes are sketchy on some items of importance for this study. The next collection of extant statutes is more than two centuries later (1566).[2] These are set forth in great detail and are about four times the length of the 1344 collection. For the fifteenth century—the whole central span of the period to be studied here—there is little in the way of guild statutes: a mere table of contents which lists the individual rubrics as they stood in 1415.[3] Additional material, however, can be extracted from the guild acts (*atti*), from some volumes of consular deliberations, as well as from the legislation and statutes of the Republic. Hence our knowledge of how the guild was organized and run must be pieced together from a variety of

[1] ASF, *AGN*, 749. All documents cited in this chapter are in the State Archives of Florence.

[2] *AGN*, 1. Published in a hopeless edition by Lorenzo Cantini, *Legislazione toscana*, vol. VI (Firenze, 1803), 171-265.

[3] *AGN*, 2, ff. 1r-4r. Folios 5r-12r are actually summaries of rubrics added to the guild statutes from 1416 to 1518.

sources. But the framework will be constructed from the elements of continuity that link the two collections of guild statutes and the table of contents of 1415.

I call attention to the statutes because they are the blueprint, so to speak, of the guild's organization and function. Keeping to the essential interest of this study—statecraft—I shall try to present a picture of the guild which highlights those features that made it stand out in public life.

A PHENOMENON of the later twelfth century, the birth of guilds in Florence, as in other Italian communes, derived in part from the debilities of the central or sovereign state. As Florence absorbed a continuous influx of men from the country, thereby showing remarkable economic vitality and capacity for expansion, new social and occupational groups gained admission to the Commune or pressed to enter it. Since the state, such as it was, seemed unfit to enhance or fully protect his opportunities and civil rights, the individual was ready to be drawn into well-organized corps. What neither state nor Commune was able to do, the corporation could. This goes far to explain the universality and boldness of the corporate spirit in Italy during the twelfth and thirteenth centuries. But it was the revival and scientific study of Roman law that facilitated the formation of the corporation, whether as guild or other association, providing its legal basis, terminology, and procuratorial forms.[4] None was to profit from this more than the guild of the legal profession, which immediately acquired outstanding authority.

In a sense all recorded legal relations in Florence came under the purview of the guild of lawyers and notaries. It exercised jurisdiction over members, and no man outside the guild was authorized to attest public instruments. This prohibition was endorsed by the Commune itself. The claim of the guild to a certain judicial competence over all its members also had the support of the Commune. This claim had particular force in all matters that touched the legal and notarial profession: every document which betrayed the official hand of a lawyer or notary was therewith implicated. With the consent of the guild consulate, the

---

[4] G. Post, *Studies in Medieval Legal Thought* (Princeton, 1964), esp. Ch. 1.

proconsul—supreme officer of the guild—could requisition any such document, calling it into his court to examine its format or validity, in some cases even to change and correct it. In this regard, accordingly, there was hardly a commercial establishment or private study which lay beyond the guild's reach. Did X claim to have a document attesting to a business partnership or a deed establishing his title to certain lands? The guild was empowered to look into its authenticity.

This was a formidable power in a city sustained by its commerce and industry, a city where one of the major passions was the stress on the written contract, the sworn testimony, the public instrument. Yet the guild does not seem to have abused its privileges. It needed a certain authority to help foil shyster lawyers, crooked notaries, and charlatans who passed themselves off as members of the guild.

Let us note some things about the guild's relation to a class of functionaries who composed the framework of a developing civil service in Florence. The statutes, papers, and records of every leading public office were in the hands of notaries who took turns holding down the city's different secretarial and recording posts. Older, experienced guildsmen and men of solid standing in the guild occupied the better posts of this type, serving as secretaries attached to the Signory, to the War Commission (The Ten on War), the Eight on Public Safety, the Monte Officials, the Treasury, the Tribunal of Six (Sei di Mercanzia), and so forth. Also prominent in the guild were the first secretary of the Republic (always a lawyer after 1459), the notary in charge of legislation, and the official who handled the lists of all Florentines drawn for office. These men were expected to have at their fingertips a knowledge of the functions and jurisdictions of the offices which they served as secretaries.

Every piece of Florentine legislation, when passed in the councils, was attested and authenticated by the *notaio delle riformagioni*, a functionary whose fitness as a notary had first been certified by the guild. From the end of the fifteenth century, every Florentine ambassador, just before starting out on his appointed mission, had to have a notary draw up an official document attesting to the facts of his departure.[5]

---

[5] Before starting out on their embassies, all ambassadors had once been required

Lawyers and notaries were the leading assistants of governors in the Florentine dominion. I could continue to enumerate examples of the many jobs performed in public life under the aegis of the Arte dei Giudici e Notai, but these suffice to indicate that of all Florentine guilds this one was nearest to the centers of public administration and the working out of policy.

There seems to have been only one guild in twelfth-century Florence, the Calimala, and it included different types of merchants and craftsmen. Toward the end of the century this *universitas* began to split up, and by 1220 the four richest of the seven major guilds already had independent existences: the Calimala (now more specialized) and the Lana, Cambio, and Por Santa Maria guilds. Two of the other major guilds came into being later in the century, the guild of furriers and that of the physicians and spicers. Davidsohn observed that a Florentine college or association of advocates existed in the middle years of the twelfth century. But it was dissolved not long after, probably with the birth of the guild of lawyers and notaries, already a vigorous organization in 1212.[6] This guild was a force in the city and had an enormous reputation from its earliest years. Indeed, down to the final demise of the Republic it was officially the highest-ranking guild. It occupied the first place of honor at ceremonies or processions in which all the guilds were represented, and the proconsul, chief officer of the lawyers and notaries, was considered the honorary head of the whole guild system.

Precisely why the lawyers' guild enjoyed such an exalted position is a question no student of the period has cared to explore. Among the main causal factors, no doubt, was the high status generally accorded to the study of Roman law, as well as the influence of this law on the growth and structure of guilds and other corporate bodies. Old and respected Florentine families gave many notaries and especially lawyers to the city. The guild also drew great prestige from the imperial office. Until

---

to appear before the Executor of the Ordinances of Justice or one of his judges and "iurare de sua ambaxiata legaliter facienda, et expedienda, et quod vere electi sint et non ficte." *Statuta*, I, 415. This job passed to the Podestà when the Executor's office was suppressed.

[6] R. Davidsohn, *Geschichte von Florenz* (Berlin, 1896-1927), I, 274-75; A. Doren, *Entwicklung und Organisation der florentiner Zünfte im 13. und 14. Jahrhundert* (Leipzig, 1897), p. 35.

about the middle of the twelfth century, all Florentine notaries seem to have been created by imperial appointment, although this power was temporarily delegated at times.[7] Up to then, too, justice in Florence had been in the care of jurists appointed by the imperial vicar. At the beginning of the thirteenth century, the entire legal profession still had about it a certain color borrowed from the office of the Holy Roman Emperor. Florence like the rest of Tuscany was a fief of the Empire.

A grasp of the law, a practical knowledge of Latin, familiarity with complex notarial formulae: such a professional preparation must have made a notable impression on the rude mind of the urban populace in the twelfth and thirteenth centuries. Offering advantages to the pocket as well as to the spirit, the legal and notarial professions easily attracted well-born and able men. They, in turn, worked to provide the guild with a distinctive place in public life.

No individual or corporate group can enjoy high place and power without provoking detractors and the enmity of men hurt in the normal course of things. The lawyers' guild was no exception, particularly as rivalries developed between the guilds on the question of their different shares in the distribution of public offices. The remarkable thing is that the lawyers and notaries succeeded in long maintaining their political prominence. In 1338, at the peak of its strength in terms of membership, the guild had 80 lawyers and 600 notaries, of whom in all probability not more than half were endowed with the right to hold public office.[8] In the same year there were more than 200 workshops affiliated with the Lana guild, whose members (*lanaiuoli*) must therefore have amounted to several times this number. The *lanaiuoli* disposed of large quantities of capital, and their economic activity directly affected the livelihood of some 30,000 Florentines.[9] If we think for a moment of the rich, powerful families of *popolani* status—the princes of the Cambio and Calimala guilds—engaged in banking and the international wool trade, we cannot avoid the suspicion that in any showdown between the different guilds

---

[7] On this and prior observations, Davidsohn, *Geschichte*, I, 662; Doren, *Le arti fiorentine*, tr. G. B. Klein, 2 vols. (Firenze, 1940), II, 274-75; G. Salvemini, *Magnati e popolani* (Torino, 1960), pp. 81-83.

[8] Davidsohn, *Geschichte*, IV, ii, 109.

[9] Figures in Giovanni Villani, *Cronica*, ed. F. G. Dragomanni, 4 vols. (Firenze, 1844-45), III, bk. xi, ch. 94.

the lawyers and notaries would have been bound to lose power and place. Yet except for two setbacks suffered by the notaries in the fifteenth century (to be discussed in due time), a showdown did not come—not during the turbulent 1290s, nor during the crises of the 1340s, 1370s, or 1380s. Throughout the fourteenth century the legal guild enjoyed political parity with the other major guilds and got its full share of seats in the offices, major and minor, of the Republic. External political conditions permitting, lawyers and notaries were too practical to alienate the other major guilds. No matter what regime won out, they had to be near it for professional reasons—serving it, acceptable to it.[10]

From the end of the thirteenth century on, and quite likely for a long time before as well, each generation produced a number of lawyers who ranked with the most influential political figures in the city. As has already been noted, every one of the Republic's leading magistracies had at least one notary attached. These observations help to explain how the guild managed to retain its exalted place in politics and in the whole system of guilds. The avenues leading to the centers of the decision-making process were always open to the guild, and its agents and spokesmen—lawyers and notaries—tended to be experienced statesmen, shrewd administrators, or persuasive speakers.

### 2. *Policies and Organization*

The guild existed to give a rule to the legal profession, to survey the professional conduct of lawyers and notaries. In some societies these functions or parts thereof have belonged to the state. This was not so in Florence, where every guild more or less regulated the services or goods of its own sphere and claimed a certain judicial competence over its members. The Commune cooperated with this system of divided authority.

Looking into the guild constitution of 1344, we find that no significant aspect of professional aims or activity was neglected. Matriculation requirements, fees, examinations, the different offices of the guild and their authority, questions of procedure, the preservation of guild records and notarial protocols, rules of professional and even moral conduct,

---

[10] Cf. Salvemini's shrewd remarks, *op.cit.*, pp. 82-83.

16

the prerequisites connected with certain jobs (e.g., that of *procurator* in the court of the Podestà): all these and other matters are summarily or extensively treated by the statutes. My plan will be to set forth only as many particulars as seem to accord with the aims of this study; if I dwell on the details of guild office, I do so in order to be able to point out, in the last part of this chapter, some striking parallels with certain forms in public life.

All members of the guild were matriculated as *giudici* or *notai*: judge-lawyers or notaries. Later on in this chapter we shall see how the two differed. I call attention here to the distinction because the offices of the guild were staffed by lawyers and notaries in certain fixed proportions.

The proconsul was the supreme head of the guild. His office survived the republican period and passed over into the duchy.[11] He was always a notary. A term as proconsul lasted six months in the fourteenth century, four in the fifteenth and sixteenth centuries. The statutes of 1344 specify that he must be at least thirty-six years old and have been in the guild not less than ten years. In the fifteenth and sixteenth centuries the age requirement varied from forty to forty-five years and the incumbent had to have been in the guild for at least twenty years. This denoted perhaps an element of growing conservatism.

Chief of the proconsul's functions were those connected with his investigative and judicial powers. The guild whip, he looked to the honor and high state of the profession, and was expected to prosecute all lawyers and notaries accused or suspected of any form of dishonesty or negligence in the exercise of their professional duties. To be guilty of an infraction, it was enough to do something which cast shame on the guild or detracted from its authority. The proconsul first ordered an investigation and then had the defendant summoned before the proconsular court for trial. Ordinarily his sentences involved fines and could not be appealed. During the fourteenth century and possibly thereafter, the proconsul seems to have been authorized to suspend lawyers and notaries from practicing, even to take this right away permanently. In

[11] Material on proconsul in *AGN*, 749, ff. 5r-6r, 8r-9r, 10r, 13v, 32v. In 1564 the Duke decreed that the proconsul was to have the first seat in the Council of Two Hundred, thus putting him before *cavalieri* and doctors of law.

the sixteenth century, however, he could do this only with the consent of the guild consuls and counsellors. On the matter of his competence in civil cases lying before the guild court, we find that these powers of his were always limited by the intervention of the consuls. According to the statutes of 1344, the proconsul had to hold court daily, mornings and afternoons. He was joined by the consuls every Friday, when civil cases were heard and determined. Subsequently this practice changed; the statutes of 1566 obligated the consuls to meet with him "at least twice each month,"[12] although he could summon them at will to get their help in expediting any pressing affairs of the guild.

The proconsul was the embodiment of the guild. His person was held in high esteem, and any guild member who dared to use dishonorable words in his regard, or indeed against any of the consuls, was liable to severe penalties. The obligations of the office required the proconsul to wear an outer garment of crimson or violet, and he was forbidden—like cardinals in our own day—to go into public unaccompanied. Two guild pages were always at his side.

The consulate was composed of eight consuls throughout the period from 1344 to 1566.[13] The office of the consuls was to hear civil cases, to entertain petitions, to keep a certain check on the proconsul, and to have a hand in guild legislation. Acting in concert with the proconsul, they had judicial competence over all civil litigation between members of the guild. Despite the proconsul's powers, the consuls could also move of their own initiative against lawyers and notaries accused of corruption in the pursuance of their profession. They were empowered to act on a variety of petitions: requests for matriculation in the guild, for the authentication of public instruments, for certified copies of instruments drawn from the abbreviatures (*imbreviaturas*) of deceased notaries, and for action against individual guild members. On October 5, 1461, for example, Messer Giovanni de' Saracini d'Arezzo appeared before the consuls, claiming that the doctorate in civil law had been conferred on him in 1454 in the presence of the Florentine College of Lawyers and of the *decretorum doctor* Messer Lazzaro Nardi d'Arezzo. Nardi had been there to represent the Archbishop of Florence, who was in-

[12] *AGN*, 1, ff. 5v-6r.    [13] *AGN*, 749, f. 6r; 1, f. 5r.

vested with the papal and imperial right to confer doctorates. The doctoral act had been attested by Ser Jacopo di Ser Antonio da Romena, who had since died and whose notarial protocols had been lost. Saracini was requesting certification of his doctorate.[14]

Another example is a petition which sought to compel a lawyer and a notary to offer a certain guarantee. In the spring of 1442, Giovanni della Casa reported to the consuls that it was two years since he had given one of his daughters in marriage to the advocate and doctor of law Francesco di Ser Piero Pucetti, providing her with a dowry of 525 gold florins.[15] The jurist's father, a notary, had promised to acknowledge receipt of the money and to guarantee it ("confexare, promettere, e sodare"); but he had so far failed to keep his promise. Della Casa wanted the dowry insured "according to the practice and custom of the city of Florence," so that if, for example, Messer Francesco died, the 525 florins would revert to the widow or, if she died, to her father or heirs. At the end of the hearings the consuls moved to make the notary observe his promise.

The requests of Saracini and Della Casa were not typical. I adduce them to suggest the variety of petitions entertained by the guild consulate, with of course the proconsul present. Really typical were two kinds of petitions which seem to have dominated the activity of the consuls: (a) petitions requesting the authentication of last wills, deeds, and contracts and (b) petitions of shopkeepers, artisans, and merchants, bringing charges of debt against individual members of the guild. For the period from 1390 to 1530 there are nearly 230 registers of guild acts, recording thousands of such petitions, many of which gave rise to cases tried in the guild court. The cases usually turned on quarrels over debt or the authenticity of instruments. Now and then litigation concerned items lent and not returned. Claims rarely involved sums of less than 2.00 florins; sometimes it was a question of several hundred. In October 1438 Cosimo and Lorenzo de' Medici brought a suit, in the form of a petition, against the heirs of Guaspare de' Bonizi, a Perugian who had moved to Florence and entered the guild in 1406. The brothers were suing for 256 florins "di camera" and 26.0 florins "direno" (sic), which they claimed

---

[14] *AGN*, 182, f. 17r.          [15] *AGN*, 129, f. 37r.

to have lent to Messer Guaspare, a doctor of law and consistorial advocate.[16] It is interesting and somewhat perplexing that jurisdiction in this case was attributed to the guild. We may suspect that the brothers for some reason considered the consulate to be the tribunal most likely to adjudicate this suit in their favor. That particular consuls were sometimes in collusion with plaintiffs is an observation borne out by evidence in the guild record itself.[17]

The guild statutes explicitly required the consuls to hear cases from two to five times a month, but the number of petitions and high incidence of civil litigation compelled them to join the proconsul in court or *in camera* a good deal more often. Taking the first three months of 1433 as a random example, we find that the consuls heard cases and entertained petitions during eleven days in January, seven in February, and sixteen in March.[18] Additional meetings were undoubtedly called for the purpose of managing other affairs of the guild. The office of consul—a term lasted four months—was therefore no sinecure and no easy task. During the period covered by this study, two of the eight consuls were always lawyers, the other six notaries.[19] The guild constitution of 1344 specified that to qualify for this office lawyers had to have been members of the guild and have practiced "in the city" for three years, notaries for ten. Both were required to be at least thirty-two years of age. The rule that a notary had to be a member of the guild for ten years before becoming eligible for the consulate lasted down to the sixteenth century and beyond, but the three years required of the lawyer were reduced to one in 1435,[20] a condition still observed more than 100 years later.

In all matters of general or grave importance to the guild, the proconsul and consuls assembled with at least one council of advisors.[21] In the middle years of the fourteenth century, and perhaps later, this council was composed of ten notaries and six lawyers. During the fifteenth and

---

[16] *AGN*, 124, f. 11v. Guaspare's family name appears as "Bonazzi" in this document. On him see the Appendix.

[17] *AGN*, 123, f. 19r.          [18] *AGN*, 114, ff. 1r *et seq.*

[19] This ratio was different up to about 1370, as will be noted in next section of this chapter.

[20] *AGN*, 2, f. 7v.

[21] *AGN*, 749, ff. 14r-15r; 1, ff. 6r-7v.

early sixteenth centuries two councils (the twelve and the thirty-two) served as advisory bodies, and lawyers here held one-fourth the places. By the 1550s these had been replaced by the councils of twelve and fifteen, where lawyers held only two and three places respectively. These bodies were regularly summoned to give their advice and votes on such matters as guild legislation, changes of policy, relations with the state, and "scrutinies" to pick out the men eligible to hold offices in the guild. When a wider representation was desired, the consulate and the advisory bodies were joined in their deliberations by a group of *arrotos,* or select guild members. Such an assembly became the supreme council of that sworn association—the guild—and wielded its final authority. If we consider that even the meanest member of this assembly enjoyed a certain status (e.g., he had to practice his profession *in* the city and come from a family which had paid taxes regularly for a continuous twenty-five or thirty years), then it appears that the guild retained a semi-oligarchical tendency even in its most democratic moments. We shall presently see the political ramifications of this.

Like other guilds and like the Florentine Republic itself, the Arte dei Giudici e Notai had, or now and then created, a number of special commissions to handle matters that either required particular care or were too taxing for the proconsul and consuls. To this class of jobs belonged the "syndication" of guild officials: the practice, at the end of terms, of conducting inquiries into the way guild offices had been managed. In the sixteenth century, for example, the consuls, the proconsul, and the guild treasurer were examined by three notaries and one lawyer, all drawn from the twelve advisors.[22]

The statutes of 1344 provided for an office of "arbiters": a commission of three lawyers and five notaries, elected every two years for the purpose of checking, correcting, improving, or otherwise emending the statutes of the guild. During part of the fifteenth century this job seems to have been done by the *correctores,*[23] but later on it may have been taken over by the consulate and advisory bodies. Two other commissions are worthy of mention: the examiners and the defenders (*conservatores*). The first of these, as the name indicates, examined candidates for entry into the

[22] *AGN,* 1, ff. 13v-14r. For a technical definition of "syndication" see pp. 143-45.
[23] *AGN,* 2, f. 6r.

guild, and was made up either of lawyers or notaries, depending on the nature of the candidacy.[24] During part if not all of the fourteenth century the examiners were recruited from the advisory council and served only two or three months. Thereafter they were a commission apart, elected for one year. The candidate was examined by the commission, but the consuls and proconsul also had a voice in whether or not he was finally taken into the guild.

The participation of the proconsulate (proconsul and consuls) was not a feature in the workings of the other commission—the defenders. Set up in 1473, this body consisted of five notaries and one lawyer.[25] They were elected by the proconsulate and served for a period of six months. Each had to have passed his thirty-fifth year and be eligible to hold public office in the city. As "defenders of the statutes and ordinances of the guild," their job was to combat the fraud, corruption, and dishonorable activity of guild members. To carry out this task they were given the authority not only to conduct investigations but also to sit as a tribunal with full powers of jurisdiction. An extension of this authority gave them the right to draw up new guild statutes in the sphere of professional ethics. It is clear, therefore, that the powers of this magistracy overlapped with those of the proconsul and consuls, who however retained a frank priority. The defenders did not have the judicial competence to touch cases already lying before the proconsular court. And in any conflict of jurisdiction between the defenders and the proconsulate, the former had to give way.

Two offices of first-rate importance were held by individuals, the treasurer and the provisor, whose terms lasted four months.[26] Each of these posts went to an experienced notary. He had to be thirty years old or more, a member of ten-years standing in the guild, and come from a family which had paid taxes in the city for not less than thirty continuous years. The treasurer saw to the accounts, took in and paid out money, recorded the letters sent by the proconsul and consuls to magistrates in the Florentine dominion, and kept a summary of all cases tried in the guild court. The provisor was in charge of guild properties, including

---

[24] *AGN*, 749, f. 39r-v.                    [25] *AGN*, 31, f. 1r; 1, ff. 7r-8r.
[26] Material on these offices in *AGN*, 749, ff. 11v-13r; 2, f. 9v; 1, ff. 9v-12v.

some shops, lands, and a small collection of law books kept in the palace of the guild. He drew up certified copies of public instruments stored in the guild archives and kept the matriculation rosters, the lists of the office-holders, and the lists of men eligible for guild office. By dividing all the debtors and creditors of the guild into several classes, entering these into different registers, and keeping a strict account of the individual sums, the provisor did some of the treasurer's work and so was a key figure in the "syndication" of the treasurer.

It is not too soon to ask whether there can have been a better training ground than these two offices, or some of the others mentioned above, for the work of regulation and administration connected with municipal and territorial government. We have seen that there were fewer posts for lawyers than for notaries, in this as in all the other guilds, where notaries also carried out much of the critical work of administration. But there were so few lawyers who qualified for the consulate or the other leading guild offices,[27] that nearly all those who won political distinction were also exceedingly active in guild affairs. I have in mind, for the later fourteenth century, Giovanni de' Ricci and Filippo Corsini; for the early fifteenth century, Lorenzo Ridolfi, Bartolommeo Popoleschi, and Piero Beccanugi; for the middle years of that century, Guglielmo Tanagli, Domenico Martelli, Otto Niccolini; for the 1490s and after, Domenico Bonsi, Guidantonio Vespucci, Antonio Malegonnelli, Antonio Strozzi, and Baldassare Carducci.

The particular curse of the guild from the fourteenth to the sixteenth centuries seems to have been the incidence of corruption and fraud among members, notaries especially. Something might be said in praise of the guild's statutory readiness to prosecute lawyers and notaries who violated their professional oaths, but this mere disposition of the guild was not a sufficient guarantee. The record, guild and otherwise, is heavy with the misconduct of men who practiced the notarial craft. At least one case shows that the Podestà himself was not safe from the depredations of a notary attached to his own staff.[28] May we conclude that there was ex-

[27] There were seldom more than about twenty-five in any year between 1380 and 1530.
[28] *AP*, 4319, by date: 27 June 1421. Not paginated.

cessive indulgence? The evidence suggests that there was.[29] Indulgence was also shown outside the guild. There were always men who practiced as notaries, especially in the county and district of Florence, who were not inscribed in the guild. Some periods undoubtedly saw more of this than others. The period of the late fifteenth and early sixteenth centuries was such a time; the palace of the archbishop of Florence one of the settings. In December 1515 a denunciation was lodged with the *conservatores* (the defenders) against the many working notaries in the archbishop's train of officials, men "who are not matriculated and therefore go against the ordinances of the guild and Commune of Florence."[30] Evidently, apart from their other duties, they were also engaged in affairs of pure temporal stamp. The guild, however, was lenient: no action was taken.

There was prudence here, the prudence of men who recognized the point at which their insistence on ordinances could become excessive and begin to go against their own corporate interests. If we judge by the way the guild sometimes suspended its rules in order to make matriculation easier for notaries,[31] it is clear that there was often a shortage of such men. Lenience was one way to overcome the shortage, to placate the demands; if this meant a falling off of professional standards in the deep country, practice within the city walls did not necessarily suffer. Competition here was keener, specimens of instruments and notarial protocols were more often under the public eye, and the officers of the guild were just around the corner—much too near. The guild's practical outlook was more evident still in its attitude toward the non-matriculated notaries in the archbishop's entourage. The proconsul and consuls might annoy this dignitary, but could they ever forget his powers, particularly in a time when the authority of the papacy stood higher than it had for two centuries and more? It was better to suffer the archbishop's notaries.

---

[29] This is denoted by the constant duplication of measures enacted against fraud and corruption. The existing laws, though vigorous and clear, seemed never to suffice. A special guild statute of 1441 raised the fine against *baratteria* (fraud) to 200 gold florins, to be equally divided by guild and state, *AGN*, 2, f. 8r. On the incidence of illegal contact between notaries and the Podestà or his judges, see statute of 1475 in ASF, *Statuti di Firenze*, 29, f. 411r.

[30] *AGN*, 32, f. 65r.

[31] *Ibid.*, ff. 26v-30r, 73v, 74r.

In this flexible or, if one chooses, indulgent application of policy, we can see that the guild sensed its limitations and recognized its self-interest. The officers of the guild took an oath: to do their jobs honestly and as best they could, to defend the guild and its ordinances, and to defend all members. Sometimes, however, it was necessary to balance parts of this oath. It was right to favor the interests of guild members, but only so far as these coincided with the advantage of the corporation as a whole. Poor relations with others, outright clashes, bad publicity, and a standing on principle which only served to make enemies in high place did not serve the interests of the guild. The *universitas* came first.

What emerges here is that element which was so much a feature of late medieval Italy—particularism: the toughness and drive of the small, clearly defined community inside the larger one, a phenomenon which cut through much of Florentine political and social life. We find it in most of the important sectors of life. The family, the faction, the guild, the class, the extraordinary political magistracy—each of these was "managed" with an eye to taking in as wide an area as possible, whether of wealth, numbers, influence, or might. The larger community was perceived, acknowledged, or accepted only when it served the lesser one, or when it was so clearly superior that to be strong-headed about resisting it was to be wrong-headed, was to invite loss rather than gain. In the practical conduct of affairs, particularism governed both the way of the guild and Florentine relations with other states.

A passage in the guild constitution of 1344 observed that there were many magnates inscribed in the guild as notaries who were ignorant of Latin and scarcely knew how to write.[32] They were not interested in practicing the notarial art (one of the charges against them was that they did not practice), but rather in holding guild office so as to have a pretext for entering the palace of the Signory. Their objectives were quite plainly the rewards of politics. Having had their political power broken by the Ordinances of Justice (1293-1295), the magnates had evidently tried in the first decades of the fourteenth century to infiltrate this most strategic of guilds, determined to retain or regain some of their former political influence. Indirect power apparently served their purposes as

---

[32] *AGN*, 749, f. 41v. Noticed by Doren, *Le arti fiorentine*, I, 132.

well as direct power, might in some instances even prove to be more effective. Yet in an age of high political passion, how discrete can their entry into the guild have been? How serious the examinations, written and oral, which they took to qualify for matriculation? We must assume that there were powerful men in the guild who tolerated and even supported the matriculation of "ignorant" magnates. Opponents were probably silenced or reduced to impotence, which fully accords with the aristocratic reaction seen in Florence during the first decades of the century. Some of the leaders of the guild were deeply involved in politics; they waited to see the outcome of things, made perhaps an occasional protest against the unlettered magnates, then fell silent. Here, for once, the interests of guild and faction were identical; surely the guild would be served if at the right moment its officers were found on the triumphant side. Then came the city's encounter with one-man rule (September 1342 to July 1343), the *signoria* of Walter of Brienne, who managed to alienate the entire political class. His expulsion was followed in the autumn by a popular reaction against the magnates; the statutes of the guild, containing the clause against ignorant magnates, were drafted shortly thereafter, most likely at the beginning of 1344. Now finally the guild began to move against those political intriguers who were notaries in name only. Once again, however, the guild did not lose its prudence; it was not going to engage in a witch-hunt. Such matters were best conducted in an orderly fashion. That this was taken for granted is borne out by the whole tenor of the statute against impostors.[33] A series of individual investigations was to precede the purge, though purge is too strong a word. First of all there would be examinations; then each suspect was to submit for inspection a volume of his protocols or abbreviatures; finally the proconsul and consuls were to examine his actual notarial license or diploma. Unfortunately, a record of the outcome of this reform does not survive.

### 3. Lawyers and Notaries

The guild was neither a mere professional organization nor just an impersonal, semi-public body. It was a brotherhood, a sworn association which the members were bound to obey and defend, just as they were

[33] *AGN*, 749, f. 41v.

bound to treat one another with a special consideration, a certain fraternal feeling which they need not express for others. This confraternal feature of the guild lost a good deal of its strength with the passage of time. It was surely different in the sixteenth century from what it had been at the outset of the thirteenth, when the guild, not yet very old, was struggling to consolidate its position and increase its influence on the destinies of the Commune. It is impossible to say how far certain rules were observed. To give an idea of the presumed bond between members, it may be noted that the statutes of 1344 and 1566 alike obligate all lawyers and notaries to attend the funerals of fellow guild members. Something here hung on of the old sentiment which undoubtedly helped to give birth to the guild. A kindred note can be detected in the rule which forbade any guild member—unless he had the previous permission of the proconsul— to take part as an advocate or procurator in any lawsuit brought against a lawyer or notary. Nor could one member bring a civil action against another save within the compass of the organization. Thus the guild court.[34]

We have seen that the guild absorbed certain judicial and regulative powers from the Commune and so was an appendage of government. A professional organization, a confraternity, and also an arm of the state, in principle it had to be somewhat demanding about its requirements for membership. Some of the requirements touched social and ceremonial matters, for the guild had a strong sense of its respectability, a sense of class or caste which left its mark on the ordinances that governed matriculation. Certain classes of men were excluded from membership. The bans are revealing.

Towncriers, undertakers, former prison wardens, actors and clowns: all these were barred from entry into the guild by the statutes of 1344. It was not only the indecorous side of these occupations which closed the doors of the guild to them but also their economic lowliness. Surveyors, music teachers, and men who taught children their ABC's were also excluded.[35] These seem to have been singled out because, of all men who hired themselves out on an hourly basis, they were the ones most likely to seek matriculation as notaries. In Florence, as in most of Europe in the

---

[34] *AGN*, 749, f. 20v; 1, f. 41r; 2, ff. 1v-2r.
[35] *AGN*, 749, ff. 37v-38r; 2, f. 67r; 1, f. 26r.

late medieval and Renaissance periods, the upper classes attached a stigma as well to manual labor as to the hiring out of oneself on an hourly or daily basis. One of the surprising things is that physicians were also declared ineligible to enter the guild. In this case, however, the prohibition probably issued from some desire to keep the two professions entirely apart, and perhaps from possible envy aroused within the guild at seeing a physican perform with ease in two different fields. Still another prohibition concerned heretics, bastards, and clerics. Heretics caused scandal and horror, and besides, members of the guild often had lucrative relations with the Church. Bastardy—whatever Bruckhardt and others may have said about its political place in the Italian Renaissance—generally carried a stain of some sort, especially in urban society, although men could be made to overlook it by the force of power and place or by means of money and a dispensation. The clause against men in holy orders is perfectly understandable: the guild wanted to be sure of its jurisdiction over members, and this disqualified clerics, who were under ecclesiastical jurisdiction.[36] A similar precaution was exhibited in one final ban: no one could enter the guild who was bound by ties of homage, fidelity, or servitude in Florentine territory. The last of these was plainly irreconcilable with the pursuit of a liberal profession.

In Western Europe, generally speaking, urban society of the late medieval and Renaissance periods was disposed to harbor a certain distrust, indeed often a dislike, of the outsider or foreigner. This was less true of the medieval commune during its revolutionary period, when men were given the prize of citizenship somewhat more easily. At Florence this communal phase came to an end in the thirteenth century. The requirements for both citizenship and guild matriculation were increasingly raised, although they levelled off in some matters before the middle of the fourteenth century. During most of the fourteenth century, the guild demanded that the candidate for matriculation, lawyer or notary, be of Florentine origin and that his father have been a resident of the city or county of Florence for at least twenty-five years. This twenty-five-year requirement remained in effect throughout the fifteenth and sixteenth

---

[36] Furthermore, the Florentine constitution excluded all clerics from office. A notary was legally and in essence a public official.

centuries. But in 1467 a new guild statute was enacted, bearing directly
on the residence requirement: thereafter the aspiring neophyte or his
family had to have paid taxes in Florence proper for twenty-five continuous years if he proposed to practice law or attest documents in the
city.[37] Shortages sometimes compelled the guild to relax this requirement,
but the consuls and other officers were always tough about exacting high
matriculation fees from foreigners and even from natives without guild
connections.

The moment we begin to talk about fees and other matters pertaining to
matriculation, we touch at once on the question of the difference between
lawyers and notaries. This question calls for detailed treatment. For when
we look to see what has previously been done with it, whether in connection with Florence or other city-states of the time, we find that institutional and legal historians have either neglected the question altogether or accorded it such vague and general treatment that they have
sown misunderstanding and a still more hopeless imprecision in others.[38]

We may start with titles. Throughout the late medieval and Renaissance periods the lawyer was called Messer or Dominus, the notary Ser.
Sometimes priests also were called Ser. The title Messer (Latin Dominus)
was more elevated than Ser and used with reference to knights, great
lords, ecclesiastical dignitaries, as well as lawyers.[39] Interestingly, official
documents often used Dominus in connection with university students.
Messer or Dominus was also accorded as an honorary title: Boccaccio,
Salutati, and Machiavelli were sometimes designated thus in chancellery
documents. Notaries in Tuscany were never called Messer or Dominus,
save through error or to acknowledge fame and distinction, as in the
case of notaries like Salutati and Poggio Bracciolini.

In many cities the lawyer ranked ceremonially with the knight or just

[37] *AGN*, 2, ff. 9v-10r. This statute was then revoked in 1470, but most probably
reintroduced later.
[38] Cf. e.g., F.-T. Perrens, *Histoire de Florence*, 6 vols. (Paris, 1877-1880), III,
283-94, where the confusion is invincible regarding the difference between lawyers
and notaries; also Piero Fiorelli, "Avvocato e procuratore," *Enciclopedia del Diritto*,
ed. Fr. Calasso (Varese, 1958—), IV, 644-70.
[39] The lawyer's claim to the title "Lord" (*Dominus*) was based on the *equiparatio*
in Roman law of the lawyer and *miles*, which the glossators translated as "knight."
E. H. Kantorowicz, *Studies*, pp. 153-54.

below; in Bologna, Perugia, and Siena he held the rank above. In Florence the lawyer came just after the knight, as in wedding ceremonies or public processions.[40] But they were equal in other matters. During the early fifteenth century, lawyer and knight were given the same stipend and number of horses when serving as ambassadors of the Republic: 5.00 gold florins per day and ten horses. On an identical mission the notary, banker, merchant or any other was allotted 4.00 gold florins and eight horses.[41] When addressing its agents in diplomatic correspondence, the Florentine Signory gave precedence to the knight over the lawyer and to the lawyer over all others.

Unlike the guild of physicians and spicers, which circumscribed a multiplicity of trades and one profession, the Arte Iudicum et Notariorum was composed solely of two professional groups, and members could be inscribed in only one of these. As the official name of the guild denotes, the two groups were the *iudices* and *notarii*, or judge-lawyers and notaries. The guild recognized no middle ground between them. Records of all sorts, public and private, nearly always refer to the notary as *notarius*, *notaio*, or *notaro*. The lawyer, on the other hand, was known by a variety of names, most often by the first five of the following: *advocatus, iudex, iurista, iurisperitus, legum* or *iuris doctor, iurisconsultus, consultor*, and *causidicus*. In the case of canon lawyers, usage called for a name like *canonista, decretista*, or *decretorum doctor*. Some notaries became skilled enough to perform the work of representation in a court of law. In this capacity they were called *procuratores*. Strictly speaking, the general term "lawyer," which the dictionary defines as a man versed in law, might be used of a good procurator. I shall return to this point in a moment. Suffice it for now to observe that the guild itself relegated the procurator of the civilians to the class of notaries, and I shall do the same, chiefly because political and guild records of the period do not and could not distinguish the notary who did things purely by formula and rote from the one who bothered to acquire a working knowledge of the law. The truth

---

[40] G. Salvemini, *La dignità cavalleresca nel comune di Firenze* (ed. Torino, 1960), pp. 386-88. When knight and lawyer were one, as often happened, the title alone, Messer or Dominus, could not reveal this.

[41] *Signori, Carte di Corredo*, 52, ff. 2v-3r, 5r; *Statuta*, ii, 706.

is that there were practicing notaries who did not know the correct forms for certain types of contracts and petitions, let alone for briefs.[42]

The word "lawyer" as used in this study may be most simply defined as any man listed in the guild rolls among the so-called judges, the vast majority of whom actually practiced law. To be inscribed among the judges meant that one had studied civil or canon law at an Italian university for at least five years. Very often, but most especially in the fifteenth century and later, the student attended law school for six to nine years and terminated his formal studies with the doctorate, frequently in both civil and canon law. In the 1340s an aspiring lawyer was received into the guild only after he fulfilled five conditions: he had to (1) produce proof of his birth and Florentine residence; (2) pay 16.0 gold florins to the guild treasurer; (3) prove—usually by means of a notarized document—that he had frequented the law faculty of a university (*studio generale*) for a period of five years or more; (4) pass a legal examination administered by a special commission of the guild; and (5) have several sponsors attest to his moral rectitude.[43] The outline of these conditions remained more or less the same down to the period of the duchy, although some changes of a non-structural sort deserve mention. At some point in the second half of the fourteenth century the matriculation fee was increased to 25.0 gold florins,[44] an extraordinary increase, which may have been occasioned by the desire to keep "new men" out of the profession, the results of the Black Death having brought many to the top. At all events, the practice was eventually introduced of letting matriculants pay their entrance fee in several installments. The guild statutes of the sixteenth century permitted settle-

---

[42] An example is to be found in Lapo Mazzei, *Lettere di un notaro a un mercante del secolo xiv*, ed. C. Guasti, 2 vols. (Firenze, 1880), I, 62. Yet most of the basic models are to be found in one of the most widely used formularies of the period, Rolandino Passaggeri's *Summa artis notariae*. Poggio Bracciolini tells the story of two men who went to a notary for a contract of sale. When asked to give their names, they said they were John and Phillip, whereupon the notary immediately said that he could not draw up the instrument for them. "If the vendor is not called Gaius, said the notary, and the buyer Titus (these were the names given in the formulary), the contract cannot be drafted nor can it have any legal validity." *Facezie*, no. 103.

[43] *AGN*, 749, f. 38r-v.

[44] *AGN*, 2, f. 2r. The date of the entry is 1415 but refers to a statute enacted before 1400.

ment of the fee in three payments. Another change was formally introduced in 1367, although there may well have been some precedent: it was
ordained that any Florentine citizen with a doctorate in civil or canon law
could enter the college of lawyers without having to undergo an examination.[45] However he had to fulfill the other four conditions and produce a
*bona fide* doctoral degree. This form of accreditation was still used by the
guild in the late sixteenth century.

Like other Florentine guilds, this one also accorded preferential treatment to the sons, brothers, and nephews of men already inscribed in
its rosters. Guildsmen knew how to look after their own. Preferred treatment, however, did not bear on the requirement that the aspiring lawyer
give proof of his having attended a law school for at least five years.
Instead, it concerned his matriculation fee and the stipulation that he
be not less than twenty-five years old on entering the guild. A man thus
favored could be two or three years younger and, in the fifteenth century, pay a matriculation fee of as little as 5.00 florins. Now and then the
fee was waived entirely.[46]

To see the Florentine lawyer from another vantage point it may be
useful to look for a moment at the "college of judges and advocates" at
Modena in the late thirteenth and early fourteenth centuries.[47] There
lawyers and notaries had separate guilds. Throughout the Guelf-Ghibel-
line struggles of the thirteenth century, the Modenese lawyers seem to
have identified their interests with those of the knights and noblemen.
Eventually, however, they passed over to the victorious popular camp
and thereby retained their prominence in public life. The lawyers' guild
took precedence over all others; the second place was held by the notaries.
To enter the guild, the prospective lawyer had to prove that he had been
a citizen of Modena for at least ten years, or that he or his family had
lived in the county or district of Modena for twenty continuous years.
Having paid his matriculation fee (20.0 *solidos mutinem*), he was ready
for the examination and went first of all before the guild consuls, who
examined him briefly on his knowledge of the law. Not more than eight

[45] *AGN*, 748, by date: 16 Sept. 1367. Not paginated.
[46] *AGN*, 2, ff. 13r-v, 14r.
[47] Material in this paragraph from *Statuta iudicum et advocatorum collegii
civitatis Mutinae, mcclxx-mcccxxxvii*, ed. E. P. Vicini (Modena, 1935).

days later, he had to present himself to an examining board of eight judge-lawyers, bringing with him two parts of the *Corpus Iuris Civilis*— the *Old Digest* and the *Code*. Opening these to any book he wished, he began to discuss one of the laws, "and once he had started none of the jurists could talk, save to interrogate and examine the candidate." He passed the examination if he obtained a majority of the eight votes. Although the statutes are not explicit about this, the guild clearly assumed that he had frequented a law school for a sufficient period of time. This was certainly expected of any man appointed to one of Modena's judgeships. A statute of 1328 declared that he must have studied law for five consecutive years in schools with qualified professors. He had to give proof of this by producing witnesses, among them a "master of laws [dominum legum]." Amusingly enough, the master was not required to take an oath: the Commune was ready, said the statute, to accept his word.

In order not to confuse the functions and preparation of the Florentine lawyer with those of the notary, let us draw professional distinctions between the two.

The lawyer was a man formally trained in jurisprudence. Additional knowledge, chiefly of the practical sort, came with experience in the law courts and with clients. But first of all he spent five or more years acquainting himself with the theory and content of the laws, civil or canon. And he learned to deal with the different classes of questions raised by the interpretation as well as by the application of the law. Once he began to practice, the lawyer was normally called on to perform three functions: those of judge, advocate, and counsel. In the first of these capacities he made binding judicial decisions; in the second he pleaded in open court or submitted written defenses; in the third he not only gave legal advice to clients but also, on requests from magistrates, examined lawsuits and submitted judicial opinions. It is when he acted as a legal consultant, and more precisely when he presented written counsel to a magistrate, that we best see the *consilium* of the lawyer as part of the judicial process. On being read out by the magistrate *pro tribunali sedens*, the *consilium sapientis* (the opinion of the jurisconsult) was transformed into a court decision.[48] This practice was widely observed

[48] On which see the excellent study by Guido Rossi, *Consilium sapientis iudiciale*

in Italy during the Middle Ages and Renaissance because many judicial posts were filled by *iudices idiotae*—laymen, men not trained in the law. But the tradition of having lawyers provide judicial counsel had a long history: it went back to ancient Rome. Medieval kings were also to employ lawyers as judges and judicial advisors. We see, therefore, why the lawyer was spontaneously associated with the judicial dignity and why in some cities he entered the guild as a *iudex*.

The notary was not as glamorous a figure as the lawyer. His place, political and social, was solid but lower. In the 1340s the would-be notary entered the guild at the age of twenty or after—at seventeen or eighteen if he could procure a dispensation. This requirement was later raised to twenty-five years (twenty-two with a dispensation) and remained in effect throughout the fifteenth century and beyond.[49] About the middle of the sixteenth century the age minimum was reduced to twenty-one years. In the 1340s the notary paid a matriculation fee of 8.00 gold florins. Later this fee was more than doubled, raised to 17.0 gold florins (18.0 for the matriculant who came from the county or district of Florence), and remained so down to the late sixteenth century.

The most trying phase of matriculation for the notarial candidate was the one which involved the examining commission, usually consisting of at least four notaries. A lawyer also had to be present at the examination. In the form given to it by the statutes of 1344, the examination had three parts: the first tested the candidate's knowledge of grammar (Latin), the second his handwriting and composition, the third his understanding of the nature and form of contracts and other public instruments.[50] If he failed the first two parts, he was not permitted to try again for one year, nor could he sit for the examination on contracts until a second year had elapsed. The third part of the examination was

---

(Milano, 1956); also Peter Riesenberg, "The Consilia Literature: A Prospectus," *Manuscripta*, VI (1962), 3-22

[49] Now and then this rule was suspended even for individuals who had no relatives in the guild. *AGN*, 32, ff. 73v, 74r (date: May 1515).

[50] *AGN*, 749, ff. 39v-40r, on this and succeeding information. Compare with examination practices at Bologna in the mid-thirteenth century: Lino Sighinolfi, "Salatiele e la sua 'ars notariae,'" *Studi e memorie per la storia dell' università di Bologna*, IV (Bologna, 1920), 67-149. See pp. 108-11.

the hardest. To prepare for it the candidate attended classes on the *ars notarie* for about two years or learned the appropriate subject matter by working in the *apotheca* of a practicing notary. The guild commission examined him in the following manner. First he was asked about the vernacular form of a given contract. Then, taking either the same contract or another, he was examined on its technical Latin form. Next the commission asked him a series of questions concerning the forms of contracts ("de hiis que in contractibus requiruntur"). At some point in the exchange between commission and examinee, the lawyer raised some questions: he conducted a brief examination on a type of contract which had not been considered. Questions could be put by the proconsul and consuls, who were also present. The candidate was finally invited to draw up "at least the first article of a public instrument." When the vote was finally taken, he needed a two-thirds majority to pass.

The form of the examination did not change much during the period covered by this study, but its application seems to have become more rigorous. Somewhere along the line the parts of the examination dealing with grammar and composition were combined, thus issuing in a more rational form. The statutes of the sixteenth century speak of two examinations: one in grammar, the other in *notarìa*.[51] Public instruments, their nature and form, remained the subject of the second of these. First the candidate was questioned by an examining commission which consisted of seven notaries and one lawyer. Obtaining their approval by a two-thirds vote, he passed on to the proconsul, consuls, and twelve advisors. They required him to deal in Latin with at least three themes. Then he dictated parts of three public instruments, being very careful to observe their correct form. A third and final round of examinations included the participation of the advisory council of fifteen. The statutes do not specify, but we may assume that the candidate was expected once more to give proof of his grasp of the nature of contracts and to dictate in Latin parts of two or three instruments.

Elsewhere in Tuscany the preparation and testing of notaries were much the same. Let us look at Pisa a moment. There, at the beginning of the fourteenth century, no one could practice the notarial craft until he

---

[51] *AGN*, I, ff. 8r-v, 27v-28r.

was twenty years old, unless he worked as an apprentice in a notary's *apotheca* and was a close relative.[52] To enter the guild he had to be a Pisan born or to have resided in the city or district for at least twenty years. He or his father had to be a registered taxpayer and the prestanzas of the household had to have been paid during the four years preceding matriculation. Some requirements were more onerous than any imposed at Florence. Thus any youth seeking entry into the Pisan guild was made to prove that he had served four years as a notary's apprentice. During that period he was required to turn a large part of his earnings over to his master, and it was the master who recommended him for matriculation by attesting to the youth's knowledge of the craft. The candidate then appeared before a board consisting of the four captains or chief officers of the guild, in addition to twenty-four notaries, six from each quarter of the city. He was supposed to have studied Latin for not less than four years. They examined his grammar, his grasp of the forms of public instruments, but especially his ability to draft the documents of his *métier* in Latin. The four captains and the six notaries from his own quarter were the judges of his performance in the examination. He needed six of the ten votes to pass, but the statute on matriculation specifically provided that if a candidate made a single mistake in his Latin, "he could be neither approved nor accepted."

At Bergamo requirements were somewhat less rigorous, at all events in the second half of the thirteenth century. The stiffest examination was administered to notaries who wished to qualify for the notarial offices of the Commune. And eligibility to sit for this examination was based on two items only: the candidate's being at least eighteen years old, and his giving proof either of having practiced as a notary for one year or of having spent one year studying for the notariate. Not surprisingly, there were some notaries in thirteenth-century Bergamo who were also barbers and shopkeepers.[53]

[52] Pisan material from *Statuti inediti della città di Pisa*, ed. Fr. Bonaini, 3 vols. (Firenze, 1857), III, 761-857, are statutes of Pisan guild.

[53] G. Poletti, *Il notariato a Bergamo nel secolo xiii* (Bergamo, 1912), pp. 31-39, 61. In the thirteenth century, generally speaking, the North Italian communes required that notaries be eighteen to twenty years old before they could be taken on as communal functionaries. Pietro Torelli, *Studi e ricerche di diplomatica comunale* (Mantova, 1915), pp. 33-34.

We must try to define the public person of the notary.[54] He performed a variety of jobs and appeared, so to speak, in different guises. Yet in most of these his essential function remained unchanged: most simply stated, it was to attest or certify human affairs of a certain kind by recording them in public form. Of all public officials he alone was invested with the authority to make those affairs legally binding. His official contact with the document which recorded a transaction brought in the seal of public law and made it a valid instrument. Deeds, wills, business agreements, emancipations from parents, marriage contracts: these were the notary's province and specialty in the field of private transactions. In public affairs his official hand was required to authenticate or certify laws, ordinances, treaties, decrees, judicial writs, and indeed all public acts. Although the statutes of the guild say nothing about this, we must assume that examinations for the notariate could occasionally touch on the correct form of different types of public acts.

The steps involved in drawing up a public instrument were these. First the notary had the contractors, testators, or donors tell him what they wanted. Raising questions to clarify points, he made a full note of the business at hand. Next he read out his summary (this was the so-called *recitatio*), noting down any changes or corrections made by the parties concerned. From two to seven witnesses had to be present, depending on the nature of the document (wills, for example, required the most). The notary then entered the summary—technically known as an abbreviature or protocol—into a register of protocols. The authentic instrument was always drawn from the original protocol. An instrument had two parts: the business at hand and the formalities of publication. It was the second of these that made an authentic public instrument; it could only be registered by the hand of a notary. Publication included and specified these formalities: year, indiction, day and month, specific place, names of witnesses, the notary's signature, and, in some parts of Italy, the name of the reigning emperor or pope.

Notaries attached to the Signory, to the chief offices of the Republic, and to the law courts were expected to have a wider, finer experience than those who made their living merely by attesting (*rogando*) con-

[54] Succeeding material from items on notaries in sources for this chapter.

tracts and other private matters. In the major law courts, the notaries who conducted the examination of witnesses were skilled in court procedure. They were recruited from among the more experienced or better-prepared men. The notary in charge of legislation (*notaio delle riformagioni*), the notaries who assisted the first secretary of the Republic, and those who took office with every new group of priors, recording their deliberations, had to have an intimate working knowledge of at least parts of the Florentine constitution and of some sectors of the city's statutory law. It seems clear, accordingly, that the class of notaries was not a homogeneous one; it included specialists as well as men with a superficial preparation.[55]

During the fourteenth and fifteenth centuries, Bologna may have been the only center where the aspiring notary was actually required to follow university courses. Significantly, the *ars notarie* came under the arts faculty, not the law school.[56] At Florence, Milan, Pisa, and elsewhere, men who aimed at a notarial career might be encouraged to enroll for some formal university courses, but this training was perhaps more easily acquired in the *apotheca* of a practicing notary. And if at Pisa the required period of apprenticeship was four years, at Milan it was only two, although three years of university work could be substituted for these two years.[57]

There is enough evidence to show that nearly everywhere in Italy the notary's education and office, at least in some of his incarnations, gradually became more complex and demanding. At Milan, by 1498, a statute already demanded—although we should be suspicious of its application—that the notary know Azo's gloss and be familiar with the chief books of the *Corpus Iuris Civilis*. In Piedmont, university courses for the notariate were not finally prescribed until the sixteenth century. The situation at Florence was somewhat more complicated and centered mainly on the figure of the procurator.

[55] This aspect of the history of the profession is the least studied, the least understood.

[56] Bologna had public instruction in *notarìa* as early as 1228. A. Anselmi, *Le scuole di notariato in Italia* (Viterbo, 1926), p. 8.

[57] Charles Dejob, *Le notaire en Italie et en France*, offprint from *Miscellanea di studi storici in onore di A. Manno* (Torino, 1912), p. 7.

By the 1550s we see quite clearly for the first time that the office of procurator had been steadily evolving at Florence for some three centuries and had now reached a point where it could only be exercised by men with some technical grasp of the law. Occasionally, lawyers undertook the simple representation of clients—that is, performed the part of procurators. But this function was normally restricted to men properly inscribed in the guild as notaries. To obtain a license to practice as a procurator in the Council of Justice, the highest Florentine court after 1502, the notary had to present himself to an examining board consisting of the proconsul and consuls, two doctors of law, and two procurators from the guild's advisory council of twelve.[58] Not only was the candidate required to have been a practicing member of the guild for three years or more, he also had to show that during that period he had served as a recorder (*scriptor*) in the designated tribunal. Furthermore, he had to present proof of having studied at a university (a *studio generale*) for three years, presumably following the basic courses offered by its law faculty. That the number of notaries qualified to serve as procurators in the Council of Justice was very limited is denoted by the fact that the guild made special provisions for ways of enlisting the two procurators for the above-mentioned examining board. If the current council of twelve happened not to include any, they could be drawn from the advisory council of fifteen; and if this council also had no procurators, then the proconsul and consuls were authorized to use their own initiative in recruiting them.

The procurator had thus come a long way since the thirteenth and fourteenth centuries, when his functions of attorney, so long as they were fully joined with those of the simple notary, were considered beneath the dignity of the trained jurist and even thought by some to be *ignobile*.[59] With an ever increasing skill and a growing fund of techniques, the procurator handled the formalities and paperwork connected with the lawsuits of his clients, gave them advice, and represented their claims in court. In time, therefore, the procurator of the civilians came to cor-

[58] *AGN*, I, ff. 30v-31r.
[59] G. Salvioli, *Storia della procedura*, in P. Del Giudice, ed., *Storia del diritto italiano* (Milano, 1925-1927), III, ii, 218.

respond to the solicitor in chancery and to the old public attorney. Probably he had the right to argue certain types of cases, at all events in some courts. In general, however, he was denied the right of audience, which properly belonged to the advocate or lawyer, a full-fledged jurist.

## 4. Political Vicissitudes and Parallels

The internal organization of the guild seems to present a tranquil countenance during the fifteenth and sixteenth centuries. Not so in the period running from the middle thirteenth to the later fourteenth century, when there was a good deal of conflict between lawyers and notaries. The differences sometimes turned on questions of status and faction, and occasionally they took an acute form, creating scissions within the guild, until such a time as political society itself became less stormy.

It is not unlikely that the earliest conflicts between lawyers and notaries were connected with the struggle between Guelfs and Ghibellines. David-sohn found that in 1254 the six guild consuls were three lawyers and three notaries, a distribution which favored lawyers because notaries outnumbered them in the guild by about eight or nine to one.[60] In 1269 the hand of the jurists was heavier still, for the consulate then had only four places and three were held by lawyers. But by 1275 the old numerical parity had been restored, though strife within the guild continued. It came to a head in 1287, when the two groups temporarily split, formed two guilds, and elected separate consuls. The Council of the People, however, soon persuaded them to reunite, undoubtedly fearing the additional political influence that a new major guild would confer on lawyers and notaries alike. The reunification was a partial victory for the notaries, and thereafter the representation of lawyers in the main offices of the guild was gradually whittled down. In 1329 the guild had five consuls, only two of whom were lawyers. Later on the number of consuls was raised to eight, with lawyers securing three of the seats. About 1370, finally, the notaries succeeded in claiming a sixth consul.[61] Although this arrangement survived the lifetime of the Republic, the overall rep-

[60] Davidsohn, *Geschichte*, IV, ii, 123. On other material in this paragraph see Davidsohn, *Forschungen zur Geschichte von Florenz* (Berlin, 1896-1908), III, 232; Doren, *Entwicklung*, p. 35.

[61] The change came between 1368 and 1372. Cf. lists of consuls in *AGN*, 92, 93.

resentation of lawyers was less than has been suggested, for in the advisory councils they held in fact less than one-fourth the seats. It has already been noted that from the fourteenth century on the proconsul (once the *capitudo*) was always a notary. Despite these observations, it would be wrong to conclude that the lawyers' hold on the guild had been excessively weakened. They set their own professional standards and either received men into their ranks or not, as they saw fit. Seldom in the fifteenth century and up to 1530 did the number of lawyers registered with the guild exceed more than about twenty-five. Notaries, on the other hand, numbered from about 400 to 420 in any given year. Hence on a proportional basis lawyers continued to enjoy a very high number of places in the guild councils. In subsequent chapters we shall see that their prominence in politics far surpassed that of the notaries.

In the fourteenth century, disturbances within the guild seem to have issued more from professional contrasts and questions of status than from social differences. Speaking of the thirteenth century, Davidsohn observed that Florentine lawyers sprang on the whole from the urban patriciate. He noted that while lawyers were conservative in their outlook, notaries were more democratic because they were "in continuous contact with people of all classes."[62] This is speculation, but it may describe what generally happened, even though there were notaries with a strong antidemocratic bias. If many notaries were recruited from old ruling families or their remnants, it was still true that the higher status and superior social ties of lawyers had the effect of drawing these closer to the Commune's more aristocratic forces. The tensions that derived from this difference vanished by the 1320s or 1330s when, as has already been noted, a noteworthy number of magnates (with the necessary connivance of highly placed notaries) sneaked into the guild with the aim of pursuing their own political ends. But even in the 1280s and 1290s lawyers and notaries had on occasion been drawn into working together. Salvemini called attention to the fact that lawyers and notaries alone, of the great guildsmen and *popolani*, had nothing to do with the establishment of the Priorate in 1282. He explained this odd and interesting abdication of influence by arguing that since they depended on the offices and oppor-

[62] Davidsohn, *Geschichte*, iv, ii, 111.

tunities accorded to them by the Commune, they had little choice but to be time-servers and to stay on the good side of the faction or class at the political helm.[63] Yet owing to their social ties and family connections, how could lawyers keep from gravitating toward the aristocratic forces? And how could notaries avoid being pulled first one way and then another—drawn by family ties, commitment to a previous regime, or the desire to be favored by the next? Salvemini concluded that these cross-currents so disoriented lawyers and notaries, created such confusion in them, that they ended by following their personal whims. Evidently they found it more opportune not to participate as a group in the establishment of the Priorate. A decade or so later, however, they did join forces in a successful operation. Here the Italian historian's narrative is perhaps less schematic and more convincing. Following one of Giovanni Villani's observations, he noted that between 1293 and 1295 lawyers and notaries entered the lists against Giano della Bella, sire and prime mover of those smart enactments against the magnates—the Ordinances of Justice. Like the magnates themselves, the Arte dei Giudici e Notai, led by its chieftains, joined those who set out to destroy the leader of the *popolani*. Salvemini shrewdly observed that as no lawyers sat in the Signory between October 1293 and February 1295, there may well have been a move to bar them indefinitely from this magistracy. Probably this frightened lawyers into thinking "that the *popolo minuto* might bring to Florence also the laws of communes where lawyers were equated with magnates or *grandi*."[64] In such an event, the Ordinances of Justice would have been turned against the college of lawyers within the guild, excluding them from all major communal offices and inflicting ruinous fines on them or their families for any violent or abusive behavior against legally recognized commoners (*popolani*). It was to prevent this, apparently, that the guild joined in the destruction of Giano della Bella.

Perhaps one can take it as axiomatic that wherever political conflict is extreme—and by extreme I mean the point at which the stakes become the political and social order itself—the strife will be carried over to many

---

[63] Salvemini, *Magnati*, pp. 81-82, 119.
[64] *Ibid.*, pp. 220-22, 244; also Davidsohn, *Geschichte*, ii, ii, 537-39.

of the private sectors of life, including the family and business associations. Up to the end of the fourteenth century the guilds of Florence were susceptible to the pressures of political controversy, the more so as they were semi-public corporations with a stipulated place in the political life of the city and with representation in the councils of government. During the 1360s and 1370s—that period which Gene Brucker has studied with exemplary insight and care—the guild of lawyers and notaries, in its internal difficulties, reflected the same lesions which marked the larger world of municipal politics. Those decades encouraged the variegated activity of strong political personalities, men whose *historical* differences finally concerned the kinds and classes of men who should rule Florence. The history of the guild in that period provides examples as well of the meanest as of the most generous side of politics: of personal favoritism and of action taken in favor of large aims and policies.

In August 1373 a lawyer, Messer Giovanni di Ser Fruosino, was denounced to the Podestà for condemning the regime. It was reported that he particularly disapproved of the government's having fallen into the hands of citizens who had banished the Albizzi and Ricci families from political office.[65] Now, among the Ricci were Messer Giovanni di Ruggero, a fellow lawyer, and Uguccione, a powerful politician who had captained the popular party until the autumn of 1371, when he had suddenly passed over to the oligarchical faction, having first sold himself "for gold." Since Giovanni di Ser Fruosino was risking his neck and had certainly been working for their political rehabilitation, he must have owed something to the Ricci—friendship anyway. The nature of one of his debts is recorded in a register of guild deliberations. On March 19, 1370, he had been condemned by the proconsul, Ser Jacopo Benintendi, to pay a fine of 200 pounds *piccioli*. Two days later a guild commission was appointed to examine the case. Why the fine was imposed does not emerge, but during the next three weeks our lawyer did a job of canvassing. On April 13 the new group of guild consuls declared that because of a petition from the wise and distinguished Uguccione de' Ricci, and by right of the

43

power invested in them, they thereby annulled the sentence against Giovanni di Ser Fruosino and ordered the treasurers, present and future, to expunge the record of both fine and sentence from all guild registers.[66] No other grounds were given for this amnesty. Yet a fine of 200 pounds *piccioli*—some 60.0 to 65.0 gold florins in this period—was a heavy sentence and could only have been imposed because of a serious infraction. Clearly, however, Uguccione's influence was an even more serious matter, at all events for the new consuls. And it says something for Giovanni's political adaptability that he had no great trouble staying in Uguccione's train when this politico passed from the leadership of the popular party into the camp of the ultraconservatives.

As has already been suggested, the most important political question of the 1360s and 1370s concerned the kinds and classes of men who should dispose of political power. Leaders of the older and more entrenched families made an effort to keep newcomers out of the top places in government. Gradually they built up a campaign against such men, articulated chiefly but not entirely through the offices of the Guelf Society. New men were secretly denounced, accused of Ghibellinism, or simply warned against accepting appointments to public office. Many of the despised upstarts were notaries in good standing with the guild, and while feeling against them probably went back some time, it was not until the early 1360s that voices began to call for their ostracism from the offices of the guild. In the late autumn of 1363 the consulate expressed dissatisfaction with the "scrutiny" of February 1348, with the men who on that occasion had been made eligible to hold office in the guild. That list of approved men was no longer acceptable. It was resolved to undertake a new review and to fill the eligibility pouches with a different series of names. Furthermore, the officials appointed to conduct this review were made to swear, by order of the proconsul, that they would refuse their favor to men who were neither true Guelfs nor qualified to hold office.[67]

To bar a man from guild office was no unimportant thing. It laid him open to charges of Ghibellinism from other sources. It tended to exclude him from public office even when no formal accusation had been made. For, not being a registered *rentier* (*scioperato*), his right to

[66] *AGN*, 748, by date: 13 April 1370.     [67] *AGN*, 28, f. 115r.

44

hold communal office was predicated on his status as an active guild member in good standing. But if he was ineligible to hold office in his own guild, how could he rightly qualify for a higher order of offices?

It took time for the ultraconservatives within the guild to mount an effective campaign. Until this group could monopolize the corporation's chief offices, their implementing of a program would be fitful; they must move in coordination with other movements against the presence of new men in government. On April 22, 1366, the consuls and a group of *arrotos* censured the proconsulate of November 1365. They claimed that many of the names put into the eligibility pouches in that month were those of "Ghibellines and men unqualified [to hold office], according to the form of the statutes of the Commune of Florence." Wishing "to remedy this for the honor and glory of the Guelf Society and guild," they enjoined the proconsul and several consuls of his choice to choose one guild member from each quarter of the city and together to review the names put into the pouches the previous November.[68] The reviewers were authorized to make any changes—presumably withdraw names—that would further "the honor and good state" of the guild. It is significant that the proconsul was Ser Niccolò de' Serragli, born into a well-known family of ultraconservative leanings and with strong ties among the magnates.[69] Furthermore, of the three lawyers among the eight consuls, at least two were exponents of close oligarchy: Filippo Corsini and Lapo da Castiglionchio. With the critical backing of several notaries from among the consuls and *arrotos*, the proconsul and lawyers were undoubtedly the authors of this more intransigent turn in guild policy. The record of guild deliberations of the time goes only as far as 1372, but the pressure of the conservatives within the guild continued. For additional appeals were made to keep the guild a society of "good Guelfs" and to open offices only to the men who "qualified." Particularly interesting was a session held on September 24, 1372; at that session the proconsulate resolved that all past and future guild consuls who were ex-captains or secretaries of the Guelf Society (the Parte Guelfa) must at-

---

[68] *AGN*, 748, by date: 22 April 1366.

[69] On the Serragli see my *The Social World of the Florentine Humanists* (Princeton, 1963), p. 230.

tend meetings of the society and of the city's legislative councils.[70] Any violation of this rule was to carry a penalty of 40.0 *soldi florenorum parvorum*. It seems clear that there was a concerted effort behind this measure to get leading Guelfs and ex-officers of the guild to bring their influence to bear on prospective legislation in the designated councils.

Social struggles of the type seen at Florence in the thirteenth century, or in the 1360s and 1370s, were not repeated in the fifteenth century or thereafter. The socio-political disturbances of the 1490s were different in both order and magnitude from the discord and troubles of those earlier times. Throughout the fifteenth century the guild seems to have been at peace, save at one point in the 1420s when two notaries, representing rival factions, created tension by their efforts to out-maneuver each other.[71] Yet one question persisted, was in fact to move into the foreground: this was the question of the extent to which notaries should have entrée into the whole circuit of government offices. There is some evidence to show that efforts were made by certain groups to downgrade the guild as a whole. But a municipal statute of the 1490s, as well as some statistical data concerning the Signory, conclusively prove that the real target of those efforts was that influential administrative class—the notaries.

At least two attacks were made on the guild in the late fourteenth century. This is established by a guild register recording the major privileges granted by the guild. Given to men who performed outstanding services for the honor, status, or authority of the guild, the privileges usually entailed free grants of guild membership and were conferred not only on the original benefactor but also on his legitimate male descendants via the masculine line. Two patents of privilege allege services done in the late fourteenth century. The first involved Ser Buonaccorso di Ser Piero, who was taken into the guild freely on October 23, 1400. This privilege was not entered into the above-mentioned register until 1440, when Ser Buonaccorso himself accounted for his free matriculation: "this was to pay back the good done for the guild by my father Piero in 1383. Serving as one of the Dodici, he alone fought to keep the guild

---

[70] *AGN*, 748, by date.
[71] G. Cavalcanti, *Istorie fiorentine*, 2 vols. (Firenze, 1838), II, 399-400.

from losing the offices and honors which some men wanted to take away from it at that time."[72] The other privilege concerned a powerful political figure of the so-called Albizzi period: the knight, Messer Rinaldo Gianfigliazzi. In 1392 a measure was tabled in the Council of the People, severely criticizing the guild and seeking to deprive its members of the right to hold public office. The measure however was defeated, due in part at least to the intervention of Messer Rinaldo, who seems to have presented an especially eloquent and forceful defense of the guild. Most of the script on the appropriate folio has been eroded by time and humidity, so that the nature of the attack on the guild does not emerge. That the attacks continued is suggested by the fact that when in March 1421 the guild was accorded its due by the officials who "celebrated" a new scrutiny of the citizens eligible for public office, grateful acknowledgment was made of the support given to the guild by the Signory, the Twelve, and the Sixteen.[73]

The attacks on the guild, aboveboard or not, did not meet with much success until the 1430s, as we shall see later. The most crippling blow of all fell on March 14, 1496. On that day the Grand Council of the Republic enacted a statute directed against notaries.[74] It was a statute in three parts, the second of which may have been a "rider." The first part stipulated that any notary who drew the equivalent of 5.00 gold florins per month from a public office could not receive additional money from any individual, directly or indirectly, "for activity connected with the documents of his office." Part two of the *provvisione* (the most important part) declared: "And because it does not seem fair that a notary should be able to enjoy the offices of [ordinary] citizens as well as those of notaries, let it herewith be laid down that every notary, whatever his grade or condition, must choose within the month to be eligible either for the offices of notaries or for those of [ordinary] citizens." The choice

---

[72] *AGN*, 27, f. 12v. The item following is on f. 4r. I made a search in *Libri Fabarum*, 44, for the measure disputed by Gianfigliazzi, but could find no trace of it as a rejected bill.

[73] *AGN*, 27, f. 7v.

[74] *Prov.*, 186, f. 212r-v, contains following quotations, including tallies of final vote on statute. Commented on by diarist Luca Landucci, *Diario fiorentino dal 1450 al 1516*, ed. I. Del Badia (Firenze, 1883), p. 127.

had to be notarized and deposited with the *notaio delle tratte*, who was the secretary in charge of the lists of Florentines drawn for public office. Any notary who violated his attested choice was liable to a fine of 100 large florins for each infraction. The fine was to be paid into the Monte treasury. Jurisdiction in these cases was specifically denied the guild and given to the Defenders of the Laws (Conservatores Legum), one of the Republic's special commissions. The third part of the statute forbade notaries to draw more than one salary at a time from the Republic. It also required every notary to tend personally to the work connected with any office in his charge. This provision was clearly directed against pluralism, for it allowed no man to have substitutes serving in his place save for reasons of sickness and just absence. Even then, however, the absence had to be approved by twenty-five votes out of the thirty-seven in the Signory and colleges.

It would be hard to surpass this statute as a specimen of redaction and legislative maneuvering. Rarely if ever had notaries been popular or well-liked figures. Although they were indispensable to the state, to the great families, to the property-owning sector of the populace, and to merchants, they were often criticized for being venal and dishonest. The extant papers of the guild reveal that the criticism was not unfounded.[75] And Savonarola's Florence, filled with the mixed desire for political and religious reform, was just the setting in which to rectify matters. Notaries presented the perfect object of criticism, taking part, as they did, in virtually every phase of Florentine public life. Sandwiched between a provision wiping out extra profits and another putting a stop to the lucrative piling up of notarial posts, the provision which excluded notaries from the ordinary circuit of offices must have been seen under the same moralistic light as the other two. If the first and third provisions were meant to make honest men of notaries, why not the second? It was not even necessary to give this provision a more reasoned or more face-saving vindication than that it was not fair for a notary to hold both the offices of his profession and those in the ordinary public circuit. The statute was

[75] This seems clear from the continuous duplication of measures directed against their fraud and corruption, as if somehow the existing guild laws never quite sufficed. But see also, e.g., Boccaccio, *Decameron*, I, nov. 1; Poggio Bracciolini, *Facezie*, n. 168.

passed by a vote which highlighted the unpopularity of notaries: 79 to 2 in the combined executive councils, and 669 to 30 in the Grand Council.

Of course notaries seem to have been given a choice: they could elect the normal run of offices or the specialized posts reserved only for members of the notarial profession. But in a period of keen economic uncertainty, as the 1490s were for Florence, notaries naturally attached greater importance to the steady income from fixed notarial posts. Their economic possibilities were seldom so plentiful that they could afford to gamble on the different mechanisms—e.g., scrutinies, drawings by lot, *divieti*—that determined appointments to the ordinary run of public offices.

The ban had long been sought in some quarters. When qualified to occupy professional as well as ordinary public offices, notaries were able—through their contacts with all the leading magistracies—to acquire a special control over key records and an influence which far surpassed that of many ordinary citizens. That the ban was finally enacted in 1496 was perhaps a by-product of the fall from power of the Medici family, with whose thinly veiled signory the leading notaries (backbone of the administrative class) must have been associated. Yet we must be clear about one thing: the political attack on notaries went back a long way, at least to the 1380s. This attack is best seen, even if somewhat obliquely, in the declining frequency with which notaries sat in the Signory.

Reviewing a complete inventory of the priors of the Signory,[76] we find that the most encouraging time for notaries was the early period, from 1282 to 1328. Established in 1282, the government of priors first consisted of seven men, one of whom was the Gonfalonier of Justice. Two priors were subsequently added and for the remaining lifetime of the Republic the Signory was made up of eight priors and the Gonfalonier. Following are the tallies of places held in the Signory by notaries during certain intervals of time. The intervals are not all identical, but the declining frequency is plainly evident:

1282–1328: 72 places

1328–1348: 10

[76] ASF, see the *Priorista di Palazzo*.

1348–1378: 9
1378–1398: 12
1398–1418: 7
1418–1438: 5

It was sometime after 1433 that the notaries, with four exceptions, were entirely excluded from the Signory. Between 1433 and 1471 only one notary attained this dignity and did so four times. He was Ser Niccolò di Michele Dini. Significantly, he appeared in the Signory not as a representative of the lawyers and notaries but as a *galigaio* (a tanner). The three notaries who entered the Signory thereafter took office in 1471, 1475, and 1492. Although it would take a good deal of research to prove the assumption, we must suspect all three of having enjoyed the favor of Lorenzo the Magnificent or of one of his close associates. For some practice or prejudice, some rule or mechanism, was certainly suspended in order to make room for them in the Signory. After 1492 the office of prior was not again conferred on a notary.

Although the political position of notaries had long been in decline, they were not effectively barred from the Signory until after 1433. I have been unable to find a statute introducing a ban or a prohibitory clause in any of the schemes for a new review (*scrutinio*) of men eligible to sit in the Signory. But if such a statute or clause was not enacted—and this is possible—then the process of exclusion went on quietly at one of two points: either when names were voted on or, once declared eligible, when the Eight on Public Safety so decided. The question arises, how did the ban affect the political influence of notaries? Their direct influence as priors in the Signory vanished; they could no longer boast of this privilege. But we should be innocent to suppose that they had been silenced, their influence broken. As long as they went on staffing the notarial posts attached to all the leading offices, their weight in administration, in the bureaucratic organization of the state, was not affected. Even so, however, they had to be placated, and so the proconsul was awarded a prominent place in the *Balìe* of 1434, 1444, and 1458.[77] Further-

---

[77] A *balìa* was a picked council of 250 to 350 men, temporarily invested with near absolute powers.

more, as happened in July 1448,[78] the proconsul and at least one other notary sometimes took part in the commissions appointed to carry out new reviews or "scrutinies" of men eligible for municipal and territorial offices, including all the notarial posts.

Meanwhile, what had happened to lawyers and their place in the Signory? The notaries lost representation but the guild as a whole did not. As fewer notaries obtained places in the chief magistracy, more and more lawyers found their way into it. Following is a periodic breakdown of the places held by lawyers in the Signory during 152 years:

> 1380–1399: 7 places
> 1400–1419: 8
> 1420–1439: 13
> 1440–1459: 14
> 1460–1479: 7
> 1480–1499: 26
> 1500–1519: 27
> 1520–1531: 15

The last of these periods involved only twelve years, but it promised to be as good a one for lawyers as the two twenty-year periods which immediately preceded. The drop between 1460 and 1479 is explained by the fact that during those years the guild had the least number of registered lawyers. Why the number of practicing lawyers in the city temporarily dropped at that time is another question, though not one connected with the vicissitudes of politics. The great increase after 1480, however, did derive in part from a grave political situation: it corresponded to a constitutional crisis.[79]

THE TITLE of this section refers to political "parallels." I have in mind some striking similarities, both functional and structural, between the government of the guild and the government of the city. Similarities also existed between Florentine government and the way in which some of the other guilds were run, but they were not as striking or as sustained.

[78] *Balìe*, 26, f. 183r-v.
[79] To be discussed from different viewpoints in Chs. V, 1; IX, 2; X.

The proconsul and the eight consuls of the Arte dei Giudici e Notai corresponded to the Gonfalonier of Justice and the eight priors of the Signory. In the guild's advisory boards were reproduced the functions and organization of the two colleges attached to the Signory, the Dodici Buonomini and the Sedici Gonfalonieri. Like the Signory, the nine men of the proconsulate had not only executive but also very important judicial powers. A parallel naturally obtained with regard to the initiative on municipal and guild legislation: all bills were first discussed and voted on by the Signory and colleges, or by the proconsulate and advisory bodies, then presented to the legislative councils, or to the whole body of guild officers and *arrotos*.

Some of the functional similarities are more remarkable than those concerning organization. One of the standard features of Florentine public life was the practice of duplicating authority. Two, three, or more offices sometimes touched on areas of identical executive and, especially, judicial competence. The guild also sanctioned this breaking up of authority, most notably in connection with its permanent campaign against the dishonesty and corruption of lawyers and notaries. Proconsul and consuls, separately or together, had the power of investigation into professional trickery, fraud, and the like. But after 1473 they shared this authority, including the power to pass sentence, with the *conservatores legum* of the guild. Still another parallel pertained to the "syndication" of offices, i. e., investigation of the way in which the duties of office had been exercised. The procedures followed were standard, used alike by the state and by most of the other guilds. Ordinarily, for both guild and state, the job of syndication was performed by one of the standing offices or by an especially created commission.

This brings up another, more significant similarity between the world of the guild and that of the Commune. In the creation of special commissions—whether investigative, regulatory, or judicial—no Italians were more experienced than the Florentines, and this practice was observed in municipal no less than in guild government. Lawyers and notaries established and abolished offices (e.g., the "correctors" and "arbiters") with ease. They often created *ad hoc* syndics and examiners. Indeed, the whole institution of *arrotos* was a variant of the *ad hoc* commission.[80] *Arrotos* were temporarily attached to the proconsulate or to one of the other standing offices of the guild. They enjoyed exceptional powers, insofar at least as they might decide the final outcome of an issue by their votes or direct influence. Florentines partly retained their exploratory attitude toward political mechanisms even in the fifteenth century. As statesmen or guildsmen, lawyers or notaries, they had few loyalties which moved them to put an end to the proliferation of new investigative, regulatory, and judicial bodies. The Defenders of the Laws, the Nocturnal Officials, the Consuls of the Sea, the Catasto Officials, the Eight on Foreign Affairs (Otto di Pratica), the Accoppiatores, and a number of other municipal offices were all established in the fifteenth century, and as many others were abolished.

I have called attention to the parallels between guild and municipal government not to engage in an academic exercise but to show that the milieu of the guild was in its way an education in statecraft, a preparation for politics. Young lawyers and notaries might have their first experience of political processes within the compass of the guild. Officials here were regularly changed, *divieti* were imposed, commissions appointed, measures proposed, acts drafted, men screened for office, violators of guild regulations secretly denounced (by *tamburazione*), all in much the same way as in government circles proper. Lawyers and notaries naturally carried over their experience of municipal politics into the guild councils. In the fifteenth century and later, formative influences were undoubtedly much stronger when moving from the state to the guild. This cannot have been nearly so true in the thirteenth and early fourteenth centuries, when there was a gradual convergence of communal government and the leadership of the major guilds and when the Arte dei Giudici e Notai was a more vital, more solidified body. Influences must have been more reciprocal then. But we need not weigh or dispute influences. The point is that Florentines fashioned both guilds and a communal polity after the same image. As it happens, lawyers and notaries produced the best "imitation," and the continuous exchange

[80] *Arrotos*: a select group of men appended to a governing body to help decide or resolve given problems. The institution was much used in Venice.

of experience between their guild and the Commune became a more coordinated, perhaps a more reflexive affair.

## 5. *The Course of Change*

The preceding sections of this chapter have given piecemeal the details of change in the organization and function of the guild. My plan here is to indicate the general course or direction of change taken by the guild, though once again I shall stay mainly on the political level.

Between the middle of the fourteenth century and the fall of the Republic (1530) the guild constitution underwent no remarkable changes. The structure of magistracies retained the same basic outlines. But often in history the veil of events temporarily conceals the work of change. We have already seen that with the passage of time the process of specialization produced different types of notaries, even though the distinctions among them were often hazy and a notary skilled in one area could, by acquiring the necessary experience, gradually pass over into another. It was the procurator who best exemplified the results of slow occupational change. By the sixteenth century he was closer in some ways to the jurist than to the simple author and attestor of documents, public or private. There is no evidence to show, however, that the dignity of the fully evolved procurator increased the political weight or influence of notaries as a group.

It has been observed that notaries came to hold more and more seats in the offices of the guild, until the lawyers' share was reduced in the consulate to only one-fourth the number of seats and in the other offices to less than this. Within the guild, accordingly, it was the notaries who prevailed. Yet the remarkable thing is that while notaries increasingly dominated the guild, lawyers entered communal politics in greater numbers. Owing to the network of well-placed notarial posts, notaries always enjoyed a political influence not easily detectable on the surface, and this influence may well have grown with the growing, insinuating rule of the Medici. Nevertheless, after the middle of the fourteenth century and even more so in the course of the fifteenth century, notaries appeared less and less often in the Republic's principal dignities; and I mean not only the Signory and colleges but also powerful magistracies like the

Dieci di Balìa and the Otto di Guardia. Lawyers, on the other hand, maintained and indeed improved their outstanding position in the city's political life. There are two explanations for this. The first relates to the special skills of the lawyer in strict connection with the political needs of the Florentine Republic during the fifteenth century and later; the second has to do primarily with social forces and factors.

In his authoritative study of the Florentine chancellery, Marzi observed that the leading offices in this department of Florentine government tended, in the course of the fifteenth century, to pass over into the hands of lawyers.[81] Noting the prominence of lawyers in other sectors of government as well, he held that this new fashion was a function of the grander, more "aristocratic" tenor of public life in Renaissance Florence. With his learning, his robes, and his degrees, the lawyer cut a more distinguished figure. Marzi's observation accords with a trend noticed by Salvemini, who called attention to the renewed passion for the dignity of knighthood and to the high incidence of knights at the summit of political society. To these observations let us add that never in the history of the Republic were citizen prelates—bishops and archbishops—to play as prominent a part in Florentine diplomacy as in the late fifteenth and early sixteenth centuries.[82] It was not merely that powerful neighbors, near and far, expected Florentines to favor political and ecclesiastical luminaries in the appointment of ambassadors, but that the great ruling families desired and expected their own members to fill these posts. Now and then patricians refused proffered embassies, but they certainly anticipated that these would go to their social peers.

The preceding trends certainly mean that Florentine public life became less easily accessible in the course of the fifteenth century and more demanding about the social place of statesmen, and certainly more dependent on the individual's immediate purse. For the Republic often took months, sometimes even years, to settle some of its accounts—for example, ambassadorial salaries. These changes in public life fully accord with the direction of style elsewhere: the more princely Florentine palaces of the fifteenth century, the fussier dress styles, the increasing ardor for

[81] *La cancelleria della repubblica fiorentina* (Rocca S. Casciano, 1910), pp. 217-18, 229.

[82] A subject worthy of a monograph.

55

costly and flashy jewelry, the inflationary dowries, and the budding collections of *objets d'art.*[83]

The notary could not keep up this pace. In the age of the revolutionary
commune, he often sprang from the higher social strata, claimed the
prestige of a certain connection with the Empire (via the imperial investment of notaries), or, having slender financial means, could benefit
from the popular currents of the early commune. But in the fifteenth
century and later, he could not keep up with the new social tenor of
high office. The fact was that he did not have the requisite social standing. Neither his income nor his profession sufficiently conferred this on
him. Conversely, the doctor of laws—and most Florentine lawyers were
*doctores*—enjoyed the rank, style, and dignity of profession and income
of one who "naturally" and traditionally merited a leading place in
society, unless, as in the case of Machiavelli's father, he was excessively
attached to leisured fecklessness.

Thus the notary's bureaucratic influence aside, it was almost part of
a natural process that in the fifteenth century he should have lost—being
excluded from the principal public offices—his former political éclat.
There were exceptions of course. There always are. But I am speaking of
trends, of the general direction of change, not of exceptional particulars.
Lawyers on embassy appointments might go six months to a year without receiving their salaries. They might complain bitterly, but they seem
always to have had the private means to get on with their tasks. The
notary, on the other hand, did not; so that to give him identical treatment was not to treat him in quite the same way. Not that notaries were
given important embassies in the fifteenth and sixteenth centuries; those
times were gone. But they often served as diplomatic agents or embassy
secretaries. The notary Ser Francesco Cappelli, secretary of the Florentine
embassy in Rome for several years around 1500, was twice thrown into a
Roman jail for debt. And the fault lay entirely with the Signory, which
had failed, because of stubbornness and neglect, to pay his salary for ten
months. The Florentine ambassador in Rome, a lawyer named Francesco
Pepi, relayed Cappelli's cries of lament to the Signory.[84]

---

[83] My *Florentine Humanists*, pp. 37-38, 290.
[84] *SCRO*, 22, ff. 25r, 8or, 256r-v.

The process of oligarchical contraction, political and even social, worked to undermine the political power of the guilds. No longer in the fifteenth century did the Florentine economy produce new men in historical numbers, that is, in numbers large enough to affect the course of things, large enough to effect significant change. From having been, in the thirteenth and early fourteenth centuries, the opponents of entrenched privilege—the agencies through which new men articulated their desires or expressed a viewpoint—the guilds were manipulated into becoming the defenders of privilege. Eventually, too, there was no longer any need to keep the guilds politicized, save insofar as they had to be ready to follow the lead of the oligarchy. Some of the intransigent men around Cosimo de' Medici—Luca Pitti and the rest—went farther: they wanted the political influence of the guilds *qua* guilds entirely dissolved, and so with the *coup d'état* of 1458 they changed the name of the officials who made up the Signory from "priors of the guilds" to "priors of liberty." The irony may even have been unintentional.

How did the Arte dei Giudici e Notai respond to the new direction of things political? Unlike the other guilds, it had never been an opponent of entrenched political and social privilege. In some periods, law and the grindstone of formula-ridden paperwork have had the effect of driving their practitioners to line up with the establishment. But be this as it may, the drift toward an ever-narrowing polity in Florence received the support of the guild. It might even be argued that the guild played a servile role, though such an allegation would be value-determined. In any event, influential lawyers and notaries prevailed upon their guild to support not only the oligarchical blows of 1444 and 1458, but also the sharp change of government in 1530.[85] There is no evidence that the guild ever took a position, feeble or otherwise, against Lorenzo the Magnificent. All indications point the other way.

## SOURCES FOR CHAPTER TWO

This statement of sources should begin with a list of the general and specific secondary works on the subject. But the institutional history of the

[85] *AGN*, 27, consult by date, including vellum insert of 1530 and last entry of register.

*profession* in Italy has been neglected by historians—neglected in its essential details. Very often, accordingly, generalizations encountered in the standard legal histories are misleading, confusing, or so thin and vague as to be of little value. Even the best student of the guilds of Florence, Alfred Doren, hardly touched on the Arte dei Giudici e Notai, and rightly so in his scheme of things, as he was almost exclusively interested in the commercial and industrial guilds.

The student may wish to begin with vol. II, i, of the classic work by Antonio Pèrtile, *Storia del diritto italiano dalla caduta dell' Impero Romano fino alla codificazione*, 8 vols. (Torino, 1896-1903); and Carlo Calisse, *Storia del diritto italiano*, 3 vols. (Firenze, 1891). A crisp treatment is Giuseppe Salvioli, *Storia del diritto italiano* (9th ed., Torino, 1930). Useful for purposes of orientation and bibliographical hints is Francesco Calasso, *Medio Evo del diritto* (Milano, 1954). In actually preparing this chapter, I found that of the general studies the following was the most useful: G. Salvioli, *Storia della procedura civile e criminale*, vol. III, i-ii, of the collaborative work, *Storia del diritto italiano*, ed. P. Del Giudice (Milano, 1925-1927). For the period from the eleventh to the thirteenth centuries there is some suggestive background material in Ernst Mayer, *Italienische Verfassungsgeschichte von der Gothenzeit bis zur Zünftherrschaft*, 2 vols. (Leipzig, 1909), I, 99-126. I have been unable to get hold of F. Oesterley, *Das Deutsche Notariat* (Hannover, 1842), part of which (I, ch. IV, 67-355) is devoted to Italy. Particularly good on notaries in the thirteenth century, though entirely with reference to the North Italian communes, is Pietro Torelli, *Studi e ricerche di diplomatica comunale* (Mantova, 1915), published under the auspices of the R. Accademia Virgiliana di Mantova.

Turning specifically to Florence, we find the best pages on the profession and on the guild proper in R. Davidsohn, *Geschichte von Florenz*, IV, ii (Berlin, 1925), 109-25; A. Doren, *Entwicklung und Organisation der Florentiner Zünfte im 13. und 14. Jahrhundert* (Leipzig, 1897), p. 35; Doren, *Le arti fiorentine*, 2 vols., tr. G. B. Klein (Firenze, 1940), *passim*; F.-T. Perrens, *Histoire de Florence*, 6 vols. (Paris, 1877-1880), III, 283-94; G. Salvemini, *Magnati e popolani in Firenze dal 1280 al 1295* (Torino, 1960), pp. 81ff., 119ff., 220ff. An interesting old work is Lorenzo

Cantini, "Dell' ufizio del potestà di Firenze," in his *Saggi storici d'anti-chità toscane*, II (Firenze, 1796), especially good on the duties of the notaries attached to the Podestà. The only pertinent articles on the guild are these: P. Minucci del Rosso, "Curiosità e particolarità del proconsolo dopo la riforma statutaria del 1566," *Rassegna nazionale*, VI (1881), 226-40; Giov. Filippi, "L'Arte dei giudici e notai di Firenze ed il suo statuto del anno 1566," *Giornale ligustico*, XV (1888); Umberto Marchesini, "Dell' età in cui poteva cominciarsi l'esercizio del notariato in Firenze nei sec. xiv-xvi," *Archivio storico italiano*, XV (1895), 92-99. An article with a fetching title and little substance is Luigi Chiappelli, "Firenze e la scienza del diritto nel periodo del Rinascimento," *Archivio giuridico*, XXVIII (1882), 451-86.

The major primary sources for the substantive parts of this chapter are in the guild archives: ASF, *Arte dei Giudici e Notai*, vols. 1-749. A good deal of material is to be found in ASF, *Provvisioni*, the registers and statutes referred to in the notes; ASF, *Statuti di Firenze*, 29 (being the statutes of 1415 with addenda up to 1494); also the *Statuta Populi et Communis Florentiae*, 3 vols. (Friburgi, 1778-1781), esp. II, bk. iv. The guild statutes of 1566 were brought out in a frightful edition by Lorenzo Cantini, *Legislazione toscana*, VI (Firenze, 1803), 171-276. Virtually every page of this edition has the most awful mistakes, which can only be explained by supposing that Cantini hired someone to transcribe the statutes for him and then did not bother to read proofs.

The structure and function of the Florentine guild should not be studied in isolation from the legal profession elsewhere in Italy. In this connection, I shall list the sources which I found most useful. Primary material first: M. E. Andrea Gloria, ed., *Statuti del collegio padovano dei dottori giuristi*, in *Atti del reale istituto veneto di scienze, lettere ed arti*, VII (Nov. 1888–Oct. 1889), 355-402; E. P. Vicini, ed., *Statuta iudicum et advocatorum colegii civitatis mutinae, mcclxx-mcccxxxvii* (Modena, 1935); Fr. Bonaini, ed., *Statuti inediti della città di Pisa*, 3 vols. (Firenze, 1857), esp. the "Breve collegii notariorum, an. mcccv," III, 761-857; *Compendium ordinum, stilatuum et aliarum scripturarum decorem, et splendorem ven. collegii d.d. causidicorum et notariorum mediolani ostendentium* (Milan, 1701); *Statuta venerandi collegii d.d. iudicum civitatis novariae* (Novara,

1513); *Statuta collegii doctorum patriae forijulii edita anno mcccclxxxxvii*, ed. G. Loschi and L. Riva (Udine, 1880). In the way of secondary works, three excellent studies are particularly worthy of mention: M. Roberti, "Il collegio padovano dei dottori giuristi," *Rivista italiana per le scienze giuridiche*, xxv (Torino, 1903), 173ff.; G. M. Monti, "Il collegio napoletano dei dottori in diritto sotto Giovanna I," *Nuovi studi angioni* (Trani, 1937), 469-500; and G. Cencetti, "Il collegio Bolognese dei giudici e avvocati e i suoi statuti del 1393," in a special number of the *Bollettino del consiglio dell' ordine degli avvocati e procuratori di Bologna* (26 Sept. 1957), pp. 16-25. Other studies deal primarily with the guilds of notaries in different parts of Italy but often throw light on the situation in Florence. I particularly recommend the following: L. Cristofoletti, "Cenni storici sull' antico collegio dei notari della città di Verona (1220-1806)," *Archivio Veneto*, xvii-xviii (1878-1879); G. Cosentino, "I notari in Sicilia," *Archivio storico siciliano*, xii (1887), 304-65; M. Roberti, *Le corporazioni padovane d'arti e mestieri* (Venezia, 1902), 157-83. Much too summary and vague is L. Zedkauer, "Sugli statuti dell' arte dei giudici e notai di S. Gimignano (1347-1525)," *Miscellanea storica della Valdelsa*, iv, i (1896), 28-35.

On the history of the Italian notariate: P. Puccinelli, *Della fede e nobiltà del notaio* (Milano, 1654); E. Durando, *Il tabellionato o notariato nelle leggi romane, nelle leggi medievali italiane, e nelle posteriori specialmente piemontesi* (Torino, 1897); Ch. Dejob, *Le notaire en Italie et en France*, offprint from *Miscellanea di studi storici in onore di A. Manno* (Torino, 1912); see also the studies by Oesterley and Torelli listed above. Especially valuable on the notariate in the papal curia are P. M. Baumgarten, *Von der apostolischen Kanzlei* (Köln, 1908); G. Barraclough, *Public Notaries and the Papal Curia* (London, 1934); and A. Petrucci, *Notarii: documenti per la storia del notariato italiano* (Milano, 1958). I have been unable in Italy to find a copy of Pappafava, *Storia del notariato* (1884). The life and work of two famous masters of *notarìa* are treated by A. Palmieri, *Rolandino Passaggeri* (Bologna, 1933); and L. Sighinolfi, "Salatiele e la sua 'ars notariae,'" *Studi e memorie per la storia dell' università di Bologna*, iv (Bologna, 1920), 67-149.

A basic reference work is the new inventory of published statutes: *Catalogo della raccolta di statuti*, brought out in several volumes under the auspices of the Biblioteca del Senato della Repubblica (Roma, 1943 —).

For some other aspects, social and political, touched on in this chapter see the sources for Chs. III, V, IX, and X.

Santi Calleri's book, *L'Arte dei giudici e notai di Firenze nell' età comunale e nel suo statuto del 1344* (Milano, 1966), appeared just as this study was going to press. It provides a partial description, with some extensive quotations, of the guild statutes of 1344. Calleri does not draw on the hundreds of other registers in the guild archives and he offers no analyses which affect the content of this chapter. But his photographic reproductions of many folios of the statutes of 1344 are very handsome.

*Chapter Three*

# Backgrounds and Foregrounds

## *1. Society*

The historian's use of straight biography to get at representative figures has its pitfalls, the most serious being his temptation to become so occupied with individuals that the larger interest, the general flux of things, is lost.

I propose to look at some representative lawyers. But rather than taking a biographical approach, I shall use the method of fixing on "events"—on social backgrounds, schooling, cases, legal fees, and careers. While various aspects of the profession and related matters will be central to the discussion, these will be illustrated by reference to particular lawyers. The representative figures will thus gradually emerge.

Where, as in Renaissance Florence, government is the affair of an oligarchy and so relies to a considerable extent on hereditary privilege and preferment, one of the keys to politics must be a study of social backgrounds, the backgrounds as well of those who run things as of those who realistically aspire to do so. At Florence, in the fifteenth century and later, families like the Ridolfi, Guicciardini, and Soderini owed their good start in politics to birth and the inheritance of place.[1] The political headway of new men—e.g., lawyers like Tommaso Salvetti and Bernardo Buongirolami—was also predicated on birth, though on birth at one remove: they needed the direct backing of great ruling families in order to climb. In this respect the Medici stood out only in that they provided the most effective support.

Florentine lawyers who achieved distinction in public life came, as can be seen in the Appendix, from three social groups: old families, new men (parvenus), and outsiders (families lately come from the Florentine dominion or beyond). The problems connected with each of these are such as to require careful analysis.

---

[1] Owed their good start only, for if in any generation they failed to produce an able statesman, their secondary political importance remained but they had to step down temporarily from the limelight of politics.

The first group in point of political and social importance was the one made up of the old ruling families. Of these the most eminent and influential had attained fortune, power, and place by about 1320. Many came up in the second half of the thirteenth century; a few—like the Acciaiuoli, Cavalcanti, Peruzzi, and Pazzi—went back in their pride to the twelfth century and before. There is a question as to whether or not this first group should include certain families that broke into politics as late as the middle years of the fourteenth century. Three leading families to which this applies are the Martelli, Pandolfini, and Niccolini, who enjoyed high political and social place during the second half of the fifteenth century and thereafter. They produced lawyers of great prominence, most especially the Niccolini, a veritable legal dynasty which gave six doctors of law to Florence between 1425 and 1530.

If we consider these three families around 1400, they look like new men. But if we consider them six or seven decades later, several things induce us to rank them with the old ruling houses: their political influence, marriage alliances, customs, and style. Quite plainly the problem is an artificial one, created by the span of time covered in this study (some 150 years) and by the decision to group Florentine lawyers according to a convenient historical standard. Artificial or not, however, the question raised by the three families has somehow to be settled. We can turn, of course, to the testimony of contemporaries, but it too is problematic, in part because contemporary viewpoints on a matter of this sort could be highly personal. It has just been noted, for example, that by 1460 or 1470 the Niccolini and Pandolfini moved in the circuit of the old ruling families. Yet the historian and lawyer, Francesco Guicciardini, very nearly considered them mere upstarts. Discussing the 1470s in about 1509, he observed that Lorenzo the Magnificent favored men whom he did not have to fear—"men naked of influential relatives and authority, like Messer Bernardo Buongirolami, Antonio di Puccio, and later on Messer Agnolo Niccolini, Bernardo del Nero, Pier Filippo Pandolfini, and the like."[2] Who were these men? Messer Bernardo was a lawyer whose father, also a lawyer, was born in Gubbio, an Umbrian town in the province of Perugia. The elder Buongirolami transferred himself to Flor-

[2] *Storie fiorentine dal 1378 al 1509*, ed. R. Palmarocchi (Bari, 1931), pp. 24-25.

ence about 1410 and obtained Florentine citizenship in 1416. The Buon-girolami were thus a family of outsiders, "naked" of all Florentine traditions, and much in need of backing from one or more of the great old families if they proposed to enter the upper ranks of political society in Florence. Antonio di Puccio and Bernardo del Nero were native Floren-tines but new men, distinctly new. The early Del Nero were second-hand clothes dealers (*rigattieri*) who entered the Signory for the first time in 1382, while the Pucci did not attain a place there until 1396, or dispose of great wealth until three or four decades later. Guicciardini's phrase—"spogliati di parenti e credito"—thus takes on a fuller meaning: by devoid of "credito," he meant individuals without the authority of a family tradition; by devoid of "parenti," men who had no close family ties with any of the city's powerful old houses.

Like their political record, the influence and strategic marriages of the Niccolini and Pandolfini families during the larger part of the fifteenth century seem to speak against ranking Pier Filippo and the lawyer Messer Agnolo with the other men named above. How, therefore, can we explain Francesco Guicciardini's lumping them all together? He descended from one of the best-known of the old ruling families, a fact which filled him with such pride that it is instructive to watch him abandon himself to it.[3] Not only did he consider the Guicciardini one of the city's principal families, he also saw them as fulfilling an historic mission, one intimately connected with the history of Florence from about the time of the *Ciompi* (1378) onward. Acutely aware of being in a long line of men who had helped to shape Florentine destiny, Francesco was determined to do the same, to have a great political career. For these rea-sons, he could not fail to apply only the most rigorous social standards to political figures like Messer Agnolo Niccolini and Pier Filippo Pan-dolfini. He was an oligarch who did not look to the already limited polit-ical class but to an even more restricted group—to the oldest and most dis-tinguished bloc of Florentine families. Neither his pride nor his sense of political right would have allowed him to invest the Niccolini and Pandolfini with honors which he reserved only for families like his own.

[3] *Scritti autobiografici e rari*, ed. Palmarocchi (Bari, 1936), esp. his *Memorie di famiglia*, pp. 3ff.

Francesco was much too involved to be impartial. Yet he was right in one sense, and we may agree with his conclusions without agreeing with his reasons. If the top of the politico-social scale belonged to the Medici, Rucellai, Strozzi, Soderini, Salviati, Guicciardini, and so on, then it is true that families like the Pandolfini and Niccolini came just after. In the Appendix these two families are ranked with the new men. In this group they were in the uppermost tier, along with the Vespucci, Cocchi-Donati, Bonsi, and Carducci, all whom produced prominent lawyers and held a very high place in Florentine political society between about 1470 and 1530.

What is the principle of classification in the Appendix? The dividing line between new and old families is the year 1350. Families are considered old if they made their debut in the Signory before that year, new if after 1350. There are two reasons for putting the dividing line there. The first is that the temporal fulcrum of this study is the middle of the fifteenth century, with some seventy-five years on either side. This is wholly artificial and would have no meaning were it not for the second reason. The period immediately after the Black Death, 1350 or thereabouts, may be seen as a watershed. In the two centuries before, the city saw its greatest period of economic and demographic expansion. After 1350 the rise of new men whose families went on to have a distinguished history was to a large extent arrested, did not again equal, in kind or magnitude, the upward movement which long preceded the Black Death. Interestingly, families that attained high status around 1320 were already considered old stock in the earlier fifteenth century, while others that came up between about 1350 and 1385 were still thought of as "new" more than 100 years later. This curious difference calls for an explanation.

The psychological processes of social assessment were critically affected in the second half of the fifteenth century by the development of a phenomenon which made social standards more rigorous and the upper classes more exigent. Under the influence of more than a generation of Medicean government and in the wake of an economy which no longer raised new men to political consciousness in historical numbers, a particular bloc of families within the circle of ruling families begins to stand

out. They mark themselves for the cardinal place in politics, for the leading diplomatic posts, and are linked by an amazing network of family
and marriage relationships. Often their marriages required special papal
dispensations, owing to close consanguinities. The leaders of this group include the Canigiani, Capponi, Gianfigliazzi, Guicciardini, Ridolfi, Rucellai, Salviati, Soderini, Strozzi, Valori, and Vettori. These are the most
influential families, politically the most alive. They have enough in common to stand out above other ancient families with strong historical
claims, above such names as Altoviti, Corbinelli, Corsini, Davanzati, Della
Stufa, Giugni, Guadagni, Machiavelli, Popoleschi, and others. The first
of these two groups constitutes the upper tier of a new nobility; it is the
core of the old ruling class now "hardening" into a nobility.[4] This internal metamorphosis is what forbids us to complicate further the
boundaries of the old ruling houses by appending to them yet another bloc
of families (e.g., the Niccolini and Pandolfini) with uncertain credentials.
The emergence or, better, the crystallization of a new nobility had the
effect of prolonging the pushy, snobbish, or unpleasant reputation of upstart families in the estimation of noblemen like Francesco Guicciardini.

Of the three social groups supplying Florence with lawyers—old ruling
families, parvenus, and outsiders—it was the first which supplied the
largest number, as well as more than half the ones who achieved the greatest political heights. That these men attained pre-eminence more easily
than other lawyers is entirely understandable. Other things being equal,
they began their careers with superior advantages. Not only were their
direct contacts better and their political eligibility vastly superior, but also
the reputations of their families provided them with an aura of reliability,
which had negotiable value. Among the most important clients of these
lawyers were communal magistracies, monasteries, hospitals, and leading
guilds. Following are mentioned thirteen lawyers of this group.

Giovanni de' Ricci and Filippo Corsini were amazingly active in nearly
all branches of government and diplomacy at the end of the fourteenth
century. Some of their legal opinions have come down to us. Lorenzo
Ridolfi and Bartolommeo Popoleschi, the first a canonist, the second a
civilian, appear and reappear in the executive consultations and diplomatic

---

[4] In light of these observations see also pp. 76, 112, 205, 389-90.

correspondence of the 1390s and the early fifteenth century. The Republic often had recourse to them in matters that required jurisprudential skills. During the 1420s and 1430s, Giuliano Davanzati won great distinction in politics, much more than in the legal profession. Rector of the Italian nation at the University of Bologna in 1416, he was fond of the limelight. Girolamo Machiavelli was a well-known lawyer of the middle decades of the century. He taught civil law at the University of Florence in the late 1430s. Unlike most other Florentine lawyers of his time, he had independent political views which went against the ruling current, and in 1458 he was banished to Avignon for twenty-five years. Then late in 1459 he was declared a rebel and his property confiscated; Vespasiano da Bisticci, the well-known biographer and friend of humanists, was called in, with another stationer, to help estimate the value of the rebel's law books.[5] Very different from Messer Girolamo, at all events in their political perceptions, were Piero Beccanugi and Guglielmo Tanagli, active right through the middle years of the century. Like Giuliano Davanzati, they passed easily, unhurt, and apparently unfluttered, through the *coups d'état* of 1433 and 1434. Did they manage this, as the canonist Lorenzo Ridolfi also did, by holding back from any real commitment to political principle? The question is tendentious. A Florentine could be an exponent of close oligarchy, of a particular line in foreign policy, yet not necessarily fall in with one faction or another. By the end of the fifteenth century, however, certain changes had crept into the nature of political risk. Five eminent lawyers of that era who sprang from old political families were Tommaso Deti, Antonio Strozzi, Niccolò Altoviti, Antonio Malegonnelli, and Francesco Pepi. Deti did some teaching at the University of Florence; all the others taught civil law for a time at the University of Pisa. These five lawyers survived the political tumults of 1494 unscathed, and three of them went on to have brilliant political careers. Had they not compromised themselves with the Medici? They had of course. But so had most other men active in politics; indeed, all the "best" part of the ruling class had been compromised—the cream of the oligarchy. There was therefore no reason to single out lawyers. With the expulsion of the Medici, prominent lawyers were prepared to do penance (like their

[5] ASF, *Capitani di Parte, num. rossi*, 65, f. 109r.

compromised compeers in the rest of society) by taking power themselves.

The fact that the old ruling families brought forth the largest number of lawyers, and among these the ones most likely to make a name for themselves, throws some light on the commonplace observation that historically in Western Europe the legal profession was one of the avenues to riches and rank. Particularly is this supposed to have been true of the late medieval and Renaissance periods. Florence challenges the simple form of this thesis. It challenges the idea that by going into the legal profession a clever man could go from rags to riches and from the meanest to the highest social rank. This did not happen in Florence, nor do I believe, generally speaking, that it happened elsewhere in Italy.

Of the forty-seven lawyers listed in the Appendix under new families, there does not seem to be one of whom it can be definitely said that he both made a fortune and established his family's place in the sun. Now and then one man might do one or the other, but rarely if ever both. The great majority of lawyers listed as new men came from families that had acquired wealth and some political estate one to three generations before there was a lawyer in the household. One of the lawyers whom Francesco Guicciardini considered a man of insignificant social parts, Agnolo Niccolini (d. 1499), had a rich merchant grandfather who held the Republic's highest office five times between 1401 and 1425—a record which none of his contemporaries surpassed. Another lawyer, Virgilio Adriani (d. 1493), was the son of a successful linen manufacturer and the grandson of a wine merchant who entered the Signory in 1395. Bono Boni, who began lecturing on the *Institutes* at Pisa in 1484 and afterward held the ordinary chair in canon law down to the 1520s, came from a family of bankers, money-lenders, and silk merchants. They did not achieve a place in the Signory until 1442. The Bencivenni were for a long time makers and merchants of wool cloth, one as early as the 1330s. Not until 1389 did they get into the Signory, when Salvi di Filippo served as a prior. One of his sons, Messer Alessandro (d. 1423), obtained a doctorate in civil law at Bologna in 1411, returned to practice law in Florence and to conduct, eventually, a series of important diplomatic missions. Another family of new men, the Bonsi, gave two lawyers to the city: Domenico (d. 1502), a pre-eminent political figure, and Antonio (fl.

1518), who lectured at Pisa on the *Institutes* between 1515 and 1518. Their great-grandfather, Ugolino Bonsi, plied the trade of the sword-maker and was the first, in 1364, to represent the family in the Signory. The lawyers Baldassare Carducci, Bartolommeo Ciai, Puccio Pucci, and two Cocchi-Donati were also born into families whose wealth and rising political fortunes preceded any connection with the legal profession by one to three generations—more often three.

Eight lawyers from new families were the sons of notaries. The observation has its interest for the reason that, owing to their proximity to lawyers, notaries were the one group capable of producing men who might use the law for the purpose of rising to positions of great prominence. Yet even so we tend to find remarkable advantages or a thorough "preparation," economic and social, behind the sons of notaries who took degrees in law and then went on to practice or to seek a name in politics. Giovanni Serristori's father, grandfather, and great-grandfather were all notaries. In the second half of the fourteenth century the family gradually came into an enormous fortune. Ser Ristoro, Giovanni's father, was the first member of the family to appear in the Signory (1383). Giovanni himself obtained a doctorate in civil law at Bologna in 1397. The Viviani and Guidi families also exemplify the point that money, rank, or some other advantage tended to precede a family's decision to send a son to law school, even when his father was a notary. Francesco Viviani's father, a leading notary, was one of the two senior secretaries in the Florentine chancellery during the period 1378 to 1414. Actually a branch of an old county family (Franchi da Sambuco), the Viviani were first represented in the Signory in 1393. Francesco obtained his doctorate at Bologna in 1407. The Guidi were a different sort but still well connected. Three generations or more of notaries stood behind Messer Bartolommeo Guidi, who took his doctorate in civil law at Pisa about 1489. Ser Giovanni, his father, the first member of the family to sit in the Signory (1471), seems to have been a protégé of Lorenzo the Magnificent. He was proconsul of the guild when his son was received into it as a member of the college of lawyers. Two other lawyers who came from a line of prosperous notaries were Grifo Grifi (fl. 1395) and Domenico Sermini (fl. 1400); neither achieved any political distinction.

It seems obvious, yet it is very frequently forgotten, that to follow a full course of study at one of the great law schools was an expensive affair. There will be reason later on in this chapter to say something about the actual costs. Here it need only be observed that keeping a youth in law school for five to eight years required the backing of a well-to-do family. The custom of many business and banking families of Florence—where manufacture, trade, and money-lending were the normal means of amassing wealth—was to use the labor and diligence of all the males in the family firm. Ordinarily, the up-and-coming family did not much relish the idea of having one of their members go off to study law for a half dozen years or more: he was needed in the counting house. This was more likely to be the case once the family had established itself; and even then a student from such a household might, while still in law school, look after some aspect of the family enterprises. As a practicing lawyer, he might continue to devote some of his time to commercial affairs in company with his father and brothers.[6]

If now and then notaries sent their sons to law school at an earlier stage in the family history than was done in other families, it is also true that they had a more intimate contact with both lawyers and the world of the law courts. The importance of this type of contact in late medieval and early-modern Europe—of one's having a direct and close view of an occupation or profession before going into it—has seldom been fully appreciated. The corporate nature of society in the cities was against the easy movement of men into economic pursuits far from those of their forebears.[7] Men were most likely to follow the art, business, or profession of their fathers—or an allied pursuit. Thus a notary was much more apt to send a son to law school than was a wealthy hosier, even if the latter's family had been hosiers for generations. But hosier, butcher, baker, or craftsman, there was a certain pattern to things. First a man moved from one of the lowlier trades to one where he handled textiles, spices, or banking deposits. Or, having piled up real estate, he might simply live off his lands. Only then were the social contacts of his family

---

[6] E.g., ASF, *Carte del Bene*, 37 (*Ricordanze* of Messer Ricciardo del Bene); *Strozz.*, *2a ser.*, 23 (*Ricordanze* of Messer Giovanni Buongirolami).

[7] Excepting, of course, the priestly vocation.

on their way to becoming "honorable" enough for one of the sons or grandsons to point toward a career in law. What else can we make of the fact that of nearly 200 jurists listed in the Appendix, only three seem to have been born into families associated with one of the humbler trades: Marco di Cenno (fl. 1380s), son of a rich innkeeper; Bartolommeo Scala (1428-1497), a miller's son; and Giovanni Battista Gamberelli (1434-1513), often called "del Lastraiuolo," indicating that his father dealt in stone for paving surfaces such as roofs and roads.

We should resist any tendency on our part to confuse modern social phenomena with what took place in the world of Renaissance Europe. On occasion the Church may have provided a surer way up for new men, though less often, I believe, than we sometimes imagine. And anyway, clerics were not normally the founders or social improvers of their families. The Church was in contact with all levels of the urban population, and its hands could reach out to draw up even the lowliest of men. But when it was a question of going to law school for a half-dozen or more years, of a long preparation with a view to moving in a world which would include great merchant-bankers, ecclesiastical dignitaries, princes, or statesmen, we can expect that the aspiring lawyer either had some direct contact with the profession or had grown up in a household where the material ease was such that he could select his dignified pursuit at will. Now and then someone without this background might have the help of a rich or influential patron. But even as a protégé of Lorenzo the Magnificent, Bartolommeo Scala, son of a miller, was the wonder of men, and his origins provided an easy handle for his enemies and detractors.

The attitude of the old ruling families toward lawyers and law schools was flattering to the profession. A career in law was "grand" enough to reflect or even gild the honor of the Acciaiuoli, Corsini, Guicciardini, Ridolfi, Soderini, and Strozzi families. They all produced extremely able lawyers. What, then, was the precise social relationship of new men to the legal profession? This has already been implied. The law served to finish or round off newly acquired status. First you attained your place, then you looked to securing it, making it more attractive, heightening its effect. A well-appointed marriage, an outstanding

office in Church or state, a doctorate in civil or canon law: these served
to solidify place, to give the family its final touches or the man his
cachet. But the law was not only decorative, it was also useful: it opened
the way to ecclesiastical honors for men from even the greatest families
and brought exalted political place within reach. Especially was this true
of ambassadorial appointments, where the dignity of the doctorate and
skill of the jurist were often explicit requirements.

The instrumental quality of a legal education is what made politics
an easier sphere for "foreign" lawyers to penetrate than for other men from
outside Florence or even from lands beyond Florentine rule. I list more
than fifty such lawyers in the Appendix. Some sixty per cent of these men
—or their fathers—were born in Florentine territory, e.g., Prato, Arezzo,
San Gimignano, Pistoia, Volterra, and some of the lesser towns. The
others came from cities and towns beyond the boundaries of the Republic: one each from Rome, Milan, Lucca, Ferrara and other places;
three from the Marches, six from Perugia, and another six from the
province of Perugia. A large number of these outsiders were the sons
of lawyers; many hailed from noble or old county families; a few were the
sons of notaries and medical men. In some cases they were political
exiles, in others they had gone to Florence to teach or to give legal
counsel, in still others they were the sons of men who had settled there.
Guaspare Accorambuoni (b. 1381) provides a good case study.[8] His father,
Ludovico di Bartolo, taught medicine at the University of Florence from
1365 on, lecturing mostly on Galen. A noble family from Gubbio (near
Perugia), the Accorambuoni furnished Florence with a number of
foreign magistrats in the course of the fourteenth century. One of
Guaspare's brothers, Bartolommeo, taught medicine at the university from
1402 on; another, Ser Jacopo, became a notary. That the family connections in Florence were remarkable is confirmed by the fact that in 1405
the Signory solicited a benefice for Guaspare up to the value of 300 gold
florins. Called a "florentine cleric," he was then a student at the University. He had not, however, taken final vows, for in April 1406 he was
awarded the doctorate in *utroque iure* and a few months later was of-

---

[8] Ensuing material from ASF, *AGN*, 101, f. 15r; *SCMLC*, 9, f. 34v; *Strozz.*, *3a
ser.*, 4, ff. 40r, 92r, 94r, 94v, 129v, 130v; A. Gherardi, ed., *Statuti della università e
studio fiorentino*, docs. 182, 341, 384.

ficially received into the guild. Thereafter, Guaspare divided his time between an active legal practice and the teaching of canon law at the University of Florence, where he lectured in 1413-1415, 1423-1424, and possibly—since the *Studio* documents are incomplete—in other years as well.

One of Guaspare's brilliant colleagues, Nello di Giuliano Martini (b. 1373), was a Cetti of San Gimignano, one of that hill town's richest families. Passing his doctoral examination at Bologna with great distinction, he took his degree in 1398 and then moved to Florence, where he practiced law very successfully, became a leading diplomatist of the period 1410-1430, and on occasion professed law at the University.[9] Ludovico Albergotti (d. 1398), Torello Torelli (fl. 1385-1415), Buonaccorso da Montemagno (*ca.* 1392-1429), and Bernardo Buongirolami (fl. 1450-1480) were sons of lawyers and all lent their services to the Florentine Republic. Though none could lay claim to Florentine traditions, they all attained some public distinction, the first three in diplomacy, the fourth, Buongirolami, in domestic politics.

The question arises of how to explain the presence of so many outsiders among the lawyers in the guild. Owing to lacunae in the guild records, it is not possible to say how many outside lawyers came to Florence to practice law in the two or three decades following the Black Death of 1348. But the figures at hand indicate that there was a shortage of lawyers in Florence during the second half of the fourteenth century and up to about the 1430s. Taking the span of time covered by this study and dividing it into three fifty-year periods, I found that the number of outside lawyers active in Florence fell off as follows:[10]

$$
\begin{array}{ll}
1380\text{--}1430\text{:} & 22 \text{ outsiders} \\
1430\text{--}1480\text{:} & 18 \\
1480\text{--}1530\text{:} & 7
\end{array}
$$

[9] On Cetti family, Enrico Fiumi, *Storia economica e sociale di San Gimignano* (Firenze, 1961), pp. 248-49; on Messer Nello, *Il Liber secretus*, ed. A. Sorbelli, 2 vols. (Bologna, 1938-42), i, 117, 121. Diplomatic correspondence of period replete with his activity and movements.

[10] A valid comparison between the three periods required that the figure for 1380-1430 exclude lawyers who were active before 1380, even if they were also active thereafter.

These figures may not include every outsider who practiced as an advocate or jurisconsult, but they are very nearly conclusive so far as the guild is concerned. There is no reason to believe that legal practice outside the guild was heavier in the early sixteenth century than in the second half of the fourteenth. The trend, therefore, is clear. What was the reason for the decline? It is likely that Florence became less and less hospitable to non-Florentine lawyers as the number coming from the city proper increased. Already by about 1500 the city may have had an over-abundance of lawyers, for, speaking of the period around 1507, Francesco Guicciardini rather commended himself on his early professional success, considering the large number of *legum doctores* in Florence.[11]

There is conclusive evidence to show that lawyers who came from outside Florence had very much the same sorts of background as lawyers whose great-grandfathers or more remote ancestors were citizens of Florence. Professional or landed families, houses of solid merchants or manufacturers or bankers, old county families, and not rarely the old nobility —all at least "respectable" and some very "grand"—produced the vast majority of lawyers who practiced in Florence between about 1380 and 1530. Recruitment for politics and public affairs was more restricted. With some exceptions, seen mainly in the field of diplomacy, lawyers from the old ruling families went furthest, were the ones most likely to attain the greatest influence and win the supreme political prizes. Lorenzo Ridolfi (1362-1443), Giuliano Davanzati (1390-1446), Francesco Gualterotti (1456-1509), Antonio Malegonnelli (1451-1506), and Francesco Guicciardini (1483-1540) are perfect examples of this type. The second best set of political credentials was that of lawyers who came from the *fior fiore* or cream of the newer families, that is, the oldest, wealthiest, and best-connected of the parvenus. This seems schematic, I know, but there it is. The exemplars of this type were Domenico Bonsi (1430-1502), Guidantonio Vespucci (1437-1501), and Baldassare Carducci (1458-1530).

In the foregoing review of social backgrounds, I have called attention to elements of variety as well as uniformity, to stability as well as change. On the subject of change, it has been shown that in the course of the fifteenth

[11] In his *Ricordanze*, in *Scritti autobiografici*, p. 57.

century there was a marked decline in the number of foreign lawyers admitted to practice in Florence. We have also seen the emergence of a nobility from the ranks of the old ruling families, a change which had the effect of raising the social premium on the law doctorate. Let us now pursue this change with figures and with speculation. Following is a breakdown of active indigenous lawyers during the three fifty-year periods mentioned above:[12]

| *from new families* | *from old ruling families* |
|---|---|
| 1380–1430: 11 lawyers | 1380–1430: 13 lawyers |
| 1430–1480: 11 | 1430–1480: 14 |
| 1480–1530: 14 | 1480–1530: 32 |

It is best not to make much of the small increase in lawyers from new families. But the increase registered by the old families during the third period was truly remarkable. I hesitate to use the word *crisis*; yet if the jump after 1480 is combined with another factor, it may suggest that the upper classes faced a critical time. The other factor centered on a process of social contraction. In the second half of the fifteenth century, Florence began for the first time to reveal a tendency toward the formation of "dynasties" of lawyers. Only two native lawyers of the first period (1380–1430) were sons of lawyers, Filippo Corsini and Tommaso Marchi. In the second period the same was true of Antonio de' Cocchi-Donati and Agnolo Niccolini; but the third period (1480-1530) witnessed six cases of sons who followed their fathers into the legal profession—cases involving the Aldobrandini, Bonsi, Deti, Gualterotti, Malegonnelli, and Niccolini families, the last of which claimed four generations of lawyers by 1530. Closely connected with this phenomenon was the appearance for the first time, again during the third period, of a number of series of two or more contemporary lawyers from the same family groups— brothers or cousins, more often cousins. This new turn was revealed by the Acciaiuoli, Altoviti, Guicciardini, Niccolini, Rucellai, Soderini, and Strozzi families. One of the brothers involved, Francesco Soderini (b. 1453), taught civil and canon law at Pisa in his youth, then plunged into an ecclesiastical career, becoming a bishop and finally a cardinal.

---

[12] Excludes lawyers active before 1380, even if active thereafter.

Another jurist who turned to a career in the Church was one of the cousins involved—Roberto di Carlo Strozzi, who professed canon law at Pisa in the 1480s and was contemporaneously vicar general of the archdiocese of Pisa.[13]

The question remains, how to explain the proliferation of jurists from old ruling families during the period 1480 to 1530. The law not only conferred honor and standing on new families, it also helped to keep up the public image of illustrious old houses: this in a time when the governing class itself was beset by a new wave of invidious distinctions, a wave brought on by the emergence of a nobility. The economic order of things was a factor in this transformation. No longer—as we noted in the previous chapter—was there an ascent of new Florentine merchants and manufacturers in historical numbers—numbers large enough to affect the course of change. Manufacture and trade took on a slower tempo. The state was racked by debt—had been so for many decades. And rich citizens insisted on their pound of flesh—on substantial returns from their investments in the government Monte (the funded debt). Public finance, moreover, had an effect on economic conditions: taxes affecting trade and industry went up. We must suppose that faith in new business enterprise declined. At the end of the century, finally, the threat to the Florentine economy was greatly increased by the French invasion and the Republic's loss of Pisa. This threat was perpetuated by the Italian wars, as well as by the adverse commercial pressure of papal and Venetian foreign policy.

It was a natural outcome of the uncertain economic situation in Florence that those who were able to in some cases turned to the legal profession. The law offered more than mere security: with the right connections, it was a guarantee of a high level of material comfort. The rewards were those of the Church or politics, so that the inducement to study law must have been particularly strong for men from the old ruling families: they had the connections and could easily "cash in" on them. From this viewpoint the specific field of activity mattered little, whether it was advocating and counselling, an academic career, the Church, or politics. In all these fields the advantage was with the lawyers

[13] On Strozzi, ASF, *NA*, R242, ff. 8v, 166r. His doctorate *in utroque iure*.

who had the support of a powerful family, of a strong man, of a group or faction at the helm of things.

To illustrate the new attraction of the law for men of a certain social type, let us look for a moment at Francesco Pepi (1451-1513), whose family had a name by 1260 and was first represented in the Signory in 1301. His mother was a Salviati, whom Guicciardini put in the first rank of the old ruling families. A pre-eminent lawyer and statesman of the 1490s and later, Francesco was haunted by the desire to have one of his direct descendants go to law school, work for the doctorate, and follow him in the profession. The desire was enunciated in his last will and testament,[14] where one of the clauses stipulates that his library of law books was to pass to his only son if and when the youth was awarded the doctorate. Otherwise, the library was to be held intact until such time as this degree was conferred on one of his grandsons or more remote lineal decendants. There is a touching insistence in this part of the will. The testator had made a name for himself in law, politics, and the academic world. He professed civil law at the University of Pisa in the 1480s and 1490s, remaining with the faculty after 1494, when the university was temporarily moved to Prato. During the academic year 1500-1501, his professorial salary of 500 gold florins was second only to that of the renowned Milanese jurist, Filippo Decio. We shall never know precisely what Francesco Pepi's private reasons were for ardently desiring to have one of his descendants succeed him in the profession. Probably there was a good deal of professional pride in the desire. But the ensemble of forces that gives historical meaning to Francesco's urgent wish derived, as we have already suggested, from the new stresses in Florentine social and economic life. In this connection, it does not seem beside the point to observe that a salary of 500 gold florins per annum was little less than half the average yearly profit of the Florentine branch of the Medici bank during one of its best periods—1420 to 1435.[15] Speak-

---

[14] *NA*, V154, ff. 73r-79v, 103r-08v. Two versions of will, for 1505 and 1512.

[15] Raymond de Roover, *The Rise and Decline of the Medici Bank, 1397-1494* (Harvard, 1963), p. 55. The average yearly profit of this branch in those years was 1,188 florins. Although the difference of seventy years matters little, a precise comparison would call for an adjustment of some sort. In the 1490s and after, salaries at the Studio were paid out on the basis of 4.00 lire per large gold florin.

ing of the middle of the fifteenth century, which he considered an opulent time for Florentine merchants, Guicciardini noted with admiration that one of his great uncles made 11,000 ducats in the silk trade during a period of twenty years. Francesco Pepi, accordingly, had done well. For his university salary was supplemented by his earnings as an ambassador and practicing lawyer. During periods when he served the Republic, whether on embassies or other official business, he received his professorial stipend in full.[16]

## 2. *School*

Latin was the linguistic basis of all subjects in the university curriculum. Through it alone could a man acquire a technical knowledge of the law, and he certainly could not practice without it. Lectures, legal commentaries, examinations, formal legal opinions—all were given in Latin, the language of the two codes of law, civil and canon. Hence the first step for anyone aiming at a career in law was to learn what the Middle Ages and Renaissance called *grammatica*.

Throughout most of the Middle Ages there were various kinds of Church schools in Europe. In Italy these went through a period of decline during the fourteenth and fifteenth centuries, just at the time the initiative in education seemed to pass to lay grammar schools and teachers.[17] Florence and other Italian cities had private grammar schools by 1300, specialized in the instruction of Latin grammar. Giovanni Villani said that in the 1330s some 8,000 to 10,000 boys and girls were learning to read. From 1,000 to 1,200 boys studied arithmetic and accounting (*l'abbaco*) in six schools, while another 550 to 600 were enrolled "in four great schools" devoted to the teaching of grammar and logic.[18]

There was also another system of lay instruction—that of the private tutor, widely used by the upper classes. A tutor either lived in, which is what the great houses encouraged, or he had students come to his own

---

[16] ASF, *UDS*, 6, ff. 60v, 65v, 72v.

[17] G. Manacorda, *Storia della scuola in Italia*, I, 149-54, 299; on Florence proper see C. T. Davis, "Education in Dante's Florence," *Speculum*, XL, 3 (1965), 415-35, where the stress is on the influence of religious schools.

[18] *Cronica* (ed., 1844-45), III, 324.

house. The children of the Albizzi, Medici, Niccolini, Strozzi, and others were taught by men who were given a stipend, as well as room and board in the family *palazzo*. Even a poor old noble family like the Rustichi—much humbled in the Quattrocento world—could afford to keep a private tutor who, however, was given only clothing apart from room and board. Machiavelli's father could not afford to keep one, and young Niccolò was sent first to a *maestro* Matteo, at the foot of the Santa Trinità bridge (a hundred meters or so from the old Machiavelli houses), then to the notary Ser Battista da Poppi. Francesco Guicciardini's Latin master was also a notary, Ser Giovanni dalla Castellina, who lived with the Guicciardini and taught grammar not only to Francesco but to all his brothers.[19]

The elementary grammatical texts were those of Donatus and Priscianus, chiefly the former. Having learned the fundamentals of Latin, the student then moved on to the elements of letter-writing and style. The study of rhetoric came last and in its more advanced phases was a university subject. During the thirteenth and fourteenth centuries, at the University of Bologna, rhetoric was normally taught by a notary of some renown. But in the fifteenth century and after, in Florence as in Bologna, the professorships of rhetoric usually went to humanists.

If candidates for the notariate were required to have studied Latin for at least three or four years, we can be sure that aspiring lawyers had to exhibit a superior preparation. Ordinarily, boys started Latin at the age of six or seven. Machiavelli was sent to Master Matteo when he was seven. But a child might begin learning to read—presumably in the vernacular—at four years. In a letter of 1470, we find Bartolommea di Tommaso Corbinelli, wife of a leading lawyer and diplomat, reminding her husband that their son Jacopo (age four) should start to learn to read.[20] At the age of twelve one of Jacopo's brothers, Girolamo, was reading Virgil, Sallust, and the letters of Ovid. With the help of his tutor, he was then going on to study Juvenal, though his father also wished him

[19] On the Rustichi item see the *Ricordanze* (1412-36) of Antonio Rustichi, *Strozz.*, 2a ser., xi; Bernardo Machiavelli, *Libro di ricordi*, ed. C. Olschki (Firenze, 1954), pp. 31, 70; Guicciardini, *Ricordanze*, p. 60.

[20] G. Niccolini di Camugliano, *The Chronicles of a Florentine Family, 1200-1470* (London, 1933), pp. 185-86, 332. Her husband was the Medicean *seguace*, Messer Otto di Lapo Niccolini.

to start in on Cicero's orations. When we read, therefore, that Giovanni di Lorenzo de' Medici (the future Leo X) was awarded the doctorate in canon law at the age of thirteen,[21] if we are surprised or amused, it is not because his grammatical preparation may have been inadequate so far as the law was concerned (in all probability it was good enough!), but because one cannot believe that he could have been competent to render a mature legal opinion, which after all is what the doctorate implied.

By the time a young man went to the university he was expected to have a full command of Latin. The practice in Florence was to send men to law school between the ages of sixteen and eighteen. A jurist of the fourteenth century, Donato Velluti, was sent to Bologna to study when he was not yet sixteen years old. Francesco Guicciardini was sixteen and a half when he attended his first university lectures in November 1498. Giovanni Niccolini was seventeen when it was recommended that he be sent to the University of Perugia.

It is not known precisely what the conditions for admission were at the various Italian universities. Stelling-Michaud has noted that "law students at Bologna were masters of arts or possessed at least a sufficient preparation in grammar, logic, rhetoric and dialectic to begin the study of the texts of Justinian and the *Decretals*."[22] Though it must have happened sometimes, I have found no evidence that it was the custom of Florentines to take an advanced degree in arts before going on to law school. What does come through is the fact that apart from grammar they studied some logic and rhetoric, and now and then some philosophy or, in the fifteenth century and later, even Greek. On entering the University of Bologna in 1329, Donato Velluti's preparation was in Latin and logic only. Up to the time he entered law school, Francesco Guicciardini studied Latin, a little Greek, a little logic, "cose di umanità" (i.e.,

---

[21] In 1488. Giovanni Prezziner, *Storia del pubblico studio e delle società scientifiche e letterarie di Firenze*, 2 vols. (Firenze, 1810), I, 166. The examiners who lent themselves to this entertainment were two lawyers very prominent in public life, Domenico Bonsi and Agnolo Niccolini, whom Lorenzo had in his pocket. Yet Bonsi passed over with great sparkle into the politics of the Savonarola period, while Niccolini made his comeback early in 1497.

[22] *L'Université de Bologne et la pénétration des droits romain et canonique en Suisse aux xiii⁰ et xiv⁰ siècles* (Geneva, 1955), p. 66.

rhetoric, history, and some poetry), arithmetic, and accounting.[23] Hence he cannot be said to have had the rudiments of a legal vocabulary when he started his university studies. A good Latin master was usually prepared to teach the fundamentals of rhetoric and logic. Some of the elements of law, or a legal vocabulary, could be learned from a well-trained notary who happened to teach part-time. For those who took advantage of it, this background of study gave Florentines and other Italians a good enough preparation for their first encounters with the *Digest* and Gratian's *Decretum*.

The Appendix shows that most Florentine lawyers took their degrees from two universities: before 1473 from Bologna, thereafter from Pisa or, for some years after 1494, from the Studio Pisano of Prato-Florence. Next in number were degrees from the universities of Perugia and Florence. There were a few Florentine lawyers with degrees from Ferrara, Siena, Padua, and Pavia. Many Florentines began their formal legal study in Florence but usually finished up somewhere else, not only because the law faculty of the Studio Fiorentino had no great reputation but also because the Studio always had an unsteady existence and on occasion was closed down altogether. The main difficulty was financial, as when the government used the funds of the Studio for military expenses.[24] But with the setting up of the Studio Pisano in 1473, the Republic's academic aims and performance were taken much more seriously, and a law was enacted forbidding Florentine citizens and subjects from studying law anywhere else than Pisa. The Florentine loss of Pisa in 1494 necessitated a reconstitution of the Studio in Florence and Prato, so that for some years there ensued another period of unsteadiness. Not until 1509 did Pisa return to Florentine hands.

The great majority of Florentine lawyers pursued their legal studies through to the doctorate: if in canon law, this normally meant six years of university; if in civil law, seven or eight years, depending on the time and place.[25] But as the first of these degrees could be got rather easily

---

[23] *Ricordanze*, pp. 53-54; on Velluti see his *Cronica domestica*, ed I. del Lungo and G. Volpi (Firenze, 1914), p. 157.

[24] Gherardi, ed., *Statuti*, p. 205.

[25] The statutes of the Studio Fiorentino stipulated eight years, but doctoral exam-

by civilians who took the "ordinary" courses in canon law and passed the requisite examinations, a very large number of Florentine lawyers had doctorates *in utroque iure*—that is, in both civil and canon law. Theoretically, as some historians have shown,[26] it took a minimum of ten years to complete the work for the double doctorate; but there were ways of lopping off requirements, bringing the minimum down to about eight or nine years. The basic courses in civil law could be completed in about five years, those in canon law—dealing with the *Decretals*, the *Decretum*, the *Sextus* and *Clementines*—in something like three. Each of the two degrees also required that the candidate teach for a year or conduct some "repetitions" and public disputations; but here again it was possible in some cases to skip these requirements. I suspect—although it would be difficult to prove—that the usual way of doing this at Bologna was to provide the College of Doctors of Law with a good face-saving excuse, followed up by a generous donation of money in the right places. A jurist from one of the great new families of Florence, Donato de' Cocchi-Donati (1409-1464), was allowed to take the examination for the licentiate in civil law at Bologna, "despite the fact that he had neither repeated nor disputed." Some three weeks later, on January 10, 1438, because "of pressing and necessary reasons," he was privately examined for a degree—the doctorate—which could ordinarily only be conferred on the basis of a public examination called the *conventus* or *conventatio*. Donato had thus been twice indulged. Interestingly, he was at that time rector of the Italian nation at the university (a most expensive dignity to hold) and was given the foregoing dispensations by the College of Doctors of Law and the Archdeacon of Bologna.[27]

All lawyers in the guild had studied at least five years at a university. This and a satisfactory performance in an examination were two of the requirements for matriculation among the guild's advocates and jurisconsults. Eventually the examination was waived for men with the

---

inations could be taken six months before. At Padua in the fourteenth century the doctorate in civil law could be awarded after six years.

[26] Stelling-Michaud, *L'Université de Bologne*, p. 67; H. Rashdall, *The Universities of Europe in the Middle Ages*, 3 vols., ed. Powicke and Emden (Oxford, 1936), I, 220-21.

[27] *Liber secretus*, II, 160.

doctorate. In five years of study a man took the basic law courses; that is, he heard all the ordinary lectures in his field. If, moreover, he had publicly discussed in some detail a legal point raised in one of the ordinary lectures, he was entitled to receive the baccalaureate, a degree which had neither the importance nor the precise delimitations of a bachelor's degree today. The most difficult degree to obtain was the *licentia docendi*; it came just before the doctorate and conferred the right to teach. The right to practice law had already been earned by the five years of university attendance and matriculation in the guild. We shall presently review the requirements for the licentiate and doctorate. For the moment let us note that the distinction between these two degrees was mainly ceremonial. Some men who prepared for the law went only as far as the *licentia*, owing to the heavy costs connected with the ceremonies for the doctorate. The professional value of these degrees may be gauged from the fact that the most responsible and lucrative judgeships in Florentine territory required the doctorate or license. Furthermore, the most important litigation between states, or between private individuals who could afford to pay, was always referred to *legum doctores*, often to a whole college of doctors, whether at Florence, Perugia, Bologna, or elsewhere.

The succeeding pages will apply primarily to the University of Bologna in the fourteenth and fifteenth centuries. For until the second half of the fifteenth century Bologna not only attracted the best professors and students of law, it also served as the model for the universities of Florence, Perugia, Ferrara, and other *studi generali*.

The doctorate in civil or canon law could be taken at the age of twenty, not before, save by special dispensation. This meant that students occasionally began their university studies at thirteen or fourteen. Most often, however, the doctorate was conferred on men in their middle and later twenties or older. The first thing a student did on arrival at the university was to pay his fees and have himself formally entered in the student rolls. He then selected his major professor (his *magister regens*) and attended this man's ordinary lectures, as well as the occasional recitations or lessons offered by the bachelors who supplemented the master's instruction. The most elementary legal manuals were two:

*De verborum significatione* and *De regulis iuris,* "which constituted the point of departure for the study of law."[28] These manuals supplied students with a nomenclature and introduced them to first rules. The rich student swiftly acquired the basic texts of the Roman or canon law or both. His poorer colleagues copied their own or were more careful about taking fuller notes in class. How full might these notes be? We can get an idea of this by observing that lectures entailed, among other things, a recitation of the laws or titles under discussion. Legal commentaries and *consilia legalia* were also widely consulted and hence collected—copied by the collector or eventually purchased from stationers, copyists, or from other lawyers. It was thus most common for practicing lawyers to have invested from 200 to 300 gold florins in law books, and we often find estimates reaching up to 600 and 1,000 florins.[29] Nevertheless, one comes on odd cases of prominent lawyers who either did not have the basic texts at hand or had them only in corrupt versions. In August 1480, Machiavelli's father, Messer Bernardo, lent his copies of the *New Digest* and the first nine books of the *Code* to Tommaso Deti, a well-known lawyer then attached to the Tower Officials (Ufficiali della Torre). Deti wished to consult these texts "on material concerning rebels."[30]

Having settled on his major professor, the law student faced five to eight years of study. There were ordinary and extraordinary courses, which seem to have corresponded partly to a somewhat arbitrary division between the basic and less basic parts of the civil and canon laws. The chief requirement laid on students was frequenting the ordinary courses. During the fourteenth century this meant, in the field of civil law, the lectures and special classes on the *Old Digest* and *Code.*[31] The

---

[28] A. Sorbelli, *Storia della università di Bologna: il medioevo,* 2 vols. (Bologna, 1940), I, 87.

[29] Best seen in tax returns for the *catasto* of 1427. E.g., *Catasto,* 66, f. 76v; 68, f. 81r-v; 69, ff. 45r, 250r, 584v; 79, f. 214v; 81, f. 430v, 481v; also L. Martines, "The career and library of a 15th-century lawyer," *Annali di storia del diritto,* III-IV (1959-60), 331-32.

[30] Bernardo Machiavelli, *Ricordi,* p. 116.

[31] The *Corpus Iuris Civilis* had four major parts: the *Digest* or *Pandects,* the *Code,* the *Institutes,* and the *Novels.* Jurists of the medieval and Renaissance periods divided the fifty books of the *Digest* into three parts: the *Old Digest,* the *Infortiatum,* and the *New Digest.* The twelve books of the *Code* were also divided: the first nine were known as the *Codico* or *Code,* the last three as the *Tres Libri* (*Three Books*).

extraordinary courses treated the *Infortiatum*, the *New Digest*, and later on the *Volumen*. Included in the *Volumen* were the *Institutes*, the *Novels* (or *Authentics*), the *Libri Feudorum* (a Lombard collection of laws), and the *Three Books* (Books x to xii of the *Code*).[32] In the fifteenth century the *New Digest* was added to the program of ordinary courses and the *Infortiatum* had to be treated contemporaneously with the *Code*.

At the beginning of the fourteenth century, the student of canon law was compelled to attend two series of ordinary lectures and lessons: one dealing with Gratian's *Decretum*, the other with the *Decretals* of Gregory IX. The extraordinary place on the canonical syllabus was held by the *Liber Sextus* (introduced in 1298) and the *Clementines* (1313). Less important was the fifth part of the *Corpus Iuris Canonici*, the so-called *Extravagants*, brought in by Pope John XXII in 1317. In the course of the fourteenth century, the *Liber Sextus* was given ordinary status at the universities of Bologna, Florence, and elsewhere. Bologna and Pisa had ordinary lectures both in the mornings and afternoons, though in the afternoons there tended to be a greater concentration on the extraordinary subject matter. Evenings, the hours from about 6:00 to 9:00, were set aside chiefly for special lessons and exercises such as repetitions.

Some professors wrote their lectures out in full; others preferred a more spontaneous approach. The method of instruction tended to be rigorous, sometimes schematic. A lecture might begin with a summary of the laws or titles[33] to be treated, carefully calling attention to the type or types of subject matter under consideration. This was followed by a recitation of the text, together with a grammatical commentary and corrections. Another summary might be presented at this point. Last of all came the analysis: here the lecturer raised the major problems presented by the text, pointed out the leading arguments on each side, and then solved the apparent contradictions. It was during his review of the problems that the lecturer was compelled, sometimes by university statute,

[32] According to Sorbelli, *Storia*, 1, 236, the study of the *Novels*, the *Institutes*, and the *Libri Feudorum*—three of the four parts of the *Volumen*—was not introduced at Bologna until the fifteenth century. Yet Donato Barbadori was already lecturing on the *Volumen* at Florence in the 1360s. Gherardi, ed., *Statuti*, p. 315.

[33] Titles: subdivisions of books of the *Digest*, *Code*, *Decretals*, etc.

to bring forth the apposite glosses and commentaries of the great thir-
teenth- and fourteenth-century jurists. Holders of the ordinary professorial chairs normally began the year (about October 10th) with some
*praelectiones*—lectures that introduced students to the more general
aspects of the work to be studied (the *Old Digest*, the *Decretum*, or
whatever) and discussed its major divisions. A most important adjunct
to the lectures were the *repetitiones*, which every ordinary professor was
expected to offer, usually about once a week, though for only part of
the year. The repetition was an exercise in analysis. Taking a specific
law or a difficult point of law from a book already treated in class, the
instructor brought out all the problems of the text in question, enumerated against it all possible objections, and then refuted these. We can see
here the use of the *pro-contra* method of argument. Still another aspect
of instruction concerned the disputations, held in the spring and summer.
The disputation was in part a public debate. Giving notice of his subject six or seven days beforehand, the instructor or one of the *laureandi*
selected a suitable topic and discussed it according to the *pro-contra*
method. His purpose was both to exemplify a technique and to provide
solutions. There was something of the *repetitio* in this, save that in the
disputation the technique of argument was much more pointed up and
the debate was an open one. Students were encouraged to raise objections, the disputant obliged to answer them.

When—after six or seven years of study—the student girded himself
to come up for his most important trial, the private examination leading
to the *licentia docendi*, he had to have presented a certain number of
repetitions and disputations, in addition to having done some teaching.
In disputations the student chose his own themes. In repetitions it was
the professor who selected the law, case, or point, and the student who
furnished the arguments, using the *pro-contra* technique.

The method of teaching law at Bologna and the other Italian universities aimed at getting the student to memorize a large part of the great
texts of the Roman and canon laws. Of cardinal importance were the
opening phrases of particular laws, glosses, or legal commentaries, including their precise place in the appropriate text. The ability to hold
on to these was the foundation of all sophisticated legal argument, and

86

the most celebrated lawyers usually possessed remarkable memories. They were expected to bring this facility to the cases turned up in everyday life, to be ready to quote not only a very large part of the Roman and canon laws but also the glosses of Accursius and Azo, as well as the commentaries and *consilia* of jurists like Cino, Bartolus, Baldo, Paolo di Castro, and half a dozen others. With some exaggeration, one historian has recently observed that "the best jurists were those who in argument cited the most possible texts and authors."[34]

No less important than argument from texts and memory was a certain type of forensic oratory and rational debate. What was the final aim, after all, of the repetition and public disputation? In the best counsel or written defenses only the most fitting texts and passages were adduced. This presupposed an eye or training for both the general and the particular. Once a lawyer had his texts, he had to know what to do with them. The hack might be content, as in a *consilium sapientis*, with merely arranging them on each side of a given case, then according right to the side with the most texts in its favor. But this was not so easy in difficult cases; the best lawyers were therefore, naturally, not the ones who looked for mechanical solutions but rather those who best exploited the resources of rational argument learned during their university days.[35] Having gathered texts and arguments on each side of a given point, a lawyer then had to call on his training in logic and dialectics to resolve the contradictions or legal difficulties. Thousands of extant *consilia*, penned by Florentine lawyers of the time, attest to the intelligent (or of course mechanical) use of the *pro-contra* method of argument. They exemplify the movement in reasoning from the particular to the general, in argument from the general to the particular. We must not forget that at the law *studium* of Bologna, the model law school, the teaching of rigorous rational argument looked to inculcating a technique which, when combined with a well-stocked memory, became the mainstay of late medieval legal science. Not that the outstanding practitioners of the method became the prisoners of a given system of dialectics and logic;

[34] Stelling-Michaud, *L'Université de Bologna*, p. 72.
[35] See the suggestive but frustratingly short study by Gino Masi, "Il Guicciardini e la giurisprudenza del suo tempo," in supp. n. 1 of *Rinascita*, XVIII (1940), 117-39, esp. 135-38.

on the contrary, they soon learned, like the greatest of the commentators, to get the best out of their rationalism by adapting it to the practical exigencies of daily life. The legal-judicial opinions (*consilia*) of Lorenzo Ridolfi and Giovanni de' Ricci, Domenico Bonsi and Antonio Malegonnelli all exhibit this virtue.[36]

When it came time to take the private examination leading to the *licentia docendi*—the most difficult trial—candidates at Florence were examined by a shadowy College of Doctors of Law, fourteen of them, not all of whom were attached to the Studio Fiorentino as professors. At Bologna examinations were in the hands of the Bolognese College of Doctors, a body of sixteen native-born professors of law, created for the purpose of conducting examinations and dispensing legal-judicial counsel. The candidate for the private examination was presented to the College of Doctors by his major professor or by another *promotor*. A day or two later he was assigned some arguments or topics (*puncta*) and given two days to prepare to deal with them. On the day of the examination he illustrated the *puncta*, took a position, and presented his arguments and conclusions. Now the examination began in earnest. The interrogation moved in turn from the youngest to the oldest of the examining doctors. At the end of the examination the candidate and his *promotor* or sponsor departed. A vote was taken and the decision on his performance was determined by a simple majority. If the candidate passed, he was awarded the license to teach and he could then come up for the *conventus* or doctoral examination within three days.

The public examination, or *conventus*, was largely ceremonial. Traditionally the candidate for the doctorate was accompanied to the cathedral by a following of student friends and relatives. This might be done with a great deal of fanfare. Along the way of the procession, shops were sometimes temporarily closed. In the cathedral the candidate delivered a lecture to the assembled College of Doctors, the archbishop or archdeacon, an audience of university students, and others. At the end of the lecture, time was allowed for debate or dispute with the candidate.

[36] E.g., BNF, *Fondo principale*, II, III, 370 (Ridolfi); II, I, 401 (Ricci); *Panciatichiani*, 138 (Ricci, Ridolfi, *et al.*); ASF, *CRS*, Arch. 98 ("Eredità Bonsi"), 234-37 (Malegonnelli and Bonsi, *passim*). For a more complete list of *consilia* see the sources for Ch. X.

Theoretically he could be put on trial by the College of Doctors and by the others. But having already given its approval at the private examination, the College usually took no active part in this ceremony, while the others in the audience, friends and acquaintances of the budding jurist, took the occasion to praise some aspect of his performance.

Taking the doctorate was the most expensive single event connected with the study of law. Up to about the middle of the fifteenth century these ceremonies were more expensive at Bologna than elsewhere, but in the sixteenth century Padua commanded a greater name and higher fees. After paying the Bolognese College of Doctors or the examiners in Florence, paying his sponsor or sponsors, the archdeacon, the recording notaries, passing out gifts of gloves, caps, rings, or other items, and after offering a sumptuous banquet, hiring horses and servants for the festivities, the student who came up for the doctorate easily spent from 20.0 to 30.0 gold florins or more. This was the annual rent for a large shop or very large private house, two to three times the annual earnings of a servant, or better than the full annual wage of a skilled worker employed in the manufacture of wool cloth. In 1338 Donato Velluti expected to spend 40.0 florins on his private and doctoral examinations at Bologna. When Francesco Guicciardini took his doctorate in civil law at the "college of the Pisan studio" of Florence in 1505, he spent 26.0 gold ducats (the ducat was worth slightly more than the large gold florin), but he refused the equivalent degree in canon law to avoid the extra expense of 12.5 ducats and because "it is of little importance."[37] Some students of the law went as far as the *licentia docendi* and then, owing to the expense, either did not come up for the public examination or put it off for years. Others, instead, obtained the license from one institution and then went for their final degree to a university where doctoral fees were somewhat lower. The Appendix shows that most Florentine lawyers attended two or more universities. Some moved around for reasons of study, physical convenience, to follow a particular master, or for other reasons. A few must have moved because of finances.

[37] Guicciardini, *Ricordanze*, p. 57. Velluti item in his *Cronica domestica*, p. 157. On workers' wages see G. Brucker, "The Ciompi Revolution," article to appear in a Faber and Faber volume of Florentine studies, ed., N. Rubinstein (London, —).

Comparing educational costs with such factors as wages, rents, and real estate values, we find that a university education in the fifteenth and sixteenth centuries was much costlier than in modern times.[38] It was therefore all the more prized by the men who had one, more highly regarded by those who did not. In the first half of the fifteenth century "the yearly expenses of a young man enrolled in a university away from home averaged about 20.0 florins."[39] If the same thing happened to university expenses as happened to other luxury items, this figure must have gone up in the course of the century. Guicciardini spent seven years (1498-1505) and more than 500 gold ducats on his legal education. This came to something more than 70.0 ducats annually: spent for books, travel, food, lodging, fees, and so on.[40] Though he was born into a rich family, his memoirs and personal reflections reveal a markedly frugal temperament and suggest that his student days were certainly not given to orgies of spending. The available evidence indicates that Florentine students, even the very rich ones, tended to be careful about expenses. Like their fathers, they were meticulous account keepers. Ricciardo del Bene, as a student at Bologna, occasionally handled family moneys but always with exemplary caution. Francesco Gaddi and Giovanni Buongirolami, lawyers both, were sticklers about their accounts.[41] There were of course students who lived on a princely basis: they arrived in Bologna with a cook, a steward, a manservant, and took a house or the entire floor of a Bolognese *palazzo*. But this was not the way of rich Florentines, who could get on with one servant. Giovanni di Messer Otto Niccolini was meant to study law at Perugia in 1470 and to take along his tutor, Agnolo, who would both coach him and prepare his food.[42] Guicciardini does not say this of himself, but when he went to Ferrara and Padua to study, he was probably accompanied by a servant, if for no other reason than to live up to his family's exalted social condition. Not surprisingly, therefore, influential Florentine families with sons at law school sometimes tried to solicit prebends for them. And a student abroad,

[38] Cf. following figures with property values in Martines, *Florentine Humanists*, ch. iii.

[39] *Ibid.*, p. 117.

[40] Guicciardini, *loc.cit.*, including doctoral fees.

[41] See their accounts and *ricordanze* cited in sources for this chapter.

[42] Camugliano, *Chronicles*, p. 186.

with only 20.0 florins a year to spend, was really cutting things close to the bone.

## 3. *Cases and Fees*

Just as Italy, generally speaking, came under the formal sway of two laws, civil and canon, so there were two kinds of lawyers, civilians and canonists. In theory there were two spheres of jurisdiction, but in practice, the distinction was not a sharp one. The two spheres faded into each other, and cases which should have been handled by ecclesiastical courts were often heard in temporal courts, although a movement in the opposite direction was much less common, at all events in city-states like Venice, Milan, and Florence. How was the indistinct area between the two laws reflected in the legal profession? We have already seen that the same man could be both a canonist and a civilian. Indeed *decretorum doctores*, like their civilian counterparts, were regularly consulted in temporal cases, although consulted of course as experts in civil and municipal law. Four outstanding lawyers of the early fifteenth century—prominent in Florentine politics—had their doctorates in canon not civil law: Tommaso Marchi, Lorenzo Ridolfi, Stefano Buonaccorsi, and Francesco Machiavelli. They were often summoned to give counsel in cases due for adjudication in secular tribunals,[43] and it is not at all unlikely that most of their clients were laymen engaged in ordinary civil litigation. For canonists were also schooled in the *pro-contra* method, in the bringing forth and juxtaposition of varieties of texts, and frequently they had devoted several years to the study of Roman law. Hence it was perfectly natural to consider them competent to act as lawyers or judges in purely temporal cases.

It would be misleading to say that the Florentine judicial system never discriminated against lay canonists. It was not, however, a matter of prejudice or ignorance but of specialization. Custom and practicality reserved the senior judicial posts for men with the doctorate or at least the license in civil law, although some of these posts were not in any case open to Florentines. One of the three major foreign magistrates,[44] on

[43] Evident from collections of *consilia*.
[44] The Podestà. ASF, *DSCOA*, 29 (1444-1454), f. 68r-v.

taking office in Florence, was obligated to arrive in the city with a full staff of aides and attendants, all of whom had to be foreign. Among these there had to be four "iudices legistas, iurisque peritos," two of whom had to have taken the doctorate in civil law not less than six and three years before taking up their tasks in Florence. Similarly, the Captain of the People and the Executor of Justice were each to be assisted by at least one foreign doctor *in iure civile*.[45] But these posts, like that of chief jurisconsult in the city's supreme commercial tribunal, could only be held by foreign lawyers who came to the city for six months and then departed. On the other hand, major judgeships in the Florentine dominion were reserved for Florentines. The Captain of Pisa was accompanied by at least one lawyer licensed in civil law, the Podestà by one with the doctorate. At Pistoia at least one judge had to hold the doctorate, while Arezzo required one doctor and one licentiate, all in civil law.[46] Apart from these requirements, it does not seem to have been anyone's wish to put office beyond the reach of lay canonists. So far as the dominion was concerned, Florentines were strict only about seeing that the major centers (e.g., Pisa, Arezzo, Pistoia) had well-trained civil lawyers among the officials sent out from the capital. Owing to their population, wealth, and economic complexity, the larger urban centers were more apt than rural areas and small towns to come up with cases whose resolution required a particular preparation in Roman law—the common law of Tuscany, the law most often reflected in the corpus of Florentine municipal law. There were divergencies of course, but Florentine statutory law took for granted many of the principles of Roman law, especially in matters regarding property, contracts, rebellion, the position of the father, and aspects of civil status.[47]

The jurisdictions of the civil and canon laws were these: canon law regulated marriage, oaths, and manifest usury; cases concerning clerics, the materially destitute, sacred grounds, and those affairs in which sin was critically involved or where lawyers were in doubt. Everything else

[45] *Statuta*, I, 26, 37.

[46] *Tratte*, 65, ff. 7r, 8r, 10r, 11r, 17r, 27r; *Statuta*, III, 516ff.

[47] It was ruled in 1346 that Roman law was to apply in the city's tribunals. L. Chiappelli, "Firenze e la scienza del diritto nel periodo del Rinascimento," *Archivio giuridico* XXVIII (1882), 454, n. 1.

fell under the aegis of civil and temporal law. This at least was the theory. In practice, at Florence and elsewhere, the state paid little attention to some of these boundaries. For one thing, Roman public law, when touching on *sacra* and priests, had long given some backing to the state's encroachments on priests and churches. Again, the same body of law treated the most important public building, the imperial palace, as a "sacred" place, which occasionally led medieval lawyers to regard the principal government buildings (e.g., communal *palazzi*) as *sacra*.[48] Accordingly, Florence often tried the violation of sacred places in temporal courts. It was the same with the sins of blasphemy, sacrilege, and the adultery of women: the Florentine state drew these under its jurisdiction, though in the middle of the sixteenth century this competence had to be vigorously defended by two ducal lawyers against the pretensions of the Inquisition.[49] Heresy, on the other hand, was left to the Church from earliest times; but sorcery was usually tried in the lay courts, even though it often bordered on heresy. The statutes of 1415 forbade Florentine clerics to refuse the competence of the Republic's tribunals.[50] In the period around 1500 the Signory often heard and determined cases involving disputes over church benefices.

Florence threatened the theoretical rights of clerics in other ways too—as when the city levied taxes on them without previous papal consent, although always adducing argument from public necessity (see Ch. VII, 2). Apart from the privilege of being tried by ecclesiastical courts only, clerics were also ensured the following rights under canon law: immunity from all public levies, the protection of their physical being and personal integrity, and the *privilegium competentiae*, i.e., a cleric's right to an income sufficient for his livelihood in cases where judicial action had gone against his or his group's income or patrimony.

[48] G. Post, *Studies*, pp. 387-88, who cites *D.* 1, 1, 1, 2 and *C.* 11, 77, 1. Cf. also Justinian's statement to Epiphanius, *Nov.*, 7, 2, 30, "utique cum nec multo differant ab alterutro sacerdotium et imperium, et sacrae res a communibus et publicis."

[49] Lelio Torelli and Francesco Vinta, two of Cosimo I's leading lawyers and counsellors. A. Anzilotti, *La costituzione interna dello stato fiorentino sotto il duca Cosimo I de' Medici*, pp. 191-93. On the adultery item see Davidsohn, *Geschichte*, IV, i, 320, who notes that male adulterers were not prosecuted.

[50] G. Salvioli, *Storia del diritto italiano* (9th ed., Torino, 1930), p. 355. On the

Although an organic feature of marriage, dowries belonged to the patrimonial order of things and so came under the jurisdiction of civil not canon law. Roman lawyers had always regarded the *dos* (dowry) in terms of the public interest and public law.[51] Of lawsuits handled by Florentine lawyers, disputes over dowries were among the most common types. For the portion brought by a woman to the expenses of the married estate was deemed so important by all social classes that dowerless marriage, we may say, did not exist in Florence. Under Roman law the protective dowry was one given by the wife's father or by another donor in her behalf. If she herself provided the dowry it was adventitious. But whatever its source, on her or her husband's death, it might be reclaimed by her protector or the protector's heirs, or by the widow or her heirs against the husband's legatees. Since dowries often attained the value of 500 to 2,000 florins, and occasionally in Laurentian Florence and later as much as 4,000 and even 5,000 florins, it followed that litigation over dowries could be extremely keen. Such a case involving the Pantaleoni family arose in 1444. The plaintiff was a certain nun, Piera, who claimed her mother's dowry. Lumped together with her father's properties, the dowry had been alienated years before by the trustees appointed over her father's bankruptcy proceedings. Evidently ruined, he had taken flight and was now dead, as was the nun's mother. Three Florentine lawyers were commissioned to submit judicial opinions on the case: Giovanni Buongirolami, a civilian with a doctorate from Padua, and two *doctores in utroque iure*, Guglielmo Tanagli and Piero Ambrosini. They decided the case in Piera's favor.[52]

The preceding commission originated with the judge in the case. In such commissions we perceive an institution which kept lawyers as busy as did defense work or requests for counsel from other sources: this was the institution or practice of soliciting judicial opinions on particular cases.[53]

---

preceding item above see the valuable piece by G. Brucker, "Sorcery in Early Renaissance Florence," *Studies in the Renaissance*, x (1963), 7-24.

[51] *D.* 23, 3, 3 and *C.* 5, 12. Any of the *consilia* collections cited in the sources for Ch. X would reveal the high incidence of Florentine lawsuits involving dowries. A few random examples are: BNF, *Fondo principale*, II, 11, 376, ff. 1r-20r; *Magl.*, cl. XXIX, 117, ff. 81r-82r, 88r, 90r, 100r; ASF, *Carte del Bene*, 54, f. 21v.

[52] *MAP*, 87, ff. 514r-520r.

[53] There are fundamental studies on this by G. Rossi, *Consilium sapientis iudiciale*

The institution had Roman origins. Confronted by certain types of cases or by a difficult point of law, a judge, a tribunal, or an executive body might have recourse to the judicial opinion of one or more lawyers. And although the final sentence could be at variance with the judgment of the experts, in practice this did not often happen. The judicial *consilia* of experts tended to be binding, sometimes by statute, more often by custom or by expediency, as in cases where the official and final judge was not a trained legist. When a group of lawyers submitted two conflicting opinions, the majority opinion triumphed or the case might be reassigned. Deadlocks were resolved by the judge.

A statute of January 1357 stipulated that Florentine lawyers must accept any request to give judicial counsel, providing of course that the request came from one of the foreign magistrates, an authorized official of the Republic, or one of the magistracies with judicial powers.[54] Continuing in effect throughout the fifteenth century, this statute opened the way for lawyers to be called on for judicial counsel from any of about forty different sources. For apart from the Podestà, the Captain of the People, the Executor and the Appellate Judge, there were the consulates (in their function as courts) of the twenty-one guilds, as well as other executive bodies and officials endowed with judicial privileges, such as the Signory, the Eight on Public Safety, the War Commission, the Defenders of the Laws, the Tower Officials, Monte Officials, Regulators, and perhaps another dozen offices. Unlike local practice in some parts of Italy, Florentine law permitted legal counsel and defense in criminal cases. If the defendant requested an advocate, the judge was obliged to provide one. This right, however, was denied to heretics; neither lawyers nor notaries could plead for or represent any man known to be tainted with heresy. Annually on the feast of St. Ivo of Chartres, the patron saint of lawyers, the guild appointed a lawyer and notary as advocate and procurator respectively "of poor, destitute, or depressed persons." The

---

(Milano, 1956); W. Engelmann, *Die Wiedergeburt der Rechtskultur in Italien durch die wissenschaftliche Lehre* (Leipzig, 1938), ch. III. In English there is only the short interesting piece by Peter Riesenberg, "The Consilia Literature: A Prospectus," *Manuscripta*, VI (1962), 3-22.

[54] *Prov.*, 44, ff. 51r-52r.

two men served for one year with a tiny honorarium from the guild.[55]

Another class of cases very often handled by lawyers of the period was occasioned by the confiscation of private property because of some act of rebellion. In the fifteenth century properties so seized were normally administered by the Tower Officials. First assessing their value, then publishing the proposed place and date of their sale, these officials were meant to alienate such goods in a wholly disinterested fashion. Predictably, this was not always the case. Family relations, legacies, and the effect of contracts and documents being what they were in Florence, the activity of the Tower Officials often gave rise to appellate proceedings.

An interesting case of this sort, involving two places of worship, came up for adjudication in the court of the Podestà in November 1401. The late Messer Niccolò di Jacopo degli Alberti had willed all his worldly possessions to his four sons. Antonio, the eldest, was made the chief executor of two chapels, one at Cafaggiolo and the other on the big Alberti estate known as "il Paradiso." Certain properties and rights were attached to these chapels in perpetuity to cover their maintenance and to pay for regular religious services. While the chapel at Cafaggiolo was to be semi-independent, being bound to some dwellings "intended for the perpetual use and service of the poor and destitute," the chapel of St. Zenobius on the Paradiso estate was meant to pass down in perpetuity through the elder masculine line of the family. At some point Antonio was supposed to appoint five men with full power to administer the Cafaggiolo chapel and properties after his death. But just then some of the Alberti became involved in grave political difficulties: they were accused of plotting against the state. In January 1401 Antonio was arrested, condemned, fined, and banished.[56] All his "properties and rights" were confiscated by the city. His brothers, on the other hand, were not implicated in the alleged conspiracy, and they took legal action to recover the two chapels with the attached rights and properties. Two prominent lawyers were invited to give judicial counsel in the proceedings: Giovanni Serristori and one of the leading oligarchs of the period, Filippo Corsini. It says something for the integrity of these two men, especially Corsini's, that

---

[55] *Statuta*, II, 154. St. Luke, however, was the particular patron saint of the guild, at all events in the sixteenth century. *AGN*, I, f. 21r.

[56] *Balìe*, 17, f. 190r-v.

they awarded the case to the brothers, despite the antipathy of the dominant political faction for the Alberti. Adducing sections both from the civil and canon laws, as well as commentaries by Cino, Bartolus, and Angelo degli Ubaldi, the two lawyers argued that as the chapels had been founded and provided for in perpetuity by Messer Niccolò, not by Antonio, the city must respect the legacy's original intent, irrespective of the crimes of any single heir. This much, they pointed out, was guaranteed by the statutes of the Republic itself. Hence there could be no confiscation of the rights of patronage over the two chapels, nor therefore of the entailed properties.[57]

In December 1409 the Tower Officials solicited a judicial opinion from the municipal lawyers Nello of San Gimignano and Ricciardo del Bene, both of whom had been trained at Bologna in Roman law. Ser Angelo di Fulgineo, a notary, was accused of pederasty while serving as an official of the Republic. Tried in the court of the Captain of the People, he was found guilty and condemned to pay a fine of 200 gold florins. Unable, apparently, to face the ensuing scandal, Ser Angelo tried to poison himself but failed; whereupon he was again brought to trial by the Captain, condemned and this time beheaded. His goods and properties were then seized by the Tower Officials, who were preparing to sell them when the heirs of the notary initiated proceedings to recover part at least of the confiscated properties. The two lawyers were called in to provide judicial counsel at this point. In a sense the attempted suicide constituted an act of rebellion, although one devoid of political content. The case has its interest.[58] Judicial and legal opinions of the Renaissance, particularly in proceedings concerning rebellion, offer a vast, unexplored field for students of political theory.

Two other classes of controversy frequently engaged the labors of Florentine lawyers: (a) litigation between religious houses or between individual clerics over benefices and (b) border disputes between local administrations in the Florentine dominion. It has already been noted that the first of these was very common around 1500. High among the Si-

---

[57] All details of preceding case in BNF, *Magl.*, cl. xxix, 117 (a volume of *consilia legalia diversorum*), ff. 35r-38r.
[58] Details of case in ASF, *Carte del Bene*, 54, f. 51v.

gnory's prerogatives were its judicial powers; it could render or influence judgments touching a variety of cases, including legal disputes over
benefices and boundary rights. Presented with an appeal, the Signory
might turn the case over to two, three, or more lawyers, who were expected to submit a *consilium sapientis iudiciale*. The practice of the
Signory was to turn the decision of the lawyers into a final judgment.

In 1512 the Signory undertook to settle a conflict between the Lana
guild and a group of Eremitani friars on one side and, on the other, the
spice merchants and Carmelite friars of the church of San Bernabò. Each
side claimed the rights of patronage over a chapel in a Fiesolan church.
Three lawyers were assigned to the case: Francesco Pepi, Bono Boni, and
Ormannozzo Deti. Pepi was subsequently replaced by Niccolò Altoviti.
Turning in their opinion late in June, the lawyers awarded the case to
the Lana guild and the Eremitani friars, although they stipulated that
the Carmelites and their backers still had some rights in the chapel.
Left thus unresolved, the case was transferred to the Council of Justice,
the Republic's highest ordinary tribunal, which on August 18th decided
the case more fully in favor of the Lana guild.[59] A few months later
Altoviti and Boni were summoned to give counsel on another "causa
ecclesiastica," also to be determined by the Signory. The case involved
two clerics—Ser Bartolommeo de' Gambassi, a Florentine, and Ser Eliseo
da Colle, both of whom laid claim to the church of San Martino at Pilli,
in the diocese of Volterra. Adhering to the judicial opinion turned in by
the two lawyers, the Signory decided the case in Gambassi's favor.[60]

As an example of a territorial dispute between men of two districts, let
us take a case heard by the Signory in February 1498. The Castle of
Biserno had a large courtyard claimed both by the Commune of Galeata
and by "the men of the mountain"—presumably the men of the high
country around. It was the contention of the hillsmen that they were part
of the Commune of Galeata, that Galeata had purchased the courtyard
from a Count Giovanni, and that they therefore had legal title to a share
in it. Three lawyers were summoned to look into the case and provide
a judicial opinion: Agnolo Niccolini, Antonio Malegonnelli, and Fran-

[59] *DSCOA*, 114, ff. 64v, 69v, 75r, 78v, 88v (pencil). The Council of Justice or
*Rota* was established in 1502.
[60] *Ibid.*, f. 132r.

cesco Gualterotti, all political figures of the first rank. Their *consilium* was prepared and drafted by Malegonnelli but countersigned by the other two. Going back to some early registers of the Commune of Galeata, Malegonnelli found that the Castle and its adjacent properties had been bought by Galeata in 1398. To show what had happened to the adjacent properties since then, he next cited a series of notarial instruments from 1401, 1454, 1456, and 1461. Until further evidence was produced, he concluded, the law was with the claims advanced by the Commune of Galeata, not with the hillsmen.[61]

In addition to the types of cases already mentioned, the surviving treasures of *consilia legalia* reveal the incidence of litigation between guilds, between guilds and one or more government offices, between guilds and individuals, and of course between government offices and individuals. All of these—the last need not even be exemplified—have their equivalents in modern times, e.g., as in lawsuits between corporations, between public and semi-public corporations, between individuals and semi-public corporations, or between local and national governing bodies. Cases of the sort less commonly found in modern societies are those in which political rights are directly related to the question of legitimate birth. Florence was by no means unique in this. The histories of many medieval communes betray an unpleasant though comprehensible distrust of bastardy, notably in connection with political rights and requirements for guild membership. It was sometimes thought that the stain of illegitimacy was transmitted from one generation to the next. Of a number of Florentine examples, one may suffice. In the spring of 1498 Dardano and Francesco di Niccolò Acciaiuoli appealed to the Signory for the right to be included in the lists of citizens eligible to hold public office. They had been banned from office because their father was born out of wedlock, although subsequently he had been legitimized by an imperial act. Probably some of the "real" Acciaiuoli had contested their claim to belong to the family and challenged their qualifications for office. Turning to two eminent jurisconsults, Guidantonio Vespucci and Antonio Malegonnelli, the Signory solicited an opinion from them. Reviewing Florentine legislation on legitimate birth and eligibility for public office,

[61] *DSCOA*, 100, ff. 14r, 19v-20r.

Vespucci and Malegonnelli went back to statutes enacted in 1404, 1428, and 1495, and found that the last of these permitted members of the political class to hold office if the incumbent, his father, or his grandfather had been legitimately born. The Signory thereupon decreed that the two brothers should be entered in the eligibility lists.[62]

To turn from classes of lawsuits to legal fees is to turn from the little studied to the unstudied. Legal historians have shown little penchant for the history of the profession and none at all for its economic underpinnings.

Speaking of the late thirteenth and early fourteenth centuries, Davidsohn found that lawyers sometimes asked 7.00 per cent of the claims involved in lawsuits.[63] He notes this in passing and adduces one document. More reliable figures are available.

Lawyers provided counsel and spoke or argued in open court. Sources give little specific information on the fees taken by lawyers for pleading at the bar, but we may assume that these fees were much like those paid for written counsel. Even if it was one thing to advise private groups or individuals and another to give judicial counsel on the request of a judge or tribunal, there is evidence to show that a similar range of fees applied to the two types of activity.

According to the Florentine statutes of 1415, the following rates applied to judicial counsel on a case awaiting final judgment ("de quaestione diffinitivae sententiae"): where claims up to 50.0 pounds silver were involved, the fee was 4.00 pounds; from 50.0 to 100 pounds, 5.00 pounds in fees; 100 to 500 pounds, 10.0 pounds; 500 to 1,000 pounds, 12.0 pounds; 1,000 to 2,000 pounds, 16.0 pounds; and for any claims whatsoever above 2,000 pounds silver, the fee was to be 20.0 pounds and no more.[64] Changing these figures into gold florins (and this can only be done roughly, owing to continuous fluctuations in the silver standard), we find that a judicial opinion could carry a fee of from 1.00 to 5.00 florins. In cases

---

[62] *Ibid.*, f. 38v.

[63] *Geschichte*, IV, ii, 112.

[64] All figures here in *Statuta*, I, 183-84. The pound was a money of account. The value of silver in relation to gold declined during the fifteenth century, went very roughly from 3.00 to 5.00 lire per gold florin. In 1472, e.g., the large gold florin equalled about 5.50 lire, by the beginning of the sixteenth century about 7.00 lire. *Strozz.*, 2a ser., 21, f. 81v; 23, f. 177v.

which entailed no material claim, as in the bid for public office advanced by the two Acciaiuoli, the fee was decided on by the magistrate or body which had commissioned the counsel, although in no case could it exceed 5.00 florins. Interlocutory counsel—counsel given to either party in the course of an action—was paid somewhat less well: the fee was 1.50 pounds silver for claims up to 50.0 pounds, 2.00 pounds for claims from 50.0 to 100 pounds, and so on up to a top fee of 10.0 pounds silver, or about 2.50 florins.

The preceding range of fees is entirely consistent with figures taken from a variety of sources. In 1393 that wily usurer, *nouveau riche*, and pious merchant, Francesco Datini, found himself entangled in a lawsuit. His friend and notary, Ser Lapo Mazzei, recommended that he have a brief drawn up and sent to two famous Bolognese lawyers for their opinions. Mazzei pointed out that if the opinions were in Datini's favor, he should present them to the court in order to help his case; if not, then he should be silent. The notary estimated that the two opinions, including postage fees, would cost about 10.0 florins. Transportation or postage on that run involved perhaps a florin or slightly more each way, so that payment would have been something like 4.00 florins *pro consilio*. Another case involving Datini came up soon after his death in 1410. He had left a testament disposing of some 70,000 florins. It was contested, and more than seven lawyers were summoned to give counsel. Each of them turned in an opinion. Filippo Corsini received a fee of 4 florins/9 lire for his; Ricciardo del Bene received 3 florins/3 lire; Bartolommeo Popoleschi, 3 florins/5; Nello da San Gimignano, 3 florins/9; Rosso degli Orlandi, 2 florins/2; the canonist, Stefano Buonaccorsi, 2 florins/2; and another canonist, the statesman Lorenzo Ridolfi, drafted three opinions for which he received respectively 2 florins/2, 2 florins/2, and 6 florins/7. The most expensive opinion was procured at Padua, very probably from the College of Doctors of Law, and cost 29.0 florins.[65]

Whenever we come on the details of payments to lawyers, we tend to find sums of from 1.00 to 3.00 or 4.00 florins. Occasionally payment was made in kind. In February 1400 the lawyer of the Del Dolce Hospital

[65] Foregoing items in Lapo Mazzei, *Lettere di un notaro a un mercante del secolo xiv*, ed. C. Guasti, 2 vols. (Firenze, 1880), I, 46-47, cxxxviii, n. 5.

of Prato received 1.00 florin "for his labors" in connection with a lawsuit.[66] On August 16, 1464, the upstart lawyer and descendant of vintners, Virgilio Adriani, received 1.00 large florin for handling a suit involving Ser Zanobi Bartolommei.[67] In April 1480 Machiavelli's father, the lawyer Bernardo, was asked by Benedetto di Goro to examine the legal particulars connected with a farm which Benedetto was about to buy from the court of the Podestà. Bernardo was to see that the form of the purchase was correct, in return for which he was promised a pair of black stockings in the Perpignon style,[68] a dressy and rather expensive stocking. Municipalities and religious houses often hired lawyers on retainer, which in some cases was paid in kind. In the 1370s and 1380s the lawyers of the charitable Society of St. Michael received a fee of 12.0 florins annually.[69] When Tommaso Deti died in 1498, his son, Ormannozzo, succeeded him as one of the three lawyers of the Commune of Prato. The other two were Agnolo Niccolini and Luca Corsini. Like his colleagues, Ormannozzo was given an appointment for life and guaranteed an annual retainer in kind: twelve sextants of grain during harvest, ten barrels of wine at vintage, and a cart of small firewood in October.[70] Between 1479 and 1494 Messer Puccio Pucci, one of the lawyers of the Misericordia Hospital of Prato, received a yearly retainer of 3.00 large florins.[71]

None of these stipends was princely, but apart from the facts that labor was divided between lawyers and that excessive service was recompensed, there was a definite prestige, as well as other advantages, attached to the foregoing offices, particularly to that of municipal lawyer in towns like Prato, Arezzo, and Pistoia. An appointment of this sort could not fail to attract other clients from those towns. Tommaso Deti, for example, one of the official lawyers of the Commune of Prato, was also counsel for the Misericordia Hospital of Prato during more than thirty years.[72]

---

[66] Archivio di Stato di Prato, *Spedale del Dolce,* 15, f. 80r. I owe this and other citations from the Pratese archives to Prof. Gino Corti.

[67] *Strozz., 2a ser.,* 21, f. 12v.

[68] *Ricordi,* p. 111.

[69] ASF, *Orsanmichele,* 9, ff. 34v, 72r; 11, ff. 69r, 71r.

[70] ASF, *CRS,* Arch. 98, Reg. 237, f. 5r.

[71] Archivio di Stato di Prato, *Spedale della Misericordia,* 1558, f. 226.

[72] Archivio di Stato di Prato, *Misericordia,* 1557, f. 4; 1559, f. 27.

We can best draw out the import of the preceding details by dwelling on some particular figure. The lawyer who best lends himself to this treatment is Ricciardo di Francesco del Bene (*ca.* 1369-1411). He left one of the fullest and most interesting accounts of a lawyer's professional earnings. Born into an old merchant family of medium rank, he read civil law at Bologna, where he presented brilliant doctoral examinations in 1395. Returning to Florence soon after, he gave himself assiduously to the profession and taught civil law for a time at the Studio Fiorentino. Among his family letters and papers, there is a small volume of *ricordanze* for the years 1397 to 1407, giving Ricciardo's professional income on a near daily basis over a period of more than three years—November 1403 to February 1407.[73] In the first year he earned 294 florins, in the second about 317, and in the third 350 florins. Although the record was left incomplete, the fourth year promised a continuing rise in his income. Of the totals listed under each of the thirty-nine months during which the record was kept, his income of 52.0 florins for the last fully recorded month (January 1407) was the highest, and the sum of 38.0 florins for December 1406 was surpassed by the earnings of only one previous month. His straight professional income of the third year excludes his teaching salary—75.0 florins.

Most of Ricciardo's clients were individual citizens, but his services were also much used by various corporate groups. Among the latter were the smiths, the second-hand clothes dealers, the Calimala guild, the guild of lawyers and notaries, the commission charged with building and repairs in the cathedral, a group of Carthusian friars, the friars of Ogni Santi, the Society of St. Michael, the Hospital of Santa Maria Nuova, and the communes of San Miniato and Florence. He received an annual retainer from the convent of Ogni Santi and the village of Vitolini of 1.00 and 2.00 florins respectively. Now and then he was paid in kind. Bernardo Portinari settled a fee by giving Ricciardo "duos stapolos panni valoris florenorum otto." Another client gave him a ring worth 3.00 florins. For the services that went into an arbitrator's award ("pro concordia facta et laudo dato"), Ricciardo received twelve silver forks worth 10.0 florins. But the great bulk of the entries recorded money payments, mostly for

[73] *Carte del Bene*, 38, ff. 6r-17r. Following data from this source.

sums of 1.00 florin; in many cases these must have been for his defense activity in open court. He often took 1.00 florin "pro consilio," but on occasion an opinion brought in 2.00 and 3.00 florins. Among his clients were men who came from the major branches of the Strozzi, Medici, Soderini, Ricasoli, and Rucellai families. Other prominent names in his accounts belonged to the Rossi, Altoviti, Martelli, Ardinghelli, and Davanzati families. Goro Dati, the silk merchant and chronicler, was a client.

One of the more fascinating features of Ricciardo's *ricordanze* is the picture given there of the social character of his clients. They were merchants, money-lenders, bankers, manufacturers, usurers, and men who lived off landed income. There was a Malatesta count, the Count of Montegranelli, and the procurator of the Cardinal of Bologna; and there were notaries, physicians, a goldsmith, a stationer, some leather vendors, and petty employers of croppers and dyers. As we might expect, men from the lowest strata of the populace do not appear among Ricciardo's clients: we find no wool carders, beaters, combers, or burlers, not to mention the wholly destitute. Litigation was never a thing for the really poor, although the Church, the municipality, and the guild tried to make legal help available to them.

Like all his rich contemporaries and like so many lawyers, Ricciardo had various sources of income apart from his profession. Chief of these were his returns on government securities, on the sale of wine and grain from his farms, and on house rents. In the twelve months beginning June 1397 this income came to something like 350 florins, about 205 of which was the earnings on government securities.[74] But owing to the Republic's changing commitments and to fluctuations in farm prices, Ricciardo's professional activity was his surest and largest source of income. Judging by what he earned as a lawyer from 1403 to the beginning of 1407, we gather that his income had been steadily increasing ever since his return from Bologna in 1395 or 1396, until, in his eleventh year out of law school, he netted about 350 florins on his straight legal practice and another 75.0 for teaching law at the Studio. He was a rich man, and we need not doubt that if he had lived beyond 1411 his professional intake, even with-

[74] *Ibid.*, ff. 33r *et seq.*

out university teaching, would have risen eventually to 500 or 600 florins per year. This projected income accords perfectly with that of another fifteenth-century lawyer, Benedetto Accolti (1415-1464), who became first secretary of the Republic in 1458. At the outset of 1461, when this office carried a yearly salary of 450 florins, a commission of experts ascertained that Benedetto's legal practice had brought in a greater income. His salary was therewith raised to 600 florins per annum.[75] This new figure presumably approximated what he had earned, or what he soon had hoped to earn, as a practicing lawyer. How did 500 to 600 florins per year compare with big business profits? Let us choose a severe standard by drawing on figures from a large operation like the Medici bank. In the twenty-three years from 1397 to 1420, the Florentine branch of the bank cleared net profits of 25,344 florins, for an average yearly profit of about 1,102 florins.[76] The years 1397 to 1420 were the period of greatest profit for the Florentine branch, second only to the branch in Rome.

Compared with a profit of 1,100 florins—the average yearly profit accruing to a major branch of one of Europe's biggest banking houses—a professional income of 500 to 600 florins was exceedingly high. And as both Del Bene and Accolti taught at the Studio, what if we also took their professorial salaries into account? But there is no reason to push these calculations. The point has been made. It is more important to try to settle the difficult question: how typical were Del Bene and Accolti? Certainly there were lawyers in the city, the younger ones at any rate, who earned less and who expected to earn less. There is the case of the Lucchese, Filippo di Andrea Balducci (ca. 1398-1458), a *legum doctor* who taught law at Siena in the later 1420s. In 1428-1429 he was invited by his friend, Averardo de' Medici, to emigrate to Florence to teach and practice law. Averardo was sure enough of his own connections to promise Filippo a teaching post and to get him admitted into the guild of lawyers and notaries. The lawyer wanted very much to move to Florence—it being, he said, one of the three greatest cities. But he pointed out to Averardo that his income from teaching and his legal practice in Siena were such that he could not make the move to Florence unless he was guar-

---

[75] D. Marzi, *La cancelleria della repubblica fiorentina*, p. 231.
[76] De Roover, *Medici Bank*, p. 47.

anteed a minimum intake of 150 to 200 florins per annum.[77] This was something like a third of the income potential of Del Bene and Accolti. Still, Filippo Balducci was an outsider and Florence was no friend of the Commune of Lucca in the late 1420s. Furthermore, a yearly income of 150 to 200 florins was the sum with which Filippo proposed to start. Residence in Florence and a growing network of friends, acquaintances, and connections would soon carry his income well beyond that. He went to Florence, entered the guild in 1431, was in the consulate by 1436, and in 1444 was appointed to a leading post in the Florentine chancellery.

To come back to Del Bene and Accolti, how typical was an income of 500 to 600 florins per annum? Financially, they were not at the head of their profession. Neither of these two men was by any means the most fashionable or sought-after lawyer of his time. They were successful without really enjoying any remarkable prominence as lawyers. Benedetto Accolti was married to Laura di Carlo Federighi, the daughter of a lawyer, but he was considered an Aretine and hence a new man in Florence. The Accolti could not lay claim to a Florentine political or social tradition. Ricciardo del Bene was a Florentine by birth and custom. His contacts were good. He enjoyed a close friendship with Benedetto Strozzi and Messer Rinaldo Gianfigliazzi, one of the leading statesmen of the day. More active, however, and far better known than Ricciardo in the period around 1400 were lawyers like Filippo Corsini, Lorenzo Ridolfi, Giovanni de' Ricci, Bartolommeo Popoleschi, Stefano Buonaccorsi, and Tommaso Marchi. Unlike Ricciardo, these men were extremely active in politics and were constantly being approached for legal counsel by the Republic's executive and judicial bodies. They would have been recognized in the streets of the city by almost every Florentine of any political or social importance.

## 4. Careers

The lawyer often appears at the forefront of things in the history of politics. This is not chance. Trained in the forms and formulae, customary

[77] *MAP*, 2, letters 69, 109, 291, 293. See *DSCOA*, 47, f. 50r, for proof of his teaching civil law at the Studio Fiorentino in 1435-36. His salary for the year was 130 florins.

and written, that govern public conduct, the lawyer seems to be the ideal public official, the perfect type of functionary to have near the decision-making process in the world of public affairs. The wisdom of this may be criticized or deplored, but no one can gainsay the ease with which lawyers may switch from law to politics if they show the slightest bit of leadership or political talent.

In Florence, as in other famous oligarchies, the best-known lawyers were those who stood out in public affairs. It is not only that the brilliant lawyer could choose to turn his talents to politics and so strike out for a new distinction; if his connections were right, if he came from one of the great oligarchical families, he might be duty-bound to go into politics, duty-bound to go after the prizes for whose competition he qualified by right of his birth and estate. If, on the other hand, his connections were modest or few and he sought to attract clients, he did well to go in search of sponsors and political place. His legal practice and political activity could go hand in hand. The more distinction he attained in politics, the more clients he attracted and the greater his legal reputation. Where there is government by oligarchy, a lawyer in the public eye is likely, more than in open societies, to win cases and draw clients. For he commands the prestige and can exert influence and pressures in any of a thousand ways. Florence, moreover, was physically a small world. A citizen could walk across it in twenty minutes. Prominent political and financial figures were immediately recognized. Executive and judicial magistracies, the chief commercial court (the Tribunale di Mercanzia), the foreign magistrates, and later on the Council of Justice, all were sensitive to the distribution of power in the city, sensitive also to the activity of lawyers who helped to captain (or were much favored by) the dominant blocs of families within the oligarchy. Justice must have been most purely realized when two such lawyers confronted each other in a lawsuit.

Who were the most widely employed jurisconsults of the early fifteenth century? Statesmen and diplomats like Filippo Corsini, Lorenzo Ridolfi, Nello da San Gimignano, Torello Torelli, Stefano Buonaccorsi, Bartolommeo Popoleschi, and Rosso degli Orlandi. At the end of the century the most important were Antonio Malegonnelli, Francesco Gualterotti, Domenico Bonsi, Guidantonio Vespucci, Antonio Strozzi, Francesco

Pepi, and Ormannozzo Deti. Vespucci was a brilliant political tactician, a powerful proponent of close oligarchy, a man hated and feared by the humbler sectors of the political class—small merchants, new men, shopkeepers, and such. Bonsi was an influential backer of Savonarola. Although finally abandoning the prophet, he was appointed Florentine ambassador to Rome and detained there during the very months when the anti-Savonarolans brought about the downfall of the friar. Malegonnelli was, in 1502, one of Piero Soderini's two leading rivals for the lifetime gonfaloniership. In the autumn of 1494 Gualterotti was a key figure in preventing the populace from sacking and setting fire to the *palazzi* of prominent Mediceans, and in 1500 he was one of the chieftains of the city's Cancellieri faction, the "sect" most committed to a closer form of oligarchy. All the others were men of remarkable political influence who constantly appeared in the leading offices and embassies. They were the sort of men to be found in the secret councils of the *optimates*.

Chapter X will take up the legal-political ideas of lawyers. The task here is to examine the link between law and politics in the careers of certain lawyers. I shall focus attention on two men: a fourteenth-century lawyer and a great figure of the Cinquecento.

Messer Donato di Lamberto Velluti (1314-1370) was born into a merchant family of decent antiquity, settled in Florence before 1244. They made their debut in the Signory in 1283, the year after its establishment, and thereafter regularly appeared and reappeared in the principal offices. Donato studied civil law at Bologna for almost nine years (1329-1338), returned to Florence, and was received into the guild in 1339. Setting in at once "to practice both privately and for the Commune, my services were much requested," he wrote.[78] His excellent family connections—he was a Ferrucci on his mother's side—must have helped to launch him in style, particularly with regard to commissions obtained from government offices. In 1342-1343 he made a play for the favor of the Duke of Athens, who had seized power in Florence, and got it. At one point he even lent the "tyrant" 400 florins. "After people saw how much favor I enjoyed, my services were in great demand; and if I had wished to make money, I could have made a great deal." But some

[78] This and following quotations from Velluti, *Cronica domestica*, pp. 159, 162-63.

dim craft in Donato gave him enough detachment to recognize the point at which the Duke began to head for trouble. Seeing him fall in the estimation of the citizenry, "I began sweetly to disengage myself from him, not in whole but in part, asking nothing of him nor going to him, save on holidays and to hear Mass and also on a few other feast days." We must suppose that the lawyer began to gravitate toward the enemies of the Duke, for in the summer of 1343, when the Duke barely escaped from Florence with his life, not only was Donato already in the clear, he had managed to get himself appointed to the ensuing caretaker government (the *balìa* of Fourteen). The man's privileged birth and estate were clearly matched by his personal cunning. In 1343, 1344, and 1345 he was sent on embassies to Siena, Arezzo, and Perugia. Other embassies followed, to Bologna, Ferrara, Pisa and elsewhere—missions which called for the use of his legal skills. Leading municipal dignities also came his way, until in March 1351, at the age of thirty-seven, he was drawn for the supreme executive office, the Gonfaloniership of Justice.

Borne by the force of his family connections and personal enterprise, Donato was able to hold high office and receive numerous legal commissions from the first years of his matriculation in the guild. Yet the two activities, politics and legal practice, could conflict. Each took a great deal of time. The point was to strike a balance—not to sacrifice one to the other but to wring the maximum advantage from each. Where was the balance? Speaking of the term he served in one of the Signory's advisory colleges during the winter of 1347-1348, Donato added, "I also held many other offices and embassies which redounded to my honor, though they hurt my pocket book and deflected me from my profession. Were it not that at the beginning of priorates I was careful to beg off being sent abroad as an ambassador, I would have been on embassies almost continuously. But the priors did not do [all they could] for me, which meant that I was abandoning my practice. Yet it is true that in another way the honors of the Commune were very useful to me. For it was owing to these and to my own efforts that I was legal consultant almost continuously to the trustees in bankruptcy [sindachi] of the Bardi, Peruzzi, Acciaiuoli, Buonaccorsi, and many others, for which I was well paid. In the same way I also served many offices of the Commune, which took on legal consultants at a salary, because at that time . . . the Commune did not have salaried legal consultants and each office could call in its own. Thus did I make up for the harm and disruption inflicted on my legal practice, although I was drawn away from it."[79]

Donato Velluti might protest against the burdens of public office but he loved politics and was a first-rate politician.[80] Later on in life he suffered much from gout and so was often allowed to turn down embassy appointments. On the domestic front, however, his political activity did not fall off. He served Florence as long as he lived, and his legal and judicial skills continued to be in great demand.

The early career of Francesco Guicciardini offers another case study. Many of his best clients were initially procured through his high political and social connections. Taking his doctorate toward the end of 1505, he started practicing law almost at once. As early as 1506, various communities and religious houses began to take him on as a legal consultant and advocate on retainer. One of the most important of these engagements started in July 1506, when he was made fourth advocate of the Hospital of Santa Maria Nuova, thus joining, in this distinction, three of the city's most eminent lawyers and statesmen: Francesco Pepi, Antonio Strozzi, and Giovan Vettorio Soderini. By the beginning of 1508 (he was only twenty-six years old) the Signory was already employing him on certain commissions. By this time he was already married. In 1507, despite his father's reluctance, he had married Maria Salviati. Her father and uncle, Alamanno and Jacopo, "surpassed every private citizen of Florence in powerful family connections [parentadi], in riches, in being well-liked, and in reputation. I was greatly attracted by these things and for this reason I wanted them [Alamanno and Jacopo] as relatives at all costs." Reflecting on this for a moment, Francesco then said, "God forgive me for having importuned Piero [my father] about this so much."[81]

From this time on his political and legal careers came under a new star, for the Salviati were the most influential spokesmen for one of the Republic's most powerful political currents. In March 1509 the Signory

---

[79] *Ibid.*, pp. 189-90.

[80] Brucker, *Florentine Politics and Society*, esp. pp. 78, 81, 151, 162, 209.

[81] This and following quotations from his *Ricordanze*, in *Scritti autobiografici*, pp. 58, 61.

summoned Francesco to participate for the first time in an executive advisory session. In April the cathedral canons made him one of their lawyers, and while this appointment carried a yearly salary of only 1.00 ducat and one goose (sic!), "it was most honorable because of the nature of the place and because the city's leading doctors [of law] had always been attached to it." In June he and another lawyer, Ormannozzo Deti, were chosen by the Signory to entertain two ambassadors of the Emperor Maximilian. In November, still 1509, the order of Santa Maria di Vallombrosa contracted for his legal services on a yearly basis. A few days later he was taken on as advocate of the Camaldolese order.

In some of these appointments the Salviati connection was crucial. And it is not difficult to see how one or two such appointments easily paved the way for others. Alamanno Salviati died in March 1510, but Francesco continued to enjoy the backing of his own father Piero and of Jacopo Salviati; he was soon to come under the care of another influential politician—Messer Piero Alamanni. This man made numerous contacts for him during the years 1511 to 1513, part of which our lawyer spent on his famous Spanish legation. From 1513 on it was Lorenzo di Piero de' Medici who best favored Francesco's political and professional ambitions. When in March 1514, after the election of Pope Leo X, a group of citizens was given rather full fiscal powers in Florence, Lorenzo was the man who persuaded Francesco to accept a place in this commission. "And I," said the youthful statesman, "took to the idea, seeing his disposition and thinking that the credit thus acquired would favor my legal practice."[82]

One outstanding appointment as a lawyer on retainer could help obtain other such appointments, but neither Francesco nor his contemporaries in the college of lawyers left things like this to chance. Throughout his early years at the bar and in politics, Francesco had the direct support of leading political personalities: his own father first, next Alamanno and Jacopo Salviati, then Piero Alamanni, Lorenzo di Piero de' Medici, and various others. When in May 1515 Francesco became the victim of a whispering campaign which turned Lorenzo against him, he resorted at once to his personal connections and swiftly enlisted the intervention of Lanfredino Lanfredini and Matteo Strozzi, both of whom were close

[82] *Ibid.*, p. 75.

to Lorenzo, undeclared *signore* of Florence. Lorenzo was importuned until the two men were successful not only in getting Francesco reinstated, but also in procuring a place for him in the inner circle of Medicean counsellors.

By such means was a great political and legal career fashioned: by a combination of personal pleading and private contact, by the exploitation of high place and influence, by the relentless and able aggregation of clients, position, and offices. To all this, like Donato Velluti, Francesco Guicciardini added his own arts and excellence.

### SOURCES FOR CHAPTER THREE

*Society.* Virtually any primary source—letter, statute, official dispatch, statement of fact or property—may be a document of social history. A direction and basis are provided by G. A. Brucker, *Florentine Politics and Society, 1343-1378* (Princeton, 1962), and L. Martines, *The Social World of the Florentine Humanists, 1390-1460* (Princeton, 1963), esp. Chs. II, VII, and the appendices. The reader may consult these books for a more complete bibliography both on the course of change in Florentine society and on its general anatomy. My stress on the crystallization or emergence of a nobility, a feature of the second half of the fifteenth century, is here given distinctive prominence for the first time. At the end of the fifteenth century the social attitudes and political outlook of the Florentine patriciate were so different from corresponding views three generations earlier—the inner oligarchy never recovered from the Medicean experience—that we need a word to summarize the change. *Nobility* best does this because it also looks forward to the dominant social "style" of the sixteenth century. Critical sources for this view are the chronicle (1476-1507) of Piero di Marco Parenti, BNF, *Fondo principale,* II, iv, 169-71; II, ii, 129-34 (a later copy, including a copy of the missing original MS. for the years 1502 to 1507); Francesco Guicciardini, *Storie fiorentine dal 1378 al 1509,* ed. R. Palmarocchi (Bari, 1931) and *Scritti autobiografici e rari,* ed. Palmarocchi (Bari, 1936). Not to be overlooked is the brilliant essay by Antonio Anzilotti, *La crisi costituzionale della repubblica fiorentina* (Firenze, 1912). Also helpful on social trends, even if not as much to the point because of their different focus, are these studies: R. von Albertini,

*Das Florentinische Staatsbewusstsein im Übergang von der Republik zum Prinzipat* (Bern, 1955); V. Ricchioni, *La costituzione politica di Firenze ai tempi di Lorenzo il Magnifico* (Siena, 1913); and A. Municchi, *La fazione antimedicea detta 'del Poggio'* (Firenze, 1911), for the political struggles of the later 1450s and 1460s. In a valuable article with documents attached, G. Pampaloni touches on the social forces behind the crisis of 1465-1466: "Fermenti di riforme democratiche nella Firenze medicea del quattrocento," *Archivio storico italiano*, cxix, 1-2 (1961), 11-62, 241-81; cxx, 4 (1962), 521-81. Although endowed with a suggestive title, an old article by A. Crivellucci is not helpful: "Del governo popolare di Firenze, 1494-1512 e del suo riordinamento secondo il Guicciardini," *Annali della scuola normale superiore di Pisa*, iii, ii, division of philosophy and philology (Pisa, 1877), 223-338.

For the social background of individual lawyers see ASF, *Carte del Bene,* the papers and letters pertaining to Messer Ricciardo; *Acquisti e doni,* 3-5 (accounts of Messer Francesco Gaddi); *Strozz., 2a ser.,* 23 (*Ricordanze* of Messer Giovanni Buongirolami); *Strozz., 2a ser.,* 21, (*Ricordanze* of Messer Virgilio Adriani); *AGN,* 677 (*Ricordanze* of Messer Sallustio Buonguglielmi); and BNF, *Cod. Panciatichiani,* 147 (*Zibaldone* of Messer Lorenzo Ridolfi). In published material of this sort there is F. Guicciardini, *Scritti autobiografici*; Bernardo Machiavelli, *Libro di ricordi,* ed. C. Olschki (Firenze, 1954); and G. Niccolini di Camugliano, *The Chronicles of a Florentine Family, 1200-1470* (London, 1933). A great mass of material is to be found in the letters to and from lawyers contained in the collection ASF, *Mediceo avanti il principato*, see esp. the indices to each catalogue volume. A full list of the names of lawyers there can only be compiled by taking them from the appendix to this book.

*School.* The principal sources are the collections of university documents: A. Gherardi, ed., *Statuti della università e studio fiorentino* (Firenze, 1881); C. Malagola, ed., *Statuti della università e dei collegi dello studio bolognese* (Bologna, 1888); A. Gloria, ed., *Monumenti della università di Padova, 1318-1405* (Padova, 1888). Of the standard studies in the field I have found the following the most useful: H. Denifle, *Die Entstehung der Universitäten des Mittelalters bis 1400* (Berlin, 1885);

H. Rashdall, *The Universities of Europe in the Middle Ages*, 3 vols., ed. Powicke and Emden (Oxford, 1936); G. Zaccagnini, *La vita dei maestri e degli scolari nello studio di Bologna nei secoli xiii e xiv* (Geneva, 1926); the Introduction to *Il 'Liber secretus iuris caesarei' dell' università di Bologna*, 2 vols., ed. A. Sorbelli (Bologna, 1938-1942); A. Sorbelli and L. Simeoni, *Storia della università di Bologna*, 2 vols. (Bologna, 1940); S. Stelling-Michaud, *L'Université de Bologne et la pénétration des droits romain et canonique en Suisse aux xiii<sup>e</sup> et xiv<sup>e</sup> siècles* (Geneva, 1955); and Pearl Kibre, *Scholarly Privileges in the Middle Ages* (London, 1961). For elementary and secondary education there is the broad treatment by G. Manacorda, *Storia della scuola in Italia*, 2 vols. (Milano, n.d.); on Florence in particular, dealing chiefly with the age of Dante, there is a chapter in R. Davidsohn, *Geschichte von Florenz*, iv, iii (Berlin, 1927), ch. iii, and now the excellent piece by C. T. Davis, "Education in Dante's Florence," *Speculum*, xl, 3 (1965), 415-35. H. Wieruszowski, "Arezzo as a Center of Learning and Letters in the Thirteenth Century," *Traditio*, ix (1953), 321-91, is especially noteworthy on a neighboring town and the *ars dictandi* tradition.

*Cases and fees.* On the jurisdiction of the two laws see the standard legal histories listed in the sources for Ch. II. Several hundred volumes of deliberations and *consilia legalia* provide a picture of the variety of cases handled by Florentine lawyers. The major sequences are these: ASF, *Signori, Deliberazioni in forza della loro ordinaria autorità*, see esp. the volumes for the period 1450-1530; ASF, *Corporazioni religiose soppresse*, Arch. 98 ("Eredità Bonsi"), vols. 234-282; *Strozz., 3a ser.*, 41, 42, twenty-one volumes of *consilia*, many of which collected by one of the subjects of this study, Messer Antonio Strozzi; BNF, *Fondo Magliabechiano*, cl. xxix, and *Fondo Panciatichiano* have about twenty-five volumes of legal opinions, dating from the end of the fourteenth to the beginning of the sixteenth century. These volumes are described and listed in detail in the sources for Ch. X.

On the subject of legal fees, retainers and the like, my notes in the text proper provide a list of the different sources consulted.

*Careers.* Regarding the link between careers in law and politics, the student may begin with these sources: ASF, *Consulte e Pratiche*, 19-73;

*Tratte*, 67-71, 78-83; *Priorista di palazzo; Manoscritti*, 265, 266 (lists, arranged by family, of the *Dodici Buonomini* and *Sedici Gonfalonieri*); also the numerous volumes of diplomatic and foreign correspondence listed in the sources for Chs. VII and VIII. Having drawn from these sources the names of lawyers who figured prominently in public affairs, one then finds that they were the ones whose legal services were most in demand. This fact is established by the collections of *consilia* listed above, by the Signory's legal and judicial commissions as recorded in the many volumes of *Signori, Deliberazioni (ut supra)*, and by the types of lawyers most often hired or put on retainer by religious houses, guilds, and other corporate bodies. For analyzing the confluence of legal and political careers, apart from that which appears in the writings of Velluti and Guicciardini, there are the many dozens of letters to and from lawyers in the *Strozziane* and *MAP* collections of the Archivio di Stato di Firenze.

*Government and Statecraft*

## Chapter Four

# Legal Aspects of Sovereignty and Magistracy in Florence

Chapters V-VIII require an introduction because of their detail and scope. The aim of these chapters is to give a full account of the different functions performed by lawyers in the whole spectrum of public affairs. We shall see lawyers confronting questions relating to the norms of political practice and to the very nature of the Florentine state. It must be said that the questions will often be implicit. Attention will be given to the specific assignments of lawyers, to particular problems and difficulties that needed immediate solutions. But looming just beyond the foreground will be the great constitutional, legal, and political questions to which the major tasks of lawyers finally referred. These are the questions that call for identification in this introductory chapter.

Identification, I say, not a full hearing, for the aim here will be to provide an orientation and some general guidelines. The technical details of legal-political theory and detailed solutions to questions raised will not be set forth until after a view has been presented of the practical workings of statecraft in Florence. Only in Chapters IX and especially X, after having represented the "real" world in which lawyers carried out their public assignments, do I turn fully to legal-political theory.

Was Florence a sovereign state? From a legal viewpoint, this is a fundamental question: on it depend a number of other leading questions.

If a sovereign political entity be one with absolutely no limitations on its authority in matters of public law and the state, Florence was not sovereign. Not all men who resided in Florentine territory were subject to the laws of that state. In the fifteenth century, neither in Florence nor generally in Western Europe were clerics normally subject to the full sway of the temporal power. Episcopal courts, possessed of an obvious public authority, stood outside the ordinary jurisdiction of the state.

Up to about the middle of the fourteenth century, Florence was subject *de iure* to the general laws of a higher authority, the Empire. While having very little if any effect in practical terms, this bond was explicitly acknowledged by Florentines. The next 100 years saw a gradual transition: the supreme authority *de facto* of the Florentine state—always with reference to temporal affairs—developed into an authority *de iure*. As late as 1414 there were lawyers in the city who could still refer to Florentines as *fideles* of the Empire,[1] but the reference leaps out of the documents anachronistically and seems capable of conjuring up no more than a vanishing or nebulous sentiment. Such references soon disappeared altogether. Having lived for 200 years and more as if without a temporal superior, Florence now acknowledged no superior even in theory. The force of custom had finally made valid *de iure*—at all events in its own eyes—the sovereign authority of the Republic in secular affairs.[2]

If we admit degrees of sovereignty and emphasize fact more than declining legal theory, it is clear that Florence was sovereign in the period included in this study. Its relations with the clergy aside, the Republic was sole master of its affairs, sole source of its laws. From about the last third of the fourteenth century, Florentine lawyers began to adopt a series of legal formulas which summed up sovereignty.[3] In the course of the fifteenth century, they drew on these formulas more and more frequently in litigious relations with lands under Florentine rule. The decades right around 1400 were still marked by confusion: legal counsel for the state sometimes adduced the formulas of sovereignty and sometimes not. Thus, in the Moncione murder case of 1421, government lawyers circumvented the rights of a community in Florentine territory not by relying on arguments from the state's superior or sovereign status, but by citing particular statutes which enabled Florence to claim competence in the case, while at the same time seeming to leave local judicial rights intact.[4] On the other hand, in a dispute over citizenship some eight years earlier, counsel for Florence overrode the claims of subject Pisa by relying on the formulas of sovereignty.[5] In 1399, in still another case,

---

[1] See p. 340.

[2] There were, however, conflicting views concerning whether or not in Roman law the powers of the prince were subject to prescriptive right. Cf. W. Ullmann, *The Medieval Idea of Law* (London, 1946), p. 182.

[3] Details on pp. 415ff.

[4] Case fully discussed on pp. 155ff.

[5] Nello da San Gimignano, p. 416.

Florence arbitrarily disregarded the rights of a regional court—rights which Florence had previously confirmed—and temporarily took these to itself.[6] No argument from law was produced: representing the state, the Signory acted extraordinarily from its presumed sovereign powers.

By the later fifteenth century, as Chapter X will show, Florentine legal assumptions about the Republic's sovereignty in temporal affairs were no longer tentative or yielding. Here and there in Florentine territory there remained a few small pockets of feudal jurisdiction. But when it chose, Florence could normally make its supremacy felt throughout its lands. What is more, Florentine lawyers readily advanced the sovereign prerogatives of the *civitas superior*, whether in questions of judicial competence out in the dominion, the imposition of taxes on subject lands, or the extraordinary revocation of privileges guaranteed by the ordinary rule of law. The power to revoke these had once pertained solely to the *princeps* of the Roman law books.

Were Florentine statutes general laws which applied to all communities under the Republic's rule? Some were, but most were not. Statutes concerning taxation, civil disorder, rebellion, and defense often bound the whole of Florentine territory. Florence occasionally stepped in and directly altered administrative procedure in a subject town. Much, however, was left to local laws and customs. Particularly were penal laws and civil proceedings the subject of local regulation. Yet the statutes of subject communes were valid only when approved and confirmed by Florence. In this sense the validity of all local law depended on the sovereign power.

Whatever the theoretical claims of the Emperor in fourteenth-century Italy, it would be unthinkable to hold that republican Florence ever conducted its foreign affairs other than as a sovereign power. In the fifteenth century, although there might be some variety in the fanfare put on at receptions, the Republic treated the Emperor as it did other princes: as one sovereign dealing with another. In its foreign affairs, Florence did all things that sovereigns do: it made war and peace, dispatched ambassadors to all the leading capitals of Western Europe (and to the Sultan), negotiated and concluded treaties of every kind, and took disputes before *ad hoc* boards of international arbitration. Evidently, the Italian city-

[6] See the Pitti incident, p. 164.

states of the Renaissance period managed their diplomatic relations in accordance with norms which enjoyed a degree of international recognition. Chapter VIII will study these norms in connection with the diplomatic functions of lawyers.

Very occasionally, in Florentine relations with the papacy, the city was put under extreme stress and the question of its internal sovereignty became an issue. At the end of the fifteenth century this question was raised by the transfer of civil lawsuits from Florence to Rome. Involved in legal disputes at home, Florentine laymen, adducing one of two or three reasons, sometimes had recourse to Rome and managed to get the Sacra Rota Romana to hear their cases in appeal.[7] The Republic knew that such action struck at its sovereign authority *in temporalibus*, and so, working through its ambassadors, it lodged protests with the holy father and sought every means to block lay litigious appeal to Rome. If Florence got less than satisfaction in this tug of war, it must be pointed out that the city, in turn, claimed and exercised jurisdiction over certain types of ecclesiastical litigious disputes. The question of the sovereignty of Florence vis-à-vis the Church, or rather some of the legal-political aspects thereof, will be taken up in Chapter VII.

Occasional violations in a given sector of the Republic's sovereignty did not necessarily affect its actions on other fronts, nor did they disturb the basic suppositions which governed its foreign and territorial affairs. To take a kindred example from our own times, deficiencies *de facto* in the sovereignty of states like Guatemala and Vietnam impugn neither their theoretical claims to an absolute sovereignty *de iure* nor the fact that on many questions their imperfect sovereignty is compelling and decisive. Sovereignty in fifteenth-century Europe presented many more problems than it does today, but this is no reason to exclude it from our historical considerations.

What I have said so far may be summed up as follows. During and before the period included in this study, Florence acknowledged—for all practical purposes—absolutely no superior in temporal affairs.[8] From the last third, roughly, of the fourteenth century, the theoretical rights of supreme lordship over Florence, hitherto belonging to the Emperor *de*

[7] Ch. VII, 3.          [8] Saving an exceptional moment in 1401, p. 414.

*iure*, were gradually claimed and taken over by Florence itself. Thereafter, expressed in a few concise formulas, these rights were increasingly and vigorously advanced by lawyers speaking for the Florentine state.

Where lay the Republic's sovereign authority, its *imperium*?[9] It had to be vested in a particular magistracy, in certain councils, or in a larger Florentine *universitas*. That one or more of these sectors held the focal points of power will be apparent to the student of Italian city-states. Yet the question of the precise locus of those points has at times been oversimplified or miscast.[10] More often it has been evaded, paradoxically, by being taken for granted. Historians have supposed the foci of Florentine political power to be contained either in the Signory, the legislative councils, the oligarchy, a dominant clique, or in assemblies of the people. As a socio-political solution to the question, emphasis on the oligarchy has made for the most realistic and satisfactory analyses. The real interest here is somewhat different. It is to get at the distribution of the public power by noting the interplay among fact, custom, and constitutional theory.

Theoretically, the final repository of the sovereign power was that *populus liber*, the Florentine people.[11] On the rare occasions of its formal assembly, it disposed of the totality of public power in temporal affairs. It could discard or revolutionize the Florentine constitution. But customarily the supremacy of power—the power of the *princeps* of Roman law— was exercised by the legislative councils and the Signory. Such was the rule in normal times. But in abnormal times, which very often punctuated the period from the fourteenth to the early sixteenth centuries, what happened then? In times of war, political tumult, and plague the full power of the state might temporarily devolve on a plenipotentiary council (*balìa*) or on the key offices of the executive complex.

Medieval theories of government did not, generally speaking, envisage a separation of powers. The legislative, judicial, and executive functions— though in part delegable—were vested in one head: king, pope, or supreme

---

[9] Cf. M. P. Gilmore, *Argument from Roman Law in Political Thought, 1200-1600* (Cambridge, Mass., 1941), pp. 20-21, on *imperium*.

[10] E.g. by V. Ricchioni, *La costituzione politica di Firenze ai tempi di Lorenzo il Magnifico* (Siena, 1913).

[11] References and discussion on pp. 423-25.

magistracy.[12] Save in moments of emergency, this arrangement was not seen at Florence, but neither did the city hallow a three-way division of authority. Florentine government was more richly appointed: it called for both a fusion and a separation of powers.

As long as the Republic lasted, the ordinary power to make laws was claimed and exercised by the legislative councils: the old Councils of the People and Commune, the Council of Two Hundred, later on the Council of One Hundred, then the Seventy, and finally the Grand Council. Here was the most clearly delineated sector of public authority—legislating—although it was always subject to the initiative of the executive. The legislative councils could vote on nothing which had not first been approved by the Signory and advisory colleges. Furthermore, the legislative competence of the Grand Council was impure; this body could sit as a vast court of appeal in serious cases of alleged political crime.[13]

Five major courts—the guild courts aside—dispensed penal and civil justice.[14] Accorded a working autonomy, they functioned vigorously up to about the early fifteenth century. Nearly all the city's important judicial business was heard and determined in their chambers. But in the course of the fifteenth century great inroads were made into their autonomy and competence. The judicial operations of the executive, especially as represented by the Signory and the Eight on Public Safety, were vastly expanded, and two or three of the five major courts were gradually made the target of executive directives which touched particular cases and often determined decisions.

On what did the executive base its authority to take part in the dispensation of justice? Although the need for such defense rarely arose, four claims could be set forth.

The most explicit and obvious claim was based on legislation. This provided limited powers. Now and then the legislative councils—always subject to the initiative of the Signory—voted to invest the executive with the authority to decide particular types of cases. The judicial activity

---

[12] On which see W. Ullmann, *Principles of Government and Politics in the Middle Ages* (London, 2nd ed., 1966), and especially M. Wilks, *The Problem of Sovereignty in the Later Middle Ages* (Cambridge, 1963).

[13] See p. 140.

[14] Described and analyzed in Ch. V, 1.

of the Eight and the Conservatores was so based. The second source of the executive's title to judicial competence was custom. There was noth-in the Florentine constitution, at least as set out in the communal statutes of 1415, which explicitly authorized the Signory to sit as an appellate judge in criminal or civil proceedings. Nevertheless, the Signory had occasionally although rarely assumed this function in the fourteenth century. The practice undoubtedly went back to the thirteenth century and was taken over from the "podestaral" commune, when the city's leading official was vested with powers of high justice. A trace of this old practice persisted throughout the fourteenth and fifteenth centuries and was reflected in the name of the Republic's chief dignitary, the Gonfalonier (or Standard-bearer) of Justice. At the beginning of the sixteenth century the founding legislation for the lifetime position of Gonfalonier of Justice designated him "the head of justice."[15]

Still another source of the executive's judicial prerogative was its authority *de facto*. This would seem, *prima facie*, not to bestow a sound constitutional or legal right. But we must free ourselves from twentieth-century assumptions in such matters. The authority of the Signory was high. Precedent provided some support. The Signory had infrequently acted as a high court of justice. If suddenly, extraordinarily, it claimed competence in a particular case, either for itself or for one of its adjuncts (e.g., the Eight or the Conservatores), there might be protests, but none could or would block its actions. The legal justification for an intervention of this sort is best seen in the principle which sometimes governed emergencies: action in the name of public safety or the community good. In such moments the *utilitas publica* seemed to call for swift, summary action; and from whence was this to come if not from the head of state, the Signory?

The common law of Italy, as summed up in Justinian's compilation, provided the fourth and final source of the executive's judicial competence. Roman law sanctioned the right of final appeal to the prince.[16] Normally, the Signory did not occupy the place of the prince in Florentine territory.[17] But when lawyers confronted an urgent problem in

[15] Reference, p. 142.
[16] E.g., the implications of *D*. 49, 3, 1.
[17] As demonstrated on pp. 439-40.

the sphere of public law, they had often to produce rapid, practical solutions. Casting around for the focal point of public authority, they most often hit on the Signory as that body which, for everyday purposes, most approximated the prince of the *Digest* and *Code*.

Approximated, for the Signory was not the prince. Was it, nevertheless, empowered to hear *any* temporal case in appeal? Could it somehow be turned into a supreme court? These questions have never been raised, perhaps because they point to one of the most obscure features of the Florentine constitution.

Down to the early fifteenth century, as I have said, the city's regular courts enjoyed nearly full autonomy. The Signory did not normally undertake to hear appeals against their decisions. Ordinary civil litigation remained beyond the reach of the executive's *regular* powers even in the later fifteenth century, although there were many exceptions and "infractions." The judicial competence of the Signory was equally self-contained, for no appeal was possible in cases subject to the jurisdiction of the Signory. This rule particularly applied to criminal proceedings. The Signory thus disposed of certain powers of high justice. But at the end of the fifteenth century appellate procedure was introduced for one class of cases tried by the Signory and its adjuncts—cases of serious political crime. In these cases the appeal was processed by the Signory but went to the Grand Council for final action, so that in this one respect the summary justice of the Grand Council was superior to that of the Signory and other offices of the executive complex. The new Council of Justice (the Rota Fiorentina), established at the beginning of the sixteenth century, was made the highest regular court. The executive could not accept appeals against its decisions, but neither, in turn, could the Rota encroach on the executive's summary judicial proceedings.

In short, the dispensation of justice in Florence belonged to two separate spheres: to a system of regular courts and to the prerogative of the executive; but a share might be accorded even to the legislature in special cases. In theory, the regular courts derived from the plenitude of power which distinguished the prince (*populus* or sovereign magistracy); in practice, they occupied a sphere apart and were held to adjudicate *de iure*.[18] The executive, on the contrary, adjudicated *de facto*; that is to say, drawing

[18] See pp. 138-39.

on its ordinary practical authority, the executive dispensed a special type of summary justice from a point outside the regular system of courts.

Although separate, there were yet certain points of contact between the two spheres. For one thing, the executive occasionally exerted pressure on the regular courts and might indirectly determine their decisions.[19] The course of the fifteenth century brought a striking increase in contact of this sort. Moreover, the Signory and the Eight on Public Safety were authorized, whenever they chose, to transfer their own cases to the regular courts.

The division between the two spheres entirely vanished when the Signory acted from its extraordinary powers. Suddenly the executive rose high above the regular courts and assumed all the judicial prerogatives of the prince. In this incarnation, the executive could undertake to hear and determine *any* cause. Such action was most often taken in the name of the public good and occasionally couched in terms of necessity or the force of circumstance. Relying on this argument, the Signory and the Eight on Public Safety once set themselves above the Grand Council and boldly blocked a controversial appeal to it.[20]

In pointing out the legal-political foundations of the executive's judicial prerogative, I have called attention to extraordinary and emergency powers. This discretionary aspect of Florentine government was usually accorded legal justification by reference to the public or community or common good. Lawyers and statesmen were to employ this type of argument *pari passu* with the rise of the modern state, and this inquiry will often note the argument. In our time, heads of state tend to dispose of a powerful discretionary prerogative, but there is usually precise machinery for deposing or trying them in cases of abuse. Not so in the Italian city-state, where deposition nearly aways depended on uprisings, *colpi di stato*, force, and where discretionary powers were so frequently brought into play that in certain respects they ended by becoming a permanent feature of the everyday political landscape. Thus the prominence in these pages of those powers.

It remains to take up a few questions concerning the magistracies of the executive complex. What was the Signory's relation to them? Was

[19] As in the Moncione murder case, pp. 155ff.
[20] Discussed on pp. 441-45.

their authority established by an act of delegation? Who resolved conflict between them? How were they regulated?

The competence of the many executive offices derived from the Signory by way of the legislative councils. These authorized the delegation and distribution of functions which, if collected, returned finally to the prerogative of the Signory. For the Signory was the head of state, the original repository—when viewed in structural terms—of the sum of executive functions. Intervening at will in all the affairs of its general competence, it dispatched directives to the Ten on War (Dieci di Balìa), the Eight on Public Safety, the Conservatores, the Monte, the Morals, and the Catasto offices. Apart from having regulative functions, these offices customarily had summary judicial powers over specific material. Their decisions could not be questioned save by appeal to the Signory, which had the last word in such matters.

With the exception of the Signory (and in some matters it also complied), the offices of the executive cluster were regulated by statute. An office had only as much authority as the law conferred.[21] This was the theory and expectation. In fact, however, the departures from this norm were many and particularly manifest in the activities of the Ten on War and the Eight on Public Safety. Consequently, one of the Signory's tasks was to demand observance of the norm, to step in, issue admonitions, and correct abuses. From time to time it also lodged apposite criticism in the prefaces of new regulatory statutes. When disputes broke out between two or more offices, the constitutional place of the Signory made it the natural seat of arbitration. The Signory was free to delegate the responsibility, but whether delegated or not, the attendant technical functions were inevitably left to lawyers. Only the Signory could turn their opinions into binding decisions.

There was one office, the Ten on War, which did not much cleave to the pattern of the others. In times of war or danger of war, it customarily held special powers, including even the right to dispatch ambassadors and confer citizenship.[22] Statutory law established the amplitude of the Ten's powers, which in practice were such as not to allow for the im-

[21] See p. 411.
[22] G. Pampaloni, "Gli organi della repubblica fiorentina per le relazioni con

position of clearly defined limits. Here was an office in some ways like the Signory because it temporarily exercised certain of the Signory's powers. Not surprisingly, we come on instances of rivalry between the two.[23] At the end of the fifteenth century, the question of the Ten's fortunes contributed to a raging controversy between the exponents of two opposed views of government.[24]

The preceding pages rather suggest that whoever controlled the key offices of the executive complex potentially controlled the state. Political opponents had little chance of survival when faced with the great discretionary powers vested in magistracies like the Signory, the Ten on War, and the Eight on Public Safety. If the Signory sometimes failed to ram its preferred legislation through the legislative councils, these in turn could not enact legislation which had not first been approved by the Signory and its advisory colleges. In the second half of the fifteenth century, with the decay of the regular courts and the ever-expanding powers of the executive, justice at times became a spoil and citizens became more docile.

## SOURCES FOR CHAPTER FOUR

As the footnotes reveal, the substance of this chapter is drawn from succeeding parts of the book. For the general legal-political background, readers should consult the detailed bibliography at the end of Chapter X, taking particular note of the books and papers by the following: O. Gierke, C.N.S. Woolf, F. Ercole, E. Kantorowicz, G. Post, W. Ullmann, F. Calasso, E. E. Stengel, B. Tierney, and D. Segoloni.

The unpublished sources given at the end of Chapter V and the opinions of lawyers listed by collection at the end of Chapter X are absolutely essential for an understanding of the Florentine constitution, its changes, Florentine political practice, and the changing legal-political outlook in the city. Studies bearing on these matters are also listed at the end of Chapter V; particular note should be taken of the books and papers by the following: R. Davidsohn, G. Antonelli, A. Anzilotti, G. Brucker, F. Gilbert, G. Pampaloni, A. Rado, and N. Rubinstein.

---

l'estero," *Rivista di studi politici internazionali*, xx, ii (1953), 261-96, and this study p. 415.

[23] Martines, *The Social World of the Florentine Humanists*, p. 146.

[24] See pp. 198-201, 211-14.

## Chapter Five

# Problems of Internal Government

## *1. The Judiciary*

No aspect of government in the late medieval and Renaissance periods is more elusive, trickier to study in its changes, than the administration of justice. For although the judiciary often had its own sphere and magistracies, the other branches of government frequently shared in the right to dispense justice. This happened in advanced city-states like Venice, Siena, Genoa, Florence, and in most states under one-man rule (*signorie*). Legislative assemblies—senates chiefly—were turned at times into high courts of justice. Supreme executive bodies and their dependent offices (e.g., permanent commissions) were frequently empowered to dole out fines, prison sentences, and capital punishment. Indeed, the executive arm of the Italian states reached out so far that in many cases no sure division was possible between the judicial and the executive functions of government. In Florence, a decision of the Podestà might be rescinded by an act of the Councils of the People and Commune. Except in Venice, however, legislative assemblies were less inclined than executive bodies to pass beyond the customary limits of their jurisdiction. Although it may be true that one of the prime causes of trouble in Renaissance Italy was nearly always a grasping executive, it is also true that legislatures—in perfect harmony with the dominant views of jurists—were too often excessively passive. During the period spanned by this study, and increasingly so in the course of the fifteenth century, the Florentine Signory sometimes took an active part in the judicial business of the city's ordinary regular courts.[1]

Davidsohn noted that in the thirteenth century the Florentine Commune had no fewer than thirty-eight different courts, apart from the special offices which enjoyed a variety of judicial powers.[2] These courts

---

[1] Such action took the form of concrete directives, at times touching the sifting of evidence and even final judgments. *Statuta*, ii, 519, bears in part on the constitutional norms of the designated intervention.

[2] *Geschichte von Florenz*, iv, i, 265.

were not organized in the relation of higher to lower bodies; they functioned autonomously—as creations of the Church, the guilds, the Commune. Created by the Commune, they might be full-fledged tribunals like the courts of the Podestà and the Captain; or, like the Defenders of the Laws (founded in 1429), they might be standing executive commissions with limited judicial powers, such as that of setting crippling fines or barring citizens from public office. This partitioning of judicial author-ity remained a feature of Florentine government for as long as the Republic lasted and even beyond.

During the fourteenth and fifteenth centuries, the ordinary regular courts were those of the *rectores forenses* (Podestà, Captain, and Executor), the Appellate Judge, the bishop (archbishop after 1420), the Mercanzia, and the twenty-one guilds. Some important additions were made from the late fourteenth century on. Florence established a series of executive offices endowed with remarkable judicial powers: such were the Eight on Public Safety, the Tower Officials, the Ten on Liberty, the Ten on War, the Defenders of the Laws, the Nocturnal Officials, and later on the Otto di Pratica, as well as more than half a dozen other offices. By 1478 the Eight on Public Safety were all but a full-fledged court, competent primarily in criminal cases, while yet retaining the constitutional status of an executive commission with extraordinary powers of justice.

Not until the outset of the sixteenth century, when the Council of Justice was established, did Florence have a high court made up of a panel of jurists, and then their jurisdiction was both original and appellate. The fifteenth-century courts of the Podestà, the Captain, the Executor, the Mercanzia, and twenty-one guilds were all courts of first instance, the first four also functioning as courts of appeal. Generally speaking, no ordinary appeal was possible in the fourteenth century against decisions handed down by the courts of the major guilds. It was not the same, however, with the minor guilds. Appeal against their decisions was normally permitted by the laws of the city in cases where claims exceeded certain sums. Yet most guilds strongly discouraged this practice, and such appeals were not very often processed in the earlier fourteenth century.[3] When they were, the cases ordinarily went to the Mercanzia. Doren observed that in the course of the fourteenth century there was a marked increase in the incidence of appeal from the guild courts. He noted that according as the guilds were weakened, the Mercanzia heard more appeals, granted first hearings to more and more cases which had once been handled by the guild courts.[4]

I have indicated that the jurisdiction of the courts of the Podestà, the Captain, and the Executor was both original and appellate. Until about the middle of the fifteenth century their active jurisdiction extended to criminal as well as civil cases. Competence in particular cases belonged to that court in whose chambers the case was first moved or to that magistrate whose guardsmen made the initial arrest. In any deadlock, the Podestà had precedence over the other two, the Captain over the Executor.[5] Appeal proceedings were equally rational but more complicated. In the second half of the fourteenth century, appeal from the courts of the *rectores forenses* went to the Appellate Judge, also a foreign magistrate whose election was conducted by the Signory and colleges. If he rendered a decision different from the original one, a second appeal could be made to the Captain or the Podestà, depending on the source of the original decision.[6] The independent office of Appellate Judge was eliminated in 1410, but revived in 1412 and integrated "in all its members, parts, and appurtenances" with the office of the Executor.[7] After 1415 and until 1477, the functions of the independent Appellate Judge passed over to the Captain of the People. But when the original cause had been adjudicated in one of the Captain's courts, the first appeal went to the Executor of the Ordinances of Justice, the second to the Podestà.[8] If the first Appellate Judge confirmed the original judgment, no further appeal was possible. In certain types of criminal cases, however, the procedure

[3] A. Doren, *Le arti fiorentine*, tr. G. B. Klein, 2 vols. (Firenze, 1940), II, 68-71. See *SCF*, 19 (statutes of Podestà, year 1355), ff. 109v-110v, for the law denying appeal against the sentences of major guilds.

[4] Doren, *loc.cit.*     [5] *Statuta*, I, 236.     [6] *SCF*, 19, ff. 15r-16v.

[7] *Prov.*, 100, ff. 131r-132r (4 Feb. 1411, Florentine).

[8] *Statuta*, I, 218-22. *Carte di Corredo*, II, f. 115v, pencil, for a provision of 1431 which permitted appeal against sentences of the Eight on Public Safety, though only by license of the Signory and colleges.

was entirely different. For, according to the statutes of 1415, when penalties in criminal proceedings were pronounced by communal officials whose authority issued from the executive sector of government, no appeal could be made to the Appellate Judge.[9] Instead, the appellant had to turn to the Signory. Thus were the judicial prerogatives of the executive protected.

The magistrates of the major regular courts—Podestà, Captain, Executor, and Appellate Judge—were all recruited from abroad. At the outset of the fifteenth century, the train of the first three of these officials included nine foreign jurists who sat as judges in the city's district courts.[10] The four who accompanied the Podestà, for example, were deployed as follows. Two were put over civil litigation, one holding court for the quarters of S. Spirito and S. Croce, the other for S. Giovanni and S. Maria Novella. The two others were assigned as judges over criminal proceedings and each, again, was given jurisdiction over two quarters of the city.[11] The court of the Mercanzia included a consulting body of six Florentine merchants, but the chief magistrate was always a foreigner, and from the second half of the fourteenth century always a doctor of civil law. There was no appeal against the decisions of this court, whose jurisdiction was rather special, as the name suggests. All cases of reprisal, whether moved by Florentines against foreigners or the converse, came before this court; so too did bankruptcy, litigation between native commercial companies, between business partners, and after 1357 between merchants and either lawyers or notaries. Where both the Mercanzia and a guild court were competent, the *actor* could move his case where he saw fit. During the second half of the fourteenth century, since the Captain too was empowered to try cases of bankruptcy and the Podestà was competent in reprisal proceedings, the Mercanzia shared sectors of its jurisdiction.[12] But in the course of the fifteenth century it fully won out, in fact acquired authority over additional judicial business, such as disputes over dowries.

---

[9] *Statuta*, I, 220.       [10] *Ibid.*, I, 13, 26, 37.

[11] *Ibid.*, I, 16, 18.

[12] G. Bonolis, *La giurisdizione della mercanzia in Firenze nel secolo xiv* (Firenze, 1901), pp. 34-41, 81, 105-107. On the post-1357 item see *Prov.*, 44, f. 57r.

Although resident and native Florentine lawyers were barred from the leading judicial posts, the city's elaborate system of courts required a class of experts apart from the foreign judges. These experts—lawyers and notaries—acted of course as agents in the courtroom proper. Lawyers also served as judicial counsellors out of court and as consultants on the statutes that regulated the life of the different tribunals. The concern of this study being statecraft, my interest here is not the obvious link—litigious business or crime—between lawyers and courts and clients. I am concerned, rather, with the agents and agencies called upon to regulate the judicial system and to work change in it.

Sources do not always reveal the names of lawyers who directed the work of establishing or redefining the functions of particular courts and of executive offices with *de facto* power to impose sentences. But the hand of lawyers is easily traceable in such reform. When in 1394 the statutes governing the court of the Mercanzia were recodified, the men put in charge of the revision were laymen.[13] Their subject matter, however, and the new changes affecting the competence and scope of this court leave no doubt that the work was carried out under the close supervision of at least one lawyer and a notary with great practical knowledge of the Florentine judicial system. Little more than 100 years later there was another full-scale review and recodification of the Mercanzia statutes. Again the final product was the work of experts: it is full of distinctions between executive and ordinary lawsuits, of descriptions bearing on varieties of petitions, and of material on commercial reprisal, on property and dowry disputes, on procedural questions, and on a host of other technical matters. Guidantonio Vespucci, one of the oligarchical chieftains of the period, seems to have been the lawyer who took in hand the working out of this reform.[14]

The reappointment of the Mercanzia in 1495-1496 was not fortuitous. This and later reforms, looking to dislocations in the Florentine judiciary,

---

[13] *Mercanzia*, 5, which includes additions up to the year 1476. The lawyer, Ludovico Albergotti, was one of the witnesses present when these statutes were confirmed.

[14] *Mercanzia*, 9-11, three copies of the statutes of 1496. *Prov.*, 186, ff. 42r. (21 May 1495), 146v (November 1495), authorized the reform of the Mercanzia statutes. On Vespucci see A. M. Bandini, *Vita di Amerigo Vespucci* (Firenze, 1892), p. 7.

sought to redress imbalances and defects that in some matters went back to the first half of the fifteenth century. The signs of a profound judicial malaise are revealed not only by the evidence of private correspondence or of writers like Giovanni Cavalcanti, Alamanno Rinuccini, and Vespasiano da Bisticci, but also and much more than these by the reform provisions themselves. They reveal that in the course of the fifteenth century an expanding and invasive executive had weakened the traditional courts by tending to dissolve the boundaries around the old judiciary. This was the long-term effect of a rash of new executive commissions endowed with extraordinary judicial powers. It was not the fruit of a conspiracy mounted by the Medici family but a by-product of the trends, economic and social, which went to draw the old and new ruling families more closely around the leading house. In tracing the rise of signorial rule in Italy, too often we concentrate on one man, one dynasty, one faction, or the cunning exploitation of a constitutional norm, forgetting that no prince of that period could long survive without the backing of a strategic sector of society: the merchant class, the landowners and feudal chieftains, or the old administrative class.

Out of the city's judicial troubles came the occasion for lawyers to play a part in the reform of the courts.

The Eight on Public Safety were created in 1378, immediately following the celebrated revolt and defeat of the Florentine proletariat.[15] A type of political and military police, they were designed to track down conspiracy, troublesome discontent, and other forms of activity that menaced the security of the state. Two provisions of the 1420s invested the Eight with very wide investigative authority. Both by law and direct onslaught their potency grew. They seem to have grabbed power wherever they could. By the 1430s they were sending directives to the foreign magistrates, instructing them on particular cases and sentences. Thereafter the competence of the Eight was especially felt in criminal proceedings. In January 1453 the legislative councils enacted a provision which protested against the fact that the Eight often interfered in civil cases. But the

---

[15] G. Antonelli, "La magistratura degli Otto di Guardia a Firenze," *ASI*, 402, 1 (1954), is the only existing treatment, though it only scratches the surface.

commission did not mend its ways, for it was again reformed in 1471, when the need was felt to stipulate all the areas in which the commission had no competence. Particularly were the Eight admonished not to tamper with civil litigation and disputes over ecclesiastical benefices. They had developed by this time into all but a full-scale criminal court, having long since absorbed—by dint of seizure and encroachment—much of the criminal jurisdiction which had once belonged to the Podestà, the Captain, and the Executor.[16]

This process of enfeeblement at the heart of the old judiciary was fostered by the growing judicial activity of the Signory, the Defenders of the Laws, the Ten on War, and a number of other standing commissions. If we turn to the Signory's ordinary deliberations of the 1390s, we find that the priors seldom interfered in civil litigation. They accepted few litigious petitions, sometimes none for months at a time. A hundred years later, the same run of documents—*Deliberazioni dei Signori e Collegi, Ordinaria Autorità*—shows that the Signory spent considerable time settling disputes which had once been adjudicated in the law courts.[17] The beginnings of this trend are already noticeable in the 1430s and 1440s, but the decisive change came after 1460.

With all these changes, the traditional courts of law could not remain unchanged. We have already seen that the independent Appellate Judge

[16] *SCF*, 29 (communal statutes of 1415 with addenda to 1494), ff. 393v-396r, for the reform of September 1471. I say "all but" a full-scale court because the proceedings of this magistracy tended to be summary. There was no ordinary defense, no extended sifting of evidence, no regular cross-examination of witnesses. The Eight favored automatic sentences, the use of "bulletins," and the dispatch of directives to the foreign magistrates. They accounted to no one save the Signory, which seldom poked into their affairs. A good sample set of their proceedings is *Otto di Guardia, Rep.*, 47 (deliberations of Jan.-April 1478).

[17] For the late fifteenth century and after, marginalia in the ordinary deliberations of the Signory and colleges show that there was once a record—another run of documents—of litigation handled by the Signory. That record having been lost, the historian must turn to the designated ordinary deliberations. E.g., *DSCOA*, 24 (July-Aug. 1389) contains no instances of the Signory's activity in litigation. But here is an example from June 1412: *DSCOA*, 30, ff. 27r-29r. The Signory wrote to the Podestà, requesting him to assume the lawyers Stefano Buonaccorsi and Nello da San Gimignano as arbiters in a dispute between Antonio Mangioni and a group of Pisan friars. This was clearly a case in appeal. Note that the Signory's intervention was consultative, did not directly touch the final decision.

was suppressed in 1410. The number of jurists which the Captain was required to bring to Florence was reduced from three to two in 1425.[18] In 1435 the Executor of the Ordinances of Justice was eliminated, his office having first been allowed to lapse for two months. The remains of his jurisdiction were transferred to the Podestà.[19] This left only two of the original four magistrates traditionally brought in from abroad. But the whittling down of their salaries and subalterns, and hence of the scope of their authority, continued.[20] In 1463 the government cut the staff of the Podestà by more than two-thirds and reduced his semi-annual salary from 11,550 to a mere 4,320 pounds.[21] Fourteen years later (1477) the office of Captain was abolished altogether and part of his old judicial authority passed to the Mercanzia.

The independent Appellate Judge, re-established in 1477, and the court of the Mercanzia got only part of the jurisdiction once claimed by the foreign magistrates. The rest had been gradually absorbed by the Signory and a variety of executive commissions, chief of which was the Eight on Public Safety.

Florence was faced with a judicial crisis. A thorough reform, root and branch, was necessary. The patriciate ought to have called for a review of all the municipal courts and their competence, and most particularly a review of the executive commissions that set fines and other penalties. But this would have meant a drawing of clearer boundaries around the executive, and the Medicean core of the oligarchy was better off keeping these limits hazy. Even after being severely admonished by the Signory in 1478, the Eight on Public Safety persisted in passing beyond their statutory limits and did so with the acquiescence of Signories. How may one explain the patriciate's failure or refusal to bring about the necessary reforms? It seems evident that where a political class is more or less

---

[18] *Carte di Corredo*, 6 (list of provisions from 1414 to 1443), f. 6, pencil, for provision of 1425.

[19] *Prov.*, 126, ff. 13r-v, 162r-v, and law of 3 Oct. 1435; *Prov.*, 127, ff. 170r-v, 183r, laws empowering Signory and other bodies to elect Captain *or* Executor for one year. The Captain won out.

[20] *Carte di Corredo*, 47, summaries of fifteenth-century legislation on the foreign magistrates.

[21] *SCF*, 29, ff. 397-405v; L. Cantini, "Dell' ufizio del potestà di Firenze," *Saggi istorici d'antichità toscane*, II (Firenze, 1796), 164. Still a useful study.

content with the existing judiciary, whatever the aberrations, no far-reaching reforms are likely to take place. Patronage, influence, and skulduggery work in the interests of the class. In short, it is most probable that the power of the Medicean oligarchy—the power to persuade and intimidate—was based to some extent on its control over the administration of justice. Reform had to wait for discontent.

By the spring of 1494 the discontent around Piero de' Medici had gone far enough to make possible the first moves toward basic reform. On June 20th the Council of One Hundred voted to set up a commission to review and reorganize the judicial system.[22] Of the twenty-three members of the commission, three were lawyers: Agnolo Niccolini, Domenico Bonsi, and Antonio Malegonnelli. A busy public figure and many times an ambassador, Niccolini was a close follower of the Medici. Bonsi and Malegonnelli were to figure prominently in the regime which outlawed Piero de' Medici late in 1494, but they had not objected to serving in high office under Lorenzo the Magnificent. The commission started out with the idea of establishing one major tribunal to do most of the work once handled by the courts of the Podestà, the Captain, the Executor, and the Appellate Judge. A plan of reform had to be drawn up which took into consideration the number of judges to be appointed, their qualifications, salaries, and prerogatives, the sorts of cases to come under their jurisdiction, the internal structure of the court (which was to have a supreme magistrate or Podestà), and the type of inquest ("syndication") to which all officials of the new tribunal would be subjected at the end of each term.

Within two months of their appointment the three lawyers and the other members of the commission submitted a plan to the government. It covered all the items mentioned above. The new tribunal was to be both an appellate court and a court of first instance. In some matters appeal was to be permitted against decisions even of the Mercanzia. One of the striking features of the plan was that it proposed to forbid the tribunal to accept appeals against decisions which issued from the executive sector of government, be it the Signory, the Ten on War, the Otto di Pratica, the Eight on Public Safety, "aut alium magistratum

---

[22] *Consiglio del Cento, Protocolli,* 2. ff. 308r-319v; also *SCF,* 29, f. 425r.

qui di iure sententiare non teneretur."[23] Nor could appeals be received against the sentences of any commission whose competence derived, in the form of a temporary delegation of power, from one of the foregoing offices. If they chose, these offices were to be free to turn cases over to the new tribunal, but it was emphasized that this did not diminish their authority or jurisdiction in any way.

The executive had won. Indeed, no serious threat had been directed against it. Although substantial, the proposed reform did not go far enough. And yet, while we may be tempted to take sides in history, let us not seem to wish for something which probably could not be. Neither in Florence nor elsewhere in Italy was the Renaissance to pare down the power of the executive, certainly not in the exercise of extraordinary or arbitrary justice.[24] This was not an objective for which the powerful urban families knew how to work, nor is it at all clear that they desired to. The great reforms of the judiciary were not to be introduced until the late eighteenth century.

On August 19, 1494, the Council of One Hundred approved the plan of reform, and it should have gone into effect soon after, but did not. The reform was blocked, we know not how, and then discarded. Sentimentality played a part: voices were heard calling for the re-establishment of the Captain of the People. The issue took hold. Representing the order of lawyers on December 20, 1495, and speaking to the Council of Eighty, Messer Domenico Bonsi recommended "returning to the old way" (that of having a Captain), as "it is something which enjoys great popularity." Then, cutting through the sentiment, he made an observation which more nearly reflected his profession. He declared that to have a civil life the city must have a judge of appeals, and he urged that they provide for the Captain to bring a well-trained jurist to Florence.[25] Bonsi seems to have been thinking of practice before 1477, when the first Appellate Judge in civil cases was ordinarily drawn from one of the two or three foreign jurists in the Captain's entourage.

---

[23] *Consiglio del Cento, Protocolli, loc.cit.*

[24] The one exception was seen in Venice, where much power was taken from the Council of Ten in the course of the sixteenth century.

[25] *CP*, 61, f. 117r.

Discontent with the judicial system continued throughout the 1490s. Obsolescence, inefficiency, and weakness in the face of a meddlesome executive were the drawbacks of the system. In May 1495 the courts of the Podestà saw a minor reform of appellate procedure.[26] We have already mentioned the reorganization of the Mercanzia in 1495-1496. Another reform sought to impose some controls on the penal activity of the executive: a law was enacted granting the right of appeal to citizens condemned by the Signory or by one of the powerful commissions for alleged crime against the state. Such appeal was to go to the Grand Council.[27] Yet discontent with the administration of justice persisted. After some years of indecision and sporadic debate, the office of Captain of the People was revived in 1498. The most important structural changes did not come, however, until 1502, when the courts of the Podestà and the Captain were at last permanently abolished. Some ten months before, a Gonfalonier of Justice, Filippo Carducci, had declared that the maladministration of justice was one of the most pressing of all public issues, and beginning with a criticism of the Signory, he spoke "of many things which are customarily done now against the laws and ordinances of the city, [most especially of] interfering with all sorts of matters, even civil cases."[28]

The scheme of reform approved in 1494, which had been ignored, was revived by a provision of the Grand Council on April 15, 1502. The pre-

[26] *Prov.*, 186, f. 43v.

[27] *Prov.*, 185, ff. 90v-92v, pencil (18 March 1495, modern). Henceforth, when any man eligible for public office (and the right applied to this category alone) was condemned for reasons of state to exile, death, or a penalty of more than 300 large florins by the Signory, the Eight, or another office by these commissioned, he could file an appeal within eight days of the condemnation. Not more than fifteen days later, the Signory was required to introduce the appeal to the Grand Council in the form of a petition for absolution. The petition could be voted on up to six times, not more than thrice in any one day. Absolution required a two-thirds vote of approval. The language of the preamble and reasons given for this reform reveal that its inspiration was Savonarolan. Cf. discussion of controversial appeal, pp. 441-45.

[28] *CP*, 66, f. 336r (14 July 1501). Most important, he said, was "la observanza della Iustitia sanza la quale niùno regno o dominio si può reggere, et comminciando dalla Signoria, che è il supremo magistrato, narra più cose che è consuete da uno tempo in qua fare contro alla legge et ordine della città, mettendo le mani in ogni cosa et insino alle cause civile."

amble of this provision avers that the reform would have been instituted "had the adversity of the times not delayed things."[29] Now finally the government fixed a day in October 1502 for the new Council of Justice to begin its work. Five foreign judges were scheduled to be on the Bench, all doctors of civil law and each to serve as presiding magistrate of the court for six months. A new panel of judges would be appointed every three years, together with a staff of recording notaries.[30] Most important from the viewpoint of this study is the fact that the new tribunal was conceived in close consultation with "many [of the city's] expert lawyers and experienced citizens."[31] It could not have been otherwise: the city had too many courts; too much judicial business fell under competing jurisdictions. Competence over a certain range of civil cases had been taken away from the Mercanzia in 1477, returned in 1497, only to be withdrawn again in 1502 and given to the new Council of Justice.[32] Shifts of this sort was the very stuff of which significant change in the judiciary was made. Competence taken from one court had necessarily to be transferred to another. And in the whole checkerboard of ordinary and summary Florentine courts, it took lawyers, or notaries with wide experience of the judicial system, to know how to shift things about.

A product of planning, of rational enterprise, the Council of Justice was the major piece of judicial reform seen in republican Florence. A large body of civil litigation came under its jurisdiction, but not cases involving commercial reprisal, business dispute, or some bankruptcy, all of which were handled by the court of the Mercanzia. The Council of Justice was also a court of appeal, although only for certain types of litigation. It could entertain no appeals against sentences in criminal proceed-

---

[29] *Prov.*, 193, f. 1r. Printed by Cantini, *Saggi*, II, 168ff. Adversity aptly summarizes the city's troubles following the expulsion of Piero de' Medici, Charles VIII's invasion of Italy, and especially the Florentine money and energies spent in trying to recover Pisa.

[30] Presumably one of the judges served as presiding magistrate for two terms or in the last term another judge was brought in from abroad.

[31] *Prov.*, 193, f. 1v, "havutone etiamdio sopra di ciò lungha praticha et maturo examine di molti vostri savi doctori et prudenti cittadini."

[32] *Ibid.*, f. 11v, for these changes. The material in question involved intestacy, certain types of disputes involving dowries, petitions of inheritance, houses having common walls, and still more claims based on public instruments.

ings, as these belonged chiefly to the competence of the Eight on Public Safety and (less so) to that of the Defenders of the Laws.

Procedure in criminal cases also underwent reform. To achieve more efficiency and promptness in the adjudication of crime, the government created a new body with some of the characteristics of a grand jury. This was the Quarantìa, to be composed of one prior, five members of the colleges, and twenty to forty men drawn from the Council of Eighty.[33] Their task was to pass sentence in criminal cases handed over to them by the Eight or the Defenders, who had a month to expedite most cases. The Quarantìa had fifteen days to take action, but it could try no case without the previous approval of the Signory and colleges by a two-thirds vote. Here, therefore, was another partial attempt to wrest cases away from the summary justice of the executive. The Gonfalonier of Justice, a lifetime position, created by a provision of August 26, 1502, was empowered "as the head of justice" to intervene with an opinion in all criminal cases.[34] But he was forbidden to exercise any influence on judicial decisions of the Podestà or the Captain, which after October 20th meant all judgments rendered by the new Council of Justice.

The boundaries laid down by the preceding reforms, which divided jurisdictions and outlined procedure in cases of appeal, were not always respected. Somewhat less so between 1502 and 1512, but once again thereafter, the executive arm of government continued to be exceedingly active in the exercise of summary justice. The early dukes of Tuscany were to give this exercise a rule and a more explicit constitutional basis.

Looking back at change in the judiciary during the fifteenth and early sixteenth centuries, we find, perhaps surprisingly at first, that Florentine lawyers seem never to appear—either as a corps or as individuals—in the vanguard of judicial reform. In vain do we search the *Consulte e Pratiche* for signs of their agitation in the name of a better or more equitable or more efficient judiciary. May we suppose that the confusions or excessive strains in the existing system were to the advantage of their pockets? This may have been true now and then of some notaries;[35] it

[33] *Ibid.*, ff. 85r-88r (29 Dec. 1502), no doubt suggested by practice in Venice, which had, however, three tribunals of forty by the end of the fifteenth century.
[34] *Ibid.*, f. 50r.
[35] This is suggested by their scoundrelly reputation (surely exaggerated by con-

seems to have been less true of lawyers, who had nothing to do with the everyday paperwork of the courts. Sometimes a consideration of where the crude financial interests lie serves to throw light on historical situations. Not here. We shall have to find another way to try to account for the failure of lawyers to take the initiative in the field of judicial reform.

In the working out of policy or in the political arena, Florentine lawyers were neither better nor worse than other men of the ruling class. As professionals, they were men trained to work with existing institutions, men ready to see that practice and living custom were observed. But as makers of public policy, such as reform of any sort, they had all the shortcomings and blind spots of their political peers. They could see many phases of procedure or technique more clearly and they could see detail. But to rearrange things entirely, to develop a new line of policy—this was something else, requiring a different kind of talent. By handing down one legal opinion rather than another, lawyers might inadvertently shift the emphasis in law or policy; but most likely they sought to keep faith with the established norms. They had learned to work with the existing courts and so they worked with them; for this reason accretions of inefficiency or worse might well be less a nuisance to lawyers than to clients. When, however, a clamor for judicial reform finally went up in the right places, lawyers either voiced a preference for the system to which they were accustomed or, in political wisdom, followed the wave of reform. Those who favored change, if summoned to give help, were in a position to turn their skills to the business at hand. It was thus late in the game that lawyers entered the lists. Taking in the advice of informed laymen or leading statesmen, they directed the work of whatever commission was appointed to devise a scheme of reform.

AN ESSENTIAL feature of the judicial system—"syndication"—might logically be discussed in the third section of this chapter, but it is better for the narrative to deal with it here.

---

temporaries), a fact connected with the embarrassments of their modest material situation in the fifteenth century. See the fascinating letter of a country notary who moved to Florence in search of a career: *CRS*, Arch. 78, filza 395, f. 93r-v (30 May 1421), brought to my attention by Professor Gene Brucker.

The late Latin verb *syndicare*, often found in Florentine state papers, meant to carry out an inquest or investigation of public officials.[36] At the end of their terms in office all the city's foreign magistrates, along with the judges and notaries who had served them, were subjected to a syndication which lasted from eight to twelve days. Ideally, syndication was one of the major safeguards of the Florentine judiciary—designed to expose irregularities, corruption, denials of just appeal, and so forth. Whatever the state of the courts, there can be no doubt that syndication served to raise their moral and legal level. But we need only concern ourselves with syndication as a feature of statecraft.

It was a device of some refinement. When a foreign magistrate and the officials of his train finished their terms in office, the Signory appointed eight "syndics" by drawing names by lot from pouches. From two other pouches the Signory drew the names of two other officials: a notary who acted as general secretary and recorder to the syndics, and a lawyer who worked as their "assessor" or legal aide. Then several other lawyers were appointed to serve as consultants.[37] It was the assessor (i.e., the lawyer) who initiated proceedings. The job of the syndics was to conduct hearings on all petitions filed against the retiring magistrate or members of his staff. Once presented, a petition could not be withdrawn; the inquiry on it had to be seen through to the end. When the Podestà or the Captain of the People was under investigation, the Executor of the Ordinances of Justice presided over the syndicating commission; when the Executor was himself the object of the inquest, the notary or incoming Executor presided. By submitting a petition or accusation to the syndics, any man from the city or territory could move an action against the magistrate on trial (for a trial is in a sense what every syndication was). Having sifted and judged the evidence relating to each petition, the commission voted to condemn or absolve the magistrate. His innocence

---

[36] G. Masi, "Il sindacato delle magistrature comunali nel sec. xiv," *Rivista ital. per la scienze giuridiche*, n.s. v, 1-2 (1930), 43-115, 331-411; also *Statuta*, 1, 72-77.

[37] Neither Masi nor the statutes give enough emphasis to the fact that it was customary for the syndics, or the assessor, to assume a group of consultants, usually four other lawyers or more. E.g., *ACP*, 1705, f. 2r and folios for 6 Sept. 1387 list the syndics, aides, and other legal consultants appointed to syndicate the Captain of the People in early Aug. 1387 and the Executor in Sept. 1387. A more complete picture is provided by the series in ASF, *Sindacati*.

was established by a two-thirds vote. Apart from initiating proceedings, the assessor also had the job of providing the syndics with any technical information or counsel requested by them. He, in turn, drew on the assistance and counsel of the lawyers who had been chosen to act as consultants. The syndics were not, however, required to follow his advice. They could have recourse to other lawyers from the city or territory. The law made it clear that the retiring magistrate and members of his staff could be absolved or condemned with or without the legal counsel of the assessor or any other lawyers. But this rarely happened in practice. Except where there was the danger of collusion, pettifogging, or some other irregularity, the chief legal aide or assessor was a key agent in the investigation and trial. Like the notary who helped to keep the commission within the bounds of established syndicating procedure, the assessor acted as a check on the system by calling the attention of the syndics to the norms of their office and the demands of the law.

Syndication illustrates a feature of public administration which we shall see again in other areas of Florentine statecraft: the phenomenon of expert and layman working together on a job. Yet syndication would not have worked—certainly could not have been the same—without the direction provided by the assessor, the notary, and the lawyers taken on as consultants. Not that the institution was handed over to the expert; on the contrary, an effort was made to keep it as much as possible in the hands of laymen—the syndics. The experts stood by to designate procedure and explain the law.

## 2. *Jurisdictional Problems*

We have seen that the traditional centers of judicial dispensation were eroded by the executive, most especially in the course of the Quattrocento. The authority thus "usurped" passed over to and was divided among the standing commissions. Hence previously existing conflicts of jurisdiction were not necessarily resolved; in some cases they were merely shifted from one sphere to another or even opened up to additional dispute. Two or three permanent commissions at the executive or administrative level of government might claim jurisdiction over the same material. It is therefore easy to see that both the parcelling out of authority and the encroachment on the old judicial preserves increased the rivalry for competence among the different commissions and courts. Conflicts of jurisdiction born of such rivalry had the effect of drawing attention to the technical skills of lawyers, giving them a new prominence. We can thus see why lawyers came to perform tasks that made them key figures in constitutional development.

My emphasis on the judicial system should not limit the meaning of the word *jurisdiction*, which may refer as well to administrative as to judicial competence. When I use the phrase "conflicts of jurisdiction," I have in mind disputes not only between judicial bodies but also between executive or administrative offices. One aspect of the lawyer's most precise work in government concerned the settling of disputes between two offices over a question of their respective authority. Now and then the need also arose to decide whether or not a given matter came under the administrative jurisdiction of any office whatsoever.

Up to about the middle of the fourteenth century, conflicts of jurisdiction in Florence seem to have been settled in an *ad hoc* fashion. Two or more lawyers were appointed to resolve a particular dispute for that one case and time. But there was an attempt to abandon this practice around 1350, when the government created the office of the *sapientes communis*. The office called for two lawyers, and a term lasted four months. Elected by the Signory, the *sapientes* were to serve the gabelle officials and any communal officials who desired legal advice.[38]

It is a pity that so few fragments of the papers of these lawyers survive. A sufficient record would have given a rounded picture and have simplified research. Of three surviving registers, one is the work of lawyers appointed on an *ad hoc* basis between 1293 and 1344 and deals with the legality of demands for commercial reprisal. The other two span the years 1378-1403 and 1410-1415, but derive only in part from the original archives of the government lawyers and contain briefs with the attached *consilia* of other lawyers.[39] When the treasury notaries were enjoined by the Signory, another magistracy, or an appellate court to expunge from their records a fine, a condemnation, or even certain taxes, they usually turned for counsel to the guild of lawyers and notaries. The proconsulate

[38] *SCF*, 10 (statutes of 1355), ff. 67v-68r.
[39] *Pareri di Savi*, 1-3.

146

then appointed one or more lawyers to examine the request, to study the brief of the case, and to submit an opinion in support of the cancellation. The science of lawyers was thus used to "cover" the treasury notaries. Now and then, on commission of the proconsulate, it was the *sapientes* who drew up the supporting opinion. Such opinions make up the content of the two registers attributed to the *sapientes communis*. This is why I have had to turn to other sources for the illustrative material in this chapter.[40]

Official communal lawyers (*savi* or *sapientes*) were more or less regularly appointed until 1449, when the Balìa of that year curtly and somewhat mysteriously suppressed the office.[41] Thereafter, the government returned to the old system of letting the different offices procure their own legal aid. But regardless of the method used, lawyers chosen to advise the Signory or other major offices were seldom obscure barristers or little provincial judges. Generally speaking, they were men who figured among the city's most influential administrators, politicians, or diplomats. Consequently, it was perfectly natural for them to draw not only on their theoretical knowledge of public law, on their working skills as advocates and judges, but also on their personal experience in politics at all levels, much of it at the focal points of power.

A fascinating and troublesome case was debated by the Signory and colleges in the late summer of 1387. It brought under question the jurisdiction of the Captain of the People, the immunity from prosecution of recent members of the Signory, and the Signory's intervention in the Captain's court.

The Bastari were one of the city's prominent political families of the second half of the fourteenth century. Filippo di Cionetto Bastari— thought to have been a political independent—openly criticized the two leading families of the period, the Ricci and Albizzi. He maintained his political status throughout the 1380s, despite the fact that he and his son, Giovenco, seem to have been good at making enemies in high places. But finally in April 1394, Filippo, his sons, and grandsons were banished

---

[40] Chiefly *Consulte e Pratiche, Deliberazioni dei Signori e Collegi in forza della loro ordinaria autorità,* and judicial records.

[41] *Balìe,* 26, f. 212r; *Carte di Corredo,* 14, f. 71r.

from Florence for reasons of state.[42] Later on Giovenco plotted to overthrow Messer Maso degli Albizzi. The family's misfortunes, however,
really began in 1387.

In the spring and summer of 1387, Giovenco was Vicar of the Castle
of San Miniato Fiorentino, a governorship which took in all the Lower
Valdarno. On August 7th proceedings were moved in the Captain's
criminal court against him and against the communal treasurer of San
Miniato, a notary named Ser Andrea di Ser Tommaso. They were accused of having stolen money from a chest in the local communal palace,
money belonging to the Florentine treasury. Apart from the fact that
they allegedly recorded less money in the communal accounts than had
actually been in the chest, it was also charged that two folios had been
torn from a particular register in order to conceal their theft. They were
therefore indicted for fraud as well as for larceny. Ser Andrea confessed
to the crime "but said that he had done it from force and fear and
Giovenco's threats."[43] On August 12th Giovenco's procurator, Ser Ricciardo di Piero, appeared in court and denied the charges. He held that
the indictment was too general, that it specified neither dates, nor sums,
nor the content of the missing folios. Furthermore, Giovenco was still Vicar
of San Miniato Fiorentino and his term in this dignity ran until October 18th next. But Ser Ricciardo's strongest legal objection was that,
since Giovenco had been a member of the September-October Signory
of 1386, no legal action could be taken against him for a year from the
time of his leaving that office.

Ser Andrea's procurator also appeared in court on August 12th. Surprisingly, he also denied the charges and took back the notary's confession. But on the 17th, probably under torture, Ser Andrea again confessed, substantiating all the charges; on the 19th a herald was sent

---

[42] Filippo was banished to Ragusa for ten years, Giovenco and the others to
points at least 100 miles from Florence for five years. *ACP*, 1988, ff. 162r-163v. Cf.
the inaccuracy in S. Ammirato, *Istorie fiorentine* (Torino, 1853), IV, 268; and M.
Rastrelli, *Priorista fiorentino istorico* (Firenze, 1783), p. 68.

[43] *ACP*, 1686, ff. 7r-14r, for this and succeeding data. Ser Ricciardo's representa-
tions on 12 Aug. were exaggerated. The charges were more specific than he alleged.
A full report of the case, including the sentences of 22 and 23 Aug., is also in
*Sindacati, Capitano del Popolo*, 41, ff. 9r *et seq.*

through the city, sounding his trumpet and announcing that Giovenco had three days to appear before the Captain. On the third day Giovenco's procurator reappeared in court, maintained that the trial was illegal, and stated that his client could neither abandon his post nor come to Florence "without the license and command" of the Signory. He had no such license, the court was told, and was unlikely to be given one. On the same day, August 22nd, the other defendant declared through his own procurator, Ser Vanni di Stefano, that he was ready to pay any fine imposed. He was condemned to pay a fine of 200 pounds *piccioli*. The sentence against Giovenco was more severe. Condemned to repay the stolen money, he was also stripped for twenty years of the right to hold public office, beginning from the day of this sentence (August 23rd). If he failed to repay the stolen money (95.0 pounds *piccioli*) within a month, the sum was to be quadrupled.

But Giovenco was not without resources and influence. The moment had come to turn the proceedings into a constitutional issue. According to Florentine statutory law, no member of the Signory could be prosecuted for a period of one year from the time of his leaving office, "save for homicide or for inflicting wounds with an effusion of blood on any person."[44] Even then, however, the tribunal which undertook to try the case had first to obtain a clearance from the current Signory and Gonfalonier of Justice.

On the day Giovenco was sentenced, the clash between the two magistrates—Giovenco, a territorial governor, and the Captain, a high officer of justice—finally broke in on the Signory and colleges.[45] The question they had to decide was whether they should let the sentence stand or step in vigorously, reprove the Captain, and insist on the full term of Giovenco's immunity. They were most uncertain about what to do. Pazzino Strozzi argued that they should not suffer the privileges of the

[44] *SCF*, 10 (statutes of 1355), ff. 66v-67v; also in statutes of 1322-25, ed. R. Caggese, *Statuti della repubblica fiorentina*, 2 vols. (Firenze, 1910-21), I, 89.

[45] *CP*, 26, f. 94r. The fact that Giovenco was invested with "merum et mixtum imperium" (i.e., with the powers of high justice) was another point in his favor; it reinforced the rule that he must not absent himself from his vicariate save with a license from the Signory and on the appearance of his replacement. On "merum et mixtum imperium" see M. P. Gilmore, *Argument from Roman Law in Political Thought, 1200-1600* (Cambridge, Mass., 1941), pp. 37ff.

Signory "to be broken," as this involved a violation of the Ordinances of Justice, but that when Giovenco's immunity expired the case should revert to the Captain so that he could discharge his functions.[46] Representing the officers of the Guelf Society, Guccio de' Nobili—like most of the other speakers—recommended that before taking any action the Signory provide itself with the advice of the *sapientes communis*. The *sapientes* and four others were therewith commissioned to submit an opinion. Six well-known jurists were assembled: Filippo Corsini, Giovanni de' Ricci, Tommaso Marchi, Rosello Roselli, Jacopo Folchi, and Ludovico Albergotti. Working swiftly, they presented their report on the afternoon or evening of the same day. They began by complaining that the point under dispute was so open to question that they would have preferred not to give counsel in the matter at all. Still, enjoined to do so by the lord priors and colleges and inclined to be lenient, in accordance as the laws admonish, they said, "the immunity of the priorate should be and ought to have been observed in this case. But neither the Captain nor his court is to be blamed for judging otherwise because the material is so dubious that one need not wonder at its eliciting other opinions."[47]

This namby-pamby formulation was not typical of lawyers like Filippo Corsini and Giovanni de' Ricci, who were accustomed to assert their views unequivocally, unless the political game called for equivocating. A month earlier, Giovanni had taken a vigorous stand against the ambitions of Pope Urban. "It is dangerous," the lawyer declared, "to let the pope do whatever he wants"—he "wants to destroy the son of the king [Charles of Durazzo] and also our city."[48] The unadorned frankness

---

[46] *CP*, 26, f. 94r, "Dominus Pazinus de Strozis dixit quod non patiatur ita et taliter quod privilegium prioratus non rumpatur. Et viso quod sit contra ordinamenta iusticie, id quod factum est contra revocetur, dimittendo tamen processum in manibus Capitanei ita quod omni tempore possit prosequi sicut ius disponit."

[47] *Ibid.*, f. 95r, "Domini Filippus de Corsinis, Iohannes de Riccis, Tomas Marchi, Rosellus [de Rosellis], Jacobus Fulchi, et Ludovicus de Aretio Albergottis dixerunt quod licet punctus iste sit valde dubius adeo quod vellemus non habere in hoc consulere, tamen ex quo . . . [illegible] nos ex precepto dominorum et collegiorum eligere inclinantes in benigniorem partem ut iura precipiunt, dicimus privilegium prioratus in hoc casu locum habere et observandum esse et fuisse. Non tamen est reprehensibile Capitaneo vel sue curie si aliter iudicavit, quia res est adea dubia quod non est mirum si alii opinioni adhesit."

[48] *Ibid.*, ff. 64r, 66v.

in the executive debates of these months throws some suspicion on the report of the six lawyers. Can it be that different influential political groups pressed for and against Giovenco and hence for the Captain or for the privileges of the Signory? We must suspect that this was so when we try to understand what lay behind the report. For if the controversy had a concrete political background, we can see why the six lawyers, probably of differing political inclinations, were unable to commit themselves fully to one side or the other. At all events, their equivocation did not pass unnoticed. On the day after their report, the first speaker to address the Signory declared that "the opinion of the lawyers is obscure." He urged that they be called back to advise the government on whether or not the Captain had violated the Ordinances of Justice. If they found he had, Giovenco should be absolved. If not, the Captain should in any case be censured for failing to observe his promises, and something should be done for Giovenco "because the lawyers say that the sentence has no validity."[49] Speaking for the other college (the Twelve Good Men), Adovardo Belfredelli supported the proposal that there be a second meeting with the lawyers. Several days passed. On August 27th and 28th the case was accorded another round of sessions. We learn that although Giovenco continued to hold his vicariate and was anxious to serve out the prescribed term, the Captain's sentence against him stood in the way. The consensus of the colleges was that the sentence should be nullified or a way found to let Giovenco complete his term of office. Interestingly, they were still waiting for the lawyers' second report. It was not finally presented until August 30th,

---

[49] *Ibid.*, f. 95v. The lawyers did not in fact assert that the sentence had no validity in law. Maestro Giovanni del Maestro Ambrogio, spokesman for the Sixteen, was the speaker. Said he, "Quod consilium sapientum super facto Giovenchi est obscurum. Et ideo habeantur de novo et cogantur consulere an factum sit per Capitaneum contra ordinamenta iusticie. Et si consulunt quod sic, tunc domini provideant ut fuerit sui honoris, offerentes se cum eorum fabis, et Giovencus absolvatur. Si vero non contrafecerit, reprehendatur de promissa non servata. Et quia sapientes dicunt sententiam esse nullam, fiat Giovenco iusticia." What had the Captain promised? A subsequent investigation revealed that Giovenco's father and many friends had made repeated efforts to procure a license from the Signory, allowing Giovenco to repair to Florence to face the charges against him. But no license was granted, I suspect because the Captain had promised, perhaps in vague terms only, to suspend his proceedings until Giovenco returned from S. Miniato Fiorentino and the full term of his immunity had expired. *Sindacati, Capt. del Popolo*, 41, ff. 9r-24r.

two days before a new Signory was to take office. The report seems to have been a dry and shifty affair, for the lawyers said that "the sentence passed against Giovenco is *ipso iure* null and void and he may discharge any office, just as if he had not been judged. But presupposing that the sentence is valid, he cannot complete his office *sine preiudicio*, unless the Captain of the People declares that it was not and is not his intention to have the sentence, if such it be, apply to the present office, a declaration he is empowered to make by law."[50] Once again, accordingly, counsel provided the Captain with a loophole, while giving way in part to the pressures of a Signory due to leave office the day after. Who could tell what the next group of priors would do?

Some factors connected with the case evade us wholly or in part. Yet the statute concerning the judicial immunity of former members of the Signory was uncommonly clear. In trying Giovenco without first having got the consent of the Signory, the Captain was violating a statute. On the other hand, his tenacity and the equivocal opinion of the lawyers suggest that there was something to be said for the legality of his position—some appeal to custom, something in the circumstances of Giovenco's alleged crime which may have been covered by another statute. Another thing is that although fully authorized to do so, the Signory does not seem to have made a point of impressing it on the Captain that he had taken action in a case which wanted the preliminary clearance of the priors and Gonfalonier.

Taking office on September 1st, the new Signory decided not to occupy itself with the case. Hence Giovenco was probably forced to give up his governorship. Nothing more was heard of the matter in the executive chambers until February 6, 1388, when we learn that Giovenco had instituted proceedings against the Captain. Having just finished his term of office, the Captain and his officials were being investigated by a group of "syndics"—the procedure to which all foreign magistrates, as explained

---

[50] *CP*, 26, f. 98v, "Sapientes alias nominati. Dixerunt quod sententia lata contra Giovencum est nulla ipso iure et tanquam si iudicatum non esset potest omnia exercere. Sed presupponendo quod sententia valeat, non posset sine preiudicio officium quod obtinet complere, nisi per Capitaneum populi declaretur quod non fuerit nec sit sue intentionis quod illa sententia si qua est se extendat ad presens officium, quam declarationem ipse potest de iure facere."

above, were regularly subjected on terminating their duties. And it was with the syndics that Giovenco had lodged a petition against the Captain—the claims of the petition resting on the disputed immunity privilege, on the rank of Giovenco's governorship, and on the necessity to procure a license from the Signory before absenting oneself from such a post. The government now, however, would not hear of an action against the retiring magistrate. Speaking for the Sixteen Gonfaloniers, Messer Francesco Rucellai declared that since the Signory of September-October 1387 "had given up the case of Giovenco Bastari, and not without cause, they [the Sixteen] felt that the Captain had administered justice and therefore the syndics should be ordered to absolve him."[51] The speaker for the other college, Messer Tommaso Marchi, one of the lawyers originally consulted, said that the Captain should be favored for the sake of the city's honor. He recommended that they send for the petitioner and persuade him to withdraw his petition; but whatever happened, Marchi encouraged the Signory to give its unreserved support to the Captain. Although no prior or "colleague" was to hold forth on the case again, a final echo was heard late in October 1388, when Giovenco was still trying to get the Signory to clear his good name. His defense was founded on the fact that eight months earlier the sentence against him had been declared null and void by the commission which conducted inquiries into his petition against the Captain—Messer Sentio of Spoleto, Count of Campello.[52] Nevertheless, Giovenco had not yet succeeded in getting himself rehabilitated for public office.

What may we conclude? The case put the Captain's competence under serious question when Giovenco appealed to the Signory, bringing into opposition the judicial and executive arms of government. The friction between the two was possible not only because of the statute on the immunity privilege, but also because the executive had a discretionary right to intervene in the judicial process. Trying for a pure legal solution,

---

[51] *Ibid.*, f. 169r.

[52] *CP*, 27, f. 41v (29 Oct. 1388), when Leonardo Peruzzi said for the Sixteen, "Quod super consilio reddito in favorem Giovenchi Filippi Bastari fiat iusticia et ponatur partitum." Inquiries into the Count of Campello's conduct in office lasted from 6 to 13 Feb. 1388. *Sindacati, Capt. del Popolo*, 41, ff. 9r *et seq.*

rather than for one more arbitrary or political, the Signory called in a group of lawyers. Some members of the Signory and colleges sought to constrain them to take a particular position, but they managed to retain a certain independence. Perhaps this independence was favored by the alignment of political groups, perhaps by the legal nature of the case itself. We cannot be sure, and it is not important to this study that we be sure. The Signory of September-October 1387 swept the whole case aside, refusing to get mixed up in it. Receiving the support of the colleges, a third Signory (that of January-February 1388) threw its weight behind the Captain and ordered the syndics to dismiss Giovenco's petition against him—a clear instance of intervention in the judicial process.[53] Did all this mean that the lawyers originally consulted had performed no effective part in the controversy? Not so, for the first Signory leaned on them, expecting that they would help resolve the dispute or at any rate help justify any intervention on its part. At the very least, the counsel of the lawyers both protected the Captain and gave the Signory a way to step directly into the proceedings. That the second and succeeding Signories decided not to interfere is another matter. So far as the *sapientes* and other lawyers were *used* to promote the interests of the executive or of an influential bloc of families, it is clear that the jurist could be called on to play a straight political part in government.

If from one viewpoint the Bastari case reveals an indecisive aspect of professional intervention by a group of lawyers, some other cases, also much discussed in the city, were more conclusively handled.[54] Such a

[53] "Syndication" was both an inquiry and a trial. Masi, "Il sindacato delle magistrature comunali nel sec. xiv (con speciale riferimento a Firenze)," *loc.cit.* The behavior of this Signory was odd. Once a petition was submitted to a syndicating commission, it had to be processed. When, therefore, the Signory intervened, the syndics could not and did not dismiss Giovenco's petition against the Captain. But having the Signory's blessing, they could more easily indulge the Captain.

[54] See *CP*, 28, ff. 49v-51r (17 March 1389, Florentine), for another case which brought the Signory into conflict with one of the foreign magistrates. The Podestà had arrested Francesco di Messer Jacopo degli Alberti, probably for alleged activity against the regime, and wished to put him on the rack. Taking the prisoner's side, the Signory sought to exercise pressure on the Podestà. Two lawyers, Giovanni de' Ricci and Tommaso Marchi, spoke up in Francesco's favor. Representing the Sixteen, Marchi urged the Signory to summon the Podestà and direct him to free Francesco; if he refused, the government was advised to take the matter to the official communal lawyers and the city's other jurists.

case, which caused a good deal of scandal in the late spring and summer of 1421, was touched off by a murder.

Moncione was a castle in the Upper Valdarno near Montevarchi, between the dioceses of Fiesole and Arezzo. Once a fief of the counts Guidi, granted to them by imperial diploma, Moncione was forcibly taken over by Florence in 1336, following the rebellion of Count Marcovaldo, who had conspired with an important Florentine—Messer Piero di Gualterotto Bardi. There ensued certain arrangements between Florence and the Battifolle branch of the Guidi, who therewith acquired Moncione and other territories, including certain jurisdictional and fiscal rights. A little later the family also came into the possession of the nearby Castle of Barbischio.[55]

Early in May 1421 Guido, Count of Moncione and Barbischio, was murdered by a group of men native to or from near the areas linked to his name and title. According to a contemporary, he was assassinated by order of the Fibindacci, a powerful county family.[56] Seven men, some of whom were *fideles* of his, caught the Count in one of the small Moncione courtyards and assaulted him with sword, dagger, and short lance. The effect of the murder was particularly felt in Florence, not only because Guido was a protégé of the Republic, but also because he was related by marriage to a prominent and influential Florentine family— the Pitti. Wasting no time, the governor of the Upper Valdarno ("Vicarius vallis Arni superioris"), Giovanni Carducci, collected 500 men and made for the castles of Moncione and Barbischio, where the crime had resulted in a good deal of civil disorder. All the men involved in the assassination were arrested. The Signory heard of these events on May 12th, sent off to have them confirmed, and then directed Carducci to send the prisoners to Florence to be questioned. Anticipating his annoyance, the priors and colleges promised that they would act with due honor

[55] E. Repetti, *Dizionario geografico, fisico, storico della Toscana*, 6 vols. (Firenze, 1833-1846), III, 251-52.

[56] Buonaccorso Pitti, *Cronica*, ed. A. B. della Lega (Bologna, 1905), p. 238. I take the rest of my information about the murder and ensuing dispute from the following sources: *CP*, 44, ff. 90r-94v, 101r-106r, 108r, 111v, 118v; *ACP*, 2772, ff. 2r-5r, 9r-20r; 2774, ff. 5r-20v; *AEOJ*, 1966, ff. 48r-51r; 1968, by date (4 Aug. 1421); Ammirato, *Istorie fiorentine*, v, 66. I could find no record of the case in the Podestà's papers, which are very fragmentary for the year 1421.

for Carducci's office, return the prisoners to him, and carry out all interrogations in the presence of his chief aide. By May 16th the prisoners had arrived in Florence. Some were put in the custody of the Podestà, others in that of the Captain and the Executor. Within a day or two the examination of the prisoners was satisfactorily concluded and it is then the controversy began.

The foreign magistrates—Podestà, Captain, and Executor—retained custody of the prisoners but refrained from trying them. Opinion in the Signory was divided. Some members insisted that the prisoners be returned for trial, as promised, to the governor of the Upper Valdarno. Others held that the Signory should send a directive to the foreign magistrates, instructing them to conduct the trial and administer justice. Recommendations made to the Signory on May 19th indicate that feeling against the prisoners was running high, that the demand for swift justice was strong. By May 20th one of the colleges (the Sixteen) had conferred with Ser Martino Martini, the chief notary on legislation (*notaio delle riformagioni*). This functionary was expected to have a thorough grasp of Florentine statutory law and a good understanding of technical matters concerning the major phases of administration. He was the type of notary whose practical experience justifies our thinking of him as a lawyer—although one who was not quite a jurist, for he would not have been able to hold forth on the ramifications and conundrums of particular cases. According to Guidetto Guidetti, Ser Martino's advice was that they return the prisoners to the governor because jurisdiction in the case belonged to him. Antonio Raffacani, however, reporting for the Twelve, announced that they had heard that the governor did not have power ("baliam") in the case and therefore they advised the Signory to send a notice to the foreign magistrates, directing *them* to apply the law and administer justice. A special meeting between the two colleges thus became necessary to iron out differences. Later on in the day (May 20th) Paolo Graziani reported for both colleges. He counselled the Signory "to have the officials of the palace, that is Ser Paolo and Ser Martino," and a selection "of doctors [of law] conduct an inquiry to decide whether or not Giovanni Carducci has the requisite judicial authority."[57] If it

[57] *CP*, 44, ff. 93v-94r.

was found that he did not, then the foreign magistrates were to be directed to get on with the trial.

By May 23rd the difficulties had been compounded. Meeting with Ser Paolo and Ser Martino, the lawyers (i.e., *legum doctores*) called in by the government decided that Carducci had no judicial competence in the case but, oddly, they failed to say who did. The colleges therewith moved that the lawyers be called back to pin down the disputed competence; if necessary, more "doctores" were to take part in the consultation. One of the speakers already hinted at the possibility that the jurisdiction might not even belong to the city's foreign magistrates.[58] Not until May 31st was the case again made the subject of executive consultation. Nothing had yet been resolved. The lawyers and the palace notaries (Ser Paolo and Ser Martino) had not yet assembled for a second meeting. But it is clear that someone in or near the Signory and advisory colleges—someone trained in law and informed about the Republic's justiciary arrangements with subject lordships—had circulated the opinion that possibly the Florentine state had no jurisdiction in the case whatsoever. Reporter for the Sixteen, the physician Cristofano Brandini recommended that the lawyers previously consulted, meeting together with the legal aides of the three foreign magistrates, examine the conditions of citizenship and protection which the city had extended to Count Guido. Their job would be to determine who had *de iure* the disputed competence. "And if it be reported that administering the law [in this case] is not the business of your [Florentine] Commune, then let there be another consultation with the body of advisors. . . . In addition, they [the Sixteen] reckon that the lawyers should also see to whom the lands [where the Count had been assassinated] belong, whether to the Commune of Florence, to one of the Bardi, one of the Peruzzi, or to the Count of Poppi, so that the recommendation can be made to apply the law."[59] The Twelve were less united. Seven members of this college

---

[58] *Ibid.*, f. 94r, Giovanni Altoviti, speaking for the Twelve.

[59] *Ibid.*, f. 101r. Report of Maestro Cristofano di Giorgio Brandini. "Et quod si dominis videtur de novo habeantur illi doctores et collaterales virorum rectorum, videlicet illi tres principales et examinetur civilitas et accomandisia comitis et videatur ad quem spectat cognitio. Et si referretur comune vestrum non spectare executionem, habeatur consilium requisitorum et quod putant bonam conclusionem inde sequi debere. Videtur etiam eis quod illi judices et sapientes etiam examinent ad quem

wanted the assassins sentenced by the foreign magistrates; the other five held out for a resolution first of the disputed jurisdiction.

On June 2nd the chambers of the Signory and colleges resounded with the complaints of worthies like Rinaldo degli Albizzi, Matteo Castellani, and Bartolommeo Valori, who grieved at the Republic's dishonor and shame for having so far failed to try the Count's murderers. A few counsellors were for taking immediate action and favored bullying the foreign magistrates; others wanted things done with due regard for whatever feudal rights Florence was committed to observe in the Moncione-Barbischio areas. The most suggestive recommendation was made by the lawyer and diplomat, Messer Alessandro Bencivenni. He proposed that while keeping faith with the obligations and agreements between Florence and the heads of the disputed areas, the government look to see "if specific competence [in the case] belongs to us, even if the jurisdiction may not."[60] Later on in the day Castellani and Valori spoke for the whole *pratica*. Deploring the assassination and the delay in the judicial proceedings, they returned to the point that a group of lawyers should establish competence in the case "respectu civilitatis, recommandigie, et prestantiarum."[61]

---

terre spectent, vel ad comune Florentie vel ad illum de Bardis vel ad illum de Peruzis vel ad Comitem Puppi ut detur expeditio et fiat ius." These families evidently possessed lands in the Upper Valdarno with attached rights of jurisdiction. On hearing of the murder, the Count of Poppi had also rushed to the disturbed areas with 500 men, so that he too claimed rights in the said region. The procurator of the prisoners in the Captain's custody was to hold that they were not subject to Florentine jurisdiction "sed fuerunt et sunt de iurisdictione dicti comitis Guidonis" and that the counts of Moncione had held court there for some thirty years. *ACP*, 2772, ff. 17r-19v.

[60] *CP*, 44, f. 120r-v, "Idem quod dominus Matheus et dominus Rainaldus, addendo quod respectu recommandigie et civilitatis examinetur si cognitio pertinet ad nos licet iurisdictione non pertineret." *Iurisdictio* should be understood as the general right to administer justice in a given area, *cognitio* as the competence (or specific right of jurisdiction) in a particular case. The right "to know" a case, once that was granted, was not different from the right "to say" (i.e., to adjudicate) where the law stood in the matter. It looks as if the appeal to some "higher" political authority was here used to vindicate an intervention not otherwise sanctioned by the law. I benefited from discussing the above passage with the legal historian Roberto Abbondanza, director of state archives in Perugia.

[61] I.e., with reference in the disputed areas to conditions of citizenship, Florentine commitments to protégés, and payment of taxes. The payment of *prestanze* helped to fix grades of civil status, which affected competence in the case.

Far from being resolved the complications grew and the government's patience became strained. On June 3rd the Signory and colleges were at last treated to a brief report submitted by four lawyers: Rosso Orlandi, Nello da San Gimignano, Alessandro Bencivenni, and Giuliano Davanzati. All were prominent in public affairs. Messer Nello had a peninsula-wide reputation in the fields of commercial and international law. They ruled that both specific competence and jurisdiction ("cognitionem et iurisdictionem") belonged to the city's foreign magistrates—Podestà, Captain, and Executor. This decision was founded on several statutes directed against conspiracy and illegal assembly, parts of which put all general disorder in the county and district of Florence under direct Florentine jurisdiction. The four also based themselves on agreements reached between Florence and the patrilineal ancestors of the dead count. They observed, however, that they could not at present discuss local rule in the Moncione-Barbischio areas, not having seen the documents showing the rights of the parties involved there ("non visis partium iuribus").[62] And so, while finally taking a clear stand, they left the way open for a possible alternative opinion.

The experts had done their job. It was the government's turn to move next—either to see that more documents were produced, thus enabling the lawyers to draft a definitive opinion, or to act on what had already

[62] *CP*, 44, f. 104r, "Quod visis statutis et ordinamentis comunis Florentie tam veteribus quam novis et maxime statuto posito in tertio libro voluminis antiqui potestatis sub rubrica de pena facientis congregationem et de pena clamantium, etc., et in tertio libro statutorum novorum sub rubrica de pena clamantium et de pena congregationem facientium et alio statuto sub rubrica de officio judicum, et reformatione edita in mccccxvi, et recommendatione assumpta per magnificum comune Florentie de Comite Guidone peravo occisi et posteris anno mccclxvii et beneficio civilitatis concesso eidem comiti Guidoni, filiis et descendentibus, anno mccclxxiiii°, et aliis ad materiam facientibus cognitionem et iurisdictionem contra malefactores existentes in fortia comunis Florentie pertinere ad rectores ipsius comunis. Omisso pro presenti per ipsos articulo dominii locorum predictorum quem discutere non possunt non visis partium iuribus." Two of the statutes referred to in the new compilation are *Statuta*, I, 278, 285. Summaries of the agreements reached with the counts of Moncione in 1367 and 1374 are in *ACP*, 2772, ff. 3r, 4r-5r; also C. Guasti, ed., *I capitoli del comune di Firenze*, 2 vols. (Firenze, 1866-1893), I, 98-99, 465. The arrangements with Guido Guidi da Battifolle in 1374 were occasioned by his selling of certain lands to Florence. Moncione was not included in the sale, and justice there, over all cases civil and criminal, remained with the Guidi. The jurisconsults believed that the adduced statutes overrode the designated rights.

159

been reported and induce the foreign magistrates to mete out justice. In the days that followed (June 5th to 7th) most advisors agreed that the Signory should direct the magistrates to get on with the trial, although there was a good deal of disagreement about whether or not to send copies of the lawyers' report to them. It was even suggested that the three magistrates be summoned before the Signory so that the report could be read out to them. The main difficulty was presented by the fact that any legal opinion acted on by the government must have the previous support of thirty-two votes out of the thirty-seven in the Signory and colleges.[63] Extra-legal pressures or uneasy consciences held things up. On June 9th the spokesmen for the colleges recommended that a few lawyers, together with Ser Martino and Ser Paolo, examine some unspecified papers connected with the controversy. But the priors who had seen the outbreak of this disrupting conflict of jurisdictions did not again have the case discussed in open council (or, if so, the minutes were not recorded) and they went out of office on the last day of June.

Since the old colleges continued in office into July and August, the new Signory would have a group of informed advisors; but it had to be oriented, particularly as the case had given so much trouble to the preceding Signory. The new priors took up the subject on their second day in office, when Bartolo Banchi, representing the Twelve, spoke of the ignominy of the government's failure so far to punish the murderers. On July 3rd Rinaldo degli Albizzi made an appeal to precedent. Speaking for the Twelve, he reminded the lord priors that on two previous occasions the Signory had moved with great swiftness to avenge murders committed in the Florentine dominion: once when the marquises Malespini were killed and another time when the Count Piero da Porciano was murdered. Why should those who had killed Guido da Moncione be treated differently?[64] The proud and impulsive *cavaliere* Rinaldo, with the Twelve supporting him, was not a man to be reduced to inaction by legal niceties. And besides, had not the legal experts already declared themselves? Only once thereafter (on July 12th) was the case

[63] *Prov.*, 104, f. 50v (date: 23 Jan. 1415). Raised to thirty-six votes in 1419, *Carte di Corredo*, 14, f. 16v.

[64] *CP*, 44, f. 108v. The Malespini murders took place in the summer of 1418, when the Marquis of Castel dell' Aquila had the marquises of Verrucola assassinated. Ammirato, *Istorie*, v, 48.

brought up for discussion in the Signory's advisory consultations. Each college delivered a curt report, advising the Signory to summon the foreign magistrates and to press them to deal out justice to the prisoners, "so as to be rid of this bother," "for the honor of the Commune," and "no longer to be kept in this confusion." Podestà, Captain, and Executor did not finally take action for another three weeks. Of the thirteen prisoners in their custody, three were found innocent, four were sentenced to prison, and the others were decapitated.[65] The state had at last acquitted itself.

About a generation apart, the Moncione and Bastari cases are suggestive enough to induce us to reflect on family interests, political currents, the relative power of magistracies (such as the relation of the colleges to the Signory), and the interplay between the ordinary judiciary and the executive. But we must try—here at all events—to keep to a focal point. In the Bastari case, the question was raised whether or not one of the foreign magistrates (the Captain of the People) was competent to try a territorial governor whose prior's judicial immunity had not yet expired and who himself disposed of the powers of justice, up to and including capital punishment, in part of the Florentine dominion. Approached by the Signory, the Captain seemed to have promised to hold up proceedings but then did not. Although the ensuing clash between Signory and Captain was not frontal, the government saw fit to call in a team of six lawyers to give counsel. In this friction between the executive and the judiciary, lawyers were the ones expected to set things right. Even later, when Giovenco appealed to the commission of syndics against the Captain, the decisive part in the hearings was played by lawyers.[66]

[65] *CP*, 44, f. 111v (12 July); *AEOJ*, 1968, by date (4 Aug. 1421); Ammirato, *Istorie*, v, 66.

[66] The Executor of the Ordinances of Justice sat in judgment on the proceedings. He and two of the eight syndics took up Giovenco's petition. They were assisted by the lawyer Messer Gianbruno Bruni (murdered in the same year). He procured opinions on the case from seven other lawyers: Filippo Corsini, Giovanni de' Ricci, Angelo degli Ubaldi, Tommaso Marchi, Jacopo Folchi, Rosello Roselli, and Rosso di Andreozzo Orlandi. All agreed—and this was the final judgment of the commission on 13 February—that the sentence against Giovenco had no validity in law, but they also absolved the Captain, owing to the complexities of the case and to the fact that there was insufficient proof of Giovenco's charges against him. Giovenco accused the Captain of spite and willful violation of the Signory's immunity privilege. *Sindacati, Capt. del Popolo*, 41, f. 65r-v.

The controversy over the Count of Moncione's murder turned on three rival claims to jurisdiction—claims advanced by the governor of the Upper Valdarno, by the Signory on behalf of its foreign magistrates, and by a medley of feudal interests with judicial prerogatives in the Moncione-Barbischio area. In this case the job of the lawyers was to assign or identify the power of justice, not to affirm or deny that a trial could legally take place.

What also emerges from the two cases is the fact that the Signory was the moving force *par excellence*. Giovenco Bastari's first appeal went to the Signory and it was the Signory which had the Count of Moncione's assassins transferred to Florence, thus opening the way for a conflict of jurisdictions. It was also the Signory which summoned the colleges and other groups for consultation, invited lawyers and palace officials to submit counsel, and took the initiative with regard to any action recommended.

In these, as in other cases, the foreign magistrates were slow to surrender to the pressures of the Signory. Weaker men would have yielded sooner. A rapacious executive and the capitulation of weak men help partly to account for why the traditional judiciary in Florence was robbed of its power in the course of the fifteenth century. But it is well to remember that when they left office, the Podestà, the Captain, and the Executor each had to submit to an investigation. If it was demonstrated that they had violated the laws of the city, they could be prosecuted, despite the fact that they had been under the strong influence of a Signory some months earlier. So no matter what pressures were exerted by an executive office, no matter how powerful, the foreign magistrates did well to show some concern for their personal and staff interests. As it happened, this concern was in the community's favor because it served to offset the pressures of a determined executive body, unless of course the Signory also exerted influence on the commission of investigation (the syndics), as happened when Giovenco Bastari appealed to the syndics in February 1388. In such a case, one Signory could "cover" or protect the actions of a former one by pressing for the absolution of a magistrate under indictment.

We may also look elsewhere to help explain the behavior of the foreign officials. It is conceivable that Giovenco's enemies acquired an influential hold on his antagonist, the Captain of the People, Messer Sentio da Spoleto (Count of Campello), and then supported his proceedings against Giovenco by maintaining majorities in the succeeding Signories. Similarly, because the Moncione case seems to have implicated the interests of the Guidi da Battifolle, the Guidi Count of Poppi, and the families Pitti, Bardi, and Peruzzi, the Signory as well as the foreign magistrates were undoubtedly subjected to strong family pressures, in part *against* summoning the prisoners to trial. For if competence in the case really belonged to an ancient feudal clan or to one of the city's great families, then they—not the Florentine state—could rightfully acquire the confiscated properties and goods of Guido's assassins. Another consideration was, as the competent party well knew, that the future of the contested jurisdiction was at stake. In all probability, therefore, this is what lay behind the Signory's reluctance to probe into feudal rights in the Moncione-Barbischio area.[67]

Amid this welter of interests, with the state pulling one way and certain families another, with the Signory desiring one thing and the judiciary another, groups of lawyers were called upon to make a detached assessment and to point out jurisdictional boundaries. In such a context, it seems clear that the Florentine lawyer was as likely to succumb to private pressures, political interests, or the frontal attack of particular magistracies, as to hold fast to an article of Roman law, an eroded right, or a principle of justice. Indeed, in the give and take of everyday life, he was more likely to find ways of justifying the dominant voice, the force hardest to oppose, than to remain in practice loyal (whatever his private sentiments) to a fuzzy statute, an old feudal arrangement, or an abstract point of law. This is why we must guard against seeing Florentine lawyers as innovators rather than as agents through whom the existing disposition of forces was justified and hallowed.

[67] The defense held, in fact, that the trial of the Count's assassins was illegal, that Florence had no competence in the case, that private settlement of old scores was permitted by the Ordinances of Justice when the person assaulted or killed was a magnate of the *contado*, and that the accused had been violently moved out of the sphere of jurisdiction which properly claimed them. That sphere, said the procurator of the defendants tried by the Captain, came under the judicial authority of the heirs of the murdered nobleman. *ACP*, 2772, f. 17r.

Buonaccorso Pitti describes an incident which marred his term as Captain of Pistoia in the autumn of 1399. Having arrested a confirmed robber ("pubblico ladro"), he was directed by the Signory to send the man to Florence. Buonaccorso refused, requesting the Signory to observe the rights and freedoms which Florence had accorded to Pistoia and so to respect the power of local justice. When the Signory threatened to teach him a lesson, he enlisted the help of relatives and friends and again refused to surrender his man, whereupon one of the priors proposed to the Signory and colleges that the Captain of Pistoia be banished from Florence for twenty years. This proposal required twenty-five votes to go into effect. It obtained twenty-three, and at this point Buonaccorso was served an ultimatum: either the criminal was to be sent to Florence or Buonaccorso's exile would be put to the vote again and again until it was passed. He yielded. On this occasion the Signory does not seem to have held consultations with lawyers. Probably, as Buonaccorso maintained, it was violating local rights,[68] but it had the *de facto* power to take such action.

In the cases considered so far, dispute centered on the nature of judicial authority. Let us turn to conflicts of jurisdiction in administrative affairs.

Here is a case which touched the fisc.[69] By an act of October 8, 1393, the *parlamento* of that autumn appointed Ser Benedetto Fortini notary of the exitus accounts of the communal treasury. The appointment was for life. Dying in 1406, Ser Benedetto was replaced in the following year by his brother, Ser Paolo, who was also given the office "pro toto tempore vite sue." In 1411 Ser Paolo became chancellor (first secretary) of the Republic. He held this post until the end of 1427, while continuing throughout to be in charge of the exitus accounts. In October 1425 the government set up the office of the Ufficiali della Masseritia—five special accountants whose job was to ferret out all money, goods, properties, and rights of the Commune of Florence which had fallen into private hands, individual or corporate. The authority of these officials particularly concerned alienations which had escaped being recorded in the communal registers.[70] Within six or seven weeks of taking office, these officials re-

[68] Pitti, *Cronica*, pp. 112-14.
[69] Reported in *DSCOA*, 40 (May-June 1432), f. 42r.
[70] *Prov.*, 115, ff. 173r-175v.

solved, among other things, to make Ser Paolo keep an official chest ("capsettam") and observe certain other unspecified regulations. The chest was undoubtedly meant to hold the exitus account books. Such an arrangement, calling for lock and key, would have given the new officials an opportunity to demand a key and so a chance to exercise some control over the exitus accounts. But they were going against a powerful official: Ser Paolo was to be chancellor of the Republic for still another two years. Furthermore, he had great experience in public administration and certainly knew how to defend the prerogatives of his office. Not, therefore, until June 1432 did the struggle between him and the Masseritia Officials break into the open and reach the chambers of the Signory. Taking a legalistic line, Ser Paolo argued that he had been made notary of the exitus accounts with all the rights, privileges, and conveniences enjoyed by his brother, who had not kept a "capsettam." Hence the officials in question were exceeding their authority. They, on the contrary, claimed to be within their rights. To settle the controversy, the Signory and colleges, on June 28, 1432, ordered the official government lawyers to bring in an opinion on the case. Stefano Buonaccorsi and Biagio Niccolini were to submit their *consilium* by July 9th, on pain of a fine of 500 gold florins.[71] We cannot be sure of the outcome of this conflict because the appropriate set of deliberations was lost. But in all likelihood—judging partly by the law which established the authority of the new officials—the notary of the exitus accounts had to yield to the five accountants. The case was almost surely darkened by an element of political intrigue. Ser Paolo was a known opponent of the Medici family and had lost the chancellorship partly because of having involved himself in political rivalries. By the summer of 1432, the claims of the Masseritia Officials against Ser Paolo were no doubt kindled by the new increase in factional differences.

Another case which touched the fisc was debated by the priors and colleges on November 8, 1420, though unfortunately the surviving record provides maddeningly little information. Two sets of officials—the communal treasurers and the officials of the Monte (the funded public debt)

[71] In communal affairs of this sort, it was customary to threaten lawyers with an enormous fine so as to make them submit their *consilia* by a certain date. The device was effective.

—had been laying claim to a given sum of money for some time. The dispute was taken to the Signory and colleges, where the consensus was to resolve the matter in law, though not in one of the ordinary tribunals. They decided to turn the dispute over to four experts: the official government lawyers and the two men who held the Republic's most prestigious notarial posts, Ser Paolo Fortini (chancellor) and Ser Martino Martini (notary on legislation).[72] In a case of this kind, any opinion turned in by them was likely to be accepted and put into effect by the government.

The conflicts produced by confused and competing authority were no less remarkable in the late fifteenth century and persisted for as long as the Republic lasted. By the beginning of the sixteenth century, in its configuration partly and in many of its details, the Florentine state had seen some notable change, but the use of lawyers to resolve conflicts of jurisdiction remained much the same. Let us take a case involving Machiavelli's famous citizen militia. The case was provoked by two commissions and came to a head in the late winter of 1511. The Nine of the Militia (Novem Militie) had judicial authority over members of the corps. This authority, according to the Eight on Public Safety, extended only to cases involving militia conscripts. The Nine, however, claimed the power of justice over certain cases involving members of the militia and others. Confronted with this dispute, the Signory and colleges turned it over to three of the five jurists who made up the Council of Justice.[73] Their decision was recorded on March 18, 1511: the clash between the two commissions was decided in favor of the powerful Eight on Public Safety, an office with a long history (founded in 1378), cherished by the supporters of close oligarchy, but often feared and hated by the proponents of government with a wider social base.

In this controversy between the Eight and the Nine, there was an easy cooperation between the Signory and new Council of Justice. But

---

[72] CP, 44, f. 42r. On Filippo Carducci's recommendation that the "Domini habeant sapientes comunis et Ser Martinum et Cancellarium et examinentur leges comunis et si pecunia de qua est differentia pertinet ad cameram vel ad officium montis. Ubi iura disponunt ibi solvatur."

[73] DSCOA, 113, ff. 26v-27r. On the judicial powers of the Nine see the founding provision, Prov., 197, ff. 34v-39r (6 Dec. 1506). Some commercial litigation aside, the Council of Justice was now the highest of all ordinary civil courts. The traditional system of foreign magistrates had been abandoned.

these two could also be at loggerheads. One of their more notorious encounters took place in the late spring of 1508 when, acting as a high court of justice *una cum collegiis*, the Signory tried the chief magistrate of the Council of Justice, Piero Saracini da Fano, deposed him from office, and had him thrown into prison. He was accused of dishonesty, "evil customs," and maladministration of justice. In the context of this study, the most interesting feature of the case is the fact that the action against Saracini was taken in close consultation with sixteen prominent citizens, no fewer than thirteen of whom were lawyers. It seems clear that the government felt it could not effectively move against this superior magistrate without first obtaining the counsel of the city's best legal minds. The least known of the thirteen lawyers, at all events in legal circles, was Francesco Guicciardini, who had taken his doctorate in civil law only some nineteen months before.[74]

Some of the foregoing cases and controversies, implicating different types of magistracies, may seem of trivial significance if we see them only in isolation from one another. The truth is that they were representative expressions of an immensely complicated polity, a whole system of state. It was a system which depended on the contemporaneous functioning of scores of offices: three or four legislative assemblies, a variety of courts, special commissions, executive organs, short-term bodies, technical-administrative posts, territorial commissions, governors, and so forth. This complex of offices prefigured much that is found in the modern state. Three features of government in Florence were, however, different. The first is that no sure divisions were laid down between the legislative, executive, and judicial functions of government. Not seldom a temporary but powerful council performed all three functions in whole or in part. Moreover, the executive and judicial functions often went together. The second difference is that with some exceptions—unlike practice in most modern states—nearly every Florentine magistracy or single post was held for relatively short periods of time,[75] usually from two to six months,

---

[74] The other twelve lawyers were Francesco Gualterotti, Giovan Vettorio Soderini, Ormannozzo Deti, Luca Corsini, Niccolò Altoviti, Antonio Strozzi, Enea della Stufa, Matteo Niccolini, Piero Aldobrandini, Ludovico Acciaiuoli, Niccolò Rucellai, and Baldassare Carducci. Saracini was deposed on 30 May 1508. *DSCOA*, 110, f. 45r. See *Statuta*, II, 520, for the Signory's constitutional right in this case.

[75] Two notable exceptions after 1480 were the Council of Seventy, abolished in

more rarely for a year, but sometimes only for a few days or weeks. This short-term tenure gave rise to the third feature that was different— the fact that Florentine statecraft called for a continuous rotation of personnel through a multiplicity of offices. The best of the office holders were highly experienced men with considerable skill in a variety of jobs, but they were always on the move from one function to another.

From time to time, even the most efficient states are faced with persistent elements of jurisdictional uncertainty. Points along the lines between the different spheres of authority suddenly become unclear. In republican Florence the movement of personnel through office was so continuous and rapid that unusual flexibility crept into the way authority was exercised. Some groups of priors (*signorie*) were tougher and more authoritarian than others, some governors more compliant, some Eights on Public Safety less invasive and arrogant (in the original sense of this word), some War Commissions more or less dictatorial. The differences went far enough to occasion obstinate uncertainties and to provoke disputes between judicial as well as legislative bodies.

The flexibility of Florentine statecraft, particularly as seen in territorial and internal affairs, had its manifest merits, and perhaps these outweighed the drawbacks; but it also meant that divisions inside the compass of public authority were fraught with more confusion and uncertainty than is common in modern states. It was this situation which lawyers were called on to clarify and make more manageable. They did not constitute the linchpin of the system—there is no need to claim that—but neither could the system quite do without them. In a world where dispute between different spheres of authority was the norm, there had to be experts to help decide things. Was it a question of settling a conflict between the Podestà and the Sei di Mercanzia (the city's chief commercial tribunal)?[76] Lawyers were called into the case. Were the Eight on

---

1494, and the dignity held by Piero Soderini from 1502 to 1512. The chancellorship and the office of *notaio delle riformagioni* were often held by the same men for years, but these appointments had to be renewed annually.

[76] *Strozz., 3a ser.,* 41, vol. 3, ff. 94r-104v. One of Antonio Strozzi's opinions (*ca.* 1500), where the dispute between Podestà and Sex Mercantiae constituted an aspect of the case.

Public Safety competent to grant a license of safe conduct to a bankrupt condemned by one of the ordinary tribunals? Again this was a matter for lawyers. Was there a question as to whether the trustees (the *operarios*) over repairs and building in the cathedral came under the jurisdiction of the Commune or the Lana guild (a semi-public entity)? Six lawyers were commissioned to submit a judgment in the dispute.[77]

The examples could be multiplied, but the point has been made. One of the key functions of lawyers in Florentine public life was to help solve the puzzles of jurisdiction created by an intricate parcelling out of authority and by a mobile system of office-holding.

## 3. Administrative Problems

*Administrare*: to help, to manage, to carry out. The administrator has the job of executing or helping to carry out policy. He may interpret it, but policy is finally determined by someone else. Hence this part of the study will emphasize procedure and procedural questions.

Daily, hourly the state system of republican Florence confronted questions about precisely how certain jobs would be done, how particular aspects of policy would be executed. And solutions presented themselves in the normal course of things. For better or worse, systems are partly self-propelling: states and offices develop their own norms and then run along the grooves that have been thus developed. Much of the business at hand is thus automatically dispatched. But according as there is more mobility in the office-holding class and more uncertainty along the boundaries between the different offices, more and more problems arise to plague administrative procedure. Florentine offices had both their norms and problems. The daily tasks of government were carried out along well-defined lines. Officials assembled and knew what they could and could not do. Syndicating commissions, for example, accepted petitions against foreign magistrates only when these were directly filed, not when they were presented through procurators; wishing to visit

[77] *CRS*, Arch. 98, vol. 237, ff. 1r-5v. A case of the later 1450s. The six lawyers were Otto Niccolini, Benedetto Accolti, Guglielmo Tanagli, Piero Ambrosini, Girolamo Machiavelli, and Bernardo Buongirolami. They awarded the case to the Lana guild.

Florence, officials stationed in the dominion had to procure beforehand a license from the Signory or the Eight on Public Safety; petitions of eligibility for office normally went to the Defenders of the Laws (after 1429); what English law calls the Abominable Crime was tried by the first of four or five commissions to receive knowledge of the case; appeals against the Tower Officials went directly to the Signory; tax indulgences were cleared first by the Signory and colleges and finally authorized by the Councils of the People and Commune; etc.; etc. But now and then the old lines no longer sufficed. The multiple duties of one office became much too heavy, or something came up which did not accord with the established lines. Then a call for help went out and the solution was often provided by lawyers.

It would be wrong to give the impression that the Republic on the banks of the Arno was run by specialists, that there was a cult of the expert in Florentine statecraft. There was too much movement through the circuit of public office for this, too much diversification in the experience which made up many a political career. Yet the state had a permanent fund of administrative competence in the notary. As a result, the most skillful and well-connected notaries were in constant demand. All top-ranking offices included at least one notarial post whose occupant was expected to be familiar with the norms of the office which he happened to be serving. Such men were the mainstay of the system and office-holding class. For although notaries moved regularly from one notarial post to another, remaining in each for periods of from two to twelve months, their duties tended to be uniform. They had to know the modes and formulae of the paperwork connected with any office they served, and this meant dealing with correspondence, deliberations, petitions, introitus and exitus accounts, and the sending out of directives and summonses. Apart from having to understand the authority of the office and its limits, they had to acquaint themselves with all legislation and executive directives concerning it. They also saw to it that this material was recorded in the appropriate registers, and a leading official (the notary on legislation) furnished them with all the new statutes or executive orders bearing on the office. In short, the notaries most often found in government service *were* specialists: they were technical experts in the field of public administration. The other citizens who normally staffed the different offices were experts alone in the original sense of the word: the best of them were men *tried* and *proved* in public affairs.

Citizens had their preferences, of course. Some exhibited more skill in public finance, others in the administration of justice; still others preferred military matters, diplomacy, or trade relations. But such specialities and preferences did not prevent the Signory or other bodies, when faced with a particular issue, from soliciting the opinions of men with more general interests. Florentine public administration drew on wide experience as well as on specialization. The office-holding class was well braced by experts: the government notaries. At the head of these stood men who held more permanent and strategic positions—the chancellery's leading officials, who from about the middle of the fifteenth century and after tended to be men with law degrees.

There is considerable evidence to show that the Florentine patriciate sought to join the expert and the layman in political matters. In 1415 the legislative councils enacted a measure which required that any judicial opinion solicited by the state *ex sapientibus communis* must, to have binding force, receive the votes of at least thirty-two of the thirty-seven men who constituted the Signory and colleges.[78] Another measure, passed in June 1432, erected a bar against permanently associating legal counsellors with any office, although the *sapientes communis* were to go on functioning as in the past. If a particular office needed legal advice, it could turn to a lawyer matriculated in the guild of lawyers and notaries, but his association with the office must end with the question he had been asked to treat.[79] Then in 1449, as has already been noted, the *sapientes communis* were eliminated, the office permanently dissolved. In these events we seem to perceive a downright distrust of the lawyer, of the expert who might bully or confuse laymen with his subtleties. It is clearer still that citizens were eager to temper the recommendations of the expert with those of laymen whose everyday experience might serve to curb the exaggerations of professional men. All the same,

[78] *Prov.,* 104, f. 50v. Raised to thirty-six affirmative votes in 1419, *Carte di Corredo,* 14, f. 16v.
[79] *Prov.,* 123, ff. 126v-127r.

there was no getting away from the utility of lawyers. Not only their legal understanding but also their practical experience at the top level of politics and diplomacy far transcended that of notaries. In the course of the Quattrocento, when notaries were increasingly and then exclusively confined to straight notarial posts, lawyers retained an active hold on the key magistracies. They made proposals there, argued, deliberated, and deeply involved themselves in the formation and articulation of policy. They could therefore envisage problems both as administrators and makers of policy, although they might be drawn by their legal experience to range themselves on the side of custom and continuity.

Something of the lawyer's administrative activity has already been seen. Wherever the articulation of policy was blocked by controversy between two or more offices and lawyers were called in to help settle the dispute, they disentangled things; they cleared the way for officials to get on with their duties. Conflicts of jurisdiction were thus resolved. We shall now take jurisdictions for granted and concentrate on the procedural problems encountered by offices in full activity. I take most of the succeeding examples from two fields—public finance and recruitment for public office.

During most of the century and a half covered by this study, there were few years when some aspect of public finance was not hotly and bitterly disputed in the executive councils of the Republic. Just as the political class hated to pay taxes, so the state hated to disburse money, whether for war, diplomacy, the University of Florence, or to foreign creditors. Public finance was always one of the city's two most divisive issues.[80] The continuing struggle for one or another system of taxation went far to undermine the Republic. More accurately, the failure to solve the problems of public finance was a symptom of the refusal or inability of the oligarchy to find a working and adaptable political arrangement. The social base of government should have been either wider or more narrow; relations with the *petite bourgeoisie* and disfranchised multitude should have been readjusted; some uniform, dogged policy ought to have been developed (as at Venice) against the anarchic influence of the powerful and bold single houses. But only the last of these was done, and only

[80] Eligibility for public office was the other.

172

partly. Social and political strains vitiated the best of Florentine policy, undermined the best resolutions on the most important internal issues. In the field of public finance the result was a shifty, inequitable, divisive tax policy—an instrument as well of political and social hegemony as of economic exploitation.

In 1427, after months of acrimonious and strained debate in the executive councils, the government introduced the *catasto*, a tax that continued to be levied in Florence in one form or another down to the 1480s. It started out as a tax of 0.5 per cent on all capital that brought in an income of some sort: farms, livestock, buildings, shops, industrial equipment, commercial stock, investments in the Monte, and even the lawbooks of practicing lawyers.[81] Occasionally collected several times yearly, the tax soon had some citizens implicated in trickery and evasion. To correct this, a penalty was introduced involving the forfeiture of all property concealed from the Catasto Officials. Where incriminating evidence was furnished by an informer, he received one-fourth the value of the property confiscated. One particular method of tax evasion, however, was hard to pin down because it involved the connivance of men in holy orders. This was the practice of falsely declaring that certain properties— lands or buildings—had been legally and fully bestowed on a church, chapel, monastery, or hospital. Too often in these cases the alleged beneficiary was ready to attest to the veracity of the donation, thus cheating the state of its revenue. But the issue was clear: the state knew it had an unequivocal tax right over such properties. The only question was how to bring them out into the open.

It was a question of procedure, and some lawyers were engaged to look into it. Exactly who they were is not revealed, but the language and form of some resolutions taken by the Catasto Officials in the 1430s leave no doubt of the fact that they were in close consultation with one or more legal minds. The gist of a pronouncement made by these officials in October 1431 was that thenceforth, by a two-thirds vote, they could declare "fictitious and fraudulent" any conveyances of property by taxpaying persons to any individual, place, *collegium* or corporation "non supportantem onera catastorum." Penalties were to be imposed as if for

[81] Martines, *The Social World of the Florentine Humanists*, pp. 101, 106, n. 54.

ordinary tax fraud: "and let the aforesaid go to enhance the authority of the Catasto Officials, not to diminish it."[82] There was something so arbitrary in this ruling that they had trouble applying it, and so another measure, more detailed and comprehensive, was brought forth in April 1434. This time the lawyers' handiwork was even more obvious. Together with the Catasto Officials, they devised a scheme which ruled that all properties taxed in the first *catasto* (1427), and later alienated or transferred to places or persons not subject to the *catasto*, belong in fact and *de iure* to those persons or that place or corporation to which the designated properties had been given, sold, or otherwise alienated. All such transfers of ownership were to be treated "as if they are true, not fictitious, despite any [secret] counter-contract or document which may have been drawn up between the parties so as to render fraudulent the contract or instrument of alienation." To cover a possible loophole, it was also provided—in apparent contradiction—that all properties alienated with intent to defraud the Commune belonged *ipso facto* "to the Commune of Florence, save the fourth which goes to the informer."[83] But before this scheme could have the force of law, it had to get the approval of the Councils of the People and Commune by a two-thirds vote. Anticipating some resistance, legal counsel persuaded the Catasto Officials to include two other articles in the projected law. The first paid tribute to the Signory's discretionary prerogative to act as a court of appeal. Calling attention to such appeal, it pointed out that the appellant was required to move his case according to forms prescribed by the Defenders of the Laws and not more than fifteen days after the confiscatory action of the Catasto Officials. The other article cut the bitterness of the proposed remedy: if a man reported his fraudulent alienations to the Catasto Officials within a month from the day the proposed measure was approved in the Council of the Commune, the embarrassed properties would not be affected, although they had to be recorded in his *catasto* forms and he had to pay the ordinary tax on them.[84]

[82] *Catasto,* 1, f. 39r.
[83] *Ibid.,* f. 55r. I say "apparent contradiction" because it seems clear that where fraud could be demonstrated, thus establishing the connivance of the second party, the first part of this measure would give way to a number of statutes against defrauding the Commune.
[84] This bill became law on 9 April 1434. *Prov.,* 125, f. 8r.

The lawyers consulted by the Catasto Officials concentrated their fire on the fraudulent use of public instruments. They sought validation in the document made public, not, of course, in the one concealed. If the trickery emerged anyway, then the officials could move in and seize the embarrassed property. This much was in aid of the procedure to be followed by the Catasto Officials. The codicils on the thirty-day clemency and on appeal were also part of the machinery to help expose tax evasion, but their special significance lay in the fact that they facilitated approval of the measure in the legislative councils. Legal counsel thus served administrative procedure on two quite different levels.

We may assume that the connivance of the Florentine clergy, or rather parts thereof, persisted. For tax evasion of the sort based on fictitious conveyances to religious places and bodies continued to worry the authorities. In still another attempt to find a remedy, the government invited two more lawyers to submit additional recommendations—Giovanni Buongirolami and Giovanni Bovacchiesi, both trained in Roman law. Their report was considered in February 1437, and although it does not survive, the records of the executive debates make clear what the two had proposed. They seem to have devised a plan to levy a graduated tax on all properties the ownership of which had been transferred to religious persons, corporations, or places since the time of the first *catasto*.[85] Here finally was a weapon against tax dodgers who had used the trick of false alienation. Unfortunately, it also affected properties which had been acquired by the Florentine church in good faith. Put into effect, the plan would have resulted in a frontal clash between Church and state. The plan naturally divided the oligarchy. Andrea de' Pazzi, for example, builder of the famous Pazzi chapel, strongly favored the scheme of the two lawyers. Relying indirectly on argument from public welfare, he declared, "I fail to see why ecclesiastical properties should bear no taxes. These are defended from enemies just as are other properties." The same view was expressed by Giannozzo Pitti. For Antonio di Tedice degli Albizzi, on the other hand, the lawyers' plan was clearly contrary to the liberty of the Church and so he opposed it. He recommended that interest payments be withheld from the numerous clerics with investments

[85] *CP*, 51, f. 86v.

in the public debt (the Monte). The knight Messer Agnolo Acciaiuoli also declared himself personally opposed to the taxation of properties which had been transferred to non-taxable organizations and persons, despite the fact that he delivered the majority report for a *pratica* of seventeen men, fifteen of whom favored the proposals of the two jurists.[86] The legal views of lawyers concerning the taxation of clerks and church property will be set forth later on in this work (Ch. VII, 2).

Buongirolami and Bovacchiesi were citizens and legal residents of Florence, but the former hailed from Gubbio, the latter from Prato. It is perhaps because they were outsiders, strictly speaking, that they were the lawyers called upon to treat the question of false alienation. Having no powerful or deep-rooted family connections in the city, they may have been expected to come up with more objective, non-partisan suggestions. If so, this expectation of neutrality was marked for failure. They were not on neutral ground: the issue was itself explosive. Social relations between key personnel of the Florentine church and some of the city's great families were too close. More was involved than a question of principle, of the liberty of the Church (though this was exceedingly important); it was also a matter of protecting the wealth of certain families, of satisfying ambitions, of not surrendering where others had escaped. Besides, were not the two lawyers running over into policy-making by recommending a tax on *all* properties made over to the Florentine church since 1427? They were of course. But it was also true that certain clerics or groups under ecclesiastical jurisdiction had encouraged citizens to break the civil law. In giving help and protection to tax dodgers, they had violated an implicit contract with the state. From what bonds, therefore, was the state released? The issue was one in which the party originally injured might have pressed for negotiation. But Florence refrained from provoking a controversy with the Church. The way proposed by the two lawyers was not adopted, and the fraudulent conveyance of property continued unabated. We may suppose that the old devices used to defraud were perfected or that new ones against detection were developed. The barrier to a more effective system of taxation was always the same. "We cannot lay hands," moaned a well-known

---

[86] *Ibid.*, ff. 86v, 87r, 89v, for the views of Pazzi, Acciaiuoli and the others.

lawyer, "on the property of the Church."[87] It was December 6, 1457. On June 10th, 1458, the legislative councils enacted a bill in which it was laid down that all properties transferred to non-taxable persons and institutions since 1407 (sic) had been transferred in fraud and that the Catasto Officials could levy taxes on them. But this was verbal bravura, for the same act went on to requisition the documents and terms of all such alienations, authorized the Catasto Officials and Signory to exempt the legal ones, and declared that they could not tax properties "freely made over to the Church."[88] Things thus were back to where they had started, and a year later all the old complaints were rehearsed once again, denouncing the high incidence of fraud committed via the false transfer of property.[89] Two prominent lawyers, Donato de' Cocchi-Donati and Otto Niccolini, were invited to treat the question, but they had to be content with pointing out administrative and legal snarls.[90]

Despite the troubles produced by the *catasto*, not all questions of public finance or related matters were so controversial that they caused political dispute and rancor without end. Some were fully settled by the intervention of lawyers. When a certain citizen fled from Florence with money which Alfonso of Aragon, on behalf of a favorite, then importuned the Republic to pay, it was a lawyer who recommended that the government publish a "provisio late sententie" against the fugitive.[91] Or again, possessions and properties confiscated because of political crime were not infrequently the subject of administrative complication. The money from the sale of these goods was meant in whole or in part for the government coffers. There was no dispute here about the state's

[87] *CP*, 54, f. 175v, Messer Otto Niccolini.
[88] *Catasto*, 2, ff. 90r-92v, pencil. It looks as if Florentines who had sold property to ecclesiastical organizations were in some cases passing themselves off as benefactors by claiming that the property had been freely donated.
[89] *CP*, 55, ff. 97r-102r.
[90] *Ibid.*, f. 99r-v. The same problem continued to afflict the officials who administered the new tax distributions of 1469 and 1480. *Catasto*, 2, ff. 106r, 137r, pencil.
[91] *CP*, 54, ff. 123v-124r, 133r (April-May 1457). The lawyer was Tommaso Salvetti, the favorite Messer Giovanni da Fossa, the fugitive Giovanni Biliotti. As Vicar of Firenzuola, Biliotti had arrested Messer Giovanni, who was carrying an illegal safe-conduct. Biliotti released his man only after imposing a "taglio" on him. He confiscated Messer Giovanni's "cloth and other merchandise" valued at 1,500 to 2,000 florins. Alfonso's claim, however, was for 3,300 florins.

jurisdiction: the statutes were clear on this. It was also the state's part to dispose of the confiscated properties. The question was, what about the priorities of creditors with claims on the said properties? A case in point involved the properties of the exile Messer Rinaldo degli Albizzi. On September 1, 1435, his brother, Luca, appealed to the Signory, seeking to put certain controls on the officials who had custody of all Rinaldo's possessions. Once these were sold and the money dispersed, Luca feared that he might himself be sued for outstanding debts or obligations contracted by Rinaldo or by their father, Messer Maso (d. 1417), who had left certain bequests binding his heirs. With the consent of the Rebel Officials (trustees over properties confiscated from rebels), the Signory appointed six men to handle the matter: three lawyers and three laymen.[92] Having examined the different claims involved, the six reported on October 29, 1435, that all the known claims on the properties had been satisfied, leaving only—if any there were—the unknown contracts and obligations. Pointing out next the remaining steps to be followed, they urged the Rebel Officials to publish a notice to the effect that all men having claims of any kind whatsoever on Rinaldo's possessions should present them by a certain time. Once that time expired, the officials were to proclaim the remaining goods and properties to be free of any and all obligations, thus putting a "perpetual silence on every person and place." We may take for granted that the three lawyers performed the technical work connected with the documents examined and procedures designated.

A similar case came up on October 15, 1495. The question was raised in the executive councils of what order to follow in disposing of the seized Medici properties. Francesco Pepi and Domenico Bonsi, lawyers both, were the first two speakers. Combining utility with a legalistic approach, they made the surest and most precise recommendations. They argued that the claims of all private citizens (i.e., creditors of Piero de' Medici) should be examined and settled first. For these are mostly merchants, said Pepi, and the city has need of them. Bonsi agreed, but he

[92] *DSCOA*, 47, ff. 4r-5r, 9r. Giuliano Davanzati, Piero Beccanugi, and Tommaso Salvetti were the lawyers. The others were Banco Bencivenni and two powerful politicians—Cosimo de' Medici and Neri di Gino Capponi.

urged shrewdly that the list of creditors be headed by all foreigners "who are in a position to move reprisals [in the courts] against us."[93]

An example of a quarrel between two offices over a question of administering the state's monies concerns the *balzello*, a particular type of tax collected at different times during the fifteenth and early sixteenth centuries. One was levied in 1527-1528. The legislation which created the Balzello Officials of 1527 does not seem to have been clear about precisely how these officials were to draw their salaries. This drew them into a dispute with the officials appointed to check the accounts relating to the public debt, the Monte Syndics. The Balzello Officials claimed that their salaries should be paid by order of the Monte Syndics, who in turn denied this. Having conducted an investigation, the Signory sided with the Balzello Officials, but only after first having held close consultations with an eminent lawyer, Silvestro Aldobrandini, with the notary Ser Lorenzo Violi, and with the two scribes of the Monte Syndics. These consultants determined in detail the plan of payment.[94]

To move from public finance and allied matters to the order of procedures connected with the screening of men for public office involved a shift which at least some lawyers negotiated with ease. Taxes, confiscated property, and government salaries entailed intricacies and hidden problems, but so did the modes of according and denying political eligibility.

Offices were usually staffed by drawing names from a series of pouches (*borse*). The names of all eligible citizens went into the pouches, and names were drawn by lot. Now and then, however, the *borse* for major office were kept *a mano* ("by hand"), meaning that they were filled according to a process ("reduction") which excluded most of the eligible.[95] Whenever the ruling faction, especially after 1434, became anxious about its security and so drew in on itself, the pouches were kept *a mano*, although the practice even then was to do this with the pouches for key office only. All told, the system was a complicated one and called

---

[93] *CP*, 61, f. 71r-v.

[94] *DSCOA*, 130, ff. 171v-172r, 189r, pencil. Aldobrandini was forced into exile in 1530 but went on to have a brilliant professorial career at Ferrara.

[95] N. Rubinstein, *The Government of Florence Under the Medici (1434 to 1494)*, pp. 34-36.

for different sets of pouches. The external or territorial offices had their pouches, the internal ones theirs. There were major and minor offices and corresponding series of pouches. To complicate things further, each full-scale review or "scrutiny" of men eligible for public office resulted in new pouches for the whole range of offices. Thus, in the first quarter of the fifteenth century, aggregates of pouches were prepared for the scrutinies of 1407, 1410, 1412, 1417, and 1421. The need arose for a new scrutiny and with it arose the question of which of the lists previously approved should be rejected or modified or used as a starting point. Sometimes in good faith and sometimes in bad, an effort was usually made to observe the norms laid down by law. Evidently, the struggle for and against political eligibility in Florence gave rise to a system of procedures hardly less elaborate than those connected with public finance, and here too lawyers lent a hand.

Could a citizen refuse to accept an important territorial office on grounds of sickness or old age? How, if at all, would this affect his eligibility for other public dignities? The notary who supervised the drawing of names from the pouches (the *notaio delle tratte*) had to have answers to questions of this sort, as it was his task to decide whether or not to recommend fines and whether or not to proceed with having other names extracted from the appropriate pouch. Such procedural snags were not uncommon and just the sort of problem for the legal mind, so that the Tratte notary sometimes turned for counsel to the communal lawyers as well as to men in private practice.[96]

Of particular interest was a complication which arose in late February 1408. The time to designate the next Gonfalonier of Justice was overdue. Ser Bonifazio Salutati (Tratte notary) and his aides had already drawn all the names from the pouch for this office, but each had been found to have a *divieto*; i.e., none of the citizens whose names had been in the pouch was eligible for the office at that particular time. Each had a

[96] E.g., *Carte del Bene*, 54, ff. 6r-7r (May 1409), an opinion of the Del Bene lawyer, Ricciardo, on a dispute between Messer Rinaldo Gianfigliazzi and the Tratte notary; *DSCOA*, 40, ff. 5r-6v, 20v-21r (May 1432), opinions of the *sapientes* on Tratte procedure and on a citizen deprived of eligibility for office. For the mechanics of scrutinies and *divieti* in the later Trecento see G. Brucker, *Florentine Politics and Society*, pp. 66-68; also Rubinstein, *The Government of Florence*, pp. 53ff., 318ff.

temporary bar against him, either because he currently held another leading post, or because he had sat in the Signory too recently, or was behind
in his taxes, or had a relative in the forthcoming Signory, or for another
reason. Yet the office had to be filled, and the deadlock was broken by
the experts whom the colleges had designated. The Sixteen advised the
Signory to let the problem be handled by the lawyers who assisted the
Podestà and the Captain, by the official communal lawyers, by the notary
on legislation, the Tratte notary, and the chancellor or first secretary.
These officials were encouraged to meet without adjourning until they
found a solution. They were then to submit their "consilium cum sigillo
clausum" to the Signory.[97] Since six of the Twelve Good Men fully con-
curred with this advice, we may assume that it was followed. The other
six proposed that only two of the lawyers attached to the Podestà and
the Captain be asked to propose a solution and that this solution next
be submitted to the palace notaries (i.e., chancellor, Tratte notary, and
notary on legislation); the final plan of procedure, however, was to be
left to the decision of these three officials. It has already been noted that
the palace notaries had a considerable grasp of legislation and practical
constitutional law, owing to which we may rightly think of them as
lawyers. A record does not survive of the solution they finally hit on in
this affair.

Whenever the question of a new scrutiny was raised in the executive
councils, the ensuing debate could go on—although with interruptions—
for months. Particularly was this true if, as in late 1422 and early 1423,
the bill on the proposed scrutiny had been repeatedly defeated in the
legislative assemblies. Political intrigue might be rampant; the flower
of the oligarchy might come out for or against a new scrutiny; eventually,
however, the colleges or *pratica* of invited counsellors advised the use of
lawyers to see that the methods of screening accorded with communal
ordinances. Sometimes, also, it was a matter of employing lawyers to
help maneuver a scrutiny bill through the legislature. For as an influential
canonist once observed to the Signory, there are many ways to draft a
bill, but some are more likely to win votes than others.[98] On March 24,

[97] A formal legal opinion. The whole question treated in *CP*, 39, f. 12v.
[98] *CP*, 51, f. 69v (28 Nov. 1436), observed by Lorenzo Ridolfi. In the succeeding
item above, Corsini was talking for the whole body of invited counsellors: *CP*,
43, f. 141r.

1417, the lawyer Filippo Corsini urged the Signory to appoint some lawyers ("doctores [legum]") and other citizens to help give suitable form to a projected bill on a forthcoming scrutiny. Several years later the Signory heard a similar proposal. Serving as the spokesmen for a *pratica* of twenty-seven men, a knight and lawyer submitted the following advice: "once the scrutiny is finished, the approved names should be reviewed by others as is called for by the ordinances. . . . And to proceed warily, let the lords draw up and appoint the provision with the help of all the lawyers they wish."[99] In September 1429 there was a move afoot, deriving from one of the factions or ruling blocs, to stymie efforts at realizing a new scrutiny. Here again those who opposed the scrutiny found it advisable to enlist the aid of lawyers. The city echoed with dissension over taxes and war and there was agitation to reform the pouches of eligibility for office. Lorenzo Ridolfi, a fashionable canon lawyer, spoke for the entire *pratica*. He recommended to the Signory that if there should be an onslaught of plague when the time came to carry out a new scrutiny, the scrutiny should be put off.[100] Much of the discord in the city concerned the current list of men eligible for office, but Ridolfi and the *pratica* opposed even "touching" the pouches. Indeed, he moved that the pouches be confirmed in their present state and that this be done by having the Signory draw on the help "of many lawyers from among the most informed" on the subject. These lawyers, he concluded, should consult with the notary on legislation so that all together could decide on the best way and means to keep the pouches unchanged.[101]

The correct or effective drafting of bills answered to a phase of administration at the highest level of government, just as did the strategy connected with negotiating bills through the legislative councils. But the alert eye will have seen that such performance also bordered on the formu-

---

[99] *CP*, 45, f. 87r (8 March 1423). Said Matteo Castellani and Giuliano Davanzati, "Sed perfecto scrutinio debeant per alios scrutinari ut per ordinamento disponitur. Et non solum pro scrutinio presenti fiat sed etiam per alia omnia scrutinia celebranda ex officiis extrinsecis, et sic per legem firmetur et provideatur. Et ut caute procedatur domini habeant omnes doctores quos volent ut provisionem ordinent et forment."

[100] The scrutiny of 1417 had been carried out, possibly illegally, in a time of plague. For years there were protests against it.

[101] *CP*, 48, f. 89v.

lation of policy, on questions of legislation and constitutional law, and on the political struggle proper. Florentine lawyers, when invited to work on delicate problems of administration, came very near the centers of power, where policy itself was determined and launched.

## 4. Legislation and Constitutional Affairs

Benedetto Varchi (b. 1503), who did not much care for lawyers, devotes a brief chapter of his *Storia fiorentina* to a bill passed by the Grand Council in December 1529. It was the bill which gave birth to the five Syndics on Rebels. Varchi points out that the five were given retroactive powers to change and "correct" recent decisions of the Tower Officials, to validate or invalidate contracts bearing on the properties of rebels, to annul "guarantees of sureties . . . donations, cessions of rights and other terms of legists."[102] They could seize properties and credits almost at will and sell these—by force if necessary—to whom they chose. Any cleric who appealed against an action of theirs was subject to the death penalty. The measure also proscribed any Florentine judge, lawyer, or procurator who brooked or aided attempts to move reprisals in answer to action taken by the Syndics.

For Varchi the Florentine Republic showed itself to be worse than a tyranny in this enactment. That the final repository of all public authority (the Grand Council and Signory) had approved it, that the city was surrounded and under attack by an imperial army, that defeat meant the end of the Republic—these circumstances did not, in Varchi's eyes, mitigate the pure wickedness of handing such powers over to the Syndics on Rebels. And he did not fail to point out that the iniquitous bill was "composed"—worked out in all its details and drafted—by Messer Silvestro Aldobrandini, a practicing lawyer who had taken his doctorate in civil law at Pisa in 1521. Banished from Florence in 1530, this man went on to profess law at the University of Ferrara, where he served on occasion as counsellor to Duke Ercole II.

Aldobrandini's work on the foregoing piece of legislation had three

---

[102] Varchi, *Opere*, 2 vols. (Trieste, 1858), I, 228-29, "in loro potestà era annullare i fidecommissi, le substituzioni o volgari o pupillari, le donagioni, le cessioni di ragioni ed altri termini di legisti, i quali, se gl' intendevano essi, non sono gran fatto intesi da altri."

parts, answering to three types of jobs performed by lawyers in the Republic's internal affairs. (1) There was the drafting of the bill, an administrative task which involved figuring out the details of the authority to be handed over to the five Syndics. Technically, this was the job of the Signory and one of the chief palace notaries, but it was often, as in this case, delegated to one or more consultants. (2) There was Aldobrandini's obligation to devise a bill consistent with the laws of the Republic or, where this was not possible because of urgent needs, to include clauses which temporarily suspended the pertinent prohibitory ordinances, so that approval by the Grand Council would make the bill legally defensible in all its particulars. This aspect of things touched on the part played by lawyers in the field of legislation and constitutional law. (3) There was the pure political part: the job of drafting a bill designed to overcome opposition in the Grand Council. Our business here is the second of these operations. Surveying the activity of lawyers in the realm of legislation and constitutional affairs, one can make out five different tasks. While the first and third were not often required, the others answered to a frequent and lasting need. The tasks were as follows: (1) directing reforms of the judiciary; (2) helping—in their formal capacity as jurists—to settle conflicts of jurisdiction; (3) reviewing, emending, and reorganizing the corpus of Florentine statutory law; (4) giving legal consultation on projected pieces of legislation; and (5) offering expert views in the executive councils on the nature and authority of particular magistracies. Since the first two of these have already been discussed in sections apart, only the others remain to be considered.

In the course of the fourteenth century the statutes of the Commune were twice (in 1322-1325 and in 1355) fully reviewed, changed here and there, and rearranged. Later on in the century other serious attempts to effect new reforms came to nothing. In 1415 the statutes were again revised and reorganized—for the last time under the Republic. The later fifteenth century, a period of relentless contraction in the political life of the city, was not a time to have a frank look at the whole body of statutes. Possibly the oligarchy felt intuitively that it had a freer hand with statutes which contained contradictions, ambiguities, and complexities fit for legal minds. More auspicious for a revision of the statutes would have been the political climate of the middle 1490s and the first years of the sixteenth century; but the contemporaries of Savonarola and Piero Soderini barely rose to the task of doing things piecemeal.

To revise the communal statutes: what exactly did this entail? A legislative measure of December 23, 1394, is enlightening. An attempt was made then—it went unrealized—to give new order to the statutes.[103] The document observes that the statutes, reforms, and provisions of the Commune had not been examined in about forty years, that there was need of a new revision and compilation. For in many parts and places "some are mutually contradictory and in part corrected by others, many are superfluous, still others are obscure and perplexing, and indeed there is so much confusion in them that they cannot be understood by the foreign magistrates, nor properly used, nor even memorized; whence it often happens that public and private right are violated and that many troubles ensue, owing to ignorance, variations [in the law], and [legal] intricacies." The measure thereupon ordained that by the end of February 1395 the government engage a lawyer to study the communal statutes with an eye to removing "the conflicts, obscurities, perplexities, superfluities, absurdities, and disorders." He was to arrange them "in harmonious and suitable sections, just as he shall see fit," giving them "unity and order and as much clarity as he can achieve." The lawyer chosen for this assignment was required to have a doctorate in civil law and be assisted by two "scribe-notaries" and two servants. Forbidden to introduce substantive changes of any kind, he could neither add nor take away things from the corpus of statutes. It was also stipulated that he carry out his assignment "with the consent and consultation of eight citizens during, before, and after" his revision. He had one year to do the job. The eight consultants were to be elected according to a plan laid out in the measure and could not include any lawyer, canonist, or notary.[104] Here again, accordingly, the government took care to see that the expert was surrounded by a group of laymen. How far he would be able to prevail over them was up to him.

The statutes were in a chaotic state. Ordinances of trivial consequence

---

[103] *Prov.*, 83, ff. 246r-249r.
[104] *Ibid.*, f. 247r.

appeared cheek by jowl with others of supreme importance. Complaints had rained in on the Signory. Particularly, it seems, had there been protests from the foreign magistrates and their judges. There may have been some notaries and lawyers who felt an interest in perpetuating the disorder, if by so doing they increased their chances to cavil or to draw up more documents. In any case, they seldom appear at the forefront of any move to review and revise the laws and ordinances of the city. Yet when the time came it was a lawyer—although one brought in from abroad—who was chosen to captain the work of revision.[105] The possibility that the presence of another lawyer or notary among the eight consultants might well disrupt or retard or flummox the others was, I presume, one reason for restricting the consulting body to laymen.

A good deal of obscurity surrounds the attempted reform of 1394-1395, of which nothing came. Another attempt, also abortive, took place during the summer of 1396.[106]

Not until 1415 were the statutes finally re-examined and reformed. Two foreign lawyers, then resident and practicing in Florence, conducted the work: Bartolommeo Vulpi da Soncino and his more able and famous contemporary, Paolo di Castro, both of whom taught law at the Studio Fiorentino. They were assisted by nine notaries, and the work was carried out in collaboration with the five Monte Officials, who were meant to keep an eye on the experts.[107] When finished, the new redaction was approved first by the Signory and colleges, then by the legislative councils in December 1415, but it was not to go into effect until the following June. Even after this reform, however, the condition of the statutes continued to elicit criticism. The new compilation—Paolo di Castro's reputation notwithstanding—retained some of the old difficulties and obscurities. Little more than two years later, the lawyer Alessandro Bencivenni, speaking for one of the colleges, urged the Signory to delegate a few distinguished lawyers and some other select citizens to meet with

[105] The editing and revising of the statutes of 1355 was headed by Messer Tommaso di Ser Puccio da Gubbio, "legum doctor." *SCF*, 11, f. 1r; 19, at beginning of text.

[106] *Prov.*, 85, ff. 84r-85v (9 June 1396), meant to be put into effect by the end of August. Two copies of the new compilation (never compiled) were ordered—one in the vernacular, the other in Latin.

[107] *Statuta*, I, 1-4; III, 714-22.

the palace officials for the purpose of examining the newly edited statutes. Those "incorrectly arranged" he wanted either corrected or suspended.[108] But nothing was done. Thereafter, down to the establishment of the duchy, the general structure and disposition of the communal statutes remained much the same.

The provision of 1394 makes clear the purpose of engaging lawyers to review and emend the Florentine statutory corpus. They were not engaged for the mere sake of compiling a more harmonious set of laws and regulations, but to iron out difficulties in the existing set so as to make for a more efficient and smoother execution of the tasks of government. Now and then in the executive councils the recommendations of lawyers touched on this theme. On May 10, 1462, for example, we find Domenico Martelli—a lawyer trained at Bologna—saying that it is the duty of the most active citizens to see that useless laws are expunged from the municipal code.[109] More commonly, however, the advice of lawyers in council concerned particular statutes or proposed legislation.

Whatever the lawyer's part in judicial and general statutory reform, his part in the enactment of specific legislation was always more prominent and he was more often called on to play it. There was good reason for this. In their capacity as active citizens, not as men of the law, two or three lawyers (sometimes more) normally sat in the supreme councils, where they could be consulted at will. We scarcely need mention notaries, who were distributed as recording secretaries throughout all the main offices.

A leading American student of Trecento Florence has called attention to an interesting consultation held at the outset of November 1366.[110] On the 3rd and 4th of November the legislative assemblies passed a measure aimed at gagging the strongly pro-papal Guelf Society—the Parte Guelfa, then very active in the political proscription of certain types of citizens. Two factions divided Florentine political society. On one side was the semi-popular faction led by the Ricci, and on the other were the oligarchs, captained by the Albizzi. Since the oligarchs controlled the

[108] *CP*, 43, f. 125v (15 Jan. 1417). The same recommendation was made by the spokesman for the Dodici, Averardo de' Medici.
[109] *CP*, 56, f. 194v.
[110] Gene A. Brucker, *Florentine Politics and Society*, pp. 208-11.

mechanisms of the Parte Guelfa, their views prevailed there, making the society an arch-conservative organization. Sire of the measure which sought to put controls on the Society was Uguccione de' Ricci, family chieftain and a member of the Signory for the months of November and December 1366. The captains of the society were to be increased "from six to eight, of whom two were to be lower guildsmen. . . . the law also provided that future proscriptions were not valid unless they were ratified by a committee of twenty-four Guelfs, chosen specifically for that purpose."[111] But the measure did not stop here. It went on to include a gratuitous clause which ordained that no communal official was to be subject to the penalties of the Apostolic Camera because of anything contained in the measure.[112] It appears that someone in the chancellery or Signory had directed a sidelong slap at the papacy. The clause created some consternation and had possibly been overlooked at the time it was rushed through the legislative councils. Three days after the measure was passed, the Signory and colleges assembled eleven lawyers, confronting them with the question, Could the government legally and with impunity put into effect the newly enacted provision, even without the disputed clause?[113] The eleven lawyers assured them that it could. They found the provision legal and valid in all respects, with or without the clause. Thus, whatever charges might thereafter be brought against those who had sponsored the measure, none could in good faith assert that they had knowingly acted unconstitutionally. At least one lawyer of the Albizzi faction was present among the advisors in the executive chambers—Messer Filippo Corsini—but even he found nothing illegal in the provision.

Do eleven lawyers seem many? Following is a measure on which no fewer than sixteen were consulted. It was first drafted on the request of the Parte Guelfa and other citizens in January 1377, but not proclaimed as an ordinance until February 15, 1382, by the Balìa of that year.[114] The

---

[111] *Ibid.*, p. 208.

[112] *Prov.*, 54, f. 67r; *CP*, 8, f. 3v.

[113] *CP*, 8, f. 3v. The eleven lawyers were Niccola Lapi, Guido Bonciani, Filippo Corsini, Luigi de Torre, Donato Barbadori, Antonio Machiavelli, Giovanni de' Ricci, Donato Ricchi Aldighieri, Francesco [Albergotti] d'Arezzo, Lorenzo di Angelo Paniche, and Giovanni [del Maestro Neri] da Poggibonsi.

[114] *Balìe*, 17, ff. 41r-42v. Partly printed in the *Diario d'Anonimo Fiorentino dal' anno 1358 al 1389*, ed. Alessandro Gherardi (Firenze, 1876), pp. 494-96.

ordinance enumerated the various crimes for which a citizen, on some-one else's petition to the Signory, could be declared a magnate or super-magnate. Any man so attainted lost his right to hold major office and was rendered—above and beyond his original offense—particularly susceptible to prosecution. The crimes enumerated by the ordinance ranged from homicide, assault, petty larceny, and vendetta to adultery, arson, illegal taxation, duress, private incarceration, and demands for ransom. Messer Donato Aldighieri, a lawyer and prominent political figure, drafted the law. He and fifteen other lawyers signed it.[115] They had been requested by the government to give their views on whether or not this law could be observed and applied according to the forms therein set forth. All sixteen attested to its legality and attached their signatures.

In view of the times involved, January 1377 and February 1382, the suspicion arises that there was a roundabout piece of political trickery or nastiness in the ordinance, but one cannot be sure. Certainly the factional alignments of this period were no longer what they had been in the middle 1360s. The Ricci family, for one, had cleared out of the semi-popular movement. Furthermore, the ordinance was endorsed by lawyers of contrasting political views, e.g., Lapo da Castiglionchio and Filippo Corsini (arch-conservatives), Giovanni di Ser Fruosino, Giovanni de' Ricci, and Donato Aldighieri (men of more flexible political views). Confronted with the political unrest of the textile proletariat and *petite bourgeoisie* during the period 1377-1382, the upper class sought to close its ranks, to suppress its own divisions, and to attract wider support by enacting a law against its more lawless members. By so doing it seemed to give proof of its praiseworthy intentions and good faith.

Moving to the second half of our period, I shall draw on two other illustrations of the lawyer's part in the drafting of legislation, and then go on to the uses of lawyers in consultation on the nature and authority of particular magistracies.

[115] Lapo da Castiglionchio, Filippo Corsini, Giovanni de' Ricci, Giovanni del Maestro Neri da Poggibonsi, Niccolò di Antonio [da Rabatta], Giovanni di Ser Fruosino, the prior Ubaldino of S. Stefano "a poncte" (*decretorum doctor*), Ludovico Albergotti, Tommaso Falconi, Benedetto di Jacopo da Empoli, Niccolò da Prato, Baldo da Fighine, Parente [di Corrado da Prato], Cino da Pistoia, and Michi Scolao. On most of these men see the Appendix.

On March 28, 1476, three influential knights reported to the Signory and colleges on the subject of three projected laws.[116] The first law concerned last wills and testaments, the second dicers and gambling, the third a particular type of fraudulent contract. Giovanni Canigiani observed that the draft of the law on last wills called for additional advice from lawyers. The other *rapporteurs* supported this recommendation. Six lawyers were present at the meeting, all of whom were to have brilliant political careers. Their subsequent report on the draft concerning last wills was not preserved, but as the final bill was not put through the Council of One Hundred until October 1476, the consultations must have been drawn out.[117] The gist of the new law was that any man who came into an inheritance either by will or *ab intestato* was responsible for all the unpaid taxes of the deceased, unless he repudiated the possessions within a given period of time. In addition, if the deceased was on the list of remiss taxpayers (the *specchio*), having thereby been barred from public office, and his heir accepted an office without first having given correct notice of the repudiation, he was liable to a fine of 500 large florins.

We turn next to a proposal acted on by the Grand Council shortly before the fall of the Republic. It was February 1528. The city had recently undergone a frightening epidemic and seemed on the verge of a relapse; Florentine society was rent by grave political dissension and discontent (the supporters of a Medicean restoration were themselves divided); there was the threat of war and the danger of possible conspiracies against the Republic. It was obvious to all men at the helm of state that the city's political destiny was soon to be decided. On the 9th of February, according to Varchi, the Gonfalonier of Justice fell to his knees before the Grand Council (1,102 voting members were present), begging God's mercy for Florence.[118] The entire assembly followed suit. Rising, the Gonfalonier proposed that they vote to make "the Lord God governor

[116] Giovanni Canigiani, Angelo della Stufa, Antonio Ridolfi. *CP*, 60, f. 154v, pencil.

[117] *Prov.*, 167, f. 164r. Bernardo Buongirolami, Guidantonio Vespucci, Domenico Bonsi, Agnolo Niccolini, Antonio Malegonnelli, and Puccio Pucci were the six lawyers.

[118] Benedetto Varchi, *Storia fiorentina*, in *Opere*, I, 94.

and king of the city," that they call the Immaculate Virgin "queen" and have "their most holy names perpetually inscribed in gold letters on the doors of the public palace."[119] Like Varchi, Jacopo Nardi would have us believe that the proposal was immediately approved by the Council, with only a few dissenting votes.[120] Such perhaps was the way observers remembered the things of that day. The truth is, however, that once the proposal was made, it had to be drawn up with regard for the correct legislative forms. There must also have been some concern about its constitutionality. For it was then the government consulted several lawyers.[121] They found the projected measure constitutional. Only then did the government proceed to call (or recall) for a definitive vote in the Grand Council. The record says nothing about the nature of the consultation with the lawyers, but it seems most likely that they were asked to consider the constitutionality of appointing a spiritual, titular king. In Roman public law a "sacred" place might certainly be inscribed with a sacred name; and certainly there could be no question of the city's occupying a subject status vis-à-vis the Empire, for the Empire had advanced no serious or even theoretical claims of lordship over the city in more than a century.[122]

I have tried to give an idea of the range of legislative questions on which lawyers were consulted. Most of the illustrations given have been drawn from the famous *Consulte e Pratiche*. Despite the fame for detail of these records, we should remember that they are sometimes summary, formula-ridden, and discontinuous. For the fifteenth century there are some significant gaps involving not only most of the Laurentian period, but also, for instance, the years 1418-1420, 1438-1446, and 1451-1452. Yet when we go through the *Consulte e Pratiche* with care, we often find lawyers holding forth in a professional capacity on particular bills or larger questions.[123] Of distinctive importance was their participation in debate on the nature and authority of individual magistracies.

[119] *LF*, 72, f. 234v.
[120] Nardi, *Istorie della città di Firenze*, 2 vols. (Firenze, 1838-41), II, 148-49.
[121] *LF*, 72, f. 234v.
[122] On the general issue see F. Ercole, *Dal comune al principato* (Firenze, 1929), esp. pp. 119-354; also G. de Vergottini, *Il diritto pubblico italiano nei secoli xii-xv*, 2 vols. (3rd ed., Milano, 1959), II, 2-3.
[123] They are constantly found as consultants in a non-professional capacity.

Late in November 1436 the government was in urgent need of money. Whether or not to raise it by ordinary methods was a question because there was also a driving need to redistribute the tax levies. On November 28th the government held consultations on the subject. The first five counsellors to speak were lawyers. They introduced the themes that were to prevail in the succeeding recommendations.[124] All the speakers who came after fell in with one or another of their proposals. Each of the five lawyers pressed the Signory and colleges to take energetic action in concert with a few of the other leading magistracies. A constitutional question arose, however, to worry the consultants. How free a hand would the Signory and colleges have to set up the machinery for redistributing tax levies? Time was of the essence.

Lorenzo Ridolfi, the first of the five lawyers to speak, urged on the Signory and the assembled group of advisors complete agreement and unity. He said that if they took a well-appointed bill into the legislative councils, and showed determination as well as unity, they would get their way. Marcello Strozzi, trained in civil law at Bologna, echoed Ridolfi. The representations of the third lawyer, Giuliano Davanzati, were more detailed. He pointed out that the *ventina* method of distributing the tax levies would take too long and that the government could not wait.[125] Hence a more expedient way was the newly suggested method which called for a ten-man commission. The ten, he submitted, should be chosen not by the legislative councils but by the Signory and colleges and other officials from the key offices, "for such was always the custom." Knowing very well that the government had to consult the legislature on any new tax, Davanzati recommended that the Signory, colleges, and other leading officials select three men for each of the commission's ten places and that the Council of the People then elect ten out of the thirty. The proposal was a clever one, as it could then rightly be held that the legislature had been consulted. A fourth lawyer, Albizzo Albergotti, noted that since the newly proposed tax method had not yet been thoroughly examined, it would be harmful to give public notice of it. He

---

[124] *CP*, 51, ff. 69v-70r. Note that urgent public necessity, although not finally adduced, often provided an overriding argument and was central to the "reason of state" concept. See Chs. IV, VII (2), and X.

[125] *Ventina*: a tax administered by a twenty-man commission.

pressed the government to return to the legislature and try again to win support for the commission of ten. We learn from another source that such a scheme had already been twice rejected, on November 24th and 27th, by the Council of the People.[126] The rejected bill prescribed the method of electing the ten tax distributors and this, it seems, is what had drawn the negative vote.

The most interesting of the representations made by the five lawyers, or at any rate the one best summarized by the recording notary, was that of Guglielmo Tanagli. Acknowledging the ticklish nature of the subject, especially because it concerned so many people, he prompted the Signory and colleges to return in unity to the Council of the People and do their best to win approval for the new method. Then came a revealing suggestion. He observed that the Signory and colleges could gird themselves with the additional political weight ("auctoritatem") of the Council of Two Hundred by taking thirty-two select citizens from this body and putting them to a vote in the Council of the People for the ten places in the commission.[127]

These consultations were recorded in too condensed a fashion in the *Consulte e Pratiche*. One would like to know in greater detail exactly what the lawyers said. Some of the outlines are missing. Yet the major issue seems clear. Although the *ventina* was one of the traditional taxes, electing the twenty commissioners to administer it took up too much time and their mode of procedure entailed too many complications for the needs at hand. By comparison, the *decina* (administered by a commission of ten) called for a swifter, more executive approach, save that in this case the government must persuade the legislature to yield on one of its prerogatives—that of having a more conclusive voice in electing the tax commissioners. As well as a matter of tactics, there was a constitutional question here. This is why five lawyers in succession were consulted first. Davanzati believed that the government would have less trouble getting its way if, in electing the commission of ten, it gave the Council of the People a limited choice. The most notable piece of advice was that the government take thirty-two men from the Council of Two

---

[126] *LF*, 57, ff. 107r-108r. Again rejected on 4 Dec.
[127] *CP*, 51, f. 70r.

Hundred and present them to the Council of the People as candidates for the ten places. Established in 1411, the Two Hundred sat for terms of six months and could be elected only from among men eligible to serve in the highest offices—the Gonfaloniership of Justice, the Signory, and the colleges.[128] Hence they made up a kind of senatorial body. Their particular legislative competence extended to declarations of war, the ratifying of treaties, the recruitment of troops above a certain number, the giving or lending of communal monies to foreign persons or states, and other related matters. No bill concerning affairs of this sort could be tabled in the regular legislative councils until it was first cleared by the Two Hundred. In time of war or foreign danger, when the state was unexpectedly faced with urgent fiscal needs, the stature and authority of the Two Hundred stood high.[129] We can thus see the shrewdness of Tanagli's proposal to have the Signory and colleges enhance their authority by selecting the thirty-two candidates (eight per quarter) for the commission of ten from the Council of Two Hundred. All the lawyers, in slightly varying ways, supported the executive's determination to step up its fiscal prerogatives in face of an urgent need. But legislation sanctioning a new tax distribution was not to be achieved for nearly another two months, and even then the government had to be content with the old *ventina* method.[130]

By "the government" here I mean the Signory and its assembly of advisors, i.e., the colleges, other leading officials, and the solid partisans of the regime who were regularly called in as counsellors. Although they were not necessarily in unity, they managed to stir up a good deal of uneasiness and resistance in the legislative councils. For it was only little more than two years since the return from exile of the Medici, and a determined faction at the head of state was set on having things its way. The Gonfalonier of Justice and priors of the Signory were drawn from

[128] The provision establishing this body and defining its competence was published by F. Pellegrini, *Sulla repubblica fiorentina a tempo di Cosimo il Vecchio* (Pisa, 1889), pp. ix-xii.

[129] From October 1436 to the following winter, the Duke of Milan's *condottiere*, Piccinino, was in Tuscany with an army, and Florence, having hired Francesco Sforza, was on the verge of open war with the Duke. Ammirato, *Istorie*, v, 234-35. Urgent public necessity, a manifestation of *Staatsräson*, enhanced ordinary prerogatives. See references *supra*, n. 124.

[130] *LF*, 57, by date (19-24 Jan. 1436, Florentine).

pouches controlled by the *accoppiatori*. This caused the legislative councils to fear what such a government might do with a new tax distribution which was not kept under a severe check. Probably, therefore, the five lawyers were summoned to give counsel not only because of their views on the prerogatives of the Signory and colleges, but also to help overcome the doubts of those advisors who worried about how far the executive could legally go in setting up the machinery for a new tax.

Holding on to the context of this discussion, let us turn to a more focused illustration of lawyers working to fix the constitutional boundaries of partitioned authority.

Apart from *balìe* (plenipotentiary councils), the *accoppiatori* provided the Medicean oligarchy with one of its chief instruments of political control. Created in October 1434, just after Cosimo de' Medici's repatriation, the *accoppiatori* were at first reconfirmed every few months and then yearly—in 1436 and 1437—by the Signory.[131] In May 1438 the question was again raised of renewing the commission's mandate, and this time the Signory had recourse to the counsel of three lawyers (all well-known partisans of the regime): Giovanni Buongirolami, Guglielmo Tanagli, and Domenico Martelli. Reporting on June 2nd, they called the Signory's attention to the "major council" recently created for three years, a council with the character of a *balìa* because it combined certain executive and legislative powers in an unusual fashion. The lawyers observed that having looked into the law which established it, their opinion was that this body had the legal power to prolong the mandate of the *accoppiatori* "until the end of December 1439," notwithstanding the acts of the Balìa of 1434.[132] The specific job of the *accoppiatori* was to limit

---

[131] Actually by the Signory and colleges: *DSCSA*, 25, f. 152r; 26, f. 10v; also N. Rubinstein, *The Government of Florence*, ch. 1.

[132] *Tratte*, 60, f. 224r, "Quod hi quibus est concessa auctoritas per dictam novam legem et reformationem . . . possunt copulatoribus scruptinii anni 1434 prorogare tempus at concedere auctoritatem eisdem inbursandi in bursis de quibus fieri debet extractio de dominis et vexillifero et reducendi ad minorem numerum imbursandos in quolibet marsupio, dummodo imbursent habiles secundum disposita in dicta balìa del 34; et hoc usque ad et per totum mensem decembris 1439, non obstantibus dispositis et nobis ostensis in dicta balìa del 34." The lawyers went on to say that the law creating the *Balìa* or "major council" for three years also authorized it to set up the machinery for a scrutiny to be administered early in 1440 (Florentine: Jan.-Feb. 1439).

the number of names deposited in the pouches from which the Signory was drawn. In fact, they decided on the names to be deposited by selecting them from the list of all names already approved (i.e., the men found eligible for major office by the scrutiny of 1434).

Taking the opinion of the three lawyers, the Signory referred it to the new "major council," which on June 11, 1438, ruled that the *accoppiatori* were to remain in office and keep the pouches for the Signory *a mano* until the end of December 1439.[133]

Somewhat more than a year and a half later, the "major council," whose mandate ran out in May 1441, was itself to raise a critical question in the field of constitutional law. Could this body legally override two ordinances of 1434 which explicitly provided that the scrutiny of 1439 was not to take precedence over the scrutiny of 1434? On this occasion the government engaged eight lawyers and again all were staunch supporters of the Medici regime.[134] Making their report on February 2, 1440 (1439 *stile fiorentino*), the eight started out by observing that owing to decrees of both the general *parlamento* and the Balìa of 1434, their initial view was that it was not legally possible to give precedence to the scrutiny of 1439. They then reversed their ground and declared the very opposite "de iure esse veriorem." A *force majeure*—the public good— was their basis in law. They argued that if the scrutiny of 1434 was allowed to prevail over the new one, the probable breakout of civil disturbances might pose a threat to the security of the state. This danger sanctioned extraordinary measures, namely, the right of the "major council" to suspend the prohibitory ordinances of 1434. To put an additional legal buttress under this opinion, the lawyers noted that since the "major council" was acting in place of the regular legislative bodies, it was invested for the time being with all their powers over material concerning scrutinies. There followed the signatures of Buongirolami, Tanagli, Martelli, Niccolini, and Salvetti.

Although endorsing the foregoing *consilium*, the canonist Francesco di Ser Benedetto di Marco—a university professor and new man on the

---

[133] Rubinstein, *loc.cit.*

[134] Giovanni Buongirolami, Guglielmo Tanagli, Domenico Martelli, Otto Niccolini, Tommaso Salvetti, Francesco di Ser Benedetto di Marco, Donato de' Cocchi-Donati, Carlo Federighi. *Tratte*, 60, f. 227r-v, contains their report.

make—saw fit to append some additional observations.[135] First he noted that the disputed ordinances of 1434 prevented the scrutiny of 1439 from taking precedence over the earlier one. This, he said, was a strict interpretation. Then, affecting to observe an equal rigor, he called attention to the fact that the said ordinances did not say that the scrutiny of 1434 could not be nullified. Accordingly, only those laws ought to be considered which concerned the abrogation of scrutinies. As to this—he pointed out triumphantly—all such competence, including the power to nullify and revoke, has been made over to the "major council" by the regular legislative bodies. Hence by simply abolishing the scrutiny of 1434, the "major council" automatically accorded full legal status to the scrutiny of 1439. There followed the signatures of Cocchi-Donati and Federighi.

The report of the eight lawyers was put to a vote in the Signory and colleges, where it was approved. The "major council" was now free to turn the scrutiny of 1439 into law.

So ticklish and technical was the question, that the government had seen fit to withdraw it from the ordinary advisory chambers. Charged with the commission, the lawyers went off on their own. They deliberated, made up their minds, and then returned to the Signory with their verdict. But no matter how technical the question, how much a matter for constitutional law, one cannot fail to see that the eight lawyers had also been used in the political struggle. For some reason, the regime no longer liked the list of men found eligible for public office in the autumn of 1434. Either the scrutiny had been too exclusive, thus causing too much discontent, or—what is more likely—voting had been too easy on candidates, the criteria too broad, and too many had been made eligible for office.[136] Whatever the trouble, the *reggimento* found a temporary remedy in the scrutiny of January 1439 (1440 modern).

To sharpen our understanding of the performance of lawyers in the

[135] *Ibid.*, f. 227v. On argument from public welfare, adduced by Francesco's compeers, and its relation to the concept of the state, see esp. Ch. X.

[136] The *consilium* of the lawyers suggests that many citizens who came of age after 1434 were excluded from office, not having been cleared by the scrutiny of that year. This is not entirely convincing. The machinery existed for processing new names and putting the stamp of eligibility for office on them.

field of constitutional law, above all with reference to the authority and scope of particular magistracies, let us return to the *Consulte e Pratiche*, to two critical questions aired in the executive councils at the end of the fifteenth century.

During the agitated years that followed Piero de' Medici's flight from Florence (November 1494), lawyers constituted a distinct order or group in the government's counselling chambers. Getting up to advise the government, men spoke as representatives of the Monte Officials, the Parte Guelfa, the Eight on Public Safety, the Sei di Mercanzia, the Ten on War, or one of the tiers of benches occupied by the Council of Eighty. One of the orders represented in this fashion was made up of lawyers, a group sometimes enlarged by including in it the knights in the Council of Eighty. Without the knights, this order usually numbered from three to six lawyers, on occasion more.

In most cases—the question of rhetorical and grammatical form aside—the speeches of lawyers in the *Consulte e Pratiche* of the 1490s and later are indistinguishable from those of laymen. When discussion concerned the recovery of Pisa, the peril from Venice, relations with France, or the wretched state of public finances, lawyers said the same things (often despairing) as other citizens. Now and then, however, topics came up which brought out the lawyer's stamp of mind.

During the late autumn of 1499, the question arose of renewing the mandate of a powerful commission—the old Ten on War, now called the "Ten of Liberty and Peace"! This commission was hated and feared by the citizens who favored the popular current in government. They were afraid that the ultraconservatives of the oligarchy would try to use the Ten as a Trojan horse to gain undisputed control of the state. At the end of 1499 and in the months following, some of the city's most prominent lawyers vigorously supported renewing the powers of the Ten. Speaking on December 7th for the lawyers who sat on his bench (*pancata*), Francesco Pepi urged the government to press for the bill on the Ten until it was approved by the Council of Eighty and the Grand Council. Then, breaking into constitutional theory, he suggested that the bill include a statement aimed at "lifting the suspicion that the

Signory cannot give the said office its authority."[137] The scribe recorded no more, but Pepi's meaning was conveyed. Someone had questioned the Signory's right to make over part of its competence to another office. Replying to this challenge, Pepi and the other lawyers wanted the bill to make it clear that with the consent of the Grand Council the Signory could *de iure* delegate part of its authority. Dominant legal theory fully supported this view. The supreme public authority—in this case the Signory and the Grand Council—was entitled to delegate some kind of *imperium*.

Francesco Pepi became Gonfalonier of Justice on January 1, 1500, and for the next two months was one of the most ardent proponents of the Ten ever to hold the supreme dignity.[138] At the consultations of February 2nd, the speaker for the order of lawyers was the doctor *in utroque iure*, Niccolò Altoviti, an expert on Florentine constitutional law who had served as chancellor on legislation from 1495 to 1499. Again the subject was the office of the Ten. The aristocrats and their adherents fought tenaciously for a bill which would win over the Eighty and the Grand Council. Knowing that there were backsliders in the consulting bodies,[139] Altoviti incited the Signory to keep pressing and fighting for the disputed magistracy. At a certain point he unleashed what seems to have been an unexpected attack based on a theory of law: he flatly asserted that he and the other lawyers reckoned that "the Signory has no authority to try to resolve things in the affairs of war."[140] This was going farther

---

[137] *CP*, 65, f. 167v, "che si seguiti la provisione ordinata insino si vegha il fine, agiugnendo per parte di qualchuno che si potrebbe agiugnere che si levassi il sospecto che la Signoria non potesse dare a decto officio la auctorità sua." The possessive pronoun is ambiguous: *sua* may refer to the authority of the Signory or of "the said office" (the Ten). If the latter, the Signory's delegation is not to be understood as a literal, concrete affair. Constitutionally, the Ten were definitely under the Signory, but their authority derived from more than just the Signory in isolation.

[138] On Pepi see the illuminating observations of Piero Parenti, *Storia fiorentina*, BNF, *Fondo principale*, II, IV, 170, f. 108r.

[139] Men like Piero Parenti, who, sitting in the colleges or Council of Eighty, sometimes gave the impression of favoring the Ten but secretly were strongly opposed. Thus the occasional disparity between what he said in the advisory councils and what he expressed in his private chronicle.

[140] *CP*, 65, f. 211v, pencil, "in nome suo e di quelli che segono nel suo ordine,

than their colleague, Francesco Pepi. What exactly did Altoviti mean?
We must try to give more substance to that which the recording notary
had time to catch only in the most summary way. Turning Altoviti's
assertion over in our minds—"the Signory has no authority to try to
resolve things in the affairs of war"—and taking into account the fact
that he represented the order of lawyers, we gather that he drew on the
principle of negative prescription and said something like the following:
Not only may the Signory delegate some of its powers, custom requires
that it do so. Indeed, in the affairs of war this is such standard procedure
and the Ten are so firmly established as an institution, that in a way
the Signory no longer has any direct competence in this area. The authority of the Ten has a broader constitutional basis than any which
the Signory may provide by means of a mere act of delegation.

The practice of appointing a war commission of Ten went back to the
1380s.[141] Thereafter the Ten became a standing commission in times of
war and great peril. During the months under discussion here, although
advocates of the Ten often appealed to custom and frequently argued that
Florentines could not go wrong in imitating their forebears, no lawyer
had hitherto gone so far, in open council at any rate, as to declare that
the Signory had no right to take decisions in affairs of war. While much
in Florentine public life was based on custom or prescription (the
principle which supported Altoviti's argument), the lawyers' challenge
was not taken up. The opponents of the Ten knew well that whatever
lawyers and the upholders of close oligarchy might say, the decision regarding the Ten rested finally with the Eighty and the Grand Council.
Toward the end of February 1500, the Signory at last persuaded the Eighty
to yield on the matter. They gave their approval to a magistracy of Ten
with full powers. More than 100 men, one after another, were then proposed for the office to the Grand Council, but not one obtained the re-

che iudicano tucti unitamente che la Signoria seguiti in proporre di fare lo officio
de X rispecto alle cose vanno atorno, et che la Signoria non ha auctorità alcuna
di deliberare delle cose della guerra."

[141] A proper study of the Ten has yet to be undertaken. A good start was made
by G. Pampaloni, "Gli organi della repubblica fiorentina per le relazioni con
l'estero," *Rivista di studi politici internazionali*, xx, ii (1953), 261-96.

quired number of votes.[142] The office was not set up for another seven months. We will discuss the political aspects of this long debate on the appointment of the Ten in the next section.

We are in a period here which had recently seen a famous debate concluded in blood and fire. The protagonist was Savonarola; the issues were all that he represented, some critical papal prerogatives, and perhaps to a degree (though in a roundabout way) the social composition of the Florentine state. Before the debate was concluded, the Signory's authority had been brought into question.

Late in March 1498 a Franciscan proposed an ordeal by fire to prove or invalidate Savonarola's claims about himself and his prophetic worth. The proposal was seized on by Savonarola's bitterest enemies, the *Arrabbiati*, who swiftly gained the support of the Signory and populace. Domenico da Pescia, a Dominican and devoted follower of Savonarola, agreed to enter the fire for his master. His rival in the ordeal was to be the Minorite, Giuliano Rondinelli. For some reason, it was taken for granted from the very beginning that the obvious place for the trial was the government square—the Piazza de' Signori. This assumption was fostered by the fact that the Signory supported and helped organize the spectacle. Very soon, however, a voice shrewdly questioned the Signory's authority to sponsor such a trial and even to offer up the government square for it. After all, were not the protagonists in holy orders?

The question of the Signory's authority to grant or deny a trial by fire was debated as part of a more general question: was it desirable or right to go through with the ordeal at all? On March 30th the government assembled a body of fifty advisors to discuss this question, one-seventh of whom were lawyers: Guidantonio Vespucci, Agnolo Niccolini, Antonio Malegonnelli, Antonio Strozzi, Francesco Gualterotti, Luca Corsini, and Ormannozzo Deti.[143] The list has its interest. Of all lawyers in the city, these were the most influential in political society, the ones most in the

---

[142] Parenti, *Storia*, BNF, II, IV, 170, f. IIIv.

[143] *CP*, 64, ff. 47r-52v, pencil. In margin: "Consigli nella audientia sopra lo offerta facta da frati predicatori et minori d'entrare nel fuoco." This *consultatio* was published by C. Lupi, "Nuovi documenti intorno a fra Girolamo Savonarola," *ASI*, III, iii (1866), 55ff.

public eye. Giovan Vettorio Soderini, brother of the lifetime Gonfalonier to be, had made his mark in the legal profession but not yet in politics. Altoviti was in charge of legislation and did not normally participate in the *Consulte e Pratiche*. Domenico Bonsi, an ex-follower of Savonarola, was the only other lawyer of the first political rank not to take part in the consultations of March 30th, and he was in Rome on an embassy.

Villari, Schnitzer, and Ridolfi all give some attention to the events of March 30th; but seeing things from a politico-moral viewpoint, none observed—understandably—that the most exact question treated that day concerned the Signory's legal right to sponsor or sanction the ordeal. This finer, constitutional question was lost in the grander political and moral one. Even the lawyers, as we shall see, surrendered to the attractions of politics and public safety. Malegonnelli, Strozzi, and Gualterotti, like most other counsellors, slipped around the legal question by regarding it purely in political terms. They favored a trial by fire, expecting that it would put an end to the politico-religious divisions in the city, although Malegonnelli probably hoped for a miracle which would vindicate Savonarola. Vespucci affected disgust at the prospect of such an ordeal (quoting the motto "gens prava et adultera signum querit"), but indicated that the question of its taking place was a matter for the friars to decide, not the Signory. A confirmed and powerful enemy of the Savonarolans, Vespucci longed to have the prophet himself enter the flames.[144] Ormannozzo Deti submitted that the present Signory would be accused of wishing to perpetuate discord in the city if the ordeal was forbidden. Observing that most Florentines wanted the trial by fire, he said that the friars themselves must have thought about questions of conscience. They were the ones who should worry about this, not the government. Luca Corsini took up a more interesting line. Would an ordeal by fire be legal? The protagonists think so, Corsini affirmed, and anyway the question does not depend on the Signory's views. "But I believe the ordeal can be held because it was done at the time of the

---

[144] *CP*, 64, f. 48r. For politico-*moral* treatments of the consultation of March 30th see R. Ridolfi, *Vita di Girolamo Savonarola*, 2 vols. (Roma, 1952, 2nd ed.), I, 356-57; and P. Villari, *La storia di Girolamo Savonarola*, 2 vols. (new ed., Firenze, 1930), II, 142-44. Much more judicious and detached is J. Schnitzer, *Savonarola: Ein Kulturbild aus der Zeit der Renaissance*, 2 vols. (Munich, 1924), I, 511.

heretics, at the time of the simoniacs, and of St. John Gualbert. So I believe it would be legal."[145] Corsini, Deti, and Vespucci thus held that the question was not for the Signory to decide. For them it was out of the government's hands. Given the tumult of popular feeling in the city, this meant in effect that the government should stand by and watch the ordeal take place. Corsini's argument from historical example was meant as a reply to Agnolo Niccolini, the only lawyer to go openly and firmly against a precipitate holding of the ordeal.[146] Niccolini recommended that they look into canon law or historical precedent so as to determine the legality of a trial by fire. He also advised the Signory to consult Pope Alexander VI, who might be persuaded to dispatch some bishops to Florence to act as witnesses. Disregarding popular pressure and the prevailing political mood, this lawyer looked frankly at the legal question involved. For him the Signory's authority in the controversy was limited by the Church and by canon law. The other lawyers overrode these barriers by favoring a rapid staging of the ordeal or alleging that the Signory's competence did not extend to such matters. As to this, the putting of limits by implication around the Signory's authority, perhaps we can say that some of the lawyers here faced the constitutional question. Yet something was wrong. They were playing politics: they knew well that the Signory and colleges had already taken an official position in support of the ordeal. Not only was the Signory offering the use of the Republic's principal square, two days before, on March 28th, "in the government palace of the most civil and refined city in Italy, the points to be put on trial, as in barbarian times," had already been "registered by the hand of a public notary."[147]

Although the ordeal was not finally held, Savonarola was executed two months later, the tide having definitely turned against him.

The lawyers who were willing to help liquidate Pope Alexander's fearless enemy were citizens first, men open to political passion, and legists only secondarily. Niccolini apart, they did not fuss about legal niceties in the face of political necessity. Almost everyone in the city

---

[145] *CP*, 64, f. 49r. Gualbert (*ca.* 990-1073), founder of the Vallumbrosan Order and very active in helping the papacy to combat simony.

[146] *Ibid.*, f. 48r. Said he, "la cosa è ecclesiastica" and "io non consiglerei che il campo s'usassi se prima non si vedessi per ragione canonica o historia (sic)."

[147] Ridolfi, *Savonarola*, I, 354.

seems to have wanted the ordeal and so it had to take place. In the actual situation, for any lawyer to hold that the Signory had no legal right to intervene in the affair was in fact to rush two friars into a trial by fire and to prevent the government or Church from looking into the legality of such proceedings. Strictly speaking, to say that denial or consent in the affair was outside the Signory's purview was to make a statement about the Florentine constitution and the Signory's powers. The three lawyers who so pronounced themselves may thus be said to have discharged their commission. This aspect of the consultation ought to be stressed. But if Niccolini's position was excessively niggling, events and political tension had the immediate effect of turning the verdicts rendered by Corsini, Deti, and Vespucci into pure politics.

There is such a political strain in the foregoing affair, that we may well pass on from here to a full-scale treatment of the varied parts played by lawyers in the political struggle.

## 5. The Political Struggle

Political struggle in Florence grew out of class and faction. During the fourteenth century the struggle between classes was relatively open, at times fierce, and strife between the factions drew much of its intensity from this. But during the fifteenth century, with the oligarchy more firmly planted, the factions were activated less by popular discontent, more by the stresses between family blocs. At the turn of the century in particular, and again from 1527 to 1530, the struggle within the oligarchy between the proponents of "restricted" and those of "wide" (more popular) government was generated by the minor political families in their determination to acquire more control over the state. From a political point of view, this conflict was confined to the ruling class—to that limited number of families and individuals possessed of the political franchise. But from an economic and social standpoint, the differences between the major and minor families were class differences, and so theirs was a struggle with a class basis. No particular significance can be attached to the fact that the minor political families in some cases attracted the support or accepted the leadership of disaffected branches and members of the great families. Political commitments are rarely schematic. Yet

204

whatever the personal, non-historic reasons for the politics of an individual, his political views make historical sense only in the context of the opposed forces or interests that derive from the social arrangements around him.

Faction in Florence meant a concert of families drawn together by consanguinity, marriage, business interests, bonds of friendship, or traditions which issued in similar outlooks. Possessed of the most influence in government, the dominant group of families made its power felt through its hold on the key magistracies. This connection between government and a certain aggregate of families resulted in a political phenomenon known as the *reggimento*. The *reggimento* was the dominant group *in* government—a concert of the most powerful families, constituting the core of the oligarchy or top tier of the ruling class. Up to about 1434 and for a time in the middle 1460s, the leading families were often split into two factions, with moderate opinion somewhere between. Each faction sought to weaken the other by disgracing or destroying its leaders. But after 1434, owing to intimidation, enforced prudence, and perhaps for economic reasons as well, the dominant families of the oligarchy became more closely knit. The foundations of the *reggimento* were thus made more secure. In the later 1490s and again from 1527 to 1530, as I have already indicated, there was a struggle for power between the minor and major families of the oligarchy.[148] The former excelled their betters in number but not in statecraft, name, ruling traditions, wealth, or strategic contacts. The increased antagonisms resulted in part from a new political and social fact of the later Quattrocento: the transformation of the major families into a self-conscious nobility, into a caste which, more than its predecessors, saw political hegemony as its special privilege and birthright. The bonds of blood and marriage, no less than other social ties uniting these families, were more closely drawn. Thus, for example, the families Rucellai, Medici, Tornabuoni, Guicciardini, Ridolfi, and Salviati were all related. All in all, in 1500, theirs was a world harder to enter than that of their grandfathers in 1380 or even 1430.

Whatever the political orientation of the *reggimento*, it always com-

[148] For this and my politico-social classifications, *vide*, e.g., B. Varchi, *Storia fiorentina,* in *Opere,* 1, 57-59.

manded the loyalty of a group of lawyers who stood out in public life. The most prominent were spokesmen for the regime, spokesmen in the way other leaders were. These are the lawyers who dominate the record: in the period around 1400, Filippo Corsini, Lorenzo Ridolfi, and Bartolommeo Popoleschi; in the mid-1430s, Ridolfi again, Giuliano Davanzati, Piero Beccanugi, Carlo Federighi, Biagio Niccolini, and Guglielmo Tanagli; in the 1450s and 1460s, Otto Niccolini, Domenico Martelli, Tommaso Deti, and Bernardo Buongirolami. The later 1490s saw an acute constitutional crisis and a remarkable number of lawyers at the top level of politics: Guidantonio Vespucci, Domenico Bonsi, Antonio Malegonnelli, Francesco Gualterotti, Francesco Pepi, Niccolò Altoviti, Antonio Strozzi, Agnolo Niccolini, and the somewhat less prominent Luca Corsini, Enea della Stufa, and Simone Uguccioni. In 1529-1530, just before the downfall of the Republic and with the ranking jurist (Baldassare Carducci) in France, the outstanding lawyers of the *reggimento* were Piero Filicaia, Marco degli Asini, Francesco Nelli, and Bono Boni. None of these, however, attained the political importance enjoyed by his counterparts of the 1490s.

During the fifteenth century, the number of citizens theoretically eligible to hold office in Florence went from about 2,000 to 3,300, finally rising to 4,000 souls before the plague of 1527.[149] When we remember that the lawyers named above ranked with the more influential Florentine statesmen and politicians, that Florence seldom had more than about twenty-five registered lawyers in any given year, it is clear that they provided the city with a percentage of statesmen out of all proportion to their actual numbers.

What precisely did lawyers do for the dominant group in government? How did they serve the ruling families in the political struggle? Much of their service can neither be weighed nor precisely defined because it depended on the prestige of their profession and the dignity of the doctoral grade. As orators alone or men of state, they would have cut no better figure in the councils, probably, than did other leaders or out-

[149] Parenti, *Storia*, BNF, II, IV, 170, f. 158r, says about 3,000 for period around 1500; the figure of 4,000 in J. Nardi, *Istorie della città di Firenze*, I, 14; see also N. Rubinstein, "I primi anni del consiglio maggiore di Firenze (1494-1499)," *ASI*, CXII (1954), 181.

standing speakers. But as *legum* or *decretorum doctores*, as authorities on the law and as university men in an age when this was a distinction, they commanded a particular esteem, and this enabled them to carry more weight in the councils. Their skills and this weight are what they put at the disposal of the regimes they served. Was the doctoral grade in fact regarded with a special esteem? It has already been shown (Ch. II, 3) that on certain occasions the city officially accorded higher honors to doctors of law. On embassies, knights and doctors were paid higher stipends than were merchants, bankers, or others. On ceremonial occasions, leading public officials aside, doctors took precedence over all others save knights and prelates. While the knightly dignity was mainly honorary and decorative, the *doctoratus* denoted a concrete preparation and competence. On an embassy to Rome in 1481, Guidantonio Vespucci was criticized by the new commission on foreign and military affairs (the Otto di Pratica) for having exceeded his mandate on a particular point. He and the Milanese ambassador to Rome had negotiated a league against the Turk with the French ambassadors. The Eight accused Vespucci of having committed Florence to 3,000 or 4,000 ducats more than they had wished. An acute and gifted speaker, soon to be one of the most influential statesmen of his period, Vespucci defended himself energetically, adding, "if exceeding his mandate were excusable in a man who was not a doctor [of law], in one who is there can be no excuse; indeed, he would deserve condign punishment and such is what I would merit, holding that grade."[150] All the more ardently, therefore, did he seek to explain and justify the arrangements he had made in Rome. Knowing that laymen had a high regard for the doctorate, Vespucci played on this.

The political value of the doctoral grade is brought out still more clearly by the following assessment. Baldassare Carducci, a well-known lawyer and professor, returned to Florence from exile in 1527 and was acknowledged at once as leader of a strong political sect, the anti-Medici intransigents. They constituted the "left wing" of a group which sought to give Florentine government a wider social base. Looking to the reasons for Carducci's leadership, Benedetto Varchi, a highly perceptive contemporary, listed three: his advanced age, his well-known opposition to

[150] *OCR*, 1, f. 159r, in a letter of April 20th from Vespucci to the Otto.

the Medici family, and "the prestige associated with the doctoral grade" ("per la reputazione che si tira adietro il grado del dottorato").[151]

Had the members of the legislative councils rejected a measure already approved by the Signory and favored by the dominant group? *Legum doctores* were called on to help change their minds. Were the colleges reluctant to give their affirmative vote to a proposal recommended by the spokesmen of the dominant group? Again were lawyers requested to do a job of persuasion. The subject might be a money bill or a proposal to tax the Church, to establish or fortify a potent commission, to reorganize the lists of eligibility for office, and so forth.

During the spring of 1420, a group of consultants in the executive councils brought the scrutiny of 1417 under fire.[152] The charge was that this review of eligibility for office was dishonest and illegal because it had been carried out at the time of an epidemic. Two leaders from the dominant circle of families, Matteo Castellani and Rinaldo degli Albizzi, urged the Signory and colleges to get some select citizens and officials to examine the matter with an eye to making recommendations. Next a group of six lawyers stepped into the consultation and each supported the two leaders.[153] The lawyers were Francesco Machiavelli, Piero Beccanugi, Alessandro Bencivenni, Carlo Federighi, Giovanni Bertaldi, and Giuliano Davanzati. It is possible—but ungenerous to suggest it—that Bencivenni and Bertaldi, new men, were bartering their support for the favor of the powerful. One speaker asserted that counsel should be given without fear,[154] thus revealing that discussion was taking place in an atmosphere of intimidation. On May 23rd a group of advisors made recommendations, but the government took no action. In July Davanzati said that there had been enough talk, that the government should now appoint some "select and outstanding citizens of mature age and high seriousness" and that their proposals should be put to the vote in the Council of the Two Hundred.[155] But resistance in the colleges continued. On November 8th twenty advisors again held forth on the sub-

---

[151] *Opere*, I, 59.
[152] *CP*, 44, ff. 10r–11v (21-23 May). First criticized two years before, as noted by Giovanni Carducci, *ibid.*, f. 41v.
[153] *Ibid.*, f. 10v.    [154] *Ibid.*, Paolo di Francesco Biliotti.
[155] *Ibid.*, f. 15v.

ject, four of them lawyers: Davanzati, Bencivenni, Beccanugi, and Filippo Corsini.[156] All referred to their discontent with the disputed scrutiny and again pressed the government to consult with leading officials and select citizens. Thus in a period of little more than five months, the influence of nearly a third of the city's registered lawyers was brought to bear on one side of the issue. Not for another four months (March 1421) was the scrutiny of 1417 to be modified and a new one administered.

It is very difficult to pin down the final aim of the ruling group's agitation against the scrutiny of 1417. The group seems to have been hurt: some of its men seem to have been omitted from the lists approved that year. This is what the debates suggest and what the spokesmen for the group wished the colleges to believe. But another interpretation is possible, and I am inclined to hold with it, namely, that the inner circle of the oligarchy was looking to the future and therefore had first to eliminate enemies and risks by trying to get a rearrangement of the names in the eligibility pouches. But the councils were reluctant to go along on this matter with men like Matteo Castellani, Rinaldo degli Albizzi, and Filippo Corsini. Such is the way the second and third ranks of the oligarchy resisted the strong group at the top.

In the 1450s the regime could count on the support of the city's six or eight leading lawyers. On November 5, 1453, executive sessions included the priors and colleges, as always, in addition to twenty outside advisors (*richiesti*), of whom nearly a third were lawyers: Guglielmo Tanagli, Otto Niccolini, Tommaso Salvetti, Girolamo Machiavelli, Donato de' Cocchi-Donati, and Tommaso Deti. The question treated was that of whether or not to prolong the authority of the controversial *accoppiatori*. Since they were the trusted men of the dominant concert of families, to continue them in office was to strengthen the political hold of the ruling group. Tanagli and Niccolini were two of the four men who reported for the whole body of advisors. They said, "So as to have a good and stable government, to preserve the harmony among citizens, and in view of present conditions and the advantages gained from having kept the pouches by hand, while on the contrary the inconveniences

[156] Ibid., ff. 42v-43r.

and damage which have ensued when these were not kept by hand, we recommend that the authority conferred on the *accoppiatori* in 1452 be prolonged for that time and in that fashion and form as will seem necessary to the Signory. And this should be done as soon as possible"[157]—a clear example of argument from the public good. On the afternoon or evening of the day this report was made, the Balìa renewed the mandate of the *accoppiatori* for five years. The political identity of the city's most prominent lawyers was thus clearly revealed: they sympathized with the Medicean ruling group and its political controls. A well-known lawyer, Domenico Martelli, was not among the advisors. He was perhaps on an embassy, or in office in the dominion, or holding down a municipal post which precluded his being able to serve as an independent *richiesto*. The Martelli were acknowledged partisans of the Medici.[158]

Conferring with representatives of offices and districts, as well as with groups of influential men, was the ordinary way for the Signory and colleges to feel out the opinion of the ruling group. Such consultation went on daily or several times weekly, depending on the issues pending, so that the contact between government and the top tier of the oligarchy was direct and continuous. In addition, the ruling group was always strongly represented in the key offices. But now and then the colleges resisted or obstructed initiatives taken by the Signory, which picked the men called in as *richiesti*. For this reason, it was well for *richiesti* to be men of persuasion, spirit, or charm—at all events of influence. This goes to help explain the pre-eminence of lawyers in the advisory councils of the Republic. Their education and skills conferred the requisite standing on them.

Normally, no measures could be introduced into the legislative assemblies without the previous approval of the colleges. When these put up resistance to the recommendations of *richiesti*, the *richiesti* were not averse to bullying. Encountering a great deal of resistance to a new tax proposed in March 1456, a group of twenty-two advisors curtly stated that the colleges should approve the recommended tax because it served the peace of

---

[157] *CP*, 53, f. 44v.
[158] See L. Martines, "La famiglia Martelli e un documento sulla vigilia del ritorno dall' esilio di Cosimo de' Medici (1434)," *ASI*, cxvii, 1 (1959), 29-43. Girolamo Machiavelli ended badly, p. 67.

the city "and because they [the colleges] should believe in the leading citizens of the *reggimento*."[159]

Once a bill reached the legislative councils, it might be necessary to use persuasion again. Here too a group of lawyers might be called into play. Of many examples to draw on, the following may suffice.

In the spring of 1445, the ruling group decided to reform the administration of the Monte, the Republic's funded debt. The new plan called for a Monte commission of twenty men. Together with the Signory, this commission was to elect five other officials to examine payments made by the state during a given period. The measure was moved in the councils and defeated seven times between April 13th and May 19th.[160] Three lawyers supported the bill on May 19th: Giuliano Davanzati (for the Eight on Public Safety), Tommaso Salvetti (for the S. Croce quarter), and Domenico Martelli (for S. Giovanni). On May 29th four lawyers addressed the legislators, urging them to approve a bill on the five treasury accountants.[161] Nearly two years later, on January 13, 1447, we find most of the same lawyers backing the government on a money bill which had already been rejected several times. Of the twenty-one defenders of the measure, four were lawyers: Federighi, Martelli, Beccanugi, and Otto Niccolini.[162] There does not seem to have been much drama in all this, even if political maneuvering with regard to taxes and changes in public finance was often accompanied by pleas about the need to safeguard the liberty of Florence. Drama in history is what chiefly appeals, but much that is historically dramatic has a plain underpinning.

Few issues that created civil discord in Florence between 1380 and 1530 saw the intervention of so many lawyers for so long a time and in such a sustained fashion as the one debated in 1500, concerning whether or not to renew the powers of the Ten on War—Decem Baliae.[163] The issue had both a technical and a political side. From January to Septem-

[159] *CP*, 53, f. 232v (7 March). The colleges considered the tax inequitable. Girolamo Machiavelli was the only lawyer among the twenty-two advisors.

[160] *LF*, 60, ff. 20v-26v.

[161] *Ibid.*, f. 27r, Martelli, Salvetti, Carlo Federighi, and Piero Beccanugi.

[162] *Ibid.*, f. 62v.

[163] See also pp. 198-201. Actually the issue was first raised on 7 Dec. 1499. *CP*, 65, ff. 167v *et seq.*; *CP*, 66, f. 7r *et passim*.

ber 1500 the different Signories and Gonfaloniers of Justice insisted again and again that they were so overburdened with work that the government could not carry on without the Ten. Not until military concerns and a sector of foreign affairs were under the direction of another office, they argued, would the Signory be able to conduct all of its other affairs properly. This was the issue's technical-administrative side. It was the political side that was controversial. As I have already pointed out in another connection, the lesser families of the ruling class and individuals with little or no family backing feared that the major families, or a certain bloc thereof, would try to use the Ten to impose a highly select, close oligarchy on the city.[164] For a powerful Ten, as in the past, would dispose of large sums of money, control the army, in addition to having enormous influence on foreign policy. These resources could be used in the city proper, not only to browbeat and intimidate, but also, in a delicate situation, to stage a successful *coup d'état* in connivance with the Signory.

Interestingly, Signories of the period sometimes started out by opposing the reinstitution of the Ten, but always ended in favor of them. As Parenti observed when analyzing the political situation in the spring of 1500, "every Signory entered the palace [took office] favoring the *popolo* [the bulk of the political class] but soon turned in favor of the magnates, so that the *popolo* did not trust the Signory nor did Signories enjoy credit with the *popolo*."[165] These changes of heart strongly suggest that each succeeding Signory found itself faced with a real administrative problem—that of being overburdened with work. But Parenti and his peers, along with all the more "democratic" political families, looked past the technical-administrative side of the issue, apprehending only the political dimension. Perhaps in the long run they were hurting themselves; this was another matter. In the actual political situation of the year 1500, they feared that the magnates aimed to snatch political power away from the broad sector of the political class. Again and again the Grand Council proved itself ready to have the Signory delegate some of its powers to a

---

[164] For contemporary reports of this see Parenti, *Storia*, BNF, II, IV, 170, ff. 107v, 108r-v; Guicciardini, *Storie fiorentine*, ed. R. Palmarocchi (Bari, 1931), pp. 177-78.
[165] Parenti, *ibid.*, 170, f. 113v.

temporary commission or to a few appointees, but not to a Ten like the one of old. The spokesmen of the great families, however, would have none of this.[166] They wanted a "real" Ten or, as they said, an office with reputation and authority.

In view of socio-political alignments, to favor the Ten was to favor the aristocrats against that sector of the middle classes (the *popolo*) which enjoyed the political franchise. Practical, custom-bound, respectful of detail, Florentine lawyers may have perceived that there was a genuine administrative need for the Ten, and those most in the public eye ardently favored the Ten in council. Could the politics of this be concealed behind a pure demand for more efficient administration? If, from the beginning of the controversy, it already appeared that to advocate the restoration of the Ten was to line up with the top tier of the oligarchy, this impression was reinforced by the fact that the aristocrats spurned proposals for temporary delegations of power that would have eased the work of the Signory.[167] It has been noted that the lawyer Francesco Pepi was one of the Ten's most tenacious exponents. He opened the campaign in earnest at the beginning of January 1500, just after he became Gonfalonier of Justice.[168] In the weeks and months thereafter, seven lawyers urged the restoration of the Ten or the establishment of another, equally powerful magistracy. They usually represented the doctors of law present in the counselling bodies. Simone Uguccioni and Guidantonio Vespucci spoke for the *doctori* in January; Niccolò Altoviti, Domenico Bonsi, and Vespucci again in February; Enea della Stufa in May; and Bonsi, Vespucci, Pepi, and Antonio Strozzi in July.[169] During these months Francesco Gualterotti and Antonio Malegonnelli, two other lawyers of exalted rank, were away on embassies. But they would also have endorsed the campaign for the disputed magistracy, being part of the select group

---

[166] E.g., men like Bernardo Rucellai, Giovan Battista Ridolfi, Antonio Canigiani, Benedetto de' Nerli, Alamanno Salviati, and Piero Guicciardini.

[167] Parenti, *Storia*, 170, ff. 107v-108v; also e.g., Guidantonio Vespucci's representations on 27 May 1500: "Item, si deputi uno magistrato che habbi auctorità di potere pensare et exeguire et fare tucto con reputatione, et monstrò con più ragioni che e deputati non potevano servire et che li antiqui si sono governati sempre con X et in quello modo hanno acresciuto lo imperio, etc." *CP*, 66, f. 12r.

[168] *CP*, 65, f. 188r-v (6 Jan.).

[169] *Ibid.*, ff. 189r, 208r-v, 211v, 214r, 220r-v; *CP*, 66, ff. 7r, 12r, 31v, 47v, 53r-54r, 55r, 63v, 69r.

of influential politicians which included aristocrats like Bernardo Rucellaı, Giovan Battista Ridolfi, and Antonio Canigiani. In 1500, accordingly, the *popolo* must have regarded the entire circle of leading lawyers with deep suspicion. The most distinguished of these, Guidantonio Vespucci, was hated by most of the ordinary citizenry ("homo in odio grandissimo dello universale").[170] The summer of 1500 saw the outbreak of civil war in a subject town, Pistoia, but it was September before the government was able to realize its desire for the controversial office, and then it got only a tame commission shorn of its ancient powers.

The years 1499-1500 seem to have posed a real threat to that part of the city's middle class possessed of political rights. No doubt the leaders of the popular current believed that arrayed against them were some of the keenest and most experienced statesmen in Florence, including all the top-flight lawyers. This fear really went back to the middle 1490s. In February 1495, Piero Parenti, a merchant of middling rank, and some other citizens accused the lawyer in charge of legislation (Niccolò Altoviti) of having tricked the Grand Council. Charging him with having misrepresented the nature of a quorum—the quorum needed for the election of men to key office—they believed that Altoviti had been put up to the trick by some of the extreme oligarchs.[171] Predictably, the election which provoked this incident concerned the old Ten or Decem Baliae, known temporarily as the "Ten of Liberty and Peace."

The controversy over the Ten saw nearly all the best-known lawyers taking a uniform public stand. Was this usual? It depended very much on the context of strains and stresses, above all on whether or not the major families were themselves united. When they were, all prominent lawyers tended to fall in with them and take identical positions on the leading public issues. Otherwise, they were often found on different sides of a given question. There was thus a certain predictableness in the political behavior of the city's most eminent lawyers: unity prevailed

---

[170] Parenti, *Storia*, BNF, ii, iv, 170, f. 117v; cf. Bartolommeo Cerretani, *Istoria fiorentina*, BNF, ii, iii, 74, f. 253r.

[171] According to N. Rubinstein, "I primi anni," pp. 170-72, the trouble grew out of a mistake made in the protocols of a provision, and Altoviti had consulted these minutes rather than the provision proper. But it was surely unbusiness-like and odd for a man of Altoviti's experience to consult a draft instead of the law itself. Besides, what if the mistake in the protocols was deliberate?

among them when the foremost families were in accord, disunity when not. This is explained by the fact that lawyers who stood out in politics were themselves *of* the dominant bloc or of families *for* it. Here, indeed, was one of the main reasons for their eminence. The great families worked for their own men. Their lawyers more easily and more often got the best offices, the most influential posts. The immediate reward of these lawyers was public luster; this in turn won clients, commissions, reputation. With their great powers of patronage, the principal political families had their pick of legal talent. Ability and ambition followed power.

For a long time the Savonarolan movement had about as many partisans as opponents among Florentine lawyers. Like other major controversies of the fifteenth century—e.g., those occasioned by the *catasto*, the war with Lucca, the reform movement of 1466—this one also started out by causing sharp divisions in the political class. These divisions, above all when entertained in the foremost ranks of political society, were faithfully reflected by differences of opinion among lawyers. But there came a point in all such disputes when the opinion of those who were important began to turn decisively in a given direction. Then opposition, as if by a natural process, was rapidly silenced or converted to the winning side. In this too the behavior of prominent lawyers was typical. At first followers of Savonarola, Domenico Bonsi and Francesco Gualterotti drew away from the friar in the last months of his life and ended by joining his enemies. Lawyers like Bartolommeo Ciai and Baldo Inghirami, new men who had found a channel for their energies in the movement inspired by Savonarola, remained loyal to him but took refuge in silence and were subsequently put under temporary political bans.

### SOURCES FOR CHAPTER FIVE

The chapter as a whole draws extensively on the unpublished statutes of 1355 (in ASF), the published *Statuta* of 1415, and ASF, *Statuti del Comune di Firenze*, 29, with addenda to the year 1494. I have also relied heavily on *Provvisioni*, which should be used in close conjunction with the *Carte di Corredo*, a much neglected but important source. Registers filed under the *Carte di Corredo* were used by the notaries of the chancellery to help them track down runs of legislative acts (*provvisioni*) on particular matters. These *Carte* are arranged in different ways: by subject matter, alphabetically, or chronologically. They are primarily from the fifteenth and early sixteenth centuries.

When it exists at all, secondary material on the Florentine judiciary is thin and spotty. There being nothing comprehensive on the subject, one must begin with statutes and *provvisioni*. The Podestà has attracted some interest, as in the standard but very old work by L. Cantini, *Dell' ufizio del potestà di Firenze*, vol. II of his *Saggi istorici d'antichità toscane* (Firenze, 1796); also A. Gherardi, "Il potestà e il capitano del popolo," *Miscellanea fiorentina di erudizione e storia*, ed. I. del Badia, 2 vols. (Firenze, 1902), I, 43-44. The few works on penal proceedings and penal law deal exclusively with the fourteenth century: G. O. Corazzini, "Cenni sulla procedura penale in Firenze nel sec. xiv," *Miscellanea*, ed. I. del Badia, I, 17-23; J. Köhler and G. degli Azzi, *Das Florentiner Strafrecht des XIV. Jahrhunderts* (Mannheim-Leipzig, 1909); U. Dorini, *Il diritto penale e la delinquenza in Firenze nel sec. xiv* (Lucca, 1923). There is nothing on the Executor in the later fourteenth century and after, nothing on the Appellate Judge, and only Corazzini's above-listed note on the Captain of the People. On the chief commercial tribunal (the Mercanzia) there is the sketch by G. Bonolis, *La giurisdizione della mercanzia in Firenze nel secolo xiv* (Firenze, 1901); and the more specialized A. del Vecchio and E. Casanova, *Le rappresaglie nei comuni medievali e specialmente in Firenze* (Bologna, 1894). The Mercanzia was also treated by A. Doren, *Le arti fiorentine*, tr. G. B. Klein, 2 vols. (Firenze, 1940), esp. vol. II, which is the standard work—and an excellent one—on the judicial power of the guilds. One of the outstanding lacunae is the absence of scholarly work on the executive commissions which disposed of the powers of extraordinary justice. So far the jurisdiction of only one such commission has been studied: G. Antonelli, "La magistratura degli Otto di Guardia a Firenze," *ASI*, 1 (1954). The Conservatores Legum, Decem Baliae, Otto di Pratica, the Rebel Officials, and several other magistracies all deserve intensive study. Even, e.g., the Mint (Zecca) Officials disposed of the power of life and death over counterfeiters (see ASF, *Prov.*, 187, f. 665r-v, law of 22 Sept. 1496).

There is no historical literature on problems of jurisdiction in Renaissance Florence. Thus my total dependence on source material, chief of which the following: *Consulte e Pratiche*, 19-73; *Deliberazioni dei Signori e Collegi fatte in forza della loro ordinaria autorità*, 22-134. These two sources, but particularly the first, often lead the historian to the records of the different courts: i.e., the *Atti del Podestà, Atti del Capitano del Popolo, Atti del Esecutore degli Ordinamenti di Giustizia*, and (rarely) the *Giudice degli Appelli*. The papers of these magistrates contain the proceedings and all the details of particular cases. A different but no less valuable source for the study of jurisdictional conflicts is the legal or judicial *consilium*, collections of which are listed in the sources for Ch. X.

Secondary literature on Florentine administration is headed by the great work of D. Marzi, *La cancelleria della repubblica fiorentina* (Rocca S. Casciano, 1910). Also praiseworthy, though devoted mainly to communal finance, is G. Canestrini, *La scienza e l'arte di stato desunta dagli atti ufficiali della repubblica fiorentina e dei Medici* (Firenze, 1862). A general work on Florentine administration is lacking—just the sort of book that would have been most useful to this study. My chief sources therefore, as the notes reveal, have been *Consulte e Pratiche, Deliberazioni, Provvisioni*, and (though less so) the papers of offices like the Octo Custodiae and Catasto Officials.

On the structure of government in Florence: for the second half of the fourteenth century there are the crisp, descriptive pages in G. Brucker, *Florentine Politics and Society, 1343-1378* (Princeton, 1962), esp. ch. II; also A. Rado, *Maso degli Albizzi e il partito oligarchico in Firenze dal 1382 al 1393* (Firenze, 1927), the first to stress the role of so-called political moderates. My own *The Social World of the Florentine Humanists* (Princeton, 1963), ch. IV, has material on public office in the first half of the fifteenth century. On the later Quattrocento see the brilliant attempt at a synthesis by A. Anzilotti, *La crisi costituzionale della repubblica fiorentina* (Firenze, 1912); also V. Ricchioni, *La costituzione politica di Firenze ai tempi di Lorenzo il Magnifico* (Siena, 1913); and G. Soranzo, "Lorenzo il Magnifico alla morte del padre e il suo primo balzo verso la Signoria," *ASI*, CXI (1953), 42-77. Anzilotti, again, *La costituzione interna dello stato fiorentino sotto il duca Cosimo I de' Medici* (Firenze, 1910), is particularly useful on institutional change in the passage from republic to duchy. Anzilotti had a genius for putting down essential details with a few rough strokes. A recent work with many pages on government and politics in Florence *ca.* 1500 is F. Gilbert, *Machiavelli and Guicciardini, Politics and History in Sixteenth-Century Florence* (Princeton, 1965). Another fundamental study, N. Rubinstein, *The Government of Florence Under the Medici (1434 to 1494)* (Oxford, 1966), was published after I had finished this book. The author allowed me to read the first chapter in manuscript. He has also brought out three articles of particular relevance here: "I primi anni del consiglio maggiore di Firenze (1494-1499)," *ASI,* cxii (1954), 151-94, 321-47; "The Beginnings of Niccolò Machiavelli's Career in the Florentine Chancery," *Italian Studies,* xi (1956), 72-91; and "Politics and Constitution in Florence at the End of the Fifteenth Century," *Italian Renaissance Studies,* ed. E. F. Jacob (London, 1960), pp. 148-83. Regarding the restoration of the Medici, there is the useful study of A. Borghesi, *La restaurazione Medicea in Firenze dal 1512 al 1527* (Siena, 1937). On the Florentine constitution in the fifteenth and early sixteenth centuries little else is really worth citing. I take for granted that the student will consult the standard histories of Florence by S. Ammirato, G. Capponi, F.-T. Perrens, and R. Caggese, as well as the histories by contemporaries like Machiavelli, Guicciardini, Varchi, and Nardi, some of whom I have amply cited in the text. Observations on the structure of Florentine office by contemporaries like Filippo de' Nerli and Donato Giannotti are too partisan or inaccurate to be used as primary sources for our understanding of the Florentine constitution. They serve best as political theory or to help throw light on the political struggle proper. Here too lies the value of the book by R. von Albertini, *Das Florentinische Staatsbewusstsein im Übergang von der Republik zum Prinzipat* (Bern, 1955). On the connection between political theory and Florentine politics I must not fail to mention two outstanding articles by F. Gilbert: "Bernardo Rucellai and the Orti Oricellari: A Study on the Origin of Modern Political Thought," *Journal of the Warburg and Courtauld Institutes,* xii (1949), 101-31; "Florentine Political Assumptions in the Period of Savonarola and Soderini," *Journal of the Warburg and Courtauld Institutes,* xx (1957), 187-214.

Political struggle: the richest of all sources for this theme is of course the *Consulte e Pratiche,* on which every serious student of the history of Florence should try himself. Now and then the records of the different courts (*ut supra*) provide the full details of particular cases. Some chronical material is also supremely important: especially Piero Parenti, *Storia fiorentina,* BNF, *Fondo principale,* II, IV, 169-71, also II, II, 129-34; and Bartolomeo Cerretani, *Istoria fiorentina,* BNF, *Fondo principale,* II, III, 74. Of fifteenth-century chronicles in print, three are especially good on political strife: Buonaccorso Pitti, *Cronica,* ed. A. B. della Lega (Bologna, 1905); Giovanni Cavalcanti, *Istorie fiorentine,* 2 vols. (Firenze, 1838-1839); and Filippo di Cino Rinuccini, *Ricordi storici,* ed. G. Aiazzi (Firenze, 1840). A famous collection of letters is very important for the middle decades of the fifteenth century: Alessandra Strozzi, *Lettere di una gentildonna fiorentina del secolo xv ai figliuoli esuli,* ed. C. Guasti (Firenze, 1877). Three Florentine histories by contemporaries are absolutely essential for the late fifteenth and early sixteenth centuries: those of Guicciardini, Varchi, and Nardi. Three other studies of political strife in Quattrocento Florence are worthy of notice; F. C. Pellegrini, *Sulla repubblica fiorentina a tempo di Cosimo il Vecchio* (Pisa, 1889); A. Municchi, *La fazione antimedicea detta 'del Poggio'* (Firenze, 1911); and G. Pampaloni, "Fermenti di riforme democratiche nelle consulte della repubblica fiorentina," *ASI,* CXIX, 1-2 (1961), 11-62, 241-81; CXX, 4 (1962), 528-81.

## Chapter Six

# Aspects of Territorial Government

## 1. *Justice and Judicial Office*

If the governors and magistrates sent out from Florence were the long hand of the state reaching into every corner of the Florentine dominion, the lawyers and notaries in their train were the mind and critical eye. Nothing which concerned the state was supposed to pass unrecorded, unseen. Every right, every prerogative claimed in its territories by the Republic of Florence had to be defended up to the limits of the law and human capacity. All leading officials sent into the dominion took an oath to this effect; and although expected to observe local law and custom, should such an official err, it was better for him to err in favor of the Signory and his masters back home.[1] At all the major urban centers—Pisa, Livorno, Arezzo, Pistoia, Prato, Cortona—he had at least one lawyer on his staff to help guide him through the tangle of local custom, Florentine municipal law, and Roman law.[2] For municipal and Roman law were sometimes in conflict with the custom of the region.

Florence did not have uniform arrangements with its subject cities, towns, and more rural or mountainous communities.[3] The latitude allowed in the exercise of self-government and the extent to which local law was allowed to prevail depended both on conditions current at the time a community came under Florentine rule and on its proximity to Florence, although there are signs that the capital city imposed stricter controls in the course of the fifteenth century. If relations with the sub-

[1] Buonaccorso Pitti was twice forced to submit to this lesson, *Cronica*, pp. 113-14, 230-35. In view of the scope of Florence's sovereignty (see Chs. IV, X), there could be no question of its legal-political *right* to a subject territory.

[2] E.g., the Florentine statute on the Podestà of Pisa accorded him full power in civil and criminal cases "secundum statuta communis Pisarum, et in casibus in quibus statuta non disponerunt . . . secundum ius commune," *Statuta*, III, 518.

[3] This is evident from the registers of the *Statuti dei Comuni Soggetti* (=*SCS*) in ASF. In the following notes I cite some of the ones consulted by me.

ject community had long been good or if its absorption by Florence had been relatively easy, then, as at San Gimignano and Carmignano, Florentine officials were expected to perform their tasks more in accord with local custom, and the right to judicial appeal was generously granted.[4] But if historical relations between Florence and the lesser community had been bad, tainted by violence and warfare, then, as in subject Pisa, the rule of the resident magistrates was much tougher, the military establishment more elaborate, local custom more thoroughly put down, and judicial appeal in criminal proceedings altogether denied.[5]

At the outset of the fifteenth century, Florence governed her territories by relying on a corps of about 120 governors—podestàs, captains, and the vicars put over whole regions.[6] Each of these officials was attended by a "family" or staff of aides, including men at arms, and such a staff might range from four to sixty-five men. Time brought a good deal of administrative consolidation to the dominion. By 1456 the number of governorships had been reduced to eighty-two.[7] Territorial accretion, however, gradually added some new posts: in the 1520s Florence sent ninety-five governors into the dominion.[8]

Not all governors were assisted by lawyers; Florence had not enough of them. Also, no citizen holding a *licentia* or doctorate in law would be willing to suspend his legal practice for six months to go with a podestà or vicar into a remote or semi-wild region. Governors dispatched to the main cities or towns were usually accompanied by several notaries and at least one lawyer, aside from other men. To the lawyer went the office of judge in the governor's court of law; the notaries took care of paper work, made an official record of all civil and criminal cases, and conducted the interrogations that went on in court. Minor governorships, including those in the most remote regions, were assigned "families" which included one notary, sometimes two. Lawsuits and criminal pro-

---

[4] *SCS*, 760 (Statutes of S. Gimignano: 1415-1417), f. 3r; 143 (Carmignano: second half of fourteenth century and later), ff. 12r *et seq.*, on procedure in civil cases; cf. also *Statuta*, III, 576-84, 608-11.

[5] *Statuta*, III, 517.

[6] This figure excludes castellans. *Tratte*, 66, lists 121 governorships for the period around 1406; *Statuta*, III, 516-683, lists 116 for the period around 1415.

[7] *Tratte*, 67 (years 1418-1456).

[8] *Tratte*, 71 (years 1505-1529).

ceedings in the courts of those regions were heard and determined by the governors proper—*iudices idiotae*, lay judges who must often have consulted their notaries and who also wrote away to Florence for advice. The Commune of Galeata, in the early fifteenth century, required its podestà to be a notary.[9] Probably there were other towns and jurisdictions with the same requirement.

At Pisa the chief official of the Captain was a judge with "at least a license in civil law." Four notaries kept the records. The Podestà of Pisa had the assistance of three notaries and a lawyer.[10] Pisa was the most important of the subject cities. In Arezzo the Captain was assisted by one lawyer and three notaries, the Podestà by one lawyer (a *legum doctor*) and two notaries.[11] At Pistoia the Podestà had three notaries and three lawyers in his entourage, though only one of the lawyers was required to have the doctorate. The Captain, on the other hand, had only one lawyer and three notaries.[12] Let us take another town—San Gimignano, where the office of captain did not exist. The magisterial functions here were all carried out by the Podestà with the help of one lawyer and two notaries.[13] Lesser towns and villages, as well as more sparsely settled regions, were assigned more modest staffs, usually without lawyers. The Podestà of Barga had only one notary on his staff. At Vallombrosa the Podestà had three notaries, at Castrocaro, Chianti, and Bibbiena two notaries. The Podestà of Montepulciano, however, had the help of two notaries and a lawyer.[14]

Generally speaking, the captains were given jurisdiction "in criminalibus," the podestàs jurisdiction over both civil and criminal proceedings. In many places the captains were absolutely forbidden to intervene "in causis civilibus." The Captain's court in Pisa was exclusively a criminal court, but activity affecting the security of the state or touching "the honor

---

[9] *SCS*, 345 (Galeata: 1411, with addenda to 1543), f. 1v.

[10] *Statuta*, III, 516, 518. By Florentine law the Podestà of Pisa was meant to have a doctorate, presumably in civil law, but this rule was not observed.

[11] *SCS*, 25 (Arezzo: 1460-1501), f. 61v, from an ordinance enacted in 1385.

[12] *SCS*, 596 (Pistoia: 1388-1487), ff. 66r, 249r, 300r; also *Statuta*, III, 561-62.

[13] *Tratte*, 67 (1418-56), f. 44r; *Statuta*, III, 576.

[14] *SCS*, 69 (Barga: 1414, with addenda to eighteenth century), f. 15r; *Tratte*, 66 (1406-18), f. 92r (Vallombrosa), f. 15r (Castrocaro), f. 68r (Bibbiena); *Tratte*, 67, f. 61r (Chianti), f. 43r (Montepulciano).

of the Florentine Commune" could only come up for trial in Florence. This highlights the fact that Florentines quite consciously assigned subversive or seditious actions to a sphere apart. In civil cases, the decisions of the Podestà of Pisa could be questioned by appealing to the Appellate Judge in Florence. Appeal "in criminalibus" was denied both at Pisa and at Arezzo. At Pontenano the Podestà was competent in civil cases involving claims up to 200 pounds of *fiorini piccioli*, in criminal cases up to 50.0 pounds.[15] All cases which exceeded these sums fell to the jurisdiction of the foreign magistrates in Florence. The designated limits (50.0 and 200 pounds) departed from a general rule. Normally, the podestàs within a radius of ten miles from Florence were competent in civil litigation up to 25.0 pounds. Beyond the ten-mile limit their competence extended to cases and claims up to 50.0 pounds.[16] The exceptions—not at all rare—were governed by particular statutes, each of which delineated the exact nature of judicial competence in the region concerned.

On the matter of appeal, practice in the territory tended to be more uniform. A general statute on the powers and duties of Florentine governors specifically provided that judicial appeal was to be granted in all civil and mixed cases,[17] and there seem to have been few exceptions to this. Some towns and jurisdictions had their own appellate judges.[18] Otherwise, all appeal against the decisions of territorial magistrates went to the Appellate Judge in Florence. Throughout the fourteenth and fifteenth centuries, this magistrate handled a large body of judicial business which originated in the dominion. The records of his court—records copious and varied—have still to be examined for the light they throw on rural Tuscany and some of the Tuscan towns.

When trying to envisage the system of governors in the territory, particularly the conduct of Florentine officials in remote areas where no lawyers were sent and the one notary might be little more than a proficient scribe with a knowledge of Latin, we must not suppose that cases were necessarily adjudicated in ignorance of the law. The varieties of crime, after all, carried fixed penalties which in many cases could be

---

[15] *Statuta*, III., 553.    [16] *Ibid.*, 621-22.    [17] *Ibid.*, 634.
[18] E.g., *SCS*, 24 (Arezzo: 1437-1580), f. 101v; 207 (Castrocaro: 1404, with addenda to 1449), ff. 80v-82r; 596 (Pistoia: 1388-1487), ff. 88r, 90r, 398r.

automatically applied. Civil proceedings were more complicated, but the important lawsuits of remote regions were heard by more experienced magistrates elsewhere—at Florence chiefly. Another feature of the system to be borne in mind, and one that cannot be stressed enough because it has hitherto escaped the notice of historians, is the fact that lay judges out in the dominion observed the practice of writing to lawyers in Florence, requesting judicial and legal counsel. If there was no one in Florence whom they especially favored, they wrote directly to the guild, which then distributed such commissions among its various lawyers.[19] It was more common, however, for judges and governors to appeal to friends or acquaintances in the profession. Following is an example concerning a rather pitiable case. The letter was written by the Podestà of Galeata to a lawyer in Florence, Ricciardo del Bene:

"My honorable senior, I cannot keep from bothering you with cases that come before me. We have arrested a man who has slept many times with his blood sister, who is now with child from him, and he has confessed everything without the application of torture. In my humble opinion, it seems that he ought by law to be put to death. But even if the case were other than important, I would never do without your counsel if it were at all possible to have it. And so I am sending you the proceedings of the trial and a copy of the statutes [of Galeata]. I beg you to advise me on whether or not this man should die, and if he should what form his execution ought to take, and whether or not I may legally confiscate his properties. I also beg you to correct and put the finishing touches on the transcript of the trial, giving it the form you think it should have. And you must advise me about all this in your letter. Christ watch over you. In Galeata, the 11th day of November, 1410. Your servant."[20]

---

[19] Evident from some of the *consilia* in *AGN*, 670.

[20] ASF, *Carte del Bene*, 52 (hundreds of loose, unnumbered letters), see by date. "Honorevole maggior mio, io non posso fare che io non vi dia faticha ne' casi mi intervenghono. E m'è venuto uno nelle mani il quale a avuto più e più volte a fare colla sua sirochia carnale e di lui è grossa e tutto a confessato sanza alchuno tormento. Et sechondo mio picholo parere mi pare di ragione de' morire. Ma pure . . . [se la] questione altro che d'importanza fusse, farei mai sanza vostro consiglio quando per niuno modo mi fusse possibile averlo. Et per tanto io vi mando il processo ella copia dello statuto e preghovi mi consigliate se costui de'

I have not come upon the lawyer's reply; perhaps it did not survive. But we can be sure that the poor devil in Galeata lost all, including perhaps his life. Probably the crime should have gone for trial to an ecclesiastical court, but often in such matters the jurisdiction of the Church was more theoretical than actual.

The distribution of magistracies in the Florentine dominion provided for the quotidian needs of justice and local government. With the pivotal help of their lawyers and notaries, the territorial governors saw to it that the law was applied and that local assemblies exercised only so much autonomy as juridical arrangements with Florence allowed. Not seldom, however, cases and questions came up, controversies broke out, which Florentine officials on the spot were not legally competent to handle. At that point Florence stepped in to adjudicate, to arbitrate, or to provide another means of settlement. Let us see how the capital city treated a number of questions that fell outside the purview of territorial governors.

## 2. *Controversy Reserved for Executive Action*

Dispute between adjacent districts, each with its own machinery of local government, often raised questions which could not be resolved by the local, interested magistrates. A neutral third party was wanted, and this office was performed by the Signory. Taking the dispute in hand, the Signory turned it over to two or three lawyers or, more rarely, to a commission of laymen headed by a lawyer. A fitting example is provided by a case brought to the Signory's attention in the late summer of 1446.

Pistoia claimed the right to permit or prohibit the holding of public markets in the small jurisdictions (*podesterie*) around Pistoia, which were still in the County of Pistoia. This claim was contested by the communities in question. The Signory referred the dispute to Tommaso Salvetti and Domenico Martelli, lawyers well known in Florentine political circles. Their findings went against Pistoia.[21] Taking for granted that

---

morire o no, e se de' morire che morte debba fare, et se io posso con ragione pubblicare i suoi beni in comune, et che voi aconciate il processo dove mancasse come vi pare voglia stare, et che di tutto quello bisongnia per vostra lectera m'avisate. Che xp̄o vi guardi. In Ghaleata a di xi di novembre 1410, per vostro servidore."

[21] *DSCSA*, 29, f. 34r.

the County of Pistoia had been absorbed by law into the County of Florence, they pointed out that the public rights had passed over with areas thus absorbed. To support this view, they adduced an old statute which ordained that the County of Pistoia was henceforth an integral part of the County of Florence and was to be treated as if this had always been so.[22] They concluded that "no public market could be or can be conceded in the County of Pistoia by judgment of the said city of Pistoia." With the concurrence of the colleges and the Eight on Public Safety, the Signory turned the opinion of the two lawyers into a binding decision.[23]

Taxes too could put adjacent communities at loggerheads. A later example may serve here. In January 1507 a certain Francesco di Guido Cattani, late of the "cortine d'Arezzo," became a citizen of Arezzo proper. The change naturally affected the destination of his personal taxes, giving rise to a quarrel over which of the two jurisdictions was responsible to Florence for Cattani's tax allotment. If he paid taxes in Arezzo, should not his ancestral community pay less to Florence and Arezzo correspondingly more? The case was heard by the Signory in 1511 and turned over for an opinion to Francesco Guicciardini, already a sought-after lawyer. Having looked into the details of the dispute, Guicciardini decided—and his decision was then made binding by the Signory and colleges—that Cattani should pay taxes in Arezzo and that Arezzo's fiscal obligations to Florence should correspondingly increase.[24]

Controversy between two communities of the same jurisdiction might also go to the Signory for settlement. Thus, in 1498, in the dispute between Galeata and its hillsmen regarding the use of the courtyard of the Castle of Biserno (already treated in Ch. III)[25] the Signory handed the case over to three lawyers, and their recommendations were decisive.[26]

In view of the observations made in the preceding chapter on the constitutional status of the Eight on Public Safety,[27] we may expect that territorial dispute of the type reserved for executive action fell in some

[22] *SCS*, 596 (Pistoia: 1388-1487), ff. 1r *et seq.*; also *Statuta*, III, 559.

[23] *DSCSA*, 29, ff. 34r, 92r, on 30 Aug. 1446.

[24] *DSCOA*, 113, ff. 92v, 96v-97v. Guicciardini was put on the case in Aug. 1511. The effects of his *consilium* were made retroactive to Jan. 1507.

[25] *DSCOA*, 100, f. 14r.

[26] *Ibid.*, ff. 19v-20r. Cf. above, pp. 98-99.

[27] See pp. 135-36.

instances to the jurisdiction of the Eight. The following case is paradigmatic.

Florentine law ordained that all communities, villages, and parishes "in the County and district of Florence" had to be joined together in *ligae* (confederations).[28] By an arrangement of August 1384, the *liga* or confederation of Antella took in the area just east of Florence and reached from Settignano to Impruneta. Hence it spread out on both sides of the Arno. Three districts (*pivieri*) made up the confederation: the *pivieri* of Antella, Ripoli, and S. Maria in Impruneta. Between 1386 and 1390 this confederation suffered extensive loss from theft and damage both to buildings and farms. The district of Ripoli, however, seems to have escaped largely untouched. This district was composed of four parishes (*popoli*) and all four refused to contribute from their "common chests" for the losses suffered by the confederation. Whereupon Antella and S. Maria in Impruneta had recourse to the the Eight on Public Safety. In March 1390 the Eight called in two lawyers to help throw light on the dispute— Giovanni da Poggibonsi and Rosso degli Orlandi. Drawing up a judicial opinion favoring the confederation, they concluded that Ripoli should contribute its share. The Eight accepted this finding.[29]

The aspect of this controversy which put it under the jurisdiction of the Eight was the fact that all the trouble resulted *ab initio* from large-scale criminal activity not far from the walls of Florence. Over such activity, above all when it bordered on civil disorder, the Eight were just beginning to develop their authority. They were therefore an obvious body for the Signory to call on, or for the litigants to approach.[30]

---

[28] *Statuta*, III, 692.

[29] All the details of the case and the opinion of the lawyers in *AGN*, 670, ff. 22v-23v. *Pivieri*: from *pieve*, a church district made up of a number of parishes.

[30] A century later the Eight operated freely in the territory, entered into criminal proceedings of all kinds, and bombarded territorial governors with executive orders. See *Otto di Guardia, Rep.*, 115 (Sept.-Dec. 1499), *passim*. By the outset of the sixteenth century their action in certain disputes was sometimes the subject of diplomatic correspondence. E.g., *OCR*, 15, f. 247r (27 Sept. 1516), a letter showing that the Eight had undertaken to settle a violent row between the subject communes of Migliana and Schignano. The row had claimed the lives of several men. Conflict continued until June 1524, when it was finally resolved by the jurist Antonio Negusanto da Fano, first appellate judge of Florence's Council of Justice. E. Repetti, *Dizionario geografico*, III, 208, s.v. *Migliana*.

Wherever the Republic was itself a party in controversy with one of the subject territories, we can be sure that adjudication or arbitration was not entrusted to a local magistrate. Taking the initiative, the Signory either appointed lawyers to work out a solution or made other arrangements to settle the differences.

In March 1450 the government invited Donato de' Cocchi-Donati to draw up a judicial opinion on a dispute between Florence and Pistoia.[31] Actually, the parties involved in the action were Pistoia and the Tower Officials of Florence. The dispute concerned the question of whether or not the owners of carts near Pistoia should pay a tax to the Tower Officials, who supervised the upkeep and use of roads, bridges, and public squares. In his report, Messer Donato pointed out that since the law required all owners of carts within twenty-two miles of Florence to pay a certain gabelle to the "provisor" of the Tower Officials, all cart owners from the outlying districts of Pistoia were bound to observe it. The lawyer based himself on the fact that much of the Pistoian *contado* or countryside lay inside the twenty-two-mile limit and was by law an integral part of the County of Florence, so that ordinances pertaining to the Florentine *contado* also bound a good deal of the Pistoian countryside.[32] This judicial opinion was adopted and put into effect by the Signory. Evidently, the Signory affected to be a neutral third party in the controversy, although the contending parties were a subject commune and a magistracy of the central or sovereign state. Nothing more seems to have been heard of the matter. We must not, however, get the impression that subject communities always acquiesced mutely in the decisions that issued from the capital city. Some years earlier (1437)— to take a kindred example—a difference of opinion had arisen between Pistoia and the officials of the salt gabelle of Florence. We know nothing about the points in question, save that on this occasion the Pistoians took their cause to the College of Jurists at Bologna and requested a judicial opinion.[33] They paid a very high fee (50.0 florins) for the opinion, which probably favored them and which they certainly meant to use in the

[31] *DSCOA*, 69, ff. 13r, 18r.

[32] *Ibid.*, f. 24r-v.

[33] The request and fee recorded in *Il 'Liber secretus iuris caesarei' della università di Bologna*, ed. A. Sorbelli, 2 vols. (Bologna, 1938-42), II, 157-58.

defense of their case. Judicial opinions of the Bolognese College of Jurists were expensive but influential, and it may be that Florence yielded on a point or two. If Florence itself had agreed to letting the College act as arbiter in the case, one may hope that the Signory let itself be bound by the decision.

Controversy was often started by the action of foreigners on the Republic's frontiers. Disturbances of this sort fell manifestly outside the jurisdiction of the territorial governors. Only the direct competence of the capital city could be fitting here. So far as the Signory represented Florentine interests, it was a party in the dispute and so could not sit in judgment. In these cases the action of the executive was limited to the negotiating phase. Acting through its agents, the Signory conducted negotiations with the representatives of the other party and made arrangements for a final settlement.

Barga, a commune under Florentine rule, lay in mountainous country some fifty miles northwest of Florence, on the western edge of lands governed by the Estensi marquises of Ferrara. In 1420 a disagreement between the Barghigiani (the men of Barga) and subjects of the Estensi became so bad that the Republic and the Marquis had to step in. Probably a good deal of friction long preceded the outbreak of troubles which were to persist for nearly half a century. Each side laid claim to land on the borders between the Republic and the Marquisate. The bone of contention in the autumn of 1420 was the "Romanesca" forest. Tommaso Salvetti, a Florentine lawyer trained at Bologna, was sent to Siena to represent Florence, Siena having been chosen to arbitrate in the dispute.[34] Together with a Sienese lawyer,[35] Salvetti and the Este agent went to the disputed area, conducted on-the-spot inquiries, and interrogated thirty witnesses for each side. Whatever the solution finally hit on, violations ensued and new trouble spots developed along the same border. The bitterest differences were to exist between Barga and Fiumalbo. Salvetti was dispatched to these areas in 1435 and again in 1444,[36] but more than a decade later the wrangling continued. In 1456-1457 Siena was again chosen to act as arbiter. When the reward or decision

[34] *SRRO*, 2, f. 67v; *SCMLC*, 6, ff. 111r, 114r; *SCMC-I*, 29, ff. 124r-125v.
[35] Messer Piero di Bartolommeo Pecci.
[36] *SCMLC*, 10, f. 30r-v; 11, f. 27r.

was finally made, the Marquis would not give his agreement and refused to ratify it. Siena had favored the Barghigiani. This was reported on April 8, 1457, by the commission which had looked into the question on appointment from the Signory.[37] The commission was composed of three Florentine statesmen, none of whom was a lawyer—a most unusual thing in such matters. But a lawyer was soon to be needed, according to the commission's report. On the day after Christmas last, the Barghigiani had attacked five buildings in the disputed area, plundering to their hearts' content. Three of the buildings were just outside the frontiers assigned to Barga by the Sienese. The members of the commission declared that the Barghigiani should make amends for the damages and loss of property, but they also urged the Signory to dispatch the lawyer "best informed about this dispute," Tommaso Salvetti, "to the Marquis of Ferrara so that he could present Barga's case, point out the wrong we feel is being done to us, and demand that the judgment handed down by the Sienese be respected."[38] The commission had undoubtedly taken counsel with Salvetti.

From about the middle of the fifteenth century on, records suggest that legal dispute along Florence's borders increased and that the deployment of lawyers in such controversy became a regular procedure. The lawyer was of little value in border disputes as long as these were settled by force of arms. But the more Florence and her neighbors looked for legal solutions to quarrels along their borders, the more critical became the role of lawyers in such disputes. How to explain this trend toward negotiated settlement is not easy. More than likely it was connected with two other developments. Culminating in the Italian League (1455), there was the growing effort of the major states of Italy to achieve a *modus vivendi*; wherefore legal solutions became more desirable. This apparently derived from the fact that by the middle of the fifteenth century the leading Italian states had more or less reached their historical frontiers—no longer operated on a land mass littered with weaker states which invited intervention, absorption, or outright conquest. The tiny states that still remained counted on the protection of one or more of the major states—existed, as it were, in their shadow.

[37] *CP*, 54, f. 6r-v. The three commissioners were Bernardo Giugni, Alessandro Alessandri, and Agnolo Acciaiuoli.
[38] *Ibid.*

The Medicean oligarchy of the period 1512-1527 was especially careful about its relations with neighbors and strongly favored the use of lawyers to help resolve border disputes. In the following examples, all the emissaries involved were practicing lawyers.[39]

Ludovico Acciaiuoli, in March 1513, was sent to conduct inquiries on a violent dispute between Foiano (Florentine territory) and Lucignano (Sienese). Three months later a row between Gargonza (Florentine) and Armajolo (Sienese) required the negotiation of Veri di Tanai de' Medici. In October the same Veri was chosen to help "resolve the border disputes, wheresoever they may exist, between the men of Lucca and us."[40] Then we skip a few years, to find that Veri was sent back to Gargonza in May 1520. Two years later Antonio Bonsi was the lawyer sent to conduct inquiries and to try to get agreement in the fight between Gargonza and Armajolo. In June 1523 Marco degli Asini and Ser Lorenzo Violi (one of the Signory's notaries) were dispatched to Cicognaja, Florentine territory in the Romagna, to try to settle "a certain controversy and border disputes outstanding between our men of Cicognaja and those of Santa Sophia, subjects of the Count Robert of Meleto." A year later Bonsi was out looking into another row along the borders. At the same time, Giovanni Buongirolami was to meet with the Sienese jurisconsult, Girolamo Ghini, and with a third lawyer, Cesare de' Nobili (the arbiter). These three lawyers were busy trying to resolve a territorial dispute between Lustignano (Florentine) and Monte Rotondo (Sienese). In 1524 and 1525, the lawyers Alessandro Malegonnelli and Silvestro Aldobrandini also travelled into the territory to help make peace between border disputants.[41]

When bypassing governors and other local officials in its dealings connected with disputes over boundaries, what exactly did the Signory have its lawyers do? The record is perfectly clear about this. Lawyers were sent to the trouble spots not only to interrogate witnesses, to collect documentary evidence, and to deal effectively with their rival peers (other lawyers), but also to press Florence's case on the arbiter (normally another

[39] See data on them in the Appendix.

[40] The quotation and missions here cited in order of their textual appearance above: *OCMLI*, 10, ff. 4v, 6v, 7r.

[41] *Ibid.*, ff. 18v, 86r, 87r, 108v, 109r, 114r, 133r, citations here follow the order of business presented above. The Aldobrandini mission involved a dispute between subject jurisdictions—Borgo S. Lorenzo and a nearby *pieve*.

jurist) who had been called in to decide the dispute. They were therefore expected to have a thorough grasp of all the papers bearing on the controversy and indeed of all the available evidence. This being so, the lawyers arrived in the troubled areas with documents gathered in Florence and proceeded to collect, if possible, additional local documents that went to establish or vindicate Florentine claims. In some cases, accordingly, the jobs of representation and advocacy could have been performed by a crack notary. But during the Renaissance—the fifteenth century and after—this was discouraged, owing to the notary's modest standing in society. The Republic was best represented by negotiators who were the professional or social equals of their rivals in negotiation and litigation. There was also another supremely practical reason for the use of lawyers rather than top-flight notaries in the inquiries and dealings connected with border disputes. No one could know when the arbiter's award in such dispute was going to depend on a difficult or controversial point of law, which lawyers alone were properly trained to handle. The notary's preparation, practical or theoretical, was not good enough.

A concluding note and generalization may put this section of the study in perspective. I have reviewed the different types of controversy over which the Signory and its adjuncts claimed judicial authority. Chief among these were disputes between contiguous jurisdictions, between communities of the same jurisdiction, and between subject communes on the one hand and magistracies of the capital city on the other. In such controversies, as in border disputes with foreign states, the Signory and other executive offices customarily depended on the judicial and legal counsel of lawyers, at times even on their capabilities as advocates. Once again, accordingly, it appears that the political pre-eminence of lawyers derived from the fact that the executive was unable to discharge some of its functions without them.

## 3. Rebellion

The themes of rebellion and treason in the Italian city-state want extensive, painstaking study, from a political as well as from a constitutional viewpoint. For the Italian states of the Renaissance, like states today, acted with great swiftness and ferocity when it came to handling threats, real or imaginary, to the central governing authority. The security of the state and of the ruling classes and their institutional power were the sole objects worthy of supreme caution. When that security was endangered, men in key places instinctively became as one, united in the belief that the less mercy shown the better. It is not that repression or punishment was always savage (though it often was), but that the state took the crimes of rebellion and *laesa majestas* from the competence of the regular courts and put them under the jurisdiction of the executive or of a special body answerable to the executive. If, as sometimes happened, a regular court was allowed to hear and determine such cases, it was immediately subjected to the constraint of the executive—Signory, prince, or powerful commission. Criminal proceedings against rebellion or treason constituted a special class of cases.

Let us return for a moment to the Moncione murder case of 1421.[42] Count Guido da Battifolle was assassinated in a courtyard of the Moncione Castle by a group of his men, who may have been put up to the crime and paid by the Fibindacci, an old feudal clan. There is good reason to believe that the assassins ought to have been locally tried, either by the regional Florentine governor, by Count Guido's family, or by another outstanding family of the district. But because some civil disorder was provoked, the Signory and colleges saw fit, under the additional stimulus of private pressure groups at home, to step in and bring the case under the jurisdiction of the capital city's foreign magistrates. This the government was able to do only by engaging a team of lawyers whom it then subjected to considerable constraint. Though somewhat reluctantly, they soon found a legal basis for holding the trial in Florence by seeing the criminal activity of the defendants in the light of an armed disturbance. At no point in the exercise of their functions were the lawyers or foreign magistrates allowed to escape from the political and moral duress of the Signory and colleges. Lawyers were in this case the instruments of policy, the Signory and colleges its makers.

In the course of the fifteenth century the Signory and colleges, the Eight on Public Safety, and other leading magistracies became more and more exigent in their relations with communities under Florentine rule.

---

[42] Fully discussed on pp. 155-63.

Racked by continual treasury deficits, Florence went from one fiscal crisis to another and increased its tax levies on subject territories. This could not be done without the imposition of tighter political and administrative controls.[43] All the more, therefore, were discontent and civil disorder in the dominion handled outside the regular system of courts (which at any rate were in decay) and put under the judicial aegis of the executive sector of government. The proceedings connected with the following case were not atypical. In October 1512 the case of some exiled Aretines was heard by the existing Balìa, a temporary dictatorial commission of sixty-two men.[44] This group turned the case over to five men headed by a prominent supporter of the Medici house—the lawyer Messer Matteo Niccolini. The five were ordered to refer their findings and recommendations to another commission, the newly revived Twelve Procurators, who were to take final action in the case. A number of bodies were bypassed: the courts of the Florentine magistrates in Arezzo, the new Council of Justice (Florence's major court), and even the potent Eight on Public Safety.

During the summer of 1500, when civil discord in Pistoia became so aggravated as almost to issue in civil war, the local magistrates, Podestà and Captain, were swept aside like leaves. It was up to the Signory or a military expedition to restore order. Two of Pistoia's most powerful families—rivals of old—were again fighting. The critical point came in late July, when the Cancellieri expelled all the Panciatichi from Pistoia, setting fire to more than 100 of their houses. Florence's political elite was divided on the question of how to restore peace, the schism running partly along factional lines. Guicciardini reported that the Panciatichi were favored by Piero Soderini, Piero Guicciardini, and Alamanno and Jacopo Salviati—a moderate group which, with some popular backing, stood at

---

[43] This trend is best visible in legislation (*provvisioni*) on the administration of the territories. I have also noticed it in the collection of *Statuti dei Comuni Soggetti*. When the collected statutes of a subject commune date from the late Trecento or early Quattrocento, they are usually followed by a series of addenda: an ever-growing number of Florentine *provvisioni* and executive orders aimed at stiffening Florentine rule in the dominion.

[44] *Balìe*, 43 (16 Sept. 1512–18 Jan. 1527), f. 21r-v. The Balìa included the Signory and an *aggiunta* of fifty-three men, four of whom were lawyers.

the head of the oligarchy.[45] The Cancellieri family had the support of a clique of intransigents who longed for a more restricted oligarchy: Bernardo Rucellai, Giovan Battista Ridolfi, Guglielmo de' Pazzi, the Nerli, the lawyers Guidantonio Vespucci and Francesco Gualterotti, and other laymen. Not only Vespucci and Gualterotti, but another lawyer, Antonio Malegonnelli, also came out for the Cancellieri.

The executive consultations on the Pistoian disorders lasted into the middle of September.[46] A revealing fact is that though the Republic's entire political class was composed of about 3,300 men, not more than 1,000 or 1,200 of whom were truly active, no less than seven lawyers (from a total of about twenty-eight) figured prominently in the meetings on Pistoia.[47] One or two of the participating lawyers were current members of executive bodies; the others were especially summoned to give counsel. Evidently, the government looked to lawyers because it expected them, with their legal skills and experience, to bring forth some workable solutions.

When looking at what the seven lawyers actually said, we must disregard their factional alignments, which do not fully accord with their explicit recommendations. Was Guicciardini wrong about the political leaders at the head of the two factions? Possibly. But it is much more likely that being caught up in the political game, some of the lawyers played one hand in public and another in private, thus giving rise to the disparity between what Guicciardini reported and what they actually said in council. After all, the oligarchical diehards could not appear to be too indulgent about the Pistoian disorders.

Taking a tough line, Guidantonio Vespucci observed on August 3rd that the "right medicine" for Pistoia was "to administer justice and to punish whoever errs. And if the power to do this be missing at present, let us send troops enough for that and at Pistoian expense." Eleven days later he returned to his advice to dole out punishment, proposing as well

[45] *Istorie fiorentine*, ed. R. Palmarocchi (Bari, 1931), pp. 204-205. On the houses burnt and other details see Piero Parenti, *Storia fiorentina*, BNF, *Fondo principale*, II, IV, 170, f. 138v.

[46] *CP*, 66, ff. 87v *et seq.*

[47] Of lawyers resident in Florence at this time, about twenty-eight were eligible to hold public office.

the imposition of a special tax ("taglia") on the guilty.[48] Domenico Bonsi drily asserted that the guilty "should be made to pay." Francesco Pepi noted that the uproar in Pistoia derived from the fact that Florence had been inadequately armed and urged more vigorous intervention, "for Pistoia means more than Pistoia: it means Volterra, Arezzo, and Cortona."[49] Luca Corsini, on the contrary, desired additional consultation first, chiefly because one of the experts on the question, another lawyer, was then in Bologna—Francesco Gaddi. Antonio Malegonnelli spoke in favor of the Cancellieri at some length.[50]

By September 1st both Vespucci and Bonsi were taking an ambiguous line. Vespucci reminded the government that "first we are lords of Pistoia" and called for a bolder use of force. Then, oddly equivocating, he added that when the use of great force was not possible, Florence "should try to limit the demands [of the Pistoians] as best it could." Bonsi also recommended a swift and ample use of force, pointing out that while rebellion had not yet taken place, a small incident could touch it off. Shifting his ground then, he went on to say that "he would try by some gentle route to bring the Pistoians back to decent behavior; nor should one despair of this, for their demands were made in hatred and they can be got to modify these if shown the reasons."[51] Antonio Strozzi and Matteo Niccolini more or less repeated what the others lawyers had said. On September 14th, in his last speech on the subject in this phase of the consultation, Vespucci argued that if the government assured the Cancellieri clan that Florence meant no harm to them in their persons or property, the disturbances at Pistoia would cease. We need resort to force, he continued, only "should they refuse to go along with honest conditions" ("se non volessino di poi assentare alle cose honeste").[52] But peace was not to be restored for months.

Although the seven lawyers did not provide counsel which was markedly different from that of the laymen who participated in the meetings, their massive presence gave a technical turn to the question of what to do in Pistoia: whether to use naked force, to impose a special tax on the

[48] *CP*, 66, ff. 87v, 92v.    [49] *Ibid.*, f. 101v.
[50] *Ibid.*, ff. 108r-v (Malegonnelli), 116r (Luca Corsini).
[51] *Ibid.*, ff. 123v (Vespucci), 124r (Bonsi).
[52] *Ibid.*, f. 140v.

guilty, to administer justice in a summary or more regular fashion, or to depend mainly on the art of sweet persuasion. Faced with large-scale disorder in a subject town, the government bypassed all local magistrates and looked to the skills of lawyers no less than to the experience of laymen.

The point of these pages has been to illustrate a technique of handling rebellion in the territory. Generally speaking, the Signory or the Eight swiftly stepped in to direct things, very often with the help of lawyers. For unless there was a summary martial intervention, the moment penal proceedings were kept out of the ordinary circuit of courts, owing to action on the part of the Signory or another powerful office, laymen found themselves moving over unfamiliar ground. This is why they depended on the assistance of lawyers. In a world where the executive was determined to have a prominent place in the settlement of jurisdictional disputes and the dispensation of justice, lawyers were appropriately called to the fore to lend a hand.

## 4. Administrative Questions

Florentine machinery for governing the territory tended to function smoothly, save when war, diplomacy, or reckless fiscal pressure from the capital city encouraged or provoked local feelings of autonomy. If the *Consulte e Pratiche* of the Renaissance period occasionally reveal a particular preoccupation with problems of territorial government, this is because war and Florence's grinding need for public revenue too often hounded men at the parish level, putting severe strains on the machinery of local government. Administrative questions, however, might come up at almost any time and give rise to situations which lawyers were best equipped to handle. A few examples must suffice, the real concern here being not territorial government *per se* but the place of lawyers in it.

The relation between Florentine law and law in the territories was a matter for administration because it was under the control of governors and their aides. According to the Florentine constitution, no subject community could enact legislation which conflicted with the corpus of Florentine statutes. When a community was drawn under Florentine rule, its legal code was studied with an eye to eliminating conflicts with the laws of the capital city. In general, podestàs or regional vicars (or their representatives) were required to sit in on the meetings of local governing bodies. It was there and then that the legislation of subject communes was controlled. When doubts or constitutional questions arose in connection with proposed legislation, the skilled aides of the governors —lawyers and notaries—were the ones who took the lead in deciding matters. Persistent doubt could always, of course, be referred to Florence, where again the job was one for lawyers or the leading chancellery notaries. In this fashion, proposed territorial legislation was screened and cleaned up, so to speak, before it came up for the final vote. Such procedure is what explains the fact that the commissions appointed in Florence to approve the statutes of subject communes were nearly always made up of laymen.[53] Very seldom were lawyers chosen to serve in these commissions. For the technical work had already been done *in situ*— the labor of lawyers and notaries—and there was little danger that subject communes would send unconstitutional legislation to Florence for approval.

Let us take a different sort of problem. When, at the outset of March 1418, the Signory and colleges failed to win approval in the Council of the People for a measure concerning the way to elect the Five Provisors of Pisa, advisory meetings were called to decide on the next move. On March 7th speakers like Niccolò da Uzzano and Agnolo Pandolfini did not conceal the fact that the Signory and the top tier of the oligarchy preferred the method of "election" used the year before. They wanted the Signory and colleges to select about sixteen men, to put these to a vote in the legislative councils, and to have the office go to the five men who received two-thirds or more of the votes cast.[54] Lesser men—i.e., the bulk of the citizenry—held out instead for the method of "extraction," which

[53] E.g., *SCS*, 207 (Castrocaro: 1404 and addenda to 1449), ff. 86r, 98r, 106r, 108r, 110r, 119r, 120r; 595 (Pistoia: 1373-1500), ff. 51r, 74r, 122r, 151r. These commissions were usually composed of four men, sometimes six, occasionally even more. The approvers of the statutes of Pistoia in 1406 were two Florentines and twenty Pistoians. Only once do I remember having seen a lawyer's name among lists of commissioners appointed to approve the statutes of subject communes.

[54] *CP*, 43, ff. 174v-175r. The whole procedure is laid out in a legislative act of 27 March 1417 and its basis is social class. *Prov.*, 107, ff. 2v-3v. Twelve of the sixteen candidates had to be major guildsmen and *rentiers* (*scioperati*), the other four minor guildsmen. This reflected the traditional social and political division between the seven major and fourteen minor guilds. The sixteen candidates repre-

meant giving the office to the five men whose names were drawn by lot from a set of pouches. This method, unlike the other, gave *all* eligible members of the political class an equal chance to be drawn for the office.[55]

Who were the Five Provisors of Pisa? The year before, they had taken over the authority and responsibilities of the Decem Pisarum, who kept a watchful eye on the use and circulation of currency in Pisa, directed the paying out of all monies from the Pisan exchequer, supervised the work of defense and fortification in Pisa, Porto Pisano, and the Castle of Livorno, and were the immediate superiors of the castellans in these areas.[56] Like all Florentine officials whose responsibilities took in a large variety of charges, the Five Provisors had great power and tended constantly to acquire additional authority whenever an opportunity presented itself. They held office for one year, resided in Pisa, and received a handsome salary—25.0 gold florins per month. A coveted office, it was high on the scale of prestige.

The major session on the question of how to elect the Five Provisors was held on March 16, 1418. Five of the eighteen men who took the floor were lawyers.[57] Evidently, therefore, the Signory was looking for a particular type of solution. The lawyer Alessandro Bencivenni, a new man of wool-merchant forebears, had already aired his views nine days before and now repeated himself: he said that the office was better filled by selection than by drawing lots, praised the Signory for having favored the former of these methods, and recommended that it be proposed again to the Council of the People.[58] Filippo Corsini called for the "election"

---

sented all four quarters of the city. Of the twelve major guildsmen and *scioperati*, three were drawn from each quarter; of the four *minori*, one from each quarter. One of the Five *Provisores*, but only one, had to be a minor guildsman.

[55] I mean, naturally, within the limits of the system. For as the preceding note shows, even the more "democratic" method of drawing names by lot was "rigged" four to one in favor of major guildsmen and *scioperati*. The point is that the other method was more selective still: it favored the leading families of the major guilds. Thus in March 1417 the four upper-class places went to prominent figures like Giovanni Soderini, Piero Baroncelli, Palla di Nofri Strozzi, and Giovanni di Bicci de' Medici. *Prov.*, 107, f. 3v.

[56] *Statuta*, III, 113ff.

[57] *CP*, 43, ff. 178r-180r.

[58] "Regimini civitatis Pisarum melius providebitur per electionem quam per extractionem et sortem," "laudes merentur domini et collegia qui non sorte sed electioni committere se voluere, et licet non obtentum fuerit, non est deserendum," *CP*, 43, ff. 175v, 179r.

of five "expert and learned men"—hence he was for selection rather than for the outcome of fortune by lot. Next to speak was the canonist and resourceful politician, Lorenzo Ridolfi. At the session of March 7th he had already proposed the drawing by lot of ten names per quarter (forty in all) and the holding of a vote on these in the legislative councils. He now reminded the assembly of his previous advice, stipulated using the pouches from which the Decem Pisarum were drawn, and went on to a new suggestion, namely, that once the names were drawn, all ensuing arrangements (the job of election!) be handled by the Signory and colleges or by another limited body. Although favoring the selective route, the Strozzi lawyer (Messer Marcello) did not think it would gain the approval of the councils and so recommended a compromise: the drawing of twelve or fifteen names from the pouches and the electing of five of these by vote. Next to Ridolfi, Strozzi was closest to the final solution. Another new man, Giovanni di Piero Bertaldi, lined up (like Bencivenni) with the views of leading oligarchs. He flatly stated that election was superior to drawing names by lot.[59]

Ridolfi spoke a second time on March 16th—the last of the lawyers to hold forth that day. This time, however, he was the spokesman for the S. Spirito quarter, among whose representatives his views had apparently prevailed. He returned to his plan: to draw ten citizens per quarter (eight from the major and two from the minor guilds) and to confer the office of the Five Provisors of Pisa on those who got two-thirds or more of the votes cast by the deciding body. One of the Five was to belong to a minor guild and each of the others to come from a different quarter of the city.[60]

Ridolfi and Strozzi came close to hitting on the final solution, which required adopting procedures consistent with municipal law and administrative practice. Above all it was necessary that the solution take something from the way things were done the year before—thus contenting

[59] *Ibid.*, ff. 178v-179r, in the order Corsini, Ridolfi, Strozzi, and Bertaldi.
[60] *Ibid.*, f. 179v, "Dñs Laurentius de Ridolfis pro quarterio S. Spiritus dixit et consuluit quod licet ipsis summe placebat ut electio quinque Pisarum fieret, tamen ut custodie Pisarum provideatur, in consilio fiat extractio VIII civium ex numero [maioribus artibus et scioperatis] pro quolibet quarterio et duorum arteficum, et facta extractione hi qui obtinebunt per duas partes, videlicet V in totum, inter quos sit unus artifex, remaneant."

the oligarchy's ruling stratum—and also pay homage to the drawing of names by lot. March 17th saw another consultation on the matter and in the next four days a shrewd compromise was worked out. Niccolò da Uzzano, Agnolo Pandolfini, or others of their ilk probably had something to do with it; the lawyers Ridolfi and Strozzi certainly did, for the plan included their suggestions but with a refinement which constituted a specimen of procedural ingenuity. The pouches to be used were those for the Decem Pisarum. Twenty names (four from the minor guilds) would be drawn. Forty (ten per quarter) would have been much preferred by the political chieftains because this doubled the chances of their own men being drawn. But having to yield somewhere, they yielded here in order to gain major advantages elsewhere. Once the twenty were drawn, the government was to proceed without hesitation to the election of the Five Provisors, giving the more modest families of the oligarchy no opportunity to focus their support or do any canvassing. This advantage for the men at the top was accompanied by still another one. The votes deciding the final election were to be cast not by the large legislative bodies but by a small executive council which exalted the principle of oligarchy—a council composed of the Signory and colleges, the Eight on Public Safety, the Captains of the Guelf Society, and the Sei di Mercanzia.[61]

The results of a "democratic" procedure (drawing by lot) were thus put into the hands of a small council made up of leading officials, the majority of whom came from leading families. They made the final selection. Approved by the Councils of the People and Commune on March 23rd, this solution was the work of men—lawyers and artful politicians—who knew how to adapt administrative resources to political necessity. They could not in this case operate above or beyond political rivalries. Faction, status, and emolument were the hidden factors in the dispute. The office of the Five Provisors was lucrative, prestigious, prized; and the leaders of the oligarchy did not propose to let it slip entirely out of their patronage.

Yet apart from all this, Pisa was in fact a key point in the expanse of Florentine territorial administration. The choice of the Five was un-

---

[61] *Prov.*, 107, ff. 334v-335v.

questionably important. For whatever the solution, it must in the end be put into effect at the level of administration, even if born of politics rather than "pure" administrative concerns.

Pisa was to pose problems now and then during the rest of the century. In July 1433 the Pisan countryside went through a moment of grave civil disorder.[62] The advisors who reported on this to the Signory and colleges included two lawyers—Guglielmo Tanagli and Carlo Federighi, the spokesman for the Sei di Mercanzia. Tanagli headed the *pratica* and reported for the group. He urged the establishment of a commission of five experienced men to handle things, and so again the small commission was the means chosen to deal with a special territorial problem.

On the administrative use of lawyers in territorial government, the following is a more clear-cut illustration. A consultation of January 12, 1459, revealed that the Pisans had sent envoys to Florence with a request concerning Florentine tax policy in the County of Pisa.[63] Apart from the fact that marauding troops, some of them "friendly," had of late devastated large parts of the country around Pisa, harvests in recent years had been bad.[64] The result was that the Pisan *contado* suffered depopulation and the remaining rural inhabitants found it next to impossible to pay their full allotment of taxes. It was with the aim of negotiating a new tax policy that Pisa had sent envoys to Florence. Having heard their representations, the Signory and colleges consulted with a group of advisors. Bernardo Giugni, a knight and prominent political figure, said that the question "ought to be put into the hands of some lawyers so that they could judge whether or not they [the Pisans] are requesting what is just."[65] Another prominent knight, Carlo Pandolfini, wanted the matter referred to the Conservatores Legum, one of the outstanding executive-judicial commissions. Three lawyers took part in the consultation. Tommaso Salvetti held that the entire question, "tam de iure quam de equitate," should be turned over to the Five on Pisa and the Defenders of the

---

[62] *CP*, 50, f. 85r.

[63] *CP*, 55, f. 93v.

[64] *Consiglio del Cento, Deliberazioni*, 1, f. 15v.

[65] *CP*, 55, f. 93v, "quantum ad ea que oratores Pisani dixerunt, dixit videri sibi ut eorum causa in peritos iuris remitteretur ut intelligerent an iusta postulent nec ne."

Laws (the Conservatores Legum).[66] Domenico Martelli thought "that the [five] officials in charge of Pisan affairs have all the authority" in the matter; hence they should take charge of things. The alleviation of the Pisan tax load could not be done, he maintained, "by means of specific legislative enactments" ("per particulares provisiones").[67] Nor did he think that the question was one which needed study from a legal viewpoint. Speaking right after Martelli, Otto Niccolini also recommended that the matter be referred to the Five on Pisa.

The Signory had been directly approached by the Pisan envoys. How was it to cope with their plea for a more humane tax policy? First there would have to be a pinning down of administrative jurisdiction or a certain delegation thereof. Some doubt existed as to the locus of authority. By January 16th a provision had been prepared, according full power in the matter to the Five on Pisa. It was unanimously approved by the Signory's body of advisors on the 18th. Two days later the existing Balìa adopted the measure, thereby making it law.[68] The Five were in effect empowered to distribute tax levies, for they were authorized to hand out tax indulgences, according as they saw fit, to the communes and men of the country around Pisa. Their authority affected present as well as back taxes. The Council of One Hundred duly confirmed the action of the Balìa.[69]

The three lawyers—Salvetti, Martelli, and Niccolini—had said this was a job for the Five on Pisa. Some question came up regarding the pertinence of the Conservatores Legum, but they were swiftly bypassed. Salvetti insisted that "by law and equity" jurisdiction in the matter belonged to the Five on Pisa. Martelli was right to point out that taxes in the Pisan countryside could not be adjusted by means of individual leg-

---

[66] *Ibid.*, f. 94r. The Five on Pisa, also called the Five Governors of the Pisans, developed out of the old Quinque Provisores Pisarum. The Five Governors were exceedingly powerful, owing especially to powers made over to them between their establishment in August 1458 and the following December. See *Balìe*, 29, ff. 21v, 53v, 66r, 73r, 80r.

[67] *CP*, 55, f. 94r. By "particulares provisiones" he meant a series of legislative bills answering to private petitions from Pisans. The custom was to request relief from taxes individually.

[68] *Balìe*, 29 ff. 96v-97r.

[69] *Consiglio del Cento, Deliberazioni*, 1, f. 15v.

islative enactments. The government thereupon took things in hand and delivered the entire matter over to the Five, at the same time including in the act of delegation a general clause which suspended any existing ordinance in conflict with such an allocation of power. In this administrative episode, the function of the lawyer emerges with unusual clarity.

Where doing a job far out in Florentine territory belonged to a certain routine, or to a clearly defined mandate, no outside help was necessary. The existing system sufficed: local officials, or the ones normally sent out from Florence, took care of things. But when a task fell outside the routine, or a question arose of such importance as to require the intervention of the capital city, then the contribution of lawyers might well be critical. Four types of events were most likely to occasion the use of Florentine lawyers in territorial administration: civil disorder, border dispute, conflict between subject communities, and the need—when it arose—to define the nature of particular offices, to create new ones, or to eliminate those fallen into near desuetude.

### SOURCES FOR CHAPTER SIX

There is no secondary historical literature on the way Republican Florence governed her territories. This is one of the field's outstanding lacunae. As the footnotes reveal, the obvious points of departure for such a study are two: the Florentine statutes of 1415 and the *Statuti dei Comuni Soggetti*. The *Statuti* make up an archive of 956 registers. Containing the written laws for several hundred different communes, these registers extend in time from the end of the thirteenth to the eighteenth century. The inventory of the registers may show one or more entries for a particular commune, each entry being a register of statutes. Pistoia alone, for example, has twenty-seven entries, Prato twenty-six, San Gimignano twenty-one. Carmignano, on the other hand, has only one. Rarely does a register provide a complete set of statutes. The advantage of many of the registers in this collection is that after presenting the statutes of the commune in question they go on to include addenda, often consisting of Florentine legislation which bears concretely on the commune or deals generally with some aspect of territorial government.

Once again I have drawn considerable material from the *Consulte e*

*Pratiche, Deliberazioni dei Signori e Collegi* (both the ordinary and extraordinary series), *Provvisioni,* and *Balìe.* The papers of the *Giudice degli Appelli* have a great deal of material on justice and litigation in the dominion. In this connection, one source which should not be overlooked is that of the *Otto di Guardia* (the Republican series), especially the registers of *Deliberazioni* for the second half of the fifteenth century and later.

A final source in Florence for the study of territorial government is the collection of *Capitoli.* This archive contains the records of treaties with feudal lords, with fortified areas, and with lands that passed voluntarily under Florentine rule. There are also records of other pacts and arrangements between subject territories and the capital city. Two volumes of *Capitoli* were edited and published by C. Guasti and A. Gherardi, *I Capitoli del Comune di Firenze* (Firenze, 1866-1893).

I hope the title of this chapter accurately designates the modest content therein, for the subject matter is one which merits several doctoral dissertations. Still, if I have indicated some of the problems of territorial government or some approaches to the study thereof, the chapter may have its uses apart from any inquiry into the political role of lawyers. But any student who undertakes to do a study of territorial government *per se* must go out to some of the towns within a radius of forty or fifty miles from Florence and get at the archival material there. Many of the provincial archives are rich in material, e.g., deliberations of local councils, public correspondence, treasury accounts, and court records.

## Chapter Seven

# Florentine Relations
# with the Church

## *1. Introduction*

The difference between spiritual and temporal affairs was not as clear
to the mind of medieval and early modern Europe as it sometimes is to
intellectual historians. Nor, when a clear difference was discerned and
one side had something to gain, the other something to lose, were the
boundaries always respected by the interested parties—clergy and laity.
But even when each side gave up trying to get as much as it could from
the other, daily life posed manifold questions about which legitimate
dispute could well arise. Spiritual and temporal concerns refused to stay
separate. Priest and statesman were sometimes one; or the statesman did
not see how he could stay out of the far-reaching affairs of the priest.

When the history of Florentine relations with the Church is finally
written, we shall find alternating periods of strife and imperfect harmony.
At the worst of times Florentine and papal armies met on the field of
battle, while priests were forced in spite of interdicts to open the doors
of churches and perform their holy offices. By and large, however, a certain unison prevailed. Like the city's top-flight public offices, the leading
dignities of the Florentine church were very often held by men of the
upper classes, less often by humbler men of administrative talent. Cleric
and statesman dealt with their own social kind. Controversy broke out
all the same, and was so common a thing that the litigants had either to
turn to negotiation and arbitration or render coexistence impossible. As
in current Soviet-American relations, necessity imposed negotiation and
peaceful settlement.

At Florence and in Italy generally, the history of relations between
Church and state issued in a body of practical norms, agreements tacit
or articulated, methods of arbitration, and suppositions more or less taken
for granted on both sides. But owing to the blurred areas between the two

jurisdictions, to the strains between past compacts and new necessities, to the emphasis put on documents and sworn testimony, and to the elaborate structures of the civil and canon laws, controversy between the ecclesiastical and temporal orders sometimes turned on fine legal or even grammatical points. The struggle for power was shatteringly real, but it was also conducted, in good faith or bad, at the level of reasoned argument. Hence dispute could arise or apparently subside with the specific interpretation of a document—a treaty, a contract, a law. Is it not clear that this was a world for lawyers *par excellence*? That the history of the dispute between the two jurisdictions would bring celebrity to many a lawyer, civilian as well as canonist? From the end of the twelfth century the law schools and legal profession gave a remarkable number of popes to the Church, some of them among the most dynamic in the history of the papacy: Innocent III, Boniface VIII, and John XXII. In the fifteenth century alone the following were trained in law: Innocent VII, Benedict XIII, John XXIII, Martin V, Calixtus III, and Alexander VI. Of these six, three—Innocent, John, and Martin—rose from the ranks of the auditors or judges of one of the leading Church tribunals, the Sacra Rota Romana.[1]

Not only popes but also other dignitaries of the Church were very often recruited from among men trained in law. It was training they would be called on to use, even though they could certainly turn to other men for legal counsel. In July 1461 there was an altercation between the Signory and the Archbishop of Florence, who seemed determined to violate some licenses of safe-conduct granted by the Eight on Public Safety (the Octo Custodiae).[2] He did not feel that he was thereby offending the dignity or temporal sovereignty of the state. Addressing the Signory and its counsellors, the lawyers Domenico Martelli and Otto Niccolini threw their weight in support of the government. Martelli touched on aspects of canon law and enviously referred to the nature of relations between Church and state at Venice. The outcome of this dispute is not revealed

---

[1] D. Bernino, *Il tribunale della S. Rota Romana* (Roma, 1717), pp. 314ff. Five of the seven Avignonese popes were trained lawyers, P. Hughes, *A History of the Church* (London, 1955), III, 156n; also the observations in B. Guillemain, *La Cour Pontificale d'Avignon (1309-1376), Étude d'une Société* (Paris, 1962), pp. 118-19.

[2] *CP*, 56, ff. 172v-174v.

by the sources, but the new Archbishop, Giovanni Neroni (born into an illustrious Florentine family), may have sought to rely on the practice of his immediate predecessor, Orlando Bonarli (1399-1461). More is known about this man. A *decretorum doctor*, Bonarli studied at Bologna and was also licensed in civil law. During the academic year 1439-1440, he taught canon law at Florence. Thereafter, he practiced law for a time. In 1440 he was matriculated in the Arte dei Giudici e Notai and in 1445 served as a guild consul. His activity in the guild indicates that he had not yet taken holy orders. But sometime in the late 1440s he went to Rome. Tonsured, he was appointed an auditor of the Rota Romana in 1451 and became Archbishop of Florence in 1459, on the death of St. Antonino, another canonist and one-time Rota auditor. Bonarli's legal skills had enabled him, as Archbishop, to pursue more demanding policies.[3]

In a letter of April 16, 1500, the Signory requested a leading statesman and professor of law, Antonio Malegonnelli, then Florentine ambassador in Rome, to try to get the Bishop of Volterra to free the vicariate of the Val di Cecina from episcopal censure.[4] The bishop was a Florentine— Francesco Soderini (1453-1524). Most of his diocese was in Florentine territory and the Val di Cecina was wholly under Florentine rule. The Signory wanted the governor (*vicarius*) of the Val di Cecina and his associates to be released from the penalty of excommunication. Malegonnelli went to work on the bishop, who at once responded by writing an indignant letter to the Signory. He protested that his antagonists were guilty of having departed from customary practice, that he, not they, was the injured party. Then he explained the nature of the conflict:[5]

---

[3] On Bonarli see my sketch in a forthcoming volume of the *Dizionario biografico degli Italiani* (Roma, 1960—).

[4] *SCMLC*, 25, f. 100v.

[5] *SCRO*, 14, f. 113r-v. "La chiesa di Volterra per privilegii antiquissimi et di Imperadori et di Pontefici ha sempre exercitata la iurisdictione inter laicos sanza alcuna contradictione, et io gia 22 anni che son suto vescovo di quella chiesa sempre la ho exercitata. Et quando Sancto Gemignano et l'altre terre del contado di Firenze et di Pisa et del territorio di Siena sanza alcuna difficultà obediscono mi parrebbe ragionevole che molto più lo facessi la terra di Ripamarance, la quale mi è subdita particularmente in temporalibus et spiritualibus, non solo per e' privilegii et consuetudine sopradecte ma per spetiale concessione di cotesta Repubblica nel mccccxxix et per iuramento della fidelità che ha prestato nelle mane mia fino dal principio che

"The church of Volterra, by right of ancient privileges both from emperors and popes, has always exercised jurisdiction *inter laicos* without any opposition; and I, bishop of that church already for twenty-two years, have always exercised it. Now when San Gimignano and other lands of the county of Florence, Pisa, and the territory of Siena all obey without causing any difficulties, it would seem to me reasonable that all the more should this be true of Ripamarance [i.e., Pomerance in Val di Cecina], a land particularly subject to me *in temporalibus et spiritualibus*, not only by right of the privileges and customs mentioned above but also by special concession of this [Florentine] Republic, made in 1429, as well as by the oath of fidelity sworn in my hands at the time I became bishop, which this land was compelled to do, as it now is, by the threat of censures. Nor did the region then make so much noise about things, and it seems to me in the interests of this city [Florence] to preserve the disputed jurisdiction so that the Sienese, moved by this example, may not also withdraw their obedience from me." The bishop then pointed out that all the men of his diocese, save those of Ripamarance, went to him to ask for absolution and that all the trouble in the recalcitrant region was being caused by public officials and "a few others." Not only, he claimed, had he refused absolution to none who had sincerely requested it, he had also served the officials of Ripamarance with a humane warning to obey. Contrary to their claims, he had not just rudely threatened them with excommunication. Nevertheless, Soderini continued, these officials jailed his representatives and sent out orders to resist his jurisdiction. To make the Signory see the full justice of his case, he reproduced in his letter the key parts of the decree of excommunication, which gave the officials under censure three months to make amends.

Ripamarance had once been subject to Volterra and so perhaps, in some remote past, to the Bishop of Volterra. The Republic took the Castle of Ripamarance and seems to have put it under the jurisdiction of the bishop in 1430 (1429 Florentine), after Volterra had rebelled against

---

io fui facto vescovo, al quale fu constracta per mezo delle censure come adesso, et non ne fece tanto romore, et parmi interesse di cotesta città conservare questa iurisditione accio e Sanesi per questo exemplo non mi subtrahessino anche loro la obedientia."

Florence in protest to the *catasto* tax.[6] According to Soderini's testimony, there was a feudal tie between himself and Ripamarance. With so much of her territory up in arms in 1500, was it possible that Florence now sought to be conciliatory by letting that bond be dissolved? This is not what the existing correspondence on the affair reveals. A month after the Signory's instructions to Malegonnelli, nothing had yet been done to remove the ecclesiastical penalties (the bishop was holding his ground),[7] and the lord priors gave no evidence of wanting to make an issue of his self-proclaimed temporal jurisdiction. Though a prince of the Church, Soderini was also one of their own. Born into one of the city's most illustrious families, a shrewd statesman with great experience in public affairs, he conducted a variety of extremely important embassies for the Republic.[8] Of greater significance for this study, however, is the fact that he read civil and canon law at the University of Pisa, where he began to teach law at the age of twenty-three. In the 1490s and up to the time he became a cardinal in 1503, he held one of the papal curia's leading judicial posts, being an "auditor audientiae litterarum contradictarum."[9] It is this we should have in mind when we think of him and Malegonnelli—they were almost exact contemporaries—confronting each other in Rome. The bishop had a perfect legal grasp of the jurisdiction in question and his letter to the Signory was formulated so as in part to exhibit this. When meeting with the Florentine ambassador in Rome, Soderini no doubt put forward the same claims as in his letter, claims which a jurist like Malegonnelli would know how to handle. Having him as ambassador in Rome thus provided Florence with an advantage, even if the Signory made no great effort to exploit it in this case. In the end the governor of the Val di Cecina and his officials were most likely compelled to bend the knee. Little more than four months after his last interviews with

[6] G. Capponi, *Storia della repubblica di Firenze*, 2 vols. (Firenze, 1875), I, 490; see also *Commissioni di Rinaldo degli Albizzi*, ed. C. Guasti (Firenze, 1867-1873), III, 184n.

[7] *SCMLC*, 25, f. 106v.

[8] *Négociations diplomatique de la France avec la Toscane*, ed. and introd. by A. Desjardins, docs. by G. Canestrini, 5 vols. (Paris, 1859), I, 639. Soderini's is one of the dominant names in the diplomatic correspondence of the period.

[9] This post must often have been exercised by proxy. W. von Hofmann, *Forschungen zur Geschichte der kurialen Behörden vom Schisma bis zur Reformation*, 2 vols. (Rome, 1914), II, 76.

Malegonnelli, the bishop received a letter of credence, designating him the new Florentine ambassador to Rome.[10]

We have seen that training in the law gave advantages to Church officials, that it was for good reasons an avenue to ecclesiastical preferment. And where a cleric in high office was without such training, we can be sure that a lawyer or two figured prominently among the assistants in his train. In a way, the recruitment of lawyers was the Church's answer to the strains produced by the coexistence of two different yet often overlapping jurisdictions. The state naturally reacted in much the same way, and in its relations with the Church frequently put the service of lawyers foremost.

The history of Florentine or any state's relations with the Church may be said to have two sides—the internal and external histories. The internal history regards the state's direct relations with ecclesiastical institutions and clerics: it may take in everything from conflicts with abbots and bishops to ecclesiastical elections and works of charity performed by the state, as in the giving of economic support to particular religious houses. The external history centers on Florentine relations with the papacy, the papacy both in itself and as intermediary in the state's dealings with the Florentine clergy.

Apart from the fact that the internal history would take me very far afield, I have elected to concentrate on the external history for three reasons: (a) because it does throw considerable light, after all, on internal problems; (b) because by fixing attention on the papacy, the center of ecclesiastical power, I can more easily and economically deal with the interplay between the two jurisdictions; and (c) because no historian will be able to treat satisfactorily the internal history of Florentine relations with the Church until the archives of the Archbishop of Florence are fully open for public consultation and catalogues of material there made readily available.

## 2. *Taxing the Clergy*

Were religious bodies, houses, and men in holy orders subject to the taxation of the laity? The question was much debated by lawyers and

[10] *SCMLC*, 25, f. 121r.

publicists in the later Middle Ages. A key argument held that as the state defended churches and priests, these were somehow bound to give the state material support. The argument was heard down to the fifteenth century and beyond.

In 1179 it was laid down with great firmness by the Third Lateran Council that ecclesiastical goods were immune to taxation by secular authorities. Never before enunciated with so much force, this ruling came as a rejoinder to the aggressive pretensions of the great Italian communes. The rejoinder was not altogether effective, for from the twelfth century on the Italian communes encroached ever increasingly on the alleged rights of churches and clergy, on their immunity from lay taxation; and often the communes had recourse to argument from public necessity, the public safety, or the public good.[11]

The Third Lateran Council admitted that in cases of evident public or common necessity, "ubi laicorum non suppetunt facultates," the laity might impose a temporary tax on the clergy, provided the bishop and clergy consented.[12] The canon was followed by a decision of the Fourth Lateran Council (1215), which ruled that the first step in all emergency taxation was the consent of the pope. Passing over into canon law, these decisions had more clarity in theory than in application. What of the delays and tergiversations of popes? How bad must an emergency be before the pope could be expected to give his approval? What if he consented and the bishops or clergy did not? Pope Boniface VIII (1294-1303) "was forced to accept the supremacy of France and England in this, that if the danger to the state was so imminent and urgent that the king must act at once, the clergy should submit without waiting for authorization."[13]

Rarely if ever was the Florentine Republic able to importune the papacy as much as did some kings of England and France. Generally speaking, it could not even demand as much as did Milan or Quattrocento Venice. Yet Florence was by no means averse to pressing its claims and

[11] On the importance and implications of such argument see especially Ch. X.

[12] L. Prosdocimi, *Il diritto ecclesiastico dello stato di Milano dall' inizio della signoria viscontea al periodo tridentino, sec. xiii-xvi* (Milano, 1941), pp. 97ff.

[13] G. Post, *Studies in Medieval Legal Thought: Public Law and the State, 1100-1322* (Princeton, 1964), p. 284.

a few times went to war with the papacy on this account. Foremost among such claims was that which derived from the Republic's need to tax the clergy in times of acute need, a need felt with developing urgency in the late fourteenth century, when the menace of Giangaleazzo Visconti and the city's growing involvement in peninsular politics resulted in public expenditure on such a vast scale that Florence was driven to seek additional sources of revenue. The treasury's grinding need was made more acute by the paying out of handsome interest rates to citizens with investments in the Monte.[14] In the course of the fifteenth century, hardly a pope who reigned for more than a lustrum escaped the Republic's urgent pleas for a license to tax the clergy. Despite canon law on this material, the Florentine Signory no longer bothered to procure the consent of the clergy —or the consent was given *pro forma*. In fact, the approval of the papacy sufficed, and once this was obtained, a tax commission was immediately set up and started in at once to levy or borrow monies on the strength of the papal license. It seems clear, therefore, that the focal point of negotiation for a license to tax the clergy was the point at which a Florentine ambassador confronted the pope and his counsellors. Though a great deal went on behind the scenes, here—at such audiences—is where art and knowledge were concentrated, where the Republic was on trial, and where the man who represented it must exhibit his talents as diplomat.

A fact that has never been observed before is that an extraordinary number of Florentine ambassadors to the papal curia were lawyers, a percentage far out of proportion to their numbers in Florence.[15] This was not fortuitous. The reasons can best be seen by our reviewing a few embassies put into the hands of lawyers. We shall see that high among their commissions was that of working to procure papal consent to tax the clergy.

[14] Some material on tax policy and on the Monte is to be found in G. Canestrini, *La scienza e l'arte di stato desunta dagli atti ufficiali della repubblica fiorentina e dei Medici* (Firenze, 1862); B. Barbadoro, *Le finanze della repubblica fiorentina, imposta diretta e debito pubblico fino all' istituzione del Monte* (Firenze, 1929); G. Brucker, *Florentine Politics and Society, 1343-1378* (Princeton, 1962); and L. Marks, "The Financial Oligarchy in Florence under Lorenzo," *Italian Renaissance Studies,* ed. E. F. Jacob (New York, 1960); M. Becker, "Economic Change and the Emerging Florentine State," *Studies in the Renaissance,* XIII (1966), 7-39, appeared as this book was going to press.

[15] My tallies suggest that it was approximately half. See p. 283.

Donato de' Cocchi-Donati (1409-1464) was born into a family of parvenus who rose to political prominence on the shirt-tails of the Medici. Rector of the Italian nation at the University of Bologna in 1437-1438, a dignity which only rich men could afford and which in a man like Donato denoted smart social ambitions, he took the doctorate in civil law at the end of his term as Rector and the year after was back in Florence, teaching at the University.[16] A member of the lawyers' guild since 1435, he gradually built up a law practice and, like others of his family, soon began to hold leading public offices. In time he was also entrusted with embassies. A major appointment of this sort came his way late in June 1451. He was sent by the Signory and the Ten on War as ambassador to Pope Nicholas V and arrived in Rome on July 2nd.[17] His chief tasks were two: to solicit papal support in the Republic's struggle against the territorial pretensions of Venice and the King of Naples, and to secure a license from Nicholas authorizing the city to levy a tax on the Florentine clergy. The tax was to involve one-fourth the annual income of the clergy and to be collected once only.

If we did not already know it from other sources, we would learn at once from Donato's letters to the Ten that Pope Nicholas was a formidable opponent in discussion. Holder of a doctorate in theology from the University of Bologna, this pope had read very widely in the field of humanistic studies and revealed some knowledge of both civil and canon law. But Donato was not a man to draw back in meekness or silence. Within six days of his arrival in Rome, he reported that the holy father "threw a sententious remark at me, saying that I had too much rhetoric."[18] Not until the end of July, however, did he get round to pleading for the pope's consent to a Florentine tax on the clergy. The mastery expected of Donato is brought out in a letter he wrote to the Ten on August 2nd.[19]

---

[16] *AGN*, 118, f. 68r; A. Sorbelli, ed., *Il 'Liber secretus,'* 2 vols. (Bologna, 1938-1942), II, 159-60. On the Cocchi-Donati see Martines, *Florentine Humanists,* pp. 71-75.

[17] *DBCR*, 22, ff. 37r, 39r; *SCMLC*, 13, ff. 21r-23r.

[18] *DBCR*, 22, f. 20r, "mi gitto uno motto, diciendo havevo troppa rethorica.

[19] *Ibid.*, f. 55r. One of his major pleas centered on the idea of the "just war," which Italian jurists had discussed and vindicated ever since the twelfth century. Such war, urged for the common welfare and involving a supreme necessity, allegedly justified emergency and special taxes. Cf. Post, *Studies,* pp. 436-40, and Kantorowicz, *The King's Two Bodies,* p. 236.

Referring to the desired tax, he reported that in his talks with Pope Nicholas he had demonstrated "that your request was licit by divine and human law and that it suited his sanctity to grant it because of the many good things that would follow." But Nicholas had rejoined that "your city abounds in wiser and more literary men than almost any other city known to him in Italy or beyond, that therefore it should be easy for you [the Ten] to realize that the request is not an honest one and that it would not be honorable for him to grant it. . . . Then he started drawing precepts from the Old Testament, moved on to the New Testament, adducing examples by which he concluded that your request is against *ius divinum*, against theological opinions, even against the [Roman] imperial laws, and that many princes had plied him with the same request but never had he wished to accede to it." The kings of Poland, Hungary, Aragon, the dukes of Brittany and Milan, the Emperor, a great French lord: all had been refused by him. "My reply to the first part," continued Donato, "was that what the pope had said and what I had said could both be true; that is, it was against divine law for the laity to impose a tax on the clergy without the license or consent of the supreme pontiff and in cases where wars were unleashed by ambition to dominate; but where such a tax was imposed by right of license and consent, as was requested by your lordships, not only was this not contrary to divine and human laws but rather, in accordance with these, his holiness should concede the license." The ambassador adduced still other reasons why the pope should give his consent: he argued that war had been imposed on Florence, stressed the great power of her adversaries (Venice and the Kingdom of Naples), the need to protect her own holy places, to preserve her liberty, and even other reasons "which I shall omit so as not to tire your lordships." Pope Nicholas, however, was adamant, and when Donato told him that he planned in his report to the Ten to say that the holy father would certainly reconsider the matter and perhaps eventually rescind his refusal, Nicholas immediately replied that under no circumstances should Donato say such a thing, that "rather would he give away a pound of his blood."[20]

[20] *DBCR*, 22, f. 55r. Donato tried to prove "che de iure divino et humano la domanda vostra era lecita et honesta et alla sua santità debita concederla pergli

For a time there was some hope that a peace could be arranged between the warring states, and Messer Donato stayed on in Rome for expected consultations (to be conducted under papal aegis) with the ambassadors of Naples, Milan, and Venice. But hopes were soon dashed; the Florentine need for additional revenue reasserted itself, and by the first week of December Donato was again working to persuade the pope to vouchsafe the requested tax. A letter of January 7-8, 1452, shows him arguing that it was customary for popes to license clerical taxation "in times even of lesser need," that the authority to tax the clergy "had been usurped by many lords and signories, especially the Venetians, and tolerated by his holiness." Not only did he remind Pope Nicholas of the fact that one-third of all immovable property in Florentine territory belonged to the Church, but also of "the fraud worked with lay properties [by falsely registering them] under the name of ecclesiastics."[21]

The collection of Donato's letters to the Ten and the Signory is very incomplete, and we are somewhat in the dark about the outcome of his negotiations.[22] But the letter of January 7-8th indicates that his manner

infiniti beni n'anno a resultare. . . . [Nicholas replied:] la vostra ciptà essere copiosa di savi et litterati huomini quanto alcun altra conosca in Italia o fuori d'Italia e per questo doversi facilmente intendere la domanda non havere in se honestà ne allui essere honore concederla et dovere rimanere bene patienti del negharla. Di poi entrò dando principio dal testamento vechio, descendendo al testamento nuovo, alleghando alcuni exempli per li quali concludeva quello si domandava essere contra *ius divinum* et finalmente secondo le oppinioni teolosice (sic) et etiamdio essere contra le leggi imperiali, et che da molti principi poi è in pontificatu gli'è suto domandato questo medesimo et mai l'a voluto concedere. . . . [Donato agreed it was] contra ragione divina el porre e' secolari a cherici senza licentia o consenso del sommo pontefice et in casi di guerra si facessino per ambitione di dominare, ma imponendosi con licentia et consentimento come si domandava per la vostra signoria non tanto non essere con[tra] ragione divina et humana ma secondo quelle dovere la sua santità prestare licentia . . . più volentieri darebbe una libbra di suo sangue."

[21] *DBCR*, 22, f. 15r, "quella [the authority to tax] essersi usurpata da molti signori e signorie et spetialmente da Vinitiani, et dalla sua santità tolerata, allegando ancora . . . la fraude si fa de' beni seculari sotto nome delli ecclesiastici, et che el terzo de' beni immobili del vostro territorio e oggidì de' cherici." On the fraud in question see pp. 173-77.

[22] There is a gap in the *Consulte e Pratiche* from 10 June 1451 to 14 Feb. 1453. Worse still, there is nothing on the matter in *DBCMLC*, 4 (26 June 1451–14 May 1454); and *SCMC-I*, 37, 38 skip from Oct. 1448 to Dec. 1452. *Prov.*, 143 (21 March 1452–24 March 1453), contains a legislative act of 5 April 1452 authorizing an

with the supreme pontiff had become franker and more insistent, which suggests that for some reason Florence now enjoyed a stronger position. Indeed, the same letter also informed the government that the pope had let it be understood that he might acquiesce if Florence finally imposed the tax without the papal license, for "then it could not be said that it was done because of its having been consented to."[23]

There is no need to make a labored commentary on Donato's mission. It is evident that the job he was doing in Rome was best done by a lawyer with "troppa rethorica." Although trained in theology, Nicholas was determined to raise legal barriers against the requested tax license: he held that the request itself was contrary to both civil and canon law. Yet he was certainly informed about the decisions of the Third and Fourth Lateran Councils and about the debates which had gone on at the time of the famous controversy between Philip the Fair and Pope Boniface VIII. He also knew that ever since that time popes had granted licenses to tax the clergy. In this connection, he himself cited his own predecessor, Eugene IV, who authorized the King of Aragon to levy a tax on the clergy of 150,000 gold florins. And still Nicholas held out. If he was in good faith, if he truly believed that the Florentine request was illegal under all lights, then it was exceedingly important for Florence to be represented by an ambassador—a lawyer—who would know how to meet the objections raised, even if he did not plunge fully into technical difficulties and details. But if the pope was merely stalling for time, or if, for whatever reason, he simply did not wish to grant the requested license, then it was still very important that the Republic's ambassador to Rome be a lawyer. For he would have to deal with the pope in audiences which usually included cardinals and other dignitaries of the Church, some of whom were well versed in law. It was before such men that Florence either did or did not acquit herself with honor.

---

official to draw up the plan for a new tax distribution, a plan to list in the appropriate records all laymen as well as clergy. But subsequent legislation does not reveal the outcome of this.

[23] *DBCR*, 22, f. 15r, "così non si potrà dire si sia facto per averlo consentito." A letter from the Signory to the pope, dated 8 or 9 Dec. 1451, seems to have made a great impression on Nicholas, the cardinals, and other curialists. Referred to in *DBCR*, 22, f. 100r.

The terms of exchange between pope and ambassador were determined by the former, who gave the interviews a legal twist by resting his refusal on canonical objections. Possibly Nicholas really convinced himself that the Florentine request was dishonest and illegal, in which case the functions of the ambassador-lawyer took on a critical importance. It would have been easier for the holy father to argue that the Republic's fiscal need was not sufficiently extreme, or that in any case Florentine citizens were not sincerely taxing themselves to the utmost. This type of objection would have offered him more room for ambiguity and hence a greater advantage. The question arises, was it known in Florence that the pope would resort to argument from law? And was this why a lawyer was sent to Rome? The government must have been informed about the pope's state of mind by Giovannozzo Pitti, who preceded Donato as Florentine ambassador to Rome and was still there when the lawyer arrived on July 2nd.[24]

During the period of his Roman embassy (nearly seven months), Donato was taken up with a variety of other official commissions. Some of these were commissions also best taken care of by an emissary trained in law—those, for example, involving questions of commercial reprisal, which will be discussed later in this chapter, in the part on litigation handled by papal tribunals.

Florence's fiscal pains continued. The need to tax the clergy recurred. Wars and the paying out of interest by the state swelled the public debt.[25] The last years of the fifteenth century were particularly hard, and the Florentine exchequer was impossibly strained. In 1498 and 1499, over a period of twenty months, agents of the Republic worked to procure a tax license from one of the most wily of Renaissance popes, Alexander VI, who had himself studied law at Bologna. Three lawyers in succession, all *doctores in utroque iure* and professors of law, were sent to Rome to deal with him. Seasoned statesmen, they went as full-fledged ambassadors: Domenico Bonsi, Francesco Gualterotti, and Antonio Malegonnelli. Of the different commissions assigned to them, let us see what they did with the most important, which was also the most protracted.

[24] *DBCR*, 22, f. 37r.
[25] Cf. L. Marks, "La crisi finanziaria a Firenze dal 1494 al 1502," *ASI*, cxii, 1 (1954).

Domenico Bonsi's initial set of instructions, dated January 9, 1497 (1498 modern), ordered him to try to win support for the Florentine reconquest of Pisa and to urge Pope Alexander to authorize Florence to tax her clergy.[26] To be collected once yearly, the tax was to be a *decima* (a tenth) of the income from all ecclesiastical properties located in Florentine territory, including the properties of "ecclesiastical persons." Hence the tax was aimed at individuals as well as corporate bodies. In coaching their ambassador, the priors of the Signory made the following observation: since all Florentines pay "for the universal defense and preservation of all . . . possessions and goods [in Florentine territory], it seems only just that all goods should contribute proportionately and *pro rata parte* to the payment of taxes." The instructions also point out that Bonsi was especially informed about the subject in question, having consulted legislation concerning it from as far back as 1407 and 1428. Provided with copies of this legislation, he was to take it with him to Rome.[27] Most probably it had been picked out and collected with the help of leading chancellery officials, but the job of making proper use of it in Rome would be Bonsi's. An expert on constitutional questions,[28] he was expected, in his interviews with the pope, to cite the legislation—old laws touching on the status of ecclesiastical property in Florence.

Bonsi successfully executed some of his commissions, but failed utterly to move Pope Alexander on the matter of the tax license. There was good reason for the failure. Florentine relations with the papacy were especially strained during the period from January to April 1498 and even before. Savonarola was still at large in Florence, went around unmolested by the civil authorities, and had even started preaching again, despite the facts that he had been under a censure of excommunication since June 1497 and that the pope had specifically forbidden him to preach. The head of Latin Christendom was in no mood to invest the Republic with the authority to levy a tax on the clergy. On the contrary,

[26] *SCMLC*, 23, ff. 14v-16r.

[27] *Ibid.*, f. 16r, "Et perchè voi siate di questa materia benissimo informato et havete visto certe provisioni factesi per il comune infino nello anno 1407 et nel 1428, di che arete copia apresso di voi."

[28] See his plan for a *consiglio maggiore*, in *Strozz.*, 2a ser., 95, folder 19, ff. 233r-236v.

in March he was on the point of putting the whole of Florence under a general interdict which would have ruined many a Florentine merchant with investments and merchandise abroad.[29] But no sooner had Savonarola been arrested on order of the Signory and tortured than Guidantonio Vespucci—statesman, lawyer, and enemy of the friar—began (April 14) urging the government to press the pope for a *decima* in perpetuity, or at least for twenty-five years, "or for as long as possible." Always the lawyer, Vespucci went on to recommend that "the arrangements [with the pope] be made clear, so that if he should die we would not stand to lose the [negotiated] money."[30] The government was not to let this advice go unheeded.

With the judicial murder of Savonarola, there was a change in the tenor of Florentine politics, and Domenico Bonsi, once associated with the wrought-up friar (though latterly an enemy), was withdrawn from Rome in May. As in modern diplomacy, so in fifteenth-century Florence statecraft already included the practice of changing ambassadors not only with changes of government but also with shifts in policy. The new ambassador, Francesco Gualterotti, was assigned the same objectives as Bonsi: to win active support for the Florentine reconquest of Pisa, to turn papal policy against Venice, and to procure the pope's consent to levy a yearly *decima* on the clergy.[31]

Gualterotti's embassy lasted a year. He was more successful than Bonsi, but the wily pope could not be expected to change his stand immediately. The ambassador, on arriving in Rome, did not rush into his commission regarding the tax license. Instead, he gradually set forth the view that Florence desired a small five-year tax on the clergy in order to help succor the University (the Studio), which had been moved from Pisa to Prato and was having financial difficulties. In October, to explain the protracted negotiations, he informed the Signory that such was the way

---

[29] Cf. esp. Giuliano Gondi's harangue in the executive consultations of 14 March 1498, C. Lupi, "Nuovi documenti intorno a fra Girolamo Savonarola," *ASI*, iii, iii (1866), 44. This part of Bonsi's mission is treated in P. Vincenzo Marchese, "Lettere inedite di fra Girolamo Savonarola e documenti concernenti lo stesso," *ASI*, viii (1850), 75-203.

[30] *CP*, 64, f. 72v.

[31] *SCMLC*, 23, ff. 19r-20r, instructions dated 12 May 1498.

things were done in Rome and that one had to adapt, but that he was already in the process of procuring the license for the tax in support of the University. By November 9th this license had been granted and the fees connected with it paid for by a Florentine firm in Rome. Meanwhile, he had finally started pressing for the *decima*. He had assured men at the curia that if the Signory was not accorded the requested license, "they [the *Signori*] will always be forgiven *apud deum et homines*, imposing it [the *decima*] by virtue of their own authority, as they will do anyway."[32] This was the line to be followed by the lawyer thereafter, especially when Pope Alexander went back on earlier promises and began to insist that he would grant the license only if there was something in such a transaction for his own coffers too. Again and again Gualterotti reminded the holy father that "where the apostolic license is missing, they [the rulers of Florence] will use their own authority in the face of such grave dangers." To one of the pope's aides, Paolo Orsini, he continually insisted that the priors of the Signory did not need a license to meet their current necessities.[33] Like any other well-informed lawyer of his time, he knew that this proposition had the support of a certain body of European legal theory. Furthermore, states like Venice and Milan offered a good deal of precedent in the matter. But the Signory could not take instruction from them nor proceed according to Gualterotti's representations. The Republic was too weak, the pope too strong. Florence was forced to negotiate. In the end, however, the law was to play its part, for the final agreement would be circumscribed, as we shall see, by some carefully enunciated legal norms.

Before the end of the previous November (1498), Francesco Gualterotti had already started reminding the Signory to begin casting round for the man who would replace him in Rome. By March he was extremely eager to repatriate. But he had to stay on in Rome until June because the new ambassador, Antonio Malegonnelli, did not leave Florence until after the middle of May. The two overlapped in Rome for a month or so,

---

[32] *SCRO*, 10, ff. 258r, 275r, "saranno sempre excusate apud deum et homines, ponendo la autoritate propria come in ogni modo faranno."

[33] *Ibid.*, f. 38r, "Io sono sempre stato in su lo honorevole con dire alle excelse signorie vostre non è necessario licentia alcuna in queste vostre necessità."

giving Gualterotti a chance to brief his successor and complete a round of meetings.[34]

In the year and a half that Florence had been trying to obtain the tax license, Gualterotti had managed to secure a definite promise, even if the pope later disclaimed the particular arrangement to which he had committed himself. But the probable outcome was already clear: if a bargain could be struck, the license would be granted. To strike a bargain was the task of the new ambassador, who was instructed to yield as little as possible. A leading light of the law faculty of the Studio Pisano, Antonio Malegonnelli was to spend nearly thirteen months in Rome. He was holder of the ordinary chair (afternoons) in civil law, and his professorial salary was second only to that of the renowned Filippo Decio, *ordinario* (mornings) in canon law.[35]

In a letter of July 3rd to the Signory, Malegonnelli confirmed the fact that his predecessor had at one point obtained papal consent for the *decima*, that the letter of authorization had even been drafted, but that the pope had then suddenly changed his mind, deciding that any such consent on his part would have to be kept secret. The reason for the desired secrecy was "purely so that the priests won't cry out."[36] Deeming this a "frivolous" reason, the Signory's suspicions were aroused and Malegonnelli was ordered to resist any proposals concerning a secret license or secret papal brief. This phase of the negotiations was handled for the pope by one of his aides, the Cardinal of Capua. He informed the ambassador that the holy father was ready to grant four levies of a tenth for a period of four years. Each year one of the four would be made public by a papal

---

[34] Gualterotti did not in fact leave Rome until 3 July. *SCRO*, 12, f. 198r; *SCMLC*, 23, f. 41v.

[35] Decio earned 650, Malegonnelli 500 florins annually. *UDS*, 6, f. 169r. On his return to Florence more than a year later, Malegonnelli was paid his full professor's stipend for the year he had spent in Rome. *UDS*, 6, f. 62v, "intellecta dispositione iuris comunis [the Studio officials] declaraverunt Dominum Antonium de Malegonellis eo tempore quo stetit orator Rome habere debuisse . . . salarium decti temporis, licet non legisset." Departing from medieval practice, the Studio Pisano offered ordinary lectures both mornings and afternoons.

[36] *SCRO*, 12, ff. 198r, 147v, "solamente perchè e preti non gridino." *SCMLC*, 25, f. 11r, on Signory's reaction. The pope's game was clear. There was already a good deal of feeling against him. He would provoke even more by openly consenting to a tax license which would be very unpopular with the clergy.

brief, but the comprehensive license itself was to be put into the hands of a third party and kept a closely guarded secret. This proposal was rejected by Malegonnelli, who argued that his government would be unable to raise the money for its pressing needs on the basis of a secret license because the merchants who might advance (i.e., lend) the necessary cash would want to see the license. How therefore could it be kept secret? In the letter informing the Signory of his interview with the cardinal, the ambassador finally added, "If this way of keeping the license secret should appeal to your lordships, then consult some of the distinguished doctors [of law] there on the form. See how it is that in their judgment the grant of the said secret brief would have the most security. And I too *ex officio* will think about it . . . but it is also most advisable to have their opinion because four eyes see more than two."[37]

For several weeks the technicalities connected with a secret license were to hold the focus of negotiation. The pope was represented by Cardinal Farnese and Paolo Orsini, both of whom—interestingly enough—intervened with their master in favor of the Republic (and they would have their reward for this in hard cash). A turn in the course of the negotiations was announced by Malegonnelli on August 2nd. Orsini reported that the pope was disposed to concede four levies (each a tenth), two to be openly announced in a public brief, the grant of the other two to be contained in a secret brief and put into the hands of a Florentine merchant. Furthermore, the trustee of the secret brief would be authorized to show it to any man who advanced money to the government. Having informed the Signory of this, Malegonnelli advised, "I would think that if the pope allows the secret brief to be held by your merchants, and if it could be shown by them to those who lent [money] and also be presented to [a group of] judges, it might not be a bad idea to accept the proposal. For the said judges could . . . publish the brief when it became necessary." Then once again he urged the Signory to consult some lawyers on the matter, to study the procedure normally followed by tax commis-

---

[37] *SCRO*, 12, f. 104v, "Et piacendo ad v. ex. S. questo modo del tenere el breve secreto, faccino pigliare forma costì da qualchuno di quelli egregii doctori come iudicassino la concessione del detto breve segreto essere più sicura. Et io ancora ex officio ci penserò, ma a ogni modo et per ogni rispetto è buono et aproposito il parere loro, perchè più veggono 4 occhi che 2." See also f. 33v.

sioners when levying a tax on the clergy, and to see "if we can make so many secret acts that there would be the greatest security in the face of every danger that might arise."[38]

In treating with the pope's aides, Malegonnelli strained to secure an agreement which would provide Florentine interests with foolproof legal protection. It was not merely that popes die too, that a secret papal brief might be disavowed, but also that a truly secret arrangement inspired little confidence, at all events with the state's prospective creditors. Thus, whereas the holder of the secret brief was originally to be a cardinal, it was finally decided that he should be a Florentine merchant. In the right to exhibit the secret brief, moreover, Malegonnelli got a concession which would satisfy not only prospective creditors but also cut Florentine fears of a possible disavowal on the pope's part or of his untimely death. The best safeguard was in the device of showing the secret brief to a group of preselected judges, who could then publish it by sudden request of the Florentine government.

Before the middle of August 1499 the government saw that the most it could hope for was the proposal last outlined by Malegonnelli. There would be four levies and two papal briefs, one public, the other secret. The depositary of the secret brief was to be Paolo Rucellai, who would be authorized to present the brief to a group of judges and to show it to prospective government creditors.[39] On August 17th the ambassador thought he would be able to send the briefs to Florence in two or three days, but his own legal acumen held things up. For little more than a week later we learn that he had delayed the briefs in protest to a certain clause.[40] The Apostolic Datary had included a tax immunity exempting the friars of the Order of Hospitallers of St. John of Jerusalem (i.e., the Knights of Rhodes) and Malegonnelli demanded that the clause be expunged.

[38] *Ibid.*, f. 370r-v, "crederrei quando il papa concedessi che il breve secreto stessi in mano de' vostri mercatanti et quella la potessino monstrare a chi prestassi et etiam si potessi presentare a iudici, forse non sarebbe male ad acceptarlo, perchè detti iudici potrebbono . . . publicarla poi quando bisognassi. Intendino v. ex. S. il parare di cotesti egregii doctori et lo stilo che soglono tenere e commissari et vedrassi se possiamo fare tanti acti secreti che ne resulti pienissima securità di ogni pericolo potessi nascere."

[39] *Ibid.*, ff. 329v, 346v.     [40] *Ibid.*, f. 293r.

He was told that his predecessor, Francesco Gualterotti, had consented to the clause, that it appeared in the retracted brief and thus bound the Republic. The point was well made and reflected no honor on Gualterotti's legal talents. There were both material and formal grounds for the claim put forth by the curia. I emphasize this incident because it underlines the critical role of lawyers in such negotiations. If even Gualterotti had been remiss, what might have happened had he not been a lawyer? The best solution for Florence was the one recommended by Malegonnelli. He held that if there was no way to avoid granting the exemption, it should be conferred "by a separate [papal] brief year by year, according as the needs of the Order of Rhodes arise."[41] The aim of this proposal becomes perfectly clear the moment we realize that other clerics and prelates would also try to claim tax immunities.[42] Furthermore, there was the possibility that in a year or two the pope might not wish to confer a tax exemption on the Hospitallers. Or again, Florence might wish to contest such an exemption in law. But if the exemption was written directly into the licensing briefs, there would be no possibility of evading or contesting it. Worse still, it would encourage other clerical orders or regional clergy to sue for tax exemptions. At length, the resouceful ambassador managed to secure a promise from the pope that he would grant no exemptions of any kind in the licenses proper.[43]

Alexander VI and his counsellors took their own legal precautions. No informed contemporary would have failed to predict this. It was agreed that papal authorization for the first and second tenths would be made public at once; the license for the third and fourth, cast in the form of a secret papal brief, was to be published only at the end of two years or on the death of the pope. All who saw the secret brief must take an oath, swearing not to make their knowledge public "on pain of excommunication *lata sententia*."[44] This included the judges or arbiters who were to be shown the brief, as well as any merchants and bankers who

[41] *Ibid.*

[42] E.g., in November the Bishop of Cortona advanced just such a claim on behalf of his clergy, *SCRO*, 13, f. 160r-v. The Archbishop of Florence was also determined to procure an exemption, *SCMLC*, 25, f. 46r.

[43] *SCRO*, 12, f. 294r.

[44] *Ibid.*, f. 291r, i.e., subject to automatic excommunication.

lent money to the Republic on the strength of the papal authorization. None who incurred censure in this matter could receive absolution save from the supreme pontiff or his "pardoners." Paolo Rucellai, trustee of the secret brief, was threatened with the harshest penalties. He bound himself as follows: "I, Paolo Rucellai, promise his holiness to hold the said brief and to observe the designated conditions, subject to a penalty of 5,000 gold ducats, payable *de iure* to the apostolic camera and subject also to the penalty of excommunication *lata sententia*."[45]

All final arrangements had been made and the two briefs had been drafted by September 3rd, when the ambassador wrote to the Signory to say that the leading agents in the transaction had already been paid off by Florentine merchants in Rome. The pope received 3,000 cameral ducats of gold, Paolo Orsini 3,000 ducats *di carlini*, and Cardinal Farnese (later Pope Paul III) 1,000 ducats *di carlini*.[46]

No Florentine ambassador to the papal curia was ever given one commission alone. Some of Malegonnelli's other jobs required legal skills, a few did not. Of those that did, one was directly occasioned by the recently authorized levies. He wrote to the Signory about it on November 23rd: "The Bishop of Cortona has given me to understand that his clerics have appealed against the *decima*, alleging that this tax comes under the privilege of immunity granted to that city by your lordships. It would be well to have the privilege looked into from a legal standpoint by some distinguished doctors [i.e., Florentine lawyers]. Then send their opinions to me along with a copy of the immunity privilege, in order that we may see how we should guide ourselves and so that they [the Cortonese clergy] will not set a bad example if they are wrong."[47] Knowing enough to expect little satisfaction from Florence, the Bishop of Cortona had immediately decided to file the appeal on behalf of his clergy in Rome. The Signory's reply to Malegonnelli was as follows: "The reasons adduced for an exemption by the clergy of Cortona are based chiefly on a pro-

---

[45] *Ibid.*

[46] *SCRO*, 12, f. 532r-v. Orsini at one point pretended that this was payment for losses he had suffered in Florence in 1494. *SCRO*, 10, f. 38r.

[47] *SCRO*, 13, f. 160r-v, pencil, "mi ha facto intendere che il clero suo ha facto appellatione dalla exactione della decima. . . . Sarà bene farla vedere di ragione da cotesti egregii doctori et mandarmi le loro opinioni et la copia della exemptione," etc.

vision enacted a few years ago. We enclose a copy so that you can use it as you see fit. Meanwhile, if the claim is pressed, we shall see here about getting legal counsel on it and give you a more detailed response later on. Speak to the bishop in our name. Make him see how much this thing distresses us because of the example it will hold up for others, and say that we urge him to persuade his clergy to be content with that which has contented the [supreme] pontiff; for he has imposed the levy, not us. This is why there is no need to adduce argument against any exemption or privilege granted to them by us . . . we cannot cancel things from the resolutions of the pope."[48]

The evasiveness of the Signory was transparent. They were not providing their ambassador with a defense which would keep the appeal from coming before the auditors of the Rota or Cameral court. For the time being they clearly counted on him to handle the matter himself, if need be by bringing all his legal skills to bear. But Malegonnelli was in a difficult position. Better informed than they, he expected a lawsuit and had reacted by setting out at once to collect data—the provision and the requested legal opinions—in support of the Republic's interests. Not that he could act as counsel for the defense in a papal court of law—this would have to be done by a consistorial advocate; but he could call for the essential data, study the *consilia legalia* sent to him from Florence, and give advice to the Republic's advocate. Malegonnelli commanded the particulars connected with one side of the Florentine case; the consistorial advocate would be thoroughly informed about procedure and current prejudice in the Rotal and Cameral courts.

The chances are that Florence was forced to submit to a lawsuit.

During an earlier period, at the time of the Avignonese Papacy (1309-1377) and the Great Schism (1378-1417), which saw the nadir of papal power in Italy, Florence had been able on a few occasions to tax her clergy without having previously secured papal consent.[49] But in the

---

[48] *SCMLC*, 25, f. 58v, pencil, "Le ragioni che adlega il clero di Corthona per la sua exemptione sua sono principalmente fondate in su una provisione facta pochi anni sono," etc.

[49] Brucker, *Florentine Politics and Society*, pp. 158-59, 196, 304, 317. Milan and the Visconti managed this much more successfully, L. Prosdocimi, *Il diritto ecclesiastico*, pp. 112-13.

course of the fifteenth century, as Florentine fiscal needs continually
grew, papal administration was consolidated and the authority of the
pope regained some of its force of old, until it would have been suicidal
for the Republic to insist on taxing the Florentine clergy at will. The
papacy had become too strong for this well before the middle of the
century. With a general interdict and special briefs sent to the right places,
popes could hound Florentine merchants and bankers abroad. This is
why in the foregoing pages we have considered the later period of this
study, when Florence went through one of its most acute fiscal crises.
During the years 1498 to 1501, Florentine ambassadors in Rome were all
men bred to the law: Domenico Bonsi, Francesco Gualterotti, Antonio
Malegonnelli, Bishop Soderini, and Francesco Pepi. Never had Florence
trained such a concentration of legal experience on the papal curia.

Florence very seldom acted unilaterally in levying a tax on the clergy
and did so only at the most critical moments. In September 1511, Pope
Julius II had put Florence under an interdict because the government was
giving support to the schismatic *conciliabolo* of Pisa. Later on that autumn,
driven by extreme military need, the Signory levied an "illegal" tax on
the clergy.[50] Julius thereupon increased his pressure. But using a mixture
of intimidation and indulgence, he refrained from striking at Florentine
merchants abroad. By December the discontent in Florence was so pronounced that the Signory and its counsellors prepared to dispatch an
ambassador to Rome to sue for a settlement. They selected Antonio
Strozzi (1455-1523), an outstanding lawyer and professor of jurisprudence. The tax on the clergy and two other matters constituted the main
items of controversy.[51] Julius demanded that the Florentines "promise via
public instrument not to collect the levy imposed on the clergy" and to
affirm publicly that they had no power to impose such levies.[52] Arriving
in Rome, Strozzi managed to tone down the demands of the fiery pope,
who refused however to remove the interdict until the "illegal" tax was
expunged from the public record (it had been approved by an act of

[50] Ammirato, *Istorie fiorentine*, ed. L. Scarabelli, 7 vols. (Torino, 1853), VI, 276-77.
[51] The Florentine appeal to the Pisan conciliabulum against the pope's interdict
and the *form* of the Republic's request for a pardon (*vènia*) were the other matters.
See Strozzi's initial set of instructions (23 Dec. 1511), SCMLC, 23, ff. 88v-90r.
[52] CP, 70, ff. 17r-18r, pencil (15 Dec. 1511), for a discussion of these demands.

the Grand Council). The ambassador's letter announcing this was read out to a meeting of the Signory and its advisors on January 12th. In great emergencies, especially when in conflict with the papacy, Florentines often turned to their lawyers for advice and leadership. On January 13th three of the four men who reported for the four quarters of the city were lawyers: Matteo Niccolini, Niccolò Altoviti, and Giovanni Cerretani.[53] Opinion was divided between the men who were ready to yield and those, the tougher ones, who urged that it was enough to suspend the collection of the tax on the clergy. Referring to the presence of papal troops in the Romagna and observing that the populace hungered for the Sacrament of the Mass, Niccolini (spokesman for the Santa Croce quarter) recommended that they suspend collection of the monies but that they not seek repeal of the levy in the Grand Council because this would widen differences in the city and delay things unduly. Niccolini's proposal was finally adopted, but the interdict was not lifted until late March, when Julius was convinced by Strozzi that repeal of the tax provision would have entailed pointless legislative delays. The pope had been on the verge of denouncing all Florentines as "heretics" and encouraging the seizure of their goods abroad, "wherever these were found, whether in Rome, Naples, England, or any other place."[54]

Between 1527 and 1530, the moribund Republic tried several times to put an unlicensed tax on the clergy, with some success but considerable papal resistance.[55] The most critical time came late in 1529 and lasted until the summer of 1530, a period during which once again some five or six lawyers moved into the forefront of debate in the supreme political councils.[56] In January there was a move afoot to confiscate one-third of all ecclesiastical properties in order to raise funds for the Republic's heroic resistance to the imperial blockade of the city. Executive consultations on the matter were especially precise in late April, just before a law authorizing the confiscation was finally enacted. Once again a lawyer,

---

[53] *Ibid.*, ff. 22v-23r, pencil.

[54] *Ibid.*, f. 36r, pencil; *SCRO*, 33, f. 9r (27 Feb. 1512), a letter to the Signory from the "università et collegio de mercanti fiorentini" in Rome.

[55] C. Roth, *The Last Florentine Republic* (London, 1925), pp. 87, 122-23, 141-42.

[56] *CP*, 72, 73, *passim*, above all Marco degli Asini, Alessandro Malegonnelli, Piero Filicaia, Lorenzo di Giovanni Ridolfi, Francesco Nelli, and Bono Boni. On these lawyers see the Appendix.

Francesco Nelli, was able to speak for the ruling group and to present its aims in the trappings of legality. Speaking for the S. Giovanni quarter, the lawyer said, "seeing that the city finds itself in so much danger that things could not be worse, they [the representatives of S. Giovanni] believe that all the canons allow that these [ecclesiastical properties] can be alienated." He therewith asked that the tax commissioners be given the power to raise the needed funds—given it in the face of any who might deny that these officials had such a right. For "it has been said that it would not be improper for things which cannot be administered ordinarily to be administered extraordinarily."[57] A dire public emergency legally vindicated the seizure of Church properties: extraordinary measures attained full sanction by right of a *force majeure*.

Throughout the period from the middle of the fifteenth century to 1530 Florentine statecraft made an optimum use of lawyers when it came to getting money out of the Church.

## 3. *Rotal and Cameral Lawsuits*

Technical subjects occasionally appear more formidable than in fact they are. Perhaps this is what has tended to keep the political historian away from the papal courts and their political consequences.[58] One result of this shyness is that a whole sector of Renaissance diplomacy has been absolutely neglected. For in the fifteenth and sixteenth centuries, much of the work done by ambassadors in Rome, above all by resident ambassadors, was connected with judicial business pending before the two highest of all Church courts—the Rota Romana and the Cameral court (or court of the Auditor of the Apostolic Camera). The efforts in 1527 of William Knight, the English ambassador to Rome, to secure an annulment of marriage for King Henry VIII concerned only the most celebrated of many thousands of cases heard in Rome during the Renaissance.

With the papal bull *Ratio iuris* (1326) John XXII gave order and system to the Rota. The Cameral court, dating from the thirteenth century,

---

[57] *CP*, 73, f. 38r, "pensano che tutti e canoni promettono che si possino alienare . . . non sarà inconveniente che le cose che non si possono governare ordinariamente si governassino extraordinariamente." Roth, *op.cit.*, pp. 268-70, discusses the beginnings of this move to seize Church property.

[58] For scholarly work on these courts see the sources for this chapter.

seems to have had a more gradual development. During the middle decades of the fifteenth century, following the reconsolidation of papal
power, these courts became very vigorous and retained an immense importance down to the seventeenth century. They were appellate courts
and courts of first instance, with competence in ecclesiastical as well as
temporal proceedings. The jurisdiction of the Cameral court extended to
all causes involving the papal treasury, prelates and personnel attached
to the curia, crime in the papal states and some litigation originating
there. While the lines of jurisdiction between the Rotal and Cameral
courts are in some instances far from clear, the Rota more often heard and
determined cases in appeal. When two litigants were willing, they could
turn to the Rota for justice. Manifest usury and forgery also provided
material for Rotal jurisdiction. Canon law admitted the right of laymen
to appeal—*in defectu iustitiae saecularis*—to an ecclesiastical tribunal,
which in practice often turned out to be the Roman Rota or the Cameral
court. Judging by the nature of Florentine lawsuits which were heard
in Rome, I believe that the last of these, appeal against the miscarriage
of temporal justice, provided the basis for the type of case most often
moved from Florence to Rome.[59]

Once the Rota or the Auditor of the Apostolic Camera decided a case,
what means were there to compel the observance of justice in Florence
or for that matter anywhere else in Italy? Two chiefly: ecclesiastical censures against persons or places, and the concession of commercial reprisals against compatriots of the defendant in the lawsuit.

Florentine material bearing on litigation at Rome (correspondence
mainly) is especially rich for the period around 1500, the decades before
and after: reason enough for us to put the focus of things there. We shall
see that so many civil cases of temporal stamp were moved from Florence
to Rome that at one point the Signory became gravely distressed. The
vigor of popes like Alexander VI and Julius II and the prestige of the
papal courts were such as to make us assume that the same thing, the

---

[59] See, e.g., *SCRO*, 27 (years 1504-1505), 31 (1508-1509), *passim*, for the types of
cases which the Signory brought to the attention of Florentine ambassadors in
Rome. I dislike the use of the convention *passim*, but in this case, as in others where
I use it, there is such an abundance of well-distributed evidence that *passim* is a
precise reference.

transfer of lawsuits to Rome, was going on almost everywhere else in Italy. Bernabò and Giangaleazzo Visconti had put up strong resistance to the invasive activity of the Rotal and Cameral courts as early as the later fourteenth century, but 100 years later the flow of lawsuits out of Milan had increased.[60]

The Florentine Republic was much concerned about the interests abroad of its individual citizens. High among these interests were those which involved litigious dispute in Rome. Of lawsuits pending in the Rotal and Cameral courts toward the end of the fifteenth century, there were sometimes as many as twenty which critically implicated citizens or subjects of Florence. To look into these proceedings, or rather to work for decisions which favored their countrymen, was one of the tasks of Florentine ambassadors to the papal curia. As I have already noted, a remarkable number of these ambassadors were trained lawyers. They were uniquely qualified to keep a sharp eye on the litigious interests of fellow Florentines. Let us watch a few such ambassadors at work.

Francesco di Chirico Pepi (1451-1513) was born into an old ruling family of modest rank in the oligarchy. But he was well connected: his mother was a Salviati and he married a Pitti. After taking a double doctorate in civil and canon law at the University of Pisa (1478), he went into university teaching and then plunged whole-heartedly into public life. He was an ambitious, determined man who took strong political stands. During most of the 1480s and 1490s, he taught civil law first at Pisa and then at Prato, and by 1499 had a salary second only to Filippo Decio's.[61] From about the middle 1490s he began to appear and reappear in leading government offices, was Gonfalonier of Justice, and conducted a number of exceedingly important embassies to Rome, Milan, Venice, France, and elsewhere. All told, he was one of the city's eminent statesmen of the period 1494 to 1512.

From late February to the middle of December 1501, Francesco served as Florentine ambassador to the papal curia. He was forced to spend much of his time consulting Rotal auditors and Cameral clerks about cases in-

---

[60] Prosdocimi, *Il diritto ecclesiastico*, pp. 302-305.

[61] *AGN*, 241, ff. 3r-4v. *UDS*, 6, f. 169r. Pepi and Malegonnelli drew identical salaries. See n. 35 above.

volving Florentines, and he had often to meet with the plaintiffs. Some-times the plaintiffs were Florentines, more often not. On June 19th, after reporting to the Signory on the fortunes of a claim made by the Cardinal of Siena against the properties of Lorenzo Tornabuoni, the ambassador tartly observed, "With all due reverence, I remind your lordships that it would be better to assign these private affairs to a private agent, so that anyone not satisfied would be compelled to complain against a pri-vate person and not against a public secretary. For it happens on occasion that such a mixture [of functions] results in harm for the city or obstructs its good."[62] There was a clean grasp here of the difference between the public and private interest. The fact is, however, that proceedings in the papal courts very often started by directly implicating the public interest, as when Alfonsina Orsini nei Medici sued the Florentine state for her dowry, or when Florentine subjects were charged with piracy on the high seas, or when the members of a Florentine magistracy were sued for decisions they had taken in office. Furthermore, although many Roman lawsuits began as private affairs, they frequently spilled over into the public domain, as when in consequence of a particular case one or more churches in the city were put under an interdict, or when reprisals were granted which led to the seizure of Florentine goods abroad.

On August 13th Francesco Pepi went into some of the details of a case which was fought for years. The plaintiff was a Florentine usurer, Giovanni di Domenico dello Strinato, who had made an appeal to the Cameral court and won. Pepi wrote, "With reference to the interdict granted at the instance of Giovanni Strinati (sic) against the two [Floren-tine] churches, your lordships order me to work for its removal because they [the curates] had Antonio Pugi, his debtor, put into jail. Yet they did not send me an official notice [fede] from the notary of the place, attesting that Antonio is there at the request of the said Giovanni. For though the letter from your lordships suffices me, it may not satisfy others, as it failed to satisfy the Auditor of the Camera and Giovanni. So have them send the designated document to me and also a certified letter from the *proconsolo*, affirming that he [the notary] is a legal Florentine public

---

[62] *SCRO*, 21, f. 67r, "Et con reverenza ricordo alle ex. S. V.," etc., "qualche volta da tale mixtura se ne causa male o impediscene bene per la città."

notary. Your lordships should know, moreover, that even then the in-terdict will not be withdrawn but suspended. This is what I am told by the above-mentioned auditor."[63] These things were promptly done. The fees to pay for the suspension of the interdict were disbursed by the curates, and at the end of August the interdict was suspended for four months. All the sacraments, not the essential ones only, could again be celebrated in the stricken churches.

During the next three months, Pepi continued to occupy himself with lawsuits and threats of lawsuits against Florentines: pleading or arguing with plaintiffs, looking for ways of circumventing their claims, con-sulting *procuratores*, notaries, barristers, tracking down legal details, and prodding or keeping the Signory informed. The pressure against the Signory and Francesco was always the same: local interdicts imposed on particular Florentine churches, excommunications, and the concession of reprisals or threats thereof. In mid-November the ambassador drew up a list of proceedings still pending or acted on since his arrival in Rome. There were twenty-one in all: eleven cases of reprisals already granted or imminent, nine cases entailing local interdicts, and one interdict-reprisal.[64] The Cardinal of Cosenza, for example, was suing for reprisals to make up for the goods stolen from him on the high seas by alleged Florentine subjects. The Bishop of Trani, a nephew of the pope and creditor of one of the Strozzi firms, was also seeking the right of reprisal but so far had been disuaded by our ambassador from pressing for a definitive judgment. A certain Cristofano da Lodi had been assaulted and robbed in Borgo San Lorenzo, one of Florence's subject towns. Get-ting no judicial satisfaction from Florence, he appealed to the Cameral court "per denegata giustizia."

More serious than the reprisal cases were some of the suits which threatened to issue in excommunications and interdicts. Three of these

[63] *Ibid.*, f. 150r, "Le ex. S. V. mi commandano che io facci qui opera che lo inter-decto concesso costi in le 2 chiese ad instantia di Giovanni Strinati si levi per havere quelle facto mettere in le stinche Antonio Pugi suo debitore," etc., "lo interdecto etiam con questo non si levera ma si subspendera, che così mi fa intendere il prefato auditore," etc. The *proconsolo* was the supreme officer of the guild of lawyers and notaries.

[64] *SCRO*, 22, ff. 168r-169r. Some of these cases also issued in personal interdicts, a censure analogous to excommunication.

directly concerned the dignity and power of the Florentine state, thus emphasizing that the preoccupation with Rotal and Cameral lawsuits was not a matter of mere administrative routine; it bore directly on the question of the Republic's sovereignty.[65] I am best informed about a case moved by Messer Giovan Francesco Bracciolini, son of the famous humanist Poggio. A cathedral canon, Bracciolini was accused of having publicly stated that the Florentine war against the rebellious Pisans was unjust, that the Pisans had every moral and legal right to struggle for their liberty against Florence. These statements were made to a crowd of people in the cathedral on July 9, 1500. Two days later the canon was arrested by the Eight on Public Safety. With the approval of the Signory and an alleged license from the vicar of the Archbishop of Florence, the Eight condemned him to be banished from the city for five years. Despite the license alleged, they seem to have usurped the jurisdiction of the Church. Turning to Rome and papal justice, the exiled canon, Francesco Pepi wrote, "obtained an authorization to proceed against the Eight who banished him and he would come to an interdict, except that I [Francesco Pepi] have held him back."[66] A layman and another cleric had also started proceedings in Rome against the particular Eight on Public Safety who had condemned them.[67] Carlo Carnesecchi, the layman, had even managed to get the Eight excommunicated and was thereupon proclaimed a rebel. He then decided to sue for a local interdict, but was discouraged from doing so by Pepi.

How did the government regard proceedings transferred to Rome, and in this connection how did it employ, generally speaking, its ambassadors to the curia? Save for when certain sectors of diplomacy passed over to the Ten on War, the day-to-day epistolary contact with ambassadors was the job of the Signory. But as signories changed every two months, we cannot say that the government had an utterly uniform policy.

[65] See p. 122 and Ch. X.

[66] *SCRO*, 22, f. 168v, "ha tracto una commissione per procedere contro alli viii che lo confinorono et verria ad lo interdecto se non che io lo ho tenuto." On the canon's condemnation by the Eight see *Otto di Guardia, Rep.*, 117 (May-Aug. 1500), ff. 151v-152v; BNF, *Fondo principale*, ii, iv, 170 (Parenti's chronicle), ff. 131v-132r. The canon's chief argument—that Florence was conducting an unjust war—had a rich and important legal background. See here n. 19.

[67] The Eight changed every four months in this period. *Tratte*, 83, f. 1r-v.

Needless to say, no Signory liked the constant threat of ecclesiastical censures against its churches and leading officials, and no Signory liked to see Florentines taking their disputes outside the boundaries of Florentine jurisdiction. Some signories reacted more vigorously than others, but none could use excessive pressure on Rome: first, because the papacy as a political entity was stronger than the Republic; second, because the administration of justice in Florence was so disorderly and confused in this period that men who appealed to Rome often had legitimate complaints;[68] and finally, because the Signory itself claimed judicial competence in certain types of dispute between clerics, more especially in litigation concerning benefices and *bona patrimonialia*. Predictably, this competence was sometimes contested by the papal tribunals.

The government's attitude toward citizens who took causes from Florence to Rome emerged clearly at the time of Antonio Malegonnelli's embassy of 1500. A case we have already touched on gave the occasion.

Sometime in 1499 Giovanni dello Strinato, a merchant and money-lender, was served a summons to appear before an executive commission, the Regulators, one of whose functions was that of hearing and determining controversy arising from usurious contracts.[69] When Dello Strinato failed to present himself, proceedings took their normal course and the case was won by the plantiff, Antonio Pugi. The Regulators condemned Dello Strinato to pay a fine "for having unjustly contracted with" Pugi. Then residing in Rome, the condemned usurer appealed to the Cameral court *in defectu iustitiae saecularis*. Here the decision was reversed by the Cameral Auditor: the case was awarded to Dello Strinato and, to enforce his claim, an interdict was imposed on two Florentine churches early in 1500—San Felice and Santa Felicità. On March 18, 1500, the Signory informed the Florentine ambassador, Malegonnelli, that they had tried unsuccessfully to have the interdict removed. They went on to say, "Make him [Dello Strinato] understand that if he does not order the re-blessing of Santa Felicità and San Felice, we shall declare him a rebel and treat him like a rebel."[70] On March 20th they sent a

[68] See Ch. V, 1.

[69] Affirmed by the Signory in a letter of 30 Oct. 1500 to the Bishop of Volterra, *SCMLC*, 25, f. 122v, specifically in connection with the Dello Strinato case.

[70] *Ibid.*, f. 87v; cf. also *SCMC-I*, 52, f. 25r, pencil (15 May 1500), letter from the Signory to Malegonnelli, proving that Pugi had been temporarily put in jail.

summons to the man, commanding him to repair to Florence and appear before them. Dello Strinato, however, not only ignored the summons, he procured a censure of excommunication against the Regulators who had fined him, although the excommunication was not actually published. Proceedings were sometimes very slow, communications were slower then, and the case dragged on for years, with Dello Strinato periodically granting suspensions of the interdict for six months at a time. As late as September 1504, he was begging the Signory for a safe-conduct to go to Florence to try to settle the dispute. In November he "granted a suspension on the interdict for another six months."[71]

In punishing the contumacious disobedience of Dello Strinato and Carnesecchi by declaring them rebels, the state articulated its attitude toward citizens and subjects who sought to escape its jurisdiction. And while Dello Strinato might menace Florentine officials with ecclesiastical censures, he too suffered a deprivation by being denied the right to put foot on Florentine territory save on pain of immediate arrest and probable condemnation. Threats and counterthreats was a game that two could play.

It was *à propos* of the Dello Strinato case that, in a letter to Malegonnelli, the Signory of March-April 1500 was driven to make a general complaint against the number of actions transferred from Florence to Rome. "We wish to know from you, and we want you to get information on, what effective remedy can be concocted there against those who take temporal cases before the ecclesiastical bar of justice. For there is today a multitude of such cases that dishonor the city and hurt individuals. We want to know whether or not it is possible to take steps against this, so that we may give you a specific assignment at another time, [after] comparing your findings with whatever we shall have thought of here."[72] One of the things the ambassador pointed out in his reply to this letter was that there was irritation and discontent in Rome with the fact that

---

[71] *SCRO*, 27, ff. 174r, 179r, 194r.

[72] *SCMLC*, 25, f. 92r, pencil (20 March 1500), "In oltre desiderremo intender da voi che remedio efficace si potessi fare di costà contro a chi riducessi le cause prophane allo ecclesiastico et che ne pigliassi informatione da qualchuno, perchè hoggi ce ne è una multitudine grande in dishonore della città et danno de' privati, et se egli è possibile provederci o non provederci per potere darvene ad altro tempo . . . [word illegible] particulare commissione, conferendo il retracto vostro di costà con quello havessimo pensato noi di qua."

the Signory exercised jurisdiction over some types of ecclesiastical cases. The Signory shot back at once, "In ecclesiastical cases, we are not for proceeding other than we have hitherto done with the permission of so many popes, for we would think it a greater error to depart from this [the established route] than to cleave to it."[73]

The conflict of jurisdictions was certainly not to be settled during the lifetime of the Republic. Hardly more than ten days after the foregoing communication, the Signory was urging Malegonnelli to use his office and skills in a case to which I have already alluded. A notary, Ser Giovanni da Montevarchi, was on his way to Rome with the particulars. All the disputants were Florentines: Gregorio del Benino and Andrea Carnesecchi on one side, Carlo Carnesecchi (then in Rome) on the other. The trouble started, observed the Signory, when Carlo "ceded all his rights in the case to a son of his, a cleric, thus converting a pure temporal lawsuit into an ecclesiastical one, and all to swindle his mother and one of his brothers." Having been informed of this, "we could not but be greatly displeased, owing to the fraud done and in the interest of the city's honor." The moment therefore that Ser Giovanni arrived in Rome with the documents, the ambassador was to request an audience with the holy father "and make him fully understand the nature of the case," persuading him "to send it back here where it deserves to be handled. For we know well that the case is not in fact an ecclesiastical one but proceeds that way only because of its having been ceded. . . . All cry out here at the injustice which this promises in similar cases."[74]

Malegonnelli was very busy. Never before had so many lawsuits been removed to Rome. It rained interdicts and reprisals; appeals to the Rota

---

[73] *Ibid.*, f. 93r, pencil (28 March 1500), "Noi nelle cause ecclesiastiche non siamo per procedere altrimenti che si sia facto infino qui con permissione di tanti pontefici perchè noi crederremo errare più partendoci da questo che perseverandoci."

[74] *Ibid.*, f. 97r-v, pencil, "ha cedute le ragioni sue a uno suo figliuolo cherico e così facto d'una causa mera prophana ecclesiastica e tucto in fraude della madre e di uno suo fratello . . . non habbiamo potuto non haverne gran dispiacere e per la fraude che è facta loro e per lo interesse del honore della città . . . et lo facciate bene intendere la natura della causa . . . e rimetterla qua dove meritamente si debba tractare perchè molto bene si conosce che la causa non è in facto ecclesiastica ma solo procedere per esserne facta la cessione . . . e qui si exclama per ogniuno della iniustitia che quella promette di simili cose."

and court of the Apostolic Camera sprouted. In May 1508 the Florentine ambassador to Rome observed, "As for reprisals, any clerk of the Camera can grant these anytime someone alleges denied justice."[75] Most of the Cameral clerks were trained lawyers—doctors of law or men licensed in law. Malegonnelli was thus dealing with experts. For this reason he knew better than to try to carry out every crude wish that the Signory turned into a commission for him. He was ready and eager to use his legal skills to favor his countrymen, but he was disposed neither to try to do the impossible nor to make a public fool of himself. In May 1500 the Signory ordered him to try to persuade the pope to invest the Florentine commissaries in Pistoia with judicial power over a certain ecclesiastical dispute. Alleging the fictitious advice of a Roman friend (a presumed lawyer), Malegonnelli wrote back, "He [the friend] replied that I certainly would not obtain it [the desired investiture], reckoned that because of my being a doctor [of law] the pontiff would strongly reprimand me for making such a request and said that the cause in question can only be taken care of by appointing an ecclesiastical judge who is neither suspect nor partial in that city [Pistoia] . . . who will move things and render a decision according to the canons and not according to temporal authorities."[76] The judge had to be a cleric and be appointed either in the papal

---

[75] *SCRO*, 31, f. 64r, "Circa le rapresaglie, ogni volta che allegino la denegata giustizia ciaschuno cherico di camera le puo concedere." The Apostolic Camera was the chief financial organ of the papacy and the Cameral clerks, extremely important officials, were very often promoted to the highest ecclesiastical dignities. It has been observed that they handled the major accounts of papal finance. "They supervised the provincial treasurers of the Papal State and the Apostolic Collectors throughout Europe. . . . They drafted the bulls dealing with nominations to consistorial benefices, and many other bulls. . . . They corrected the letters of the [Apostolic] Chamberlain." P. Partner, *The Papal State Under Martin V* (London, 1958), p. 133. Soon they also acquired the right to act as judges in the Cameral court. In 1485 Innocent VIII formally invested them with the power to decide summarily all cases in their competence. He also forbade appeal against their decisions. G. Felici, *La reverenda camera apostolica, studio-giuridico* (Vaticana, 1940), p. 29. From about the middle of the fourteenth century and even before, most Cameral clerks tended to be trained lawyers, on which see F. Baix, "Notes sur les clercs de la Chambre Apostolique," *Bulletin de l'Institut Historique Belge de Rome*, XXVII (1952), esp. 35ff.

[76] *SCRO*, 15, f. 65r, "Il quale mi rispose che per niente la obterrei," etc., "il quale proceda et iudichi secondo i canoni e non secondo li arbitri secolari." I say "fictitious" because Malegonnelli needed no such advice. The point made is ele-

curia or by the Archbishop of Florence. Knowing that his letter would displease the Signory, Malegonnelli added, "If a few of your distinguished lawyers give some thought to this matter, perhaps they will find some device or way other than the one mentioned above. Forgive me, your lordships, if I put off talking with the pope [about this], as I am certain we would suffer a loss and not gain." The ambassador had his way.

Busy running a state, the Signory often had an oversimplified view of the details connected with operations and events abroad. This was unavoidable (thus their deployment of experts); otherwise executive bodies at the head of states could not confront and conduct the daily tasks of government. In fact, the procedural complexities of the papal courts were such at times as temporarily to confuse hardened lawyers. Was this not a reason, even if the Signory did not always observe it, to favor jurists for embassies to Rome? In a letter of August 9, 1499, Antonio Malegonnelli informed the Signory that a number of men at the curia, having suffered from the raids of a pirate who flew the Florentine flag, were pressing the pope for reprisals against Florentine merchants. The pope, said the ambassador, neither assents to these requests nor rejects them. "He commits the request to law; the adversaries [i.e., plaintiffs] then bring about the dispatch of certain general summonses which are incomprehensible, and decisions are passed down because no defense is offered. Should they wish to cite even your lordships, they [would] have a summons drawn up consisting of apparent entreaties and encouragements. It is sent out under the name of the [Apostolic] Chamberlain and they do not say that the case has already been taken to court."[77]

It looks as if papal courts, in Alexander VI's time at any rate, were not above the sort of legal trickery which enhanced their own prerogatives and favored the lawsuits of curialists. Occasionally, however, the trouble derived from the Signory's innocence or the ineptitude of others at home. An example from 1512 will serve. The Florentine ambassador,

---

mentary enough and our man was a crack lawyer. Pretending to quote a friend was merely a device to make himself seem less rudely self-sufficient.

[77] *SCRO*, 12, f. 359r, "Ma commette la causa di ragione et li adversarii di poi fanno certe citatione generali che non s'intendono et dassi la sententia per non si difendere. Et se pure voglono fare citatione ad v. ex. S., fanno scrivere in nome del camarlingo quasi sotto nome di prieghi et di conforti et non dicono che la causa sia commessa."

Antonio Strozzi, was a brilliant lawyer. He reported to the Signory on May 29th, "You remind me of the lawsuit between the men from Barga and Lucca, which is the first I have heard of the case since my arrival here [in Rome]. Nor would it have been in my power, nor in the power of others, to stop the Lucchesi from going to law with the dispute. Having however been served a summons, the men from Barga should certainly have sent a copy of it to me, or told me which auditor was hearing the case, so that there would be no need to go in search of fifty notaries in order to find the judge in the dispute."[78] Strozzi had located the judge by June 14th, when he informed the Signory that the dispute was going to require several lawyers and take a great deal of litigation.[79]

BRINGING details into focus has the effect of distorting the surrounding area, and I have focused on certain commissions of the ambassadors Pepi and Malegonnelli. This calls for some adjustment in perspective.

Turning back to the late fourteenth century and just after, we find that instructions of the Signory to Florentine ambassadors in Rome include very little in the way of commissions to intervene in Cameral and Rotal litigation.[80] It was not that the Signory of that period had a rule about not using its influence abroad in favor of individual citizens, for it was generous about seeking preferment for Florentine clerics and in striving to protect the foreign interests of its merchants and bankers. Instead, it was the disorder produced by the Great Schism which held down judicial appeal to Rome and kept papal courts from becoming excessively interfering. States had certainly resisted papal interference in temporal affairs long before the Great Schism, but there is little evidence, at least with reference to Florence, that lay judicial appeal to papal courts was much of a problem in the earlier fourteenth century or before. Even in the late 1430s, the appropriate correspondence issuing from Florence reveals no real preoccupation with the course of private lawsuits in

---

[78] *SCRO*, 33, f. 142r, "mi ricordano la lite delli Barghigiani con quelli di Luccha, della quale non ho mai inteso cosa alcuna," etc., "accio non si havessi a ricercare 50 notari per ritrovare dinanzi a chi fussi la causa."

[79] *Ibid.*, f. 163r.

[80] *SCMLC*, 1-5 (years 1395-1430), *passim* in instructions for embassies to the papal curia.

Rome.[81] It shows, like the earlier correspondence, an overriding concern with the great affairs of state—with treaties, alliances, conferences, military questions, and the policies of foreign governments. But from the middle years of the century a gradual change sets in: Florentine ambassadors to Rome begin to divide their time between the great but conventional foreign issues and curial action at law—action capable of affecting the entire Florentine community because it often issued in reprisals and interdicts. Thus in the summer of 1451 we find the lawyer, Donato de' Cocchi-Donati, using his ambassadorial dignity to help Florentines implicated in three different lawsuits.[82] By the end of 1455 an action was pending which could not but disturb relations between Florence and the curia. Claiming investments in the Florentine Monte, a number of men in Rome took court action against two groups of Florentine magistrates—the Monte Officials and the responsible group of priors. The occasion was the Republic's failure to disburse interest payments due on foreign investments in the Monte. At the end of December the creditors in question (among whom were some members of the Orsini family) won reprisals against Florence and in January procured the excommunication of the responsible magistrates. On January 4th the Signory wrote to the Florentine envoy (*mandatario*) in Rome, the notary Ser Giovanni Bargellini, directing him to try to get the reprisals blocked or suspended.[83] He succeeded in having them temporarily suspended, but the censures of excommunication remained. On the 12th Antonio di Messer Lorenzo Ridolfi—recent ambassador to the papal curia—was dispatched to Rome. The excommunications were published before the end of January. To try to have these revoked and to ward off the threatened reprisals were among the chief tasks of the ambassador. But foreign pressure on the Signory and its counsellors was "escalated." For the next two months the dominant subjects of executive consultation were the Monte, the economic damage wrought by reprisals, and the imperative need to settle the claims of foreign creditors of the Monte.[84] The evidence at hand suggests that

---

[81] *SCMLC*, 10 (years 1435-1441), *passim* in instructions for embassies to the papal curia.

[82] *SCMLC*, 13, ff. 23r, 27r, 29r.

[83] *Ibid.*, f. 179r.

[84] On foregoing data *CP*, 53, ff. 194r-234r; *SCMLC*, 13, ff. 181r, 188r.

from this time on it became less difficult for the papal courts to strike at Florentine officials.

The rise of curial litigation involving Florentines reached a peak at the end of the century and seems to have held that level for as long as the Republic lasted.[85] Racked by internal dissension, faced with rebellion in her territories and the menace of foreign armies, the Republic was much weakened in the later 1490s and early years of the sixteenth century, with the result that the papal courts were able to increase their jurisdictional claims over Florentine subjects and citizens. Pepi and Malegonnelli spent so much time on litigious matters that they were the obvious subjects for this part of the study.

I have not said and I have not wished to suggest that all Florentine ambassadors to the papal curia were lawyers. Nor, indeed, were lawyers always entrusted with those embassies whose success was partly to depend on the working out of legal problems. This was the rule, but exceptions abounded. What I have said is that lawyers figured much more often and prominently among ambassadors sent to the papal curia than did representatives from other groups. Trying for a rough estimate, I should say that during most of the fifteenth century the business of negotiation in about half of all such embassies was carried out in part or in whole by lawyers. Between January 1411 and December 1426 there were twenty-one embassies to the pope: two were conducted by leading clerics, nine purely by laymen (knights, merchants, and *rentiers*), and ten in part or in whole by lawyers.[86] Toward the end of the fifteenth century, lawyers came in for still more preferment of this sort. Between January 1498 and November 1512 there were no fewer than sixteen full-scale embassies to the papal curia. Eleven were entirely handled by trained lawyers, one

---

[85] It remains to be seen whether or not there was a notable decline in such action during the pontificates of the Medici popes, Leo X (1513-1521) and Clement VII (1523-1534).

[86] Figures compiled from *SRRO*, 2 (16 Jan. 1411–11 Dec. 1426), *passim*. I do not count two purely ceremonial missions. In one case the envoys were to accompany John XXIII from the outskirts of Bologna to Siena, in the other they joined Martin V on his journey to Florence in 1419. Knights were very often favored for embassies of ceremony. Better still, of course, were the ambassadors who combined the dignity of knighthood with that of the doctorate in law: e.g., Lorenzo Ridolfi, Giuliano Davanzati, Otto Niccolini.

by a lawyer and five other men (two of whom were prominent ecclesiastics), and four by laymen.[87]

When an ambassador to the papal curia who was not a lawyer came up against legal questions or tricky procedures, what then? An ambassador in need of legal counsel could only obtain it from two sources: from home via the Signory or from a lawyer or lawyers in Rome. We have already seen that ambassadors to Rome, even when they were men who practiced law, often solicited the opinions or advice of lawyers back home. This was done on the principle that three or four heads were better than one, particularly in matters touching controversial or delicate questions. The Signory then dispatched the written counsel to the ambassador. But a great deal of counselling also went on at the curia. For Florence—and the same must have been true of other Italian states—employed the services of an advocate who gave counsel and defended clients in the Rotal and Cameral courts.[88] The first such lawyer to come to my attention is Guaspare Accorambuoni (b. 1381), who served Florence during the 1430s. We may assume that his affiliation with the city was part of a growing tradition. In a letter of March 21, 1431, the Signory called him *"procuratore* and advocate of the Commune." A six-man mission had been sent to the new pope, Eugene IV. Three of the six were lawyers: Lorenzo Ridolfi, Giuliano Davanzati, and Zanobi Guasconi.[89] Their first assignment was to lodge a strong protest against the pretensions and treacheries of the Duke of Milan. They were also commissioned to sue for the return of certain castles near Forlì, claimed by Florence as well as by the Bishop of Sarsina. Since the prelate had urged his case on Pope Eugene, the Signory ordered the ambassadors "to get the views of Messer Guaspare del Maestro Ludovico [Accorambuoni], procurator and advocate of the Commune, and find out if

---

[87] Based on *DSCSA*, 40 (21 Feb. 1498–5 Sept. 1512), ff. 5r, 6v, 17v, 16r/v, 28v, 39r, 42r, 45v-49r, 52r, 57v, 58v, 60r, 63r, 67r. The jurists were Bonsi, Gualterotti (twice), Malegonnelli (twice), Bishop Soderini, Pepi (three times), Giovan Vettorio Soderini, Matteo Niccolini, and Antonio Strozzi. Only one of these embassies, that of Francesco Soderini (Bishop of Volterra), is missing from *DSCSA*, 40.

[88] In the 1420s the Venetian Republic already had a *procuratore* in Rome to look after its legal business. G. Mattingly, *Renaissance Diplomacy* (London, 1955), p. 79.

[89] *SCMLC*, 9, f. 32r. The other three were Palla di Nofri Strozzi, Ridolfo Peruzzi, and Lorenzo di Giovanni de' Medici.

anything in particular has to be done [to favor our case]."[90] The same
letter orders them to recommend him for preferment to the pope; this
was apparently done with some success, for that very year Guaspare was
made the "advocatum fisci camerae apostolicae."[91] The son of a man
whose father taught medicine at Florence in the 1360s and 1370s, Guaspare studied at the Studio Fiorentino and in 1406 was awarded the
doctorate *in utroque iure*. In minor orders at the time, he renounced
these to enter the guild, civilian life, and the practice of law. He taught
canon law at the Studio between about 1413 and 1428 or 1429, then went
back into the Church, taking full orders this time and moving on to
Rome, where he joined the order of consistorial advocates.[92] But he kept
up his close connections with Florence, and when the government sought
counsel or legal representation in Rome, he was the person best suited
to give help. The Signory, in turn, promoted his ecclesiastical preferment.
Perhaps this was his retainer.[93]

One of the regime's favorites in Rome in the 1450s was the Florentine
canonist, Orlando Bonarli, "doctore famosissimo e auditore della Ruota
Apostolica," eventually to become Archbishop of Florence. Now and
then, via its ambassadors, the Signory intervened in his favor by bringing
him to the attention of the sovereign pontiff.[94] As a judge in one of the
foremost Church tribunals, he undoubtedly offered legal counsel to
Florentine emissaries or referred them to lawyers whose friendship and
skills he could endorse.

Later on in the century and for some time thereafter, when curial
litigation involving the Republic and its citizens became very intense,
Florentine ambassadors easily obtained legal counsel on the spot. In
his dispatches to the Signory, Giovanni Acciaiuoli, ambassador to Rome
in 1504-1505, often refers to the Republic's attorneys there—an advocate

---

[90] *Ibid.*

[91] W. von Hofmann, *Forschungen zur Geschichte der Kurialen Behörden*, ii, 94,
counsel for the defense in causes before the Auditor of the Apostolic Camera.

[92] There were about seven consistorial advocates in this period. Sixtus IV in
1472 raised the number to ten. Hofmann, *op.cit.*, i, 130; F. Egon Schneider, *Die
Römische Rota* (Paderborn, 1914), p. 152. It was from the ranks of the consistorial
advocates that defense lawyers were drawn for the Rotal and Cameral courts.

[93] On Guaspare see *AGN*, 101, f. 15r; *SCMLC*, 9, f. 34v; A. Gherardi, ed.,
*Statuti della università e studio fiorentino* (Firenze, 1881), docs. 182, 341, 384.

[94] *SCMLC*, 13, f. 140r.

and a procurator.[95] Not himself a lawyer, he was in constant touch with these men on the subject of lawsuits brought to his attention by the Signory. The ambassador to Rome in 1508-1509, Roberto Acciaiuoli, was another diplomat who had no legal training. He also was compelled to give considerable time to litigious business and was therefore often in need of legal aid. Owing either to a friendship or for some other reason, he usually procured counsel from one of the twelve Rotal judges, Piero Accolti, a protégé of the Republic and a distinguished jurist of Aretine-Florentine ancestry.[96]

In this consideration of Florentine relations with the Church, we have seen the work of lawyers abroad in connection with curial lawsuits and problems of taxation. What these men did with regard to the holding of Church councils will provide a picture of their activity at home, where their labors were no less distinctive and important.

### 4. Church Councils

In the spring of 1376, with Florence and the papacy at war, many of the city's political leaders were excommunicated, orders went out from Avignon which called for the seizure of Florentine goods in foreign lands, and a general interdict was laid on Florence and her territories.[97] Religious services were suspended. Only the essential sacraments—baptism and penance—could be administered. Extreme unction was forbidden. And Mass could not be publicly celebrated—this was the most traumatic spiritual blow. In March a leading lawyer, Donato Barbadori, had been dispatched to Avignon as ambassador and defense attorney. His mission was to go before the consistory as tribunal to defend Florence and ward

---

[95] *SCRO*, 27, e.g., ff. 7r, 16v, 20r, 165r. Furthermore, he relied heavily on his secretary, Ser Francesco Cappelli, a highly skilled notary who served Florentine ambassadors in Rome from about the time of Malegonnelli's embassy of 1499. During these years, when Florence was without ambassadorial representation in Rome, the Signory employed Cappelli as the resident Florentine *mandatario* in Rome.

[96] *SCRO*, 31, e.g., ff. 20r, 174r. Piero or Pietro (1455-1532) was Bishop of Ancona (1505, absentee) and later Cardinal (1511); see *Dizionario biografico degli italiani*, I (Roma, 1960), 106-10. In 1498 he was responsible for having interdicts imposed on three communes under Florentine rule—Monte Carlo, Pescia, and Fucecchio. The Signory ordered him to have the interdicts suspended. A strained exchange ensued. See *SCRO*, 10, f. 287r.

[97] Brucker, *Florentine Politics and Society*, p. 310.

off the impending interdict.[98] He failed, and in May, when the interdict went into effect, the government considered sending another lawyer to Avignon, first Niccolò Cambioni and then Donato Aldighieri.[99] At the same time a group of magistrates met with three lawyers to decide whether or not it was lawful to have Mass said in public. They concluded that it was not, "that the interdict ought legally to be observed."[100] Two other times in the course of the war the Signory and colleges called on lawyers to produce opinions on the legality of Pope Gregory's interdict. At the end of September 1376, having been invited to draw up a *consilium* on the interdict and even on the consistorial trial itself, the *sapientes* or government lawyers returned the opinion—apparently in written form, endorsed and sealed—that the interdict should be respected.[101] A year later, on October 6, 1377, a new group of lawyers departed from the two previous decisions; finding that the interdict was not perfectly valid in legal terms, they assented to the public Sacrifice of the Mass.[102]

Was this deployment of lawyers a mere public gesture, an act of propaganda made in bad faith? Or was the Signory, moved by an obscure sense of right, sincerely trying to determine the legal validity of Gregory's interdict? The Great Schism had not yet taken place, so that Florence could not play one pope off against another. But whatever the rejoinder to the questions raised, in this frontal collision between Florence and the head of the Church, the high political estate of lawyers stands out. We need not know whether or not their counsel was seriously intended to dispute the decisions of a pope and his advisors or merely to achieve certain political and propagandistic ends.

It has been pointed out that relations between the Church and the different European states were subject to an elaborate body of law and

---

[98] R. C. Trexler, *Economic, Political, and Religious Effects of the Papal Interdict on Florence, 1376-1378* (Inaugural-Dissertation zur Erlangung des Doktorgrades der Philosophischen Fakultät der Johann Wolfgang Goethe-Universität, Frankfurt am Main, 1964, p. 33).

[99] *CP*, 14, ff. 42v, 43v.

[100] *Ibid.*, f. 43v. Filippo Corsini was one of the lawyers.

[101] Dissatisfied with this opinion, two speakers urged that some other lawyers be summoned to see if a different view could be obtained. *Ibid.*, ff. 87v, 88r, 90r.

[102] *CP*, 15, ff. 41r-42v. Three of the lawyers, prominent backers of the regime, were the statesmen Donato Barbadori, Donato Aldighieri, and the canonist Ristoro Canigiani.

287

legal theory, which was why students and practitioners of the law were summoned to take a decisive part in the resolution of conflicts between the ecclesiastical and temporal jurisdictions. Already common before 1200, this use of legal talent came into its own in the thirteenth century and remained a feature of European history down almost to modern times. In 1376, accordingly, it was the most normal thing in the world for the Florentine Signory to recruit the help of lawyers in its clash with the papacy. Princes and other city-states had long since done the same in similar situations. The result was that the presence of lawyers near the centers of power invested them and their learning with remarkable authority. After 1378 the controversies that raged round the Great Schism made this phenomenon still more common. France, for example, produced many theologians and jurists, civilians as well as canonists, who stepped into the forefront of the movement to restore unity to the Church. In February 1405 Florence received an embassy of three men from the King of France. They were in Italy to conduct consultations on the question of reunifying the Church. Guillaume de Meuillon, the royal chamberlain, headed the mission. But it was the jurist Guigon Flandrin, "a very able doctor of decretals who defended their side with numerous reasons, arguing that Benedict [XIII] was the true pope and showing in a long, effective speech that this was so," as the Signory put it. "He finally beseeched us to put ourselves on the side of Benedict and so be one with the crown of France as we always had been."[103]

Let us see how Florence finally responded to this and to other pleas regarding the reunification of the Church. The Council of Pisa (1409) was, after all, to be held on Florentine territory, and five or six of the Republic's lawyers were to take a leading part in the debates and con-

[103] *SCMLC*, 3, f. 56r-v, in a letter of 13 Feb. 1405 from the Signory to the Florentine ambassadors in Rome. "Poi in conclusione venneno alla terza parte e per lo detto Guigon, che è uno valentissimo dottore in decretali, chon infinite ragioni si venne a giustificare la parte loro e come Benedetto era veramente papa," etc. On this mission see N. Valois, *La France et le Grand Schisme d'Occident*, 4 vols. (Paris, 1896-1902), III, 390-91, 396-97. Flandrin was a royal counsellor who taught canon law at the University of Toulouse. He served as a protonotary under Benedict, became a Rotal auditor of the Avignonese obedience before 1407, then a judge in the court of "audience of disputed letters." P. M. Baumgarten, *Von der Apostolischen Kanzlei* (Köln, 1908), pp. 132-35. He was highly connected, the nephew of an Avignonese cardinal.

sultations which drew Florence into the heart of the conciliar movement. That unusual set of minutes, the *Consulte e Pratiche*, will serve as our major source.

Late in 1387 and early 1388 ambassadors from Avignon and Paris arrived in Florence to request, among other things, that the Republic come out in favor of the Antipope, Clement VII. They argued that France had supported Clement only after the present king's father had consulted "the most learned men in canon law."[104] Florence however refused to abandon Urban VI, although at the outset of 1388 the government held some meetings on the question with a group of lawyers and theologians.[105]

Between February 1405 and April 1408, Florence sent out six or more embassies aimed partly or wholly at persuading the contending popes, chiefly Benedict XIII, to come together in a Church council for the purpose of healing the schism. Two lawyers were prominent in these negotiations: Filippo Corsini and Lorenzo Ridolfi.[106] But not until the summer of 1408 did Florence begin to go through a real crisis of conscience, and then only because the political class was forced by the relentless advance of the conciliar movement to reorient its thinking. The papers of the executive consultations register the first major signs of the coming change at the end of May 1408, a few days after France had withdrawn her allegiance from both Benedict XIII and Gregory XII. Entitled to dispose of certain Florentine benefices, Gregory had just made appointments to some of them, only to find that they had already been filled without his consent. The incumbents were thereupon threatened with dismissal. Florence refused to yield. The colleges resolved to resist Gregory and recommended that the government apply to lawyers for advice and support.[107] On the 9th of June the colleges and other counsellors hurled a second challenge at Gregory: they moved that no major Florentine benefice could be given *in commendam*. The spokes-

---

[104] Ammirato, *Istorie*, iv, 188; Valois, *op.cit.*, ii, 132-35. Clement himself sent three ambassadors, one a doctor of law; two others were envoys of the uncles of the King of France.

[105] Meetings recommended by the colleges on 15 Jan. *CP*, 26, ff. 163r-164v.

[106] *SCMLC*, 3, ff. 56r *et seq.*; 4, ff. 10r, 14v, 26v, 45r, 50r.

[107] *CP*, 39, f. 53r.

man for the Sixteen, Vannozzo Serragli, urged that some canon lawyers meet with the council of advisors (*richiesti*) to draft a bill on this motion.[108] Two lawyers supported the challenge to Gregory: Bartolommeo Popoleschi, speaking for the Parte Guelfa, and Ricciardo del Bene for the quarter of Santa Maria Novella.

This toughening on Florence's part heralded a direct involvement in the conciliar movement. The independent or united cardinals—six from Benedict's train and eight from Gregory's—were already getting ready to meet at Livorno, where on July 14, 1408, they called for a universal Church council, to be convened on March 25, 1409. Almost immediately the question came up in Florence as to whether or not the city should allow the council to be held on Florentine territory. The question was discussed in the executive sessions of July 30 and August 3, 1408, and while opposition was very strong, the conciliar group prevailed.[109] Lorenzo Ridolfi, Ricciardo del Bene, Piero Beccanugi, and Bartolommeo Popoleschi were the four lawyers who took part in the consultations. Although recommending additional discussion, all four were in favor of having the Republic lend a meeting place to the independent cardinals. The idea of letting the council assemble at Pisa, the city finally chosen, was not seriously entertained in the executive chambers until August 21st. For the next four months almost nothing went into the *Consulte e Pratiche* on the subject of the council. Then quite suddenly on December 20th a discussion broke out which was to occupy the Signory for more than two months and which, in the course of its unfolding, was to rack the religio-political conscience of the ruling class.

The independent cardinals and the French governor of Genoa, Boucicaut, had applied to the Republic with the request that it declare itself neutral on the question of the two obediences. This meant denying Pope Gregory, a prospect which immediately divided the oligarchy and plunged the city into discord. Certain Florentines calmly held that they should give their full backing to the independent cardinals and so disavow

---

[108] *Ibid.*, ff. 55v, 57r. *Prov.*, 97, shows that no legislation was enacted on the matter. A benefice was held *in commendam* when a cleric or layman was made the recipient of its revenues during a vacancy.

[109] *CP*, 39, ff. 77v-83r; then also ff. 85r-86v, 87v, 88r.

Gregory; others argued that they dare not withdraw their obedience from him because no one had yet shown that he was not the true pope; still others were confused and uncertain, or urged that Florence wait until King Ladislaus, Venice, England, and the German princes had declared their neutrality.[110] The government had assembled a large body of advisors for the occasion (December 20, 1408), and the different currents became apparent as men rose from their benches to present their views. Outstanding political figures like Bartolommeo Valori, Cristofano Spini (for the Sei di Mercanzia), and Jacopo Salviati (for S. Maria Novella) all proposed that the government consult with key officials and lawyers, civil and canon. Four lawyers also pressed for additional consultations. The canonist Lorenzo Ridolfi revealed the clearest head, and his representations won the approval of most of the advisors from two quarters of the city, S. Spirito and S. Croce. Coldly rational, Ridolfi knifed through the counsel already given, pointing out that the entire debate came down to two questions: (a) what should Florence do according to law and good conscience, and (b) if the answer to the first question called for abandoning Pope Gregory, would such a course of action favor the Republic's *libertas* and *status*—i.e., its political and worldly advantage?[111] It was clear from Ridolfi's statement of the problem that debate must continue and that in all probability the second question would dominate the consultations.

Prodded by Boucicaut and the independent cardinals, the Signory and colleges returned to the subject three weeks later (January 11th), when it appeared that private and informal discussion had already gone on long enough to crystallize opinion.[112] But the uncertainty and conflict of views still prevailed. Certain counsellors even argued that they opposed abandoning Gregory so as not to sow scandal in the city, presumably among the sectors known for their conservative opinions. The lawyers Popoleschi and Corsini took part in the sessions of January 11th, but once again it was Ridolfi who cut through the immobilizing refinements, this time with a tougher statement of practicality. He asserted that whatever they did, the only real question was that which concerned

---

[110] *Ibid.*, ff. 108v *et seq.*     [111] *Ibid.*, f. 111r.
[112] *Ibid.*, ff. 115r-120v.

Florence's advantage.[113] We must infer that conscience and right, in his eyes at least, now were abstract or secondary matters.

On January 23rd there was a third full-scale session "super materia unitatis ecclesiae."[114] The most important speeches that day were five: made by Maso degli Albizzi and Niccolò da Uzzano, powerful politicians, and by three lawyers—Corsini, Ridolfi, and Stefano Buonaccorsi. Corsini, the first speaker of the day, boldly argued that Florence could and should withdraw its obedience from Gregory, that this was entirely in accord with divine law, civil custom, and the public good. The second speaker was Ridolfi, who took a seemingly softer line which in the end was nearly as tough and shrewder. Noting that the Signory had not asked for counsel on whether or not neutrality was possible *de iure*, he observed, all the same, that many universities had decided it was—Paris, Pavia, Bologna, and Oxford. He did not advocate the immediate repudiation of Florentine allegiance to Gregory; on the contrary, he thought they could go on observing it for the time being. But he urged the government to support the independent cardinals, to encourage important Florentine ecclesiastics to go to Pisa, and to see to it that no one was molested on his way to the Council.[115] Like Ridolfi, the third jurist, Stefano Buonaccorsi, was a prominent canon lawyer and professor of canon law at the Studio Fiorentino. He told the Signory and colleges, according to the minutes, "that we can and should withdraw [our] obedience in accordance with God, that unless we make ourselves neutral we offend God and we sin. As for the second point, whether such a disavowal would be to our Republic's advantage, [he said] that once this is in accordance with God it would doubtless profit us and also [that we should repudiate Gregory] on account of the temporal advantage . . . unless we do, we will arouse many suspicions in the other peoples and princes. He did not see how our prelates can go to the Council save by being neutral."[116]

[113] *Ibid.*, f. 118v.   [114] *Ibid.*, ff. 124v-131v.   [115] *Ibid.*, ff. 124v-125r.
[116] *Ibid.*, f. 125v, "quod nos possimus et debeamus secundum deum tollere obedientiam et quod ni faciamus nos neutrales nos offendimus deum et peccamus. Quantum ad secundam partem, si utile sit rei publice nostre, quod postquam est secundum deum sine dubio utile est et etiam propter utilitatem temporalem et quod ni faciamus nos dabimus multas suspitiones ceteris populis et principibus, et quod non videt quomodo nostri prelati vadant ad concilium ni fiant neutralitas."

If Maso degli Albizzi, Niccolò da Uzzano, Cristofano Spini, and others of their ilk, all of whom strongly advocated Florentine neutrality, provided an indication that the top men of the oligarchy were now wholeheartedly in the conciliar camp, the three lawyers provided the legal and doctrinal justification for this shift in allegiance. As minutes, the *Consulte e Pratiche* are far from complete. The recording notary did not take down everything that was said and when he came to the representations of the lawyers, he missed or skipped a good deal—special terms, technical details, refinements. His principal aim was to summarize. Nevertheless, there is no reason to believe that Corsini, Ridolfi, and Buonaccorsi delivered formal legal arguments. Owing to their reputation and authority in the city, it sufficed the government to have them come out in favor of the Council of Pisa, even if they kept their recitation of the reasons on a general level.

The above-mentioned lawyers and statesmen had this in common: they were informed about the great issues being debated beyond Florence's frontiers; they were accustomed to looking at events on an international scale. Men like Uzzano and Albizzi had acquired that vision in and through politics, most especially diplomacy. Corsini, Ridolfi, and Buonaccorsi could also claim much diplomatic experience, but they gained their international outlook also from their study of the Roman and canon laws. The same legal texts were used everywhere, and in Italy, at least, the methods of instruction and study were much the same. Bologna, Padua, Perugia, Florence, and Siena all depended on the same methods. Not surprisingly, therefore, lawyers no less than leading statesmen came forth to endorse the Council of Pisa from the outset of the Florentine debate on the question. But being men of the world, conscious of sentiment in the city and versed in politics, they did not at once give full vent to their views. In a world in which the only practical remedy to the schism was a universal Church council, too many of the simpler or more provincial men of the Florentine ruling class still feared the consequences, temporal or spiritual, of repudiating Pope Gregory. It was to ease their consciences that the executive consultations of January 24th ended with a resolution to convoke a special assembly of all Florentine lawyers as well as men learned in theology and authoritative local officials of the Church.[117] They were to meet in the episcopal palace. Their task was to decide, once and for all, whether or not Florence could legally and doctrinally abandon Gregory and adopt a neutral position. The most cautious of the four spokesmen for advisory groups that day was an insignificant figure, Simone della Fioraia, who spoke for the Sixteen. But a civil lawyer (Bartolommeo Popoleschi) and two oligarchical chieftains (Vanni Castellani and Maso degli Albizzi) frankly supported the Council of Pisa and Florentine neutrality.[118]

The assembly of lawyers, learned clerics, and ecclesiastics was held sometime before the 9th of February. According to one report,[119] 120 men attended meetings which went on for three days. It was the final decision of this assembly that Gregory was "a heretic and promoter of schism, that as an enemy and destroyer of the Christian faith he should be deposed from the papacy and in future no longer be called Pope Gregory but Angelo Correr, as he had been before."[120] The judgment of this little-known assembly thus preceded by about four months the identical judgment of the Council of Pisa. As a sentence, however, it seemed so harsh that the government of Florence, for reasons of conscience or political strategy, could not immediately bring itself to act on it. This is clear from the consultations of February 9th.[121] Speaking for the Twelve, the lawyer Popoleschi still favored the repudiation of Gregory, while Uzzano, speaking for the *pratica*, encouraged the government to summon a large body of advisors for the purpose of reading out to them the conclusions reached by the assembly of 120 churchmen and lawyers. But the Signory rejected this course of action for the time being, deciding instead to dispatch an ambassador to Gregory in one final attempt to persuade him to cooperate with the cardinals and other prelates

---

[117] *Ibid.*, ff. 129r-130r.

[118] Popoleschi spoke for the Twelve, Castellani for various magistracies, Albizzi for the *pratica*. Della Fioraia counselled "quod domini deputent omnes doctores decretorum et iuris civilis et omnes professores sacre pagine in uno loco extra domum hanc et ibi examinent quid sit faciendum secundum bonam conscientiam et tunc deliberent." *Ibid.*, f. 129r.

[119] Ammirato, *Istorie*, IV, 411-12.

[120] *Ibid.* Ammirato does not cite the document he used and I have not come on it.

[121] *CP*, 39, f. 134r-v.

soon to meet at Pisa. The man picked for the embassy was one of Gregory's most learned opponents in Florence, the canon lawyer Stefano
Buonaccorsi.[122] Buonaccorsi left Florence for Rimini on February 11th,
having been instructed to spend no more than three days in negotiations;
his mission was a failure and he was back home eleven days later.

The government had no choice now but to convoke an assembly of
advisors and have one of the notaries read out to them "that which was
concluded in the episcopal palace" by the churchmen and corps of lawyers civil and canon.[123] Stefano Buonaccorsi was asked to report to the
same assembly on his unsuccessful mission. On February 25th the
Signory and colleges finally resolved to allow Gregory about a month
to give his backing to the Council of Pisa or forfeit the Republic's obedience.[124] Two weeks later, when the Signory requested advice on the subject of how to handle a new embassy from Gregory, the Sixteen recommended that the Republic's position be explained and justified to the
ambassadors by lawyers and professors of holy writ.[125] When on June 26,
1409, the Council of Pisa elected a new pope, Alexander V, Florence
was among the first states to recognize him.

Never again was the city to be so divided and troubled by a recognized
Church council. For this one time too, in the act of lending Pisa, the
Florentine ruling class put itself at the forefront of an international
movement. Florence could not have done this without the leadership and
thrust provided by her top statesmen, lawyers, and churchmen. In the
Republic's dealings with Gregory, with the independent cardinals, with
the Council of Pisa, and with the newly elected pope, the work of
diplomacy fell mainly to civil and canon lawyers—Corsini, Popoleschi,
Ridolfi, Buonaccorsi, and Giovanni Serristori.[126] Working both in and
out of the executive councils with influential men like Uzzano, Albizzi,
and Vanni Castellani, two civil and two canon lawyers edged Florence

---

[122] *SCMLC*, 4, ff. 87r-88r.
[123] *CP*, 39, f. 144v, "illud quod fuit determinatum in palatio episcopali."
[124] *Ibid.*, f. 147v.
[125] *Ibid.*, f. 159r (11 March 1409).
[126] Serristori led embassies to the Council of Pisa (July 1409) and to the new
pope, Alexander V, in Oct. 1409 and Feb. 1410. *SCMLC*, 4, ff. 107v, 118v; *SCMC-I*,
28, f. 124v. Ridolfi represented Florence at the Council of Pisa. *SCMC-I*, 28, ff.
120r, 124r.

gradually into the front lines of the conciliar camp. They had the help of churchmen and other lawyers as well. Together with men like Uzzano and Albizzi, they were the bridge between the conciliar movement in the world abroad and that large part of the Florentine political class which was provincial, shortsighted, or merely small-minded. They were the men who brought the conciliar views of Paris and Bologna to Florence. The tradesmen and small merchants who sat in the governing councils and would not abandon Gregory were afraid, were troubled in conscience, were tormented by uncertainty. But students of the law and holy writ were just the men to confront the questions raised by the existence of two obediences. In the end, tradesmen and their kind and stay-at-home *rentiers* and their kind had to yield. The Council of Pisa and the break with Gregory were defended in Florence with the arguments, legal and doctrinal, prepared by lawyers and learned clerics. It took time for the humbler and more parochial sectors of the political class to catch up with the vanguard, but the gap was finally closed in the Republic's actions.

The place of lawyers in Florentine statecraft is in some respects epitomized by their part in converting Florence to the Council of Pisa.

With one exception, later councils or discussions of councils were not to weigh on Florence nearly as much. The subject, however, always moved the government to seek the advice of lawyers. In the case of the Council of Constance (1414-1418) this need did not arise; Florence had committed herself at Pisa and kept faith. But in the autumn of 1421, when there was talk of another council and Martin V had not yet drawn in his horns, Florence was not ardent in its support. The conciliar tide was ebbing. On October 2nd the Signory heard counsel on whether or not Florence should again offer a site to the conciliarists. Five lawyers— three civilians and two canonists—participated in the consultations: Francesco Machiavelli, Alessandro Bencivenni, Carlo Federighi, Piero Beccanugi, and Giuliano Davanzati.[127] More than in the discussions occasioned by the Council of Pisa, one is struck by the worldliness of these. The paramount question was whether holding a council on Florentine territory would be advantageous or not, risky or not. There was no unity

---

[127] *CP*, 44, f. 128v.

among the lawyers. Beccanugi seemed indifferent. The two canonists expressed conflicting views: Machiavelli recommended additional debate, but he was rather more against having Florence act as host to the council, while Federighi favored a Florentine site because it promised advantages for the city "and because the citizens and artisans earn nothing."[128] Davanzati also took the view that Florence should welcome a council because it would bring economic gain. He favored a council strongly supported by the secular authorities and attended as well by laymen as by clergy. This view was fully shared by Alessandro Bencivenni. In the consultations of October 3, 1421, the *decretorum doctor* Francesco Machiavelli was the only lawyer to speak out strongly against permitting a council to be held on Florentine territory.[129] Possibly he anticipated trouble from the pope. But with the lawyers Davanzati, Federighi, and Bencivenni on the side of those—and they were not few—who wanted Florence itself as the site for the council, it is likely that the Republic could again have been won for the conciliar camp. Conditions abroad, however, favored a different course of things.

At the end of May 1437, when the question was first raised in Florence of holding the East-West Council in the city, the government included four lawyers among the men summoned to give advice: Piero Beccanugi, Giovanni Buongirolami, Guglielmo Tanagli, and Albizzo Albergotti.[130] A prominent doctor of medicine, deemed a highly informed figure, Gallileo Gallilei, also took part in the consultations. Once again discussion turned on the utility for Florence of such a council.

The subject of Church councils came up two other times; the first time the government was not directly involved. Early in 1498, at the height of Pope Alexander VI's fulminations against Savonarola, the friar prepared to call for a universal council to reform the Church and depose its head. Some partisans of the friar wrote letters to ambassadors and princes, with the aim of persuading them to begin working for the council's realization.[131] In so doing they clearly went over the heads of the Signory and holy father. What to do about this, once Savonarola

---

[128] *Ibid.*, f. 130v, "et quia cives et artifices nil lucrantur."
[129] *Ibid.*, f. 132v.
[130] *CP*, 51, ff. 103v-104r.
[131] R. Ridolfi, *Vita di Girolamo Savonarola*, 2 vols., 2nd ed. (Roma, 1952), i, 346.

was under arrest and feeling in high place had turned against him, was succinctly pointed out by the most political of Florentine lawyers— Guidantonio Vespucci. Addressing the Signory and the Council of Eighty, he observed that the men who had written the letters merited punishment "because I think there are statutes which forbid writing [by private citizens] to princes."[132]

More serious was the Republic's involvement in 1511. Set off by papal fear of French power in Italy, a feud between Pope Julius II and Louis XII of France resulted in the king's determination to call a Church council in order to harry the pope. The French cardinals fell in with the scheme, which at first also attracted the Emperor Maximilian. A close ally of France and the weakest of the major states of the peninsula, Florence was more or less compelled to offer its support, and so, on a request from the schismatic cardinals, offered them the hospitality of Pisa. It was announced that the council would commence on September 1 (later November 1), 1511. Julius retorted by calling an assembly of his own, the Fifth Lateran Council, to be convened in April 1512. In August 1511 he dispatched an auditor of the Rota Romana to Florence with the commission to dissuade the Florentines from letting the schismatic council meet at Pisa.[133] But the Republic, with Piero Soderini at its head, refused to abandon the French, whereupon the incensed Julius hit at Florence with a general interdict. It was published in September. Soderini then did two things which increased the pope's exasperation. Bypassing the Council of Eighty, "but with the advice of some lawyers, he had an order issued to six convents of mendicant friars, directing them to perform their holy offices despite any unjust command to the contrary, or to get out of Florentine territory altogether."[134] It was the second action, however, which particularly offended Julius: Soderini's government appealed to the schismatic council against the "unjust" interdict. This was heresy. Not only had the Republic agreed to let the "diabolical conciliabulum" meet at Pisa; by appealing to it, the

[132] Lupi, "Nuovi documenti," p. 73, in a consultation of 28 April. The "I think" was ironical. Vespucci knew perfectly well that there were such statutes.

[133] Ammirato, *Istorie*, VI, 274.

[134] *Ibid.*, p. 275. I have been unable to identify his legal advisors.

rulers of Florence were according it the status of an ecumenical council which stood above the pope himself.

Viewed as a general council, the conciliabulum of Pisa was a wretched failure. The Pisan clergy fled and the burghers accorded an icy reception to the council's handful of French dignitaries—four cardinals and eighteen bishops and abbots.[135] Even Florence made no effort to get its leading churchmen to attend. Realizing that the Republic was partly the victim of its foreign policy, Julius did not release the full force of his powers against it. Neither Florentine merchants nor goods in foreign lands were seized. But in December—the schismatic council having already been moved to Milan—the pope sharply insisted not only that the priors of the Signory withdraw their appeal to the conciliabulum, but also that they have a statement drawn up, fully attested and notarized, declaring that they could impose no further levies on the Florentine clergy.[136] As in October and early November, when the regime was preoccupied with how Florentine officials in Pisa should behave toward the council,[137] so now again a number of lawyers stepped forth to take the lead in discussion. Florentines at the head of state, once they got into grave political difficulties, were always inclined to turn to lawyers for help, as if in a frenzy of rationalism.[138]

The major consultation on the demands of the pope was held on December 15th. Julius was willing to suspend the interdict, but only for a single month. Florence, in return, was required to withdraw the appeal to the conciliabulum and publicly renounce in perpetuity its pretended right to tax the clergy. Speaking for the Sixteen, Manno degli Albizzi observed, "Concerning the appeal, because it is based on law, which they [the Sixteen] neither understand nor practice, it ought to be left to the counsel of our lawyers, who do understand these things and whose profession this is."[139] The spokesman for the Twelve, Piero

---

[135] L. Pastor, *Histoire des Papes*, tr. F. Raynaud, vi (Paris, 1898), 363-66.

[136] *CP*, 70, f. 17r, pencil.    [137] *Ibid.*, ff. 3v-4v, 14r, pencil.

[138] Cf. the observations of a contemporary, B. Varchi, *Storia fiorentina*, in *Opere di B. V.*, 2 vols. (Trieste, 1858), i, 105.

[139] *CP*, 70, f. 17r, pencil, "Quanto al caso della appellatione, perch' è cosa che sta in sul fondamento delle leggi, di che loro non hanno cognitione nè ne fanno professione, che si dovessi questa cosa rimettere al consiglio di questi nostri doctori che intendono di queste cose et è loro professione."

Scarfi, also said that the question of the appeal should be referred to lawyers (to the "consiglio di questi doctori che fanno professione delle leggie"). Next came the recommendations of the men who represented the four quarters of the city in the Council of Eighty. Five of the *rapporteurs* were lawyers: Ludovico Acciaiuoli for S. Maria Novella, Piero Aldobrandini for S. Giovanni, Giovan Vettorio Soderini for S. Spirito, Niccolò Altoviti also for S. Maria Novella, and Bartolommeo Ciai also for S. Giovanni.[140] Acciaiuoli stated that as Julius proposed to suspend the interdict for a mere month, they should defer any decision about the appeal or tax renunciation until after the new Florentine ambassador arrived in Rome, was received by his holiness, and had assessed the prevailing mood at the curia. Aldobrandini reported that while a few councillors from his quarter were ready to yield, most of the others were not. The sovereign pontiff was asking too much and giving too little. Soderini—appropriately enough—made the boldest statement of policy: he submitted that the councillors from S. Spirito were not disposed to yield, not only because a month's suspension of the interdict was too small a return, but also because the appeal could not be retracted "without diminishing the dignity of the council."[141] They were equally opposed to making a public statement renouncing in perpetuity the right to tax the clergy. Altoviti said that the *pratica* from S. Maria Novella was disposed to withdraw the appeal to the conciliabulum but not to surrender all future right to tax the clergy. Ciai spoke for the *pratica* from S. Giovanni. They were more divided but especially eager to work through the Florentine ambassador, who was due to arrive in Rome late in December. Ciai declared that some members of his group were inclined to withdraw the substance of the appeal; others wanted the interdict removed first; some were willing to yield on the tax question; still others felt that the ambassador should hold out for the tax on the clergy and impress on the pope the city's urgent fiscal needs.

We are in the dark about succeeding consultations on the question of the appeal, the appropriate set of minutes having been lost. But since the colleges, when expressing a perfect unity of views, usually got their way, it may be assumed that the disputed appeal was referred to a group

[140] *Ibid.*, ff. 18r-19r, pencil.     [141] *Ibid.*

300

of lawyers, just as the colleges had recommended. These lawyers then advised the only sensible course of action, withdrawal of the appeal—advice which the Soderini government did not long resist, for the utter failure of the French conciliabulum had been uncomfortably obvious for some time. The appeal was retracted before January 12th. This action had the undoubted blessing of the new Florentine ambassador to the papal curia—a lawyer, predictably, and professor of jurisprudence, Antonio Strozzi. Only the tax issue remained.[142]

The practical legal difficulties created by Church councils have been revealed in the narrative and speak for themselves. Could the state intervene in ecclesiastical affairs? Must councils act with the consent of the pope or could they act without him? Could the state declare a pope to be no true pope? Was it possible to sanction an ambiguous legality (*viz.*, the Pisan Council of 1409) by drawing on the consensus of the political class? What about offering hospitality to a council: could a state do this without at the same time according it formal, juridical recognition? Could lawyers, civil or canon, be called on by the state to question ecclesiastical censures; and if so, how valid were their judgments? When menaced by a temporal power on one side and the sovereign pontiff on the other, could a state be effectively vindicated by its lawyers? Or was the use of lawyers in such circumstances merely a political device, a means of providing excuses or palliatives to those who wielded power?

In all affairs which brought these questions out into the open, Florence—like other Italian states—relied on the assistance of lawyers. But it did not bully them in matters pertaining to Church councils. Troubled in conscience, lawyers could come forth with views which they knew would not be to the government's liking, or they could refuse to give council. They were not hounded for this. The state, even in 1511, always found some lawyers ready to stand by it.

## 5. *A Note on Papal Power*

When treating a subject like political or ecclesiastical power, it seems important to draw generalizations from legal practice no less than

---

[142] Strozzi was given his instructions in Florence on 23 Dec. *SCMLC*, 23, f. 88v. On the tax issue see pp. 268-69.

from legal theory. Roman imperial law took for granted the supreme value of monarchy as a form of government; but Florentine lawyers, though trained in this law, lived in a merchant republic governed by an oligarchy and preferred it. Perhaps, like Bartolus, they found that this was the polity which best suited the city-state. With two or three exceptions, Florentine lawyers were not outstanding theorists.[143] When they taught law, they taught accepted theory. So, at least, do we infer from the fact that they never produced their own school of jurisprudence, as did the doctors at Bologna and Perugia. Their formal legal opinions teem with approving references to the great commentators of the fourteenth century and the leading fifteenth-century jurists in the same tradition. One may go through hundreds of *consilia* of Florentine lawyers with an eye to eliciting a political theory and a theory will emerge. But it must be extracted from a variety of *consilia*, any one of which may provide fragmentary intuitions or ideas that add up to a comprehensive theory only when they are viewed together. One may also study the actions of lawyers in the political assemblies, noting what they said, what they opposed, and what they favored. Here too something emerges: a series of assumptions which may be seen as the components of a theory. In a study of statecraft and political technique, this is the prior route because it is closer to practice.

Legal historians and students of political theory make much of advanced conciliar theory. Dietrich, D'Ailly, Gerson, and others provided the theoretical basis for the councils of Pisa, Constance, and Basel. The last of these (1431), however, was already not nearly the success that Constance had been. Though a large body of conciliar theory remained and more was added, merely to enunciate or promote it did not suffice to bring about the holding of Church councils, especially since the new tide of events went to favor the papal monarchy. Florentine lawyers endorsed "progressive" conciliar theory of the late fourteenth and fifteenth century as long as events and the force of circumstances favored the conciliar movement. But when the power of events began to work in opposition to conciliar theory, lawyers returned to more traditional

[143] The exceptions, I believe, would be Lorenzo di Antonio Ridolfi, Nello da San Gimignano, and Antonio Strozzi. They enjoyed peninsula-wide reputations.

views of the Church as a mystic body, a church in which "the members of the hierarchy, and the pope at its head, were there by divine appointment."[144]

Judging by their behavior in the political councils, we may say that Florentine lawyers did not publicly question the authority of the sovereign pontiff in spiritual matters, save in moments of extraordinary crisis,[145] and even then they did so with protestations of faith. Such caution does not seem to have been imposed by the sharpness of religious feeling in the city, which after all was also found in states like Milan and Venice, but by politics and expediency. The prestige and might of the papacy were too great and Florentines, with their commercial and banking interests abroad, were too vulnerable. Hence any limitations imposed on Florentine sovereignty by the papacy was a function of the opposition between two unequal powers, not a by-product of ardent religious feeling in the city. Only once, in 1409, did lawyers help downgrade a pope in spiritual matters and then they went all the way, declaring that he was not the true pope, and threw their weight behind the independent cardinals and prelates at Pisa. Two other times, in 1377 and 1511, lawyers engaged by the government were bold enough to deny the legal validity of papal censures, but in each case client and defense attorneys were compelled to beat a retreat. If in 1421 there were lawyers in Florence who ardently favored a universal council with or without Pope Martin V's consent, there were others who drew away from defying Martin. The conciliar movement, in Italy at all events, no longer had the massive support of men in high place. The reunification of the Church at Constance and the passage of just a few years had already changed the course of things.

An executive consultation of March 14, 1498, highlights the traditional views of Florentine lawyers on the question of papal power. The controversy over Savonarola was approaching its climax. Excommunicated in June 1497, the friar had also been ordered by Pope Alexander VI to stop preaching. He was silent until February 1498 and then plunged into another succession of public sermons. At that point the pope

---

[144] P. E. Sigmund, *Nicholas of Cusa and Medieval Political Thought* (Cambridge, Mass., 1963), p. 116.

[145] E.g., in 1376-1377, 1408-1409, 1498, 1511-1512.

brusquely demanded that the Signory stop him from preaching, order his arrest, and have him sent under guard to Rome. If the friar continued to preach, the pope threatened to lay the city under a general interdict and to encourage the seizure of Florentine goods and properties in foreign lands. Among the citizens invited to give counsel on the pope's imperious letter were nine lawyers. Five opposed Savonarola and four supported him—a split which perfectly reflected the division in the city, most especially in the political class. Speaking for the lawyers who desired Savonarola's silence, Guidantonio Vespucci took refuge in traditional theory on papal power, in part at least because it favored the case against the friar. Antonio Malegonnelli, spokesman for the lawyers who backed the friar, also made an assertion in keeping with traditional theory: it was lip service he knew he must render. But apart from going on to cast a fleeting doubt on the validity of Savonarola's excommunication, he also sought to give the forces against the cleric an unsavory political import, as if to suggest that the pope's competence in the case was not so total that it excluded all other judges. Fully aware of dominant theory on the disputed material, Malegonnelli was sacrificing theory to politics. Vespucci and his group were also moved by suspect motives, for in the actual situation their expression of orthodox theory had an explicit political objective: to destroy Savonarola, discredit his followers, and in a roundabout fashion strike at the opponents of close oligarchy.

Let us consider the words of the two lawyers.[146] Vespucci used both political and legal arguments. His strongest political point was that the Signory was angling at that very moment for a papal license to tax the clergy, "which if it be not obtained we cannot meet expenses." Then he observed that while some citizens made light of the pope's threats, he (Vespucci) did not. "For [ecclesiastical] censures are the weapons of the Apostolic See. Take these from them [from the pope and his courts] and you take away their dignity as well as their power to command obedience. Censures therefore are worthy of great respect because these are held in great esteem by them—who have no other weapons. . . .

[146] *CP*, 64, ff. 30v-31v; the consultation was published by Lupi, "Nuovi documenti," pp. 39-41.

*Item,* it has been said that we should honor God, and for myself I judge that this should go before all other things. But this is equivocal talk, for the pope is the vicar of Christ on earth and has his power from God. I believe[147] that he who shall want to obey the supreme pontiff and his censures, just or unjust, which in no way would I wish to judge, will deserve more than by not obeying. . . . The Apostolic See has supreme power over censures and every man ought to obey these." Sufficiently provoked, continued Vespucci, the pope has every right to call for the assistance of the secular arm. Should it ever be established that the friar is sent of God, then he could preach. "But not being sure of this, it seems to me more profitable in all ways for this city to satisfy the supreme pontiff."

This doctrinal representation was clear, orthodox, and vigorous. Coming from a statesman and lawyer like Vespucci, the allusion to the remote possibility that the friar might have something divine in him was meant for no other purpose than to smooth down Savonarola's partisans and perhaps disengage a few of their votes.

Malegonnelli was unable to present a view as self-consistent and unflinching as Vespucci's. He was much too near the quicksands of heterodoxy. Admitting first that Florence was in serious trouble and in need of the pope's benevolence, he started out with an orthodox statement: "there is no doubt that among Christians no greater power exists than the pope's, for he is put among us in place of God." But from this point on Malegonnelli departed from the beaten path: "I do not want to dispute the validity of the excommunication nor the question of whether or not he [Savonarola] should preach, though what we have to do here is to make up our minds . . . we see that [his] doctrine and life are

[147] To be consistent, I have transposed "crede lui" to the first person singular. Rushed, the scribe-notary kept shifting his pronouns, striving to keep up with what was being said. The passage reads: "l'arme della Siede Appostolica sono le censure, et levate queste è levata loro la dignità et obedienza loro, et sono da stimare assai perchè loro le stimano assai perchè non hanno altre armi. . . . Item, s'è decto d'avere cura a l'onore di Dio, et io per me giudico sia da mandare inanzi ogni cosa; ma questo è parlare ambiguo perchè el papa è vicario di Cristo in terra et da Dio ha la sua potestà, et crede lui che chi vorrà obedire al sommo pontefice e a sue censure o giuste o ingiuste, che non lo voglio in nessun modo giudicare, meriterà più che non obediendo. . . . La Sede Apostolica ha la somma potestà nelle censure et ognuno debbe obedire a quelle." *Ibid.*

good, that there is great wisdom in him. His doctrine, however, was slandered even before his disobedience. The rulers of Italy seek nothing more than the way to generate division in your city and they seek this way through friar Girolamo. It is unlikely that our citizens are responsible for this, nor would I wish to look for such a thing. I believe rather that this [the effort to divide us] comes from those who seek our misfortune and who have led the pope into doing what he has done. Nor do I believe that by listening or not listening to the sermons of friar Girolamo we stand to lose paradise, for we can have another. When he says he is doing God's will, I am constrained to believe him." Once again he praised the saintliness of Savonarola's life and concluded that if the friar really spoke for God, the papal censures should not prevent him from preaching, as Florence might then run the risk of a graver malediction.[148]

Not Malegonnelli's confused theology but the form of his argument is what catches our interest here. He moved from an orthodox statement of papal power to a dark suggestion about political machinations and on to doctrine which bordered on heresy. Unless the scribe distorted the gist of what was said, it was not a performance worthy of Malegonnelli's political and forensic abilities. The break was complete: on the one side— with their loyalty to Savonarola—was the group he represented, on the other the ultimatum of the pope. It seems clear that Malegonnelli's poise was shaken by his own awareness of the awfulness of the dilemma.[149]

---

[148] *Ibid.*, "et nonè dubbio che tra cristiani non ci è maggior potenza che quella del pontefice perchè è in luogo di Dio lasciato ad noi. Hora e' richiede da voi quello che vi chiede, nè non voglio disputare se la scomunica vale o non vale o se puo predicare o non predicare, ma noi ci habbiamo a risolvere qui. E' si vede pure la doctrina et la vita esser buona et in lui esser prudenza grande, ma inanzi alla sua disubedienza si vede che gl'era la sua doctrina calumpniata. Et i potentati d'Italia non cerchano altro se non in che modo nasca divisione nella cictà vostra et cerchano questo modo di frate Hieronimo, et non è da credere ch' e' cictadini nostri procurano questo nè non lo voglio cerchare, ma crede [transposed in translation] piùtosto sia da quegli che ci vogliono male et hanno condocto el papa insino a qui, et non crede lui [transposed] che udire o non udire le prediche di fra Girolamo, che per questo noi habbiamo a perdere el paradiso perchè ne possiamo avere un altro. Io sono constructo quando lui dice che gl'è volontà di Dio a credergli a ogni modo."

[149] The next two weeks were to unnerve him to such an extent that he ended by advising the government to take the same course of action as was recommended by the friar's declared enemies. See pp. 201-04.

A bolder stand was taken by the one lawyer sitting in the Council of Eighty that semester—Enea della Stufa, who taught civil law at the University of Pisa in the 1480s. After the representatives of the various commissions and special groups had presented their views, the spokesmen for the Eighty addressed the Signory. Speaking for the men from his bench (eight out of fifteen) who supported Savonarola, the lawyer declared, "it does not seem to redound to the honor of your lordships for the pope to command you; his authority is in spiritual not in temporal things, and friar Girolamo's case ought to be considered rather more a temporal case because of its effect on [the] minds [of men]. Since the supreme pontiff has paid no attention to the proper methods, they [Della Stufa's group] do not feel that he has any right to use you [the Signory and colleges] as his ministers in this." Della Stufa then suggested that civil strife in the city might get out of control if the friar was silenced and Florence would thus be playing into the hands of the other Italian powers. If you give in on this, he concluded, the pope "would make it the occasion to demand some other, more dishonest thing."[150]

Della Stufa recognized the full legal power of the pope in spiritual matters and drew the necessary inferences—which is why he insisted on reducing the fight over Savonarola to a political issue. Only then might the controversy (and so the friar?) be taken out of the reach of Rome's jurisdiction. The law provided no other loophole.

I have put this discussion under the rubric of papal power. What it really does is to exemplify a mode of statecraft: the use of legal theory and legal talent for political ends. For whatever side was legally in the right, each aimed at a political victory; and lawyers employed their forensic skills, whether in good faith or bad, to gain it.

### SOURCES FOR CHAPTER SEVEN

Getting at Florentine relations with the Church at the time of the Renais-

---

[150] *CP*, 64, f. 32, "non pare honore della S. V. che il papa v'abbi a comandare perchè gl'a auctorità nello spirituale, non nel temporale. Et questo caso di fra Girolamo è da reputare piùtosto caso temporale pel fructo delle anime; ma non havendo el sommo pontefice observato e' debiti mezi, non pare loro che el papa v'abbi adoperare circa questo come suoi executori . . . piglierebbe occasione di richiedervi d'un altra cosa più disonesta."

sance is a job of piecing together items taken from books and articles on the papacy and from some of the standard histories of Florence. The result is necessarily incomplete and fatally impressionistic—a picture of many highlights and little worth. Were it a little leaner in legal theory and richer in political fact, the following would be a model of the sort of book one would like to see for Florence: L. Prosdocimi, *Il diritto ecclesiastico dello stato di Milano dall' inizio della signoria viscontea al periodo tridentino, sec. xiii-xvi* (Milano, 1941).

Too early for the Renaissance period but suggestive and still useful is G. Salvemini, "Le lotte tra stato e chiesa nei comuni italiani durante il sec. xiii," in his *Studi storici* (Firenze, 1901). There are two noteworthy studies on concrete questions of the 1340s and 1350s: F. Baldasseroni, "Una controversia tra stato e chiesa in Firenze nel 1355," *ASI*, lxx (1912), 39-49; and especially A. Panella, "Politica ecclesiastica del comune fiorentino dopo la cacciata del duca d'Atene," *ASI*, lxxi (1913), 271-370, which provided some material for the piece by M. Becker, "Some Economic Implications of the Conflict between Church and State in Trecento Florence," *Mediaeval Studies*, xxi (1959), 1-16. There is new material and a fresh look at things in a recent doctoral thesis: R. C. Trexler, *Economic, Political, and Religious Effects of the Papal Interdict on Florence, 1376-1378* (Frankfurt am Main, 1964). G. A. Brucker, *Florentine Politics and Society, 1343-1378* (Princeton, 1962), has illuminating pages on Church-state relations and pp. 408-12 list additional books and articles on the subject.

For the later period most scholarly work on the theme in question centers on Savonarola. I have footnoted the articles by C. Lupi and P. V. Marchese. These and a few other pieces are repeatedly cited in the standard biographies of Savonarola by P. Villari, J. Schnitzer, and R. Ridolfi. Also useful is J. Schnitzer, *Quellen und Forschungen zur Geschichte Savonarolas*, 4 vols. (Munich, 1902-1910).

Florentine taxation of the clergy: another scholarly lacuna. The bulk of my material is drawn from archival sources, to be listed below.

The literature on Church councils is so extensive that it would be pretentious to affect authority here by adducing even a select list of titles. I found the standard works by N. Valois especially helpful: *La France et le Grand Schisme d'Occident*, 4 vols. (Paris, 1896-1902); and *La Crise Religieuse du XVᵉ siècle. Le Pape et le Concile* (Paris, 1909). The best recent treatment, done both by region and theme, is E. Delaruelle, E.-R. Labande, Paul Ourliac, *L'Église au temps du Grand Schisme et de la crise conciliaire (1378-1449)* (Tournai, 1962), vol. 14 of the *Histoire de l'Église*, ed. by A. Fliche and V. Martin.

There is a good deal of scholarly literature on the Sacra Rota Romana and the Apostolic Camera. Much of it, however, particularly the German material, is marked by an obsession with the structural outlines of these institutions, with the way they were organized and were *meant* to work. The result is that we know very little about the day-to-day functions of the Rotal and Cameral courts, though a great deal about their theoretical jurisdictions and the kinds and numbers of officials who ran them. Always very helpful on material of this sort is the great work of reference by G. Moroni, *Dizionario di erudizione storico-ecclesiastica*, 103 vols. (Venezia, 1840-1861). The old works by D. Bernino, *Il tribunale della S. Rota Romana* (Roma, 1717) and G. Bondini, *Del tribunale della Sagra Rota Romana* (Roma, 1854) have been superseded by two modern studies: F. Egon Schneider, *Die Römische Rota* (Paderborn, 1914); and E. Cerchiari, *Capellani Papae et Apostolicae Sedis Auditores Causarum Sacre Palatii Apostolici seu Sacra Romana Rota*, 4 vols. (Rome, 1921). In three recent studies, a German scholar has been getting down to particulars, away from the old habit of fixing attention purely on the institutional aspects of this court: H. Hoberg, "Die Amtsdaten der Rotarichter in den Protokollbüchern der Rotanotare von 1464-1566," *Römische Quartalschrift für Christliche Altertumskunde und Kirchengeschichte*, 48 (1953), 43-78; "Register von Rota Prozessen des 14. Jahrhunderts im Vatikanischen Archiv," *Römische Quartalschrift*, etc., 51 (1956), 54-69; "Der Informativprozess des Rotarichters Dominikus Jacobazzi (1492)," *Ibid.*, pp. 228-35.

On the workings of the Apostolic Camera and Cameral court, the following books and articles are to be recommended: A. Gottlob, *Aus der Camera Apostolica des 15. Jahrhunderts* (Innsbruck, 1889); E. Göller, "Der Gerichtshof der päpstlichen Kammer un die Entstehung des Amtes des Procurator fiscalis im kirchlichen Prozessverfahren," *Archiv für*

*Katholisches Kirchenrecht*, xciv (1914), 605-19; G. Mollat, "Contribution à l'histoire de l'administration judiciaire de l'Église Romaine au xiv^e siècle," *Revue d'Histoire Ecclésiastique*, xxxii, 4 (Oct., 1936), 877-928; F. Baix, "Notes sur les clercs de la Chambre Apostolique (xiii^e-xiv^e siècles," *Bulletin de l'Institut Historique Belge de Rome*, xxvii (1952), 17-51; B. Guillemain, *La Cour Pontificale d'Avignon (1309-1376)*, *Étude d'une Société* (Paris, 1962), see the appropriate sections on the Camera and the administration of justice. A book which I did not find very useful, despite its ambitious title, is G. Felici, *La reverenda camera apostolica, studio storico-giuridico* (Vatican, 1940). But two other books contain some first-rate treatment of the material in question: W. von Hofmann, *Forschungen zur Geschichte der Kurialen Behörden vom Schisma bis zur Reformation*, 2 vols. (Rome, 1914); and P. Partner, *The Papal State Under Martin V* (London, 1958), published by the British School at Rome.

As the notes show, most of my material on the taxation of clerics, on Church councils, and curial litigation comes from the following sources in the Archivio di Stato of Florence: (1) *Consulte e Pratiche*; (2) *Signori-Carteggi-Missive: Legazioni e Commissarie*; (3) *Signori-Carteggi, Responsive Originali*; (4) *Dieci di Balìa-Carteggi, Responsive*; (5) *Dieci di Balìa-Carteggi-Missive: Legazioni e Commissarie*; (6) *Signori-Carteggi-Missive: I^a Cancelleria*; (7) *Signori-Carteggi, Rapporti e Relazioni di Oratori*.

## Chapter Eight

# Problems of Diplomacy

### *1. Outlines of a Tradition*

When we find a large number of lawyers among diplomats, we can assume that there is a need for their specialized knowledge and ability to use sophisticated techniques. This in turn suggests a regularity in the conduct of international relations and a definite substructure of international law.

Before the twelfth century, generally speaking, Europe saw little specialization in negotiation among states and peoples, save in the sense that certain men were favored for the tasks of diplomacy, owing to their experience and high estate. Among such favorites were ecclesiastics and literate laymen of great rank. For unimportant missions the political and social estate of diplomatic agents mattered less.[1]

It is well known that the most dramatic political changes of medieval Europe came first to Italy and took place there more swiftly. Papal legates of the late eleventh century were the earliest agents of an institution that was to have ramifications outside the Church. It was in Italy too that treaties first attained specialized, complex, and more or less standard forms—treaties of peace, of alliance, of commerce, of boundaries.[2] Burckhardt was not wrong in seeing Italy as the laboratory for the European development of subsequent political and legal forms. Living in close proximity and in continuous contact, trading on land and sea, expanding by whatever means came to hand, the city-states of

[1] Material on these themes in F.-L. Ganshof, *Le Moyen Âge* (Paris, 1953), vol. 1 of the *Histoire des Relations Internationales*, ed. P. Renouvin; and B. Paradisi, *Storia del diritto internazionale nel medio evo* (Milano, 1940).

[2] This is a fact not always realized by students of international law, some of whom have shown little or no real interest in the history of their subject matter: e.g., P. Fauchille, *Traité de droit international public*, 8th ed., vol. 1, i (Paris, 1922), 71-74, where the significance of the Italian experience is scarcely appreciated. But see the excellent pages in G. Post, *Studies in Medieval Legal Thought: Public Law and the State, 1100-1322* (Princeton, 1964), pp. 103-108, on the derivation from Roman law of the expression of the powers enjoyed by diplomatic agents in Italy during the twelfth and thirteenth centuries.

Italy were driven by their inner needs and ambitions to seek political arrangements abroad, sometimes at their very boundaries, at other times far from home. It was this that gave a new direction to the nature and style of interterritorial and then international relations.

A leading student of the early Italian communes has noted that as early as the thirteenth century embassies often included notaries who took care of the paperwork—correspondence and the redaction of treaties.[3] The agents chosen for work of this sort were more than mere Latin scribes. They were men with experience of contracts and communal administration. We may assume that in Italian diplomacy, generally, other highly skilled agents—trained legists—also helped at home and in the field to work out arrangements and draft short-term covenants or treaties. For well before the end of the twelfth century, when consuls of the Commune of Florence rode out of the city to conduct negotiations with a neighboring town, they were ordinarily accompanied and assisted by men versed in law. The first recorded example of this is from 1172, when two Florentine lawyers (*causidici*) were arrested and put in chains on order of the Archbishop Cristiano di Magonza.[4] By this time too the intense movement of trade between Florence, Lucca, Faenza, Siena, and Bologna was regulated by a series of treaties. There is no reason to believe that Florence was ahead of other Italian communes in the practice of calling on lawyers to help in diplomatic negotiation.

Throughout the thirteenth and early fourteenth centuries, when the need arose, Florence continued to rely on the expert hand of its lawyers in relations with the Empire and with other communes and city-states, but there are not enough data available to cast a detailed study around this observation. Not until the middle of the fourteenth century, in the diary of Donato Velluti, do we begin to see in some detail the career and activities of a lawyer who was widely employed by the Commune in its foreign relations.[5] And only toward the end of the century—with the mag-

[3] P. Torelli, *Studi e ricerche di diplomatica comunale* (Mantova, 1915), pp. 102-104.

[4] R. Davidsohn, *Geschichte von Florenz* (Berlin, 1896), 1, 673.

[5] D. Velluti, *Cronica domestica*, ed. I. del Lungo and G. Volpi (Firenze, 1914), pp. 168-89.

nificent collection of instructions to Florentine ambassadors, of recorded verbal and written reports, of official replies from diplomatic agents, and the professional-biographical material provided by guild and other sources—may we begin to study the role of lawyers *as a group* in foreign affairs. By that time, however, most of the norms of treaties—norms concerning their form, negotiation, and interpretation—had long since been articulated, and relations among the Italian states had been put on a more explicit footing of international law. In this chapter, accordingly, we shall be looking more at the application of fully evolved norms, above all as manifested in the performance of lawyers, than at the emergence of new ones in relations between states. What is revolutionary in Florentine diplomacy of the Renaissance period is the intense commitment to these norms—the insistence upon them and the degree to which they were applied.

It has sometimes been observed in literature on the history of diplomacy that men trained in law took a prominent part in the diplomacy and international relations of the late medieval and Renaissance periods,[6] but this observation has not served as a focus for further study. Students of early diplomacy have been more interested in exploring formalistic matters—types of embassies, of diplomatic agents, of treaties; credentials; practice in the drafting of instructions and of *relazioni*; the development of the resident ambassador; and so forth. No one has studied precisely what the lawyer, as lawyer, did on embassies; what his part was in debate on diplomatic matters back home, in the work of preparation that preceded and accompanied all diplomatic activity, or in other work connected with controversy between states.

If by the end of the fourteenth century the tradition of Italian diplomacy called for the widespread use of lawyers and other highly skilled agents, it also favored recruiting these men from among the most privileged sectors of society, especially for embassies of the first importance. It was effective statesmanship for governments to consider the impres-

---

[6] Ganshof, *Le Moyen Âge*, pp. 266, 268, 270; M. de Maulde-La-Clavière, *La Diplomatie au temps de Machiavel*, 3 vols. (Paris, 1892-93), I, 352, 355, 394; G. Mattingly, *Renaissance Diplomacy* (London, 1955), p. 116; but overlooked by A. Reumont, *Della diplomazia italiana dal sec. xiii al xvi* (Firenze, 1857).

sion made abroad by their diplomatic agents. A man known to be prominent and influential at home was more apt to command respect. It was easier for him to mix socially, to join hunting and dinner parties, to receive company—all with an eye to collecting as much information as he could. He was his government's eyes and ears far from home.

This social requirement was another factor that went to make the rulers of cities favor knights and doctors of law for the leading embassies. The two dignities, as I pointed out in Chapter III, conferred social rank where there was little to start with or enhanced it when it was already there. Moreover, it was neither the obscure country knight nor the unknown lawyer who led the great foreign missions; it was the knight and lawyer in the public eye—men influential in the political councils, men of repute. Yet to have been an ambassador also conferred distinction. Machiavelli was making a statement of fact—nothing more—when he told Raffaello Girolami, "Embassies in a city are one of those things which do honor to a citizen, nor can any man be thought eligible for the affairs of state who is not competent for this grade."[7]

Even if the archives of Siena, Genoa, Milan, Venice, and some of the other Italian cities did not exist, we would still know from Florentine sources that by the end of the fourteenth century most of the states of the peninsula relied on their lawyers to help in the tasks of foreign affairs, particularly those concerning treaties, disputes between states, and arbitration. For Florentine records often give the names of foreign ambassadors or provide precise indications of their grade or rank—e.g., *cavaliere, legum doctor, giurista, vescovo, signore naturale.* In a setting where diplomacy was frequently the business of lawyers, no major state could afford to rely on diplomatic agents whose formal preparation for the tasks of negotiation was inferior to that of agents from other states. Trained at the same law schools, or exposed to the same texts and methods, Italian lawyers had a common ground. They took for granted that a contract, public or private, must accord with certain standard forms, have so many parts, meet so many requirements. Dispute about

---

[7] "Le imbascerie sono in una città una di quelle cose che fanno onore a un cittadino, nè si può chiamare atto allo stato colui che non è atto a portare questo grado." N. Machiavelli, *Le Opere,* ed. P. Fanfani, L. Passerini, and G. Milanesi, 6 vols. (Firenze, 1873-77), VI, 375.

articles in contracts or treaties was conducted in much the same way everywhere. Argument over treaties and private contracts very often turned on fine points—indeed, such argument was a feature of the age. Sent out on a mission to draw up a treaty, a merchant or banker, whatever his experience, could have no sure knowledge of the questions that might arise with respect to form and phrasing. Thus his need of a trained secretary or of help from home. An experienced lawyer was far less likely to be at a loss, at any rate in the redaction of documents.

Although figures are sometimes as treacherous as impressions or even more so, the following, taken from two registers in the State Archives of Florence, provide some obvious and fair indications. One source shows that between January 16, 1411 and December 11, 1426, Florence was represented in the field by 175 short-term embassies.[8] Forty of these were conducted in part or in whole by lawyers, five by expert notaries. The other source records the dispatch of 236 embassies during the twenty years from October 12, 1408, to November 20, 1428.[9] Of these, forty-eight fell in part or in whole to the lot of lawyers, ten to that of notaries. The two sources thus reveal that at some point a fourth of all these missions became the responsibility of men with considerable legal experience. This simple average does not go far enough to bring out the pre-eminence of lawyers in Florentine diplomacy, and it neglects the work of deliberation and guidance that went on behind the scenes. For there were major and minor missions, and lawyers were seldom wasted on the latter. If we define a major mission as one to be taken up with the drafting or concluding of an important treaty, then we may say that such negotiation rarely went on in the absence of lawyers and perhaps never without previous legal consultation.

[8] *SRRO*, 2 (16 Jan. 1411–11 Dec. 1426). Short-term embassy: a mission with specific objectives, sometimes lasting a few days, more often several weeks or even months; carried out by full-fledged ambassadors, not *nuncii* or *procuratores*. On these see D. E. Queller, "Thirteenth Century Diplomatic Envoys: *Nuncii* and *Procuratores*," *Speculum*, xxxv, 2 (April 1960), 196-213.

[9] *SDO*, 8, "Registro di elezioni e remozioni di ambasciatori della repubblica dal 1408 al 1428," see especially the section on the record of payments, ff. 65r-87v. There are lacunae both in this register and in the one cited in the preceding note. Perhaps another two or three dozen embassies in each case would be nearer the actual historical totals.

## 2. The Negotiation of Treaties

Except that the records of the period lack the color which is added by private memoirs and letters of statesmen, we can know Florentine diplomacy of the period 1385 to 1530 nearly as well as that of France or England in the nineteenth century and down perhaps to the First World War. Such is the state of Florentine sources for the diplomacy of the Renaissance.[10] One of the problems of this chapter, therefore, will be to pin things down to the most apposite examples without cluttering the narrative. The general features of the Republic's foreign policy may be sketched in as follows.

During the fifteenth century, Florence faced four or five successive threats from abroad. The first and in some ways the most memorable came from Giangaleazzo Visconti, Lord of Milan, who sought to conquer northern and central Italy. His expansionist drive started in the late 1380s and lasted until his death in 1402. This struggle was followed by Florentine resistance to the aggressive policies of King Ladislaus of Naples, whose death in the summer of 1414 suddenly freed the Republic from danger, precisely as Giangaleazzo's had a dozen years before. Between about 1418 and 1447 Florence was again menaced from the north: another Visconti, Filippo Maria, entertained schemes of dominion over central Italy. After his death Florence found she must resist another king of Naples—Alfonso, who sought to change the *status quo* in Lombardy and central Italy. But the real danger in the eyes of Florence derived from Venice rather than from Naples, and it was a danger felt along the banks of the Arno for the duration of the century. Statesmen in Florence believed that the Venetians longed to rule northern Italy and that they would then move south.

Florence itself, when given the opportunity, expanded into Tuscany as far as it could. In 1429 the Republic tried to take Lucca by force of arms. Even in the 1490s, at the time of the revived Republic, Florentines were prepared to blunder into Sienese politics and even to overturn

---

[10] On Italian sources in general see the very useful piece by V. Ilardi, "Fifteenth-Century Diplomatic Documents in Western European Archives and Libraries (1450-1494)," *Studies in the Renaissance*, IX (1962), 64-112.

that government.[11] Nonetheless, throughout most of the fifteenth century nearly everything spent abroad by Florence in the way of money, mind, and energy went to foil the great Italian powers from establishing themselves in Tuscany by means of subversion or military violence.

Though evolved in the thirteenth and early fourteenth centuries, the diplomatic arts used by Florence against Ladislaus were perfected during her fifteen-year struggle with Giangaleazzo Visconti of Milan. We see those arts at work from the outset of the struggle.

Seizing Milan from his uncle in 1385, Giangaleazzo had taken Verona and Padua by the summer of 1388 and was soon in a position to strike south toward Tuscany. By the time Padua fell Florence had been working for some months to achieve an alliance with other cities and rulers, and now this policy was intensified. At the end of December 1388 Giangaleazzo sent two ambassadors to Florence to justify his movements and to propose the formation of a league. For the next nine months negotiations with the "Viper" of Milan were not to be conducted save in the sight of lawyers. Two prominent Florentines, the knight Luigi Guicciardini and the lawyer Giovanni de' Ricci, were sent as ambassadors to Giangaleazzo in January. They were succeeded in April by another knight and another lawyer, Gherardo Buondelmonti and Ludovico Albergotti[12]—the latter was to be one of the city's outstanding lawyers and diplomats of the next decade. The instructions for each of these embassies rigorously ordered the ambassadors never to negotiate separately, never to let themselves be enticed into separate conversations regarding the subject of their mission. Their business was to secure agreement on a league that would include the lords of Lombardy, the Romagna, the Marches, and the cities of Tuscany as well as Venice and Genoa. But while Giangaleazzo pressed for a league of simple nonintervention in Tuscany and Lombardy, the Florentines not only resolved to confine him strictly to the other side of the Secchia River, they also wanted the league to be an alliance of mutual defense: one which

[11] CP, 61 (consultation of 7 Jan. 1496), f. 140r-v.

[12] DBLC, 1, ff. 164r-167v, 171r, 185r, 188r, 191r, 196r. The diplomacy of these years is brilliantly narrated from the Milanese viewpoint by F. Cognasso in the new work of synthesis, *La storia di Milano*, vol. v, *La signoria viscontea, 1310-1392* (Milano, 1955), brought out under the auspices of the Fondazione Treccani degli Alfieri.

would denounce aggression and unite all members of the league against any who violated the articles concerning the spheres of influence. Thus the differences did not concern the form of the treaty in question but the type. Lawyers, like others in Florence, soon began to censure Giangaleazzo's proposals, which issued from a council of advisors composed of men like the brilliant Niccolò Spinelli, a ruthlessly ambitious lawyer.[13]

In March 1389 Guicciardini and Ricci sent home a copy of the articles of the league desired by the Lord of Milan. Addressing the Signory and colleges on March 22nd, the lawyer Filippo Corsini said that the articles were insidious, deceitful, full of snares and traps.[14] The denunciations continued on the 23rd and 24th, and included one by the canon lawyer Lorenzo Ridolfi. Giangaleazzo was asking that his sphere of influence be allowed to reach as far south as Modena. On the 26th Messer Biagio Guasconi urged resistance to this article and went on to say that "the other articles are also very dangerous." He encouraged the government to delegate "two Guelf captains, two members from each college, two from the Ten on War, and some lawyers [doctores] to hold consultations on the same articles and to get up a draft of them as they should be."[15] In April the Signory and the Ten turned against Guicciardini and Ricci, accusing them of sponsion, of letting themselves (especially the knight, Guicciardini) be drawn into separate consultations, and of not getting information to Florence fast enough.[16] Buondelmonti and Albergotti,

---

[13] See esp. G. Romano, "Niccolò Spinelli da Giovinazzo, diplomatico del secolo xiv," *Arch. stor. per le prov. napoletane*, vols. XXIV-XXVI (1899-1901). A *meridionale*, Spinelli professed law at Padua and Bologna between 1351 and 1360. He entered Giangaleazzo's service late in 1387. Two other professors of law, Uberto Lampugnano and Bartolommeo Benzoni, stood out among the Lord of Milan's counsellors. Romano, *ibid.*, XXVI, 414ff., 427, n. 2.

[14] *CP*, 27, f. 94r.

[15] *Ibid.*, f. 101r, "Et quia etiam alia capitula sunt multum periculosa et ideo domini habeant duos ex capitaneis partis et duos per collegium et duos ex decem balie et aliquos doctores qui praticent ipsa capitula et capitulent ut oportet." The draft was composed and soon sent out to Giangaleazzo, who rejected it. On 22 April the Signory prepared to send another to him "with clear, most equitable and candid articles which we hope will please your magnificence." *SCMC-I*, 21, ff. 98r-99r.

[16] *DBLC*, 1, ff. 185r-186v, 188r. On the Signory's grave preoccupation see the letter to Bologna of 20 April, calling for still more diplomatic teamwork and co-ordination, *SCMC-I*, 21, f. 97r-v.

who arrived in April to succeed them, stayed on in Milan until the fourth week of May.[17] But negotiation with Giangaleazzo and his Secret Council continued by letter and messenger. Representing the S. Giovanni quarter on June 25th, the lawyer and recent ambassador to Milan, Giovanni de' Ricci, deplored the treaty of alliance requested by the Milanese because of its being "obscure and full of uncertainties."[18] Such a statement was manifestly based on Giovanni's close familiarity with the articles of the proposed league. In August, on the arrival of a new draft of the treaty, Filippo Pandolfini recommended for both colleges that the articles be studied "by the [official] communal lawyers, by Messer Ludovico [Albergotti], or by some other lawyers."[19] Not until October did Florence finally conclude a treaty with the Lord of Milan, and then it was not one to her liking. Giangaleazzo's sphere was to extend as far south as Modena. The course of events and the failure to stiffen the resistance of friends abroad had more or less compelled the Republic to yield. Like the "tyrant" himself, however, Florence too was prepared to use the treaty in order to gain time.

In the years that followed, the part played by Florentine lawyers in the negotiation of treaties continued to be as prominent as in the Florentine-Milanese negotiations of 1389. Again and again, during the years that saw Giangaleazzo's agents and armies trafficking in central Italy, we find lawyers at the head of the Republic's embassies—Albergotti, Ricci, Filippo Corsini, Lorenzo Ridolfi, and Bartolommeo Popoleschi.[20] Again and again, when combing the debates of the executive councils, we come on evidence showing that lawyers were commissioned to study the drafts of treaties.[21] Wily, fastidious phrasing, and carefully articulated legalistic

[17] *DBLC*, I, f. 196r (29 May 1389), a letter from the Signory summarily dismissing them because of their having conducted negotiations in Milan and Pavia for several days after they had been ordered to start for home.

[18] *CP*, 27, f. 130r, "Quod liga cum comite in forma que petitur est obscura et dubiis plena." Giangaleazzo was still a count. He was made Duke of Milan by imperial charter in May 1395.

[19] *Ibid.*, f. 153r, "pro utroque collegio dixit quod capitula videantur per sapientes comunis, D. Ludovicum, aut alios sapientes."

[20] *SCMLC*, I, ff. 14v, 73r, 76r, 80v, 101r, 115r; 2, ff. 13r, 28r, 45v; *DBRA*, I, ff. 4v, 22v, 28r, 33r; *SRRO*, I, ff. 7v, 10r, 12v, 19v, 26v, 36r, 37v, 38v, 39v, 40v, 43r; *DBLC*, 2, ff. 23r, 25r, 46r, 46v, 68v.

[21] *CP*, 27, f. 153v; 29, ff. 36v, 40r, 107v; 34, ff. 91v, 176v; 40, f. 154r.

barriers written into formal documents were more a part of the foreign affairs of the period than military violence, though this was seldom absent for long.

What we have inferred about the attitude toward lawyers in Florentine diplomatic practice is also explicitly stated in the documents. In November and December 1399 there were four Florentine ambassadors in Rome, striving to conclude an alliance with Naples and the holy father against Giangaleazzo.[22] The four were Tommaso Sacchetti (knight), Filippo Magalotti (knight), Lorenzo Ridolfi (*decretorum doctor*), and Niccolò da Uzzano (merchant). Deciding to withdraw two of the ambassadors, the Signory informed them of this in a letter of January 4th and named the two who should remain in Rome. There was no ambiguity about the rules that determined the Signory's choice: "You know that the league cannot be negotiated without a lawyer [*doctore*] . . . it is sensible and redounds more to our honor for us to have a knight and lawyer there, rather than a lawyer and merchant. And so, for the sake of the Commune's honor and needs, we want you Messer Tommaso and Messer Lorenzo to remain there."[23] It was clear that the lawyer must stay; the only real question had been whether his colleague in Rome should be a knight or merchant.

This embassy to Rome was in line with the principal aim of Florentine foreign policy during this period—to contain Giangaleazzo. Provided that he was clever at oratory or merely a persuasive talker, any outstanding knight or merchant could conduct legations aimed at toughening the resistance of cities like Siena, Bologna, Genoa, and Venice against the pretensions of the Lord of Milan. Such missions required no legal preparation; thus the political prominence in those years of a knight like Rinaldo Gianfigliazzi, a brilliant orator sent out by his native Florence on numerous embassies. But it took a lawyer to present arguments from law and to conclude treaties *a ragione*. There was

---

[22]*SCMLC*, 3, ff. 13r, 19r. Giangaleazzo was often referred to as "the tyrant" in records and official correspondence.

[23]*Ibid.*, f. 19r, "Sapete la lega non si puote praticare senza dottore . . . e cagionevole e più honore nostro è che costà si ritruovi uno cavaliere e uno dottore, che'l dottore e'l mercatante. Sichè per honore e necessità di comune vogliamo costà rimagnate voi messer Tommaso e messer Lorenzo come detto abbiamo."

no keener awareness of this than at Bologna and Florence, where states-men regarded even the Venetians as innocents for not having the same developed awareness. Proof of this appears in a set of instructions (dated February 1400) for two ambassadors-elect to Venice, the lawyer Barto-lommeo Popoleschi and the merchant Andrea di Neri Vettori. On the way, they were to stop off at Bologna to tell the Anziani (that city's chief executive body) that they were going to Venice to see about "the peace we desire," to see "what form has been given to the contract,"[24] and to improve the existing league against Giangaleazzo. They were also to encourage the Anziani to send ambassadors to Venice so that all to-gether could work to strengthen the league, whether or not a peace with the Lord of Milan was finally signed. Tell the Anziani, continued the Signory in its instructions, "that they know well that the Venetians are not skilled in contracts [arguable] at law, so that some slight errors may have been committed against their will." Once they got to Venice, Popoleschi and Vettori were to press for a peace with honor—that formula again!—telling the Venetians "that we are sure they have sought and concluded a peace with all due faith and prudence, but that owing to the wickedness of the adversary and shrewdness of those in whose care he puts such matters, it might be [discovered], once things are subjected to an examination and to the subtlety [rigor?] of the law, that something was allowed or done clean contrary to their intention. [Then], even if the peace treaty has been finally agreed on, ask to see the articles, and if there be some way to improve the conditions accord-ing to the form of the arrangements [previously] made at Venice, a copy of which you have, try to improve them."[25]

[24] *SCMLC*, 2, f. 28r, "E che voi andate per vedere che forma fia data a questo contracto e per vantaggiare la lega loro, noi e tutti gli altri." The "contract" was the draft of the peace treaty being negotiated in Venice between the Duke of Milan and the anti-Viscontean league. As it turned out, Popoleschi went to Venice, Vettori to Bologna. Vettori's instructions, dated 5 March, repeat verbatim the ob-servation concerning Venetian inexperience with contracts arguable at law. *Ibid.*, f. 29r.

[25] *Ibid.*, f. 28r, "Et che sanno bene li Vinitiani non sono pratichi di contratti a ragione, sichè leggiermente si potrebbe contro loro intentione essere commesso errore. . . . E che noi ci rendiamo certi che chon ogni fede e prudentia essi l'abbino cerca[ta] e chonchiusa, ma per le malitie de l'aversario e astutia di coloro a chui simili cose commette si potrebbe essere consentito e fatto cosa non sarebbe punto

There was no mistaking the assumptions of the makers of Florentine foreign policy. They took for granted that while Giangaleazzo and his advisors (lawyers and consummate statesmen) were cunning, unscrupulous negotiators, the Venetians were somewhat careless and innocent, at all events in the drafting of treaties and other contracts. This picture of Venetian naiveté seems also to have been entertained at Bologna. But Florentines, unlike Venetians, were so familiar with the ways of the Milanese chancellery that they always checked and double-checked documents bearing on their relations with Giangaleazzo. Not only did the Signory and colleges cleave to the practice of having one lawyer and sometimes two conduct the negotiation of major treaties, they also insisted that ambassadors send treaty drafts and other documents to Florence, where these were again studied by lawyers.

Thus when sent on their mission to Bologna and Venice, Popoleschi and Vettori were instructed to sign nothing until they had sent a copy of the articles to Florence and received a reply. We have already seen that the treaty signed with the Lord of Milan in October 1389 was subjected to the scrutiny of lawyers at home, even though two lawyers, first Ricci and then Albergotti, had helped conduct negotiations in the field. In February 1392 lawyers were invited to examine the articles of a prospective treaty with Genoa.[26] In August the Signory consulted five lawyers on whether or not Florence could enter into a pact with the Lord of Mantua, a possible legal barrier being Florentine treaties with Pisa and Genoa.[27] The year after, in November, the government called on lawyers to study the articles of the league against Giangaleazzo so as

---

di loro intentione, riducendosi le cose ad examine e sutilità di ragione. E stipulato o no che sia la pacie, chiedete di vedere e capitoli, e se modo fusse di megliorare le conditioni secondo la fo[r]ma della pratica e le domande fatte a Vinegia delle quali averete la copia, fate di megliorarle." All the fears of the Signory were borne out, as is attested by the instructions of 7 April 1400 for the two new ambassadors to Venice—Filippo Magalotti and Niccolò da Uzzano. The first man they consulted in Venice was Popoleschi. Not only was Florence dissatisfied with that to which the Venetians had agreed, "ma pure el formare de' capitoli ci'è suto occulto, ne' quali come si vede et in facto et in ragione sono commessi non piccoli errori e tutto è intervenuto per non essere noi alla pratica." Ibid., ff. 30v-32r.

[26] CP, 29, ff. 36v, 40r.

[27] Ibid., f. 107v. Filippo Corsini, Rosello Roselli, Niccolò Cambioni, Stefano Buonaccorsi, and Lorenzo Ridolfi.

to see if the lords of Ferrara and Padua were guilty of having violated it.[28] Meanwhile, there were always participants in the executive consultations who saw to it that the critical embassies included a lawyer among the ambassadors.[29] A few years later (January 1410), we find two lawyers reporting to the Signory and colleges on whether or not Florence could make a separate peace with King Ladislaus, despite an alliance with Siena and the papacy which seemed to bar the way.[30] In May 1414 a similar question was referred to lawyers.[31]

These examples make clear that the negotiation of treaties was preceded by considerable discussion at home. In some cases discussion centered on whether or not a treaty was possible *de iure*. For a treaty then— as now—often existed in a field of treaties, of mutual obligations; it might come at the end of a series or somewhere within a series, or it might be connected in parallel, so to speak. In this simple but neglected observation we see another reason which moved governments to favor the recruitment of lawyers for the tasks of diplomacy. Neither the Florentines nor their contemporaries treated with other states in a hit-and-miss fashion. Having definite ends in mind, they treated with documents in hand and with a precise knowledge of their commitments all around. The bonds of those commitments were a legal network; the sanctions were such things as war, reprisals, and adverse public opinion.

At the end of January 1424 the Signory dispatched three ambassadors to Ferrara to negotiate a peace with Filippo Maria Visconti's diplomatic representatives.[32] As was often the case, the three Florentines were neatly balanced—being Rinaldo degli Albizzi (knight), Giuliano Davanzati (lawyer), and Veri Guadagni (merchant). We may gauge the technical level of certain aspects of the embassy from the fact that they went to Ferrara armed with five documents: (a) a copy of the peace treaty between Florence and Genoa, dated April 27, 1413; (b) a copy of the peace treaty between Florence and Filippo Maria Visconti, February 8,

---

[28] *CP*, 30, f. 83r.

[29] *CP*, 27, f. 106v; 28, f. 6r-v; 30, f. 41v; 32, f. 44v; 33, ff. 67r, 80v; 34, f. 2v; 38, ff. 102v, 109v, 111r; 39, f. 88v; 40, ff. 120r-v, 154r.

[30] *CP*, 40, f. 99r-v. Bartolommeo Popoleschi and Giovanni Serristori. The subject was first raised on 4 Jan., *ibid.*, f. 96r.

[31] *CP*, 42, ff. 138r, 141r.

[32] Albizzi, *Commissioni*, II, 8.

1420; (c) the instrument of the Florentine purchase of Pisa, August 27, 1405; (d) a document authorizing the cession of Pisa, August 28, 1405; and (e) the papers attesting to the Florentine purchase of Livorno, June 27, 1421. It was the Signory's intention to have the new treaty of peace negotiated in the context of the peace of 1420. The other four documents were meant to bear on a number of Florentine claims against Genoa, which was then under Milanese domination. Florence accused the Genoese of having illegally seized the goods of many Florentine merchants, of disturbing her shipping, and of insisting that Florentine goods acquired or sent overseas could only be transported on Genoese boats.

A Florentine embassy to Genoa late in June 1404 was assigned to five ambassadors: two knights, two merchants, and one lawyer (Filippo Corsini, the senior member of the mission).[33] There were hostilities between Florence and Pisa, and the highway linking these cities was closed. Wanting it re-opened for reasons of trade, the Pisans had sued for a truce, and their protector, Boucicaut, the French governor of Genoa, was to act as arbiter in the negotiations. The five ambassadors started out by holding that the Florence-Pisa road could not be re-opened because of a legal barrier issuing from a five-year treaty between Florence and Siena. But bullied by Boucicaut, who authorized reprisals against Florence because of its military activity in the Pisan Maremma, the commission which sponsored this embassy (the Ten on War) was compelled to compromise. A copy of the last treaty between Florence and Pisa was sent to the ambassadors.[34] Working from this treaty and presenting the Florentine demands to a group of "auditors" appointed by Boucicaut, Corsini and his colleagues were to agree to a three- or four-year truce, provided certain conditions were met. Not only had the Pisans to make reparations for having carried out illegal reprisals against Florentine merchants, they also had to assent to an agreement giving Florence the same rights ("franchigie") accorded by the last treaty—one concluded "at the time of Messer Piero Gambacorta," late *signore* of Pisa. Here,

[33] *DBLC*, 3, ff. 67v-68r, pencil.
[34] *Ibid.*, f. 69r, pencil. See also Piattoli, "Genova e Firenze al tramonto della libertà di Pisa," *Giornale storico e letterario della Liguria*, VI (1930), 214-32, 311-26, for relations between Florence, Pisa and Genoa in 1405-06.

then, was a truce which our ambassadors—with current and past documents in hand—had to put into line with the last treaty between Pisa and Florence. They also had to contrive it in such a way as to make it legally concordant with the five-year treaty between Florence and Siena.

I have talked about the care taken by Florentine statesmen with the articles and details of treaties under negotiation. If we ask what sorts of things were especially watched, the answer is that no detail was too unimportant to be neglected. This was supremely true of the language of treaties, of the pains taken with words and phrases. In its treaties with the Visconti and with Ladislaus and Alfonso of Naples, Florence always aimed at clarity of expression. The ideal in these cases was to use language which would not allow any subsequent twisting—to use words and phrases that would not be found ambiguous by a court of arbitration; for the stronger position of the enemy inevitably turned the discovery of such ambiguity into a defeat for Florence. Nor was it enough for the negotiator to have a thorough grasp of the Latin of treaties and current usage, he also had to understand the legal meaning of certain words and expressions, know their judicial weight and their possible shiftiness under the scrutiny of jurists.

In April 1403 a knight and lawyer were sent on an embassy to Rimini to meet with Carlo Malatesta and the Cardinal Baldassare Cossa, papal legate. Together with the pope, Florence was to assume the expense of keeping 500 "lances" under the command of Malatesta for a period of six months. It was to conclude the arrangements for this that Tommaso Sacchetti and Lorenzo Ridolfi were dispatched to Rimini. A draft of the agreement had already been drawn up, so that the instructions of the Ten on War were very detailed. One request concerning the draft is particularly interesting. The ambassadors were told, "First of all, in the line which begins *Se pure volesse il tutto*, etc., where it says *non solo in parole ma in facto e in scriptura*, we want it understood that the words *in facto e* have been expunged so that it says *non solo in parole ma in scriptura*."[35] I have been unable to find a copy of the pact in question

---

[35] *DBLC*, 3, f. 10v, pencil. "Prima nel versiculo che commincia Se pure volesse il tutto, etc., dove dice non solo in parole ma in facto e in scriptura, vogliamo s'intendano levate quelle parole in facto e e dica non solo in parole ma in scriptura."

and cannot fill out the meaning of the passage quoted, but it appears that the phrase *in facto e* was considered too ambiguous in its context to have a precise meaning in the eyes of a panel of experienced judges. Indeed, in order fully to realize the objectives of this embassy, the canonist Ridolfi did not scruple to have a lateral document secretly notarized contemporaneously with his and Sacchetti's signing of the pact with the pope and Malatesta. The secret instrument bore testimony to the fact that the two ambassadors had lodged a protest saying that Florence was not to be liable for more than six months (including time past) of the expenses required to maintain 500 "lances" under Malatesta's command.[36] Shifty or not, acceptable to a court of arbitration or not, here was a document which any Florentine government would be able to produce at the appropriate time. Ridolfi and Sacchetti had overlooked no margin of safety.

Although Florentines were sometimes victimized by the wiles and snares of the Visconti, they also on occasion tried their own tricks and had their victims. In early December 1396 a leading knight and lawyer, Rinaldo Gianfigliazzi and Ludovico Albergotti, were dispatched to Bologna to negotiate the final stages of a defensive alliance against Giangaleazzo. It was called "the French league" and had been ratified by Florence and the Crown of France at the end of the previous September. The Republic set out to include Bologna and the lords of Padua and Mantua in this alliance. The comprehensive treaty was finally concluded and signed in December.[37] But no sooner had the Lord of

---

The instructions then go on to lay down other very detailed conditions. I have no evidence showing that Florentine lawyers and ambassadors were aware of the old principle in Roman and canon law whereby *dolus* was *bonus* when used against the enemy. See G. Post, *Studies in Medieval Legal Thought*, p. 305.

[36] *SRRO*, 1, ff. 44r-45r. Ridolfi said in his report to the Signory: "Et quando venimmo affare la promessa di nuovo, venimmo a protestare simigliantemente e in quella forma che si contiene nel rogo fatto per ser Ticie [di ser Giovanni Tici da Empoli], il quale di tale protesto fu rogato, con tucto che el Cardinale nel vero niente sa che noi facissemo rogare o vogliamo dire fare carta al decto nostro notaio. Et però non è il decto protesto nello strumento della obligatione."

[37] *DBRA*, 1, f. 33r. On the background to this treaty see M. de Boüard, *La France et l'Italie au temps du Grand Schisme d'Occident* (Paris, 1936), pp. 213-21; also E. Pastorello, *Nuove ricerche sulla storia di Padova e dei principi da Carrara al tempo di Gian Galeazzo Visconti* (Padova, 1908), pp. 90-91.

Padua seen the instrument of the treaty than he sent a vigorous protest to Florence, whose promise to cancel a Paduan money tribute to Milan had not been kept and whose obligations to the Italian allies seemed weakened by her commitments to France. Florence immediately answered by dispatching an ambassador, the expert notary Ser Piero da San Miniato, who had spent the previous spring in France on an embassy of prime importance.[38] Ser Piero's *relazione* to his masters, the Ten on War, is in part a fascinating report on the technique of negotiation employed by Gianfigliazzi and Albergotti. Francesco Novello II da Carrara, Lord of Padua, complained that they had deceived him: they had promised him one thing—before an obligation had called Francesco away—but in the final papers of the treaty they had given his ambassador something else. "I left it to my ambassador," the notary reported Francesco as saying, "to ratify the treaty. But he has not ratified it in accordance with my mandate, for the words of the agreement [contracto] ring such that they do not please me. Indeed, it seems to me that I have been tricked, that they are equivocal and litigious words rather than solid promises." Then reading out some letters which he had just received, confirming him in his distrust of the treaty, the prince observed to Ser Piero, "just as you [Florentines] have lawyers, the others also have lawyers who know the words of contracts. If we must actually perform deeds, these equivocal words are unnecessary; they even tend to undermine our deeds." Not until the following morning did Ser Piero get to see the instrument of the treaty. "I saw the contract and debated it with Messer Arrigo [Galletti] in the presence of [Francesco Novello] and of Messer Michele da Rabatta."[39] The lawyer Galletti ended his representations by maintaining that the treaty had not yet gone into effect,

[38] *DBRA*, 1, ff. 37v-40r; M. de Boüard, *op.cit.*, p. 212.

[39] *DBRA*, 1, f. 39r-v, "Et lasciai al mio ambasciadore che facto questo ratificasse la legha. Hora il mio ambasciadore l'a ratificata fuori di mio mandato, però chè le parole del contracto suonano in forma che non mi piacciono. Anche me ne pare essere ingannato, e che elle sieno piùtosto parole doppie e di litigio che di promesse ferme . . . però chè come voi avete de' giudici che gl'altri ancora n'anno che cognoscono le parole de' contracti. Se noi dobbiamo fare facti queste parole doppie non sono necessarie; anche sono piùtosto guastatrice de' facti nostri. . . . Io vidi il contracto e fecine disputatione con messer Arrigo [Galletti] in sua presenza e di messer Michele da Rabatta." Most of this report was published by Pastorello, *Nuove ricerche*, pp. 224-25.

despite the signature of the Paduan ambassador. Ser Piero replied and concluded "that wanting to live well and to do things rightly, there would be no need of lawyers and notaries, who are always wrangling over doubts and points. It is with the sword that we now must deal, yet we stand around debating the [different] rights [of the allies], and if the sword renders them good, they will become clear however murky they were; but if it makes them issue in being wrong or bad, then all the laws of Lycurgus, of Athens, of Lacedaemon, or of Justinian will not be worth two cents."[40]

Dealing much with cunning men, it appears that Florence had learned their ways. The Lord of Padua was not himself contriving to get out of an honest commitment. He truly needed the alliance. He knew that the "Viper" of Milan, who was soon to strike at Mantua, was merely waiting for the right moment to attack Padua. Francesco Novello therefore did not break faith with the league.

This diplomatic exchange between Florence and Padua effectively underlines the importance assigned to the language of treaties and in the same connection brings out the critical role of lawyers—in this case Ludovico Albergotti, Messer Arrigo Galletti, Ser Piero da San Miniato (who stood far above the ordinary run of notaries), and Messer Pietro Paolo Crivelli, the Paduan lawyer who signed the treaty and who represented Francesco Novello in the closing stages of negotiation. Crivelli was also the ambassador sent to Florence with Francesco's protests.[41]

An excellent treaty to study from the viewpoint of the foregoing pages is one concluded about a hundred years later: the historic treaty between Florence and Charles VIII of France, ratified on November 25, 1494.[42]

[40] *Ibid.*, f. 40r, "che vollendo bene fare e ben vivere non si vorrebbe ne giudici ne notari però chè sempre stanno in su dubbi e puncti. Abbiamo teste a fare colla spada e noi stiamo nelle disputationi delle ragioni e se la spada le fara buone, quantunche fussono turbe, saranno chiare; ma se ella ce la fara cactive, tucte le leggi di Ligurgo, d'Atene, di Lacedemonia, o di Justiniano non ci varranno due danari."

[41] On Crivelli, see Guasti, ed., *Capitoli*, II, 411; Pastorello, *Nuove ricerche*, p. 227.

[42] Published by G. Capponi among the documents appended to Jacopo Pitti's *Istoria fiorentina*, in the first volume of the *Archivio storico italiano* (1842), pp. 362-75. Arts. 1 and 7 were the most humiliating. Excerpts of this treaty, with a commentary, were published in *Négociations diplomatique de la France avec la Toscane*, ed. A. Desjardins and G. Canestrini, I, 602-06.

It was negotiated for the Republic by four leading statesmen—Guidantonio Vespucci, Domenico Bonsi, Filippo Valori, and Piero Capponi. Vespucci and Bonsi figured among the city's best-known lawyers. Despite the fact that Florence was practically at the mercy of the French army, nowhere in the instrument of the treaty is the city made to suffer a striking defeat. Everything yielded is offset by a compensation. For if the document surrounds the king with the airs of majesty, making him generous and forgiving, requiring all subsequent signories to name him in their oath of office, calling him "pater patriae," yet he is also designated "protector, defensor, et libertatis nostrae conservator," and he swears to defend the city against any tyrant (Arts. 1-2). It is true that according to the treaty Livorno and Pisa were for the time being to remain militarily occupied by the French, but the Florentine negotiators saw to it that the Republic retained the powers of justice and administration in those cities (Art. 3). Furthermore, the French captains left in charge there and in command of three other fortresses were to take an oath committing themselves to return all those places to Florentine hands after the king's expedition to Naples (Art. 6). That during the expedition two royal officials were to reside in Florence and participate in deliberations affecting the interests of France (Art. 7) was counterbalanced not only by the fact that the king promised his protection to Florentine shipping and trade in and around Genoa (Art. 12), but also by his according Florentines the full right of free trade in France and all his lands— the right to contract, to buy and sell, to draw up last wills according to Florentine law, and in fact to obtain profit and favors as if they were French. To this end he promised all Florentine citizens and subjects, present and future, "plenum, liberum et perpetuum salvum conductum." The act which guaranteed these privileges was to be published in all the lands of the king and registered with the regional parliaments, "maxime ut notum sit omnibus suis subditis, de plenitudine potestatis suae Florentinos, et eorum subditos, vere naturales Gallos effectos esse" (Art. 13). Even Florence's new heraldic right to show the golden fleur-de-lis on a blue field, accorded as a favor and in sign of the king's protection, called for an added band carrying the inscription "Libertas" (Art. 14).

Some of these assurances may now seem laughable to a student of the period, but only because of the facile superiority conferred by hindsight. Vespucci and Bonsi circumscribed the king's obligations with legal safeguards. They negotiated a treaty with the best possible legal terms for Florence. If in the years that followed, the Republic had sometimes to buy off Charles VIII and his successor, while Pisa returned to Florentine hands only after vast expenditure and not until 1509, it was because Florence suddenly found itself, like all the Italian states, in a new world become the plaything of France and Spain and the Empire. Interregional politics became European politics. All the old peninsular balances, diplomatic and military, however imperfect, however hard on the weakest, which had been developed by the Italian states now collapsed. International law and international relations had to be put on a new footing. But meanwhile, far more than in Quattrocento Italy, states were to live by the rule that *ius in armis est*. And the value of lawyers in the tasks of diplomacy was to depend mainly on a non-legal factor: the force of arms.

### 3. The Interpretation of Treaties

From one point of view, negotiating treaties is inseparable from interpreting them. The diplomat puts things down, or assents to their inclusion in a treaty, presumably with a clear sense of what they mean. And in having the final document stipulate sanctions, he attests to having also thought about violations, thought about the weight and meaning which a prospective panel of judges might assign to the individual articles. Yet being different processes in diplomacy, different both as to ends and in time, negotiation and interpretation call for separate discussion.

Before two Italian states took a dispute to law, they went through a stage of wrangling. On the basis of the treaty in question or of past relations between the two states, each tried to convince the other of the right embodied in its claims. The history of Florentine foreign affairs bristles with numerous examples of this, and here again the Republic, like the other Italian states, relied heavily on its lawyers. These alone, or highly trained notaries, could argue from law about the points of a treaty, so that embassies with such objectives were always put into the care of trained legists. If negotiations with the offending or accusing state were carried on by letter, lawyers at home were summoned to draft *consilia*, recommendations, rebuttals, and so on. In cases where the Republic was the accusing part, Florentines examined the documents in question and then pointed out the obligations of the other part. A simple action of this sort took place in August 1390 when, in the midst of a war against Giangaleazzo, the Bolognese took fright and seemed on the verge of negotiating a separate peace with Milan. With another lawyer present (Giovanni de' Ricci), Filippo Corsini immediately prompted the government to take a legalistic line with the ambassadors from Bologna. He declared that Florence must dissuade the Bolognese from any intention to sue for a separate peace "because by law they cannot and should not."[43] Corsini was referring to the multilateral defense treaty of October 10, 1389, which included Florence, Bologna, Pisa, Lucca, and Perugia.

In November 1393 Rinaldo Gianfigliazzi called attention to the fact that a number of citizens suspected the lords of Padua and Mantua of having violated the defensive league of Bologna (April 11, 1392) and recommended that they investigate this as well as other questions together with a group of lawyers.[44]

By a peace between Giangaleazzo and the allies, concluded at Genoa on January 20, 1392, Francesco da Carrara retained Padua but was compelled to cede Bassano, Feltre, and Belluno to the "Viper" and to promise him, in addition, a yearly indemnity of 10,000 florins for a period of fifty years. The peace was a humiliating defeat for the Paduan, and although he assented to it, having no other choice, he did so with an eye to seizing the first way out of the commitment. His moment seemed to have come in the late spring of 1394, when he resolved not to pay the 10,000 florins of tribute. In June, to explain his actions, Francesco sent an ambassador to Florence—the lawyer Arrigo Galletti, appointed so as to lend some color of right to his master's decision to back out of an agreement

---

[43] *CP*, 28, f. 91v, "Et auferantur Bononienses ab intentione pacis petende quia nec possunt de iure ne debent."

[44] *CP*, 30, f. 83r. The dispute had already started over Giangaleazzo's efforts to deflect the waters of the River Mincio. See pp. 352-55.

legally concluded. Uneasy, knowing that Giangaleazzo was always on the lookout for excuses to invade and seize, Florence rejected the Paduan representations and prepared to follow up its rejection with legal arguments. Executive consultations were held on the question the morning of June 22nd.[45] Through their spokesman (the canon lawyer Ridolfi), the Eight on Public Safety advised the government to have the matter discussed and narrowed down by the Captains of the Guelf Society, a group of select citizens, and some lawyers. More definite views were expressed in the afternoon. All the speakers held that the Lord of Padua should meet his obligations—pay the tribute "because peace ought to be preserved." Matteo Arrighi said that if the ambassador resisted, then lawyers should look into the legal arguments favoring the Florentine view. Recommending that any such findings be kept secret "for now," he warned against letting the lawyers first confer with the ambassador. Arrighi's proposals were seconded by Rinaldo Gianfigliazzi, who emphasized and strengthened the advice against allowing the lawyers to hold a preliminary conference with the Paduan envoy. Alessandro Arrigucci repeated the views of Gianfigliazzi and Arrighi. Andrea Minerbetti also encouraged the Signory to have lawyers draft a legal opinion holding the Lord of Padua to his contractual obligations. Lorenzo Ridolfi, finally, spoke again for the Eight on Public Safety. Supporting what all the others had said, he named the lawyers best fitted to draw up the Florentine argument in the case—Giovanni de' Ricci and Ludovico Albergotti.[46]

The skill of the Florentines is not at first obvious in the case just described; it lay in their determination not to have a preliminary confrontation between the Florentine lawyers and the Paduan lawyer-ambassador. Such a meeting would have had the character of a dispute arranged and sanctioned by the rulers of the city, and this they were not prepared to allow. The issue for Florentines was not one to be met with doubts, and an arranged debate would have made the entire question

---

[45] *CP*, 30, ff. 134v-135r, "in consilio requisitorum super relatis per dominum Arrigum Galletti ambaxiatorem domini paduani." The Paduan situation discussed by Pastorello, *Nuove ricerche*, pp. 77ff.

[46] *CP*, 30, *loc.cit.*, "et quod domini habeant dominum Johannem de Riccis et dominum Lodovicum de Albergottis et cum eorum consilio fiet iusta et dulcis."

litigious from the outset. Instead, the government meant Ricci and Albergotti to provide a legal basis for the Florentine insistence that Francesco da Carrara pay the promised indemnity. Their representations would then be used to inform Francesco of the question's status in law, as if merely to remind him of a responsibility which he knew to be binding. If after this he still held out, then dispute might ensue. With the aid of the pressures exercised by Giangaleazzo himself, Florence— censor of the league against the "tyrant"—managed for the time being to make the Lord of Padua observe his obligations.[47]

Always concerned about the designs of the Visconti in central Italy, where the weakness of some city-states appeared to invite conquest or interference, Florentines were sticklers about having the allies as well as the Visconti keep faith with treaties. If in politics the Republic stood for the independence of states and the survival of republican liberty, in law it stood for the observance of international agreements and "the comity of nations." Florence thus came to be the guardian of pacts and agreements concerning Tuscany and all the bordering regions. In this work of surveillance, as we have seen, lawyers were called on to per- form a distinct function, even when the trouble issued from as far away as Padua. Florence continued to play the role of censor long after Giangaleazzo was dead. In April 1422, having recently taken Genoa and some northern cities, while also being on the move in the Romagna, Filippo Maria Visconti sent ambassadors to Florence to smooth down republican anxieties. One of the colleges—the Sixteen—immediately called for special consultations and requested the Signory to have three or four "of the more capable lawyers [*doctores*]" study the articles of the last peace treaty (February 8, 1420) to see if the duke had committed a breach. At an important executive session three days later, six of the twenty-four outside advisors were lawyers.[48] The duke's ambassadors were still wait- ing for a reply, and the government had yet to decide whether or not

---

[47] Francesco, meanwhile, had actually been in secret contact with Giangaleazzo, hoping to strike a bargain of some sort. Cognasso, *Storia di Milano*, vi, 15-16.

[48] *CP*, 45, ff. 5r, *et seq.* (23, 26 April 1422): Francesco Machiavelli, Francesco Viviani, Alessandro Bencivenni, Carlo Federighi, Giovanni Bertaldi, and Giuliano Davanzati. In the session of 23 April, the speaker for the Twelve opposed assigning preliminary "auditores" to the ambassadors "nam satis nota est intentio ducis mediolani."

the Lord of Milan had broken the peace. All the advisors urged a policy of caution.

In this as in some other cases the report or *consilium*—if that it was—of the lawyers has not survived. Generally speaking, legal reports concerning the infractions of other states were not recorded in the *Consulte e Pratiche*, but some reports concerning prospective Florentine action were. Approached by a prince or commune desiring to negotiate a compact, Florence, if receptive, had usually to look into its other foreign commitments to determine whether or not new ones were possible *de iure*. When Florentines took up a question like this, we see them often striving to fulfil all their obligations in good faith. But they could also strain to give a legal face to the breaking of a burdensome contract or to the negotiation of a more attractive one—one to which by law they should not have consented. In a world where weaker states had to depend on the norms of international law, particularly as expressed in formal alliances, Florence had to do everything in its power to tint its rare contractual violations with the color of right.

One of the chief disturbers of the peace during the early years of the fifteenth century was King Ladislaus of Naples. In 1408 he took Rome and the territory around. Before the end of the year, "all Umbria, including Perugia, Assisi, and many places in the northern papal provinces were under Neapolitan sway. . . . By the spring of 1409 Cortona, southern outpost of Tuscany, was in Ladislaus' hands; his troops were stationed near Arezzo and Siena."[49] Then in June and July, treaties were negotiated drawing Florence, Siena, the papacy (via the Cardinal of Bologna), and King Louis II of Anjou into an alliance. This stroke arrested the invader's northern advance. Indeed, the army of the league took the offensive and, moving south, was in Rome by October. For the next few months Ladislaus was in trouble. In December he made overtures of peace to Florence, soon following these with specific proposals. On January 4, 1410, the Signory had the subject discussed by its advisors, who said at once that the alliance with Siena and the others might present a barrier and encouraged the Signory to explore the matter

[49] H. Baron, *The Crisis of the Early Italian Renaissance*, 2 vols. (Princeton, 1955), I, 318.

more thoroughly with a select group of citizens.[50] This was done. But finding no loopholes in the documents concerned, the Signory decided to have lawyers study the question of Florence's legal right to sign a separate peace with Ladislaus. The assignment went to Bartolommeo Popoleschi and Giovanni Serristori. They presented their report to the government and to a select group of advisors on January 7th.[51]

First they had studied the treaties separately concluded by Florence with Siena and with the Cardinal of Bologna (the papal legate, Baldassare Cossa). The obligations there were clear. Without the express consent of the other party, none could officially end a war in which both were involved. The two lawyers had next examined the instrument of the league among King Louis of Anjou, Florence, Siena, and the Cardinal of Bologna. Here again the way to the conclusion of a separate peace was blocked. They pointed out that this league did not dissolve the earlier compacts with Siena and the papal legate, that it had the juridical character of a partnership, and that it was based on mutual trust. There was only one way to withdraw from the league before the date of its expiration: if one of the members violated the contract, the others were thereby released. Now it seems that Louis of Anjou had broken the bonds of the league by having failed to contribute a promised sum of money—about 30,000 florins. Therefore, observed the lawyers, "we may withdraw from this league, saying that because the

---

[50] *CP*, 40, ff. 96r-99r; also, more generally, A. Cutolo, *Re Ladislao D'Angiò-Durazzo*, 2 vols. (Milan, 1936), I, 350ff.

[51] *CP*, 40, f. 99r-v. They observed that as the league was a "societas" founded on mutual trust, the law provided for a way to withdraw from it, "Et quod presupo[si]to sic, verum esse quod rex Lodovicus defecerit in non faciendo solutiones pecuniarum quas debet, que esse dicuntur circa xxx milia florenorum, quod possumus discedere ab hac confederatione dicendo quod cum non serventur premissa et deficiatur in substantialibus, quod non est pro nobis persistere in tali societate et quod volumus discedere et renuntiare. Sed non possumus discedere nisi notificemus regi Lodovico vel habenti sufficiens mandatum ab eo, quod velimus discedere ab hac societate quia ipse defecit. . . . Et quod tamen non dicunt hoc precise et assertive sed su[b]mittunt se saniori iudicio et rogant dominos quod de hac re habeant savius consilium ne onus tante rei incumbat eis. Nec profitentur se sumpturos hanc rem in summa hoc verbo usus est, maxime cum in illa confederatione sit unum capitulum per quod disponitur quod si de inobservantia lige oriretur questio inter partes, non procedatur ad represalias etc. sed fiat commissio de re de qua esset questio in arbitros comunes."

promises have not been kept and some material commitments have not been observed, that it is not for us to remain in such an association and that we want to go our separate way and repudiate the league. But we cannot draw away without first notifying King Louis that we want to get out of the alliance because of his failure [to pay the money], or unless we have a sufficient mandate from him." Since the alliance, moreover, was "reinforced by an oath," Popoleschi and Serristori did not think that Louis could salvage it by now deciding to meet his obligations. Even then however, the way to a unilateral peace with Ladislaus would still be legally barred by the Republic's separate compacts with Siena and the Cardinal of Bologna. Only the express consent of these could clear the way and there was not much hope of that.

Far from affecting to have said the last word on the matter, the two lawyers were ready to submit to "sounder judgment" and urged the Signory to solicit further legal counsel so that the two would not have to carry so much responsibility themselves. They were particularly moved to say this by the implications of the statement which concluded their report, namely, that one of the articles of the quadripartite alliance stipulated that if a question arose among the parties concerning the failure on the part of one to keep faith with the league, they were not to proceed with reprisals but to refer the question to a group of arbitrators selected by common consent. Evidently, if the signing of a separate peace with Ladislaus could be viewed in law as a retaliatory action, then the Republic's quarrel with Louis of Anjou would have to be submitted to arbitration.

Florence was baffled. The ensuing consultations show that majority opinion took for granted that Popoleschi and Serristori had pretty much exhausted what might be said from a legal point of view.[52] Another lawyer, Filippo Corsini, summarized the impasse by stressing the "confederationem" allying Florence to Siena and the papacy. A peace with Ladislaus, he noted, would require the consent of the allies—of the pope above all. The only alternative was to conclude a secret, and hence illegal, peace. But Florence was not willing to take such a risk. Guided quite as much by a sense of the potential dangers as by what the lawyers had said,

[52] *Ibid.*, ff. 100v *et seq.*

the Signory, the Ten on War, and the colleges held the city to its alliances.

This was not the only time Florence was to seek the help of lawyers in its relations with King Ladislaus. A year later, acting together with Siena, Florence finally concluded a treaty of peace with him (January 9, 1411).[53] He promised not to meddle in Roman or Tuscan affairs. While disapproving of the treaty, both the pope and Louis of Anjou acquiesced, although they carried on with hostilities. Then in May Ladislaus transferred his allegiance to this pope (Cossa, John XXIII), and in 1412 the two finally reached an agreement. Pope John imagined that he would be able to make use of the king, who pretended to be on John's side until the late spring of 1413, when he was again ready to march. Starting out after the *condottiere* and ex-commander of papal forces Paolo Orsini, Ladislaus suddenly changed direction and made for Rome in May. The Florentine Signory and colleges met on June 3rd with a special group of twenty advisors to discuss the military movements of their old antagonist.[54] Speaking for the twenty, the canon lawyer Lorenzo Ridolfi encouraged the government to negotiate a peaceful settlement between king and pope, if need be by public instrument ("per viam promissionum et obligationum"). He observed that another consultation was needed in order to pin down the nature and extent of the promises and obligations to be exacted from both sides, especially since it was not in the interests of Florence to draw the two into a true league or alliance. Meanwhile, Florentine obligations were to be kept to a bare minimum. Only when these different points were decided on could instructions be sent to the Florentine ambassadors in Rome. Still speaking for the entire *pratica*, Ridolfi advised the Signory to have a group of lawyers examine two questions: was King Ladislaus violating the articles of the peace concluded with Florence (January 9, 1411) by leading soldiers toward Rome and interfering in Roman affairs? Could Florence dispatch troops to Bologna for the sole purpose of defending that city without violating the same articles? Taking swift action on this advice, the Signory turned to five lawyers: Corsini, Ridolfi, Stefano Buonaccorsi,

[53] N. Valeri, *L'Italia nell' età dei principati* (Verona, 1949), p. 362, says 26 Jan.
[54] *CP*, 42, f. 30v; more generally, Cutolo, *Re Ladislao*, I, 397-99.

Guaspare Accorambuoni, and Jacopo Niccoli (brother of the humanist, Niccolò). They presented their report to the government on June 4th. The gist of it was as follows.[55]

(1) By interfering in Roman affairs, King Ladislaus did violence to the articles of the peace. But if Rome or her governor had done him injury, if the city was in the hands of one of his foes, or if one had taken refuge there or was given aid or comfort—openly or in secret—by the Romans, then the king could intrude into the affairs of Rome and not be charged with violating the peace with Florence. (2) If the pope was not an enemy of the king and had no intention of hurting him, it would not be a breach of the designated articles for Florence to send 200 "lances" to Bologna; otherwise, the contrary. Was the pope the king's enemy and did he aim to hurt him? The answer to these questions depended on fact, not on probabilities or speculation. That the two were not enemies was evident not only from the fact that the peace between them still obtained, but also from the content of one of the king's letters, where he expressed his desire to continue in peace with the pope and claimed that he was marching toward Rome in the general interest. The pope, for his part, also affirmed that he wanted his peace with the king to remain inviolate.

Five days after the delivery of this report, three other lawyers gave it their endorsement: Torello Torelli, Giovanni Serristori, and Nello da San Gimignano. They added a minor observation purporting to show that the king would be breaking the articles of the peace if he meddled in Roman affairs.[56] Already moving toward a rupture with Ladislaus, Florence was soon given more ample ground for action than the lawyers' report. For the king had pushed into Rome on the 9th of June, causing Pope John to flee. On the 15th Florence set up a War Commission (a Decem Baliae) for one year, and at about the same time the king's soldiers began seizing the goods of Florentine merchants in Rome.

---

[55] CP, 42, f. 31r. The text begins and goes on in this style: "Ad primum, quod rex impediendo se de civitate Rome venit contra capitula pacis, salvo quod si dictus rex offenderetur a dicta civitate Romana vel a tenente illam vel illa existente in manibus inimici dicti regis vel si in ipsa receptaretur aliquis inimicus dicti regis vel illi favor vel auxilium in ea quoque modo daretur palam vel occulte, tunc non veniret contra capitula pacis impediendo se de civitate Romana."

[56] Ibid. The endorsement of Torelli and the others was recorded on 9 June.

Almost exactly a year later, with Ladislaus driving north in an unnerving fashion, the Republic was again moved to seek a peace with him, and again the need was felt to obtain the counsel of lawyers. On May 27, 1414, Alessandro Bencivenni—recently awarded the doctorate in law (1411)—recommended to the Signory that it consult with the colleges, some lawyers, and other citizens to see if by examining the existing treaty with Pope John they could find something in it which would allow Florence to conclude a unilateral peace with Ladislaus.[57] On May 28th the Signory heard a number of advisors, among them two canon lawyers—Lorenzo Ridolfi and Francesco Machiavelli.[58] Ridolfi alluded to the fact that a group of lawyers was supposed to prepare a report on the question of a peace with Ladislaus *vs.* the Republic's obligations to the pope. Messer Francesco said that he would bypass the question of whether Florence could legally sign a peace without papal consent or "sine macula fidei" because he had not seen the "scripturas" (i.e., a copy of the treaty with the pope). But he made a point of observing that when a "societas" is set up and one of the contracting parties fails to observe the terms of the partnership, then the party of the other part is released from the bonds of the contract and may legally do as he wants.[59]

The report expected by Ridolfi and others was never drawn up, and with good reason: the oligarchy was completely divided. While some citizens were ready to conclude a unilateral peace with Ladislaus, others were passionately opposed because they profoundly distrusted the king.[60] The split was dramatic. It cut through the top stratum of political society and was perfectly reflected in the differences of opinion among the lawyers who stood out in public affairs. It is not surprising that the legal profession did not produce an official report on this occasion. The peace party—bent on having an "illegal" peace—swiftly gained the upper hand. It was able to rely on a favorable Signory and got the support of power-

[57] *CP*, 42, f. 138r-v.  [58] *Ibid.*, f. 141r-v.

[59] On partnership in Roman law see *D.* 17, 2; *C.* 4, 37; *Inst.* 3, 25, *Corpus Iuris Civilis*, eds. P. Krueger, T. Mommsen, R. Schoell (Berlin, 1904-08). On breaking faith, *C.* 2, 12, 21; *D.* 16, 3, 1 and *glos. ord.* (Ed., Venice, 1591-92).

[60] A. Dainelli, "Niccolò da Uzzano nella vita politica dei suoi tempi," *ASI*, xc (1932), 81-82; Ammirato, *Istorie*, v, 34-35; the division of opinion in Florence was not taken into account by Cutolo, *Re Ladislao*, I, 420-22.

ful backers like Agnolo Pandolfini and the Gonfalonier of Justice, Maso degli Albizzi. On June 1st instructions were drafted for two ambassadors, Pandolfini (merchant) and Torelli (lawyer), who were dispatched to Assisi to arrange a peace with Ladislaus.[61] But the debate in Florence continued, even if no recorded consultations were held until June 14th. On that day the venerable old jurist Filippo Corsini argued that it was not possible for Florence, without the consent of Pope John or the Emperor Sigismund, to sign a separate peace with Ladislaus. Apart from the legal obstacles contained in Florence's treaty with the pope, Corsini observed, "we are *fideles* of the Empire, we have privileges and other things from it, and it did a great deal for us in these parts in 1368."[62] On June 15th Corsini came back to this theme, but most of the outside advisors—picked representatives of the city's four quarters—seemed to favor a peace with Ladislaus.

The peace party prevailed. On June 22nd a peace was signed at Assisi. On June 26th, however, discussion in the *Consulte e Pratiche* continued, for the peace had yet to be ratified, and there was still no unanimity among the lawyers present, although they argued with a copy of the treaty in hand. It was in this exchange that political debate among Florentine lawyers reached a high point.[63] Five lawyers participated: Lorenzo Ridolfi, Francesco Machiavelli, Filippo Corsini, Giovanni Serristori, and Alessandro Bencivenni. Although seeing the dangers, Ridolfi, Machiavelli, and Serristori came out in favor of ratifying the treaty. This, they believed, was the lesser evil. Corsini, on the other hand, ardently opposed ratification, and while Bencivenni weakly stated that he favored Ridolfi's counsel (i.e., ratification), he stressed and dwelt on the great dangers of the treaty. All five lawyers went into some of the legalistic details of the peace, but the disagreement among them was decisive. Ladislaus promised not to molest Bologna

---

[61] *SCMLC*, 6, f. 36r-v.

[62] *CP*, 42, f. 143v. Ladislaus had opposed Sigismund in Hungary. Not only were they sworn enemies, they were at war in Italy, though at the moment Sigismund was more taken up with the forthcoming Council of Constance. On Florentine relations with the Emperor Charles IV in 1368 see Brucker, *Florentine Politics and Society*, pp. 236-38. Corsini was exaggerating the alleged benefits of 1368.

[63] *CP*, 42, ff. 151r *et seq*. Bits published by Guasti in Albizzi, *Commissioni*, I, 239.

and the territory around, and for three of the lawyers this article of the peace treaty was clear enough. For Corsini and Bencivenni, however, it looked as if the Malatesta were to be given a free hand in Bologna. Again, Corsini insisted that the Florentine ambassadors had violated their mandate, that they should not have signed the treaty, and that in fact this doubtful peace drew Florence into action against the pope and Emperor Sigismund, whose forces Ladislaus was preparing to attack. Ridolfi admitted that there was something irregular about the conditions under which the ambassadors had signed the treaty (possibly a final approval had not been obtained), but he maintained that they had negotiated an agreement fully in accord with their mandate from the Signory, colleges, and War Commission.[64] Serristori also upheld the ambassadors, held that they had not exceeded their mandate. For in the consultations on the treaty of peace, he observed, it was never prescribed that either pope or emperor should have a part in it. He thus suggested that their exclusion did not constitute an act against them, as Corsini had indicated. Indeed, it must have been intimated by Serristori or someone else that pope and emperor would be able *de facto* to associate themselves with the peace, for Bencivenni deemed it necessary to assert that since neither of these princes was actually mentioned in the instrument of the peace, they were not included in it *de iure*.[65]

There is no point in trying to summarize the other details of the debate. The essential point has already been made: when an issue was so thoroughly political that the oligarchy split on it, the solutions were not likely to be, could not indeed be, in the resources of the law. Starting from conflicting political premises, the lawyers consulted by the government came to fairly different conclusions about the legal resonances and legal safeguards of the treaty in question. For Corsini and Bencivenni legal right militated against ratification of the treaty because three things had been mishandled: the mandate of the ambassadors, the status of Bologna, and the nexus of Florentine relations with the pope and

---

[64] *CP*, 42, f. 151v, Ridolfi "dixit et consuluit quod a veritate discederet si assereret pericula non esse in pace et liga conclusa, tamen conclusum est per oratores cum mandato dominorum et collegiorum et decem; quod ad reputationem et famam multum importat, licet non legitime secundum ordinamenta nostra," etc.

[65] *Ibid.*, f. 152v.

emperor. The other lawyers, while taking an opposing view, also claimed some support in the law, although they did not dare hold that the separate peace with Ladislaus was legally consistent with the Florentine-papal alliance. If the controversy had not turned on a question of political survival, on conflicting views concerning the best policy to follow with a king whose armies had twice threatened Florence, we might have been able to see the rift between the lawyers more purely in legal terms—a rift or division of judgment reflecting different legal inclinations.[66] But everything connected with the dispute over Ladislaus' intentions indicates that lawyers, like other citizens, *began* with a political view of this young, vigorous, and clever king. Their legal views of the peace treaty were constructs which came *after*; and in the case of the lawyers who favored the treaty, we may almost say that those views were legal rationalizations of politically committed positions.

The passions generated by the controversial peace and the questions raised by the lawyers were not lasting, for, having concluded his peace with Florence on June 22nd, Ladislaus fell sick in July, and was dead on August 7th, thus healing the divisions within the oligarchy and silencing the disputants. Never again, not even when faced with the machinations of Filippo Maria Visconti, was Florence compelled to cope with a prince the equal of Ladislaus. Yet in the years immediately following, there were to be other treaties and foreign agreements that posed problems of interpretation and which lawyers would be called on to resolve.

In August 1415 three lawyers were commissioned by the Signory to study a Florentine agreement with the Count of Urbino in order to see if he was legally right in claiming further cash payments from the Republic.[67] During the first half of 1417, commercial difficulties with Genoa resulted in the government's appointing a group of lawyers to draft a report on the relevant articles of an old treaty with the ex-governor of Genoa, Boucicaut.[68] In March 1418, when the Council of Two Hundred

---

[66] Ironically enough the two *decretorum doctores*—Ridolfi and Machiavelli—were not concerned to defend papal interests vis-à-vis King Ladislaus.

[67] *CP*, 43, f. 63r (13 Aug.). Filippo Corsini, Stefano Buonaccorsi, and Guaspare Accorambuoni. Having studied the articles of the agreement, they found that "de iure vero nil comes petere posset et contra eum ius comune haberet."

[68] *Ibid.*, f. 155v (25, 26 June). Among those consulted were the official communal lawyers. The report was not entered in the minutes.

refused to approve a certain cash payment to the Count of Urbino, the Signory had lawyers examine his claims. They reported—in the teeth of strong legislative opposition—that Florence was legally bound to pay.[69] In April a similar dispute broke out in connection with claims advanced by the *condottiere* Braccio da Montone. Once again lawyers were asked to examine a set of instruments, in this case those of the Florentine agreement with Braccio, and to persuade the merchant oligarchy that "de iure nos esse obligatos ad solvendum florenos 23,000."[70] A more interesting legal intervention was upheld by the government in October 1428. Florence, Venice, and Pope Martin V were trying to work out the details of a treaty of alliance. Martin insisted that under papal sponsorship Bologna and its appurtenances in the Romagna be included in the treaty. By the articles of a peace with Filippo Maria Visconti, however, Florence and Venice were forbidden to interfere in the affairs of Bologna. For this reason, and fearing what the Duke of Milan might do to profit from such a violation, Florentine statesmen wanted the tripartite treaty not only to exclude Bologna and its appurtenances but also to stipulate the exclusion in an article. To buttress this line of policy, the Signory and colleges had recourse to five lawyers: Lorenzo Ridolfi, Nello da San Gimignano, Francesco Machiavelli, Giovanni Buongirolami da Gubbio, and Zanobi Guasconi.[71] The five drew up a report and presented it to the government. They defended the point in question by offering a strict interpretation of the pertinent articles both in the peace treaty with Filippo Maria and in the draft of a treaty agreed to by Pope Martin late in 1425. These articles stipulated that Florence was not to meddle in Bolognese affairs. The lawyers argued that the Republic was herewith provided with a legal claim to have the prospective treaty specify that Bologna was to play no part in the alliance. Venice agreed. But since the Church claimed Bologna, Pope Martin was offended by the stand of the two republics, which seemed to deny his dominion there.

[69] *Ibid.*, ff. 181r-184v (21, 30 March), especially Lorenzo Ridolfi's representations, which refer to the opinion of the lawyers.

[70] *Ibid.*, f. 188v.

[71] *CP*, 48, ff. 32v-33r. On facts as presented above see also *SCMLC*, 5, ff. 39r-40v, 47r-52r, 54v-56r, instructions for ambassadors to Rome and Venice, Agnolo Pandolfini and Ser Paolo Fortini respectively.

He therefore persisted in his demand that the treaty include Bologna, and in November the two republics prepared to let the dispute be referred for arbitration to a college of jurists.[72]

We have seen lawyers at work in the executive councils—debating, making recommendations, drawing up reports. The government then acted on these, either through Florentine ambassadors, by conferring with foreign ambassadors in Florence, or by means of letters and dispatches. But what happened abroad? What happened when a Florentine ambassador was faced with having to interpret the points of an agreement in a foreign city? In important cases he was nearly always a trained lawyer and knew how to handle himself.

In the course of 1428 Florentines began to persuade themselves that Paolo Guinigi, Lord of Lucca, was too friendly with their shifty enemy, Filippo Maria Visconti of Milan. They were soon to convert their suspicions into a hankering for Lucca itself, a flourishing Tuscan city. But first Florentine relations with Guinigi were strained by a dispute over an outstanding debt.

Buonaccorso da Montemagno, lawyer and humanist, was sent as Florentine ambassador to Lucca and Genoa in July 1428.[73] In his first official contacts with the Lucchese, he was to call attention to the fact that by an agreement of August 31, 1422, the lord of that city, Paolo Guinigi, had promised to share military expenses with Florence, whose leading stipendiary at that time had been the soldier of fortune, Braccio da Montone. Guinigi had committed Lucca to paying up to one-fifth of these expenses for a period of four years, although the yearly total was at no point to exceed 6,000 florins. Braccio served Florence and Lucca for twenty months after the conclusion of the August pact and then died. Owing, however, to the Duke of Milan's designs and armies, Florence had gone on hiring other men at arms; wherefore the city now claimed payment for the remaining twenty-eight months. Reckoning Guinigi's share at the maximum rate, Florence claimed an unpaid bal-

---

[72] CP, 48, ff. 32v-33r. The report begins: "Primum, alla parte di Bologna si puo difendere la exceptione che si domanda essere ragionevole oltra le ragioni assegnate per l'ambasciadore nostro e quello di Vinegia per tre altre ragioni, le quali paiono fare molto al facto," etc.

[73] SCMLC, 5, ff. 26v-29r.

ance of 14,000 florins. The lawyer's diplomatic instructions continued: "If the Lord of Lucca should wish to deny the truth of your representations or want to argue that he was not liable for the said quantity, you will have with you a copy of the instrument and be able, moving from point to point and employing your customary good judgment and diligence, to bring out its meaning, to defend it, and to show him that he is bound to pay the amount demanded by this Signory."[74]

Buonaccorso da Montemagno's July embassy to Lucca was followed in August by another with identical objectives and this one was put into the hands of Giovanni Buongirolami, a lawyer from Gubbio who had obtained citizenship and won favor in Florence. The Lord of Lucca had refused to acknowledge the debt, alleging, among other things, that he had not been informed of the Republic's remedial military commitments after Braccio's death. Buongirolami was instructed to argue that Florence was not bound by the articles of the pact to communicate such information to him.[75] Had not everyone in Italy known that Florentines were spending more and more money on troops? The law ("ragione") was with Florence; but if Guinigi persisted in holding the converse, he might in the end have to disburse a good deal more than the sum in question, as violation of the agreement called for penalties of 50,000 florins. Besides, other charges might also be preferred against him. For by the pact of August 31, 1422, Guinigi had promised to give help against any prince who took hostile action against Florence, but he had defaulted in this; he had promised to "enter into no union or alliance in Lombardy"— this too had gone unobserved; and he had promised to have the same friends as Florence and the same enemies, but here again he had broken his word.

Buongirolami's embassy ran through the second and third weeks of August. Returning to Florence on the 21st, he drew up his report.[76] It is there we learn that he had confronted both Guinigi and his lawyers. Though the minutiae of the ensuing exchanges are denied us, the

---

[74] *Ibid.*, f. 27v, "Et se il signor di Lucca volesse dire non essere vero quanto per voi si spone o veramente vollesse difendere che non fusse obligato a la detta quantità, voi arete la copia delo instrumento con voi et di parte a parte il potrete fare chiaro," etc., "usando intorno acciò la vostra usata prudentia e diligentia."

[75] *Ibid.*, ff. 31v-33v.    [76] *SRRO*, 3, f. 111r-v.

themes and some particulars are not. The Lord of Lucca rejected the Florentine claim to 14,000 florins, insisting that his liability concerned "a time of peace and not of war, in accordance with the article that speaks of Braccio, and that he [was] thus counselled by lawyers." The ambassador invited him to submit the dispute to arbitration and recommended the College of Lawyers at Bologna, but he was told that Bologna was not a good venue because it had just suffered a change of government and was still much occupied by it. Buongirolami replied that this was no reason to suppose that the good judgment of those lawyers had also changed. Keeping to the Signory's instructions, he then suggested that Lucca and Florence have recourse to the College of Lawyers at Padua. But hedging or suspecting prejudice there, Guinigi would not have this proposal either, alleging three reasons: all the famous lawyers of Padua were now dead; there was currently an attack of the plague in that university city; and it was not good for the more unpleasant aspects of the quarrel between them to become widely known. But he expressed his readiness to have the Cardinal of Santa Croce, Niccolò Albergati, act as arbitrator. Buongirolami's rejoinder was to the point: he observed that there was certainly no shortage of "very able" lawyers at Padua and that he "was well informed about this."[77] The plague, he continued, was not bad there; Florence was not in a hurry; and Florentines were not afraid of the whole world's knowing about their dispute—indeed, having nothing to fear, they would like such publicity. In any case, he would inform the Signory of Guinigi's readiness to submit their disagreement to the Cardinal of Santa Croce.

What happened in Buongirolami's interviews with Guinigi's lawyers does not emerge. Most probably Buonaccorso da Montemagno had also gone before the same lawyers and one may imagine the exchange of views, the give and take of dispute. We know well enough what lawyers did on missions whose essential business depended on the interpretation of treaties. An ambassador might be told what to say by his government and even be provided with set rejoinders, but a good deal depended on him, as Montemagno's instructions show. He would be expected to interpret the treaty in question, a copy of it in hand—expected to

[77] *Ibid.*

elucidate points, to defend or refute statements of substance, to call on his speed of mind and aptness of expression.

Whether or not the dispute finally went for arbitration to Cardinal Albergati—himself trained in law—is not clear. The quarrel was finally composed in 1429, when Guinigi had his ambassadors pay the disputed sum into the Florentine treasury.[78]

Dispute about the meaning of treaties constituted a certain phase in relations between states; arbitration was the next phase.

## 4. Arbitration

Italians of the late medieval and Renaissance periods laid great emphasis on the certified document, in public as well as in private affairs. Why was this? The emphasis is first recorded in the course of the twelfth century and is part of a complex of concurrent phenomena: the booming expansion of cities, a vast increase of rights in property, an ensuing rise in the incidence of litigation, the revival of Roman law, and the "scientific" training of lawyers.

Jacob Burckhardt stressed the political lawlessness of Italy in the fourteenth century. Less easily controllable but equally prevalent, the lawlessness was there in the thirteenth century as well—the product of a vigorous peninsula which teemed with tiny states and half states. As each of these pushed out to conquer or absorb everything on its horizons, the Emperor, the only sovereign lord, was gradually stripped of his power and authority. Burckhardt stressed the illegitimacy of political power, but he failed to point out that Dante's contemporaries—petty lords or corporate personalities (the communes)—were not lawless every day. Between one period of political violence and another, most of them lived peacefully. Individuals carried on their workaday tasks—as peasants, textile workers, merchants, noblemen, clerics, or whatnot. Here surely was the dominant note. Yet political violence abounded and, like the immense increase of rights in property, must have been a factor leading men to assign great importance—possibly an exaggerated importance—to the use of certified public instruments. Where the leaders of communities were often driven to break the law, it was only natural that "hard"

[78] Ammirato, *Istorie*, v, 153.

evidence should be preserved, especially when the ordinary citizen did look to the law and right title. It seems clear, therefore, that the violence and illegal acts of the Burckhardtian generalization should be seen against a vast network of contracts, public and private, and of solemn agreements between states. Lawlessness was measured by its opposite—the observation of contracts—and so in speaking of late medieval and Renaissance Italy, we dare not stress one without also remembering the other.[79]

Perhaps the preceding observations serve to give a rough idea of why arbitration became a standard feature of Italian diplomacy. The incidence of lawlessness, combined with an ardent commitment to public instruments, issued in the search for impartial third parties. Also, the diplomacy of the Italian states was put into the hands of lawyers very early. Eminent and influential, they doubtless had much to do with bringing arbitration into remarkable currency.

When arbitration was the business or outcome of Florentine diplomacy, there were three points where the services of lawyers were often necessary: when Florence was presenting a case for arbitration; when it was acting as an arbitrator; and when it was attempting to persuade another to submit to arbitration. Presenting a case for arbitration was *prima facie* no part of diplomacy. Agreeing to refer a dispute to arbitration, the Signory had a group of lawyers prepare the Florentine case. The defense, like the brief, was ordinarily presented in written form. In such circumstances, it was no longer a question of sending an ambassador to a foreign government to negotiate. Nevertheless, there was on occasion critical information to be collected or something else to be done abroad. Then the Signory sent out diplomatic agents, often instructing them to try to influence the arbitrators. If the ambassador was a lawyer, his legal skills became a weapon—anyway a fact—in diplomacy. When in September 1420 Siena was chosen to act as arbitrator in a border dispute between

---

[79] The play or tension between the lawful and the lawless in Trecento Italian politics is strikingly reflected in one of the period's outstanding legal treatises— Bartolus of Sassoferrato's *De tyrannia.* Only the practice of tyranny, scrutinized by the cool eye of a lawyer who insisted on the law, could have brought forth such crisp definitions and such a lucid analysis of the anatomy of tyranny. For the English reader there is a translation of this text in E. Emerton, *Humanism and Tyranny, Studies in the Italian Trecento* (Cambridge, Mass., 1925).

Florence and the Marquis of Ferrara, the lawyer Tommaso Salvetti was dispatched as an ambassador to the Sienese. He was instructed to get them to send a referee to the disputed region (Barga) and to try to persuade them of the justice of the Florentine claims.[80] Salvetti was therefore expected to unite diplomacy and legal skills. And the practice continued. To show this let us look ahead a hundred years.

In 1524 certain lands around Pietrasanta (Florentine) were claimed by both Lucca and Florence. They chose a papal protonotary, Calisto da Maletica, to serve as arbitrator. Alessandro Malegonnelli, son of a famous lawyer and a lawyer himself, was sent out in September as Florentine envoy to Messer Calisto. His instructions directed him to meet the protonotary in Poggibonsi and to travel with him from there to Pietrasanta, "being good company to him along the way so as to win him over [to our side] as much as possible."[81] Was the lawyer not expected to combine his legal and other skills? He had also to make further use of his credentials: in treating with the protonotary and the agent from Lucca (Nazario Arnolfini, another lawyer), he was directed to try to get their consent to discuss openly all outstanding border disputes between Florence and Lucca.

Settlements reached by means of arbitration were sometimes questioned or violated after a few years. At that point the job of grasping and representing the arbitrator's decision in all its details became the responsibility of an ambassador, and here again lawyers were necessary. Florence purchased Arezzo in 1384 and at the same time absorbed Lucignano, a commune along the frontier between Arezzo and Siena. In 1386 Siena and Perugia laid claim to Lucignano. The dispute was referred for arbitration to the Commune of Bologna, which confirmed Florence's title but ruled that it must pay 8,000 florins to Siena.[82] In May 1388 Montepulciano, a commune in the same region, rebelled against the Sienese in favor of Florence. Reacting violently, the Sienese apparently considered turning Siena over to Giangaleazzo Visconti and lashed

---

[80] *SCMLC*, 6, ff. 111r, 114r; *SRRO*, 2, f. 67v; *SCMC-I*, 29, ff. 124v-125v, pencil (Oct. 1420), four letters to Salvetti from the Signory.

[81] *OCMLI*, 10, f. 114r-v (27 Sept.), "facendoli per il camino la buona compagnia acciochè ve lo guadagniate più che sia possibile."

[82] E. Repetti, *Dizionario geografico, fisico, storico della Toscana*, 6 vols. (Firenze, 1833-1846), II, 921.

out against the Republic's pretended title to Cortona, Montepulciano, and Lucignano. Florence promptly dispatched three ambassadors to Siena: Rinaldo Gianfigliazzi, Andrea Vettori, and the lawyer Giovanni de' Ricci, who was particularly commissioned to handle the question of Florence's title to Lucignano. The instructions said, "You, Messer Giovanni, are informed about how [the dispute over] Lucignano was referred to the Commune of Bologna by common consent. We got Lucignano by a decision legally arrived at ... but before this happened, Bologna wanted to see and examine the facts diligently, just as should have been done according to the law."[83]

Now and then the Florentine Republic was itself invited to help settle the disputes of others. This office drew Florence into a new relation with the contending states and in delicate situations put the city itself on trial. After all, the award of an arbitrator could hurt, hold, or create friends abroad. Seen in this light, arbitration belonged as much to diplomacy as to the judicial process. For this reason, when Florence agreed to serve as an arbitrator and the task arose of selecting the men who would actually perform the work of arbitration, the Signory was careful to call on lawyers who combined their practice of the law with great experience in the affairs of state. This seemed the best way to try to satisfy the exigencies of both the law and Florentine foreign policy.

The year 1395 saw parts of Emilia and the Romagna disturbed by war and the movement of soldiers, owing mainly to the ambitions of the pretender to the marquisate of Ferrara, Azzo d'Este. Azzo was secretly and then openly supported by the Count of Cunio (Giovanni da Barbiano), who had actually been paid to liquidate Azzo. The payers backed the Marquis of Ferrara (Niccolò d'Este), who was a member of the anti-Viscontean league of Bologna. With the encouragement of the Florentine Republic, this prince was given help by the Lord of Faenza (Astorre Manfredi I), then a Florentine stipendiary. These details are complicated enough and we need not go into the ensuing claims and counterclaims. The fact is that during the late summer of 1395 the contending parties

---

[83] *DBLC*, 1, f. 107r. "Di Lucignano voi messer Giovanni sete avisato come di concordia si commise nel comune di Bologna. E abbiamlo avuto per sententia data legitimamente dal detto comune di Bologna, il quale anzi che la desse volle vedere e examinare la verità del fatto diligentemente secondo di ragione si dovea fare."

agreed to submit their differences to arbitration. On one side was the Marquis of Ferrara and the Lord of Faenza, on the other the Count of Cunio. Interestingly, they selected a board of arbitration representing Giangaleazzo Visconti, Florence, and Bologna. In view of the forces at play, Giangaleazzo's representative would most likely favor the Count of Cunio, whose family were just then developing a tradition of military service to the Visconti. But Florence would favor the other part; possibly it was hoped that Bologna would be somewhat less partial. Hence the three probably had to aim at a compromise of some sort. The man who first went out to represent Florence in the work of arbitration was a rising young lawyer from a family of lawyers—Torello Torelli,[84] soon to win distinction as one of the city's prominent diplomats. Sent out in the second half of September to help initiate the job of inquiry and cross-examination, Torelli was replaced in October by two older men—the knight Filippo Adimari and the tough older lawyer, Filippo Corsini, whom none in Florence surpassed when it came to breadth of political experience.[85] The Republic was determined not to let Giangaleazzo worm his way into Ferrara and that part of central Italy.

Circumstances or the city's attitude occasionally caused litigants to agree on Florence as the sole arbitrator. Although the exact details escape us, we know that the Catalonians seized a number of Venetian vessels in the winter of 1447. A controversy ensued. Asked to arbitrate, the Florentine Signory immediately called for special counsel. The report of the advisory group was delivered by two leading statesmen—Neri Capponi and Puccio Pucci.[86] They wanted the dispute to be looked into at once, but they were careful to say that Florence should seek to avoid being drawn into any discord with either the Catalonians or the Venetians, for Florentines had extensive commercial relations with both. Three lawyers were chosen to arbitrate the dispute: one enjoyed an outstanding reputation as a jurist (Giovanni Buongirolami), the other two were top-ranking political figures (Otto Niccolini and Domenico Martelli). Neither

---

[84] *DBRA*, I, ff. 4v-5r, instructions to Torelli, dated 14 Sept. The Torelli were an old family from Prato, a neighboring town which had been under Florentine rule since 1350.

[85] *Ibid.*, f. 5r-v.

[86] *CP*, 52, f. 9r, report of 4 March. No further details of this controversy in *SCMC-I*, 36, 37.

of the contending parties would be able to say that Florence had failed to assign the job of arbitration to the best available men.

I have said that the Republic relied on lawyers both when it was a party in a dispute submitted for arbitration and when it agreed to discharge the office of arbitrator. But much closer to the ends and methods of diplomacy was the task—which often came up—of trying to persuade a foreign state to submit its differences with Florence to arbitration. This type of undertaking frequently required the dispatch of ambassadors— agents sent out to discuss, to argue, to threaten, to wheedle, to cozen. Whenever Florence elected to refer differences to arbitration, there must have been some conviction on the government's part that its claims were just. And since differences very often concerned alleged treaty violations, it is clear that Florence in these cases was taking a specific stand, i.e., holding that a given contract meant one thing rather than something else, or that the other party had done X and that X, according to the contract in question, had a given legal significance or a particular consequence in law. For this reason Florentine statecraft favored lawyers for embassies that had the aim of getting a prince or another city-state to accede to arbitration. Legal matters played a primary part in such missions. We have already seen something of this in the affair that took Montemagno and Buongirolami to Paolo Guinigi, Lord of Lucca, in 1428. We must try to get a sharper picture of this type of embassy, which required that the ambassador combine diplomatic and legal skills in a distinctive fashion.

One such embassy concerned Giangaleazzo's efforts (1393-1395) to deflect the waters of the River Mincio. In 1392 the Lord of Mantua, with the help of Florence, began to build a bridge on the Po River at Borgoforte. The bridge was meant to block the passage of Milanese vessels "and facilitate the entry of troops of the [anti-Viscontean] league into the Milanese state."[87] Giangaleazzo's reaction was to order the building of a dam on the Mincio and a canal to deflect its waters into the River Adige. Mantua would thus have been deprived of its river and lakes, putting it at the mercy of Giangaleazzo's cavalry and foot soldiers. The frightened Lord of Mantua, a member of the anti-Viscontean league of

[87] F. Cognasso, *Storia di Milano*, v, 566.

Bologna (April-July 1392), applied to the league for aid. Florence at once provided help, first along diplomatic lines. Negotiations on the subject of the dam were carried on, though with interruptions, for more than a year. The principal round of negotiations took place in the spring of 1394. Florence, Bologna, and the Lord of Mantua prepared in March of that year to send ambassadors to Giangaleazzo. Their aim was to get him to assent to arbitration. The Florentine Signory elected Ludovico Albergotti, a lawyer and expert on foreign questions, to go as one of its ambassadors. Early in April, however, he fell ill, and when it appeared that he would not be able to travel, the Signory wrote to the Bolognese to inform them of this.[88] Stressing the fact that the objectives of the mission would require the skills of an agent trained in law, the Signory urged them to confer their embassy on a lawyer. The letter even named the man. For as he should be "not only acute in law" but also fully informed about the matters to be treated, the Bolognese lawyer Messer Carlo Zambeccari was the best man for the job—"no other can be sent who would be more suitable."[89] Two weeks passed. Unexpectedly, Albergotti's health improved and by the end of April he was ready to start out for the coming meetings with Giangaleazzo's representatives. His companion and co-ambassador was one of Florence's most brilliant orators and diplomats—Rinaldo Gianfigliazzi.[90]

They received a set of instructions providing them with their general themes, but they had to develop and illustrate the specific arguments. The themes were these. To divert the course of the Mincio River was

[88] *SCMC-I*, 24, ff. 14v-15r, letter of 9 April.

[89] *Ibid.* "Ceterum, electus erat per nos egregius legum doctor dominus Lodovicus de Albergottis ut in Lombardiam deberet cum aliis oratoribus proficisci. Verum quia de morbo iliaco tandem in febres gravissimas est coniectus, non posset munus hoc sicut decreviumus expedire. Cumque necessarium sit doctorem unum ad hoc legationis negocium destinare, placeat de vestris unum eligere ne quantum ad ius pertinet contingat legationem hanc mancam et minus utilem reperiri. Et quoniam expedit quod transmittendus non solum perspicax sit in iure sed etiam in facto et de cunctis colloquiis informatus nedum accommodatius, sed necessarium arbitramus quod egregius legum doctor dominus Carlus de Ianbeccariis legationis huius onera debeat supportare. Nam cum de iure peritissimus sit et cuncta noverit in quibus quasi cardinibus controversia tota versetur cumque presens fuerit ubi cuncta tam in iure quam in facto discussa sunt, nullus alius posset magis idoneus destinari."

[90] *SCMLC*, 1, ff. 14v-16v, instructions drafted for them on 29 April 1394.

contrary both to law and to the articles of the peace (of January 20, 1392). Mantua and the allies had already promised not to use the Borgoforte Bridge against Giangaleazzo or to let it be used by anyone else with designs against him. Nature and "eternal evidence" had accorded the waters of the Mincio to Mantua; this benefit was backed up by the civil and canon laws, by laws human and divine. It was no good making promises by word or document: construction of the dam at Valleggio must not continue. As for the promise of the allies not to use the Borgoforte Bridge against Milan—Florence and the others had offered to seal this promise with a guarantee from King Charles of France. Was there a lord or prince anywhere in the world who was not afraid to break faith with the crown of France? The instructions then came to the plea for arbitration. It was not right for Giangaleazzo or the allies to set up as judges in the dispute over the damming of the Mincio. Nor could Giangaleazzo, respecting either the law or the articles of the peace, refuse to submit the matter to arbitration. It was at this point that the legation became most delicate. Florence and the allies were willing to have the Borgoforte Bridge and two other points put into the hands of a neutral third party. But they held that the contending parties must eventually have recourse to arbitration, and Venice—not included in the league of Bologna—seemed best qualified to fill the office of arbitrator. In fact, Florence would have this office go to no one else. It was the job of the Florentine ambassadors to convince Giangaleazzo and his advisors that Venice would make the best arbitrator for various legal and other reasons. Their instructions dwelt on this matter: "Thus with every worthy means known to you, strive to have it [the part of arbitrator] devolve upon the Venetians. Disguise your aims, beat around the bush, first establishing the characteristics which the referee ought to have, then narrowing things in such a way as almost by necessity to end up with the Venetians . . . allege all the rights and reasons you think will serve, employing all the skills and all the words which strike you as being worthy and useful enough to bring about results in line with our final aims."[91]

[91] *Ibid.*, "Sichè chon tutti quelli honesti modi che saprette adoperate venga ne' Vinitiani, dissimulando et faccendovi dalla lunga, mettendo prima in sodo le

We may take for granted that Albergotti and Gianfigliazzi made use of all their arts, even if with little success. Giangaleazzo was determined to seize Mantua, though his plan to dam and divert the Mincio failed: the force of the waters destroyed the dam in 1395.

In their representation that it was not right for Giangaleazzo or the allies to set up as judges, Florentines were adducing a juridical principle often emphasized by them in their foreign relations, above all when trying to persuade a prince or another commune to submit to arbitration. By this principle, no one who lived in accordance with justice could be both judge in a dispute and party to it.[92] In the spring and summer of 1409 Florence used every means provided by diplomacy to try to impress this rudimentary element of juridical procedure on the French governor of Genoa—Jean Le Meingre, Count of Beaufort and Alais, known as Boucicaut. The legal details of the conflict between them implicated a number of diffrent contracts.

Gabriele Maria Visconti, Giangaleazzo's natural son, inherited the lordship of Pisa on his father's death in 1402. Taking an oath of fidelity to the crown of France (1404), he obtained in return a promise of protection, including Boucicaut's promise to come to his aid if the need arose. In the summer of 1405 a confluence of circumstances compelled Gabriele, under pressure from Boucicaut, to sell Pisa to Florence for 80,000 florins. At the same time he made Livorno and Porto Pisano over to Boucicaut. Paying out only part of the money due for Pisa, Florence still owed 35,000 florins on the account in 1409, when the governor of Genoa, Boucicaut, claimed this money in the name of France. The particulars of the ensuing dispute were rehearsed late in May 1409 in a set of instructions drafted for the lawyer Messer Nello da San Gimignano, Florentine ambassador-elect to the governor of Genoa.[93] On November 22nd of the previous year, Gabriele Maria's procurator had signed an

---

qualità debbono essere nel mezano e restrignendo per modo che quasi per necessità si venga ne' Vinitiani . . . allegando tutte le ragioni vedrette facino alla materia e usando tutte l'arti e tutte quelle parole vedrette sieno honeste e utile per venire ad effetto della nostra intentione."

[92] Most crisply stated in *C.* 3, 5, 1. "Generali lege decernimus neminem sibi esse iudicem vel ius sibi dicere debem."

[93] *SCMLC*, 4, ff. 100v-101v.

agreement with Florence to accept payment of the 35,000 florins in the form of government (Monte) securities—shares in the funded public debt of Florence. Actually, only 23,000 florins of Monte had been inscribed in Gabriele's name; the balance had been put under another name. Unknown to the Signory when the agreement of November 22nd was concluded, Gabriele had run foul of Boucicaut and had already been taken prisoner; he died not long after. All his goods had thereupon been declared the property of the French crown, and early in 1409 Boucicaut had dispatched an agent to Florence, claiming title "not to the monies inscribed in the Monte but to the 35,000 florins, in addition to damages and interest, and alleging that the agreement [payment via the ascription of Monte credits] was invalid because of Gabriele Maria's arrest. But the truth is," continued the instructions to Messer Nello, "that Gabriele's arrest was not known in Florence when the agreement of November 22nd was signed with the Signory."[94] Nor, indeed, was Florence afterwards officially informed of this. And although the Signory had told Boucicaut's envoy that they had wanted to refer the matter to law, the offer had been turned down. The next move of the governor of Genoa had been to order the seizure of all Florentine goods found on a Genoese vessel named the *Squarciafico*. Florence had reacted to this retaliatory action by sending an ambassador to Genoa. The ambassador had then returned to Florence with a report that Boucicaut was claiming the Monte credits made out in Gabriele's name alone but that he wanted the dispute adjudicated in Genoa. The lawyer Nello da San Gimignano was now being sent as ambassador to the governor to complain first of all of the abusive treatment suffered in Genoa by Florentine merchants, men whose safety had been guaranteed by a standing agreement with Boucicaut. The final purpose of his embassy was to arrange to have the dispute legally settled ("noi v'abbiamo mandato perchè questo caso si chiarischa di ragione"). "Yet it does not seem fitting to us that the action should lie in Genoa but in some neutral

---

[94] *Ibid.*, "non e danari scritti in sul monte ma le xxxv mila fiorini con pene et danni et interessi, allegando che lla fine fatta non valeva per la sua presura di Gabriel Maria. Ma la verità è che non era noto a Firenze la presura del detto Gabriello quando fu fermata la concordia colla Signoria, che fu a dì 22 di Novembre."

place . . . and we shall be content to observe whatever judgment is passed down." Nello was to offer the choice of Bologna, Ferrara, Padua, Lucca, or Siena—"and who shall be the ones to sit in judgment will be the doctors of those cities, that is, the doctors of the civil and canon laws."[95] The Signory then frankly informed Nello that it would most like to have the case referred "to the lawyers of the papal Rota, to be set up at Pisa any day now."

Messer Nello set out on his mission sometime in June. He stayed on in Genoa until late July, treating and striving to get an agreement with the French governor. Boucicaut's claim rested mainly on the fact that Gabriele Maria had violated his oath of fidelity to the crown of France, thereby bringing about his imprisonment and justifying the confiscation of his goods. The French lord was adamant, with the result that the lawyer-ambassador had to inform the Signory that Boucicaut would neither restore the Florentine merchandise taken from the *Squarciafico* nor agree to let the cause be heard outside Genoa. These facts come from one of the Signory's letters (dated July 18th) to the ambassador.[96] In this letter they tell Nello that to recover the merchandise they are ready to pay Boucicaut a given sum of money, but not in the form demanded by him. "And meanwhile, adducing the reasons which you think will be the most effective, try to make him see that his request is not honest but that we shall go along with him if he wants to agree to let the dispute be adjudicated in a place selected by common consent."[97]

A week later the Signory wrote the Florentine ambassadors to the newly elected pope in Pisa, narrated the details of the quarrel with Boucicaut, and commissioned them to request an audience with King Louis II of Anjou, who was also in Pisa.[98] The ambassadors were a knight and a lawyer—Maso degli Albizzi and Giovanni Serristori. Louis was already aware of the dispute, but they were to tell him that "the

[95] *Ibid.*, "ma non ci pare convenevole che la commissione si debba fare in Genova ma in luogho comune et che noi siamo contenti d'observare quanto fia giudicato . . . et chi l'abbia a vedere sieno i doctori delle dette terre, cioè di ragione civile e canonica . . . saremo più contenti che questa rimessione si venisse a fare ne' dottori della ruota del sommo pontefice che a questi dì si debbe fare a Pisa."

[96] *SCMC-I*, 28, ff. 125v-126r.

[97] *Ibid.*

[98] *SCMC-I*, 28, f. 127r-v, letter of 24 July.

governor refuses to submit to the law [in this matter], that he preys on
our goods and merchandise without any right whatever, that it is not
the fashion for those who live by justice to want to be judges unto themselves, and ask that his majesty condescend to get the governor to agree
to let our quarrel be adjudicated in a neutral place."[99] About three weeks
passed. The ambassadors Albizzi and Serristori were replaced at Pisa by
the *legum doctor* Marcello Strozzi. Still at loggerheads with Boucicaut,
the Signory wrote to Strozzi on August 17th, directing him to obtain an
interview with Louis of Anjou. The legist was told to urge the Florentine case on him, to say that the Signory was ready to submit to arbitration "in one of these places: Bologna, Ferrara, Padua, Lucca, Siena,
before the lawyers of the papal Rota," or if need be even at Marseilles.[100]

But a settlement with Boucicaut was never to be arranged and the
Monte credits of the ill-fated Gabriele Maria Visconti reverted, it seems,
to an original designee. Ambitious, arrogant, and short of funds, an
instrument in Louis II of Anjou's plans to wrest the crown of Naples
from Ladislaus, Boucicaut set out in August to take over Milan—the first
move in the Angevin's bid for the Neapolitan crown. On his arrival in
Milan, however, he learned that he had just lost Genoa to a brilliant *condottiere*—Facino Cane. He thereupon hastened back to Genoa, only to receive
confirmation of his loss. Florentine negotiations to retrieve the merchandise taken from the *Squarciafico* would have to be carried on, if at
all, with the new rulers of Genoa. The mad Charles VI of France was
too remote literally and mentally from these things.

In the course of this quarrel with Boucicaut, Florence was made the
victim of what international lawyers sometimes call "retorsion"—retaliatory action. Although the dispute initially concerned only Boucicaut's
claim to the unpaid balance of the price fixed for the purchase of Pisa,
the ensuing confiscation of Florentine merchandise went to complicate
things and to intensify the differences. The result was that any court
of arbitration which agreed to settle the altercation between Florence

[99] *Ibid.*, "dineghi volersi sottomettere a la regione, ci predi le robe nostre senza
niùna ragione, et che non è d'usanza di chi vive con giustitia di volersi fare ragione
egli medesimo et che la sua maestà si degni da operare che'l governatore sia con-
tento a rimettere questa differentia in luogho comune."
[100] *SCMC-I*, 28, ff. 131v-132r.

and Boucicaut had also to resolve the questions raised by the governor's retaliatory measures. We come on a new topic here. When reprisals became part of a dispute, they sometimes ended by dominating it. Then diplomacy was faced with a new set of difficulties. How it met these merits an independent examination.

## 5. Reprisals and Trade Agreements

Reprisal could be provoked by a variety of actions—political, military, diplomatic. It was not necessarily the outcome of commercial conflict; yet it nearly always ended by affecting trade. This is reason enough to juxtapose the two subjects here—acts of reprisal and trade relations.

We may define acts of reprisal as any means, short of war, used by one state against another to procure redress for unrequited injury. Ordinarily, such action is directed by the aggrieved state against the subjects or citizens of the other state. For this reason, reprisal is sometimes defined as "the right granted by a government to a subject to seize the persons and goods (up to a certain value) of citizens of the foreign state where the subject had suffered some offense without being able to obtain due satisfaction."[101] The city-states of late medieval and Renaissance Italy often teemed with colonies of merchants from abroad. Hence reprisal in cities like Genoa, Milan, and Venice meant that police and magistrates pounced on the property and merchandise of these foreign citizens living in their midst. Arresting and actually imprisoning foreigners was less common than merely confiscating their property, at all events in Florentine experience with other states.

Reprisal, as I said, might be justified on a variety of grounds. In 1285, for example, Pavia closed its roads to Florentine merchants because no indemnity had been forthcoming for a death penalty inflicted more than twenty-five years before on the Abbot General of Vallombrosa, Tesoro Beccaria, a citizen of Pavia.[102] About 1300 Parma enacted reprisals against Florentines because of penalties imposed on Ugolino da Corregio, a citizen of Parma condemned to pay a heavy fine by the "syndics" who

---

[101] A. del Vecchio and E. Casanova, *Le rappresaglie nei comuni medievali e specialmente in Firenze* (Bologna, 1894), p. 1; on reprisals see also G. Arias, *Trattati commerciali della repubblica fiorentina* (Firenze, 1901), pp. 155ff.

[102] This and Parma case in Davidsohn, *Geschichte von Florenz*, IV, i, 281.

investigated his official conduct as Podestà of Florence. On his return to Parma, Corregio had instituted reprisal proceedings. Moving up to the period of this study, we have already seen that in 1409 the French governor of Genoa, Boucicaut, to pay himself for an unsatisfied claim against the government of Florence, ordered the confiscation of Florentine merchandise on a Genoese vessel, and that a large investment in the funded public debt of Florence was at the heart of this affair. Later on in the century, disputes concerning foreign investments in the Florentine Monte were often to elicit acts of reprisal—from Genoa, from the papacy, and from lesser lordships. In such cases Florentine subjects or citizens living abroad suffered reprisals because of the Republic's financial policies. At the end of the century, as noted in the chapter on Florentine relations with the Church, the official acts of powerful commissions like the Eight on Public Safety were sometimes responsible for the imposition of interdicts —a form of ecclesiastical reprisal—on particular Florentine churches. In 1511-1512 we saw Pope Julius II come close to despoiling Florentine merchants in Rome and ordering their spoliation everywhere else in Italy and outside. This was perhaps the most effective way for him to handle the Republic's appeal to an illegal Church council and the determination of Florentine legislators to levy an unlicensed tax on the Florentine clergy.

Any reprisal was a serious affair, particularly when it entailed measures that fell just short of war. Ideally, the aggrieved party first applied for redress to the appropriate magistracy of the state where the wrong had been done or at the hands of whose citizens he had suffered injury. His request was either satisfied or denied. If the latter, there was presumably a valid reason for the denial; therefore when the plaintiff next turned for redress to his own government and got it by winning the right of reprisal, the state which had ruled against him had to advance its claims and try to get a rescission, a recovery of the confiscated goods, or a bilateral settlement. Now in important cases, particularly when the state itself had occasioned reprisal by its politics or public finance, proceedings passed into the hands of diplomatic agents—in fact, very often all the resources of diplomacy were required. We shall see that as the subject of diplomatic exchange, retorsion had the effect of making negotiation a very demanding exercise in precision, in the mastering of technical details, and in dexterity.

The power in Florence to grant reprisals was taken over a few times by the Signory (at one point in the Trecento even the Podestà had it), but it was exercised for the most part by the supreme commercial tribunal, the Tribunale di Mercanzia, a court consisting of one foreign jurist (the judge) and six merchant advisors.[103] When injury to a foreigner was the result of action taken by the Republic (as represented, e.g., by the Signory or the Monte Officials or the Eight), then application for redress was made to the Signory. Ordinarily, however, foreign suitors applied to the court of the Mercanzia. Two students of the subject and period have said that because of the impulse to safeguard its trade, Quattrocento Florence led all other Italian and European states in the movement to cut down on the granting of reprisals.[104] Florence made serious and sustained efforts to get its relations with other states to the point where differences could be settled *de iure* and where taking justice into one's own hands—as in the granting of reprisals—was strongly discouraged. This meant that the court of the Mercanzia had to be chary of granting reprisals, while being most concerned to see that the claims of foreign suitors were carefully examined and, where right was demonstrated, fully satisfied. Only thus could Florence hope to have the decisions of this court respected abroad. In May 1394 we find one of the colleges advising the Signory to have the foreign judge of the Mercanzia examine the court's old and new statutes with the help of two lawyers. Next, meeting with some experienced merchants, they were "to discuss the rights of the parties" involved in an action moved by French plaintiffs and see to it that justice was done.[105] It is true that Giangaleazzo Visconti's wars of conquest led Florentines to seek the support of the crown of France, but their keen interest in the just functioning of the court of the Mercanzia was persistent. In April 1436 the lawyer Francesco

[103] On this court see G. Bonolis, *La giurisdizione della mercanzia in Firenze nel secolo xiv* (Firenze, 1901); G. Arias, *Studi e documenti di storia del diritto* (Firenze, 1902), pp. 131ff.; Davidsohn, *Geschichte*, iv, i, 281ff. The activity of this court in the fifteenth century and after has yet to be studied.

[104] Del Vecchio and Casanova, *Le rappresaglie*, p. 86.

[105] *CP*, 30, f. 123r.

Marchi was sent to Venice on an embassy regarding this court. Questions had been raised about its impartiality, and Marchi was sent to persuade the Venetians of its scrupulous care with foreign lawsuits.[106]

An illustration of the Republic's parsimony with retaliatory action was seen in May 1447. Owing to friction between some citizens of Florence and Siena, certain shipments of Sienese goods were seized by Florentines from Florentine vessels. When this matter was brought to the attention of the Signory and colleges, they referred the matter to a committee headed by two lawyers—Domenico Martelli and Otto Niccolini. There was a law according a blanket safe-conduct to foreign merchants who shipped goods on Florentine galleys. Martelli and Niccolini examined "the said law, its general preface, the rights there given, and its general words."[107] Basing themselves on this and on procedure normally followed at Florence in the granting of reprisals, they ruled that the Sienese goods should be returned to their owners. The government acted accordingly.

I have said that when reprisals, actual or pending, were the subject of diplomatic exchange, the practice of negotiation called for great precision, technical mastery, and dexterity. This was surely to be expected of the agents of a city supported by trade. Let us, in this connection, review the transactions of two embassies.

When in May 1421 Filippo Maria Visconti prepared to launch an attack on Genoa, Tommaso di Campofregoso, Genoese Doge, immediately applied to Florence for support. To hold the sympathy of the Florentines he sold them the Port of Livorno for 100,000 florins. Nevertheless, Genoa soon succumbed and passed under Viscontean rule late in the year. Although the peace between Florence and Filippo Maria was to continue for nearly two more years, Florentine shipping and trade along the Ligurian coast suffered from the threats and attacks of Genoese boats. The government of Florence tried to get Filippo Maria to grant a safe-conduct to all Florentine merchants with goods and interests in Genoa and along that coast, but he refused, adducing Genoa's semi-autonomy and

---

[106] *SCMLC*, 10, f. 52v.

[107] *CP*, 52, f. 18r (17 May), "la decta legge et la sua generale prefatione et la ragione in essa assegnata et le sue parole generali."

alleging Florence's violation of treaties with Genoa.[108] To narrate the details of the Florentine differences with Genoa would require a chapter apart. The differences impinged on three or four treaties and particularly touched the question of Florence's right to Livorno on the basis of the purchase from the former Doge, Tommaso di Campofregoso.

As a subject of negotiation, these differences came to a head in the spring of 1423. An expert notary, Ser Piero di Francesco Calcagni, was dispatched to Genoa, where he was to act both as Florentine envoy to the Milanese governor of the city (Count Carmagnola) and as procurator of the Florentines whose goods had been seized by the Genoese. Apart from the fact that Ser Piero was an expert in matters of contracts and civil procedure, as revealed by his concluding *relazione* to the Signory,[109] he was carefully advised by a group of lawyers and merchants back home and kept under their scrutiny, as is shown by their report to the Signory on March 12th.[110] This report directed Ser Piero to take particular pains with two items in his commission: (1) under no circumstances was he to compromise the status of Livorno, or even allow Carmagnola or the Podestà of Genoa to raise the question of whether or not Florence had had the right to buy it; (2) as procurator of the Florentines who were seeking to retrieve their confiscated goods, he was to inform the Podestà that his mandate permitted him to sue for summary proceedings only—ordinary civil procedure was out of the question. This limitation highlights the shrewd discernment of Ser Piero's legal advisors: if his negotiations in Genoa involved his clients in a prolonged lawsuit, they could refuse to acknowledge proceedings by simply calling attention to his limited mandate.

In his final report to the Signory, Ser Piero casually reveals the skills

[108] *SCMLC*, 7, ff. 10r-12v top right. The Signory's instructions of 30 Aug. 1422 for the ambassadors to Milan—Nello da San Gimignano and Averardo de' Medici.

[109] *SRRO*, 2, ff. 162v-163r, dated 31 March. Ser Piero was in Genoa from about 21 Jan. until late March.

[110] *CP*, 45, f. 89v. The report was presented by the lawyer Alessandro Bencivenni. Nello da San Gimignano and Guglielmo Tanagli were the other lawyers in the advisory group. See also another six letters (18 Feb.–24 March) from the Signory, *SCMC-I*, 31, ff. 13r-14v. The third letter (28 Feb.) said among other things: "ti mandiamo certa nota fatta per nostri excellenti dottori sopra la materia decta, la quale intende et nota bene et con le allegationi loro et ragioni che chiaramente dimostrano," etc.

which he was compelled to draw on in his interviews at Genoa. The burden of his mission as procurator concerned goods seized by the Genoese captain Jacopo de' Fornari from the boat *Roviera*. Admitting the confiscation, Fornari justified the action by maintaining that the *Roviera* belonged to enemies of the Commune of Genoa, that Florentines had provided many such vessels with aid and supplies, and that they had violated Art. 18 of the peace signed between Florence and Genoa in 1413.[111] The Genoese thus proposed to rest their case on a plea which cut into the sphere of international public law, putting the Florentine state itself under an indictment. Carmagnola chose the Podestà of Genoa to be the "auditor" in this dispute. Ser Piero, in his report, then described the ensuing events: "We appeared before the Podestà during many days, I striving to get the matter dispatched without litigation or a formal civil declaration, the other part striving for nothing else than that I should present my claim in writing. I offered great resistance to this as well before the Podestà as with the Count [Carmagnola]. In the end they decided that they wanted me to state my business not in a formal declaration but simply, in a short written narration of the facts. This I did, having no other choice, whereupon they answered by wanting to move things on to the tortuous path of ordinary civil proceedings. They even wanted to wait for a formal civil declaration, for special pleas, replications, and the long delays of lawsuits. They conducted examinations, laid down terms, and all in all sought to envelop me in a regular lawsuit. I made every effort to divert the Podestà away from this, representing our rights and reasons to him, giving our replies to their alleging that article of the peace, and arguing against the meaning which they imputed to it."[112]

---

[111] The article referred to the security of boats going into Porto Pisano. Archivio di Stato di Genova, *Materie Politiche* (years: 1402-1419), filza 2730, insert 15, a copy of the peace treaty, much damaged.

[112] *SRRO*, 2, ff. 162v-163r. "Fummo più dì dinanzi al podestà, cercando io dello spaccio sanza litigio o libello, et l'altra parte in altro non stava se non ch'io dessi la mia domanda per scriptura. Feci a questo assai resistenza et col podestà et col conte. In ultimo vollono che non per via di libello ma di semplice expositione per brieve scriptura io dichiarassi quello volevo. Così feci, non potendo altro, et essi risposono pigliando la via lunga del piato, et volevono pure attendere a libelli, exceptioni et replicationi et lunghezze di piati, et feciono positioni et capitoli et in

Ser Piero went on to provide further details, but we have seen enough to realize what he was up against. Moving back and forth between the Podestà and the governor, one the chief justice and the other Filippo Maria Visconti's highest representative in Genoa, Ser Piero as procurator bickered with one and sought as diplomatic envoy to persuade the other to intervene in favor of Florence. He had thus to perform the functions of both attorney and diplomat and to do so amid the adverse conditions produced by the machinations of Filippo Maria, who encouraged his diplomatic and administrative agents to foil and confound the rulers of Florence at every turn.

Needless to say, when Ser Piero returned to Florence on March 31st, he did not have a victory in hand. In May Filippo Maria's soldiers entered Forlì, and the Florentines immediately reacted by setting up their special war office, the Ten on War. Negotiations with the Genoese were cut off. In the autumn hostilities broke out; war was to go on sporadically for several years.

We have seen what happened in one case in which negotiation concerned a reprisal already in effect. The following example involves a threat of reprisal. In this case, the information comes entirely from the instructions to the ambassador; they are sufficiently detailed to give a clear picture of what awaited him in the field.

The ambassador was again an expert on contracts—the notary Ser Mariotto Bencini.[113] His instructions were drawn up on July 20, 1447. The embassy was to take him to Ludovico I, Duke of Savoy. Drafted in close consultation with some lawyers, the instructions begin with a recitation of the events leading up to the legation.[114] By special grace of the Balìa of 1434, the Bishop of Recanato, Giovanni Vitelleschi, had been made a citizen of Florence. Among the privileges conferred on him, there was one giving him the right to acquire credits of up to 20,000 florins in the Republic's regular funded debt—the Monte Comune, "on

---

tucto cercavano avilupparmi in piato. Sforzami levare il podestà da questo, monstrandogli le nostre ragioni et risposte contro il capitolo della pace allegato per loro," etc.

[113] See the fourteen volumes of his notarial protocols, *Notarile antecosimiano*, B 202-208, under the name of Mariotto Bencini Baldesi. The extreme dates of the acts here contained are 1389-1458, but Ser Mariotto's go from *ca.* 1412 to 1458.

[114] *SCMLC,* 12, ff. 22r-23v.

which he could draw the interest payments, just as did other citizens with similar credits." In return for "this favor and privilege," Vitelleschi was to be "content with the simple good faith of the Commune and no more." He was not to demand more, and if it ever happened that interest payments were late or held up, he was never to sue for reprisals, nor otherwise molest any citizens or subjects of Florence, "as is more amply stipulated in the said privilege." The bishop acquired his 20,000 florins of Monte and collected interest on the investment as long as he lived. Dying, he left a universal heir—Messer Bartolommeo da Corneto, one of the cardinals of the Council of Basel (i.e., an appointee of the anti-Pope, Felix V). On the eve of the embassy in question, this man had already been angling for some time to collect interest on the 20,000 florins of Monte. Turned away by Florence, Messer Bartolommeo had recourse to the Duke of Savoy (son of Felix V), petitioning him to withdraw the right of safe-conduct from all Florentines in his lands and to authorize reprisals against Florence. Reprisals were promised and the safe-conducts were revoked. The purpose, therefore, of the embassy assigned to Ser Mariotto Bencini was to lodge a complaint and to ward off actual reprisals.

When it came to the arguments Ser Mariotto was directed to employ, the instructions from the Signory and lawyers became remarkably precise. The subject matter was treated point by point. Messer Bartolommeo was not one of Duke Ludovico's native subjects and hence had not the right to sue for reprisals in Savoy. Presupposing that he did have this right, the fact remained that his benefactor, Vitelleschi, had obligated himself never to molest Florence or Florentines in connection with the Monte investment and to be satisfied with the Republic's word and good intentions. Even if it could be established that Messer Bartolommeo was Vitelleschi's legal heir with regard to the disputed shares in the Monte, yet he could not be heir to the interest payments "because the said privilege [to buy into the Monte] was and is a personal one and cannot pass on from Messer Giovanni [Vitelleschi's] person but perishes with it, so far as the said payments are concerned, as is contained in the words of the privilege." Again, with respect to the capital proper, should that belong to Messer Bartolommeo by law, it would still not be his to keep but only to sell or otherwise alienate. He could not, however, dispose of it this way

366

either, nor draw it into a contract of any kind, "because of being the heir of Messer Giovanni and Messer Giovanni being a debtor of our Commune for the sum of 10,000 florins, which he received from the cashier of [our] treasury in payment for entering our service; and not having [entered our service], he remained and is an outstanding debtor of the treasury and is so listed in our records. So before he [Messer Bartolommeo] can implicate the [Monte] credit in a contract, this debt must be cancelled."[115]

At this point Ser Mariotto's instructions observed that the representations made so far would be challenged by the other side and then proceeded to summarize the arguments which it was thought Messer Bartolommeo would allege. (1) Felix V was the true pope, hence he, Bartolommeo, a true cardinal of the Church, had a perfect legal right to petition Duke Ludovico for a grant of reprisals. Was not every lay lord obligated to defend the Church and its clerics? (2) *Si de quo magis ergo de quo minus*—i.e., if Bartolommeo was granted the major thing (the capital), then so much the more had he a right to anything less (the interest payments). (3) The act of buying into the Monte constituted a free investment, so that moneys invested this way, particularly when belonging to foreign creditors, could not be blocked. (4) By stopping him from drawing the 20,000 florins of Monte into a contract, the Commune was breaking its word, "et frangenti fidem, fides frangatur eidem." The original contract having thus been broken and so dissolved, the heir was released from it and could therefore make application for reprisals against Florence.

The last part of his instructions provided Ser Mariotto with a reply to each of these pleas. To the point about Felix V, he was to say that it was not up to the Florentines "to discuss the facts of the Church."

---

[115] *Ibid.*, "perchè decto privilegio fu et è personale et della persona d'esso messer Giovanni non esce ma con quella si extingue quanto a decte paghe, come per le parole d'esso si comprende ... perchè essendo herede di messer Giovanni et messer Giovanni essendo debitore del nostro comune di fiorini diecimila, e quali ebbe et prese dal cassiere della camera per venire a nostri servigi et non lo fece, ne rimase et è debitore acceso in camera in su libro della stella. Et però bisogna prima tal debito si cancelli che lui possa contractare nel credito." Viewed as a contract, the privilege referred to at the outset of this quotation could well come under the Roman legal formula, "nam socii mei socius meus socius non est." *D.* 17, 2, 20.

This was a necessary diplomatic dodge, Florence being of the Roman persuasion. The second and third objections had a single rejoinder: a privilege could not be given an interpretation different from that "contained in the words" of the contract which accorded the privilege. As to this, the words of the privilege in question clearly stated that no one other than Vitelleschi was to be competent to enjoy the accorded right. Ser Mariotto's reply to the fourth "plaint" repeated a previous observation: Vitelleschi had put his money into the Monte under the same conditions and with the same obligations which bound other Florentine citizens; "there is a [Florentine] law which expressly states that the [Monte] credits and interest payments of any man who owes money to the treasury should be held up, and he [Messer Bartolommeo] surely may not be taken to enjoy a better condition [in Florence] than our citizens."[116] The instructions concluded by directing Ser Mariotto to agree to refer the dispute to a court of arbitration, but limited him to the choice of the lawyers' colleges at Rome, Padua, or Bologna.

There is no need to go into the final outcome of this embassy.[117] Our immediate interest here is the technique or manner of negotiation, not the mission itself. It is therefore most important to remember that Ser Mariotto's destination was not a court of law, though it might seem so. He was a fully accredited ambassador sent out to confer with the Duke of Savoy and his advisors, to get the right of safe-conduct restored to Florentine merchants, to hold back the threatened reprisals, and to make arrangements for a bilateral settlement of the dispute. To achieve these aims, he had to prepare for a series of interviews and exchanges that would touch a variety of legal questions. Here again was an embassy which depended on the double skills of law and diplomacy. Back home a group of lawyers had primed Ser Mariotto. The Florentine case was fully

---

[116] *Ibid.*, "et che expressa legge c'è che chi è debitore in camera gli sia arrestato il credito et le paghe, et però lui non debba essere di migliore conditione che i nostri cittadini." The rule "Si de quo magis," etc. is from the *glos. ord.* on *D.* 50, 17, 110, "In eo, quod plus sit, semper inest et minus." (*Lex* 111 in the Venetian ed., 1591-92). On the rule "frangenti fidem," etc. see *D.* 13, 5, 1, *in mar.* ad. v. *Nota hic*: "quod frangenti fidem," etc. (edition, *idem*).

[117] *SCMC-I*, 36 (5 April 1444-13 March 1448), 37 (26 Oct. 1447-28 Oct. 1448), contain no letters or directives throwing additional light on the controversy; and the Monte records in ASF have not been inventoried and made properly available for consultation.

rehearsed for him in his instructions. But much of the mission's effectiveness would spring from the fact that he himself was trained in the law of contract and had considerable experience in the redaction of records connected with civil proceedings.

ONE result of Florentine expansion in the late fourteenth century was that the Republic, on its western frontiers, pressed nearer to the sea, until in 1406 and 1421, with the conquest and purchase of Pisa and Livorno, Florentines planted themselves on the coast. The triumph of a vigorous city, this advance to the Mediterranean worried and nettled the major sea-power along that western coast, Genoa. Commercial conflict ensued, and although the two cities tried again and again to settle their differences by means of arbitration and negotiation (Florentines continued on occasion to use Genoese shipping facilities), the first quarter of the fifteenth century saw them often locked in trade disputes or exchanging counter reprisals. During those years, Florence dispatched dozens of embassies to Genoa or on business concerning relations with Genoa. Indeed, of all the Italian powers, Genoa seems to have been the one which then most occupied Florence in the field of interstate commercial relations. For this reason, the principal illustrations in the following discussion will be drawn from the network of trade relations that linked Florence and Genoa. If only in passing, we should note that Genoa too had its circle of crack lawyers who were active in political affairs, domestic as well as foreign.[118]

Just as Florence had lawyers who were particularly adept at handling straight political matters when sent on embassies—e.g., Corsini, Ridolfi, Albergotti, and Popoleschi—so it had others who developed a special competence in the field of trade relations with other states. Of these, the following were perhaps the outstanding ones of the early fifteenth century: Ricciardo del Bene, Alessandro Bencivenni, Ridolfi again, and Nello da San Gimignano.

In April 1410, when it appeared that Florence might reach an agree-

[118] This is revealed by a number of Genoese sources: Archivio di Stato di Genova, *Paesi*, 1/341 (on activity of Genoese "College of Judges"); *Politicorum Regesti*, 1647, fasc. 1 (act of 23 June 1383, confirming privileges of College); *Archivio Segreto Diversorum*, 6/501 (dates: 1403-05), brings out prominence of lawyers in councils.

ment with the Genoese over a series of trade disputes, there was unanimity in the executive councils on the need to send a lawyer to Genoa to help conclude things.[119] Ricciardo del Bene was sent. The preliminary work of negotiation had been done by the merchant Francesco di Messer Alessandro de' Bardi, who was waiting for Ricciardo on the latter's arrival in Genoa. Ricciardo was instructed to tell the Genoese that he had been sent to them "to conclude the agreement together with Francesco . . . according to the form of the articles which you [Ricciardo] have with you—corrected, re-defined, and with the additions which you know about."[120] In January 1420 Alessandro Bencivenni and the merchant Vieri Guadagni spent more than two weeks on a mission to the Doge of Genoa, treating a variety of questions relating to mercantile and shipping disputes, free access into the Port of Pisa, Florentine trade rights in Genoa, the subject of Genoese rebels, and other matters. In one way or another, most of the themes treated touched on a previous treaty of peace and trade between Florence and Genoa.[121]

A mission to Genoa which I shall consider in some detail was carried out during the winter and spring of 1417.[122] It was the work of the merchant Francesco Tornabuoni, who initiated negotiations around the middle of February, and of the lawyer Nello da San Gimignano. Messer Nello was dispatched to Genoa at the end of March, when the two governments prepared to enter the final stage of negotiations. Late in February, one executive consultation on Francesco Tornabuoni's dealings in Genoa had already started with a report presented by twenty-one special advisors, of whom six were lawyers.[123] The business of Messer Nello's

---

[119] *CP*, 40, ff. 154r.

[120] *SCMLC*, 4, f. 135v (instructions dated 5 May 1410), "a concludere la concordia insieme con Francesco . . . secondo la forma de' capituli e quali portate et da noi avete correcti et limitati et con le aditioni che sapete."

[121] *SRRO*, 2, ff. 60r-61r.

[122] *SCMC-I*, 29, ff. 101v-102r, instructions to Nello da San Gimignano and Francesco Tornabuoni, dated 27 March.

[123] *CP*, 43, f. 132r. Alessandro Bencivenni, Filippo Corsini, Lorenzo Ridolfi, Stefano Buonaccorsi, Torello Torelli, and Nello da San Gimignano were the six lawyers. A completely different source, Lorenzo Ridolfi's third book of *consilia*, proves that these very lawyers were then asked by the Signory to draft a legal opinion against Genoese claims. These claims concerned shipping in Porto Pisano and the Florentine use (the subject of Nello's embassy) of Genoese boats during

legation will make clear the Florentine need to have a lawyer at the center of these transactions.

The instructions to the lawyer point out that Florentine merchants paid a customs ("dogana") of four per cent on all Florentine goods brought into Genoa from England and Flanders.[124] Lately, the Doge of Genoa, Tommaso di Campofregoso, had been demanding such an arrangement in perpetuity. The government of Florence opposed this but was willing to treat. We are willing, said the instructions, to pay import duties of up to three per cent, only we want the right to bring our goods into Genoa "on whatever vessels we wish." If the Genoese agreed to a "dogana" of three per cent or less, Messer Nello and Francesco were to try to secure an arrangement preventing any future increases. Failing this, they were directed to work for an agreement which included a clause stating that if the Genoese ever demanded or got more than three per cent, Florence would be "free from all the contracts and obligations entered into with the Genoese at the time of Messer Boucicaut." If the Genoese refused this too, continued the Signory, say that we are willing to put our goods on their boats in England and Flanders during the months of December and January, paying all the requisite fees and customs [i.e., four per cent]. Should it happen that for some reason our goods are put on the vessels of others, then it shall be as if these are Genoese, thus obligating us to pay the same fees and customs. But if their vessels are not available in December and January, we must have the right, lasting through June, to load our goods on any vessels we choose, "without paying any customs." And let the same thing hold for the period up through November, should it happen that Genoese boats are not available in those ports in July and August. Again, if Genoese boats do come in and are available during the months specified, Florentine merchants must employ them for the transport of their goods, unless they have already hired another boat. In this case, proof of such hire must be in the form of a public instrument. When Genoese boats are available in Flanders and England during the months of December-January and July-August, the owners must communicate this fact to at least one of the major Florentine com-

the past ten years. BNF, *Fondo principale*, ii, iii, 370, ff. 226v-228r, a *consilium* of 5 March 1417.

[124] *SCMC-I*, 29, ff. 101v-102r.

panies there. They must notify the said company via public instrument "that the boats will be there, that they want to transport their [Florentine] merchandise and goods to these parts [Italy] and for the usual fee."

At this point—the end of the substantive part of the instructions— the Signory had a note inserted into the margin, though it must have appeared in the final set of instructions. The note directly addressed the lawyer: "In working out and drawing up the written agreement, you, Messer Nello, see to it that our general objectives are realized."[125]

The instructions in question were drafted on March 27, 1417. A letter of April 24th from the Signory indicates that the negotiators had ironed out all the initial differences.[126] A draft of the treaty, with each of the articles intact, had been put together and a copy sent to Florence for the Signory's scrutiny. The Signory's letter to the two ambassadors is a commentary on the articles. Confirming some and modifying others, the Signory told the ambassadors exactly what had to be done in each case. Sometime in early June, if not before, the treaty went into effect. But before the end of the month a dispute broke out with the Genoese Captain of Livorno. To decide on a course of action, the Signory held consultations with the official government lawyers, with the recent ambassadors to Genoa, and with some other officials. A report delivered on the next day was entirely the work of lawyers.[127]

The embassy to Genoa, with the dispatch first of Francesco Tornabuoni and then Messer Nello, draws together some of the points made in the preceding sections of this chapter. First, the lawyer started out for Genoa only as negotiations reached the point at which the parties were ready to begin putting the articles of their tentative accord down on paper. Second, by prodding Nello to cleave to Florentine objectives when in the actual process of formulating the articles, the Signory was calling attention to the language of the prospective agreement and to the trickiness of interpretations. The care taken with this aspect of the transactions would be intensified when the treaty drafts were studied and checked at home. Next, it is clear that the stress on public instru-

[125] *Ibid.* "Et nel distendere et acconciare le scripture voi, messer Nello, abbia avertenza sichè l'effeto che desideriamo segua."
[126] *SCMC-I*, 29, f. 102v.
[127] *CP*, 43, f. 155v, consultations of 25 and 26 June.

ments looked to the legal verifiability of things, to potential legal disputes and arbitration. Here again, when reviewing the treaty drafts, the Signory and its advisors would recommend further precautions. And finally, the great detail of commercial treaties, the multiplicity of small points that went into their formulation, increased the risks of imprecision and the likelihood of mistakes. All the more reason to have an able lawyer actively participating in the last stages of negotiation.

It may be added that the tandem, merchant and lawyer, was a typical arrangement in the conduct of embassies whose business was the negotiation of trade agreements. The skills of the merchant and lawyer were complementary, thereby providing the Republic with a higher margin of safety at the conference tables.

Trade dispute in fifteenth-century Italy and the incidence and forms of interstate and international commercial litigation are themes which have yet to be satisfactorily studied by legal and economic historians. Yet one general observation may be hazarded from the vantage point of Florence. Although acts of reprisal against individual Florentines would always remain the business of Florentine diplomacy and its agents, the Republic's diplomatic and foreign correspondence show trends which indicate that in the course of the fifteenth century there was, generally in Italy, a growing effort to get local settlement in the trade disputes which broke out between citizens of different states. The aim was to keep such conflict from provoking reprisals and counterreprisals; so the foreign grievances of individual Florentines passed increasingly under the protection of the consuls and procurators of Florentine merchant colonies abroad. This is why, at the end of the fifteenth century, Florentine merchants in Rome were pressing the Signory to grant them the right to appoint a consul who would represent them in commercial litigation and perform a variety of other tasks. Florentine communities elsewhere, they said, already benefited from this right. The request was finally satisfied in 1515.[128]

[128] *SCRO*, 10, f. 276r, letter to the Signory, 9 Nov. 1498, from the Florentine ambassador in Rome, the lawyer Francesco Gualterotti. On the concession of 1515 *vide* J. Delumeau, *Vie économique et sociale de Rome dans la seconde moitié du xvi^e siècle*, 2 vols. (Paris, 1957), I, 209.

## 6. Open Questions of International Law

International public and private law divide the field. The former refers to the sum of rules which determine the respective rights and responsibilities of states in their mutual relations. International private law is the aggregate of rules applicable to the resolution of conflicts arising somewhere along the line between the private laws of two states. The sources of international law for late medieval and Renaissance Italy were very much what they are for European nations in our own day: treaties, the custom and practice of states, the general principles of law as recognized by "civilized" peoples, Roman law, and the product—opinions, commentaries, judicial decisions—of the most eminent lawyers.[129]

In the following pages, I propose to touch briefly on a variety of questions that are not easily classified and which entered into the business of diplomacy far less often than those already treated in this chapter. Raised by events that offered ample room for interpretation, the questions I have in mind, or rather their final settlement, often depended on political solutions.

Among the privileges reserved to the Empire were the following: the right to create notaries, to legitimize bastards, to make general laws, to arbitrate in disputes between princes and lordships immediately under it (hence many of the Italian states), and to confirm or overrule in the last instance the judicial decisions of magistrates. These rights belonged in theory to the prerogative of the Emperor, who was also King of Germany and King of Italy; in fact, most were usurped by the Italian states in the course of the thirteenth century, with the result that Florence, for example, claimed and exercised the right to make general laws which bound the whole of Florentine territory.[130] Yet something of the Emperor's prestige abided, of the respect paid to his high dignity. Though the connection with the Empire was nebulous, there were lawyers in Florence at the beginning of the fifteenth century who still felt that Florentines were in some fashion *fideles* of the Empire.[131] One

---

[129] *Vide* e.g. E. Nys, *Les origines du droit international* (Brussels, 1894); and P. Fauchille, *Traité de droit international public*, 8th ed., I, i (Paris, 1922).

[130] See esp. p. 121, and Ch. X. On the Emperor's theoretical rights, B. Paradisi, *Il problema storico del diritto internazionale*, 2nd ed. (Napoli, 1956), p. 171.

[131] In fact I have only come on one such example, p. 340.

historian has observed, "The Empire was the wellspring of law and sovereignty: outside it there was only tyranny. From it, therefore, men expected the restoration of legality and justice wherever violence held sway, the restoration of the popular will where tyranny triumphed, the restoration of beneficent and fecund peace."[132] Taken in the context of the fifteenth century, these observations lay an exaggerated emphasis on theory, on a theory which in any case was well on its way out. Yet owing in part to the residual sentiment for the idea of Empire, when the Emperor journeyed into Italy and sought to intervene in Italian affairs, he could be an embarrassment. And at times he had to be placated, bought off, even courted, especially when his backing promised to be valuable in the play of alliances, the fortunes of war, or in resistance to the conspiratorial activity of political exiles.

Though dimmed by fact and circumstance, the Emperor's prerogative to act as arbitrator in disputes between Italian states was a right recognized in international law (as was the Roman pontiff's). For this reason, when the Florentine Republic had outstanding differences with a foreign power and the Emperor communicated his desire to act as judge in the dispute, if the controversy had already been submitted to arbitration or if there was opposition to his coming in as peacemaker, Florentines might well feel the need to explain why it was not possible or practicable to employ his services. In the drawing up or delivery of such explanations, the Signory often solicited the counsel of lawyers, but the need to explain issued from expedience and protocol, rather than from any substantial links between the Emperor and the Republic.

In February 1432 the Emperor Sigismund sent ambassadors to Florence to request that he be made arbitrator in the prospective peace talks between Florence, Milan, and Venice. Since the Marquis of Ferrara had already been called on to arbitrate, the Signory quickly held a consultation with twenty-seven advisors, six of whom were lawyers.[133] Their

---

[132] F. Ercole, in the famous essay, "Impero e papato nel diritto pubblico italiano del rinascimento," reprinted in his *Dal comune al principato: saggi sulla storia del diritto pubblico del rinascimento italiano* (Firenze, 1929), pp. 309-310.

[133] *CP*, 49, f. 219v, consultation of 28 Feb. The lawyers were Lorenzo Ridolfi, Piero Beccanugi, Stefano Buonaccorsi, Carlo Federighi, Guglielmo Tanagli, and Zanobi Guasconi.

report to the government was presented by a committee of four, one of whom was the canonist Messer Zanobi Guasconi. They told the Signory to excuse itself to the imperial ambassadors for not having sent envoys to Sigismund at the time of the last round of dealings with him. In answer to his request for the part of arbitrator, the Signory was advised to say that this would have been most welcome but that the Duke of Milan was the one who suggested the Marquis of Ferrara, that the ambassadors had already been selected and Ferrara fixed on as the site, that Venice had been informed of this and was sending representatives there, so that "we cannot do other than stand by the said lordship [Venice], with which we are allied." In this way the Signory was encouraged to evade the Emperor's rightful request by setting it up against an alleged obligation to Venice and implied commitments to the lords of Milan and Ferrara. Not satisfied that there was enough here to save appearances, the advisors added one other observation which seemed to question the Emperor's right to act as arbitrator in the dispute: "if [when coming to Italy] he had come to other lands than those of the Duke of Milan, our enemy, we would have done our duty as true sons and servants of his."[134] There was the strong suggestion here that Sigismund's objectivity as judge or mediator had been compromised. Florence thus seemed to have a case for denying his request. The point was a weak one legally, but it could be argued.

Twenty years later, when Florentines acceded to Emperor Frederick III's request to act as mediator in a raging dispute between Florence and Venice, the Signory dealt with him through a prominent Medicean lawyer, Guglielmo Tanagli.[135]

If Roman and international public law were clear about the Emperor's right to act as arbitrator in disputes between Italian states, this clarity dimmed when the question was viewed with reference to the diplomatic

---

[134] *Ibid.*, "noi non possiamo altrimenti fare che confermarci colla decta signoria con la quale siamo collegati . . . se fosse venuto in altre terre che in quelle del duca di Milano, nostro inimico, aremo facto nostro debito e dovere come suoi veri figliuoli e servidori." On 6 March the Signory sent out an apologetic letter to the Emperor, *SCMC-I*, 33, ff. 61v-63v. The designation "sons and servants" was of course rhetorical.

[135] *DBLC*, 4, f. 22r-v, instructions of 9 May 1452.

practice of the fifteenth century. New facts and new institutions had long since entered the field of relations between states, with the result that while the Emperor's claim to the office of arbitrator still had theoretical legal and moral grounds, the practice of states—and so a rising current in international law—gave it little actual support.

Even more open to question than the Emperor's right to arbitrate in given circumstances was the matter of exactly when, according to international law, a given political community acquired enough external sovereignty to dispatch ambassadors. At what point, in other words, did it take on the characteristics of a state? And to whom did the decision belong—to the surrounding states? What if some of these decided that a certain community was a state while others denied it such recognition? In January 1500, Antonio Malegonnelli, lawyer and Florentine ambassador in Rome, did not hesitate to refuse the chance of a meeting with the ambassadors from Pisa. Having rebelled against Florence in 1495, thereby throwing off a rule of almost ninety years, Pisa reclaimed its autonomy and was treated as a state by both Venice and Rome, though not of course by Florence. When invited by Pope Alexander to confront the Pisan ambassadors, Malegonnelli politely refused; in a letter to the Signory he denounced the holy father's "duplicity."[136] In this instance, Florence was under no diplomatic pressure from the papacy. The 1420s saw a reverse and more complicated situation.

Claimed as papal territory, Bologna went through many changes of government during the first forty years of the fifteenth century. Rival factions and families fought for control of the city, doing so under cover of the struggle arising from papal determination to rule the Bolognese and the Commune of Bologna's determination to rule itself. In this contest Florentines tended to favor the Commune. During the wars against Giangaleazzo and Ladislaus, with the temporal power of the papacy at its nadir, Florence and the Commune of Bologna had developed a tradition of mutual alliances. In the 1420s the Florentine Republic still hoped to keep up this tradition—a defense against the new menace from Lombardy, Filippo Maria Visconti. Friction between Florence and the papacy was therefore difficult to avoid. The issue was the

[136] *SCRO*, 11, f. 54r, "non poteva meglio chiarire la sua duplicità."

political status of Bologna. A noteworthy outbreak of differences took place in the spring of 1420. Ordering the captain of papal forces, Braccio da Montone, to Bologna, Martin V resolved to make the Commune submit. The Commune appealed to Florence which, while encouraging the Bolognese, tried to set itself up as arbitrator. This so angered Martin that he hinted at his readiness to strike at Florence with an interdict.[137] Sounding out opinion in the more authoritative sectors of the oligarchy, the Signory held its major consultation on April 22nd. The speakers were five lawyers and sixteen laymen. Agreeing that Florence should support the Bolognese in some of their claims but not in others, the lawyers seemed to look for a clear distinction between the rights of Bologna on the one hand and its legitimate obligations to the pope on the other. Although wishing to avoid a clash with the holy father, Bencivenni, Corsini, and the other lawyers saw the Commune of Bologna as a state within a state. Thus, on the pivotal question of whether or not Florence was diplomatically correct in receiving the ambassadors from Bologna, they all replied in the affirmative "because," they insisted, "the [said] ambassadors cannot be legally turned away."[138] Yet Martin had "refused to renew Boniface IX's grant of the vicariate to the Commune."[139] As this vicariate had been run much like an autonomous state, with the power to wage war, levy taxes, send out ambassadors, and conclude treaties, Pope Martin's denial had the effect of putting Bologna's international status into question. The legal stand of the lawyers in the consultation of April 22nd presupposed a political decision regarding the status of the Commune, and a final agreement with the pope would be contingent on political solutions.

Late in 1425, in a series of negotiations at Rome, the pope insisted that Florence commit itself not to interfere in the affairs of Bologna. Three years later and again in 1429,[140] calling attention to this fact and leaning

---

[137] CP, 44, ff. 7v-9r.

[138] Ibid., f. 8v. The lawyers were Bencivenni, Federighi, Davanzati, Beccanugi, and Corsini.

[139] C. M. Ady, The Bentivoglio of Bologna (London, 1937), p. 13; and F. Sani, Quattrocento bolognese: l'agonia del libero comune (Bologna, 1933), pp. 5-8.

[140] CP, 48, ff. 32v-33r, 83v-84r. On the negotiations of 1425 see Abizzi, Commissioni, ii, 328 ff., conducted by three ambassadors: Rinaldo degli Albizzi, the lawyer Nello da San Gimignano, and Agnolo Pandolfini.

on the advice of lawyers, the Florentine government refused to support Martin in his efforts to recover the obedience of Bologna, where rebellion had overthrown papal rule. Such support, it was argued, would have been interference.

At the beginning of September 1447, discussion in the executive consultations returned—though in another connection—to the subject of the credentials of ambassadors. The Duke of Milan had died in August and King Alfonso of Naples, like the Venetians, contrived to bring Lombardy or parts thereof under his sway. Florence made every effort to discourage this and to maintain a balance of power in northern Italy. Sending troops into Tuscany, King Alfonso also sent ambassadors to Florence to announce his peaceful and good intentions. There was considerable disagreement in the city on the sort of reception to accord the royal ambassadors. Among the group of special advisors summoned by the Signory for consultation were four lawyers. A legal solution of some kind would have been highly desirable. But two of the lawyers—Guglielmo Tanagli and Tommaso Salvetti—refused to commit themselves. They asserted that the question of whether or not the ambassadors should be trusted was one for the Signory and colleges to decide. The decision, in other words, must be a political not a legal one. Otto Niccolini and Tommaso Deti, on the other hand, baldly stated that Alfonso's agents were not worthy of trust, "as they are not proper enemies but thieves."[141]

When the matter came up for discussion in the executive councils, the nature of diplomatic credentials usually posed questions on which the government liked to have the views of lawyers. In December 1422 the Signory became suspicious of the safe-conduct promised to Florentine ambassadors who were on their way to the Duke of Milan. Headed by the lawyer Nello da San Gimignano, a special group of government advisors reported that they disapproved of the safe-conduct and recommended that the Signory delegate "some lawyers and other expert citizens" to examine the words of the communication sent to the Florentine ambassadors by one of the Duke of Milan's secretaries. Although no conclusion was recorded, the question was taken up again six days later

---

[141] *CP*, 52, f. 24r, consultation of 6 Sept., "non servandam fidem cum non sint iusti hostes sed latrones."

and discussed by an advisory group of five lawyers and seven laymen.[142] Whatever its intentions, the Signory was often made to bend to political necessities. In September of the year following (1423), with hostilities between Florence and Milan not yet come to the point of a diplomatic rupture, Filippo Maria had two Florentine ambassadors arrested and kept at Lodi for forty days on the pretext that they had just come from lands infected by plague.[143] The Duke was not one who sought to win distinction by an excessive attachment to the norms of international law. Surely exaggerating, but also partly reflecting the spirit of the Duke's court, one of his private counsellors once said to two Florentine ambassadors with regard to certain of the Duke's claims, "Right is might." And another added: "These are not matters to be adjudicated [by law]."[144]

Although it is true that in its foreign relations the Republic of Florence, like other Italian states, looked to its own self-interest, it is also true that Florentines ordinarily tried to keep within the bounds of international law. And although, like other Italian states, Milan included, Florence often called on its lawyers to vindicate policies and to avoid clashing outright, this was not so as to play fast and loose with the law, to slip around it, but to use its resources to the utmost and to find *within* it the greatest possible freedom of political movement. Exploiting the law for political ends may not have looked very different from finding subtle ways to evade or break it, and often the material results were much the same. Nonetheless, by keeping to the law, however loosely or circuitously, a certain standard of conduct in foreign affairs was maintained, and international claims might be expected to take recognized forms. When in November 1501 lawyers encouraged the government to provide the

---

[142] *CP*, 45, ff. 67v, 69r (12, 18 Dec.). Ridolfi, Bencivenni, Davanzati, Tanagli, and Nello da San Gimignano were the lawyers.

[143] F. Cognasso in the collaborative *Storia di Milano*, VI, 206; Ammirato, *Istorie*, V, 84-85.

[144] The ambassadors were Lorenzo Ridolfi and Cosimo de' Medici, on a mission to Milan in May and June 1420. The report to the Signory was drafted by Ridolfi, who observed that on reminding the Duke's counsellors that their lord had expressed his willingness to go to law with the claims in question, "rispose messer Taddeolo, Ius est in armis, et l'altro disse queste non sono cose da giudicare in tale forma o maniera." Interestingly, the tougher of the two, Taddeolo (or Taddiolo) da Vicomercate, was a canon lawyer.

Florentine ambassadors to France with two different mandates at one and the same time, each with separate dates, one to be presented first and the other sometime later, depending on the course of negotiations,[145] they were straining to make up for the Republic's inequalities in a setting where unsteady and grasping allies, as well as enemies, disposed of greater material reserves and more powerful armies than Florence. Moreover, these were allies and enemies who were not squeamish about breaking agreements.

In fairer times, Florentine governments and their lawyers had often been sticklers about the Republic's keeping faith with its foreign obligations, not alone with regard to matters where immediate self-interest was in play. At the end of 1481 King Ferrante of Naples was the arbitrator in a territorial dispute between Siena and Florence. The award favored Florence but fixed no deadline for Siena's surrender of the territory in question. In February 1482 it was already clear that the defeated party might try to get around the decision by having the Cardinal of Siena solicit the intervention of Pope Sixtus IV, who had promised the year before to leave the decision entirely up to King Ferrante. Yet on February 13th, sure of Florence's rightful claims, Guidantonio Vespucci, lawyer and Florentine ambassador to Siena, prompted the Eight on Foreign Affairs (the Otto di Pratica) to take the most reasonable course of action. He advised them to have a special Florentine emissary apply to the Signory of Siena "to return to you the lands involved in the [King's] decision, and I say this because, no time limit having been put on the said restitution, it is necessary to claim these lands officially and to put in a proper request so as to place them in default. Such is what I think, while always submitting to [whatever is] . . . advised by my seniors, the lawyers there [in Florence]."[146]

---

[145] *CP*, 66, ff. 363v *et seq.* (22 Oct.), 368v-369v (16 Nov.). The lawyers were Domenico Bonsi, Francesco Gualterotti, and Antonio Malegonnelli. The lawyers Antonio Strozzi and Luca Corsini also endorsed the plan.

[146] *OCR*, 2, f. 247v. "Perchè *inter alia* che si contengono nelle mie commissioni si è che io vi advisi quello mi occorre di fare *de jure post latam sententiam, quamvis* io sappia che costì sia chi meglio di me vi potra consigliare, *nihilominus* a me parrebbe v. s. dovessino per vostro sindico o mandatario richiedere decta signoria di Siena che vi dovessi restituire le terre che si contengono nella sententia et questo dico perchè, non essendo posto tempo a decta restitutione, è necessario

We have already noted that in May 1447, on commission from the Signory, two leading lawyers ruled that the government should make restitution of a shipment of confiscated Sienese goods.[147] The question here was not an open one. Taken from a Florentine boat, these goods were protected by a Florentine safe-conduct—a guarantee to foreigners and foreign goods. This was a commitment binding on Florence by international law.

At the end of September 1428 Florence was about to take Guidantonio Manfredi, Lord of Faenza, into its military service, when news arrived of his occupying a land just beyond Tuscany in the Romagna—Gattaja—to which Florence seems to have had some claim. In the ensuing consultations (October 1-2),[148] far from recommending hurried or impulsive action, the Signory's advisors encouraged the government to seek a conscientious legal solution. Particularly wedded to this line of conduct were the lawyers Lorenzo Ridolfi, Albizzo Albergotti, Giuliano Davanzati (for S. Maria Novella), and the city's foremost notary, Ser Paolo Fortini (for S. Giovanni). All counselled the government to work for the recovery of Gattaja only if Florence was legally entitled to have it. They agreed that the question should be decided by a team of lawyers and other practiced citizens, according to the terms of a standing pact with Manfredi.

## SOURCES FOR CHAPTER EIGHT

On diplomacy as an art and institution in this period, the most important, if curious, book ever written is still M. de Maulde-La-Clavière, *La Diplomatie au temps de Machiavel*, 3 vols. (Paris, 1892-1893). The earliest full-scale treatment is the clear-sighted study by A. Reumont, *Della diplomazia italiana del secolo xiii al xvi* (Firenze, 1857). Much more restricted to Machiavelli's period and more limited as a study is E. Dupré-Theseider, *Niccolò Machiavelli diplomatico* (Como, 1945). An

---

interpellarli et richiederli per constituirli *in mora*. Questo occorre a me, rimettendomi sempre a quello v. m. fussino consigliate da cotesti doctori mia maggiori." Vespucci was to go on from Siena and serve as ambassador in Rome, *ibid.*, ff. 262r, 278r-v, 288r.

[147] See p. 362.

[148] *CP*, 48, ff. 27r-29r; also Ammirato, *Istorie*, v, 143-44.

outstanding work of synthesis is the best-known book on the subject: G. Mattingly, *Renaissance Diplomacy* (London, 1955), where see also the references (p. 299) to articles by Willy Andreas (1942) and Fritz Ernst (1950).

Most of these studies, it seems to me, give an excessive emphasis to the emergence of the resident ambassador. More important was what he inherited: a fully developed technique of diplomacy, which is what I have sought to bring out in this chapter.

For material on international law and international relations, I can do no better than to refer the reader to the massive bibliography compiled by Sir Thomas Barclay for *The Encyclopaedia Britannica*, 11th ed., s.v. "International law." That even today students of international law are not aware of the critical performance of lawyers in medieval and Renaissance diplomacy is clear from recent work in the field. See, e.g., *The Times Literary Supplement* (12 Aug. 1965), pp. 689-90, an expert's review of *A British Digest of International Law*, ed. C. Parry, vols. 5-8 (London, 1965), and of D. P. O'Connell, *International Law*, 2 vols. (New York-London, 1965). I have made particular use of E. Nys, *Les origines du droit international* (Brussels, 1894); E. Levi Catellani, *Il diritto internazionale privato e i suoi recenti progressi*, 2 vols. (Torino, 1895-1902); G. Bonolis, *Questioni di diritto internazionale in alcuni consigli inediti di Baldo degli Ubaldi* (Pisa, 1908); P. Fauchille, *Traité de droit international public*, 8th ed., vol. I, i (Paris, 1922); B. Paradisi, *Storia del diritto internazionale nel medio evo* (Milano, 1940); Paradisi, *Il problema storico del diritto internazionale*, 2nd ed. (Napoli, 1956). The most useful general work in the field is F.-L. Ganshof, *Le Moyen Âge* (Paris, 1953), vol. I of the *Histoire des Relations Internationales*, ed. P. Renouvin. Each of Ganshof's chapters is followed by a rich bibliography.

Of works on reprisal and commercial treaties, not in general but of the sort which I found helpful in preparing this chapter, there are the books cited in my notes, as well as three other noteworthy studies: G. Bonolis, "Due consigli inediti di Baldo degli Ubaldi," *Il diritto commerciale*, XXI, fasc. 5-6 (Pisa, 1903); G. Arias, "La base delle rappresaglie nella costituzione sociale del medio evo," *Atti del Congresso Internazionale di scienze storiche*, IX (Roma, 1904), 347-67; and G. I. Cassandro, *Le rap-*

*presaglie e il fallimento a Venezia nei secoli xiii-xvi* (Torino, 1938). A standard work of reference for Renaissance lawyers was the famous *Tractatus Repraesaliorum* of Bartolus.

Perhaps the most useful diplomatic histories on general lines are these: N. Valeri, *L'Italia nell' età dei principati dal 1343 al 1516* (Verona, 1949), whose concern—one might almost say obsession—with the problem of Italian unity is, however, anachronistic; a better study is L. Simeoni, *Le Signorie,* 2 vols. (Milan, 1950). Best of all, though from a Milanese point of view, are the treatments by F. Cognasso and F. Catalano in vols. v-vii of the *Storia di Milano* (1955-56), whose notes give references to more detailed studies.

Five important collections of treaties and other documents are the following: J. C. Lünig, ed., *Codex Italiae Diplomaticus* (Frankfurt, 1725-1732); I. Dumont, ed., *Corps universel diplomatique du droit des gens,* 9 vols. (Amsterdam, 1726-1731); A. Theiner, ed., *Codex Diplomaticus Dominii Temporalis S. Sedis,* 3 vols. (Roma, 1861-1868); L. Osio, ed., *Documenti diplomatici tratti dagli archivi milanesi e coordinati,* 6 vols. (Milano, 1864-1877); and especially C. Guasti, ed., *Commissioni di Rinaldo degli Albizzi per il comune di Firenze,* 3 vols. (Firenze, 1867-1873). Many Florentine treaties are summarized and quoted at length by C. Guasti and A. Gherardi, *I Capitoli del comune di Firenze,* 2 vols. (Firenze, 1866-1893).

Again, the fundamental sources for this chapter are in the Archivio di Stato of Florence: *Capitoli, Consulte e Pratiche,* but above all the different series of letters and instructions that passed between Florence and her diplomatic agents. A full list of the series used is given in the table of abbreviations at the beginning of this book.

*The State*

## Chapter Nine

# The Florentine State

## *1. Lawyers and Oligarchy*

The pre-eminence of lawyers in the political life of the Republic was largely a function of the exalted state of legal science and of the type of oligarchy Florence was. Unless we try to understand the precise fashion in which government by the few was the polity of this city, we shall not clearly understand the place of lawyers in Florentine statecraft.

In the 1,700 years or so between Aristotle and Bartolus, aristocracy was often defined as government by "the good" or "the best" for the welfare of the entire community. Aristocracy of this pure type cannot have made many appearances in history. Its Aristotelian corruption, oligarchy—government by the rich where the rich seek their own good—seems to have had more historical fortune. Used in this fashion, the words *aristocracy* and *oligarchy* are value ridden—which is not to our purpose here.

By oligarchy I mean government where only the few have a voice and where among these the rich tend to hold the most authoritative positions. No thought is given here to the question of whether those few were "the best" or whether or not they ruled for the universal good. In a work penned shortly before he died, the prince of fourteenth-century lawyers, Bartolus (d. 1357), observed that Venice and Florence were governed by "aristocracies," by the few "rich and good men."[1] As he saw it, the ruling class in each of these cities was large enough to hide or mask internal strife, to permit a neutral bloc of families to stand between existing or prospective factions, and to create the illusion of a polity with not too narrow a social base. The lawyer's assessment was astonishingly shrewd. Yet he missed something essential. Some distinctions were wanting. For in the following century the two cities had very different destinies, although even at Venice the leading agencies of public power were to undergo some contraction.

[1] *Tractatus de regimine civitatis*, in his *Commentaria* (Venice, 1596), x, f. 153.

At the outset of the fifteenth century, according to the best scholarship on the subject, Florence ruled over a total territorial and urban population of about 150,000 souls.[2] Of these, some 55,000 lived in Florence proper; the rest were inhabitants of the dominion. By 1427 the stable population of the city had fallen to about 40,000, owing mainly, it seems, to the plague of 1417 and partly to the fact that some families had moved into the country to escape the city's onerous, often discriminatory taxation. The urban population increased later in the century, but not by much.

The pattern of Florentine political authority consisted of a series of concentric circles. The territory was ruled by local magistrates and assemblies, these in turn by the capital city, the capital city by a select political class, the class by several hundred families,[3] and the families by about 500 men. The smallest of these circles may be delineated in some detail.

The full-fledged citizen of Florence was the man entitled to hold public office. He alone had the right to influence political decisions and to dispose of the public authority. With the exception of the Emperor[4]— and his claim was nebulous and ineffectual—no one else, directly or indirectly, could lay a claim to this privilege, for a privilege is what it was and what the political community called it. In 1382, from a list of about 5,000 names, 750 men were finally cleared by the scrutiny of that year and made eligible for the city's major executive body—the Signory. In 1391, from a total of nearly 6,000 names, 671 were approved for the Signory; and the scrutiny of 1393 ended with the approval of 619 men.[5] In these years and for two or three decades following, the total number of men eligible for all regular offices, including the legislative councils,

---

[2] E. Fiumi, "Fioritura e decadenza dell'economia fiorentina," *ASI*, cxvii (1959), 501; and cxvi (1958), 465-67.

[3] Some 365 in the 1450s, according to the chronicler Benedetto Dei and repeated by G. Pampaloni, who now considers the figure much too high. The figure of 200 *effective* families, also given and fully listed by Dei, seems much closer to the true mark. *Vide* Pampaloni, "Fermenti di riforme democratiche nella Firenze medicea del Quattrocento," *ASI*, cxix (1961), 48, 53.

[4] On which see esp. Ch. X.

[5] I owe these figures to the courtesy of Mr. Anthony Molho. They appear in his doctoral thesis (pp. 104-105), "The Florentine Oligarchy of the Late Trecento: 1393-1402," submitted to the History Department of Western Reserve University, Cleveland, Ohio, 1965.

probably stood at around 2,000 or 2,500. These men—and we ought to keep this in mind—made up the political class of Florence; they constituted the social base of the city's "broad" polity. At the end of the fifteenth century the total figure rose to 3,300 and in the late 1520s to about 4,000.[6] But it was not the *universitas* as a whole which wielded effective power. This was the privilege, instead, of an even smaller group, a sort of inner oligarchy whose members enjoyed the supreme grade of citizenship.

The supreme grade of citizenship—citizenship "in the fullness of right" —was that which afforded the possibility of election to the city's principal offices, not to the Signory only. For offices like the Ten on War and the Eight on Public Safety were at times more difficult to enter, more oligarchically appointed, than the Signory itself. But the Signory may be taken as a standard.

We have already seen that at the end of the fourteenth century the number of men eligible for election to the Signory fell from 750 to 619. This decline seems to have been temporarily arrested in the opening decades of the fifteenth century, as rival family blocs angled for advantage and looked about in search of allies. According to a contemporary, these divisions made for the entry of "new men" into government—to him a distasteful phenomenon.[7] But after the palace revolutions of 1433-1434, political power began again to concentrate. And later on in the century a number of different administrations were to reveal that they considered the whole peace, safety, and political future of the city to depend on about 400 men from the leading families. In late January and early February 1429, the government sponsored a political oath calling for civil harmony, for the suppression of faction and vendetta, and for a renewed dedication to the "good, honor, and greatness of the Republic."[8] The oath was administered to 647 men, a group which even included a sprinkling of cutlers, smiths, vintners, hosiers, and the like. Never again, however, was the inner oligarchy to include such a variety

[6] *Ricordi storici di Filippo di Cino Rinuccini*, ed. G. Aiazzi (Firenze, 1840), pp. clvi-vii, gives the figure 3,200; the figure for the 1520s in J. Nardi, *Istorie della città di Firenze*, ed. L. Arbib, 2 vols. (Firenze, 1838-1841), I, 14.

[7] Buonaccorso Pitti, *Cronica*, ed. A. B. Della Lega (Bologna, 1905), p. 135.

[8] *CP*, 48, ff. 54v-57r, 58r-v, 60v.

of men and so many. In 1466 a similar oath, with an added promise to live by the old constitutional norms, was taken by less than 400 men, again in the main government palace—the Palazzo della Signoria.[9] Early in January 1500, wishing to address "the best part" of the citizenry, those "to whom the good and bad of the city most pertained," the Gonfalonier of Justice, Francesco Pepi, assembled 400 citizens "from the principal houses."[10]

By Pepi's time the dominant families of the early fifteenth century—the surviving ones—had undergone such a metamorphosis, had so hardened in their outlook and numbers, that the change is best summarized by saying that they had become a nobility. One of the most significant results or by-products of this change was that after the creation of the "democratic" Grand Council (1494), all practical schemes for the reform of the Florentine constitution tended to pivot on the establishment of an aristocratic senate. It was assumed that the senators would sit for life and number, depending upon the scheme, between 200 and 400 men.[11]

Perception of the link between citizenship and oligarchy provides us with a clearer notion of what oligarchy meant in Florence. Not only did it mean government by the few, it also meant their exercise of public office: their direct control over the factual disposition of the public power. This is why Florentine memoirs, letters, and chronicles of the fifteenth century, and reflections on politics in Machiavelli's time, speak of "having," "holding," "occupying," "taking," "acquiring," "drawing to oneself," or "losing" the state (*lo stato*). To enter into an important office was like taking a piece of the state into one's hands,[12] or like walk-

---

[9] BNF, *Fondo principale*, II, 1, 106, f. 60r.

[10] *CP*, 65, ff. 182v, 188r.

[11] Cf. the reform schemes in *CP*, 66 (May 1500–May 1502), ff. 384v-386r; those also of Luigi Guicciardini (for a senate of 200 men), Alessandro de' Pazzi (for senate of 100 men), Francesco Guicciardini (for senate of only seventy or eighty), all in *ASI*, 1 (1842), 420ff.; and schemes in R. von Albertini, *Das Florentinische Staatsbewusstsein im Übergang von der Republik zum Prinzipat* (Bern, 1955), pp. 345ff.

[12] E.g., A. Strozzi, *Lettere di una gentildonna fiorentina del sec. xv ai figliuoli esuli*, ed. C. Guasti (Firenze, 1877), pp. 3-4, says of the Parenti family, "e hanno un poco di stato, ch'è poco tempo che'l padre fu di Collegio." This is common Florentine usage of the period: "stato" here refers to "status" and "state," having no meaning apart from politics.

ing into one's shop.[13] It is not that Florentines were unaware of the difference between public and private affairs. They were keenly aware of it, but it was a difference perceived in terms of the distinction between theory and practice. As an abstraction, the state in their eyes was the public good wedded to authority, or it was the manifestation of high civic and moral purpose in the traditional aggregate of magistracies which disposed of all public rights and powers. But as a concrete reality, as that public thing which invaded the daily life of Florentines, the state was sometimes viewed as an object (the reification of political authority), sometimes as a relationship or "marriage" between the oligarchy and the city's aggregate of leading magistracies.[14] The Florentine citizen, taken as a practical man of affairs, did not ordinarily think of the state as something separate from those who "held" it. And if one lost it, it is not that the state ceased to exist but that someone else had taken it. The real state, the state felt all around one in the form of potent commissions or as a source of income (via speculation in the Monte), existed *in* the corporate and individual holder.[15]

This conception of the state did not spring from the mind of Florentines as the fruit of instantaneous generation, like Athena from the head of her father; it issued from—was a faithful reflection of—the practice of oligarchy in Florence. Later on in this and in the following chapter we shall get at some of the other consequences of this practice, particularly with reference to legal attitudes and to the distinctive relation between lawyers and the power of the executive. Keeping here to our immediate aim, let us see how the realities of oligarchy worked for the political pre-eminence of Florentine lawyers.

[13] The metaphor is L. B. Alberti's, *I primi tre libri della famiglia*, ed. Pellegrini and Spongano (Firenze, 1946), p. 278, "che io volessi, come quasi fanno tutti, ascrivermi lo stato quasi per mia richezza, riputarlo mia bottega," etc.

[14] Marriage: see the political poem written in 1426 by a leading Florentine statesman. The central image of the poem is a *donna* who represents the state, office, the *reggimento*, the public power. E.g., three verses warn the old ruling families: "E non lasciate più in alto montare/L'orgoglio dell'ingrate e nuove genti,/che voglion *vostra donna* trasmutare." See "Versi fatti da Niccolò da Uzzano predicendo la mutazione dello stato," ed. G. Canestrini, *ASI*, iv (1843), 297-300.

[15] The medieval legal background to this idea of the state as an entity *in* something is treated by G. Post, *Studies in Medieval Legal Thought: Public Law and the State, 1100-1322* (Princeton, 1964), esp. ch. vii.

The only way a citizen of Florence—*ipso iure* a member of the oligarchy—could actively discharge his full range of civic responsibilities was to serve in public office, where he was directly involved in exercising the civil power. Nothing in the Florentine constitution emphasized the principle of indirect representation. The contact with power was direct, immediate, sensory. If today a citizen gave his approval to a bill in one of the legislative councils, tomorrow or the next he might well be helping to put it into effect by his activity in the colleges, in the Rebel or Monte or Catasto offices, in the Eight on Public Saftey, the Defenders of the Laws, the Grain or Morals commission, or one of the many other internal or territorial offices.

This direct contact with office is what led the lawyer—provided he enjoyed the privilege of citizenship—into the forefront of politics. Unless he sought to avoid public life, he was fated, as a member of the oligarchy, to be caught up in political affairs. For Florence, physically, was a small city, and its active political society was a small circle of men whose way of life was indivisible from the Florentine system of state. Thus were citizens made to feel the obligation to move operatively through the circuit of public office. But the lawyer had this advantage: everything else being equal, his prestige and legal skills gave him a strong edge over his lay compeers. Where a merchant or *rentier* would have been doomed to secondary offices, owing to his modest financial or family standing *within* the oligarchy, the lawyer from the same class—overcoming his poor connections by his skills and the dignity of his profession— was picked or drawn for the highest administrative offices, for leading governorships, for embassies, for commissions appointed to work out territorial problems, for assignments concerning relations with the Church, and for the *pratiche* which counselled the Signory. Furthermore, if, as often happened, a lawyer exhibited some political talent and was also heir to one of the city's great names—Corsini, Davanzati, Ridolfi, Gualterotti, Guicciardini—then few men in Florence could attain to his influence or stature. Florentine statecraft—it has been shown again and again—made a practice of combining the experience of experts and laymen. The distinction of the lawyer with experience in public life was that he alone embodied the combination.

Of course, lawyers could show by their manner and habits that they were not interested in public affairs. Matteo Corbinelli (fl. 1440s) and Bernardo Soderini (1451-1534) were men of this type—although there were remarkably few others. Rarely were such men sent on embassies or drawn for service in the major offices. But then it followed, strikingly, that they were most apt to be the very men who were not concerned to have much of a legal practice. Machiavelli's father, Bernardo (1428-1500), was this sort of man: he turned as much away from politics and office as from the legal profession. If one judges by the surviving papers of lawyers and by the thousands of legal *consilia* and *allegationes* that come down to us from Renaissance Florence,[16] it is absolutely clear that the volume of legal business handled by Florentine lawyers was in direct proportion to their activity and prominence in public life. A citizen trained in the law might stand out in politics and yet show no great interest in his profession. Giuliano Davanzati (1390-1446) seems to answer to this description. But any lawyer who had a large following of clients, or who easily attracted requests for judicial opinions, was most likely to be a leading public figure. The link between success in the two fields is explained by the practice of Florentine oligarchy, which is what determined the direction and flow of legal business. Let us see how this worked.

The thriving, fashionable law office bred on the political and social effects of oligarchy. For as the highest grade of Florentine citizenship signified active membership in the oligarchy and this, in turn, brought immediate contact with the public power through the exercise of office, the lawyer who gave proof of his solid standing in the oligarchy by constantly appearing in the chief magistracies was the one to whom clients turned. He was, after all, one of the city's rulers. Did he not hold a piece of the state? Clients rightly assumed that he understood the workings of the potent executive commissions, that he commanded the esteem of the Signory, and that he knew the shifty ways of courts which were in the habit of succumbing to the influence of the executive. Indeed, the executive itself disposed of extensive judicial powers. With the administra-

[16] Those, e.g., of Lorenzo Ridolfi, Alessandro Bencivenni, Antonio Strozzi, Domenico Bonsi, and Niccolò Guicciardini. Listed in the sources for the next chapter.

tion of justice appointed in this fashion, the lawyer-oligarch could not fail to invite a large volume of legal business from private suitors, guilds, religious orders, and rural communes or larger towns. In addition, there were the numerous cases and questions referred for legal or judicial counsel by territorial magistrates or by offices and courts in the city proper. It was therefore entirely natural for foreign lawyers to settle in Florence only when they were accorded at least some of the rights of citizenship, or when they were called to the city to profess law.

Here was another activity which lent stature and attracted clients—the teaching of law. Not surprisingly, university appointments were also in the donation of the oligarchy. Professors were appointed by the Studio Officials, among whom the powerful could exert their influence and the modest feel it. As is shown by the Appendix, Florence produced few lawyers of political standing or good connections who were not at some point invited to teach at the universities of Florence or Pisa. To their list of public offices they also added law professorships.

The bond which existed between oligarchy and the political pre-eminence of lawyers who enjoyed the privilege of citizenship is thus clear. Their civil status pressed them, as it pressed other citizens, into public office. The essential difference was in this: the lawyer who resolved to develop a flourishing legal practice had an additional and more urgent reason to take up politics and find a place in the limelight. Such renown is what a leading law office depended on. The bond was a circular one: the greater a lawyer's political success, the more he attracted clients and requests for judicial counsel; and the greater his professional reputation, the more he ensured or raised his place in political society.

But once he achieved public distinction, there was no turning back, no possibility of retiring from politics. Only political disgrace or self-imposed exile could intervene, and then he lost everything: his friends, his practice, his family *palazzo*, his place in the world, *Fiorenza*.

Need we ask what Florentine lawyers thought of oligarchy? Those who could not claim the supreme grade of citizenship sought it; the others enjoyed it. In one sense, much of this book is a study of the ways in which lawyers put their skills at the service of the oligarchy. For we have seen that they were often the instruments of the oligarchy's foreign policy, the tutors of its relations with the Church and with subject communities, and the moderators in conflicts arising from its internal structure of offices. Far from seeking to reform or modify the judicial system, they served it. And far from opposing the inner oligarchy's narrowing system of controls after 1434—the use of *accoppiatores,* the periodic renewal or establishment of plenipotentiary *balìe*—they contributed their skills and authority to help impose and justify these. As holder or incarnation of the state, the oligarchy was the wellspring of Florentine statutory law. This body of law laid down the essential norms governing citizenship, the organization of magistracies, the way these were filled, the levying of taxes, territorial rule, the subject status of the minor guilds, and the exclusion of most men from a voice in government. Justified, interpreted, and made with the help of Florentine lawyers, statutory law took precedence over the common or Roman law.

No doubt lawyers were under the influence of prevailing theories of citizenship, which encouraged putting effective political power into the hands of "the better part." Like their master Bartolus,[17] Florentine lawyers supposed that government was best managed when controlled by the few: the 2,000 or 3,000 citizens who formed the absolute social basis of the constitution, or the several hundred who tended to monopolize the city's principal offices. Lawyers were called upon to perform well-defined tasks in a world ruled, legitimately or illegitimately, by oligarchies and princes. What sense would it have made, where would have been the profit, for them to take up political views which would have been not so much in conflict with dominant opinion as out of touch with it or merely irrelevant? Casting a glance over the period of this study, we light upon statements and actions which reveal the oligarchical point of view of lawyers.

In a letter written to his son in the 1370s, the canon lawyer and statesman Lapo da Castiglionchio observed, "when appearing in high office, no citizen—least of all if he be a small businessman or a member of the middle classes—should press his views or presume too much. Instead,

---

[17] As represented in his *De regimine civitatis,* even the most democratic of his polities, that of the small city-state, excluded the lower classes from the sovereign people, i.e., from the class of citizens.

he should listen to the two or three [authoritative] voices in council."[18] In 1384-1385 the city's best-known lawyers (Filippo Corsini, Giovanni de' Ricci, and Tommaso Marchi) strongly endorsed plans to overthrow the semi-"popular" government of Siena. Their desire was to put power "in manibus bonorum civium"—into the hands of an oligarchy headed by rich and ancient families like the Salimbeni, Tolomei, and Malavolti.[19]

Turning to the fifteenth century, we may note, of the many examples involving collective action taken by lawyers, the ruling group's decision in November 1453 to continue "keeping" the pouches for the Signory "by hand." This was the government's chief instrument of close oligarchy in Florence. The decision was supported by six prominent lawyers, two of whom—Guglielmo Tanagli and Otto Niccolini—helped to captain the committee which urged the resolution on the government.[20] Skipping fifty years, we find Simone Uguccioni, spokesman for the lawyers at a particular executive consultation (18 January 1502), telling the Signory that government was better run according as the "moltitudine" (i.e., the Grand Council) had less to do with it. Only several days before, in two major executive consultations, four lawyers had represented a series of reform proposals which sought to reduce the power of that "moltitudine." The most drastic proposal, outlined by the lawyer Francesco Pepi for the Santa Croce quarter, called for the establishment of a new, select council. It would consist of from 200 to 400 men, absorb the Grand Council's control over taxation, and assume the power of major political appointment.[21]

With few if any exceptions, Florentine lawyers were committed oligarchs. For though we have examples of two or three who resisted new drives to narrow the circle of the established oligarchy,[22] even these were merely for one type of oligarchy (loosely composed) rather than another (smaller and more caste-like).

[18] *Epistola*, ed. L. Mehus (Bologna, 1753), p. 116, "che nullo cittadino, e massimamente popolano o uomo di piccolo affare, quando ha signoria, non deve essere troppo ardito, nè presontuoso, ma udire le due e le tre voci in consiglio."

[19] *CP*, 24, ff. 14v, 15v, 23r (27 Dec. 1384, 13 Jan. 1385).

[20] The other four lawyers were Tommaso Salvetti, Girolamo Machiavelli, Donato de' Cocchi-Donati, and Tommaso Deti: *CP*, 53, f. 44v.

[21] *CP*, 66, ff. 384r-386r, 391v.

[22] See pp. 432-33.

## 2. *The Executive Power*

Down to the early fifteenth century, the Republic's regular courts had a working autonomy; they were not intended to be under the aegis of the executive. Relying on Roman public law, lawyers might derive the judiciary from the *imperium* of the prince, but the Florentine constitution accorded the law courts a sphere of their own. Only by calling on its discretionary and special powers could the Signory overrule the decisions of the regular courts. These observations will help us to understand the following discussion of the executive power.

If Florentine oligarchy made for a society which favored the professional fortunes of citizen-lawyers, it was the executive—used and organized in a particular way—which came to rely heavily on the legal profession. I propose to examine this link between lawyers and the power of the executive, viewing the link not as a feature isolated from the oligarchy, but as an expression of the way authority was increasingly concentrated in Renaissance Florence.

There was nothing unusual *prima facie* about the fact that certain executive or administrative offices in fifteenth-century Florence disposed of special judicial powers. This phenomenon went back to the twelfth century, although the combination was less often seen then at the level of full-scale administrative offices. In his analysis of the Florentine constitution, Davidsohn drew attention to seven offices which combined regulatory or police with judicial powers in the thirteenth and early fourteenth centuries. To this sector belonged the Official over the Properties of Rebels, the Official on Sumptuary Laws, the Gabelle Commission (six officials and a foreign judge), the Grain Commission (*idem*), the Communal Surveyors, the Office over Public Rights and Properties, and the Zecca or Mint Officials. Three of these offices were put on a regular basis for the first time between 1302 and 1330,[23] so that even the thirteenth century was not much given to the fusion of the executive and judicial powers.

The fourteenth century saw a pullulation of executive offices—the birth

[23] R. Davidsohn, *Geschichte von Florenz*, IV, i (Berlin, 1922), ch. II and pp. 91-92, 138, for the officials on rebel goods, on sumptuary laws, and on public rights and properties.

of the Regulators, the Tower Officials, the War Commission, the Monte Commission, the Defectuum Officials, the Conductae Officials, the Eight on Public Safety, the Grascia Officials, the Officials over Orphans, the Ten of Liberty, the Officials of the Gabelle on Contracts, the Abundance Officials, and still others. Some of these offices combined regulatory with police functions; most were founded with certain limited powers of summary justice in their respective spheres. In the course of the fifteenth century, by means of encroachment or express statutory license, nearly all these offices stepped up their judicial activity. A few others were added to the total cluster: the Catasto Officials, the Morals Commission (Honestatis Officiales), the Consuls of the Sea, the Defenders of the Laws, the Five on the County, and the Nocturnal Officials.

A process that started in the fourteenth century, this partitioning and redistribution of the executive authority was also carried on early in the following century, which subsequently, however, was marked by a consolidation of power. It is not merely that with the enlargement of their judicial spheres the new offices took authority away from the traditional judiciary, but that four or five of these soon towered above all the others. At the vanguard of this trend was the Signory itself, which became more hammer-like in its contact with the legislative councils, more receptive to the petitions of civil suitors, and so in one sector of its activity more like a judicial commission. The result was that whole areas were lopped off the jurisdictional map of the old judiciary. First the independent Appellate Judge was suppressed, then the Executor of the Ordinances of Justice, and finally the Captain of the People.[24] The Podestà remained— a ghost of the figure he had been even as late as the third quarter of the fourteenth century.

It is the executive power's invasion of the judiciary—as often by statute as by encroachment and prescription—that put a higher value on the participation of lawyers in government. The early Commune employed *iudices idiotae* (lay judges) who often had recourse to the judicial advice of trained lawyers. In the exercise of territorial government this practice survived the Renaissance. But the fifteenth century was different in that it tended to make lawyers the indispensable aides of every potent office—of

[24] See pp. 132, 136-37.

every office which mingled administrative with special judicial functions. The judicial power of the executive, exercised by laymen, generated an enormous volume of legal business which was passed on to lawyers. To see this, we have only to go through the rich collections of fifteenth- and early sixteenth-century *consilia*.[25] There we find a large quantity of opinions penned by lawyers in answer to questions and cases referred to them by the Signory, the Eight on Public Safety, the Defenders of the Laws, the Rebel Officials, the Grascia Officials, the Officials of the Gabelle on Contracts, the Regulators, the Five on the County, the Officials over Orphans, the Monte Officials, and—though much less so—the War Commission and the Otto di Pratica. The Signory, for example, could claim jurisdiction over crimes against the state; the Defenders of the Laws handled malfeasance in public office; the Rebel Officials defined rebel property and made decisions on all private claims advanced against confiscated goods; the officials charged with the gabelle on contracts decided in particular cases whether or not the tax was to be paid; the Five on the County sometimes handled conflicts of jurisdiction between communities in the territory; and the Monte Officials often settled conflicting claims to credits in the Republic's funded debt.[26]

These offices were all assumed to function under the aegis of the Signory. Constitutionally, their authority derived from this highest of all magistracies, although only with the explicit consent of the legislative councils. Appeal against the decisions of these offices was permitted solely with approval of the Signory and colleges.

Continually invited to offer judicial counsel, the ambitious lawyer profited enormously from the development of executive-judicial offices. The constant demand for such counsel provided him with one obvious benefit, but there was another which went to make him a key functionary in government.

[25] Excellent examples in BNF, *Magl.*, XXIX, 186, 187, two volumes of *consilia* and pleas by Alessandro Bencivenni, most of them dating from the second decade of the fifteenth century; see also the volume of *consilia* by Lorenzo Ridolfi, BNF, *Fondo principale*, II, III, 370, on cases from *ca.* 1412 to 1420.

[26] Such credits were a species of capital which lawyers distinguished from both movable and real property. See *Strozz., 3a ser.*, 41/9, f. 451r (Antonio Strozzi). This volume of opinions, mainly from the first fifteen years of the sixteenth century, concerns scores of cases referred to Strozzi and to other lawyers by some of the offices named above.

We have seen that lawyers were frequently summoned to help resolve conflicts of jurisdiction.[27] The rise of new executive offices and the shifting duties in some of the older ones changed and complicated the whole checkerboard of jurisdictions. Duplication of authority was common. The boundaries between offices were sometimes uncertain.[28] Among the major beneficiaries of the developing complex of offices were those notaries who qualified for election to the highest notarial posts—the posts attached to the powerful offices. In the best of cases, these men sometimes revealed some working knowledge of administrative and constitutional law. Such notaries made up the skeletal framework of the office-holding class. They provided administrations with an element of continuity; or, if they were moved around from office to office, they soon dominated the routine of notarial work that was common to all major offices. Charged with keeping the records of all directives and legislation bearing on whichever office they happened to be serving, they had to know its powers, procedures, and the limits of its competence. By contrast, the men who had frequented the law schools (fully trained lawyers) came on the scene only as final experts, i.e., when an issue was so unclear, so disputable, or so important, that it was necessary to turn to formal legal argument to resolve the conflict or problems in question.

In short, the rise of executive-judicial offices resulted in a system of state whose smooth functioning depended on a class of experts—lawyers and notaries. Operating on two different levels, these were the men who worked to unravel the recurrent administrative and judicial snarls. The notary performed his tasks on an immediate, quotidian level; the lawyer at irregular intervals, on a more removed and more complicated level, where he was apt to be concerned with the very nature of the office or offices involved in dispute.

Carried out in the fourteenth and early fifteenth centuries, the partitioning of the executive authority had the appearance of conforming to a new democratic trend. It seemed to put power into the hands of more and more men. If this was true, then the lawyer, by helping to keep the

---

[27] In Ch. V, 2-3.

[28] As attested by the extraordinarily high number of legal *consilia* dealing entirely or principally with the question of competence. See e.g. the first two volumes of Strozzi's collection, ASF, *Strozz., 3a ser.*, 41/1, 2, *passim*.

emerging system of offices working smoothly, would appear to have been an instrument of democratic republicanism.

Nothing could be more illusory. Florence was more than its ruling group, more than its office holders. There was the bulk of the city's population (a multitude without political rights), as well as the territories and subject peoples lying beyond the city walls. If at a certain point, therefore, those who wielded effective power in the city added a few more to their numbers, far from being a move toward democratic republicanism, the change merely involved a shift of emphases, a rearrangement of forces within the oligarchy. The shift was achieved by putting the executive power on a more rotatory basis. This phase of oligarchical development was marked by a readiness to see the state as a thing to be taken, held, acquired, possessed. By increasing the number of offices and thereby making the power of the executive circulate more uniformly, the oligarchy seemed to exhibit a greater fairness in providing each of its members with a piece of the state. In these circumstances, the state had its unity in their unity.

The executive power so clearly served the Republic that the public good was unthinkable without it. In a sense, the executive and the *utilitas publica* could not be separated. Yet the redistribution of the executive power did not mean redistributing an abstraction. It meant distributing a real participation in the exercise of authority. It meant the opportunity to influence, to coerce, to enjoy, to be important, to make fateful decisions. Hence it was the redistribution of the executive power which enabled the ruling families, by their continuous contact with the major offices, to realize a closer identity with the state. Wherefore it follows that the redistribution signified an entrenchment, a reaffirmation of oligarchy, not a departure from it. Two consequences bear this out. For one thing, the preserves of the traditional judiciary were "raided" by the executive. Here was evidence of the determination to take over more and more of the public power,[29] which the oligarchs could only accomplish through the exercise of office. The result was that in the course of the fifteenth

---

[29] By the end of the century the lawyer Guidantonio Vespucci could announce with an easy naturalness: "egl'è a ognuno acquistare, e a signori acquistare dominio." *CP*, 62, f. 2v (March 1496). He was speaking for the order of lawyers.

century this process of appropriation made a wreck of the old judiciary and put the administration of justice into a state of profound crisis.

The other consequence was even more fateful. In a setting dominated by faction and clusters of powerful families, the enlargement of the executive, through the partitioning of its operations, went *pari passu* with a remarkable growth in the power of certain offices. By an indirect control over scrutinies and office pouches, the dominant families managed to earmark most of the places in those offices for themselves, the men who enjoyed *de facto* the highest grade of citizenship. The circuit of prized offices included the War Commission, the Eight on Public Safety, the Monte Commission, the Six of the Mercanzia, the Defenders of the Laws, the *accoppiatores*, the periodic special *balìe*, the colleges, and of course the Signory. These were the offices manipulated by the inner oligarchy (the Medicean circle after 1434) in the course of its political consolidation. The prince was also to follow this course.

Lawyers contributed directly and indirectly to the transformation of the executive, to a change which brought the constitution into line with the regrouping of political and social forces. Up to about 1434, they revealed no obvious inclination to strengthen the hand of the executive. As shown at the time of the Bastari (1387) and Moncione (1421) cases,[30] lawyers seemed inclined to keep the authority of the Signory within existing bounds. But after 1434 they repeatedly gave their support in council to the growing and more pressing initiatives of the executive, to keeping the pouches for major office "by hand," and to renewing or prolonging the mandates of plenipotentiary councils (*balìe*). This was their direct service to the concentration of power in the executive sector of government. In the long run, however, their indirect service was to be more decisive and lasting. For by aiding and facilitating the executive's invasion of the judicial realm, and by adducing legal argument to defend *balìe* which disrupted and weakened the old legislature, lawyers turned the ensuing fusion of powers into a working instrument: they helped to pave the way for absolute government. By standing as arbitrators over the whole range of such instruments, or rather, by articulating the guidelines for governing the working arrangements among offices,

---

[30] Described on pp. 147ff, 155ff.

lawyers became the caretakers of the new executive configuration. They worked to make possible a political system which occupied that intermediate stage in the transition from commune to principality.[31]

The reconstitution and reaffirmation of the executive—historical change of this magnitude does not occur in isolation. A more flexible and open political interlude in the middle decades of the fourteenth century, noteworthy for the presence of new men in government, offered the opportunity for the rise of new offices and the redistribution of the executive power. Gradually, however, from the early 1380s, in a reaction against that interlude and against the still more infamous one set off by the workers' revolt of 1378, the upper-class families moved to reverse things, partly by fostering the concentration of power in certain offices.

These changes can be rightly appreciated only as parts of a more comprehensive whole. Enrico Fiumi has convincingly shown that following a long period of tremendous expansion, the Florentine economy, from the middle of the fourteenth century, entered a long period of stasis—actually declined in some sectors during some years.[32] The consequences of such a cycle of change seem self-evident: a dynamic, flourishing society with plastic political institutions and a great deal of mobility before the middle of the fourteenth century; thereafter, a society whose vigorous tradition of institutional plasticity was gradually undermined by a hardening of the different social strata. The final result, in view of the oligarchical establishment, was a sharp narrowing of the agencies of public power.

Consonant with these observations is the fact that during the fifteenth century the number of new men who made their way into political society radically declined.[33] The depopulated Tuscan countryside no longer fed new men into the political ranks of the city in historical numbers. Politics became much more exclusive socially. Understandably, more men went into the legal profession. In a time of economic difficulty, the law

[31] On the details of which see Ch. XI.

[32] "Fioritura," *ASI* (1957-1959).

[33] Indeed, though with some exaggeration, Fiumi says that he knows of no leading family which achieved fortune by its own commercial and industrial activity after the fourteenth century. *Ibid.*, cxvii (1959), 502. I can think of five: the families Gaddi, Pucci, Martelli, Bonsi, and Cocchi-Donati, though all five actually began their rise in the second half of the fourteenth century. They reached the top level of political society only in the second half of the fifteenth century.

provided security; and in a time of oligarchical contraction, it brought the city's highest offices within reach—an easier prize for citizens who possessed this critical skill. As was pointed out in Chapter III,[34] the last period of this study (1480-1530) produced the largest number of Florentine lawyers, above all from the households of ancient families. When discussing the events of the late 1520s in his *Storia fiorentina*, Benedetto Varchi (1503-1566) rails against the evil influence and great political estate of lawyers under the Republic.[35] He insists that lawyers and rival political blocs were what caused so many of the Republic's chief magistracies to be tyrannical and badly appointed.

### SOURCES FOR CHAPTER NINE

The literature offers no full-scale study of oligarchy in Florence. Pertinent studies have been listed in the sources for Chs. III and V: i.e., the books by A. Municchi, A. Anzilotti, G. Brucker, A. Rado, and N. Rubinstein. Also relevant are the articles by G. Antonelli (*ASI*, 1954) and G. Pampaloni (*ASI*, 1961-1962).

My analysis of the executive is a result of the research invested in this book. Here again the subject is one without a bibliography. Years ago the article on the Eight by G. Antonelli (above) seemed adequate to me; in fact, it only scratches the surface. The reader may wish to consult the pertinent material listed in the sources for Ch. V. One of the conclusions of this study is that the achievement of lawyers in Florentine public life was closely related to oligarchy and especially to the distinctive development of the executive. Part of the last chapter also calls attention to an aspect of this.

[34] Pp. 74-75.
[35] Bk. vi, 5 of the *Storia*, in *Opere*, 2 vols. (Trieste, 1858), i, 105.

## Chapter Ten

# Lawyers Look at
# the State

Formal political reflection was not a habit of Florentine lawyers. They served the state and the oligarchy; they helped to wield the public power; but they were not given to holding forth on the nature and ends of these institutions.[1] Only occasionally, in their legal opinions or when speaking in the councils of the Republic, did they touch on broad public questions or on political ideas. The appropriate sources of study are therefore discontinuous and often summary, making hazardous any attempt to get at a faithful representation of the state as viewed by lawyers. We have therefore first presented a detailed discussion of the concrete performance of lawyers in the tasks of statecraft. Most of the lawyers who appear and reappear in these pages were caught up in the flux of politics. They were political through and through. Even when dealing with general questions of public law, they were still Florentines and men of experience in Florentine public life.[2]

Did the state exist in Florence at the beginning of the fourteenth century? It would be strange to deny that it did.[3] Gaines Post and others have rightly protested against writers who have maintained that the state is a product of the sixteenth century and later.[4] If we begin with a fixed idea of "the State," making its foundation block a particular conception of sovereignty, we shall find it only where we have previously

[1] The two exceptions, wholly atypical, were Francesco Guicciardini and his cousin, Niccolò di Luigi.

[2] This is shown even by the two exceptions (see preceding note). The political reflections of Francesco and Niccolò Guicciardini were occasioned by a keen preoccupation with Florentine government. See Francesco's *Dialogo e discorsi del reggimento di Firenze*, ed. R. Palmarocchi (Bari, 1932), and the pieces by Niccolò in R. von Albertini, *Das Florentinische Staatsbewusstsein im Übergang von der Republik zum Prinzipat*, pp. 377-99.

[3] Cf. discussion of Florence as sovereign state, pp. 119ff.

[4] Post, *Studies in Medieval Legal Thought*, pp. 3ff., 241ff.

decided it is. It seems better to admit the existence of different types of "the State."

As LATE as October 1387, Florence empowered the Lenzi family to assault at will and even kill the males of a certain branch of the Strozzi clan. Pagnozzino Strozzi had attacked and wounded Piero Lenzi at a time when the latter was one of the Sixteen Gonfaloniers, a body which counselled the Signory. By an act of the legislative assemblies, Piero's family was invested with the right to seek satisfaction, or rather vengence, by preying on Pagnozzino, on his brother Nofri, and on their family and descendants.[5] Though the government was waging a vigorous campaign in the fourteenth century against vendetta and private warfare, in this instance the law was used to legalize it. The rulers of the city were here administering justice—such is what it was *de iure*—by making the power of punishment over to private individuals. Did this concession suggest a peculiar confusion of public authority with private right? To raise a question of this sort reveals a readiness to promote a model: to lay down, by implication, a rule about what is "natural" and "proper" when public and private affairs are handled as they should be—that is to say, as we handle them.

The Lenzi-Strozzi feud resulted in a complication which serves to introduce this analysis of the state as viewed by lawyers. A dispute arose in June 1392 implicating the two families. By the provision of 1387 no assault of the Lenzi on Pagnozzino's family could be treated as a criminal offense, or so it appeared at first. It was soon discovered that the act had some inconsistencies which were so striking as to raise a constitutional question and block proceedings. The Signory called in five lawyers.[6] Looking into the provision of 1387, they found not one act but two. According to the Florentine constitution, a bill became law only after being approved first by the Council of the People, then by the Council of the Commune. When a bill was passed in the first of these councils, the law allowed it to be introduced into the Council of the

[5] *Prov.*, 76, ff. 121r-128r.

[6] The whole affair is reported in a volume of legal opinions kept by the guild: *AGN*, 670, ff. 43v-45r.

Commune with slight "subtractions"; but the substance of the bill must remain the same, and it was explicitly stipulated that nothing new could be added.[7] This rule had been violated by the provision in question. For the bill approved by the second council was so different from the one approved by the first that in the opinion of the lawyers there were two bills, not one. The bill passed by the Council of the People was more general, giving the Lenzi broad freedom of movement to strike at Pagnozzino's family; but the one passed by the Council of the Commune included some limitations, even providing the Strozzi with the right to appeal to the Signory in cases of wanton killing.

Reviewing the statutes on the making of legislation, the five lawyers ruled that the *provvisione* against the Strozzi family was invalid in its present form. For the two councils had not approved one and the same bill. If there was to be any legislation in the matter, the only solution was for the Council of the Commune to go back and approve the original bill.

In view of the opportunity given them to make some general observations on the nature of the provision, it is significant that the lawyers refrained from taking it. Instead, they kept solely to the task at hand. There was no question in their mind about what the Signory and colleges could do when joined with the legislative councils. Law and practice hallowed the authority of this complex of councils to enact statutes, ordinances, and private bills; to affect the life of particular individuals, of all the laity, or in emergencies even of the clergy.

The tacit concurrence of the five lawyers with what these councils could do was backed by a comprehensive body of assumptions: older medieval ideas, legal and philosophical, fused with some of the newer, instrumentalist notions of lawyers like Bartolus and Baldus.[8] In this

---

[7] *Ibid.*, where this constitutional procedure is reviewed by the five lawyers.

[8] I have relied *inter alia* on L. Chiappelli, "Le idee politiche del Bartolo," *Archivio giuridico*, XXVII (1881), 387-439; C. N. S. Woolf, *Bartolus of Sassoferrato* (Cambridge, 1913); the papers in *Bartolo da Sassoferrato, studi e documenti per il vi centenario*, 2 vols., ed. D. Segoloni (Milan, 1962); and E. E. Stengel, "Kaisertitel und Souveränitätsidee," *Deutsches Archiv für Geschichte des Mittelalters*, III (1939), 1-49. On Baldus there is the fifth centenary collection of papers, *L'Opera*

*ensemble*, the law was an instrument. The end was the peace of the community, harmony among social classes, punishment of the wicked and reward of the virtuous: in short, man himself. And if the government of Florence saw fit to teach the unruly Strozzi a lesson, then harsh though the means might seem, the end was a good one—the good of the community. When men did violence to public officials and refused to respect the dignity of public authority, one effective method of correcting them, and also of teaching others by example, was to deprive them of their civil rights, not by incarceration, but by means of exile, loss of citizenship, or merely by separating them from the protection of the law courts. Where Aristotle and Roman law were regnant in politico-legal discussion and where the citizen as *political* animal stood foremost in society, as in the world of the city-state, to strip a man of his civil rights meant almost to strip him of his humanity.

Historical literature is still without a satisfactory study of political fugitives and exile in late medieval and Renaissance Italy. The foregoing paragraph—possibly in too compressed a fashion—points to the guiding principle in the legal background of the phenomenon. Ideally, the aim of all political proscription was peace and the public good. But law was the means, and Bartolus urged its use as a device to destroy or humble citizens who became too powerful in their city-states.[9] Men of this type sought not the good but the oppression of their fellow citizens. The way to stop them was by having recourse to the community's most authoritative arm—the law, which only the *suprema potestas* (the state) disposed of.

The instrumental nature of the law, with its high civic and moral ends, is amply brought out in a Florentine treatise of the first quarter of the fifteenth century—the *Tractatus de bannitis*, written by Nello da San Gimignano, a leading lawyer and one of the period's outstanding diplomats. Treating the whole range of legal problems connected with

---

*di Baldo*, ed. O. Scalavanti (Perugia, 1901), vols. 10-11 of the *Annali dell' università libera di Perugia*; and W. Ullmann, "Baldus's Conception of Law," *The Law Quarterly Review*, ccxxxi (July 1942), 386-99.

[9] In the *De regimine civitatis*. Cf. the discussion of G. Salvemini, "La teoria di Bartolo da Sassoferrato sulle costituzioni politiche," in his *Studi storici* (Firenze, 1901), pp. 137ff.

fugitives, outlaws, and the consequences of proscription, this treatise, the major Florentine work on the subject, was very often cited by Florentine and other lawyers in the fifteenth and sixteenth centuries.[10]

It is laid down by statute that a man proscribed "pro maleficio" may be killed with impunity by any private party. Nello asks, has such a statute any validity in law? And he replies that it does, adducing customary opinion, Bartolus, Baldus, and others. He finds the jurisprudential validation of the statute in its purpose: by discouraging men from crime and by providing a way to keep fugitives from going unpunished, it aims at the public good ("publicam utilitatem").[11] Another defense of the statute is also given, but we shall note it later on in a different connection. Nello goes on to a related question. Is a statute valid which orders that the "plaints" of fugitives should not receive judicial hearings ("querelas bannitorum audiri non debere")? He replies in the affirmative, again citing Bartolus and Baldus. If the statute ordained, says Nello, that justice was not to be done, then it would be invalid, for it would run counter to divine law. But if it says that right ("ius") is not to be rendered, then it may have the force of law, "quia sive iuste sive iniuste dicitur ius reddi."[12] Thus a particular right is here sacrificed to a general or greater right. The defense of the statute depends on a definition of the just, where that which is just turns on the good of the community.

In its rigor and plenitude, law against political and other classes of fugitives was already in full sway by the middle of the fourteenth century and was to become no broader or stricter when serving the absolute state of the sixteenth century and after. The papers of Antonio Strozzi, a well-known lawyer and statesman, show that between 1490 and 1520 he defended a number of men who had killed Florentines listed in the city's "book of proscribed men."[13] His defense in these cases depended on the statute which allowed private parties to kill fugitives with impunity. In a related case his argument ran as follows: I cannot privately agree not to offend

[10] There are three editions. The first, preceded by Mariano Sozzini's *Tractatus de oblationibus*, is stamped "Pisciae, 1486." There is a Lyon edition (1550), and the other is in the *Tractatus universi iuris* (Venice, 1584), XI, i, 357-406.

[11] Ed. Pisciae, f. 43v.

[12] *Ibid.*

[13] *Strozz, 3a ser.*, 41/6, f. 410r, on case tried by the Eight; also *ibid.*, 41/8, ff. 201r, 362r, on cases from Pistoia and the Val d'Elsa.

a man who has been proscribed by Florence, for I am obligated to this city, "my principal." Florence wants him treated as an enemy and, indeed, a statute exists which allows anyone to assault or even kill him. We are here, concludes Strozzi, in the realm of public law and no private agreement is valid which violates that.[14]

The step from using the law as an exact instrument to using public office in the same way was a short one. It is this similarity of functions which sometimes led legal-political theorists to identify the law with the state, the state here understood as the highest and most general expression of office.[15] Francesco Guicciardini's view of the Eight on Public Safety exemplifies the habit of seeing law and office as agencies whereby a concrete political good was ensured, not merely some abstract virtues. Speaking of the conduct of the Eight during the months following the Pazzi conspiracy (1478), Guicciardini observed, "That magistracy, created at an earlier time, had been established with immense authority in criminal matters and was subject in adjudication, though not in procedure, to the laws and statutes of the city. Given a free and absolute power over crimes concerning the state, it was restrained by no laws in this sphere of things. The men who held the regime in their hands devised the office of the Eight so as to have a club for smashing the head of anyone who might wish to vilify or change the government. And though it was born in violence and tyranny, yet the outcome was very salutary. For as anyone in this land knows who has experience of things, if the fear of this magistracy—a fear caused by its swiftness in discovering and judging crimes—did not hold back the wicked, one could not live in Florence."[16]

Guicciardini was four years out of law school and a very busy lawyer when he wrote these lines (c.1509). Putting aside for now the fact that they reveal a thoroughly modern conception of the state—where the state rides somewhere above the ordinary law—we note that with a

---

[14] *Strozz., 3a ser.*, 41/10, f. 59r. Strozzi cites *D.* 2, 14, 38 (private contracts cannot affect public law), and *D.* 50, 17, 45, 1 (public law cannot be abrogated by a private agreement).

[15] On the general medieval background to the state-office nexus see G. Post, "Status, Id Est, Magistratus: L'État, C'est Moi," ch. VII of his *Studies in Medieval Legal Thought*.

[16] *Storie fiorentine dal 1378 al 1509*, ed. R. Palmarocchi (Bari, 1931), pp. 41-42.

single movement of his mind he posits the instrumental nature of law and office. But where the law, in matters of state, is insufficient to achieve certain ends, he condones the use of arbitrary power. There was nothing novel in this view. Law and statecraft are assumed to be linked, but statecraft is not subservient. The link is a flexible one. Florentines had conducted their affairs in this fashion for two and a half centuries, producing generations of lawyers who were cognizant of a doctrine to go with the practice. The doctrine was based on the idea that in emergencies the ordinary rule of law may be suspended. What was an emergency? A situation or a set of circumstances which involved a threat to the "public good," to the "reggimento," to the peaceful order of the community, to the very source of statutory law—the state. Gaines Post has shown that this was really the doctrine of "reason of State," already found in Italian, French, and English legal thought of the thirteenth century.[17] How easily and naturally Florentine lawyers resorted to argument from public utility will be presently shown.

Continually occupied with immediate practical problems, the Republic's lawyers took the law to be a highly instrumental and flexible construct. Thus, they were better able to take hold of the city's mobile constitution; they could more satisfactorily deal with the new efflorescence of offices and the partitioning of the executive authority. Later on, for the same reason, they would have little trouble explaining the concentration of power in certain offices. For in this realm of things—the powers of the Signory and Ten on War excluded—the statute stood over all. As Antonio Strozzi held in about 1505, dealing with a dispute which had brought the authority of the Grascia Officials into question, ". . . in our time officials have no authority save that which is found to be conferred by statutes."[18] And in another case, "Clarus est quod nullus officialis habet aliquam iurisdictionem nisi illam quam sibi conceditur per statuta civitatis."[19]

When combined with an intensely acquisitive executive, the emphasis of lawyers on the precise instrumentality of the law supplied any existing

[17] Post, *Studies*, esp. chs. v and x.

[18] *Strozz., 3a ser.*, 41/12, f. 69r.

[19] *Ibid.*, f. 318r; also observed by another lawyer, speaking for the Regulatores, in *CRS*, Arch. 98, 266, f. 305r.

regime with a marked political advantage. Such a jurisprudential view made it easier for the oligarchy to convert the law into a scourge wherewith to flail the opposition. Where the law in its expression as statute was envisaged as a flexible tool, it was more readily converted into a political weapon. This danger was, moreover, greatly intensified by the fact that the Florentine constitution did not provide for the existence of an organized legal opposition.

Law in Florence was constantly made, re-made, modified, and abrogated by means of statutes. Moreover, the fifteenth century saw a rise in the incidence and sway of temporary plenipotentiary councils. The changeability associated with this phenomenon pointed up the utilitarian and variable nature of the law. As a result, the more the ruling families realized an identity with the state, the less difficult it became for them to use the law for political ends, though the ends were given a high civic and moral tone. If lawyers were ready to draw with ease on that aspect of the law which was adjustable to circumstance, they were prepared *a fortiori* to do the same with public office.

By calling attention to a way of perceiving law and office, I have tried indirectly to get at the way in which lawyers looked at the state. On this evidence, it appears that they took the state to be a forceful and adaptable institution, the creator of statutory law, changeable in many ways, but not in that which concerned the social basis of its power. This was not the state in its manifestation as a passive thing which men grabbed and held,[20] but as a reality *already* possessed and therewith transformed, a reality inseparable from the groups or class which disposed of the public power.

THE modern conception of the state seems to begin with the legal idea of sovereignty, of political *majestas*. And the idea goes back in European history to the twelfth and thirteenth centuries—the great period of the revival of Roman law. The *princeps* or Emperor of the Roman law books was *dominus totius mundi*. He was a source of law: *quod principi placuit, legis habet vigorem*. And he could stand outside the law: *legibus solutus*, though ordinarily and hopefully he was *legibus alligatus*. The

---

[20] This view too was current, however, as has been shown; or rather, it was a way of looking at the state from a different standpoint.

formulas and conceptions are famous. French and other lawyers of the thirteenth century and later sought to associate their kings with a kindred authority by holding that a king in his realm was Emperor: *rex imperator in regno suo*. It was argument by analogy but the lead was taken from Roman public law.[21] In this fashion lawyers tried to give a legal and theoretical underpinning to a developing factual situation. The method was also used by canon lawyers—indeed used by them first— in their defense of papal prerogatives. The pope, they argued, in the affairs and lands of the Church was as the *princeps* of Roman law in the affairs of the world. In one major current of legal and political thought he stood above even the *princeps*.[22]

In the 1340s and 1350s Bartolus transferred this line of argument to the Italian city-state, seeking thereby to explain its legal and political foundations. It was a revolutionary stroke. In his commentaries on the *Digest* and *Code*, he developed the notion that customary law had the binding force of positive or written law.[23] The first issued from the tacit consent of the *populus*; the second, based on express consent, was the work of the prince. But since customary and written law were equally binding, tacit and express consent had an equal validity.[24] A people could thus make all its own laws, as in certain city-states. Here was the reasoning which enabled Bartolus to set forth a series of ob- servations regarding the "civitas per se sufficiens et sibi princeps," the city as an "universitas superiores non recognoscens."[25] Such a city was a

---

[21] Literature on the preceding subject matter is extensive. The central themes and references may be got in F. Ercole, *Da Bartolo all' Althusio*; F. Calasso, *I Glos- satori e la teoria della sovranità*; Post, *Studies*, esp. chs. v, x, xi; Stengel, "Kaiser- titel"; W. Ullmann, "The Development of the Medieval Idea of Sovereignty," *EHR*, LXIV (1949), 1-33; and B. Tierney, " 'The Prince is Not Bound by the Laws.' Accursius and the Origins of the Modern State," *Comparative Studies in Society and History*, v, 4 (1963), 378-400.

[22] Cf. J. A. Watt, "The Theory of Papal Monarchy in the Thirteenth Century, The Contribution of the Canonists," *Traditio*, xx (1964), 179-317.

[23] *Viz.*, as in *D.* 1, 3, 35.

[24] A detailed exposition of this aspect of Bartolist thought is in W. Ullmann, "De Bartoli Sententia: Concilium repraesentat mentem populi," in *Bartolo* (vi centenary papers, n. 8 above), ii, 707-33.

[25] The development of his thought is systematically treated by Woolf, *Bartolus*, pp. 112-207. See also the outstanding papers by Ullmann (preceding note) and Stengel (n. 8).

state, in this sense no different from a sovereign kingdom. Sovereign in its own territory, the city-state which acknowledged no superior exercised the "plenitudo imperialis potestatis." And although this might not be entirely true *de iure,* it was true in fact. Or was all fact of this type to be written off as usurpation? Was it not a consideration that the emperor was too weak and distant and that the daily business of government had to go on? In the fourteenth century, *de facto* government was often backed up by imperial diplomas which turned the rulers of some Italian cities into imperial vicars. Their exercise of that highly prized "fullness of power" was thus given a formal grounding in law. The Signory of Florence was twice invested with this official recognition, in 1355 and 1401.[26]

Like the publicists of kings, Bartolus took political fact as he found it—fact confirmed by custom—and sought to give it an explicit legal basis. The attempt was successful. For the conception of the city-state as *princeps,* as a superior with no authority above it, was widely circulated and often adduced by Italian lawyers of the later fourteenth century and after.[27] Yet if one judges by what went on in Florence, it appears that the Bartolist conception was called upon much less often to stand up to the Emperor, King of the Romans, whose real power was ineffectual, than to vindicate and make stronger the claims of the city-state over its subject territories. Actually, therefore, the argument that the city-state was "prince unto itself"—a political unit which owned no superior—became more a claim to lordship than a defense of political independence. Florentines of the fifteenth century never said to the Emperor: you are not Emperor and we do not recognize you. On the whole, they merely ignored him. Their lawyers, however, very often said to subject communities: ours is "the superior city"; in these lands we are "in loco

[26] G. Capponi, *Storia della repubblica di Firenze,* 2 vols. (Firenze, 1875), 1, 405, 570-75.

[27] In a Pistoian case of the late 1360s the brief already speaks of Pistoia as being like other Tuscan cities, "quae non recognoscunt in temporalibus superiorem." A Florentine (Giovanni de' Ricci) and a professor of law at Bologna (Bartolommeo da Saliceto) submitted opinions in the case. BNF, *Magl.,* xxix, 161 (a collection of *consilia legalia*), ff. 17r-18r. An early reference to Florence as *princeps* appears in an opinion of *ca.* 1410 by Nello da San Gimignano. The opinion questions the validity of the statutes of Pescia, a subject commune. *CRS,* Arch. 98, 277, ff. 239r-240r.

supremi principis";[28] you are under our "dominion, empire, government, and power."[29] Although relying excessively on the formal pattern and direct impact of ideas, Francesco Ercole rightly intuited, years ago, that with the idea of the *civitas superior* or *sibi princeps*, Bartolus laid down the legal foundations of the Italian territorial state.[30]

The idea sometimes turned up unexpectedly. In an early Florentine reference, the affair which brought it forth was as follows. Messer Piero Gaetani, a Pisan by birth, cooperated with the Florentines during their take-over of Pisa in 1405-1406. He turned a Pisan fortress over to them. To reward him, a powerful commission (the Decem Baliae) made him a full-fledged citizen of Florence in 1406. In 1412-1413 Florence imposed a special tax on the Pisans and authorized the priors of Pisa to appoint sixteen Pisans to distribute the individual tax levies. Claiming that he was a "natural" and "original" citizen of Pisa, they levied a tax on Gaetani, whose fixed residence in Florence dated from 1406. Denying their authority over him, he appealed to Florence. Before the dispute was finally settled in his favor, three Florentine lawyers had been com-

---

[28] Phrase used by Antonio Malegonnelli in case of 1502, *Cod. Vat. Lat.*, 8067, i, f. 138r.

[29] *Strozz., 3a ser.*, 41/14, ff. 127r-129v. Case from about 1460 referred for adjudication to Piero Ambrosini and Bernardo Buongirolami. They point out Florentine jurisdiction over Pisa and hence over two rural communes (Montecchio and Fabbrica). Once "sub dominio, imperio, regimine, et potestate pisarum," these communes in 1406 passed over in perpetuity "sub dominio communis florentie et sub ipso communis obedientia, imperio, regimine, et ghubernatione."

[30] *Da Bartolo all' Althusio*, p. 118, though Ercole's main debt on this point is to Woolf, *Bartolus*, who dwells on the idea of the territorial state yet does not, I think, use the phrase. But cf. D. Segoloni, "Bartolo da Sassoferrato e la Civitas Perusina," in *Bartolo* (vi centenary papers, n. 8 above), ii, pp. 662-65, where the stress is on the Empire's enduring rights *de iure*. In this view, Bartolus never meant the *civitates superiorem non recognoscentes* (even those at the vanguard) to be considered "miniature empires" with a full sovereignty of their own. Thus, Segoloni argues, the great jurist continued to allow for their expected "*debitum fidelitatis* verso il *Princeps*" and for the fact that the *civitas sibi princeps* could therefore be guilty of rebellion against the Emperor. In correcting Ercole, and so by implication Woolf and others, Segoloni is driven to take too theoretical a position and to slight the revolutionary implications of Bartolus's views for the political theory and history of the Renaissance period. As we shall see, by speaking of the city-state as *sibi princeps*, whatever the remaining ties with the Empire, Bartolus provided lawyers with a doctrine enabling them to defend and further the claims of "the superior city" or *populus liber* over its subject lands and peoples.

missioned to provide judicial counsel. Torello Torelli and Alessandro Bencivenni ruled that because Gaetani was a true citizen of Florence in the fullness of the law and because Florentine citizens could not be taxed by Pisa, he was not subject to the tax in question. To support this view they also emphasized the fact that Florence had long been his fixed place of residence.[31] In a second opinion, delivered under formal seal and dated September 1415, Nello da San Gimignano repeated these arguments but added others which, being more fundamental, went to conclude the case. He noted that Pisa had passed under Florentine rule, that is, that Florence had acquired dominion over all of Pisa's former jurisdictions. Then he made a point of the fact that Gaetani enjoyed his disputed privilege of citizenship by authority of Florence, "the superior of the Commune of the Pisans [est privilegiatus a superiore comunis pisarum]."[32] These observations reduced the controversy to an affair between ruler and ruled. With Bartolus and Roman law providing the basis of argument, the highest authority was the one that must prevail *de iure* in the matter of citizenship.[33]

The authority of Florence, more than the rights of its fisc, is what was put to the test here. Generally speaking, when holding out for a prerogative (a claim in the realm of public law), Florence tended to be toughest about those matters which concerned public finance and crime against the state. But as proceedings of the latter type were nearly always summary, legal *consilia* which touch on public law most often involve fiscal dispute and questions of judicial or administrative competence.

In about 1417 Castiglion Aretino, a fortified community in Florentine territory, made claims to the effect that it was a land under Florentine protection, not under Florentine rule. By this means the "Castilionenses" sought to escape paying certain taxes and gabelles to the Republic. They

---

[31] BNF, *Mss. Landau Finaly*, 98, ff. 75r-84v, 85r-86r, 330v. The opinion was endorsed by Bartolommeo Vulpi and Giovanni Buongirolami.

[32] *Ibid.*, ff. 376r-378v.

[33] Actually, on the subject of citizenship, that which had been implicit in Bartolus was made explicit by Baldus, who applied corporation theory to the creation of citizens. Viewed as an *universitas* or corporation, a *populus* was entitled to choose its own members. See Ullmann, "De Bartoli Sententia," pp. 725-26, and his *Principles of Government and Politics in the Middle Ages* (2nd ed., London, 1966), pp. 285-86.

banked on a covenant with Florence which assured them of a number of fiscal privileges. Leading counsel for Florence, Alessandro Bencivenni, denied their case. Speaking of the particular gabelle which provoked the dispute, he observed that even foreigners paid it: "si ergo forenses multo magis Castilionenses."[34] He also tried to prove that it was an ordinary not an extraordinary gabelle. From a legal-political viewpoint, however, the most suggestive and far-reaching of his representations involved the assertion that the Commune of Florence "blooms" among its subjects as prince ("quoniam Commune Florentie floret ut princeps inter suos subpositos"). Going on to explain this concept, he pointed out that the people of the land in question are subject to Florence, which "in eos iurisdictionem exercet, eosque astringere posset et in ipsos merum et mixtum imperium et gladii potestatem exercere."[35] The formula was Roman, the conception contemporary. Bencivenni drew up three other *consilia* overruling the claims of the men from Castiglion Aretino.[36] Two were endorsed by Filippo Corsini and Giovanni Buongirolami, the third by Bartolommeo Vulpi and Stefano Buonaccorsi—prominent lawyers all. The *consilia* held that Castiglion Aretino had been under Aretine rule for more than a century, that Arezzo and all its jurisdictions were legally acquired by Florence in 1384, and that the covenant alleged by the suitors did not eliminate their status as subjects of the Florentine people. In expounding these views, Bencivenni adduced not only the authority of Bartolus but also that of near contemporaries—Giovanni de' Ricci and Ludovico Albergotti, Florentine jurisconsults who in the later 1380s dealt at length with the status of Arezzo.[37]

In the course of the fifteenth century Florentine lawyers learned to use the Bartolist formulas of sovereignty with greater freedom and aggressiveness. Supported by Piero Ambrosini and Domenico Martelli, Otto Niccolini held, in an opinion of 1455, that the imperial *iura fiscalia* in Florentine territory had passed by prescriptive right to Florence, which "acknowledges no superior *de facto*."[38] One of Ambrosini's opinions of

---

[34] BNF, *Magl.*, xxix, 186, f. 46r.
[35] *Ibid.* The reference is to *D.* 2, 1, 3.
[36] *Ibid.*, ff. 155r-156v, 199v-202r, 219r-223r.
[37] *Ibid.*, ff. 199v-202r.
[38] *Strozz., 3a ser.*, 41/14, f. 139v. The case was occasioned by a cluster of feudal

about 1460, endorsed by Bernardo Buongirolami, casually refers to Florence as a "superior civitas" and equates its temporal position in Florentine territory with that of the pope inside the Church. Florence could unite two communes under its rule, just as the pope "can make two episcopal sees from one."[39] In June 1502, when Arezzo rebelled against Florence, Antonio Malegonnelli sustained that it therewith lost all its own statutes and other privileges. Even if the Aretines chose to own the Emperor as their lord, he argued, the nature of their rebellion was such that they still incurred forfeiture of all the privileges and powers confirmed on them "by the largess and permission of the Florentine people."[40] At about the same time, in a conflict occasioned by the Val di Cecina's refusal to pay a customs fee to Volterra—the two lands were under Florentine rule—the former adduced a privilege of immunity accorded by Florence. Two Florentine lawyers, Antonio Strozzi and Guidantonio Vespucci, settled the dispute in favor of the men from the vicariate of the Val di Cecina, "nam immunitas concessa eis per dominos florentinos fuit multum generalis et larga." And citing Roman law (*D.* 1, 4, 3.), they observed that benefits and privileges conferred by "the prince" ought to be broadly interpreted.[41] The *consilia* and *allegationes* of Antonio Strozzi, penned between about 1490 and 1522, show him arguing, again and again, that the statutes of subject communities were not valid, could not be applied, save with the periodic and proper approbation of "the superior city"—Florence.[42] No such approval, how-

---

rights once held on Pisan territory but now claimed by Florence on the strength of its acquisition of Pisa. The argument from prescription was used to strengthen the Republic's title. Legally, there was some question as to whether or not *iura fiscalia* were subject to prescriptive right. Cf. Ullmann, *The Medieval Idea of Law*, p. 182.

[39] *Strozz.*, *3a ser.*, 41/14, f. 129v. The equation actually appears in Buongirolami's endorsement and attached commentary.

[40] *Cod. Vat. Lat.*, 8067, Part 1, f. 138r. "Sed etiam si imperatorem recognovisset, tamen civitas aretina quae se subtraxit a iurisdictione populi florentini cui erat subdita, ipso iure intelligitur perdidisse omnia privilegia et omnem iurisdictionem quam habebat ex largitione vel permissione populi florentini a qua defecit." Also on the Aretine rebellion, *Strozz.*, *3a ser.*, 41/1, f. 81r.

[41] *Strozz.*, *3a ser.*, 41/4, ff. 175r-176v. *D.* 1, 4, 3 says "Beneficium imperatoris, quod a divina scilicet eius indulgentia proficiscitur, quam plenissime interpretari debemus."

[42] *Strozz.*, *3a ser.*, 41/5, ff. 225r, 229r, 320r; 41/6, ff. 1r, 270r; 41/9, f. 218r, 506r; 41/14, ff. 387r, 390r.

ever, could lead to the derogation of any Florentine statute, for the general authority conferred on the commissions of approval did "not extend to the cancelling of the statutes of that self-same superior."[43] If the *princeps*, says Strozzi, gives the authority to confirm local statutes, that mandate may not be used to prejudice or damage his prerogative.[44]

The direction of these views was unmistakable. There was no law, no legitimacy in the Florentine dominion save by authority of the Florentine state, which had drawn to itself, in fact and under the seal of its lawyers, the powers of the *princeps* of Roman law. Florence made the law for all subjects in the dominion: its touch raised local practice, custom, and preference to the level of the law. The state thus was creative: out of the fullness of its being, it brought forth the law and legitimated all local custom, which otherwise remained a body of arbitrary norms, whatever its theoretical status in natural law.

There is no suggestion here that Florentine rule outside the city walls was arbitrary. The nature of that rule was made clear by Florentine lawyers. Since Florence had agreements with nearly all its subject communities, lawyers assumed that the Republic would and should observe its obligations. When "the superior city" approved a body of local statutes, whether Prato's or Pistoia's or another's, local civil litigation and most crime had to be tried in accordance with these. And if these ordained that the "common law" must apply in cases where statutory insufficiencies appeared, Florentine lawyers did not hesitate to say that Roman law is what was meant, not the law which was common to Florentines, namely their own municipal law.[45] On at least one occasion Antonio Strozzi, a strong advocate of sovereign over local claims, defended a subject commune in a dispute which implicated the superior city's judicial competence. Fucecchio had a statute which ruled that litigation between

---

[43] *Strozz., 3a ser.*, 41/14; f. 387r, "quia talis auctoritas generalis non se extendit ut possint tollere statuta ipsius superioris." Cites Bartolus on the *lex Ambitiosa, D.* 50, 9, 4.

[44] *Ibid.*, f. 387v, "si daret princeps auctoritatem confirmandi statuta, non se extendit tale mandatum ut fiat preiudicium ipsi mandanti per talem confirmationem."

[45] E.g., the 1520s' opinion of Alessandro Malegonnelli, BNF, *Fondo principale*, II, II, 378, ff. 429r-434r. Endorsed with a supporting comment by Silvestro Aldobrandini. Malegonnelli observes that such was the accepted view and cites Bartolommeo Sozzini's opinion no. 271.

local parties could not be taken out of that commune for adjudication. Though having been approved by Florence, it seemed to deny the "cognitionem universalem" of the Florentine Podestà, presiding magistrate of the Republic's Council of Justice. Strozzi defended the statute by holding that the Podestà's jurisdiction was in practice neither unlimited nor universal. He also observed that other subject communes had laws with like provisions, and while admitting that the *princeps* could abrogate the disputed statute "de plenitudine potestatis," he saw no reason for this. The case in question, he assumed, should be treated from the viewpoint of the prince's "ordinary power."[46]

But by the end of the fifteenth century the marked tendency of Florentine lawyers, and of Antonio Strozzi himself, was to accord very strong favor to the "city, prince unto itself."[47] In about 1515 a case arose which questioned the validity of one of the statutes of Castiglion Aretino. The statute specifically provided that only the local podestà, no other rector or official, was competent to administer justice there. Even the authority of the Florentine Signory seemed to be challenged, for this was the body which sought to intervene. The question raised by the statute was turned over to Strozzi, who submitted that while other rectors and officials were excluded, the Priors and Gonfalonier of Justice were not. Having the supreme power ("habentes supremam potestatem"), they were not included "under the name of rectors or officials" because it did not seem right that the *princeps* should want to renounce his own jurisdiction.[48] Strozzi's famous contemporary, Francesco Guicciardini, reached a kindred decision in a case which fixed attention on a statute from Cortona. The statute said that there could "be no other com-

---

[46] *Strozz., 3a ser.*, 41/14, f. 390r, "et licet forte posset princeps revocare de plenitudine potestatis, tamen non praesumitur princeps velle uti potestate tali sed potestate ordinaria."

[47] In a case of *ca.* 1412 Nello da San Gimignano and Ricciardo del Bene drew up conflicting opinions regarding the validity of the statutes of Pescia, a subject commune. Nello argued that they had no validity, not having been submitted for approval; Ricciardo defended the applicability of the statute which pertained to the case. ASF, *CRS*, Arch. 98, 277, ff. 239r-241r. By the end of the century Ricciardo's position was a rarity.

[48] *Strozz., 3a ser.*, 41/9, f. 260r, "quia non videtur princeps velle a se ipso abdicare suam iurisdictionem neque se excipere." Cites *C.* 8, 43, 18, and Bartolus on *D.* 1, 9, 1.

petent judge in dispute between Cortonenses than the Captain of Cortona."[49] Owing to the details of the case, this statute seemed to deny the jurisdiction of the Florentine Council of Justice. It was Guicciardini's contention that the judges of this court ordinarily qualified as "the universal judges of all the Florentine territory, so that anyone from the territory can appear before them." He used a variety of arguments to resolve the apparent conflict between the subject statute and Florentine law, citing Bartolus and other lawyers, as well as different passages from the *Digest* and *Code*. But there was one argument to which he returned several times because it provided him with his strongest point. The Podestà of the Council of Justice, he insisted, "est iudex universalis in toto territorio florentino," whereas the Captain of Cortona is a particular judge in that city "and so a lower judge [et sic iudex inferior]." Consequently, the words of the Cortonese statute "nullus alius"—that "no other" judge is competent—should not be understood to rule out the Podestà, "as there is no resemblance between" this leading magistrate and that particular judge ("cum inter eos non sit similitudo") and because the Council of Justice is superior to the Captain's court in Cortona.[50] Guicciardini did away with the apparent conflict by conceptualizing the issue in terms of a sovereign versus a subject or regional court. To give himself additional backing, he cited two of the Florentine court's past decisions (nos. 218 and 456), which also acknowledged the jurisdictional pre-eminence of "the superior city."

If by the end of the fifteenth century lawyers vigorously defended the competence of the city's tribunals in the dominion, they gave even stronger support to the claims of Florentine fiscal authority. The immunities of the Church constituted the sole exception to this. When kept on retainer by a church or monastery, lawyers were occasionally called on to defend ecclesiastical privileges against the pretensions or demands of the Republic or even of the archbishop. Yet in times of critical public need Florence inevitably turned to its lawyers for help and sometimes got its way with the Church. It may be that Florentine lawyers

---

[49] BNF, *Fondo principale*, II, II, 374, f. 344r, "stante statuto Cortonensi quo caveat quod inter Cortonenses nullus alius sit iudex competens praeter capitaneum Cortonae."

[50] *Ibid.*, ff. 344r-345v.

infrequently favored the special tax privileges of subject communes against the claims of the capital city, but few if any examples of this—I have found none—survive in the extant opinions and pleas. The contrary evidence is profuse. Foolproof though an immunity or privilege might seem, counsel for the superior city always managed to find some loophole, some legal principle, some ambiguity in the phraseology of the privilege, which enabled Florence to advance its claims. And the claims—let it be stressed—had to be made on legal grounds. As I said, Florentine rule outside the city walls was not arbitrary. The oligarchy bound itself, at least in this respect, to do things in accordance with accepted procedure.[51] But we must be careful not to draw unwarranted conclusions, not to suppose that Florentines and their lawyers were more high-minded and just than other contemporaries. The tyrant was not born in Renaissance Italy who did without lawyers or without striving to give the color of right to the most tyrannical of his actions.

Resolving to collect a certain gabelle or tax in the dominion, Florence and her lawyers, when in despair at being unable to find a cogent legal claim, could always turn—as will be seen—to argument from public utility or urgent public need. Perfectly consonant with the way Florentine lawyers envisaged relations between territory and superior city is the judgment expressed *circa* 1519 by Ormannozzo Deti on a dispute between a tax office and a private party. Should the gabelle on a certain contract be paid? Deti ruled that it should, concluding: "where some doubt exists, let the interpretation be rendered in favor of the fisc and for the payment of the gabelle."[52]

*Princeps* in its territories—such was the Florentine state and such the

[51] E.g., early in the sixteenth century, the Tower Officials took a case involving them in a clash with the Commune of Fucecchio and turned it over for adjudication to the lawyer Ludovico Acciaiuoli. The dispute concerned a road which the Fucecchians, by a Florentine law of 1461, seemed obligated to maintain. Acciaiuoli ruled that Fucecchio was not affected by that law and so in this matter was not under the jurisdiction of the Tower Officials. *CRS*, Arch. 98, 238, ff. 1r-5r. Another check prevented the Signory from writing to territorial magistrates except with reference to matters in which these were competent. *Strozz.*, *2a ser.*, 95, folders 2-3, but no doubt this check could be dispensed with in emergencies.

[52] *Strozz.*, *3a ser.*, 42, f. 79r, "ubi esset aliqua dubitatio fiat interpretatio in favorem fisci et pro solvenda gabella."

image entertained by lawyers in their legal-political views. What was the nature of the *princeps* in Florence proper?

Now and then lawyers said of certain magistracies, or of combinations thereof, that these had "as much power and authority as does the Florentine people."[53] They saw this "mystic body,"[54] the Florentine people, as the final reference point in any question concerning the Republic's "plenitude of power." The view was well grounded. According to the Florentine constitution, all power in ordinary times was finally vested in the legislative councils and Signory. These were empowered to take legislative action in areas affecting the constitution itself. Extraordinary provision, however, was also made for the official assembly of the Florentine people; and indeed, it was from this *universitas* that the legislative councils originally drew their authority, presumably in delegated form. It follows that an assembly or *parlamentum* of the Florentine people could suspend or, in theory, even revoke that authority.

Under the direction of the Signory, the assembly of the people decided things by acclamation. It was a *populus liber*, a free people, which is what made it *sibi princeps* in fourteenth- and fifteenth-century public law.[55] Theoretically, therefore, all political power in Florence resided ultimately with "the people." Yet when touching questions of public law in their judicial opinions and pleas, lawyers were nearly always concerned with specific offices or functions, not with the theoretical question of consent. Their sole reason for calling on the "baliam et auctoritatem" of the Florentine people was to show that certain offices, certain functions, or certain decisions had the fullest possible sanction in law.

As the wellspring of Florentine public law, was the *populus florentinus*

[53] *Strozz.*, *3a ser.*, 41/11, f. 79r (Antonio Strozzi); 41/14, ff. 138r-139r (Otto Niccolini).

[54] Baldus defined a *populus* as a collection of "men assembled in one mystical body [hominum collectio in unum corpus mysticum]." Cited by E. H. Kantorowicz, "Pro Patria Mori in Medieval Political Thought," in his *Selected Studies*, pp. 319-20.

[55] See Woolf, *Bartolus*, pp. 156-57; Kantorowicz, *King's Two Bodies*, pp. 298-301; Ullmann, *Principles of Government and Politics*, pp. 283-86. This point is usually overlooked in the standard histories. No mention of it in E. Besta, *Il diritto pubblico italiano dagli inizii del secolo decimoprimo alla seconda metà del secolo decimoquinto* (Padua, 1929), or A. Marongiu, *Storia del diritto pubblico, Principi e istituti di governo in Italia dalla metà del ix alla metà del xix secolo* (Milano-Varese, 1956).

more than a legal fiction?[56] Florentine lawyers did not say. They provided no definitions. If they had, they would have turned, in all probability, to corporation theory of the late medieval period and so to a corporate conception of the Commune. Legally and historically, the Commune issued from a sworn association of men who had pooled their rights and jurisdictions. These they had put *in comune*. Thenceforth the Commune had continually grown, although it is difficult to see how, as a legal entity, it could ever have taken in more than those men possessed of the right to hold office in the Commune. Full membership in the corporation was indivisible from the right to hold office in it. We may accordingly conclude that the legal expression, "the Florentine people," referred to citizens in the fullness of right: at the outset of the fifteenth century, about 2,500 men; at the end of the century, from 3,000 to 3,300; and in 1527, about 4,000. It is true that when the Signory called a *parlamentum*, more than the designated number of men—citizens *and* their followers or employees—might assemble in the main government square. But in the period from 1380 to 1530 the direction of such assemblies never passed from the control of the class of citizens; it was difficult enough, and usually impossible, to wrest it from the control of the principal families.

It has been suggested that the full power of the *princeps* ordinarily lay with the legislative councils and Signory. In the course of the fifteenth century an increasing passivity overtook the legislative councils, where an organized legal opposition had never in any case been tolerated.[57] The vital, dynamic center of the Florentine political system was the executive: the Signory and the cluster of offices around it. This is where much of the prince's power tended to be concentrated, although in the later

[56] I exclude from the notion of *populus* those moments when, in an atmosphere of stultifying intimidation and with the piazzas full of soldiers, "the people" were assembled in the main government square. As G. B. Picotti, writing in the heyday of Fascism, courageously observed: at such times "the people" turned out to be the triumphant faction imposing its will in the name of the people. "Qualche osservazione sui caratteri delle signorie italiane," *Riv. stor. ital.*, XLIII, iv (1926), 15.

[57] On which my forthcoming paper, "Political Conflict in the Italian City States," *Government and Opposition: A Quarterly of Comparative Politics*, III, 1 (Winter 1968), 69-91.

Laurentian period the executive was more closely coordinated with the tight new Council of Seventy (1480-1494).[58] If in formal legal argument lawyers occasionally cited the power of "the Florentine people," it was to the Signory and its adjuncts, no less than to the vision of a *populus florentinus*, that they looked for the majesty and force associated with the *princeps* of the law books. In 1355 and 1401 the imperial vicariate was conferred on the Signory, not on the Florentine people. We get a sense of the feeling sometimes associated with the office from a representation of January 1429, when the canon lawyer Lorenzo Ridolfi, giving counsel to the government, observed that just as the one God should be adored, "so you the lord priors [of the Signory] ought to be venerated by all citizens."[59]

Can it be said that the Signory had some of the characteristics of a standing *balìa*? Had it such great powers that when these passed to an extraordinary council, a dictatorship was thereby created? One student of the Florentine constitution has maintained that the Signory was a quasi-dictatorial institution, that it adumbrated a tyranny, paving the way for one-man rule.[60] The assessment is not altogether wild. But then why did the Signory in 1421 have so much trouble pinning down judicial competence in the murder of Count Guido da Moncione?[61] And the lawyers consulted in the case—why were they so reluctant to give a decisive endorsement to the judicial prerogatives of the *civitas superior*? There were several reasons for this. Opinion in the Signory and colleges was divided. The hidden influence of strong family blocs complicated the issues, so that the lawyers consulted must have been subject to conflicting interests. Furthermore, dominant legal theory held that the *princeps* of the law books was normally bound by contracts, and Florence had apparently conferred the right of jurisdiction in Mon-

[58] This council was the very embodiment of close oligarchy. Needless to say, the veiled influence of Lorenzo the Magnificent was then considerable and no doubt often decisive.

[59] *CP*, 48, f. 51r, "ut unus deus est adorandus sic vos domini priores venerandi estis ab omnibus civibus."

[60] G. Masi, "Verso gli albori del principato in Italia," *Rivista di storia del diritto italiano*, IX (1936), 161-63.

[61] See pp. 156 ff.

cione on the local branch of the Battifolle family. But apart from this, the Signory and its adjuncts had not yet acquired the power for which the inner oligarchy was to strive in the period after 1434.

Once realized, this new concentration of power gave sharper outlines to the state, drew increasing attention to the executive, and enabled or encouraged lawyers to be more decisive in their claims respecting the *plenitudo potestatis* of the executive complex (Signory, Eight, etc.) or of the superior city. How far this trend had gone, at least in some minds, by the end of the fifteenth century may be perceived in the remarkable words of a lawyer and influential statesman, Domenico Bonsi. It was June 1501; the government was having trouble raising money to pay troops and to pay off its commitments to the king of France. Having first expressed considerable resistance, the colleges had finally been won over to the support of a money bill. Speaking in an executive session for the order of lawyers, Bonsi urged the colleges to be more unstinting in their support of the Signory's initiatives. Then he declared that "the Signory should be trusted, that to want certitude in everything is impossible, that affairs must be conducted according to accident and circumstance, and that one should not will the ruin of the city by [always] insisting on the observance of the laws."[62]

These words were the more surprising in that they came not from a shrewd and ardent politician like Guidantonio Vespucci, but from one who had been a moderate in politics—a moderate Savonarolan who in the end had turned against the friar. Furthermore, the words were those of the spokesman for the lawyers present at the session. What precisely did he mean?

While implicitly recognizing the necessity of laws, he avers that there are moments when men at the head of state must be allowed to step outside the ordinary written laws in order to save something more precious—the city itself. But "the city" is a figure of speech. Bonsi does not mean the physical city; he is not saying that Florence might vanish, crumble, or go down in flames. There was no danger of that. He means

---

[62] *CP*, 66, f. 331r, "et che si debbi prestare fede alla Signoria et che il volere certezza di ogni cosa è impossibile et che bisogna governarsi secondo li accidenti et non volere la città ruini per volere stare in sulla observanza delle leggi."

something less tangible: "the city" stands for a political way of life, a polity. This alone is what was threatened in 1501. The Republic was immensely vulnerable in its foreign affairs, owing both to military debilities and to gnawing fiscal shortages; and a defeat in this realm might well have resulted in an overturning of the state. Bonsi's point was that in moments of danger Florentines must be ready to protect their political system, if necessary by running their affairs in accordance with expedience ("secondo li accidenti") rather than law. This is pure *Staatsräson*, "reason of State." It is argument from "public utility" and in this form—pleas for irregular action in the name of the public good— is found throughout the fifteenth century. There is nothing revolutionary in Bonsi's words. Only the stark expression of the doctrine is uncommon. Let us look for a moment at two earlier examples.

One of the interesting features of Lorenzo Ridolfi's *De usuris*, written in 1403, is that it defends the Republic's paying out of interest to Florentine citizens with investments in the Monte, the funded public debt. If not compensated, Ridolfi argued, citizens who financed the government might "be driven to desperation and would plot against the Republic to the serious loss of body and soul and danger to the Republic. And if it be said that in such a case, and not otherwise, if the law benefits, it is well, I reply that the law ought to be common for the utility of the republic"—that is, the law should be made to serve the good of the republic as well.[63] A decade or two later, in his *De bannitis*, Nello da San Gimignano justified the severest of the statues against fugitives and disobedient exiles (that they could be killed with impunity) by drawing on the following arguments: because such a statute sees to it that crime does not go unpunished, because it serves the "publicam utilitatem" by discouraging men from crime and disobedience, and because a man at large may be guilty of rebellion against his prince ("etiam propter eius contumaciam et inobedientiam factam suo principi").[64] The last of these seems to invest the supreme public authority with a value which is its own justification.

[63] In vol. VII of the *Tractatus universi iuris* (Venice, 1584), pp. 15-50, passage rendered by J. T. Noonan, Jr., *The Scholastic Analysis of Usury* (Cambridge, Mass., 1957), p. 124. Cf. *D.* 1, 42 and 1, 3, 1.
[64] (Ed. of 1486), f. 43v. Cites *lex Omnes populi, D.* 1, 1, 9.

Like most of their professional contemporaries, these lawyers took for granted that the "thing public" was a good in itself. The "republic," "the city," the "public utility," the *princeps*—all represented a supreme temporal good and indeed something more, for the canonist Ridolfi suggests that a man may conspire against his native land only by risking eternal perdition.[65] This ethico-legal view of the *res publica* as a cardinal good had its obvious intellectual sources (for lawyers at all events) in the *Corpus Iuris Civilis*.[66] Aristotle, Cicero, and other classical writers were cited to develop a parallel line of discourse, moral and philosophical, which also went to help build and fortify a tradition of thought. But a sufficient historical explanation is to be found in the quotidian life of the Italian city-states. If the legal doctrine of the new state was drawn from Roman law, from the glossators and great postglossators, what was there in the everyday affairs of these men that made them receptive and provided a direction? The state as a "fact," the corresponding attitudes of men, and their capacity to see the *res publica* in a new way were all related to the actual conduct of government in the city-states.

The propensity for seeing the state as a good in itself is partly traceable to the link between law and the state. This is why the present chapter begins with a stress on the instrumental rather than the final value of the law, in opposition to the view of Lorenzo Ridolfi's imagined critic. Florentines at the head of state presumed that laws could be devised to make men live in a civil fashion. Faith in coercion was not lacking. In July 1497, speaking for one of the colleges, Antonio Strozzi advised the Signory on the problem of civil discord in the city. He said that there were only two ways to realize civil harmony, "by love or force." Seeing little love, he recommended "the use of force, that is, of the laws," and he made a plea for "the law and your lordships [the Signory], who stand over the laws, to make citizens meet their obligations; for the observance of the laws and of justice is what can make citizens come

---

[65] Thus suggesting an affiliation with the *crimen laesae majestatis*, which the Middle Ages took to be a form of sacrilege or religious crime. Ullmann, *Principles*, p. 136.

[66] See Post, *Studies*, chs. v, x.

together in unity."[67] Three weeks later another lawyer told the Signory, "the law maker aims at nothing if not at uniting the citizenry by means of the law, which is what brings forth justice, and justice brings harmony and harmony every prosperity, as Aristotle maintains in the *Ethics*."[68]

The two lawyers assume a close tie between law and office, law and the state. This perception of an immediate relation between the two was facilitated by the practice of oligarchy. The Florentine constitution gave each citizen of the highest grade a direct contact with power through his exercise of office, so that all the human intervals between law, the legislative process, and the enforcement of the law were cut to a minimum. There was little space, so to speak, between the citizen and the making, effacing, or enforcing of the law. Hence we are back to the theme of a mobile system of state, a system which made for an easier grasp of the relation between law and the state. The grasp was facilitated by the direct relations between the lawmaking process and the small class of citizens.[69]

Strozzi and Bonsi conceived of law and the state—at least in one phase—as instruments. Using the law to achieve civil harmony and the fruits thereof, the state itself is a means. Yet the law is made: statutory law appears to be made *ex nihilo*, while custom—territorial or municipal—becomes law only when those who speak for the state put their seal on it. So far as it could make the law, the state, whether as *populus* or *princeps*, was over the laws and perhaps above them. Yet normally and in their best moments, the agents of the state observed the laws in order to make law: they did things in accordance with the constitution. In critical moments, however, acting *de plenitudine potestatis*, the state could ride above the ordinary laws. It was therefore associated with a higher law, with *ius* rather than *lex*, and might sometimes appear to be

[67] *CP*, 63, f. 56r, "o per amore o per forza . . . et per questo gli pare sia d'adoperare la forza, cioè le leggi," etc.

[68] *Ibid.*, f. 75r (28 July), Domenico Bonsi: "il lattore della leggie non intende se non è a unire e cictadini per mezzo della leggie," etc.

[69] The relation is even more easily perceived under monarchy, where the *princeps*, at times identified with the state, may seem to have the law in *scrinio pectoris* ("in the shrine of his breast").

one with it. Again, although the state had an end beyond itself (the making and enforcing of the laws for the sake of peace, justice, and the fruits thereof), because it made the laws and stood as guardian over them, it could easily be looked upon as an end *per se*. Its very presence ensured the possibility of peace and justice. The existence of these virtues was unthinkable without the state. Consequently, any threat to the state was *ipso facto* a threat to civil harmony and the reign of justice. The state became its own end.

This reasoning gives us a better understanding of why Florentine statesmen of the fourteenth and fifteenth centuries were inclined to see the state as a high temporal good, an end in itself. The dialectical interplay between public agents, agencies, and civic purposes gave the appropriate legal and rational arguments. But it is clear that the timeliness of the conception, its applicability, the readiness to foster it, and the capacity to "feel" it, depended entirely on the factual existence of a state: a political entity which acknowledged no superior in temporal affairs, at the same time claiming a *fiscus*,[70] a subject territory, and an unlimited right to make its own laws, whatever the place of ecclesiastical immunities under or beside it.

In October 1382, speaking to the Signory in an advisory capacity, the canon lawyer Jacopo Folchi observed that all citizens should keep their particular interests and desires down, "heeding the good of the Republic [attendant ad utilitatem Reipublice]," while "the Commune should care for subjects equally and watch over all, just as the guardian protects his wards."[71] "Republic" and "Commune" refer to the state and its official expression. Folchi's use of the word "tutor" reveals a common habit of lawyers. They very often referred to the civil authority as guardian, custodian, protector, tutor, or father. In these moments, theirs was a view of the paternalistic state. The guardian existed to look after the ward, but the safety and good of the ward were inconceivable without the guardian. Hence we come back to the good of the guardian, the good

---

[70] Imperial power over all public monies within its jurisdiction. Woolf, *Bartolus*, pp. 115ff.; cf. M. Wilks, *The Problem of Sovereignty in the Later Middle Ages* (Cambridge, 1963), pp. 178-79.

[71] *CP*, 20, f. 92r, "Et quod comune equaliter debet subditos respicere et omnes tueri ut tutor pupillos."

of the state, and the state as an end—the state having been merged with civic ends, which in a Christian society were theoretically indivisible from Christian ends.

But the passage from theory to practice easily ended by giving short shrift to obvious, traditional moral ends. In everyday affairs, the particular or private good must give way to the state, which in practice became a higher moral entity. The larger community took precedence. Florentine lawyers, when holding forth on a case in public law, did not question the good of the Signory, of the offices around it, or of the *civitas superior*. They either did not think about this or took it all for granted, which came to the same thing. Their concern was to defend the superior city's prerogatives in the dominion and to justify or guide the government's actions in Florence proper.

The identification of the public good with the good of the state—a union promoted by princes and oligarchies all over Italy—is exceedingly important in the history of politics, political theory, and public law. For it enabled lawyers and statesmen to defend the use of extraordinary or irregular measures in the exercise of government. By this means, minor civil disturbances or the slightest threat permitted men in power to suspend the ordinary rule of law, to override constitutions, and to pounce arbitrarily on groups and individuals. When the public welfare was threatened, any means to protect it was defensible and just. And when the state was threatened, threatened too were the peace, justice, and prosperity of the community; whereupon any means to protect the state, including action outside the written law, also became defensible and just.

A test of the new state's solidity depended on three features: its ability to impose irregular or extraordinary measures, its long-term success with these, and the uniform readiness of citizen lawyers to come to its defense. In none of these was Florence deficient. Inevitably, the pivotal legal argument in support of extraordinary measures was the argument from public safety or public utility. Now and then—though far less often—the *plenitudo potestatis* of the prince was also adduced.

It is in this light that the Signory and the Eight on Public Safety, the most dreaded of all Florentine magistracies (like the Ten in Venice), are best seen. The Quattrocento saw their authority swell, most especially

431

in connection with all activity which touched on the security or prerogatives of the state. An efficient employer of spies, the Eight, as Guicciardini
noted, observed no laws in procedural matters when striking at political
crime; and constituting a permanent office, they were able to make a
fixed principle of the assumption that the state could defend itself by all
means, fair or foul. Guicciardini defended the office because, as he said,
a civil life in Florence would have been impossible without it. On the
whole, lawyers approved of the Eight.

During the middle decades of the fifteenth century, the short-term
establishment of plenipotentiary councils, appointments to key office from
pouches held or kept "by hand," and the prorogation of the "tyrannical"
*accoppiatores* were actions occasionally taken with the endorsement of
lawyers, who based their defense on the imperatives of public safety and
civic peace.[72] Opposition was thus silenced by intimidation and with the
backing of lawyers. Rarely did a lawyer break with opinion in the inner
oligarchy. In June 1448 Giovanni Bertaldi called the Signory's attention
to the civil discontent in the city, observing that it derived from the fact
that the pouches for leading office were being held "open"—which meant,
he observed, living not "popularly" but "tyrannically."[73] Poor Bertaldi
utterly failed to make his way in politics, though he was trained in law
at Bologna and had first entered public life more than thirty years before. Of greater interest was the shifting behavior of another lawyer,
Domenico Martelli, a leading member of the inner oligarchy and a
staunch partisan of the Medici. Early in July 1458, in the face of an impending move on the government's part to employ emergency measures
and establish a new plenipotentiary council, Martelli observed, ". . . if
there be agreement between the principal citizens, all things will be
obtained in the ordinary fashion, nor will there be any need of extraordinary measures."[74] But he despaired of the prospect and ended by favoring the emergency proposals. In early June and September 1465, the year
after Cosimo de' Medici's death, the government held a debate on the
powers and mandate of the Eight on Public Safety. Caught up in a

[72] See pp. 195-97, 209-10.

[73] *CP*, 52, f. 49v. On pouches held "open" or *a mano* see pp. 195-96.

[74] *CP*, 55, f. 38r, "quod si cives principales uniti sint, per viam ordinariam
omnia obtinebuntur nec opus esse extraordinariis modis."

veiled struggle involving personal factors and conflicting ambitions, the leaders of the inner oligarchy were themselves divided.[75] Domenico Martelli spoke out against concentrating additional power in the Eight. Warning the Signory that citizens already lived in fear, he maintained that "the ordinary judges and other officials [pretores]" had ample regular power to move against the criminal element and administer justice. But the Eight were not short of defenders. Another lawyer of the first political rank, Otto Niccolini, took up much the same line that Guicciardini was to follow: ". . . he praised the power and office of the Eight for many reasons" and urged their necessity in the struggle against criminal activity.[76]

Martelli's stand on this occasion is one of the very rare examples in the *Consulte e Pratiche*—indeed, the only one I have found—of a lawyer's questioning the power of the Eight. It was a year (1465-1466) of marked divisions within the ruling group, and Martelli was preeminent enough to speak out.

The Pisan revolt against Florence (1495) resulted at the very end of the century in dramatic criminal proceedings. On August 6, 1499, the Florentine army, under the command of the soldier of fortune Paolo Vitelli came very close to recapturing Pisa. A breech had been made in the Pisan walls, with the result that the Florentine commissaries in the field urged the troops to press forward and take the city by storm.[77] But Vitelli brusquely halted the advance and ordered his men back. Not for another ten years was Florence to have as good a chance. The government reacted with a paroxysm of rage but said nothing to the *condottiere* until the end of September, when he was suddenly and unexpectedly arrested by the commissaries, who rushed him to Florence. Reports from ambassadors indicated that he had been in contact with the Duke of Milan,[78] who allegedly persuaded Vitelli to hold back from taking Pisa.

[75] *CP*, 57, ff. 9v-16r, 35v-38r, 42r-45r. A bill prolonging the mandate of the Eight for five years and extending their powers was thrice rejected in June. In September a similar but more modest bill was also rejected: *LF*, 67, ff. 233r-235r.

[76] *CP*, 57, f. 10r, "Baliam multis rationibus laudavit et magistratum octo virorum per necessarium esse ob removenda scelera et facinora quae perpetrari solebant."

[77] Jacopo Nardi, *Istorie della città di Firenze*, ed. L. Arbib, 2 vols. (Firenze, 1838-41), I, 176; Ammirato, *Istorie fiorentine*, VI, 208-11.

[78] Vittorio de Caprariis asserts that there are documents which prove that Vitelli

Florentines also accused him of having been in secret touch with their arch-enemies, the Pisans. By custom and contract, *condottieri* were bound to be loyal to their employers. Rebellion or connivance with the enemy was treason liable to the severest penalties. Vitelli was brought to trial on October 1st. His judges were the Eight on Public Safety, the Signory, and a group of prominent citizens especially summoned to take part in the trial. Although the Eight had important military powers, this was not a regular court martial, owing to the presence and decisive voice of both the Signory and the assembled advisors. Tortured, Vitelli does not seem to have made much of a confession.[79] One or two of the advisors felt that it might be well to observe more regular procedure in the trial, but the prevailing mood was tersely expressed by one of the lawyers present, Messer Niccolò Altoviti, a doctor *in utroque iure* trained at the University of Pisa. Speaking for the lawyers and citizens in his group ("ordine"), he declared, ran the report, that "under no circumstances should Paolo Vitelli be let off with his life: first because of his contacts with your rebels [the Pisans], which he denies not and for which he deserves by law to die; next, in view of the man's rank, place, and what he could do to hurt your Republic, [Altoviti] reckoned that for these reasons also [we] should not proceed according to ordinary legal forms. For this is not the way things are usually done in the affairs of states. He concluded that [Vitelli] should forfeit his life and quickly."[80]

Vitelli was beheaded. Nothing in the way Roman and canon law were taught at Pisa had impressed on Niccolò Altoviti the view that reason

---

had a secret understanding with the Venetians on the matter of restoring the Medici family to Florence, in his edition of Francesco Guicciardini, *Opere* (Milano-Napoli, 1953), p. 554, n. 1.

[79] Nardi, *Istorie*, I, 181-82.

[80] *CP*, 65, f. 116r, "che in nessuno modo non sia da perdonare la vita a pagolo vitelli: la prima per le pratiche che lui ha tenuto con i vostri rebelli, el che non nega et per questo secondo la leggie lui merita la morte. Apresso considerato le qualità del huomo, il luogho donde è et quello potrebbe fare in danno della vostra repubblica, et per questo judichò anchora non si proceda secondo e termini di ragione chè così non si suole nelle cose delli stati, et concluse che non sia da perdonarli la vita et da farlo presto." My translation of the phrase "termini di ragione" differs slightly from Professor Felix Gilbert's in his *Machiavelli and Guicciardini, Politics and History in Sixteenth-Century Florence*, p. 43. On Vitelli's execution see: *Otto di Guardia, Rep.*, 115 (Sept.-Dec. 1499), ff. 73v-76v.

("ragione"), as manifested in regular legal procedure, should hold sway at all times. Like most Florentine lawyers who plunged into politics, he was ready to disregard the niceties of the law when the issue concerned the security of the state. His was a call for swift, summary action. He defended his plea by holding that Vitelli's very existence was dangerous to the Republic, and he pointedly suggested that in such matters states should cleave to a distinctive mode of action—action determined not by ordinary procedures and laws but by a *sui-generis* political logic. Weighing Altoviti's words in their late fifteenth-century context, we find it difficult to imagine a more incisive, informal statement of the doctrinal foundations of the new state.

Although privileges to favorites, individual and corporate, were to be accorded by the dukes of Tuscany, they could be rescinded. For the new state affected the whole sphere of special privileges and immunities which had characterized the early Commune. Before the demands of the state, especially in fiscal matters, some of the old immunities and semi-autonomous jurisdictions gave way. In a lawsuit of around 1417, already touched on earlier, Castiglion Aretino tried to escape paying a new Florentine gabelle by alleging a fiscal immunity in a covenant with Florence. Among the different arguments used by the lawyer Alessandro Bencivenni against this Aretine suburb was one which held that such immunities may be suspended in times of urgent public need.[81] At the end of the century, Antonio Strozzi tersely observed that the privilege of immunity is understood to be set aside by public necessity.[82] There was also another argument, not perhaps readily applicable in the dispute with Castiglion Aretino. Strozzi entered it into his legal *repertorium*: the *princeps*, he noted, may revoke the privileges and graces granted by him.[83] Yet in some cases the argument from public welfare or public necessity carried more weight. This was certainly true in moments when the Florentine state resolved to ignore ecclesiastical immunities. In the spring of 1530, with foreign armies at the gates of Florence, the struggling Republic undertook still heavier, unlicensed confiscations of ecclesi-

---

[81] BNF, *Magl.*, xxix, 186, ff. 46r-47r.
[82] *Strozz.*, *3a ser.*, 41/16, s.v. *Immunitas*, f. 198v.
[83] *Strozz.*, *3a ser.*, 41/16, s.v. *Princeps*, f. 298v.

astical properties. On April 25th the Signory heard the advice of the lawyer Francesco Nelli, who spoke for the San Giovanni quarter. Owing to the emergency, he said, "all the canons allow that the properties [of the Church] can be alienated." Hence he urged that the appropriate magistracy be given the power to seize and sell the goods in question. For "it has been said," he added, "that it is not wrong for those things which cannot be governed in the ordinary manner to be governed extraordinarily."[84]

There was no subtlety in the doctrine. Its sole purpose was to provide a sufficient defense of action which seemed to contravene the ordinary laws. These were matters of state, not intellectual exercises. In 1495-1496, after Florence had moved its Studio (University) from Pisa to Prato, owing to the rebellion of the Pisans, a number of religious houses began to claim that this transfer released them from having to pay the tax licensed by the pope for the subvention of the Studio Pisano. Adopting a strictly literal interpretation, they held that the tax had been licensed for the Studio in Pisa, not Prato. Counsel for Florence, the law professor Antonio Strozzi easily refuted this claim by arguing that the papal license had been granted not in the name of a given place but for the sake of a public good. Moreover, the transfer to Prato, he observed, had been necessitated by an emergency—rebellion, plague, and the threat of war.[85]

By THE sixth decade of the fourteenth century, Bartolus of Sassoferrato had made in his *Commentaries* on the Roman law a series of observations tending, in legal theory, to turn the Italian city-state into a sovereign political unit. From the standpoint of its sovereignty, this state was deemed in no wise inferior to the kingdoms of northern Europe and Naples. The achievement of Bartolus was his transformation of fact into legal argument, custom into higher or more positive law. He started with the

[84] *CP*, 73, f. 38r, "È stato detto che non sarà inconveniente che le cose che non si possono governare ordinariamente si governassino extraordinariamente." With the consent of the cathedral chapter, bishops were empowered by canon law to alienate church properties in moments of necessity; but the Republic had certainly not got episcopal clearance.

[85] *Strozz., 3a ser., 41/4,* ff. 238r *et seq.*

given, the city-state which owned no superior *de facto*, and looked for its sanctions in Roman law. Drawing on the implied values in the principle of tacit consent, he turned the people of such a *civitas* into a "free people" and attributed to it the powers and rights of the *princeps*. *Civitas* or *populus liber* thus became *princeps* unto itself; to an even greater degree, however—and how far Bartolus saw this is open to question—it became "prince" to its subject territories.

In the 1360s and 1370s, lawyers from Florence and Bologna were already employing the phrases which summed up the Bartolist view of the new state. And they could be sure of getting some response. The master of Italian lawyers, or rather his work, was known to all Italian students of the law. But it was to take time before Florentine law-yers—and one presumes other Italians—could make the new vision fully their own, could learn to draw on it with naturalness and impose it on others, particularly on subject territories which had stubborn local tradi-tions as well as convictions about their own autonomy. The Republic's ability to give currency to the new conception was directly related to its own political success: it had only to persuade sovereign peers and ter-ritorial subjects of its dignity and might. Theory bred on fact. By waging war against the papacy (1375-1378), by standing up to Giangaleazzo Visconti (d.1402) and King Ladislaus (d.1414), Florence established her-self as one of the major Italian powers, and her lawyers soon began to apply the Bartolist formulas with a growing ease and liberty.

At the end of the fifteenth century, lawyers like Antonio Malegonnelli and Ormannozzo Deti argue that the Signory, in its manifestation as *princeps*, has the right to dispose of minerals found in the Florentine dominion and to grant or revoke privileges of monopoly regarding their excavation.[86] A little later Antonio Strozzi and Niccolò Guicciardini, holding forth on disputes over the gabelle on salt, submit that all rights pertaining to revenue from salt belong to the prince, and "as experience teaches, not only the Florentine people but all princes of Italy proceed with the maximum force and the gravest penalties against those who interfere *in materia salis*."[87] Of all prerogatives, as this quotation sug-

[86] *Strozz., 3a ser.*, 41/14, ff. 540r, 546v.
[87] *Ibid.*, f. 388r.

gests, those connected with public monies were among the most important, and this had precise implications for the judiciary. In a plea from around 1505, Francesco Gualterotti observed that the Podestà of Florence, "who has all jurisdiction," is especially competent in the type of case which touches the exchequer ("in qua fiscus habet interesse").[88]

During the second half of the fifteenth century, the Eight on Public Safety greatly stepped up their activity and ended by operating freely in criminal matters throughout the Florentine dominion. With the establishment of the Council of Justice or Rota Fiorentina (1502), the superior city began to insist on the judicial competence of this court's presiding magistrate in every corner of the territory. The insistence was usually sounded in response to cases which directly challenged his authority. Florentine lawyers now began to draw up pleas and opinions which on occasion seemed uncommonly speculative or even appeared to border on the arbitrary. In July 1516, dealing with a case which turned on a question of judicial competence, Antonio Strozzi asseverated, "there is no doubt that the Florentine people, *non recognoscente superiorem*, can make a statute in its territory, ordaining that the sentences of some judges cannot be appealed, even on grounds of defective jurisdiction."[89] In another case dating from the same period, the following details emerge. By a law of 1514, Volterrans were given the right to appeal against decisions in criminal or civil proceedings by having recourse to the Signory, the Ten on War, and the Eight on Public Safety. The law thus seemed to turn these officials into "ordinary judges." If true, then a Volterran could appeal against their decisions also, even when these were relayed as directives and read out in the court of the Captain of Volterra. Such appeal would go to the first appellate judge of Florence.[90]

After running through this argument, Antonio Strozzi presented his refutation. He affirmed that no ordinary appeal could be lodged against

---

[88] *Ibid.*, ff. 506r-507v.

[89] *Strozz.*, *3a ser.*, 41/9, f. 518v, "et cum simus in statuto condito a populo florentino non recognoscente superiorem, non est dubium quod potest facere statutum in suo territorio quod sententie late per aliquos iudices non possint impugnari etiam ex defectu iurisdictionis." The lawyer was thinking not of the ordinary or regular magistrates but of those executive bodies which disposed of special judicial powers.

[90] *Strozz.*, *3a ser.*, 41/11, f. 79r.

the decisions of the Signory, the Ten, and the Eight. For while "I do not know whether there be a law on this, yet it is so because they [the magistracies in question] have as much power and authority as does the Florentine people."[91] Strozzi meant that because they constituted the city's highest executive and judicial authority[92] there was no dignity above them to which ordinary appeal could be made. The Grand Council never tampered with such appeal. In this affair, the three bodies apparently disposed of the power of the prince. The case brought into question the executive's judicial prerogative in the resentful town of Volterra, where the Florentine patriciate was determined to maintain its controls.

It must not be concluded from the foregoing case, or from anything else said earlier, that the Signory ordinarily exercised the power of the *princeps*. Being the Republic's supreme magistracy, when acting in concert with the Ten and the Eight, it was very powerful indeed. In legal theory, however, it did "not hold the place of the prince, save by the consent of the other general councils."[93] Only, therefore, in unusual circumstances or in *some* of its manifestations did the Signory wear the garments of the prince.

The jurisprudence of the period taught that the *princeps* could assign a case to any judge he wished;[94] so too could the Florentine people acting through its magistracies. Like the prince, Florence could adjudicate its own causes ("esse iudex in causa propria") so far as concerned its proper subjects ("quantum ad suos subditos").[95] Ordinarily, neither the prince nor Florence could revoke a privilege bestowed under the seal of contract ("per viam contractus").[96] Yet if Florence, in its guise as prince, granted a privilege which damaged or hampered any of its prerogatives or essential jurisdictions, that privilege was *ipso facto* null and void.

---

[91] *Ibid.*, "nescio an sit aliqua lex, sed forte est ex eo quia ipsi habent baliam et tantam auctoritatem quantam habet populus florentinus."

[92] The Signory could undertake extraordinarily to hear any case in appeal, thereby rising above all tribunals.

[93] *Strozz., 3a ser.*, 41/19, f. 222v. "Priores florentini non sunt loco principis nisi habita deliberatione et partito ab aliis consiliis generalibus."

[94] *Strozz., 3a ser.*, 41/17, f. 197r, "Princeps potest causam delegare cuilibet." Cites *D.* 2, 1, 1 and 5.

[95] *Strozz., 3a ser.*, 41/16, s.v. *Imperator*, f. 199r.

[96] *Ibid.*, s.v. *Privilegium*, f. 299r.

439

Again, even where guaranteed by contract, a privilege lapsed when in conflict with dire public necessity. Normally, the *civitas superior* acted in accordance with its regular powers, making use of the ordinary written and common laws.[97] Only in very exceptional cases might its "free people" act *de plenitudine potestatis.* This power in temporal affairs seems to have been unlimited. Antonio Strozzi—from whose notebooks most of these observations come—could find very few situations which appeared to warrant the superior city's acting "from the fullness of power."

Before concluding this analysis, we must go back for a moment to the subject of *utilitas* and *necessitas publica.* It underlies much that characterizes the modern state, whether of the totalitarian or liberal-bourgeois brand, and in the fourteenth and fifteenth centuries already held a prominent place in Italian and Florentine public law.

What sort of a device were lawyers fashioning when they put forth arguments in the name of the public good or public necessity? The import of these arguments may be grasped *politically* only in concrete political situations. Florence, after all, was neither a democracy nor a kingdom ruled by a philosopher-king. It was a faction-ridden oligarchy until the fourth decade of the fifteenth century. Thereafter, an inner oligarchy acquired ever more control over the state. The political and social outlook of the ruling group underwent gradual but decisive change; and when the principal family was expelled from Florence in 1494, though political tension and civil discord returned to engulf the city, struggle took a new turn. Conflict between the major and minor families of the oligarchy began to dominate the scene. The old ruling group, now hardened into an aristocratic caste, brought forth intransigents of vast political experience who set themselves against the lesser or minor families of the oligarchy. Modest in their experience of public affairs and less rich, these families could not claim long and continuous contact with the top offices of government.[98]

---

[97] *Ibid.,* s.v. *Princeps,* f. 298v.
[98] Speaking of the period 1495-1496, Bartolomeo Cerretani, *Storia fiorentina* (BNF, *Fondo principale,* II, III, 74), noted that there were three types of citizens: (1) supporters of Piero de' Medici, mainly from the rich and great noble houses; (2) rich noblemen who had supported Lorenzo the Magnificent but who drew away from Piero; (3) citizens of more middling rank and wealth who now pressed

It seems obvious that when developed and refined in a setting where struggle between the conflicting groups was nothing if not struggle for the control of the state, argument from public necessity (utility, advantage, etc.) could be transformed into a device for destroying or humbling the opponents of the families that "held" or seemed to incarnate the state. The best proof of this may be seen in the political uses to which the power of the Eight on Public Safety was put and which lawyers like Otto Niccolini and Francesco Guicciardini defended, alleging argument in the name of the public good. A legal principle could thus be turned into a political weapon. But there was another, trickier ambiguity. Just as the designated principle might be used for political ends, so—paradoxically—the refusal to adduce it might also derive from partisan politics. Nothing reveals this double facet of the principle more clearly than a political case which greatly disturbed the city at the end of the fifteenth century.

In March 1495 the Grand Council enacted a law which derived in part from Savonarolan inspiration.[99] The law concerned only those Florentines who were eligible for public office; more particularly, it directly affected any citizen who, for reasons of state, might be condemned by the Signory or the Eight on Public Safety to exile, death, or a penalty of more than 300 large florins. Henceforth, any citizen so condemned could lodge an appeal with the Signory within eight days of his conviction. The Signory was obligated to accept the appeal and in the next fifteen days must present it to the Grand Council in the form of an appeal for absolution. The appeal could not be put to a vote in the Grand Council more than three times in any one day, or more than six times in all. Absolution required the vote of two-thirds the councillors.

Guicciardini observed that this law was extremely unpopular with "many of the most influential men."[100] No doubt they feared that it was the first step in a movement to increase greatly the powers of the Grand Council. Henceforth the largest of all Florentine councils would be sitting

---

for public office, having held only a minor place in public affairs under the Medici. See the Cerretani selections in J. Schnitzer, *Quellen und Forshungen zur Geschichte Savonarolas,* 4 vols. (Munich, 1902-1910), III, 40.

[99] *Provvisioni,* 185, ff. 90v-92v, pencil.

[100] *Storie fiorentine dal 1378 al 1509,* ed. R. Palmarocchi (Bari, 1931), p. 111.

in judgment on the most important cases of alleged treason, political agitation, and sharp criticism of public policy. A check had been put on the executive, the agency which provided the inner oligarchy with its most effective controls.

It was to this law that five leading citizens had recourse on August 17, 1497, when the Signory and the Eight sentenced them to death and the forfeiture of all their earthly goods.[101] Bernardo del Nero, Niccolò Ridolfi, Lorenzo Tornabuoni, Giannozzo Pucci, and Giovanni Cambi were charged with conspiring to overthrow the government and to restore the fugitive and "tyrant," Piero de' Medici. Their plot, it appears, was to buy the support of the lower classes ("plebe," "popolo minuto"— Parenti) by importing a large quantity of grain and bread for cheap sale in Florence. Meanwhile, Piero would approach the city with a troop of armed men. Enough evidence seems to have been gathered to prove that the conspiracy was a full-blown attempt against the new republican regime—a regime associated with the name of Savonarola and much disliked by an important sector of the inner oligarchy. Beset by political passion, the city broke out in bitter controversy when the five conspirators made application for appeal. Feared because they were rich and had powerful connections, closer in politics to the extreme oligarchs than to most citizens, they had the sympathy of certain leading families but implacable hatred from Savonarolans like Francesco Valori, the Gonfalonier of Justice. Unfortunately for the five, most of the top places in government were then occupied by supporters, more or less ardent, of the new regime. Instead of processing their appeal, as the law required, the Signory and a special commission of twenty advisors took the question and referred it to a group of 160 citizens. The group was not entirely hand picked: it included the Council of Eighty, all the principal magistracies, a number of *ad hoc* advisors (*arroti*), and the Signory itself.[102]

---

[101] These and following details from: Piero Parenti, *Storia fiorentina*, BNF, *Fondo principale*, II, IV, 170, ff. 15v-19r; Bartolomeo Cerretani, *Storia*, selections in Schnitzer, *Quellen*, III, pp. 47-49; J. Nardi, *Istorie*, pp. 116-17. The chief source in ASF is *CP*, 63, ff. 83r *et seq.* The register, *Otto di Guardia, Rep.*, 107, which recorded at least part of the proceedings is curiously missing.

[102] Cerretani says that this *pratica* included 200 citizens but that 300 were finally consulted. My figure comes from Parenti and *CP*, 63, *loc.cit.* As there were several consultations, it may be that Cerretani's is a total figure. The shrewdness of the

Consulted on August 21st in an atmosphere of intimidation, the members of this assembly were individually asked whether or not the accused should be put to death, the alternative being to permit appeal to the Grand Council. Replies were given *viva voce* and then recorded. Undoubtedly men were watched. The verdict went almost unanimously against the accused, whereupon the Signory denied them the right of appeal and had the Bargello get on with their execution.

In the context of this study, the chief interest of the trial centers on the differences which it produced among lawyers. When condemned on August 17th by the Signory and the Eight, the conspirators not only appealed, they picked as their defense attorney an extremely prominent lawyer—Guidantonio Vespucci, one of the four or five most authoritative statesmen in Florence. Agreeing to defend them, Vespucci intensified the bitterness of dispute and widened the cleavage of opinion among lawyers. Of the ten or twelve lawyers who stood out in public life, the available evidence shows that four supported the appeal, while more than four others opposed it. The argument of the lawyers who defended the appeal is known to us from second-hand sources only.[103] With Vespucci as their spokesman, they insisted on the application of the appeal law. When the opposition declared that the crime of the conspirators was manifest enough and much too wicked, that they sought the right of appeal for dishonest ends and so as to rally the support of their relatives and friends in the Grand Council, Vespucci replied that to take action in accordance with such representations was to put the city beyond the rule of law and under the arbitrary rule of men.

---

group which sought to deny the appeal is revealed by the fact that they brought the whole executive complex into the trial and then broke out of it by including the Council of Eighty and some *arroti*. In this fashion they gave themselves the widest possible support, while yet keeping to a restricted group. This was one way to circumvent the appeal law, as it might then be argued that the law could not apply because part of the legislature had actively participated in the trial. Nevertheless, there remained the question of whether or not the constitution had been violated. The Eighty were a consultative-legislative body and could not normally act *de iure* as judges in criminal cases.

[103] *Viz.*, the chronicles of Parenti and Cerretani. Francesco Gualterotti, Domenico Bonsi, Luca Corsini, and Antonio Strozzi definitely opposed the appeal. Cerretani says that four favored it, but gives only the name of Guidantonio Vespucci. Judging by their stand on other matters, I would suppose Niccolò Altoviti and Ormannozzo Deti to have been among the supporters.

Neither Vespucci nor any of the other lawyers who favored the appeal were present at the combined trial-consultation of August 21st, where the fate of the conspirators was finally sealed. Cerretani asserted that if Vespucci had been present, he would have been thrown from the upper windows of the government palace, so violent was the feeling against him and the accused.

Of the four lawyers whom we know to have opposed the appeal, only one, Antonio Strozzi, did not speak at the session of August 21st. The other three, drawing on argument from public safety and stressing the danger to the city, spoke against the Signory's acceptance of the appeal. Francesco Gualterotti, representing the Ten on War suggested that the request of the condemned was dishonest. He feared the outbreak of a tumult if, in undertaking to process the appeal, the Signory was then unable to assemble a quorum of the Grand Council.[104] Speaking for the order of lawyers, Domenico Bonsi noted that the appeal law provided "for some exceptions, above all when such delay threatens to put the city into imminent danger. In this case the law would dispense with appeal."[105] Luca Corsini spoke for the Eight on Public Safety and expressed the toughest of the views presented. He began with a statement about how ever since "liberty" had been "returned to this people, . . . the city has been besieged and hated by those who want to live tyrannically." Then moving to the question of the appeal, he declared, "the Eight and I are of this opinion. Things should be speeded up, particularly because danger presses on the Republic . . . the law appears to grant the right of appeal, but if this [exposes] the city to an obvious danger, then such appeal must be denied to avoid a danger which would bring ruin to the city."[106]

Whatever the pretensions of the lawyers on either side of the question, it is clear that their views were drawn up along political as well as

[104] *CP*, 63, f. 83v, pencil.

[105] *Ibid.*, f. 84v, pencil, "benchè la legge facta paia che dia l'appello, questa legge patisce qualche exceptione e maximamente quando questo indugio possa mettere la cictà a pericolo eminente, perchè in questo caso la legge dispenserebbe."

[106] *Ibid.*, ff. 84v-85r, "Et io e quegli miei padri degl' Octo . . . sono in questa sententia: d'accelerare le cose e maximamente quando soprasta pericolo presentaneo alla repubblica . . . qui si vede che la legge pare dia l'appello, ma se per quello . . . [illegible] alla cictà manifesto pericolo, e da dispensare a tale appello per fuggire maggior pericolo, che sarebbe la ruina della cictà."

jurisprudential lines. The men accused were rich, powerful, and highly connected. Piero de' Medici was said to be in Siena with an armed body of men. For Luca Corsini and for the others who spoke on August 21st the Republic was in manifest danger. Delay would give the enemy time to organize their forces and drum up support in the Grand Council. In short, the public good—the security of the Republic—called for swift action, even at the expense of overriding a particular law.

Vespucci's position was much the more honorable legally. He insisted on the applicability of the appeal law.[107] Unlike most men in the highest offices of government, he saw no clear danger to the Republic, to a state whose most novel feature, the Grand Council, he heartily disliked, though he was willing on occasion to let its judicial powers be superior to those of the principal offices of the executive complex. In that August of alarm for upper-class Florence, it was politics—as well as his view of the law—that made Vespucci dismiss the alleged dangers, reject argument from public safety, and cleave to the letter of the law.

Around the major offices of the Republic was collecting that majesty (*majestas*) which once attached to the prince and *populus Romanus* in Roman public law and which still attached to the prince wherever he was an individual ruler. Majesty was a quality which went beyond dignity to touch on something great and almost sacred. Lawyers were associating the state with this quality, at least so far as they gave it the name, prerogatives, and powers of the prince. In the 1420s Buonaccorso da Montemagno already referred to the *maestà* of the Florentine Signory.[108] The vein was rhetorical but Buonaccorso, a practicing lawyer trained at Bologna, knew perfectly well that in Italian public affairs this appellation was most fittingly applied to the *princeps* of his day. Strictly associated with the word was the most reprehensible of crimes—treason, "the crime of injured majesty." Appropriately, legal thought gradually brought this crime back into prominence in the course of the fourteenth and fifteenth centuries.[109]

---

[107] And oddly, he had supported this law even at the time of its enactment. *CP,* 61, f. 5v.

[108] *Prose del Giovane Buonaccorso da Montemagno,* ed. G. B. Giuliari (Bologna, 1874), p. 49.

[109] C. Ghisalberti, "Sulla teoria dei delitti di lesa maestà nel diritto comune," *Archivio giuridico,* CXLIX (1955), 100-79.

But even at the end of the fifteenth century, though legal theory commonly spoke of Florence as *princeps* in its territories, the inclination to assign these powers to the principal offices of the executive cluster was not yet so overriding as to make for an irreversible trend, at any rate in the minds of lawyers. Florence was at a crossroads. A final solution had been hit on with respect to its territories. But the political and institutional changes of the second half of the fifteenth century, by strongly favoring the executive, had opened to question the real locus of the fullness of power *within* the city. Not always dramatically evident, the question was, nonetheless, supremely important; and it was to be settled by the course of political events, not by the opinions of lawyers. For lawyers could with equal facility draw on two contradictory lines of argument in legal-political theory. Something else therefore—in this case politics—had to determine the winning line. Moving from the aspect of consent implied in the *lex regia*,[110] lawyers could lodge the powers of the prince in "the Florentine people" and general councils; or, looking instead to the autocratic ingredient in the same and other laws, they could stress the authority and force of the executive.

The two lines of argument were revealed, obliquely but interestingly, in the executive consultations on the appeal law of March 1495.[111] Guidantonio Vespucci and Luca Corsini, the two lawyers who were to figure prominently in the case discussed above, entered the lists strongly in favor of legislation which would, in cases of serious political crime, admit appeals to the Grand Council against decisions of the Signory. Although they stood on the same side of the issue, each represented his views in such a way as to point up the two contrasting conceptions of government. Both deplored the fact that the Signory could take a man's life with six votes and that the decision could not be appealed. Suggesting that this power had been improperly acquired, Vespucci observed that the denial of appeal had been the cause of many wrongs. Next he equated the Signory with the *princeps* but denied that the sentences of princes were above appeal, be the prince King of France, Emperor,

[110] *D.* 1, 4, 1; *C.* 1, 17, 1, 7. On the ambiguity of this law see Kantorowicz, *King's Two Bodies*, p. 103; Ullmann, *Principles*, pp. 296-97.
[111] *CP*, 61, f. 5r-v.

Pope, Duke of Ferrara, or other. Who judges himself may be subject to correction, "and though the prince is not bound by the laws, yet he willingly submits to them."[112] Somewhat inconsistently, Vespucci then referred to the Signory's "superior, or rather to the Grand Council." But the sense of his argument was unmistakable: though the Signory held the place of the *princeps*, it should rule in accordance with the laws, not from the fullness of its authority, which in some ways set it outside the laws.

Vespucci insisted on the ordinary rule of law; he feared the exercise of arbitrary power; yet he perceived the Signory in terms of the *princeps*, a sovereign authority which he admitted could be *legibus solutus*. Not so Luca Corsini, who viewed the whole question entirely from the viewpoint of consent.[113] Equating the state—in good corporate fashion—with the whole body of the *populus*, he noted that this multitude may set up a government to administer its affairs. The *populus* brings, as it were, the ruling magistracy out of itself. Here precisely was the suitability of licensing appeal to the Grand Council, from which the Signory held its authority. Corsini concluded that the Signory was not like the *princeps* in any pure sense because the *populus*, while appointing and obeying him (i.e., the Signory), also possesses greater authority. The intent was clear: if the *princeps* was identified with the Signory he had less than

[112] *Ibid.*, "Nam talem constituere auctoritatem dominorum a qua provocari non possit, multorum fuisse causam malorum, nec reperiri principem aliquem a cuius sententia non appelletur. Nam ab ea quam tulit . . . ran [Francie?] . . . ad concilium parisiense, ab imperatore ad pontificem, et ab pontificis sententia appellatur ad alios. Idem servatur in sententiis aliorum dominorum et ducum, nam a sententia ducis Ferrarie etc. Nec est quisque qui indignetur corrigi quod ipse properam iudicaverit, et quamvis princeps solutus sit legibus, illis tamen se sponte subicit. Itaque nec esse nec debere videri incongruum si a sex fabarum dominorum sententia ad superiorem, immo ad maius consilium appelletur."

[113] *Ibid.*, "Nam cum res publica corpus sit universus populus isque propter multitudinem non facile possit ad administrandas res suas convenire, creat ex se dominantes cui rem omnem statumque suum credit regendum sperans id fare secundum justitiam ac rectitudinem. Itaque non esse incongruum immo plurimum conveniens ut ad magnum consilium appelletur a quo auctoritatem illam dominatio recipit ut siquid non bene actum sit emendetur. Nec est dominatio ut merus princeps quia populus qui eum constituit paret illi et majorem habet auctoritatem." Cf. F. Gilbert, "Florentine Political Assumptions," p. 212.

447

absolute powers; but if he was more readily associated with the *populus* and the Grand Council, the true repositories of the supreme authority in Florence, he was to be viewed in the fullness of his powers.

Signory or Grand Council, executive or *populus*: which would triumph? The final fall of the Republic (1530) and the return of the Medici house would leave no room for doubt.

### SOURCES FOR CHAPTER TEN

There are many scholarly studies, legal and political, that touch on the background material contained in this chapter. I list therefore selected works only.

My debt to the scholarship of the following men is, I hope, self-evident: Gaines Post, C. N. S. Woolf, Walter Ullmann, Ernst H. Kantorowicz, and Francesco Ercole. Particular note should be taken of these works: Post, *Studies in Medieval Legal Thought: Public Law and the State, 1100-1322.* (Princeton, 1964); Woolf, *Bartolus of Sassoferrato: His Position in the History of Medieval Political Thought* (Cambridge, 1913); Ercole, *Da Bartolo all' Althusio: saggi sulla storia del pensiero pubblicistico del rinascimento italiano* (Firenze, 1932); Kantorowicz, *The King's Two Bodies: A Study in Mediaeval Political Theology* (Princeton, 1957); and *Selected Studies* (Locust Valley, New York, 1965). Also the following five items by Ullmann: *Principles of Government and Politics in the Middle Ages* (London, 2nd ed., 1966); *The Medieval Idea of Law as represented by Lucas de Penna: A Study in Fourteenth-Century Legal Scholarship* (London, 1946); "De Bartoli Sententia: concilium repraesentat mentem populi," in *Bartolo da Sassoferrato: studi e documenti per il vi centenario*, 2 vols., ed. D. Segoloni (Milano, 1962); "The Development of the Medieval Idea of Sovereignty," *English Historical Review*, LXIV (1949), 1-33; and "Baldus's Conception of Law," *Law Quarterly Review*, CCXXXI (July 1942), 386-99.

Additional guidelines are provided by O. Gierke, *Political Theories of the Middle Age*, tr. F. W. Maitland (Cambridge, 1900); F. Calasso, *I Glossatori e la teoria della sovranità: studio di diritto comune pubblico* (Milano, 3rd ed., 1957); F. Gilbert, "Florentine Political Assumptions in the Period of Savonarola and Soderini," *Journal of the Warburg and*

*Courtauld Institutes*, xx (1957), 187-214; M. P. Gilmore, *Argument from Roman Law in Political Thought, 1200-1600* (Cambridge, Mass., 1941); D. Segoloni, "Bartolo da Sassoferrato e la civitas Perusina," pp. 513-671, in centenary collection listed with Ullmann's third item above; E. E. Stengel, "Kaisertitel und Souveränitätsidee," *Deutsches Archiv für Geschichte des Mittelalters*, iii (1939), 1-49; B. Tierney, " 'The Prince is not bound by the laws.' Accursius and the Origins of the Modern State," *Comparative Studies in Society and History*, v, 4 (1963), 378-400; J. A. Watt, "The Theory of Papal Monarchy in the Thirteenth Century, The Contribution of the Canonists," *Traditio*, xx (1964), 179-317; M. Wilks, *The Problem of Sovereignty in the Later Middle Ages: The Papal Monarchy with Augustinus Triumphus and the Publicists* (Cambridge, 1963). Two noteworthy papers dealing with the early fourteenth century are N. Rubinstein, "Marsilius of Padua and Italian Political Thought of His Time," *Europe in the Late Middle Ages*, eds. Hale, Highfield, Smalley (Evanston, 1965), pp. 44-75; and "The Beginnings of Political Thought in Florence," *Journal of the Warburg and Courtauld Institutes*, v (1942), 198-227. E. Besta, *Il diritto pubblico italiano dagli inizii del secolo decimoprimo alla seconda metà del secolo decimoquinto* (Padua, 1929), and A. Marongiu, *Storia del diritto pubblico, Principi e istituti di governo in Italia dalla metà del ix alla metà del xix secolo* (Milano-Varese, 1956) offer general treatments of the major problems of Italian public law in the late medieval and Renaissance periods.

Nearly all printed treatises by Florentine lawyers were published in 1584 in that great Venetian series, the *Tractatus universi iuris* (29 vols.). There we find the following works by Florentines and by men who lived and worked in Florence for several years or more. Angelo degli Ubaldi da Perugia, *De sequestris* (iii, ii, 142-43), *Quaestiones circa materiam testium* (iv, 76-77), *De societatibus* (vi, i, 130-33), *De sindicatu* (vii, 126-27), *De inventario* (viii, ii, 155-56). Nello da San Gimignano, *De testibus* (iv, 79-88), *De bannitis* (xi, i, 357-406). Benedetto Barzi, *De guarentigiis* (vi, ii, 340-49), *De filiis non legitime natis* (viii, ii, 24-29). Lorenzo Ridolfi, *De usuris* (vii, 15-50). Antonio Roselli, *De usuris* (vii, 66-71), *De successionibus ab intestato* (viii, i, 357-71), *De legitimatione* (viii, ii, 75-90), *De indiciis et tortura* (xi, i, 290-91), *De indulgentiis* (xiv,

147-57). Gaspare da Perugia, *De beneficiorum reservationibus* (xv, i, 244-48).

Three famous lawyers, each associated with Florence for a number of years, produced opinions and commentaries which were separately edited and published in the sixteenth century. Paolo di Castro, *Consilia*, 2 vols. in fol. (Venice, 1509-1511); *Commentaria in Digestum vetus, Infortiatum, Digestum novum et Codicem*, 6 vols. in fol. (Venice, 1568-1569); *Consilia seu responsa*, 2 vols. in fol. (Venice, 1617). Filippo Decio, different *Commentaria* published at Venice in 1523, 1535, 1540, 1593, and 1609; *Consilia* (Venice, 1552). Bartolommeo Sozzini (or Soccini), *Commentaria super Digestis*, 2 vols. (Venice, 1572).

Being a study of statecraft, government, and social functions more than a formal study of political and legal ideas, this inquiry gives less emphasis to formal treatises than to judicial opinions and pleas, where the practical activity of lawyers is more in evidence. But there is such a sea of *consilia* and *allegationes* from Florentine sources, that it would be surprising for me or others to claim to have studied them all or even a large part thereof. Opinions of Florentine and other Italian lawyers of the Renaissance turn up in the manuscript libraries of large Italian cities, in those of smaller towns like Lucca and Siena, in episcopal archival collections, and in private collections (e.g., the Niccolini and Martelli papers in Florence, to which I have not had access). Not only Florentine but all Italian *consilia* and pleas of the late medieval and Renaissance periods should be inventoried. The job would take a team of researchers several years.

The bulk of the extant judicial opinions and pleas is in the realm of private law and so of little interest to the historian of politics, political theory, public law, and the state. Even so, however, the appropriate material remains vast and unwieldy. I have used four major collections only: three in Florence and one at the Vatican Library.

(1, 2) Archivio di Stato di Firenze: there are two large collections here.

*Corporazioni religiose soppresse* (CRS), Archivio 98, *Mss.*, 237-280, make up part of the so-called "Eredità Bonsi" of the suppressed monastery of Santa Maria a Monticelli di Firenze. The collection was most likely started by a lawyer who often turns up in the pages of this study, Domenico Bonsi. Though many of these manuscripts contain opinions and other items from the second half of the sixteenth century, the student of fourteenth- and fifteenth-century Florence must go through them all. For they often contain opinions, copies or originals, by lawyers who lived from fifty to 150 years before. With this collection, as with the others, the historian should pay no attention to inventories or markings on the manuscripts proper, which are nearly always a miscellany. A single manuscript sometimes contains opinions by as many as thirty or forty different lawyers, usually but not always Florentine. *Mss.*, 237-240 of this collection are particularly rich for the period 1480-1520. But *Ms.* 240, e.g., includes more than thirty opinions by Bartolommeo Vulpi and nearly seventy by Nello da San Gimignano, early fifteenth-century lawyers. The lawyers most often represented in this collection are Marco degli Asini (see the Appendix), Giovanni and a later Domenico Bonsi (second half of the sixteenth century). *Mss.*, 250, 252, 257, and 263 contain a notable number of opinions by lawyers who lived in the second half of the fifteenth and early sixteenth centuries.

*Carte strozziane, 3a ser.*, 42, 41/1-20. Twenty-one volumes in all: sixteen of *consilia* and *allegationes*, five of legal glossaries. The collection was started by Antonio Strozzi. Markings on the registers attribute all the material contained therein to him, but the series includes numerous original papers and copies of opinions of dozens of fifteenth- and early sixteenth-century lawyers.

The above are the two major collections in the Archivio di Stato. There is a vast legacy of decisions rendered by the Council of Justice, set up in 1502, but the appropriate registers have never been inventoried or catalogued. This is a major lacuna. Some of Ricciardo del Bene's opinions are preserved in the *Carte del Bene*, 54. There is also an important run of *consilia* in *AGN*, 670, penned by different Florentine lawyers of the period 1388-1436.

(3) Biblioteca Nazionale di Firenze. Although filed under different series, I think of the legal manuscripts here as forming one collection. *Fondo principale*:

II, I, 401. An opinion (*ca.* 1388) of Giovanni de' Ricci. Endorsed by Filippo Corsini.

II, II, 374. Marked "Consigli di Francesco Guicciardini," but most of these are by his contemporaries: e.g., Francesco Pepi, Antonio Strozzi, Matteo Niccolini, Ormannozzo Deti, Niccolò Altoviti, Antonio Malegonnelli, Giovan Vettorio Soderini, Puccio Pucci, Baldassare Carducci, Ludovico Acciaiuoli, etc.

II, II, 375. *Consilia legalia diversorum. Circa* 1500-1520. Important here, e.g., is a case in which Francesco Guicciardini rules "quod iudex mercantie contra Pistoriensem non habet imperium sive iurisdictionem" (f. 130r). He could not have said this of the Signory or Council of Justice.

II, II, 376. *Diversorum*, though attributed to Niccolò Guicciardini. Most of these *consilia* are from the early sixteenth century and nearly all Florentine. Ormannozzo Deti is prominent.

II, II, 377. Rough drafts of *consilia* and pleas by Niccolò Guicciardini, 1520s and after. Contains some opinions (*autografi*) by others, including fifteenth-century lawyers like Sallustio Buonguglielmi and Piero Ambrosini.

II, II, 378. Marked "Consigli di Messer Niccolò Guicciardini." Actually by a number of fifteenth- and early sixteenth-century lawyers, including, e,g., Puccio Pucci, Antonio de' Cocchi-Donati, Francesco Guicciardini, Bono Boni, Luigi Velluti, Alessandro Malegonnelli, etc.

II, III, 361. An anonymous treatise on appellate procedure. Concludes with an opinion by Otto Niccolini.

II, III, 370. Lorenzo Ridolfi's third volume of *consilia*, 1412-1420. The first two and any subsequent volumes may have been lost. On ff. 15r-17r he deals with a fascinating case in the realm of public law. The *consilium* is endorsed by Torello Torelli, Francesco Machiavelli, Nello da San Gimignano, and takes up *inter alia* the question of relations between the Signory and Gabelle Officials.

II, IV, 434. Tommaso Salvetti's commentaries, written in 1448, on parts of Bk. II of the Florentine statutes. With *consilia* by numerous fifteenth-century lawyers, many of Perugian provenance (e.g., Angelo and Baldo degli Ubaldi).

II, IV, 435. Some of Alessandro Bencivenni's observations on Florentine statutes. Excellent on civil proceedings. Holds, e.g., that the foreign official of the Mercanzia court "is not an official of the city but of the *universitas* of merchants" (f. 1r). There is frequent reference to the opinions of contemporaries and near contemporaries. A Florentine notary copied the manuscript in November 1476, probably from Bencivenni's original.

*Fondo Magliabechiano*, Cl. xxix:

117. *Consilia legalia diversorum.* Has many opinions by lawyers of late fourteenth and early fifteenth century. Filippo Corsini prominent.

161. *Diversorum.* Mainly Florentine and Perugian, second half of fourteenth and early fifteenth century. Torello Torelli predominates. Many *consilia* of Bartolus, Baldus, and Bartolommeo da Saliceto.

164. *Diversorum.* Mostly Umbrian-Perugian, fourteenth and fifteenth century. Rare examples of *consilia* from pen of Florentine, Ristoro Canigiani.

165. *Diversorum.* Almost entirely Perugian. I list it because some of the lawyers here represented, e.g., Sallustio da Perugia (Buonguglielmi), also lived and practiced in Florence.

167. *Diversorum*, mainly fifteenth century. But some items by Francesco Guicciardini and Alessandro Malegonnelli.

171. *Repertorium iuris* of Lorenzo Ridolfi. Glossary of terms, rules, references.

172. Opinions, repetitions, and treatises, both Florentine and Perugian. Second half of fourteenth and early fifteenth century. Of non-Florentines, Bartolus and Baldus predominate; of Florentines, Nello da San Gimignano, Torello Torelli, Alessandro Bencivenni, and Giovanni Buongirolami.

173. *Diversorum.* Mainly second half of fifteenth century. But some items by both earlier (Filippo Corsini, Michele Accolti) and later (Piero Filicaia) lawyers. Rare example of an opinion by Orlando Bonarli (f. 107r), afterwards Archbishop of Florence.

174. *Diversorum.* Fourteenth and fifteenth century, going back to Oldrado da Ponte. Mainly Florentine, Perugian, and Bolognese. Rare examples of opinions by fourteenth-century Florentine lawyers like Donato Aldighieri, Antonio Machiavelli, and Antonio da Romena.

186-187. Two registers of opinions and pleas by Alessandro Bencivenni. Mainly from second decade of fifteenth century. Like most of the other manuscripts listed above, these also are extremely important.

193. *Diversorum*. Mainly fifteenth century. Opinions ranging in time (*ca.* 1400) from Filippo Corsini and Giovanni Serristori to Alessandro Malegonnelli and Marco degli Asini in first half of sixteenth century. Some rare examples by Zanobi Guasconi and Giovanni Bovacchiesi da Prato.

196. *Diversorum*. A few opinions by Angelo and Matteo Niccolini, Niccolò Guicciardini, and Antonio Bonsi. Otherwise, most of the items are late sixteenth century.

*Codici Panciatichiani*:

138. *Consilia legalia diversorum*. Mainly early fifteenth century, with a sprinkling of items by Perugian lawyers.

139. *Diversorum*. Mainly fifteenth century. Some rare examples of opinions by Lapo da Castiglionchio and Virgilio Berti. Otherwise, the important names prevail: Otto Niccolini, Bernardo Buongirolami, Domenico Bonsi, etc.

140. *Diversorum*. All fifteenth century, mainly second half. But some opinions by Marco degli Asini, Alessandro Malegonnelli, Ludovico Acciaiuoli, Filippo Corsini (*ca.* 1395), Bardo Altoviti, Niccolò Guicciardini, and Francesco Gualterotti.

147. *Zibaldone* type manuscript of Lorenzo Ridolfi. No *consilia*.

*Manoscritti Landau Finaly*:

98. *Consilia legalia diversorum*. Florentine-Perugian provenance, fourteenth and fifteenth century. Has some original *consilia* with doctoral seals. Nello da San Gimignano is prominent. Rare examples by Buonaccorso da Montemagno, the humanist-lawyer.

(4) The Vatican Library. The following manuscripts were first brought to my attention by Professor Roberto Abbondanza, Director of the Archivio di Stato in Perugia.

*Vat. Lat.*, 8067, i. A collection of legal opinions, second half of the fifteenth and early sixteenth century. Almost entirely Florentine. All the great Florentine lawyers of the period are here represented. Rare examples of opinions by Paradiso Mazzinghi and Niccolò de' Nobili.

*Vat. Lat.*, 8067, ii. Legal opinions, late fifteenth and early sixteenth century, mainly Florentine. Again the important figures predominate: Francesco Pepi, Domenico Bonsi, Francesco Guicciardini, etc.

*Vat. Lat.*, 8068. Legal opinions from Florence, Perugia, Bologna. Fourteenth and early fifteenth century. The great names prevail.

*Vat. Lat.*, 8069. Some legal opinions from Florence, fourteenth and fifteenth century. Francesco Albergotti and Filippo Corsini much in evidence.

*Vat. Lat.*, 10726. Entitled "Consultationes Baldi et Bartoli." Contains a few opinions by Florentines (Bencivenni, Torello Torelli) and others (Paolo di Castro, Angelo degli Ubaldi) who lived in Florence for a time.

*Vat. Lat.*, 11605. Described by J. Ruysschaert, ed., *Bibl. Apostolicae Vaticanae, Cod. Vat. Lat. 11414-11709* (Vatican, 1959).

*Ottob. Lat.*, 1726. Some *consilia* by Francesco Albergotti, Sallustio da Perugia, Otto Niccolini, Giovanni Buongirolami, Girolamo Machiavelli, Benedetto Accolti, and Piero Ambrosini.

*Ottob. Lat.*, 1727. A collection of *consilia*, mainly Perugian, fourteenth and fifteenth century. Some items from Florence by Piero Ambrosini, Torello Torelli, Alessandro Bencivenni, Nello da San Gimignano, and Paolo di Castro.

*Urb. Lat.*, 1132. Marked "Consilia varia." Fourteenth and fifteenth century, mostly Perugian and central Italian, but with a dozen opinions from Florence.

## Chapter Eleven

# Florence and Milan: Toward the Modern State?

It remains to put the major findings of this study into perspective. Two ways of doing so present themselves: to single out the performance of lawyers elsewhere in Italy and to fix the historical place of the Florentine state. By looking at lawyers in another part of Italy, we avoid the distortions that may arise from leaving the Florentine scene in isolation. I propose, therefore, to focus on Milan, a city-state different enough from Florence to invite comparison. The other proposal, fixing the Florentine state in its historical place, will call for movement back and forth in time and for some risky but necessary generalization.

Roman public law as seen in the *Corpus Iuris Civilis* has considerable material on the rights of cities, on local governing bodies, on corporate as well as individual rights;[1] it was normally assumed that the sovereign state would respect these. But the guiding principle of Justinian's compilation is monarchical, despite the evident ambiguity of the *lex regia*. The *imperium* or fullness of the public power is associated first and foremost with the prince. For this reason, it has sometimes been suggested that because of being trained in Roman law, medieval and Renaissance Italian lawyers, sitting at the right hand of the prince (*signore*, lord, despot), were the natural and necessary accessories of the men who brought the Italian city-states under one-man rule. Nothing, it seems to me, could be more misleading. Despite his training in Roman law, the lawyer was an agent who could adapt himself to any of the various and many political settings found in Italy. Where regional autonomies and local rights were at stake and there was sufficient actual power to give him support, the lawyer might well argue for these. Roman law could provide the grounds. Did not Bartolus and others, using some of the formulas of Roman law, give a juridical basis to the *civitas sibi princeps*,

---

[1] E.g., on local custom and law: *D.* 1, 3, 32-40.

the city-state which separated itself *de facto* from the jurisdiction of the Empire? But where the lawyer was associated with a prince or a "superior city" and the prevailing trend involved the erosion of local rights in favor of centralization, this too he could help accomplish. In short, lawyers could serve a variety of masters. Where one power won out over another, there too the appropriate principle could be made to triumph. The lawyer who was commissioned to look for right on the prevailing side encountered fewer difficulties.[2] Ultimately the law follows the direction of affairs—reality—but at the same time may help to guide affairs. The same law school, Bologna, turned out lawyers who went off to practice in their native republics of Siena, Florence, and Genoa, or in states ruled by so-called despots—Ferrara, Milan, Padua, and so forth. If the trend at Florence in the fifteenth century was toward centralization, the evidence suggests that this was because of political and socio-economic factors first, and because of grinding fiscal strains, not because of the legal opinions of lawyers. Though enormously important, these opinions caused neither the concentration of power in the executive, nor the drift towards signorial rule. They aided and promoted the course of events, certainly that; but they also tended to come after the fact, or when movement in a general direction had already been set off. The outstanding importance of the opinions of lawyers lay in the fact that they provided a necessary legal rationale—as necessary to the Republic, with its elaborate civil mechanisms, as to the subject territories, where suspicion and fear could at times get out of hand and be transformed into rebellion or civil disorder.

## *1. Milan*

On the death of the Emperor Henry VII, in 1313, the Lord of Milan's title to the imperial vicariate was thought in some quarters to have lapsed. Was the vicariate which Henry had granted valid for his own lifetime alone or for the lifetime of Matteo Visconti, *signore* of Milan?

---

[2] B. Paradisi, *Il problema storico del diritto internazionale* (2nd ed., Naples, 1956), p. 173, says that from the fourteenth to the sixteenth century lawyers sought to reconcile legal-political theory with reality, but often ended by "reducing the former to the latter." They based themselves principally on *consuetudo* and prescription.

Milanese lawyers split on the question. Some held that the vicariate terminated with the life of Henry. Others argued that Matteo had been invested with the dignity for life. Matteo thereupon called upon the latter
and sought to base his claims to the title upon their arguments. In September, when the general council of Milan (the Council of Twelve Hundred) proclaimed him "dominus et rector generalis," it was the lawyer
Alberto Taverna who offered a defense of Matteo.[3]

It appears, therefore, that from the beginning of their permanent
*signoria* in Milan the Visconti called lawyers to their side, employed
them to help formulate and vindicate their signorial claims, and indeed
were never to do without them.[4] As in Florence, in Milan too the wielders
of public power sought legitimacy. And so the Visconti used the services
of lawyers in every sector of government and statecraft: in the study
and codification of Milanese statutes, in all branches of public finance, in
the regnant communal councils, in the administration of justice, in territorial government, in diplomacy and relations with the Church, and in
the Consiglio Segreto—the privy council which discussed and decided
all the most important affairs of state.

In 1348 Luchino Visconti had Milan's chief executive body, the Council of Provisions (Consiglio delle Provvisioni), elect a commission to
check over the statutes of 1330. Eleven men were given the job, five of
whom were lawyers. The statutes were re-examined in 1351 by four laymen and two lawyers, Roggero Biffi and Arasmo Aliprandi. These
statutes remained in effect until 1396, when they were again reformed
and reorganized, this time by the Consiglio delle Provvisioni working
together with several lawyers. The statutes of 1396 changed the composition of this very important Consiglio, chief instrument of Viscontean
rule in the capital city itself. The vicar, the presiding official of this
twelve-man body, had to be a foreign lawyer, and two of the twelve had

[3] F. Cognasso, "Le basi giuridiche della signoria di Matteo Visconti in Milano,"
*Bollettino storico bibliografico subalpino*, LIII (1955); and his "L'atto fondamentale
della signoria di Matteo Visconti," *ibid.*, L (1952). In fact, no imperial vicariate
was ever supposed to survive the lifetime of the Emperor who conferred it.

[4] E. Besta, *Il diritto pubblico italiano dagli inizii del secolo decimoprimo alla
seconda metà del secolo decimoquinto* (Padua, 1929), pp. 319-20.

always to be drawn from the Milanese College of Jurists.[5] We may suppose that the initiative in this matter issued from Giangaleazzo's chancellery and circle of advisors, where—as we shall see—lawyers held a prominent place.

From the fourteenth century on, Milanese lawyers always sat as a group in the Council of Twelve Hundred (reduced to 900 after 1329),[6] just as Florentine lawyers, in the late fifteenth and early sixteenth centuries, constituted a distinct group of advisors in the executive consultations conducted by the Signory and sometimes involving 150 to 200 men.

Milanese municipal finances were managed by the Six of the Treasury (Sei della Camera del Comune). The law required that two of these be lawyers, whose stipend was nearly double that of the laymen.[7] But even this ratio does not do justice to the prominence of lawyers in Milanese public finance. For they often stood out as leading financial officials in the immediate entourage of the duke. Thus in the middle 1390s Bartolommeo Benzoni, a doctor of laws from Crema, was master of extraordinary entries, and Uberto Lampugnano, also *doctoratus in utroque iure*, was receiver for the acquisition and sale of ducal goods. In the 1420s, under Filippo Maria Visconti, the first treasurer for some years was another lawyer, Oldrado di Uberto Lampugnano. Niccolò Arcimboldi, a famous lawyer of humanist leanings and a man of encyclopedic knowledge, was master of the ordinary entries in the 1430s.[8]

Appropriately, lawyers also had a large part in the administration of justice. Like Florence, Milan had a multiplicity of courts and executive dignities endowed with special judicial powers, so that here too juris-

---

[5] On this and foregoing items see F. Cognasso in the collaborative *Storia di Milano*, VI (Milano, 1955), 458, 465-66. The *signore* himself elected the twelve.

[6] *Ibid.*, VI, 457.

[7] *Ibid.*, VI, 463. In the course of the fifteenth century two *sindaci* took over some of the powers of the Six: C. Santoro, *Storia di Milano*, VII, 534.

[8] G. Romano, "Regesto degli atti notarili di C. Cristiani, dal 1391 al 1399," *Archivio storico lombardo*, 3rd ser. (September 1894), pp. 34-35, on Benzoni and U. Lampugnano. On the others see the gloss of Butti, Fossati, and Petraglione for the *Vita Philippi Mariae* of P. C. Decembrio, *Opuscula historica*, in RRIISS, XX, fasc. 1-5 (Bologna, 1925-1935), 165ff., 184ff.

dictions often overlapped. There was a special judge on questions connected with roads and rivers, a judge on disputes over customs, and a judge on *vettovaglie* (provisions and victuals).[9] The Podestà of Milan, charged with both civil and penal justice, had six lawyers in his train. From the middle years of the fifteenth century, a foreign lawyer (the Captain of Justice) was the chief judge in criminal cases. Also occupied with the handling of civil proceedings was a court appointed by the Consiglio delle Provvisioni—the Six Consoli, of whom two were lawyers. The Six performed a variety of functions; e.g., they assigned guardian to wards, accorded or denied approval to the lawsuits of women, and certified copies of lost notarial instruments.[10]

But the outstanding tribunals of the later Visconti and Sforza, claiming competence in all the lands of the duchy, were the Consiglio Segreto and the Consiglio di Giustizia. The first of these claimed jurisdiction over crime concerning matters of state; the second was particularly active in civil proceedings which, for whatever reason, the executive elected to draw under its tutelage. Again, the Secret Council could receive cases in appeal from the Council of Justice, but no further appeal was possible. Being directly under the dukes of Milan,[11] these two councils also enjoyed great executive powers. Indeed, the Secret Council was the duchy's supreme magistracy, equivalent to the Signory in Florence. Just as Florence saw the judiciary subjected to the invasion of the executive in the course of the fifteenth century, so too in Milan the Consiglio Segreto and the Consiglio di Giustizia tended "to invade the field which belonged to others"—mainly to ordinary judges. There was a growing wave of complaints, and the duke, in February 1473, was at last forced to decree that any councillor who heard and determined a case lying outside his jurisdiction was to be fined the enormous sum of 1,000 gold ducats, unless he had obtained a special license to deal with it.[12] More will be said about the Secret Council in another connection. Of the Con-

---

[9] Santoro, *Storia di Milano*, VII, 534.

[10] E. Verga, "Le sentenze criminali dei podestà milanesi, 1385-1429," *Archivio storico lombardo*, 3rd ser., XVI (1901), 101-02; Santoro, *Storia di Milano*, VII, 537-38.

[11] D. M. Bueno de Mesquita, *Giangaleazzo Visconti, Duke of Milan (1351-1402)* (Cambridge, 1941), p. 57.

[12] Santoro, *Storia di Milano*, VII, 522-23. The words "to invade the field," etc., are Professoressa Santoro's.

siglio di Giustizia, a tribunal more than a political body, we may note that it was composed of three to five judges who were ordinarily appointed for life. Leading churchmen and outstanding lawyers were the sort of men most often called to serve in this council.[13]

The holding of inquests into the conduct of officials, at the end of their term in office—called "syndication"—seems to have had a slightly more professional organization at Milan than at Florence.[14] In fifteenth-century Milan, the men who held these inquests were known as Vicars General. Required to have a degree in law, they were nearly always six in number and were recruited from the principal families.[15] Vicars General made up a court which fell directly under the jurisdiction of the executive. Apart from conducting their ordinary inquests and trials, on commission from the duke (or his secretaries and Secret Council) they also proceeded summarily in civil, criminal, and mixed cases.

There is no need to dwell on the critical place of lawyers in Milanese diplomacy. They were men not easily surpassed in diplomatic negotiation or in the shrewd drafting of treaties and other types of documents. This, at least, was their reputation in Florence. The lawyers and *condottieri* of the later Visconti were the Florentine Republic's most dangerous and persistent antagonists, at the conference tables no less than on the field of battle. Again and again, when confronting Giangaleazzo's counsellors and diplomats or those of Filippo Maria,[16] the Florentine Signory had to take the most precautionary measures, rely on the acumen of its lawyers to a remarkable degree, and strive to obtain arrangements or agreements which expressed things with the utmost clarity. Otherwise— such was the assumption—the Republic ran the risk of being entangled in damaging ambiguities and delays. Moreover, since the Visconti rarely if ever failed to have brilliant lawyers among their leading diplomats, Florence, in its dealings with the Lombard "tyrants," could not fail to strive in the same fashion, Niccolò Spinelli, a Neapolitan lawyer of international fame, was Giangaleazzo's leading counsellor on questions of foreign policy in the late 1380s and 1390s. He professed law at Padua,

[13] *Ibid.*, p. 523.
[14] On syndication in Florence see pp. 143-45.
[15] C. Santoro, *Gli uffici del dominio sforzesco, 1450-1500* (Milano, 1948), p. xxix.
[16] See Ch. VIII.

Bologna, and finally Pavia.[17] Two other lawyers of note who conducted many embassies for the same lord were Piero da Corte and Bartolommeo Benzoni.[18] In the 1420s and 1430s, Taddiolo da Vicomercate, Niccolò Arcimboldi, and Franchino and Guarnerio Castiglione were four of Filippo Maria Visconti's top diplomats and experts on foreign policy. All four practiced law. Taddiolo professed canon law at Padua and Pavia; Franchino and Guarnerio also held professorships at Pavia; and Arcimboldi, who took his doctorate at Pavia *in utroque iure*, probably studied under Guarnerio.[19]

Even in moments when these men were not actually at the site of negotiations, the diplomacy of the later Visconti can never ultimately have been conducted beyond the scrutiny of lawyers. For by a decree of August 1385, Giangaleazzo ruled that henceforth all incoming foreign ambassadors must present themselves to his Secret Council, which would provide them with answers "ad plenum."[20] Furthermore, important treaties and other diplomatic agreements were drawn up in this council or had to be discussed and approved by it; and it was a council which nearly always claimed two or three lawyers among its members.

Made into a regular organ of government by Giangaleazzo Visconti,[21] the Secret Council was to remain the supreme executive and judicial body of Milan until the later fifteenth century, when a still smaller advisory council branched off from it. It was to the Secret Council that the later Visconti and Sforza regularly turned for advice and guidance on all the gravest questions of state, foreign and domestic. In the 1440s this council numbered ten members; in 1402, under Giangaleazzo, there were twelve.

[17] G. Romano, "Niccolò Spinelli da Giovinazzo, diplomatico del secolo xiv," *Archivio storico per le provincie napoletane*, xxiv-xxvi (1899-1901).

[18] E.g., *I Capitoli del comune di Firenze*, ed. C. Guasti and A. Gherardi, 2 vols. (Firenze, 1866-1893), ii, 114; Romano, "Regesto," p. 22.

[19] On the foregoing men and facts: G. Romano, "Contributi alla storia della ricostituzione del ducato milanese sotto Filippo Maria Visconti (1412-1421)," *Archivio storico lombardo*, xxiv (March, 1897), 118, 134; Decembrio, *Vita Philippi Mariae* (ed. cit.), pp. 184ff., 175ff., 362ff.; *Memorie e documenti per la storia dell' università di Pavia e degli uomini più illustri che v'insegnarono* (Pavia, 1877-1878), p. 29.

[20] Cognasso, *Storia di Milano*, vi, 489-90.

[21] P. del Giudice, "I consigli ducali e il senato di Milano," *Nuovi studi di storia e diritto* (Milano, 1913), pp. 227-28.

But between 1450 and 1499 the number of secret councillors rose from twelve to a peak of thirty in 1481, and then fell to seven at the end of the century. During this fifty-year period, a total of 263 men were officially connected with the Secret Council.[22] Most of them were soldiers of fortune and noblemen bred to the profession of arms. Some were prelates; others still were politically talented favorites. But more than fifty, or about one-fifth the total, were lawyers, many of whom held or had held law professorships: for example, Alberico Maletta, Francesco Accolti, Giovanni da Vicomercate, and Otto de Careto. Giangaleazzo's circle of prominent secret councillors juxtaposed soldiers and noblemen like Antonio Porro, Jacopo dal Verme, Guglielmo Bevilacqua, and Francesco Barbavara with lawyers like Niccolò Spinelli, Bartolommeo Benzoni, Uberto Lampugnano, Piero da Corte, Filippo Casoli, Giovanni da Carnago, Riccardo Villani, and Filippo Millio.[23] Five of the lawyers in Filippo Maria's train of advisors have already been named: Arcimboldi, Franchino and Guarnerio Castiglione, Oldrado Lampugnano, and Taddiolo da Vicomercate. There were at least three others: Antonio Gentili da Tortona, Jacopo Isolano, who taught law at Pavia and was cardinal deacon of St. Eustachio, and Giovanni Feruffini, ordinary professor of canon law at Pavia from 1424 on. Two of Filippo's secretaries and closest advisors were notaries: Gian Francesco Gallina and Giovanni Corvini d'Arezzo. They disposed of enormous influence.[24]

Taken in the context of this study as a whole, the foregoing summary review of names and key functions may suffice to point up the critical place of lawyers in Milanese statecraft. A careful count would undoubtedly reveal that lawyers were more massively deployed by the Milanese state (and probably also by other states under one-man rule) than by the

[22] This and the following figure drawn from the immensely valuable lists in C. Santoro, *Gli uffici*, pp. 3ff., who tries to indicate all who had degrees in law but misses a few: e.g., Niccolò Arcimboldi and Oldrado Lampugnano, whom I add to her forty-eight jurists. Hence the figure fifty is an absolute minimum. Perhaps another ten or twelve of Santoro's total of 263 secret councillors were also trained in law.

[23] Romano, "Niccolò Spinelli," xxvi (1901), 429; Bueno de Mesquita, *Giangaleazzo Visconti*, pp. 180-82, 235-36; on Casoli (Caxolis), Millio (Milleis), Carnago, and Villani see Romano, "Regesto," pp. 22, 31, 33, 70.

[24] Decembrio, *Vita Philippi Mariae*, gloss on pp. 180-89, 370ff.; also Romano, "Contributi," p. 131.

Florentine Republic. Often *déracinés*, these men became the pliable civil servants of despotism, which might seem to acquire a more convincing aura of legality by involving teams of lawyers. It was for this reason that Florence was chosen as the focus of this study. For where all important officials were appointed by the *signore* and his leading counsellors, and where conduct in public affairs was more securely under a central, continuous guidance, there the political activity of lawyers was bound to be more cut and dried, and a study of their achievement much easier to organize. By contrast, Florence offered a more open, more challenging field. Yet one result of the comparison with Milan is already obvious: the emerging evidence of a similarity between the two states, at all events in connection with the role of lawyers in public affairs. The parallelism is not accidental. As we shall see in what follows, though with regard to another set of problems, structural-functional similarities between Florence and Milan provided the ground for the political prominence of lawyers in both places.

## 2. *The Course of Change*

What kind of a state were Florentine lawyers helping to mold? Where did it stand with reference to the medieval commune and the modern state? What were its distinguishing features? These are hard but unavoidable questions—hard because all the information is not yet in. The preceding chapter refers to Renaissance Florence as a "territorial state." The designation is correct, but the description will have to be more precise.

The Commune of medieval Florence was a loosely appointed *universitas*, consisting of a multiplicity of corporations: trade guilds, merchant societies, associations of noblemen and burghers, sometimes secret and sometimes not, but usually with a large stake in public affairs. Privileges and immunities, judicial and fiscal, abounded. The country around Florence, *contado* and beyond, was also infested with immunities and local customs; and the capital city's controls there were often so minimal that it seems premature to speak of that land as "subject territory," when we are thinking of the twelfth and thirteenth centuries. Again, our loosely appointed *universitas* not infrequently had more than one head *de facto*: associations of noblemen and burghers, consuls and Podestà, Podestà and Captain of the People, or supreme communal officials and leading guilds—signs of the social struggle within the Commune and of the rivalry between powerful corporate bodies.

Some elements of judicial privilege and a good deal of local custom survived the Republic and passed over into the principate. But it would be unreasonable to hold that fifteenth-century Florence was identical in these matters with the thirteenth-century Commune. The differences between the two were on a scale which requires that the new state of the fifteenth century—the Renaissance state, the territorial state, call it what we will—be seen as neither medieval nor modern but as *sui generis*: a state somewhere between, having certain of the features of each and yet really answering to the description of neither. For by the end of the fourteenth century, the old nobility had been destroyed or domesticated and the new nobility, not fully to emerge until the end of the fifteenth century, would regularly make its influence felt by using the Republic's established agencies—the leading offices, executive consultations, special *pratiche*, and embassies.[25] The powerful guilds of the later thirteenth century were now wholly subject to the Florentine state. A special republican commission, the Approvers of the Guild Statutes, saw to it that all guild regulations, old and new, fully accorded with the laws and ordinances of the Republic. From the late fourteenth century, even the greatest of the *arti* (the Cambio and Lana guilds) no longer had any independent political weight. Semipublic corporations, they retained their guild courts, but much of their earlier competence was whittled away. Appeal against their decisions, especially those of the minor guilds, was legal and more easily granted; and in the realm of commercial litigation, a good deal of consolidation and higher authority was introduced by the flourishing Tribunale di Mercanzia, a supra-guild court which also had jurisdiction over international lawsuits.[26]

[25] When there was the serious threat of conspiracy, as in 1497, 1512, and the late 1520s, we must remember that it always centered on the princely family—the Medici. Besides, we cannot use the touchstone of conspiracy to distinguish the medieval or Renaissance state from the modern state. Or are conspiracy and *coups d'état* something unknown to modern states?

[26] F. Valsecchi, *Comune e corporazioni nel medio evo italiano* (Milano, 1949), pp. 96-114, is good on Florentine guilds in the thirteenth and early fourteenth centuries, though he tends to exaggerate their *independent* power. But he says

The corresponding growth in the authority of public magistracies was not in the first place the work of lawyers. On the contrary, in a certain sense the lawyer as a dominant figure in statecraft was the work of the state. The state gave the lead and kept the initiative. As the authority of the state and its offices grew, becoming more complex, lawyers were called on to help justify the new trend, to help iron out conflicts of jurisdiction and administrative snarls, to settle constitutional questions, to protect the rights already won by the state and to defend the new ones being wrested from the strongholds of particularism.

Custom and some privileges persisted in the territory. But these rights were carefully watched in the fifteenth century by the "superior city" and in some places and sectors reduced or suppressed, occasionally by a stroke, more often by a process of erosion. The direction of change was toward centralization, and if this trend in Milan was at times less institutional than personal (being associated with the person of the prince), in Florence the process was more truly organic, more securely absorbed into the constitution. If up to a certain point Milanese lawyers in government were engaged in carrying out orders, lawyers in Florence were more nearly the "instruments" of an impersonal trend, were more in tune with the times.

Centralization provided the direction of change, but change took place in concrete matters. During the fifteenth century, the Florentine dominion was drawn more fully under the control or government of the capital city. As at Milan,[27] so at Florence the statutes of all subject communes had periodically to be submitted to the *civitas superior* for approval. This rule had not been much observed even in the fourteenth century, but

---

absolutely nothing about their status in the fifteenth century. As late as about 1420 the lawyer Alessandro Bencivenni did not consider the foreign magistrate of the Mercanzia court "an official of the city but of the *universitas* of merchants." BNF, *Fondo principale*, II, II, 435, f. 1r. This was pure *de iure* argument. In fact, the court was under the control of the Signory and legislative councils, which in the fifteenth century periodically enacted legislation changing its jurisdiction and functions.

[27] G. Barni, "La formazione interna dello stato visconteo," *Archivio storico lombardo*, NS, VI, i-iv (1941), 48-51, where he also points out that the decrees of the Visconti princes could and did overrule the statutes of subject communes; see also F. Cognasso, "Note e documenti sulla formazione dello stato visconteo," *Bollettino della società pavese di storia patria*, XXII, i-iv (1923), 113.

now it was; and when a violation occurred, either from neglect or for another reason, Florence did not hesitate to impose her own statutes, as the *consilia* of Florentine lawyers clearly show. Surrounded by lawyers, the lords of Milan had no trouble getting competent officials to run through collections of statutes awaiting the approval of the *princeps*. The Republic delegated this job to *ad hoc* commissions, but a preliminary on-the-spot review was almost certainly carried out by the podestàs and vicars sent out from Florence with attendant lawyers and notaries.

Again, a man proscribed in Florence was under the same ban everywhere in Florentine territory. A similar law obtained in lands under Milanese rule, though there seems to have been more trouble there with men proscribed. Another feature of centralization concerned exiles. Florence alone claimed and jealously enforced the right to banish men from her territories. When subject towns and communes tried to usurp this right, they were reprimanded and the sentences revoked.[28]

The Florentine Republic and the dukes of Milan dispatched governors and judges into their subject lands. These men administered justice, were especially charged to beware of civil disorder, policed the areas under their jurisdiction, relayed orders from above to local councils, and were also in other respects the eyes of the capital city in the provinces. In addition, Florentine vicars and podestàs presided over the meetings of local communal assemblies. Observing a policy of expedience, Florence tolerated small pockets of feudal jurisdiction along its borders. But survivals of this type were not nearly as extensive and tenacious as their counterparts in Lombardy, where ancient and new feudal lords occasionally lived lawlessly and resisted or merely ignored public authority. The problems raised by these *signoroni* were to plague the Milanese state for as long as the Visconti and Sforza ruled the duchy.[29] On this score—as

[28] There was a statute on this and it was applied. Cited in a case of *ca.* 1415 by the lawyer Alessandro Bencivenni, BNF, *Magl.*, xxix, 186, ff. 22v-23r, and substantiated by Tommaso Salvetti's *Commentaria* (*ca.* 1450) on Florentine statutes. Salvetti was cited on this by Antonio Strozzi in a ruling of November 1516, *Strozz.*, *3a ser.*, 41/9, ff. 571r *et seq.*

[29] See especially D. M. Bueno de Mesquita, "Ludovico Sforza and His Vassals," *Italian Renaissance Studies*, ed. E. F. Jacob (New York, 1960), pp. 184-216. But it is also important to note that the Visconti fought the old feudal nobility, tore down their castles, and ruined the most powerful of the Milanese families (e.g.,

well as others—Florence was in advance of the most authoritarian of the Italian states. Its territories exhibited greater unity; they were more centralized. The Florentine dominion never disintegrated overnight, owing to internal particularisms, as did the empire of the Visconti in 1402 and again in 1447.

Both Republic and duchy imposed tax quotas on their subject lands. The lords of Milan developed a fiscal agent who had no parallel in republican Florence. The *referendario*—there was one in every city under Milanese rule—was at first a checker of accounts. He was often chosen locally. In the course of the fifteenth century his powers grew: he auctioned off customs and gabelles, received ducal revenues, and licensed payments made by the local treasurer. In some places he was also a magistrate, his office having been united with that of judge in disputes concerning customs and gabelles.[30] Although there was no Florentine equivalent of this official, it has yet to be proved that the Milanese system was more efficient. Relying on its local governors and messengers, the Republic, generally speaking, did not have excessive trouble collecting its territorial tax quotas, save when these were ruinous.

If the *consilia* of its lawyers are any sure indication, Florence was strongly inclined to support and defend the rights, fiscal and otherwise, of lesser subject communities against larger ones, thereby keeping down the strength of the major territorial units. Milan also observed this practice.[31]

Neither Florence nor Milan suffered their citizens or subject lands to promote activity which disturbed the civil order or to display unruly resistance in matters concerning the fisc. Under the later Visconti and Sforza, the Secret Council (or other officials deputized by it) moved with the maximum severity, usually employing summary proceedings, against seditious activity wherever it occurred in Milanese territory. The same fusion of executive and judicial powers also dealt with serious out-

---

the Torriani and Pusterla). Then they set about creating a new group of feudatories whose loyalty and obedience they meant thereby to hold. See Barni, "La formazione," p. 40; Cognasso, *Storia di Milano*, VI, 482-84.

[30] Santoro, *Gli uffici*, pp. xxxi-xxxii.

[31] Cognasso, *Storia di Milano*, VI, 511.

breaks of civil disorder. In this and in other respects there was a close parallel between the Milanese Secret Council on the one hand and the Florentine Signory, when acting together with the Eight, on the other. For the Signory and the Eight on Public Safety often took concerted action against treason, subversion, or disorder in the dominion. In fact, from the second half of the fifteenth century—and here is another sign of the drive toward a unitary state in Renaissance Florence—the Eight entered freely into criminal affairs all over Florentine territory. Well before the end of the century, they are to be found sending directives and summary sentences on even minor criminal and mixed cases to captains and podestàs in all parts of the dominion. It is not at all clear that the lords of Milan disposed of an equivalent magistracy, although their Secret Council had powers which in theory admitted such intervention.

One far-reaching Florentine innovation was wholly an achievement of the regenerate Republic: the Florentine Rota or Council of Justice established in 1502. First composed of five foreign lawyers and then six, one of whom served as Podestà or presiding magistrate, this civil tribunal survived the Republic and continued to be extremely important under the principate. It was something of a cross between the Vicars General and the Council of Justice in Milan, but with these differences. The Rota's organization and functions were more regular; it observed ordinary rather than extraordinary procedure; and it was perhaps more impartial and more rigorously professional, for unlike its Milanese correspondents, it was made up entirely of foreign lawyers. The Florentine Rota made few inroads on the judicial powers of the executive. But as the preceding chapter shows, it was in the name of the Rota's chief magistrate, the Podestà, that the opinions and decisions of Florentine lawyers were dispatched into the territories, where they promoted the judicial prerogatives of the capital city in ways and to a degree which had never been seen before.

Emphasis has been given to the movement toward political centralization in Renaissance Florence, the movement to bring certain sectors of public life under a more unitary control. The fractionalism of the medieval Commune was not vanquished by the rising new state, but it was so reduced, undermined, or otherwise changed that new names and adjectives must be used of Florentine political forms at the time of the Renaissance.

Having looked back to the early Commune and then to the movement toward centralization, we must look forward now to see whether or not the course of change was toward the modern state.

The modern state has sometimes been described as follows: a sovereign juridical order, tending to claim exclusive jurisdiction and to be, by means of its legislative activity, the sole source of law. Adopting unitary and centralizing mechanisms, it puts an end to particularism. Its constitutional organization inclines to accord with the theory of the separation of powers—legislative, judicial, and executive. One of its fundamental principles is that of the absolute sovereignty of the law, which goes with the view that legislation rather than custom should regulate the affairs of men. Owing to the supposition that the reform of society is one of the chief ends of political organization (a legacy of the French Revolution), the executive sector of the modern state has undergone an unparalleled development, entailing the rise of a large bureaucracy and a massive corpus of administrative law.[32]

Some European states did not accord with this model until the late nineteenth century or even after. That sovereign nation, the United States of America, which leaves some exceedingly important matters to the rights and legislation of individual states, does not answer to the above description in at least that one respect. In England customary law still holds a very critical place in the legal order of things. As for Nazi Germany, whether or not the law there was absolutely sovereign is a question, one which may also be raised in connection with South American military dictatorships.

Evidently the model does not fit fifteenth-century Florence or Milan.

---

[32] Modelled on the description in G. Astuti, *Lezioni di storia del diritto italiano: la formazione dello stato moderno in Italia* (Torino, 1957), I, 21-31. Looking back from the modern period, Astuti stresses (pp. 50ff.) the multiplicity of local rights, jurisdictions, and autonomies in sixteenth-century Italy. Had he been looking at the sixteenth century from the standpoint of the twelfth and thirteenth centuries, his emphasis would have been otherwise. The play of viewpoints here introduces an insoluble dialectical problem, unless we admit the existence of a distinctive Renaissance state.

For within the boundaries of these two states, as in other European states of the Renaissance, lived a large number of men in holy orders who were governed, at least in part, by a separate law. In this respect, even France and Spain were not sovereign states in the sixteenth century, though Spain was at the peak of its powers. Again, in authoritarian Milan, the prince not only disposed of full judicial powers, he also made laws by means of decrees. Hence the three functions of government could be performed there by a single body—the prince and his counsellors, or even by the prince alone. At Florence, except at times when extraordinary *balìe* temporarily held absolute power, there were signs of a tripartite division of authority, and certainly the power to legislate was cleanly divided from the executive power. During the fifteenth century, the tribunals of the Podestà, the Mercanzia, and the guild courts would have constituted a distinct judicial sphere in Florence, had it not been for the fact that the executive, breaking all precedent, invaded the judiciary, above all in the area of penal justice. The separation of powers had been much sharper in the fourteenth century, when the foreign magistrates—Podestà, Captain, Appellate Judge, and Esecutore—were leading dignitaries who presided over a vigorous and forceful system of courts.

In other respects, however, the direction of institutional change at Florence and Milan was toward the modern absolute state. The medieval Italian commune harbored a rich fund of legislative initiative and a ready talent for the drafting of statutes. An old and practiced facility was thus waiting to be harnessed by a state with a tougher center: the new territorial or Renaissance state. In fifteenth-century Florence, hardly a sector of economic, social, or political life was left untouched by statutes. Even marriage was taxed. And if large areas of economic activity came under the regulation of the guilds,[33] we must not forget that these in turn were

[33] P. J. Jones, "Communes and Despots: The City State in Late-Medieval Italy," *Transactions of the Royal Historical Society*, 5th Ser., xv (1965), p. 92, says that "in Milan and certain other towns, the powers of the courts merchant were actually increased." He cites F. Valsecchi, *Comune e corporazioni nel medio evo italiano*, pp. 60-72, and G. Salvioli, *Storia della procedura civile e criminale*, pt. 2 (Milano, 1925), pp. 97-103, but the pages cited actually emphasize the state's growing control over guilds, and Salvioli (p. 99) notes that merchant courts at Venice and Milan had a "scarso sviluppo." G. Barbieri, *Economia e politica nel ducato di*

under the close surveillance of the state. Not custom but legislation is what directly governed the public life of Florentines, who had an ardent belief in the power of laws to regulate and modify the affairs of men and even to make them live in a civil fashion. Only on rare occasions, when for some reason there happened not to be a covering statute, did Florentines revert or resort directly to custom, to procedure whose very nature required that it be put into the hands of lawyers. The customary or common law was a written law—the *Corpus Iuris Civilis,* and whenever Florence elected to accept its contingent validity, it did so by legislative enactment.[34] Regarding temporal affairs, in Florence as in Milan, there was no higher authority *de iure* or *de facto,* no other maker of the laws, than the state itself.

A review has been presented of some of the unitary, more centralized features of the new state. The trend was manifest in the field of public finance, in the administration of justice, in the stricter controls imposed on the lawmaking powers of subject communities, and in the executive's readiness and ability to police the territories and to conduct inquests there.[35] Subject statutes had no validity if they contradicted statutes made by the organs of the state, and all disputes between subject lands had to be heard and determined by judicial bodies which belonged to the jurisdiction of the executive, unless the executive elected to turn such cases over to one of the state's regular courts.

One of the most remarkable features of the new state—a feature born of the drive toward centralization—is best appreciated by noting one aspect of the performance of lawyers in statecraft. In Milan, as in Florence, the executive acquired more and more judicial powers and pre-

---

*Milano, 1386-1537* (Milano, 1938), pp. 37ff., 97ff., also cited by Jones, says that the court of the *lanaioli,* which had already lost some power, acquired additional jurisdiction in the fifteenth century; it did so, however, not at the expense of the state but of the guild of *grandi mercanti.* Moreover, as Santoro has noted, all *lanaioli* cases involving claims above a certain sum required the intervention of that powerful official, always a lawyer, the *vicario* or president of the Consiglio delle Provvisioni.

[34] See pp. 92n, 419.

[35] This is not to say that peace reigned in all subject lands. Civil disorder got out of hand at Pistoia, e.g., in 1499-1501. But interestingly, Milan seems to have had much more of this type of trouble than Florence. We may attribute this to Lombard feudatories.

rogatives, thereby moving toward the absolute state. The result was that laymen (the lords of Milan, the Florentine Signory and adjuncts) were increasingly confronted with judicial business which required experts to be in attendance. In Milan and Florence, as in other city-states, this problem was immediately solved by calling lawyers to the forefront of government. They served as the prince's counsellors in Milan; in Florence they counselled the officials belonging to the executive cluster and served directly in all the top offices of state.

The question is, why did the executive branch of the new state draw a growing and then a massive volume of judicial business under its jurisdiction? Why the many judicial commissions and *ad hoc* teams of lawyers which operated under the sponsorship of the executive? To my knowledge, this question has never been asked in the context of the route travelled by the new state. One answer has already been given in other parts of this inquiry. A narrowing and progressively bolder oligarchy used all the resources at its disposal to fortify its position and seize additional power. An obvious device was to fuse regulative, police, and judicial functions. Behind this trend toward narrowing oligarchy were critical economic and social determinants.[36] At Milan in the fourteenth century, the developing union between executive and judiciary was a function of the rising fortunes of the Visconti, faced with the need to develop tighter controls. The personal ambitions of family were a factor here.

But the question raised may also be considered from a strict constitutional viewpoint, one involving the very nature of the emerging state.

In evolving from the medieval commune—a stronghold of immunities, autonomies, and special rights—how *was* the new state to take form, if not at the expense of these? How was it to develop a system of centralized controls, how really have any superior authority, save by waging war, however guardedly, against some of the old privileges and particularisms? An undertaking of this magnitude could only devolve upon the executive —that branch of government where the quotidian power of the state was most focused. And thus, as in the modern state, although from

[36] See pp. 55-57, 403-04.

different causes, Renaissance Florence and Milan saw a tremendous burgeoning of the executive. As every student of the period knows, the corporate privileges of the communal age were tenacious in the extreme. Many were not to be removed until almost modern times. In the face of such resistance, the state needed every resource. On occasion—particularly when threatened—it reacted with violence. More often it resorted to legal pretense. Normally, however, it moved gradually, cautiously, in accordance with legal forms and accepted procedures. This meant bringing urban privileges and provincial autonomies into question. And because these were stubbornly defended, the attack on them, judicial and political, was best conducted by the most forceful sector of the public power—the executive.

The question may be asked, why was legislation not used? It *was* used, though with better results at home than in the territories, where resistance was natural, coming from subject lands with strong local traditions and with absolutely no political representation in the councils of the prince or of the *civitas superior*. Furthermore, apposite legislation could be neither thorough nor systematic; this would have required not only that lawmakers have a long-range policy but also that they have a clear-cut conception of the emerging new state. This was clearly not possible. Problems were handled as they arose, and oftentimes the executive alone was there to do the handling. Apart from urging the application of old and new laws concerning the priorities of the state, the executive also sponsored or conducted its own inquests and trials. Although the sovereign power of the Florentine people was normally in the legislative councils, the offices belonging to the executive cluster were the most mobile and could most easily focus their authority. They freely investigated and adjudicated matters that reached from the highest affairs of state to the lowliest individual. By this means, guided by both legislation and Roman public law, the Florentine state tamed the guilds, reduced unruly families to obedience, harnessed the power of the Parte Guelfa, and brought clerical privileges under a stricter surveillance. In the same way subject lands were gradually stripped of tax immunities, of supreme appellate courts, of jurisdiction over civil disorder and crime against the state, and of the power to legislate at will. The rights of these lands over lesser communities were also sharply curtailed and in many cases entirely eliminated.

In the foregoing work of readjustment and eradication—which, contrary to all scholarly opinion, in some ways went farther at Florence than under despotic states—the most important single figure was the lawyer.[37] He was called on not only to defend and extend the sovereign claims of the Visconti and the *civitas sibi princeps*, but also to help appoint and govern their territorial empires.

Coming up against other rising entities with sovereign pretensions, the new state brought forth or perfected norms of international conduct and a new diplomacy. To this the fifteenth-century papacy made a contribution, primarily because its growing power put increasing diplomatic strains on the Renaissance state. These were developments which served to make the lawyer a strategic agent in the statecraft both of the Visconti and of republican Florence.

Modes of government at Milan and Florence were more alike than has hitherto been thought. Many of the same problems and the same resistance to authority were met in both Lombardy and Tuscany, and the development of the new state form was along similar lines, resulting eventually in similar doctrines. Perhaps the essential general difference is that the machinery of the Florentine state was more organic and self-sufficient. With the possible exception of the periods 1480-1494 and 1512-1527, Florentines had no single hand which descended from on high and settled things as if with a stroke.

In the sixteenth century the dukes of Tuscany, pursuing a policy of absolutism, were to surround themselves with a large number of lawyers, often *déracinés*.[38] Casting back and forth in time and weighing things, we may wish to say that lawyers were the architects of the absolute state in northern as in central Italy. But they were also its issue. In the thirteenth

---

[37] The notary in the circuit of major notarial offices ran him a close second.

[38] The foreign lawyers around Cosimo I were powerful figures: Cristiano Pagni (from Pescia), Jacopo Guidi (Volterra), Jacopo Polverini (Prato), Alfonso Quistelli (Mirandola), Francesco Vinta (Volterra), and Lelio Torelli (Fano). They were ducal counsellors, fiscal auditors, special consultants, judges, auditors on legislation, and secretaries (Torelli). See especially A. Anzilotti, *La costituzione interna dello stato fiorentino sotto il duca Cosimo I de' Medici* (Firenze, 1910), pp. 35, 44-46, 80, 119-20, 134-39, 158-59, 173.

century, the classical age of communal strife, certain lawyers already called for an extension of the executive's effective public authority. Actual movement in this direction, however, had to await the rise of signorial rule or the toughening and narrowing of oligarchies. From this time on the executive enlisted the services of lawyers and consciously turned them to its uses. So called upon, the lawyer as a key figure in statecraft was the product of the developing new state. But as an instrument of the executive, he also fashioned the things within his sphere of competence: he helped to make and bring forth a new polity. In the course of the fifteenth century, though the trend was not yet irreversible, Florence experienced the opening phase of the absolute state. Relying on the guidance and backing of lawyers, it is then that the executive began to sweep all things public under its jurisdiction.

### SOURCES FOR CHAPTER ELEVEN

The aims of this inquiry demanded that I consider Milanese government and statecraft in connection with the problems that arose from studying Florence. A gradual realization of the many similarities between the two cities and their territories is what has led me to speak of the "new state." The conclusion was arrived at independently; only by accident does it touch on the articles of F. Chabod, "Y a-t-il un état de la Renaissance?," *Actes du Colloque sur la Renaissance* (Paris, 1958); W. K. Ferguson, "Toward the Modern State," *The Renaissance: Six Essays* (New York, Harper Torchbook ed., 1962); G. Mattingly, "Some Revisions of the Political History of the Renaissance," *The Renaissance: A Reconsideration*, ed. T. Helton (Wisconsin, 1961); and Mattingly "Changing Attitudes Towards the State During the Renaissance," *Facets of the Renaissance* (New York, Harper Torchbooks, 1963). A richer, more comprehensive article (monograph really) is G. Masi, "Verso gli albori del principato in Italia," *Rivista di storia del diritto italiano*, IX (1936). Suggestive and fresh in approach, but polemical and too condensed, is the piece by P. J. Jones, "Communes and Despots: The City State in Late-Medieval Italy," *Transactions of the Royal Historical Society*, 5th Series, XV (1956), which argues against the idea of a "Renaissance state" and seems to end, oddly, by equating the fifteenth-century territorial state with the thirteenth-century commune. There is too much reliance in this article on secondary works, which in turn rely excessively on statutes. But practice might be one thing and statutes something else.

On the modern state I have found G. Astuti, *Lezioni di storia del diritto italiano: la formazione dello stato moderno in Italia* (Torino, 1957) especially useful.

Some superb work has been done on Milan in the past two generations, principally by G. Romano, F. Cognasso, and C. Santoro. Students of their work will recognize my debt. The labors of Cognasso and Santoro are best seen and synthesized in vols. v-vii of the new *Storia di Milano* (Milano, 1955-1956), published under the auspices of the Fondazione Treccani degli Alfieri.

Two important articles by Cognasso are: "Note e documenti sulla formazione dello stato visconteo," *Bollettino della società pavese di storia patria*, xxiii (1923), and "Ricerche per la storia dello stato visconteo," *ibid.*, xxv (1925). A book which I have found immensely valuable is C. Santoro, *Gli uffici del dominio sforzesco, 1450-1500* (Milano, 1948).

The publications by G. Romano of particular importance for this study are the following: "Regesto degli atti notarili di C. Cristiani, dal 1391 al 1399," *Archivio storico lombardo*, 3rd ser., xxi (September 1894), 5-86; "Contributi alla storia della ricostituzione del ducato milanese sotto Filippo Maria Visconti (1412-1421)," *ASL*, xxiii (December, 1896), 231ff.; xxiv (March, 1897), 67ff.; "Niccolò Spinelli da Giovinazzo, diplomatico del secolo xiv," *Archivio storico per le provincie napoletane*, xxiv-xxvi (1899-1901).

There is a treasury of biographical information in the gloss for the most recent edition of P. C. Decembrio's *Vita Philippi Mariae*, ed. A. Butti, F. Fossati, and G. Petraglione, in *RRIISS*, xx, i-v (Bologna, 1925-1935).

In addition to the works by Cognasso and Santoro on the Milanese state and Milanese institutions, there are the following important books and articles: D. M. Bueno de Mesquita, *Giangaleazzo Visconti, Duke of Milan: 1351-1402* (Cambridge, 1941); G. Barni, "La formazione interna dello stato visconteo," *ASL*, vi, i-vi (1941), 3-66; G. Barbieri, *Economia e*

477

*politica nel ducato di Milano, 1386-1535* (Milano, 1938); and P. del Giudice, "I consigli ducali e il senato di Milano," an article first published in 1899 and reprinted in his *Nuovi studi di storia e diritto* (Milano, 1913). On the Milanese church there is the outstanding study by L. Prosdocimi, *Il diritto ecclesiastico dello stato di Milano* (Milano, 1941).

*Appendix*

# Lawyers in Florence: 1380-1530

There are four groups of lawyers in the following profiles: (1) men from old Florentine families, (2) new men, (3) "outsiders"—lawyers from the dominion or beyond, and (4) a miscellany. The first three answer to a social classification explained in Chapter III, 1. Though the list of outsiders reflects a geographical factor, social concerns are also present there. To be a practicing foreign lawyer in Florence was to come up against a bulwark of social and political obstacles, unless a few of the great families (or the Medici house) made it their business to provide introductions and a forceful, sustained backing.

The fourth category of lawyers, designated "A Miscellany," does not have a social basis and includes Florentines as well as outsiders. I collected their names and the attached information from a variety of sources. Some of these men taught law for a few years at Florence or Pisa and then passed from the Florentine scene. They were not matriculated in the guild of lawyers; the civilians among them (e.g., Machiavelli's father) did not practice law; and about a third or more were in holy orders. They have a place in this Appendix because of their Florentine connections. The list is not complete, but nearly so: it more than amply represents the men at the edges of the profession and the outsiders who temporarily professed law in Florentine territory. I would have included men like Filippo Decio and Bartolommeo Sozzini in the fourth rather than the third classification, but the fact is that they practiced law in and around Florence for a number of years. All the same, neither took any part in the political life of the city and their stature was Italian, not Florentine. They were professors of jurisprudence first and it is that, not their legal practice, which associated them with Florence and the Studio Pisano for many years.

A quick examination of the profiles will show that each of the four classifications lists lawyers chronologically: in order of their matriculation in the guild or of the first Florentine notice of them as lawyers to come to my attention. An alphabetical listing will occur to the reader; it would have made things easier for me and for students in search of particular references. But nothing apart from comfort warranted such a listing. An historical inquiry means looking at things in time and with an eye to change. This called for a chronological arrangement of the profiles, which had the advantage of showing up increases or declines in the number of men who went into the profession at given periods. Behind such change there was the play of critical social and political factors.

The first few names in each of the first three classifications have no certain chronological arrangement, the condition of the guild records before about 1390 being much too spotty and incomplete for that.

In the case of a few lawyers—most of them listed under classification II—there was some doubt about the information concerning their social backgrounds. Having some evidence to go on in each case, I classified such lawyers anyway, at the same time entering my doubts into the summary descriptions.

The question arose (e.g., in connection with the Buongirolami family), when did a family of outsiders become Florentine and so pass over into the category of new men? After two, three, or four generations? Generally speaking, original place names hung on to personal names for at least two generations. The line between the second and third generations seemed the decisive one. Hence Giovanni di Bernardo di Giovanni Buongirolami da Gubbio appears under the class of "New Men."

Family names are listed first, unless they were unavailable or doubtful.

## I. Lawyers from Old Families

1. *Corsini, Filippo di Tommaso*: 1334-1421. Had a doctorate in civil law before 1365, most likely from Perugia or Bologna. Taught law at Florence, 1365-1369, 1388-1389, and very probably at other times. One of the leading political figures of his time. Had a flourishing legal practice.

2. *Ricci, Giovanni di Ruggero*: ca. 1342-1402. Doctorate in civil law before 1365, probably from Padua. Taught law at Florence 1366-1369, 1388-1389, and very likely at other times as well. Powerful political figure. Flourishing practice.

3. *Aldighieri, Donato Ricchi*: d. 1382. Doctorate in civil law. Place and date of degree unknown. Good practice. Outstanding political figure.

4. *Villani, Filippo di Matteo*: d. 1405. Studied and practiced law. No doctorate. In guild before 1366. Modest participation in public life.

5. *Marchi, Tommaso di Messer Marco*: d. 1403. Doctorate, canon law. Studied or taught away from Florence *ca.* 1370. Practiced first as notary. In guild by 1372. Major political figure.

6. *Buonaccorsi, Stefano di Giovanni*: 1353-1433. Doctorate, canon law, place and date unknown. In guild by 1384. Taught canon law, Florence, 1388-1389, 1402-1403, 1413-1414. Politically influential in second and third decades of Quattrocento. Flourishing practice.

7. *Orlandi, Rosso di Andreozzo*: fl. 1400-1420s. Doctorate, civil law, Bologna, 1381. Guild matriculation, *ca.* 1382. Of medium stature in public affairs. Excellent legal practice.

8. *Covoni, Tommaso di Bernardo*: fl. 1380s. Doctorate in civil law, Bologna, 1381. Taught law at Florence in 1380s, at Siena in 1387-1388. Modest political standing.

9. *Ridolfi, Lorenzo di Antonio*: 1362-1443. Canon lawyer, doctorate from Bologna, 1388. Lectured there on the *Liber Sextus* and *Clementines* in 1387-1388; at Florence *idem*, 1388-1389, and on the *Decretum* and *Decretals* in 1402-1403, 1413-1414. Advocate for the Camaldolese friars. A powerful political figure. Flourishing practice.

10. *Popoleschi, Bartolommeo di Tommaso*: d. 1412. Doctorate from Bologna in civil law, probably obtained just before 1393, when he was matriculated in the guild. Taught law at Florence, 1401-1403. Major political figure. Had a medium to good practice.

11. *Del Bene, Ricciardo di Francesco*: *ca.* 1369-1411. Doctorate, civil law, Bologna, 1395, and unanimously approved by nine examining jurists. Taught law at Bologna for year or so, at Florence in 1396 and 1405. Political figure of medium rank or less. Married a Guasconi. Had excellent connections and a good practice.

12. *Strozzi, Marcello di Strozza*: b. 1374. Doctorate, civil law, Bologna, 1401. Lectured on the *Digest* and *Code* at Florence, 1401-1403. Married a Cavalcanti. In guild by 1409. Thereafter lived for many years in Rome, where he often served as the Signory's contact. Periodically returned to Florence up to 1440s.

13. *Empoli, Francesco di Jacopo di Vannozzo*: b. 1378. Canon lawyer, studied at Bologna and Florence. Doctorate, Florence, 1398, examined by "universorum doctorum collegii dicte civitatis florentie." Taught canon law, Florence, 1402-1403, 1416-1417, 1422-1426, 1431-1433. Was in guild and practiced. Not very active in public affairs. The Empoli were a branch of the old Siminetti family.

14. *Machiavelli, Francesco di Lorenzo*: d. 1428. Had doctorate in canon law. From Bologna? Taught law at Florence, 1402-1403, 1413-1414. In guild by about 1404. Had good practice. Relatively active in public affairs.

15. *Beccanugi, Piero di Lionardo*: 1377(79?)-1460. Doctorate in civil law. Date and place of degree unknown, but not from Bologna. Padua, Perugia, and Ferrara are the possibilities. In guild by about 1405. Moderate legal practice. Figure of some political importance.

16. *Federighi, Carlo di Francesco*: 1382-1449. Doctorate in canon law, possibly from Padua, where he studied, 1410-1411. Taught at Florence, 1419-1420, and perhaps thereafter. In guild by 1415. Good practice. Enjoyed some political prominence, being Gonfalonier of Justice in 1444. His brother Benozzo was Bishop of Fiesole.

17. *Davanzati, Giuliano di Niccolò*: 1390-1446. Studied civil law at Padua, 1409-1412, but obtained doctorate from Bologna, 1416, when he was also rector of Italian nation there. Knighted by Pope Eugene IV (1436) on request from Florence. An outstanding, influential political figure. Active in guild but had modest practice.

18. *Tanagli, Guglielmo di Francesco*: 1391-1460. Doctorates in civil and canon law, possibly from Padua, where he studied, 1412-1413. Taught law at Florence, 1425-1426. In guild by about 1424. Excellent practice. Knighted by city, 1451. A major political figure.

19. *Boscholi, Giovanni di Giachinotto*: d. 1448. Doctorate, canon law, Bologna, 1422. Cameral clerk and papal governor of Bologna in 1431. Entered guild in 1435 and took up legal practice. Not very active in Florentine public affairs. That the Boscholi were an old family is confirmed by a letter from the Signory. They sat in Signory only once (1484).

20. *Guasconi, Zanobi di Jacopo di Messer Biagio*: 1397-1464. Canon

lawyer, doctorate from Siena, 1425. Later took doctorate in civil law. Entered guild in 1425 and took up practice. Lectured on *Decretals* at Florence, 1431-1433. Ran into political trouble with Medicean faction in 1434.

21. *Bonarli, Orlando di Giovanni*: 1399-1461. Canon lawyer, doctorate from Bologna, about 1428. Studied civil law seven years at different places, passed private examination, Bologna, 1428. Professed canon law, Florence, 1439-1440. Guild matriculation, 1440. Practiced for nearly a decade. Took holy orders next. Made Auditor of Papal Rota, 1451. Archbishop of Florence, 1459-1461. Bonarli family first entered Signory in 1347.

22. *Ubaldini, Benedetto di Bartolommeo di Antonio*: d. 1460. Entered guild, April 1432. Doctorate, civil law, but place and date not indicated in matriculation. Practiced law. Not much engaged in public affairs. Son, Antonio, became a notary.

23. *Foraboschi, Bartolommeo di Baldassare*: d. 1474. Doctorate, civil law, Bologna, 1430. Active in guild, somewhat less so in the profession. Modest political standing. Changed name to Ormanni (1435-1436).

24. *Martelli, Domenico di Niccolò*: 1404-1476. Doctorate, civil law, Bologna, 1435. Rector of the Italian nation there, 1434-1435. Matriculated in guild, 1435. Built up excellent practice. Taught law, Florence, 1435-1436. Had brilliant political career. The Martelli, partisans of the Medici, were among newer of established families, having started their rise late—in the 1340s.

25. *Machiavelli, Girolamo di Agnolo*: 1415-1460. Doctorates *in utroque iure*, dates and place unknown. Taught law, Florence, 1435-1436, 1439-1440. Active in guild and profession. Very active in public affairs. Had determined political views, angered ruling group and in 1458 was banished to Avignon for twenty-five years. He and brother declared rebels in 1459. All their possessions confiscated.

26. *Corbinelli, Matteo di Giovanni*: b. 1414. Doctorates *in utroque iure*, Padua, 1440. Guild matriculation, April 1438. Practice slight. A shy or sickly man, took little part in public affairs.

27. *Deti, Tommaso di Guido*: 1414-1498. Doctorate, civil law, Bologna,

1445. Guild matriculation, August 1446. Taught law at Florence in later 1440s. Very active in public life. Enjoyed political authority and excellent standing in profession.

28. *Strozzi, Michele di Piero di Pagnozzo*: 1428-1498. Doctorate, civil law, Ferrara (1455), where the Strozzi had family connections. Also studied at Siena, Perugia, Bologna. Guild matriculation, 1463. Modest to middling legal practice. Not much involved in public affairs. Had a chair in civil law at Pisa, 1496-1497.

29. *Uguccioni, Simone di Bernardo*: d. 1514. Had doctorate in civil law but place and date unspecified in guild matriculation (September 1456). Good legal practice. Very active in public affairs, enjoyed high political standing. Uguccioni, an old consular family.

30. *Malegonnelli, Antonio di Piero di Niccolò*: 1451-1506. Doctorates in civil and canon law, Bologna, 1473. Guild matriculation, November 1473. Professed law at Studio Pisano (moved to Prato after 1494) throughout the 1490s. In 1500-1501, he and Francesco Pepi drew professorial stipends second only to that of Filippo Decio. A brilliant lawyer and statesman, one of most important political personalities in Florence during 1490s and after.

31. *Firidolfi da Panzano, Rinaldo di Matteo*: fl. 1470s. Doctorate, in civil law from Ferrara, 1473. Also studied at Florence and Siena. Active as lawyer in later 1470s. Took no part in politics. May not have been in guild.

32. *Pepi, Francesco di Chirico*: 1451-1513. Doctorates in civil and canon law, Pisa, 1477. His *promotor*, Bartolommeo Sozzini. Guild matriculation, September 1482. Flourishing practice. Professed law, Pisa (later Prato), 1484-1485, 1492-1493, 1496-1497, 1499-1502. Had brilliant career in politics. A Salviati on his mother's side, he was favored by the Medicean *balìa* of 1512.

33. *Soderini, Bernardo di Messer Niccolò*: 1451-1534. Doctorate in civil law, place and date unknown—Pisa most likely. Active in guild by about 1486. Built up no remarkable practice. Minor involvement in public affairs.

34. *Strozzi, Antonio di Vanni di Francesco*: 1455-1523. Doctorate, civil, law, Pisa, 1480. Doctorate in canon law also. Taught at Pisa in 1480s,

at Prato and again at Pisa later on. Matriculated in guild, November 1488. Enjoyed brilliant professional reputation and outstanding practice. Active in politics and diplomacy, disposed of ample political authority.

35. *Altoviti, Niccolò di Simone di Giovanni*: 1455-1518. Doctorates, civil and canon law, Pisa, 1482. Guild matriculation, October 1482. Did some teaching at Pisa. Politically ambitious and influential. Chancellor on legislation, 1495-1499. Had good legal practice. Favored by the Medicean *balìa* of 1512.

36. *Della Stufa, Enea di Giovenco*: fl. 1480s-1530s. Doctorate, civil law, Pisa, 1482. Taught law at Pisa, 1484-1487. Entered guild, December 1488. Had a middling practice. Took relatively prominent part in public affairs. Favored by the Medicean *balìa* of 1512.

37. *Gualterotti, Francesco di Lorenzo*: 1456-1509. Doctorate, civil law, Pisa, 1483. Bartolommeo Sozzini his *promotor*. Taught at Pisa, 1485-1486. In guild by 1486. Built up flourishing practice, excellent name in the profession. Extremely active in politics and diplomacy. Like colleagues Malegonnelli and Bonsi, he was a powerful political figure.

38. *Cerretani, Giovanni di Niccolò di Matteo*: 1458-1522. Doctorates, civil and canon law, Pisa, April 1484. Lectured at Pisa on *Liber Sextus* and *Clementines*, 1484-1486. Entered guild, December 1488. A Savonarolan, moderately active in public affairs. Modest to middling practice. Favored by the Medicean *balìa* of 1512.

39. *Bechuto, Deo di Felice*: fl. 1480s. Doctorate in civil law, most likely from Pisa. Date unknown. Taught law at Pisa for short time in 1480s. Active in guild, but no sign that he practiced much. Little involvement in public affairs. Possibly took holy orders in early 1490s, so may be Pietro Paolo di Felice Bechuto, *legum doctor* and friar in the Convent of San Marco, 1493. The Bechuto first entered Signory in 1348.

40. *Soderini, Giovan Vettorio di Messer Tommaso*: 1460-1528. Doctorates, civil and canon law, Pisa, *ca.* 1485. Professed law at Pisa (later Prato), 1485-1487, and throughout most of 1490s. Attracted clients easily. Took prominent part in public affairs, especially during brother's ten-year term (1502-1512) as Gonfalonier of Justice.

41. *Corsini, Luca di Bertoldo di Gherardo*: 1462-1511. Doctorate in civil law from Pisa, *ca.* 1486. Taught law at Pisa, 1486-1487, and in Studio

Pisano at Prato, 1497-1498. Entered guild, November 1488. Had good practice. An ardent republican, at times an influential public figure. Checkered political career.

42. *Deti, Ormannozzo di Messer Tommaso di Guido*: b. 1464. Doctorates from Pisa, civil and canon law, about 1488. From 1487 on taught law at Pisa, then at the Studio Pisano in Prato (1496 and following), then at Pisa again (1515-1522). Very active in guild, had leading legal practice, stood out in public affairs, was statesman of some influence. Favored by the Medicean *balìa* of 1512.

43. *Beccanugi, Piero di Simone di Messer Piero*: fl. 1490s. Held doctorate in civil law from Studio in Florence. Date of degree not specified in guild matriculation of December 1494, when he succeeded Bartolommeo Scala as first secretary of the Republic. Otherwise, slight participation in public affairs. Modest legal practice.

44. *Aldobrandini, Piero di Silvestro*: d. 1519. Doctorate in civil law from Pisa, 1490. Lectured on *Institutes*, Pisa, 1488-1489. Entered guild, 1497. Build up modest to medium practice. Moderate activity in public affairs, although favored by Medicean *balìa* of 1512.

45. *Medici, Veri di Tanai*: 1469-1522. Doctorate, civil law, Studio Pisano, *ca.* 1494-1495, when he did some teaching. First guild date, 1505. Probably not much interested in the profession, had modest to middling practice. Favored by the Medicean *balìa* of 1512, but did not stand out in public affairs.

46. *Nelli, Francesco di Giovanni di Stefano*: b. 1465. Took doctorate in civil law, 1495, probably at Ferrara. Studied at Pisa and elsewhere. Lectured at Studio Pisano, 1495 and following. Matriculated in guild, 1501. Occasionally counselled Signory. No outstanding practice.

47. *Rucellai, Niccolò di Pancrazio*: 1467-1527. Doctorate, civil law, Pisa. Date uncertain, but probably about 1495, when he lectured on the *Institutes* at Studio Pisano. Matriculated in guild, 1500. Some interest in public affairs. Modest legal practice.

48. *Acciaiuoli, Ludovico di Agnolo di Adovardo*: 1471-1527. Obtained doctorate in civil law from the Studio Pisano (then at Prato), 1496. Professed law there, 1496-1497, and at Pisa proper, 1515-1516. Matriculated in guild, 1498. Very active and influential in public affairs after 1500.

Had leading law office. Became member of the standing Medicean *balìa* in 1524.

49. *Velluti, Luigi di Piero di Andrea*: 1481-1526. Obtained doctorate in civil law about 1504, from either Pisan Studio or Bologna, where he held a public disputation in 1504. Taught law, Pisa, 1515-1516. Matriculated in guild, November 1507. Not much seen in public affairs. Had law office which attracted a medium volume of business.

50. *Guicciardini, Francesco di Piero*: 1483-1540. Obtained doctorate in civil law from college of the Studio Pisano at Florence, 1505. Also studied at Ferrara and Padua. Lectured at the Studio Pisano, 1505-1506. Would have had one of city's leading law offices, but from 1515 on devoted himself entirely to political-administrative career. A favorite of the Medicean government, 1512-1527. Date of guild matriculation unknown.

51. *Asini, Marco di Giovan Battista*: *ca.* 1484-1575. Doctorate in civil law from Studio Pisano at Florence, 1506. Matriculated in guild, October 1507. Very active in public affairs up to at least 1530. Had leading law office. The Asini were an old branch of the Uberti.

52. *Capponi, Giannozzo di Cappone di Bartolommeo*: 1482-1563. Doctorates, civil and canon law, Bologna, 1511. Taught both civil and canon law at Pisa, 1515-1522. Matriculated in guild, May 1512. No great involvement in public affairs. Possibly had modest legal practice.

53. *Soderini, Niccolò di Tommaso di Messer Lorenzo*: b. 1484. Doctorates, civil and canon law, 1512, either from Bologna or Studio Pisano at Florence. Also studied at Pavia and Padua. Taught law at both Florence and Pisa, 1512, 1515-1522. Entered guild, August 1512. Was advocate for the Calimala guild from 1528 on. Seems to have had good legal practice, though few of his *consilia* and pleas survive. Somewhat active in public affairs.

54. *Filicaia, Piero di Berto*: d. 1564. Doctorates in civil and canon law from the college of the Studio Pisano at Florence, 1512. Taught civil and canon law, Pisa, 1515-1520. Matriculated in guild, June 1513. Stood out in political affairs during late 1520s. Good practice.

55. *Malegonnelli, Alessandro di Messer Antonio*: 1491-1555. Doctorates in civil and canon law, Pisa, about 1516. Taught civil and canon law there, 1515-1522. Had an extremely successful practice in 1520s and after.

Deeply involved in public life. Gonfalonier of Justice in 1522; became member of the standing Medicean *balìa* in 1524.

56. *Gualterotti, Bartolommeo di Messer Francesco*: b. 1491. Doctorates in civil and canon law, obtained in 1516, almost certainly at Pisa. Studied at Perugia, Bologna, "et alibi." Lectured on *Institutes* at Pisa, 1516-1518. Stood out in public affairs; had leading law office. Guild matriculation, August 1516. In exile after 1530; lived in Rome; much employed by Pope Paul III. Governor of Città di Castello, 1559.

57. *Ridolfi, Lorenzo di Giovanni*: fl. 1520s. Doctorate in civil law, most probably from Pisa about 1517. Taught law at Pisa, 1517-1522 and possibly thereafter. Active in the profession, though not many of his *consilia* or pleas survive. First guild date, 1525. Prominent in public life, especially in late 1520s.

58. *Cappelli, Buono di Barone*: b. 1487. Doctorate, canon law, most likely from Pisa about 1519. Taught canon law there, 1519-1522. Was in guild by 1524. Probably practiced.

59. *Rucellai, Luigi di Piero*: fl. 1520s. Doctorate in civil law, most likely from the Pisan college in Florence. First recorded guild date, February 1509.

60. *Guicciardini, Niccolò di Luigi*: 1500-1557. Doctorates *in utroque iure*, 1521, from Pisa. Profoundly interested in politics and much involved in public affairs. Practiced law with great success. Many of his *consilia* survive.

61. *Aldobrandini, Silvestro di Messer Piero*: d. 1558. Doctorate in civil law from Pisa, 1521. Brilliant lawyer. Held committed republican views. Exiled on fall of Republic. Lived in Ferrara after 1530, teaching at university and sometimes counselling Duke Ercole II.

62. *Altoviti, Bardo di Giovanni di Bardo*: 1498-1546. Doctorates in civil and canon law, Pisa, 1523. Matriculated in guild, May 1528. Very active in public life. Practiced successfully.

63. *Soderini, Ormannozzo di Messer Tommaso*: fl. 1520s. Doctorate, civil law, probably from Pisa. First recorded date in guild, January 1528.

64. *Giugni, Galeazzo (or Galeotto) di Luigi*: b. 1497. Held doctorates in civil and canon law, place and date unknown. No trace of him in

guild, but definitely practiced as lawyer. Active in public life, e.g., conducted embassy to Duke of Ferrara in July 1529.

65. *Accciaiuoli, Niccolò di Giovanni di Piero*: 1499-1565. Doctorates in civil and canon law from Pisa, August 1529. Entered guild in September.

## II. New Men

66. *Giovanni di Messer Scolaio di Ser Berto da Petrognano*: fl. 1350s-1380s. Very active in guild, practicing law by 1355. Official advocate for Commune at different times.

67. *Giovanni di Ser Fruosino*: fl. 1360s-1380s. Practiced as notary before 1364, as jurist from 1366 on. Very active in guild and public affairs.

68. *Folchi, Jacopo di Simone*: fl. 1360s-1390s. Canon lawyer, place and date of doctorate unknown. Taught canon law at Florence, 1360s and 1380s. Had very active political life and successful practice. Consulted in 1392 by Duke Alberto d'Este on the Ferrarese statute, "De modo et forma concessionum usum rerum ecclesiasticarum." The family never appeared in Signory. Donato Velluti considered them new men.

69. *Falconi, Tommaso di Messer Michele*: fl. 1350s-1390s. Canon lawyer, place and date of doctorate unknown. Professed canon law at Florence, 1390-1391. A practicing advocate, was in guild by 1372. Active in public life. Origins obscure. Father probably a lawyer.

70. *Marco di Cenno di Marco*: fl. 1380s-1390s. Canon lawyer, place and date of doctorate unknown. Active in guild and legal practice. Held a number of leading public offices. His father an innkeeper.

71. *Bruni, Gianbruno di Messer Francesco*: d. 1388. Canon lawyer, doctorate possibly from Pavia, date unknown. May have been the *decretorum doctor* dismissed from Pavia faculty in 1387. Active in both guild and public life. His father started as a notary. Murdered in 1388.

72. *Palarcioni, Jacopo di Angelo*: fl. 1380s-1390s. Studied civil law at Bologna and Florence, where he obtained doctorate in 1391. Taught at Florence, 1388-1389. In guild by 1392. Good practice. Little evidence of activity in public life. There seems to be no documentary evidence that the Palarcioni were an old noble family, as some authorities think. Do not appear in Signory until 1473.

73. *Grifo di Ser Guidone di Ser Grifo*: fl. 1390s. Doctorate in civil law from Bologna, 1393. Active in guild and profession during late 1390s, then vanishes from sight. Born into family of notaries.

74. *Serristori, Giovanni di Ser Ristoro di Ser Jacopo*: d. 1414. Doctorate in civil law from Bologna, 1397. Entered guild, September 1398. Practiced law, but with no striking success. Preceded by three generations of notaries. Inherited an enormous fortune. Great grandfather started out from land (Fighine) under Florentine rule. Giovanni relatively active in public life.

75. *Niccoli, Jacopo di Bartolommeo*: *ca.* 1370-1425. Doctorate in civil law from Bologna, 1398. Lectured on *Volumen* at Florence, 1402-1403. Developed medium to good legal practice. Tended to avoid public affairs.

76. *Sermini, Domenico di Ser Mino*: b. 1375. Doctorate, civil law, place and date unknown. In guild by 1404. Moderately active in public life. Medium or average legal practice. From family of notaries. Still alive in 1436.

77. *Viviani, Francesco di Ser Viviano di Neri*: 1379-1430. Doctorate in civil law from Bologna, 1407. Taught law at Florence, 1425-1427. Active in guild and profession from about 1410 on. Had modest practice. Did not stand out in public life, though active. It is thought the Viviani were branch of the old Franchi di Sambuco family, but they did not sit in Signory until 1393 and probably continued to have close ties with their native ground in the *contado*. Still, Francesco might have been put under the first classification.

78. *Muscini, Bernardo di Arrigo di Ser Piero*: fl. 1410 and after. Doctorate in civil law from Padua, 1410. Entered guild soon after but had mediocre legal career. Active participation in public life. Father a wool merchant, brother and grandfather notaries.

79. *Bencivenni, Alessandro di Salvi di Filippo*: 1385-1423. Doctorate in civil law from Bologna, 1411. Brilliant legal reputation. Prominent in political affairs and influential. Had large following of clients. Born into family of wool merchants. Family first entered Signory, 1389.

80. *Bertaldi, Giovanni di Piero*: 1385-1458. Doctorate in civil law from Bologna, 1414. Entered guild soon after. Developed middling legal

practice. Possibly taught at Florence. Was relatively active in public affairs. The Bertaldi entered Signory in 1381, were then in linen.

81. *Francesco di Ser Benedetto di Marco*: 1393-1443. Doctorate in canon law from Bologna, where he was rector of the Italian nation, 1418. Lectured on *Clementines* at Florence, 1425-1426, 1431-1433, 1439-1440. Was active in guild and profession. Modest participation in public affairs.

82. *Niccolini, Biagio di Lapo*: 1396-1467. Held doctorate in civil law, place and date unknown. Studied law at Florence, Bologna, and Padua. Taught law at Florence, 1425-1426, 1431-1432. Entered guild before 1426, was moderately active in public affairs and profession. The Niccolini definitely derived from old county family—the Sirigatti—but entered Signory late (1356) and had upstart reputation. Ranked with most authoritative of newer families.

83. *Albergotti, Albizzo di Niccolò di Messer Francesco*: b. 1395. Doctorate in civil law, place and date unknown. Padua likely. In guild before 1432. Had good practice. Relatively active in public life. Descended from old and distinguished Aretine family. Albizzo's branch moved to Florence, 1349. Tradition of legal study in family.

84. *Puccetti, Francesco di Ser Piero*: b. 1407. Studied civil law at Siena and Florence, where he received doctorate, 1432. Professed *notarìa* at Florence, 1435-1436, 1439-1440. Seems to have had modest practice. Revealed little active interest in public life.

85. *Cocchi-Donati, Donato di Niccolò*: 1409-1464. Doctorate in civil law from Bologna (1438), where he was rector of the Italian nation, 1437-1438. Taught law at Florence, 1439-1440. In guild by 1435. Very active in politics. Had relatively successful practice. The Cocchi-Donati, well-known followers of the Medici, were among most authoritative of new families.

86. *Niccolini, Otto di Lapo*: 1410-1470. Doctorate in civil law from Perugia, 1438. Matriculated in guild, December 1438. Taught law at Florence, 1439-1440. Was leading public figure, very influential. Enjoyed flourishing practice. Was official counsel for subject Commune of Pistoia.

87. *Biffoli, Simone di Ser Niccolò*: b. 1417. Doctorate in civil law, place and date of degree unknown. Active in the guild but had modest pro-

fessional standing and was probably barred from public office. His father banished to Forlì by Medicean faction, 1434. Of somewhat troublesome character, Simone was in custody of Mercanzia officials in 1478.

88. *Adriani, Virgilio di Andrea di Berto*: d. 1493. Doctorate in civil law, place and date of degree unknown. Matriculated in guild, March 1451. Had slight practice. Not much engaged in public affairs. Was in linen business with father in 1470s. Adriani start as family of vintners. He married a Strozzi.

89. *Gaetani, Francesco di Benedetto di Messer Piero*: d. 1474. Guild matriculation, 1453, when he produced the privilege of his doctorate in civil law, a "doctorate by mandate of the emperor." Little evidence of professional or public activity. Grandfather a Pisan who settled in Florence (1406).

90. *Lionardo di Ser Giovanni di Ser Taddeo da Colle*: 1430-1497. First matriculated in guild as notary, 1463. Then matriculated as lawyer, December 1481, in support of which he produced documents of doctorate in civil law. Place and date of degree unspecified. Had good practice. Relatively active in public life. Family of notaries.

91. *Vespucci, Guidantonio di Giovanni*: 143(?)-1501. Doctorate in civil law from Ferrara, 1462. First studied at Bologna. Guild matriculation, July 1465. Brilliant lawyer. Had leading law office. Was profoundly political. One of most influential statesmen of his time. The Vespucci first entered Signory in 1350. Were vintners first, then smiths, notaries, silk merchants. Highly connected in second half of fifteenth century.

92. *Bonsi, Domenico di Baldassare*: 1430-1502. Doctorates in civil and canon law, Bologna, 1465. Guild matriculation, November 1466. First-rate professional standing, very successful practice. One of most important political figures of 1490s. The Bonsi a leading family of new men. Started out as sword makers.

93. *Niccolini, Agnolo di Messer Otto*: 144(?)-1499. Doctorate, civil law, obtained *ca.* 1466. Place of degree unknown. Guild matriculation, 1467. Much more taken up with politics than legal practice. Very influential under Piero di Lorenzo de' Medici, 1492-1494.

94. *Battista di Bartolommeo di Antonio di Ser Bartolommeo di Ser Nello*: 1443-1484. Doctorates in civil and canon law, Bologna, 1470. Taught

494

canon law at Bologna for short time, then at Pisa, *ca.* 1474 and after. Guild matriculation, October 1475. Little evidence of activity in public affairs. Modest legal practice. Family were notaries in mid Trecento but said to descend from old Ghetti family or the Sinibaldi of Montecuccheri. Doubtful.

95. *Pucci, Puccio di Antonio*: 1451-1494. Doctorate in civil law from Pisa, 1475. Taught law, Pisa, 1474 and after. Guild matriculation, February 1476. Had successful practice. Official advocate for Commune of Prato. Very active in public affairs. Died as ambassador to Rome. The Pucci were well-known adherents of the Medici and among the more influential of new families.

96. *Cocchi-Donati, Antonio di Messer Donato*: 1451-1491. Doctorates in civil and canon law from Pisa, 1474. Also studied at Perugia and Siena. First taught law at Pisa, 1474-1475 and after; held ordinary chair in canon law there, 1485-1486. Guild matriculation, February 1476. Active but did not stand out in public affairs or legal practice. The Cocchi-Donati were well-connected supporters of the Medici.

97. *Redditi, Bartolommeo di Andrea*: 1455-1523. Rector of the Italian nation at the University of Bologna, 1475. Took doctorates in civil and canon law there, *ca.* 1475. Guild matriculation, March 1484, oddly both as judge-advocate (lawyer) and notary. Savonarolan, active in public life. Had a modest to medium legal practice. Older brother a notary in guild.

98. *Gaddi, Francesco di Agnolo di Zanobi*: d. 1504. Matriculated in guild first as notary, 1478. By May 1486 already paying lawyer's guild fees. Seems to have taken a doctorate in civil law, place and date of degree unknown. Made second chancellor of Republic, 1494-1498(?). Prominent in public affairs. Legal practice probably slight. The Gaddi first entered Signory in 1437. Rich bankers in later fifteenth century with key financial connections in Rome.

99. *Gamberelli, Giovanni Battista di Bernardo*: 1434-1513. Doctorate in civil law from Florence, date of degree unknown. Guild matriculation, October 1482. Lectured at Pisa, 1481-1482, and at Studio Pisano in Prato-Florence, 1498-1499, 1505-1506. Modest legal practice. Not in circuit of public office. Father was a *lastraiuolo* (he worked with or made paving surfaces).

495

100. *Ciai, Bartolommeo di Ridolfo di Jacopo*: fl. 1480s and after. Doctorate in civil law from Pisa, 1482. Held doctorate in canon law also. Taught at Pisa, 1484-1485. Guild matriculation, June 1486; matriculated as notary in 1494 to qualify for post of *Tratte* chancellor, held until 1498. Practiced law. Very active in public life. Ardent Savonarolan, deprived of *Tratte* chancellorship, 1498, and forbidden to enter government palace for three years.

101. *Boni, Bono di Giuliano*: fl. 1480s and after. Doctorates in civil and canon law, Pisa 1484. Taught both laws at Pisa, 1484-1485, early 1490s, at Prato-Florence in later 1490s, again at Pisa, 1517-1522. Guild matriculation, December 1509. Moderate practice. At times much involved in public affairs. Favored by Medicean *balìa* of 1512. Active in government throughout late 1520s. First entering Signory in 1442, the Boni were family of bankers, money-lenders, silk merchants.

102. *Carducci, Baldassare di Baldassare*: 1458-1530. Studied law at different universities. Doctorates *in utroque iure* from Pisa, *ca.* 1484. Taught canon law at Pisa, 1485-1486, and at Pisa Studio during most of 1490s. Brilliant lawyer, had flourishing practice. Turned to public life in first decade of Cinquecento. In and out of Florence, 1512-1527, sometimes teaching at Padua. Vigorous opponent of Medici. Captained ardent republican movement in late 1520s.

103. *Guidi, Bartolommeo di Ser Giovanni di Ser Bartolommeo di Ser Guidone*: 1462-1518. Doctorate in civil law from Pisa, *ca.* 1489. Taught law at Pisa, 1489-1492. Guild matriculation, April 1491. Not notable for his legal practice. Ardent supporters of Medici family, he and brother deprived of civil rights in 1494 and confined to Florentine territory until 1507. From family of notaries.

104. *Buongirolami, Giovanni di Messer Bernardo*: 1464-1542. Took doctorate at Pisa in civil law, 1492. Taught at Studio Pisano in Pisa and Prato-Florence, 1492-1494, 1500-1502. Guild matriculation, August 1492. Good legal practice; active in public life; married into Ridolfi family. Descended from line of lawyers, backers of Medicean faction. Grandfather from Gubbio.

105. *Inghirami, Baldo di Francesco di Ubaldino*: d. 1504. Doctorate from Pisa, civil law, 1493. Taught law at Studio Pisano from 1492 on.

Guild matriculation, December 1494. No evidence of notable legal practice. Rather active in public affairs. Strong supporter of Savonarola, in 1498 barred from public office for three years. The Inghirami first entered Signory, 1388. Seem to start out as money-changers.

106. *Niccolini, Matteo di Messer Agnolo*: 1473-1542. Doctorate in civil law, Pisa, 1494. Taught at Studio Pisano, 1495-1496. Guild matriculation, January 1498. Practiced very successfully. Stood out in public affairs. Favored by Medicean *balìa*, 1512. Treasury cashier, 1512, but licensed by Signory to plead cases *viva voce* before any magistracy or court in city. From this point on the Niccolini might well be listed under old families. But I prefer not to arbitrate so openly.

107. *Niccolini, Carlo di Messer Agnolo*: 1474-1509. Doctorates in civil and canon law, Ferrara, 1495. Taught there, 1496-1497. *Ordinario* in canon law, Studio Pisano, 1498-1499. Guild matriculation, 1501. Practiced law. Little evidence of commitment to public affairs.

108. *Pandolfini, Francesco di Bartolommeo di Messer Carlo*: fl. 1490s and after. Doctorate in civil law from Studio Pisano, probably taken in *sala* of that Studio in Florence, about 1498. Taught law at Studio Pisano, 1498-1499, 1505-1506. Very active in guild, but had no remarkable practice. Mildly active in public affairs. Like the Niccolini, the Pandolfini family were among the oldest and most distinguished of newer ruling families.

109. *Bonsi, Antonio di Bernardo di Baldassare*: 1490-1533. Studied at Pavia, Bologna, Pisa. Doctorates in civil and cannon law, 1515, obtained through Pisan Studio at Florence. Taught at Pisan Studio, 1515-1518. Guild matriculation, December 1515. Practiced for a time. Somewhat active in public affairs. Then took holy orders. Elevated to episcopal dignity (Terracina) by Clement VII. The Bonsi among richest and most powerful of newer ruling families.

110. *Borromei, Vincenzo di Carlo*: fl. 1520s. Active as lawyer in guild before 1521. The Borromei possibly a branch of old county family (Franchi) from S. Miniato al Tedesco.

111. *Niccolini, Agnolo di Messer Matteo di Messer Agnolo*: 1502-1567. Had doctorate in civil law from Pisa, *ca.* 1523. Guild matriculation, 1530. May have practiced law early in career. Became leading public official

under Duke Cosimo I. Took holy orders, made Archbishop of Pisa (1563), later Cardinal.

112. *Leoni, Leone di Giuliano*: fl. 1520s. First notice of his membership in guild, 1527. Active as lawyer.

## III. Outsiders

113. *Giovanni del Maestro Neri da Poggibonsi*: fl. 1360s-1390s. Already in guild and a practicing lawyer by 1366.

114. *Niccolò di Antonio da Rabatta*: fl. 1360s-1390s. In guild and practicing law by 1368. Some participation in public affairs. Still alive in 1403.

115. *Baldo da Fighine*: fl. 1370s-1380s. Had doctorate in civil law, place and date of degree unknown. In guild and practicing by 1372.

116. *Parente di Corrado da Prato*: fl. 1370s-1380s. Had doctorate in civil law, place and date of degree unknown. In guild and practicing by 1372.

117. *Albergotti, Ludovico di Messer Francesco di Messer Albizzo*: d. 1398. Had doctorate in civil law, place and date of degree unknown. In guild and practicing by 1380. Prominent in public life, especially diplomacy in the 1390s. From distinguished Aretine family. Father and grandfather also lawyers.

118. *Roselli, Rosello di Ser Fino*: fl. 1380s and after. Doctorate in civil law from Bologna, where he taught with distinction in 1380s. Taught law at Florence, 1387-1388, and in 1390s. In guild and practicing by 1393. Born into Aretine family. Not in main circuit of public office at Florence. Served as government lawyer.

119. *Orlandi, Tommaso di Michele*: fl. 1380s and after. Doctorate, civil law, place and date of degree unknown. In guild, practicing law, by 1385. Still active in 1404. Occasionally served as official government lawyer. Family from Pescia.

120. *Cambioni, Niccolò di Messer Francesco*: fl. 1380s. Took doctorate in civil law from Bologna, 1386. Was in guild by 1385. Practiced successfully. Periodically served as government lawyer. Family from Prato.

121. *Montemagno, Giovanni di Messer Buonaccorso*: fl. 1380s-1420s. Took doctorate in civil law, Bologna, 1386. In guild by 1392. Practiced

with some success. Born to rich old family from Pistoia. Kept up ties with that commune. Not active in Florentine public life.

122. *Ubaldi, Angelo del Maestro Francesco*: *ca.* 1325-1400. Held doctorates in civil and canon law from Perugia, *ca.* 1349. Professed law at Perugia, Padua, Bologna, and Florence from 1388 on. Entered guild and was made Florentine citizen by special act. Practiced law in Florence. Brother of the famous Baldo degli Ubaldi. Perugian family; political exiles. Angelo enjoyed peninsula-wide legal reputation. Left treatises and *consilia*.

123. *Antonio di Giovanni da Romena*: fl. 1390s and after. Took doctorate in civil law from Bologna, 1390. Paid guild fees, 1404. Ample evidence of his practicing in and around Florence. Family from subject land of Romena. Not in circuit of public office.

124. *Ambrogio di Guidone da Volterra*: fl. 1390s. Doctorate in civil law, place and date of degree unknown. In guild by 1393. Practiced.

125. *Torelli, Buonaccorso di Messer Niccolò*: b. 1363. Held doctorate in civil law either from Florence or Bologna, having studied at both universities. Date of degree, late 1380s. In guild by 1392. Practiced but seems to have been somewhat retiring. Still active in late 1420s. Family from Prato.

126. *Torelli, Torello di Messer Niccolò*: fl. 1400. Held doctorate in civil law from Florence or Bologna. Date of degree about 1390. Taught law at Florence 1396-1397, 1402-1403, 1415-1416. In guild by 1392. Brilliant lawyer. Had very successful practice. Took part in public affairs. Often served as official government lawyer. Brother to Buonaccorso (above).

127. *Cetti, Nello (da San Gimignano) di Giuliano Martini*: b. 1373. Performed brilliantly on his doctoral examination in civil law, Bologna, 1398. Taught law at Florence, 1421-1423, 1431-1432. In guild by 1404. Stood out in Florentine public life, especially diplomacy. On friendly terms with Medici. Often served as official government lawyer. Had peninsula-wide reputation and large following of clients. His legal treatises and *consilia* were collected and esteemed. Descended from rich, distinguished Cetti family of San Gimignano, though Cetti name not used in Florence.

128. *Paolo di Ser Angelo di Castro*: *ca.* 1360-1441. Held doctorates in

civil and canon law, Avignon, dates uncertain. Taught law at Bologna, Padua, Florence, Ferrara. Lectured on *Digest* at Florence from 1401, 1413-1424 with some interruptions. Practiced law in Florence from about 1414. Matriculated in guild, where still active in 1424. Brilliant lawyer, leading practice, received legal commissions from all over Italy. His *commentaria*, treatises, *consilia* widely collected. Occasionally counselled Florentine government. He and Bartolommeo Vulpi (n. 134) reviewed and edited Florentine statutes of 1415. Hailed from Imola.

129. *Bonizi, Guaspare (da Perugia) di Piero*: *ca.* 1375-1436. Obtained doctorate in civil law, 1402, probably from Perugia. Doctorate also in canon law. Guild matriculation, November 1406. Taught at Florence, 1413, 1431-1433. Moved around much, teaching. Finally got Florentine citizenship, 1435. Family from Perugia.

130. *Accorambuoni, Guaspare del Maestro Ludovico*: b. 1381. Doctorates in civil and canon law from Florence, 1406. Entered guild, September 1406, though close to becoming cleric. Practiced and taught canon law at Florence, 1413-1415, 1423-1424, and probably thereafter. Then went to Rome and became consistorial advocate. Possibly took holy orders. Legal counsel for Florence in papal courts, 1430-1431 and after. His father and brother taught medicine at Florence. Distinguished family from Gubbio. All obtained Florentine citizenship. Their surname rarely used in Florence.

131. *Roselli, Antonio di Messer Rosello*: 1381-1466. Doctorates in both laws from Bologna, 1407. Degree in canon law taken earlier. Owing to "poverty," he presented his *publica* in old sacristy of St. Peter (Bologna). Taught civil law at Florence, 1422-1423, canon law in 1435-1436. Moved around some, though in guild and practiced at Florence in 1430s. From 1438 on taught at Padua almost continuously. Outstanding lawyer, Italy-wide reputation. His treatises and *consilia* collected and much esteemed. Family from Arezzo.

132. *Antignalli, Ruggero di Niccolò*: fl. 1390s and after. Held doctorate, civil law, most likely from Perugia. Date unknown. Made initial Florentine contacts in 1394, serving as judge in court of Capitano. Back in Florence practicing law, 1412. Obtained Florentine citizenship, De-

cember 1415. Born into distinguished Perugian family. Possibly expelled from Perugia in exile.

133. *Buongirolami, Giovanni di Girolamo di Messer Matteo*: 1381-1454. Had doctorate in civil law from Padua, 1412 (January). Guild matriculation in October. Obtained Florentine citizenship, October 1416, but not made eligible for public office until 1434. Very active in public affairs. An outstanding lawyer, built up excellent practice. Often counselled government. Founder of Florentine legal dynasty. Family from Gubbio—the "Herpiti."

134. *Vulpi da Soncino, Bartolommeo*: *ca.* 1359-1435. Had doctorates in both laws, probably from Bologna, where he passed private examination, 1384. Taught at Florence, 1413-1414, and practiced law there for a time. Edited Florentine statutes (1415) with Paolo di Castro. Taught civil law at Pavia, 1421-1435, with distinction. In 1427 made citizen of Milan, Pavia, Cremona by Filippo Maria Visconti.

135. *Montemagno, Buonaccorso di Messer Giovanni*: *ca.* 1392-1429. Doctorate, civil law, Bologna, *ca.* 1415. Taught law at Florence, 1422-1423. In guild by 1425. Began appearing in public office in late 1420s. Born of illustrious Pistoian family. See father (n. 121).

136. *Accolti, Michele di Santi*: fl. 1415 and after. Doctorate in civil law, place and date unknown. Taught law, Florence, 1435-1436, and possibly as early as 1415. Entered guild before 1427. Modest legal practice. Not in circuit of public office. Accolti were well-known Aretine family. Father to famous humanist-lawyer (Benedetto, n. 146) and lawyer (Francesco).

137. *Salvetti, Tommaso di Ser Jacopo*: 1390-1472. Doctorate, civil law, Bologna, 1418. Entered guild before 1425. Had leading law office and very high standing in profession. Left commentaries (now possibly lost) on Florentine statutes. Especially prominent in public life after 1435. Kept on retainer by Pistoia and Camaldolese friars. Family from Pistoia.

138. *Bovacchiesi, Giovanni di Bernardo di Ser Migliorato*: b. 1397. Doctorate, civil law, Bologna, 1423. Professed civil law, Florence, 1430-1433, 1435-1436, 1439. First guild date, 1436. Had modest to middling legal practice. Did not stand out in public affairs, yet provoked Medicean ruling group and suffered exile in November 1439. Taught law at Padua

from *ca.* 1441 into 1450s and perhaps beyond. Well-known family from Prato, almost certainly affiliated with the Migliorati.

139. *Leoni, Leo di Francesco*: d. 1461. Doctorate, civil law, place and date unknown. In guild by 1425. Modest practice. Came from Prato.

140. *Ubaldi, Angelo di Messer Alessandro di Messer Angelo*: fl. 1420s-1450s. Doctorates, civil and canon law, Perugia. Date of degrees unknown. Guild matriculation, August 1428. Practiced in Florence, but seems to have moved around much. Not in circuit of public affairs. Grandfather active in Florence but not father. Kept up Perugian connections.

141. *Bruni, Lionardo di Francesco*: *ca.* 1370-1444. Guild matriculation, late 1427 or early 1428, to go with his appointment to Republic's leading chancellery post. A famous humanist, he studied and perhaps practiced law for a time but did not have doctorate. Born in Arezzo.

142. *Buonguglielmi, Sallustio di Messer Guglielmo*: *ca.* 1373-1461. Doctorates in both laws, Perugia, *ca.* 1395. Taught law at Perugia, Bologna, Siena, and probably Florence. Political exile. Moved to Florence in 1431. There active in guild and profession until death. Had good practice. Some *consilia* survive. Buonguglielmi name assumed in Florence. Born in Perugia of distinguished stock.

143. *Balducci, Filippo di Andrea di Antonio*: *ca.* 1398-1458. Doctorate, civil law, Siena, about 1424. Taught law, Siena, 1429-1431. Moved to Florence, entered guild, November 1431. Enjoyed backing of Medici family. Teaching at Florence, 1435-1436. Was Florentine chancellor on legislation, 1444-1457. Practiced. Came from Lucca.

144. *Colucci, Pagolo di Giovanni di Tommaso*: fl. 1430s-1440s. Doctorates in both laws, Florence 1434. Rector of Studio Fiorentino, 1433-1434. Little evidence of professional activity. Still alive 1447. Not active in public affairs. Came from Rome.

145. *Buonfigli, Buonfiglio di Giorgio*: fl. 1400-1440s. Doctorate, civil law, Bologna, 1407. Guild matriculation, July 1435. Not notable for professional activity. Had no place in public affairs. Possibly an exile. Came from Fermo.

146. *Accolti, Benedetto di Messer Michele*: 1415-1464. Doctorates in both laws, Bologna, the civil law degree in 1437. Taught law at Flor-

ence and Volterra, 1435-1436. Also studied at Florence. Taught again at Studio Fiorentino, 1439-1440, 1448-1449, 1450-1451, 1458-1460. Guild matriculation, 1440. Practiced successfully. Some *consilia* extant. First secretary of Republic, 1459-1464. Came from Arezzo.

147. *Ambrosini, Piero di Jacopo*: 1403-1472. Doctorates in both laws, Bologna, the civil law degree in 1428. Doctorate in canon law confirmed at Rome, 1432. Guild matriculation, April 1437. Taught canon law at Florence, 1439-1440. Practiced law with considerable success. Came from Iesi (Umbria).

148. *Bracciolini, Poggio*: 1380-1459. This celebrated humanist matriculated among judge-advocates of guild by 1438. Called "doctor" in guild records but did not hold doctorate of laws. Studied law, though practiced little if at all. Papal secretary for many years. Appointed to Republic's leading chancellery post, 1453-1459. Came from Terranuova, land subject to Florence.

149. *Bargi (Barzi), Benedetto di Paoluzzo*: fl. 1440s-1450s. Studied civil law at Bologna, Perugia "et alibi." Place and date of doctorate unknown. Guild matriculation, 1440. Practiced in Florence for a few years. Excellent professional standing. Writer of legal treatises. Did not enter Florentine public affairs. Taught civil law, Ferrara, 1455-1459.

150. *Migliorati, Giovanni di Messer Michele di Messer Lapo*: fl. 1440s. Inscribed in Florentine guild, but practiced in and around Prato. Probably had doctorate in civil law. Not a Florentine citizen.

151. *Marsuppini, Carlo di Messer Gregorio*: 1398-1453. Matriculated among judge-advocates of guild, April 1444, in connection with his appointment to Republic's chief chancellery post. Studied law but took no degrees. Knew the Roman law books. Did not practice. The Marsuppini an illustrious Aretine family.

152. *Felcari, Piero di Francesco di Messer Jacopo*: ca. 1424-1478. Doctorate, civil law, Pisa, 1451. Taught at Studio Fiorentino, 1451-1452. Practiced law in Florence. Guild matriculation, November 1466. Not in office circuit. Came from S. Angelo in Vado.

153. *Saracini, Giovanni di Cristoforo*: fl. 1450s-1460s. Doctorate in civil law, Florence, 1454, as attested by guild document of October 1461,

when he petitioned guild for authentication of doctoral instrument. Doctorate confirmed. No evidence of his practicing in Florence. Came from Arezzo.

154. *Buongirolami, Bernardo di Messer Giovanni*: d. 1484. Doctorate, civil law, Bologna, September 1464. Guild matriculation, same date. Had outstanding legal practice. Enjoyed warm backing of Medici family. Attained political prominence. Father (n. 133) came from Gubbio. Buongirolami name taken in Florence.

155. *Scala, Bartolommeo di Giovanni di Francesco*: 1428-1497. In guild by 1463. Studied law and practiced for a time. Possibly had doctorate. Constantly referred to in guild records as "doctor" and "jurisconsult." Famous humanist, enjoyed powerful support of Lorenzo the Magnificent. Held leading chancellery post, 1464-1494, then shared it, 1494-1497. Was knighted. Came from Colle in the Valdelsa (Florentine). Born into poor miller's family.

156. *Cappucci, Antonio di Niccolò*: fl. 1460s. Doctorate, civil law, Perugia, 1460. Matriculated in guild, 1470. Not in circuit of public affairs.

157. *Landino, Cristoforo di Bartolommeo*: 1425-1498. Very active in guild between about 1471 and middle 1490s. Sometimes referred to in guild documents as "doctor of laws." Studied law, but probably neither practiced nor really had doctorate. Held chancellery posts. Enjoyed patronage of Lorenzo the Magnificent. Born into humble family from Pratovecchio in Casentino (Florentine).

158. *Ambrosini, Francesco di Messer Piero*: b. 1448. Doctorate, civil law, Siena, June 1473. Also studied at Florence and probably Pavia. Guild matriculation, July 1473. Had good legal practice. Often held public office. An ardent Savonarolan. Cashiered from territorial office in May 1498 and barred for three years from Grand Council. His father (n. 147) from Iesi.

159. *Sozzini, Bartolommeo*: 1436-1507. Doctorates in civil and canon law, from Siena or Bologna, taken *ca.* 1462. Professed law at Siena, Pavia, Ferrara (1473-1474), and Pisan Studio from 1474 to middle 1490s. Not in guild, but practiced law in Florence and vicinage. Took no part in public affairs. One of great fifteenth-century lawyers. Came from Siena.

160. *Passetti, Cosimo di Ludovico*: d. 1518. Doctorate, civil law, Ferrara,

1466. Professed law at Ferrara at various times, 1474-1502; also at Studio Pisano, 1490s. Guild matriculation, 1484. Practiced in Florence with some success. Not active in public life. Came from Ferrara.

161. *Decio, Filippo*: 1454-1535. Doctorates in civil and canon law, the former from Pisa, November 1476. Taught both laws at Studio Pisano, 1484-1489, during most of 1490s, 1500-1501 and following, and again in 1515-1521. Also taught at Siena, Padua, Pavia. Not in guild, but practiced in Florence and vicinage. Had brilliant reputation. Came from Milan. His *consilia* and *commentaria* collected and greatly prized.

162. *Modesti, Jacopo di Ser Michele*: b. 1463. Doctorates in civil and canon law. Examinations sustained in college of Studio Pisano at Florence, July 1496. Taught law at Studio Pisano from 1503 on. Guild matriculation, October 1515. Had moderate legal practice. Enjoyed strong support of Medici. Made Florentine citizen, 1519, and activated for public office. Was secretary for time of Cardinal Giulio de' Medici. Came from Prato.

163. *Mazzinghi, Paradiso del Maestro Ugolino*: 1491-1563. Doctorate in civil law, Pisa, *ca.* 1518. Taught at Pisa, 1518-1522. Entered guild in late 1520s. Built up moderate practice. Took no part in public life of Republic. The Mazzinghi, an old family from Signa, moved to Florence in later fifteenth century.

### IV. A Miscellany

N.B. The following men were not inscribed in the guild rolls. With two or three exceptions, they did not practice law in Florence. The few who did (e.g., Roberto Strozzi) were ecclesiastics.

164. *Del Pozzo, Filippo di Giovanni*: fl. 1415. Doctor of laws, born in Sicily. Obtained Florentine citizenship, December 1415. Then passes from sight.

165. *Zacci, Marco di Rosso*: fl. 1420s. Lectured on *Decretals* at Florence, 1422-1423. Came from Pisa.

166. *Cavalcanti, Roberto di Piero*: d. 1449. Had doctorates *in utroque iure*. Taught canon law at Florence, 1431-1433. Took holy vows. Subsequently became Rota auditor, then Bishop of Volterra.

167. *Della Bordella, Tommaso di Petrino*: fl. 1430s. Taught canon law

at Florence in 1430s. Probably in clerical orders. Came from Argenta. Some relatives previously served as foreign magistrates in Florence, thus his contact.

168. *Lazari, Filippo di Sinibaldo*: fl. 1430s. Taught canon law, Florence, 1435-1436. Came from Pistoia. Probably a cleric.

169. *Mignanelli, Giovanni*: fl. 1430s. Taught canon law, Florence, 1435-1436. Came from Siena.

170. *Narni, Bernardo di Francesco*: fl. 1430s. Taught civil law, Florence, 1435-1436. Native ground unknown.

171. *Giugni, Ugolino di Filippo*: 140(?)-1470. Already had doctorate in canon law, 1433, when still studying civil law at Florence. A cathedral canon and in Florentine "college of jurists" by 1444. Died as Bishop of Volterra. Born into old Florentine family.

172. *Banducci, Niccolò del Maestro Giovanni*: fl. 1440s. Doctor of laws, sat on doctoral examining board, Florence, 1444. Background unknown.

173. *Benzi, Andrea del Maestro Ugo di Andrea*: fl. 1440s. Doctorate in civil law, Bologna, 1442. Already held doctorate in canon law. He and four brothers made full-fledged citizens of Florence, 1447. Father a famous doctor of medicine who professed at Studio Fiorentino. Family from Siena.

174. *Roselli, Giovan Battista*: fl. 1440s. Taught law at Florence before 1451. One of the Aretine Roselli.

175. *Agolanti, Jacopo di Giuliano di Bartolommeo*: fl. 1450s-1460s. Obtained doctorates in civil and canon law, February 1453. Place of degrees unknown. Petitioned guild, October 1463, to confirm his degrees. The Agolanti were Florentine.

176. *Machiavelli, Bernardo di Niccolò*: 1428-1500. Studied civil law. Had library of law books and perhaps doctoral degree. Apart from simple notarial work, no trace of his practicing.

177. *Tifernati, Lelio*: fl. 1470s. In letter to Lorenzo the Magnificent, 1471, he signed "legum doctor et civis florentinus." Most likely came from land in Florentine dominion.

178. *Soderini, Francesco di Messer Tommaso*: 1453-1524. Studied civil and canon law. Taught at Pisa in middle 1470s. Bishop of Volterra from

1478. Later cardinal. Extremely prominent in Florentine public life, especially diplomatic affairs, from later 1490s to 1512.

179. *Guasconi, Francesco*: fl. 1470s. Doctorates, civil and canon law, place and dates of degrees unknown. Wrote from Milan to Lorenzo the Magnificent, April 1479. The Guasconi an old and prominent Florentine family.

180. *Strozzi, Roberto di Carlo*: fl. 1470s-1490s. Doctorates, civil and canon law, probably from Pisa. Dates unknown. Taught canon law, Studio Pisano, 1470s-1490s. A leading ecclesiastic. Vicar general of Archbishop of Pisa. Very influential at Studio Pisano.

181. *Poliziano, Angelo*: 1454-1494. Doctorate, canon law, Florence, December 1485. In clerical orders. His father, Messer Benedetto, a well-known jurist. Commented on law books but never practiced law. Humanist, poet, etc., famous protégé of Lorenzo the Magnificent. Family from Montepulciano.

182. *Del Maino, Giason*: 1435-1519. Doctorates, civil and canon law, Pavia, *ca.* 1467-1471. Taught at Pavia, Padua, and Pisa (1488-1489). Eventually became counsellor to Duke of Milan. Difficult personality. Enjoyed brilliant reputation. Born into old Milanese family.

183. *Malchiostri, Francesco*: fl. 1490s. From Parma. Held ordinary chair in canon law, Pisa, 1492-1493 and following. Probably in orders.

184. *Domenico di Bartolommeo da Prato*: fl. 1490s. From Prato. Lectured on *Decretum*, Studio Pisano, 1492-1493 and following.

185. *Matteo di Neroccio da San Gimignano*: fl. 1500. Doctorates in civil and canon law. Place and dates unknown. Taught canon law at Studio Pisano during 1490s, civil law from 1515. Came from San Gimignano.

186. *Buonaccorsi, Giovanni*: fl. 1490s. Taught civil law part-time, Studio Pisano, 1492-1493, and probably took his doctorate then. Hailed from Pistoia.

187. *Castellani, Castellano di Pierozzo*: fl. 1490s-1520s. Doctorate, canon law, Studio Pisano, *ca.* 1492. Taught canon law, Studio Pisano, 1490s; held ordinary chair, 1515 to 1520s. In holy orders. Born into illustrious Florentine family.

188. *Jacopo di Vanni da Pisa*: fl. 1490s. Taught civil law part-time, Pisa, 1492-1493. Probably took doctorate there. Hailed from Pisa.

189. *Lambertelli, Vincenzo*: fl. 1490s. Taught canon law, part-time at first, Studio Pisano, 1492-1493 and after. Probably took his doctorate in canon law at Pisa. Came from Arezzo.

190. *Leonardo di Cesano da Pisa*: fl. 1490s. Taught canon law part-time, Studio Pisano, 1492-1494. Probably took his doctorate there in canon law. A Pisan.

191. *Romolini, Francesco*: fl. 1490s. Taught canon law part-time, Studio Pisano, 1492-1493. A Spaniard.

192. *Tommaso di Garofolo da Sicilia*: fl. 1490s. Taught civil law part-time, Studio Pisano, 1492-1493. Sicilian.

193. *Albizzi, Giovan Francesco*: fl. 1490s. Taught canon law, part-time, Studio Pisano at Prato-Florence, 1497-1498. Almost certainly took doctorate in canon law, *ca.* 1497. In holy orders. From old Florentine family.

194. *Antinori, Carlo di Tommaso*: fl. 1490s. Taught canon law part-time, Studio Pisano at Prato-Florence, 1499-1500, when in all likelihood he took doctorate in canon law. Probably in holy orders. From rising Florentine family.

## SOURCES FOR APPENDIX

Listed in order of importance:

*AGN*, 91-340, guild acts. Information on individual lawyers, when available, may be found by year of matriculation (as given in Appendix), checked against appropriate register in catalogue of guild material, Archivio di Stato, Florence.

*AGN*, 28, 748. For biographical data before 1390.

*UDS*, 1-11. On universities of Florence and Pisa. In ASF.

*Statuti della università e studio fiorentino*, ed. A. Gherardi (Firenze, 1881).

"Gli atti degli ufficiali dello studio fiorentino dal maggio al settembre 1388," ed. R. Abbondanza, *ASI*, cxvii (1959), 80-110.

*DSCOA*, 47. Folios on faculty of Studio Fiorentino, 1435-1436. In ASF.
*SCRO*, 8. Has sprinkling of letters bearing on Studio Pisano, 1480-1490s. In ASF.

*Il 'Liber secretus iuris caesarei' dell' università di Bologna*, ed. A.

Sorbelli, 2 vols. (Bologna, 1938-1942). Lists doctorates in civil law up to 1450.

Archivio Arcivescovile, Firenze. *Filze di Cancelleria*. Papers of notaries attached to the episcopal chancellery, especially those of Ser Jacopo da Romena, Vaconda, Paganucci, Cioli, Cortesi, Roncini, Ballesi.

Archivio Arcivescovile, Pisa. *Miscellanea e Dottorati*, 1-2.

*Catasto*, registers for 1427, 1430, 1433, 1458. For birth dates. Indices for first *catasto* rather good. In ASF.

*Tratte*, 39 (1378-1456), 442bis. On ages of citizens. Very incomplete. In ASF.

*Medici e speziali*, 244-253. "Books of the dead." In ASF.

*Grascia-morti*, 1-8. Also on dead. In ASF.

*Tratte*, 65-72, 78-85. Elaborate lists of men in different offices. When one died in office, his name was deleted and the date recorded. In ASF.

*Carte Passerini, Necrologio Cirri*, in the Biblioteca Nazionale of Florence. On dates of birth and death.

Finally, there are some relevant printed lists (never complete) of professors and *laureati* at other universities:

F. Borsetti, *Historia almi ferrariae gymnasii*, 2 vols. (Ferrara, 1735).

G. Secco Suardo, *Lo studio di Ferrara a tutto il sec. xv*, ii, in *Atti della deputazione provinciale di storia patria*, vi (Ferrara, 1894), 27-294.

G. Pardi, *Titoli dottorali conferiti dallo studio di Ferrara nei sec. xv e xvi* (Lucca, 1900).

*Memorie e documenti per la storia dell' università di Pavia* (Pavia, 1877-1878).

*Codice diplomatico dell' università di Pavia*, i (1361-1400), ed. R. Maiocchi (Pavia, 1905).

*I rotuli dei lettori legisti e artisti dello studio bolognese dal 1384 al 1799*, ed. U. Dallari (Bologna, 1888).

*Monumenti della università di Padova, 1318-1405*, ed. A. Gloria, 2 vols. (Padua, 1888).

*Acta graduum academicorum gymnasii patavini ab anno mccccvi ad annum mcccl*, ed. C. Zonta and G. Brotto (Padua, 1922).

Still a great cache of information on leading jurists of the second half of the fifteenth century is the old book by F. Gabotto, *Giason del Maino e gli scandali universitari nel quattrocento* (Torino, 1888).

# Index

Abbondanza, Robert, 158, 454

Abominable Crime, 170

Abundance officials, 398

Acciaiuoli, family, 63, 71, 75; bankruptcy, 109; Agnolo, 176, 230n; Dardano di Niccolò, 99-100, 101; Francesco di Niccolò, 99-100, 101; Giovanni, 285; Ludovico di Agnolo, lawyer, 167n, 231, 300, on public law case, 422n, profile, 488-89; Niccolò di Giovanni di Piero, profile, 491; Roberto, 286

Accolti, Benedetto di Messer Michele, lawyer, 105, 106, 169n, profile, 502-503; Francesco, 463; Michele di Santi, profile, 501; Piero, 286

Accoppiatores (accoppiatori), 53, 395, 402, 432; functions of, 195-96; and support of lawyers, 209-210

Accorambuoni, family, 72; Bartolommeo, 72; Guaspare del Maestro Ludovico, lawyer, 72, 284, 285-86, 338, 342n, profile, 500; Ludovico di Bartolo, 72

Accursius, 87

Adige River, 352

Adimari, Filippo, 351

administration, problems of, 169-82; and specialization, 170-71

Adriani, family, in Signory, 68; Virgilio di Andrea di Berto, lawyer, 68, 102, profile, 494

Agnolo, tutor, 90

Agolanti, Jacopo di Giuliano di Bartolommeo, profile, 506

Alamanni, Piero, 111

Albergati, Niccolò, Cardinal of S. Croce, 346, 347

Albergotti, Albizzo di Niccolò, 192, 297, 382, profile, 493; Francesco, 188n; Ludovico di Messer Francesco, lawyer, 73, 150, 189n, 317-19, 322, 326, 327, 328, 332, 333, 353-55, 369, 417, profile, 498

Alberti, family, 96-97; conspiracy, 96; Antonio di Niccolò, 96, 97; Francesco di Messer Jacopo, 154n; Niccolò di Jacopo, 96, 97

Albizzi, family, 43, 79, 187; faction, 188; Antonio di Tedice, 175; Giovan Francesco, profile, 508; Luca di Maso, 178; Manno, 299; Maso, 148, 292, 293, 294, 295, 296, 340, 357-58; Rinaldo, 158, 160, 178, 208, 209, 323, 378

Aldighieri, Donato Ricchi, lawyer, 188n, 189, 287; profile, 482

Aldobrandini, family, 75; Piero di Silvestro, lawyer, 167n, 300, profile, 488; Silvestro di Messer Piero, lawyer, 179, 183, 231, 419n, profile, 490

Alessandri, Alessandro, 230n

Alexander V, Pope, 295

Alexander VI, Pope, 203, 247, 271, 280, 297, 377; and Florentine tax license, 258-66; and Florence, 303-307

Alfonso of Aragon, King of Naples, 177, 255, 316, 325, 379

Aliprandi, Arasmo, Milanese lawyer, 458

Altoviti, family, 66, 75, 104; Bardo di Giovanni di Bardo, lawyer, profile, 490; Niccolò di Simone, lawyer, 67, 98, 167n, 202, 206, 213, 214, 269, 300, 443, on Ten, 199-200, on Vitelli trial, 434-35, and doctrine of new state, 434-35, profile, 487

ambassadors, requirements, 13; stipends, 30

Ambrogio di Guidone da Volterra, profile, 499

Ambrosini, Francesco di Messer Piero, profile, 504; Piero di Jacopo, 94, 169n, 417, on public law case, 415n, profile, 503

America, South, 470

America, United States of, 470

Ancona, Bishop of, 286n

Andrea di Ser Tommaso, notary, 148

Angelo di Fulgineo, notary, 97

Antella, confederation of, 227

Antignalli, Ruggero di Niccolò, profile, 500-501

Antinori, Carlo di Tommaso, profile, 508

Antonio di Giovanni da Romena, profile, 499

511

Apostolic Camera, *see* Camera

Apostolic Datary, *see* Datary

appeal, judicial, 126, 132-33, 140, 142, 438-39; from guild courts, 131-32; to Signory, 132n, 133; and executive power, 138; in tax fraud, 174; in territories, 223; to Rome, 271ff, 281-82; law of, 441-42

Appellate Judge, 95, 132-33, 136-37, 138, 223, 398, 471; eliminated, 132; reestablished, 137

Appendix, 89; social classifications in, 62; and classification, 65

Approvers of Guild Statutes, 465

Aragon, King of, 255

arbitration, in foreign relations, 347-59

Arcimboldi, Niccolò, Milanese lawyer, 459, 462, 463

Ardinghelli, family, 104

Arezzo, 72, 92, 102, 109, 155, 220, 222, 223, 226, 236, 334, 349, 417; rebellion, 418

argument, *pro-contra* method of, 86, 87; legal, 87-88

aristocrats, 212-13

Aristotle, 387, 408; *Ethics*, 429

Armajolo, 231

Arnolfini, Nazario, Lucchese lawyer, 349

*Arrabbiati*, 201

Arrighi, Matteo, 332

Arrigucci, Alessandro, 332

*arrotos*, defined, 52-53

Arte dei Guidici e Notai, *see* guild of lawyers and notaries

Asini, Marco di Giovanni Battista degli, 206, 231, 269n; profile, 489

Assisi, 334, 340

Athena, 391

Athens, 328

Athens, Duke of, *see* Brienne, Walter of

Avignonese Papacy, 267

Azo, glossator, 38, 87

Baldo, *see* Baldus

Baldo da Fighine, lawyer, 189n; profile, 498

Balducci, Filippo di Andrea, income, 105-106; profile, 502

Baldus, 87, 407, 409; on citizenship, 416n; defines *populus*, 423n

*balìe*, 50, 147, 188, 195, 234, 243, 365, 395, 402, 471; and oligarchy, 195

Balzello officials, 179

Banchi, Bartolo, 160

Banducci, Niccolò del Maestro Giovanni, profile, 506

baptism, 286

Barbadori, Donato, lawyer, 188, 286, 287n

Barbavara, Francesco, 463

Barbischio, Castle, 155

Bardi, family, 157; bankruptcy, 109; and Moncione murder, 163; Francesco di Messer Alessandro, 370; Piero di Gualterotto, 155

Barga, 222, 229, 230, 281, 349

Bargellini, Giovanni, notary, 282

Bargello, 443

Barghigiani, 230

Bargi (Barzi), Benedetto di Paoluzzo, profile, 503

Baroncelli, Piero, 239n

Bartolommei, Zanobi, 102

Bartolommeo da Corneto, Cardinal, 366-68

Bartolus of Sassoferrato, 87, 97, 302, 407-409, 421, 456; *De tyrannia*, 348n; *Tractatus repraesaliorum*, 384; *Tractatus de regimine civitatis*, 387, 395n, 408n; concept of *civitas sibi princeps*, 413-15; *Commentaries*, 436; on city-state, 436-37

Basel, Council of, 302, 366

Bassano, 331

bastardy, in Renaissance, 28; and political rights, 99-100

Bastari, family, 147-48; case of, 147ff, 402; case and syndication, 161n; Filippo di Cionetto, 147, 148n; Giovenco, 147ff, 161, 162, and Signory's license, 151n, absolved, 161n

Battifolle, counts, 155, 163, 426; Guido, Count of Moncione, 155ff, 233; Guido Guidi, 159n

Battista da Poppi, notary, 79

Battista di Bartolommeo di Antonio, profile, 494-95

Beccanugi, Piero di Lionardo, lawyer, 23, 67, 178n, 206, 208, 209, 211, 290, 296, 297, 375n, 378, profile, 484; Piero di Simone di Messer Piero, profile, 488

Beccaria, Tesoro, 359

Bechuto, Deo di Felice, profile, 487

Belfredelli, Adovardo, 151

Belluno, 331

Bencini, Mariotto, notary, embassy of, 365-69

Bencivenni, family, 68; Alessandro di Salvi, lawyer, 68, 159, 186, 208, 209, 239, 296, 339, 340, 341, 363n, 369, 370, 378, 380n, 393n, 399n, 466n, 467n, and Moncione murder, 158, on public law cases, 415-17, 435, profile, 492; Banco, 178n; Salvi di Filippo, 68

Benedetto di Goro, 102

Benedetto di Jacopo da Empoli, lawyer, 189

Benedict XIII, Pope, 247, 288, 289, 290; and Florence, 289

Benintendi, Jacopo, notary, 43

Benzi, Andrea del Maestro Ugo di Andrea, profile, 506

Benzoni, Bartolommeo, Milanese lawyer, 318n, 459, 462, 463

Bergamo, notaries in, 36

Bertaldi, Giovanni di Piero, lawyer, 208, 240, 333n; on office pouches, 432; profile, 492-93

Bevilacqua, Guglielmo, 463

Bibbiena, 222

Biffi, Roggero, Milanese lawyer, 458

Biffoli, Simone di Ser Niccolò, profile, 493-94

Biliotti, Giovanni, 177n; Paolo di Francesco, 208n

biography, and history, 62

Biserno, Castle, 98

Bisticci, Vespasiano da, 67, 135

Black Death, 31, 65, 73

Boccaccio, 29, 48n

Bologna, 30, 34n, 38, 80, 109, 248, 283n, 292, 293, 296, 302, 312, 318n, 320, 322, 326, 331, 337, 349-50, 351, 357, 358, 437, 457, 462; notaries in, 38; University, 67, 81, 83, 86, 87, 88, 89; University and Italian nation, 254; Archdeacon, 82; College of Lawyers or Doctors of Law, 82, 89, 228-29, 346, 368; Cardinal, 104; league of, 350, 352-53, 354; and treaties as contracts, 320-21; and Florence, 321, 343-44; and Ladislaus, 340-41; status of, 377-79

Bonarli, Orlando, lawyer and prelate, 248, 285; profile, 485

Bonciani, Filippo, lawyer, 188n

Boni, family, 68; Bono di Giuliano, lawyer, 68, 98, 206, 269n, profile, 496

Boniface VIII, Pope, 247, 252, 257

Bonizi, Guaspare (da Perugia) di Piero, lawyer, 19-20; profile, 500

Bonsi, family, 65, 68-69, 75, 403n; in Signory, 69; Antonio di Bernardo, lawyer, 68-69, 231, profile, 497; Domenico di Baldassare, lawyer, 23, 68, 74, 88, 107, 108, 138, 139, 178, 190n, 202, 206, 213, 215, 236, 268, 284n, 329, 330, 381n, 393n, 429, 443n, 444, embassy to Rome, 258-60, and *Staatsräson*, 426-27, profile, 494; Ugolino, 69

books of law, value, 84

border disputes, 97-99, 229-32

Borgo San Lorenzo, 274

Borgoforte Bridge, 352, 354

Borromei, Vincenzo di Carlo, lawyer, profile, 497

*borse* (office pouches), 179-80, 432

Boscholi, Giovanni di Giachinotto, lawyer, profile, 484

Boucicaut (Jean Le Meingre), Count of Beaufort and Alais, 290, 291, 324, 342, 360, 371; and Florence, 355-58

Bovacchiesi, Giovanni di Bernardo, lawyer, 175, 176; profile, 501-502

Braccio da Montone, 343, 344, 345, 378

Bracciolini, Giovanni Francesco, 275; Poggio, 29, 31, 48n, 275, profile, 503

Brandini, Cristofano di Giorgio, physician, 157

Brienne, Walter of, 26, 108, 109

Brittany, duke of, 255

Brucker, Gene, 43, 143n

Bruni, Gianbruno di Messer Francesco, lawyer, 161n; profile, 491

Bruni, Lionardo di Francesco, profile, 502

Buonaccorsi, bankruptcy, 109

Buonaccorsi, Giovanni, lawyer, 417; profile, 507

Buonaccorsi, Stefano di Giovanni, lawyer, 91, 101, 106, 107, 136n, 165, 293, 295, 332n, 337, 342n, 370n, 375, 417; and opposition to Gregory XII, 292, 295; profile, 483

Buonaccorso di Ser Piero, notary, 46-47

Buondelmonti, Gherardo, diplomat, 317-19

Buonfigli, Buonfiglio di Giorgio, profile, 502

Buongirolami, family, 64, 482; Bernardo di Messer Giovanni, lawyer, 63, 73, 169n, 190n, 206, on public law case, 415n, profile, 504; Giovanni di Bernardo di Giovanni, lawyer, 482, profile, 496; Giovanni di Girolamo, lawyer, 90, 94, 175, 176, 195, 196, 231, 297, 343, 351, 352, 416, embassy to Lucca, 345-47, profile, 501

Buonguglielmi, Sallustio di Messer Guglielmo, profile, 502

Burckhardt, Jacob, 28, 311, 347, 348

Cafaggiolo, Alberti villa at, 96

Calcagni, Piero di Francesco, notary, 363-65

Calimala guild, 14, 15, 103

Calixtus III, 247

Camaldolese, 111

Cambi, Giovanni, 442

Cambio guild, 14, 15, 465

Cambioni, Niccolò di Messer Francesco, lawyer, 287, 322n; profile, 498

Camera, Apostolic, 188, 266, 279; court of, 267, 270, 284, 285n; Auditor, 270, 273, 276, 285n; court and jurisdiction, 271; clerks of, 272; Chamberlain, 279n, 280

Cameral court, *see* Camera

Campofregoso, Tommaso di, Doge of Genoa, 362, 363, 371

Cancellieri, family (Pistoia), 108, 234, 235; "sect," 108

Cane, Facino, *condottiere*, 358

Canigiani, family, 66; Antonio, 213n, 214; Giovanni, 190; Ristoro, 287n

canon law, 84, 87, 271, 293, 326n, 434; doctorate, 81-82; courses, 85; *vs.* civil law, 91; jurisdiction, 92-93; and certain crimes, 93

Cappelli, Buono di Barone, profile, 490

Cappelli, Francesco, notary, 56, 286n

Capponi, family; Giannozzo di Cappone di Bartolommeo, profile, 489; Neri di Gino, 178n, 351; Piero, 329

Cappucci, Antonio di Niccolò, profile, 504

Captain of the People, 92, 95, 97, 131-33, 138, 139, 142, 162, 163n, 181, 398, 465, 471; jurisdiction, 132; and Eight, 136; changes, 137; eliminated, 137; revived, 140; and syndication, 144; and Bastari case, 147ff; Sentio da Spoleto and Bastari case, 148ff; and Moncione murder, 156, 159, 161

Capua, Cardinal of, 262

cardinals, independent, 290ff, 303

Carducci, family, 65; Baldassare di Baldassare, lawyer, 23, 69, 74, 167n, 206, 207, profile, 496; Filippo, 140, 166n; Giovanni, 208n, and Moncione murder, 155ff

Careto, Otto de, 463

Carmagnola, Count, governor of Genoa, 363-65

Carmelites, 98

Carmignano, 221, 221n

Carnago, Giovanni da, 463

Carnesecchi, Andrea, 278; Carlo, 275, 277, 278

*Carte di Corredo*, described, 215-16

Carthusians, 103

Casoli, Filippo, 463

Castel dell'Aquila, Marquis of, 160

Castellani, Castellano di Pierozzo, profile, 507; Matteo, 158, 182, 208, 209; Vanni, 294, 295

castellans, 221n

Castiglion Aretino, and public law cases, 416-17, 420; and fisc, 435

Castiglionchio, Lapo da, lawyer, 45, 189, 395-96

Castiglione, Franchino, Milanese lawyer, 462, 463; Guarnerio, lawyer, 462, 463

Castrocaro, 222

Catalonians, *vs.* Venetians, 351-52

*catasto*, tax, 173, 215, 250

Catasto Officials (Office), 53, 128, 173-77, 392, 398

Cathedral canons, 111

Cattani, Francesco di Guido, 226

Cavalcanti, family, 63; Giovanni, 135; Roberto di Piero, profile, 505

censures, ecclesiastical, 304

centralization, *see* state

Cerretani, Bartolomeo, chronicler, 440n, 442n, 444; Giovanni di Niccolò, lawyer, 269, profile, 487

Cetti, family, 73; Nello (da San Gimignano) di Giuliano Martini, lawyer, 73, 97, 101, 107, 136n, 159, 302n, 338, 343, 355-56, 363n, 369-72, 378n, 379, 380n, *Tractatus de bannitis*, 408-409, 427, on Florence as *princeps*, 414n, on public law cases, 415-16, 420n, profile, 499

chancellor, 38, 181

chancellorship, 168n

Charles IV, Emperor, 340n

Charles VI, King of France, 354, 358

Charles VIII, King of France, 141, 328, 329-30, 426

Charles of Durazzo, 150

Chianti, 222

Church, 458; and social mobility, 71; and Florence, 122, 367; courts, 131; and tax fraud, 173ff, 256; and lay taxation, 175-77, 251ff, 360; and state, 176, 246ff; *vs.* Signory, 203-204; and lawyers, 247ff; property, 256; councils and lawyers, 288ff; councils and Florence, 295-97; censures, 304-307; papal legates, 311; immunities, 421-22, 435-36; and privileges, 474

Ciai, Bartolommeo di Ridolfo, lawyer, 69, 215, 300; profile, 496

Cicero, 80

Cicognaja, 231

Cino da Pistoia, postglossator, 87, 97

Cino da Pistoia (another), lawyer, 189n

*Ciompi*, 64

citizens, number of, 5, 206

citizenship, Florentine, 388-89

city-state: and discretionary powers, 127; juridical basis, 456-57

*civitas sibi princeps* (or *civitas superior*), 121, 413ff, 456, 475; and ordinary powers, 440; and *plenitudo potestatis*, 440. *See also* city-state; state (Renaissance)

Clement VII, 283n, 289

*Clementines*, 82, 85. *See also* canon law

clergy, and lay taxation, 251ff, 262, 299

Cocchi-Donati, family, 65, 403n; Antonio di Messer Donato, 69, 75, profile, 495; Donato di Niccolò, 69, 82, 177, 196n, 197, 209, 228, 282, 396n, embassy to Rome, 254-58, profile, 493

*Code*, 33; parts of, 84n. *See also* Roman law

College of Lawyers, 18

colleges, 194, 233, 336-37, 402; and legislation, 124; and criminal appeal, 142; and Bastari case, 147ff; and Moncione murder, 155ff; and taxation, 192. *See also* Twelve (Good Men); Sixteen (Gonfaloniers)

Colucci, Pagolo di Giovanni di Tommaso, profile, 502

Commune (Florence), 41-42; and *sapientes communis*, 110; defined, 424; and corporate privileges, 464; as *universitas*, 464. *See also* Florence; state

Conductae Officials, 398

Conservatores Legum, *see* Defenders of the Laws

*consiglio maggiore*, *see* Grand Council *under* Councils

*consilia legalia*, 84, 87, 88, 99, 399, 467, 468; collections listed and identified, 450-55

*consilium sapientis*, 94-95

consistorial advocates, 267, 285

Constance, Council of, 296, 302, 303

constitution, Florentine, 28n. *See also* Councils; Florence; state

*consuetudo*, 457n

consuls, *see under* guild

Consuls, Sea, 53, 398

*Consulte e Pratiche*, 142, 191, 193, 198, 237, 289, 293, 334, 340, 433
*conventus*, public doctoral examination, 82, 88-89
Corbinelli, family, 66; Bartolommeo di Tommaso, 79; Matteo di Giovanni, lawyer, profile, 485
corporation privileges, 474
corporation theory, and *populus*, 424
*Corpus Iuris Canonici*, 85
*Corpus Iuris Civilis*, 33, 38; parts of, 84n. *See also* Roman law
Correr, Angelo, Pope Gregory VII, 294
Corsini, family, 66, 71; Filippo di Tommaso, lawyer, 23, 45, 66, 75, 96, 101, 106, 107, 150, 161n, 181n, 182, 188, 189, 206, 209, 239, 287n, 289, 291, 293, 295, 322n, 324, 331, 336, 337, 340, 341, 342n, 351, 369, 370n, 378, 392, 396, 417, on treaties, 318, 319, profile, 482; Luca di Bertoldo, lawyer, 102, 167n, 201, 202, 203, 206, 381n, 443n, on appeal of Medicean plotters, 444-45, on *populus* and state, 447-48, on *princeps* and Grand Council, 447-48, profile, 487-88
Corte, Piero da, Milanese lawyer, 462, 463
Corti, Gino, 102n
Cortona, 220, 236, 266, 334; Bishop of, 265, 265n, 266; and Florence, 349-50; Captain of and jurisdiction, 420-21; and public law case, 420-21
Corvini d'Arezzo, Giovanni, 463
Cosenza, Cardinal of, 274
Cossa, Baldassare, Cardinal of Bologna, 325, 334, 335, 336. *See also* John XXIII
Council of Justice (Florentine), *see* Justice, Florentine Council of
Council of Ten (Venetian), 139n
Council of Two Hundred (of duchy), 17
Councils of Republic (legislative):
Council of Commune, 124, 406-407
Council of Eighty, 198, 298, 300, 442, 443n; and criminal cases, 142; and Ten on War, 199-200

Council of One Hundred, 124, 138, 139, 190, 243
Council of People, 40, 47, 124, 192, 193, 194, 406-407
Council of Seventy, 124, 167n-168n, 425
Council of Two Hundred, 124, 193, 342-43; powers of, 194
Grand Council, 47, 49, 124, 126, 183, 190, 191, 198, 259n, 269, 390, 396, 439; and appeal, 127, 140, 441-42; and Ten on War, 199-200, 212-13; and quorum, 214; and Medicean plotters, 443-45; and *princeps*, 447
"major council," 196-97
*See also* legislative councils
courts, Florentine, 130ff; composition, 133; lawyers and reform of, 142-43. *See also* judiciary
courts, guild, 95, 131, 471; appeal from, 131-32
Covoni, Tommaso di Bernardo, profile, 483
credentials, diplomatic, 379-80
Crema, 459
crime, political, 441-42
Cristiano di Magonza, Archbishop, 312
Cristofano da Lodi, 274
Crivelli, Pietro Paolo, Paduan lawyer, 328
custom, and new state, 472

D'Ailly, Pierre, 302
Dante, 347
Datary, Apostolic, 264
Dati, Goro, 104
Datini, Francesco, 101
Davanzati, family, 66, 104; Giuliano di Niccolò, lawyer, 67, 74, 159, 178n, 182n, 192, 193, 206, 208, 209, 211, 283n, 284, 296, 323, 333n, 378, 380n, 382n, 392, 393, profile, 484
Davidsohn, Robert, 11, 14, 40, 41, 100, 130, 397
Decem Baliae, *see* Ten on War
Decem Pisarum, 239, 240, 241
*decina*, tax, 193
Decio, Filippo, lawyer, 77, 262, 272, 481; profile, 505

*Decretals*, 80, 82, 85. *See also* canon law

*Decretum*, 81, 82, 85. *See also* canon law

Defectuum Officials, 398

Defenders of the Laws, 48, 53, 95, 125, 130, 142, 242-43, 392, 398, 399, 402; and Signory, 128; and judicial crisis, 136; competence of, 170; and tax fraud, 174

Dei, Benedetto, chronicler, 388n

Del Bene, Ricciardo di Francesco, lawyer, 90, 97, 101, 105, 106, 180n, 224, 290; his clients, 103-104; professional income, 103-105; on public law case, 420n; profile, 483

Del Benino, Gregorio, 278

Del Maino, Giason, profile, 507

Del Nero, family, 64; Bernardo, 63, 64, 442

Del Pozzo, Filippo di Giovanni, profile, 505

*Deliberazioni dei Signori*, source, 136

Della Bella, Giano, 42

Della Bordella, Tommaso di Petrino, profile, 505-506

Della Casa, Giovanni, 19

Della Fioraia, Simone, 294

Della Stufa, family, 66; Angelo, 190n; Enea di Giovenco, lawyer, 167n, 206, 213, on papal power, 307, profile, 487

Dello Strinato, Giovanni di Domenico, 273; appeal to Rome, 276-78

Deti, family, 75; Ormannozzo di Messer Tommaso, lawyer, 98, 102, 108, 111, 167n, 201, 203, 204, 443n, on fisc, 422, on mineral deposits, 437, profile, 488; Tommaso di Guido, lawyer, 67, 84, 102, 206, 209, 379, 396n, profile, 485

*Dieci di Balìa*, *see* Ten on War

Dietrich of Niem, 302

*Digest*, 81; parts of, 84n. *See also* Roman law

Dini, Niccolò di Michele, notary, 50

diplomacy: prelates in, 55; Renaissance, 270; and legal counsel in Rome, 284-86; language of, 319-20; and arbitration, 347ff. *See also* treaties

disputation, 86

*divieto*, defined, 180-81

doctorate: examination for, 88-89; expenses, 89; social value, 206-208

Dodici, *see* Twelve (Good Men)

*dolus*, as *bonus*, 326n

Domenico da Pescia, friar, 201

Domenico di Bartolommeo da Prato, profile, 507

Dominus, use of title, 29

Donatus, 79

Doren, Alfred, 11, 132

dowries: and litigation, 94; in Roman law, 94

East-West Council, 297

Eight on Foreign Affairs (Otto di Pratica), 53, 138, 207, 381, 399; and judicial powers, 131

Eight on Public Safety, 13, 55, 95, 125, 129, 137, 138, 142, 198, 211, 226, 233, 247, 275, 332, 360, 361, 389, 392, 398, 399, 402, 409n, 431-32, 441, 469; and judicial powers, 124, 127, 131; and Signory, 128; and statutory controls, 128; appeal from, 132n; development, 135-36; procedure, 136n; *vs.* Nine of Militia, 166; variability, 168; powers, 168-69, 170, 438-39; in territorial affairs, 226-27, 438, 469; and rebellion, 237; scholarship on, 404; defended and criticized, 410-11, 433; and Paolo Vitelli, 434; and Medicean plotters, 442-45

Eliseo da Colle, cleric, 98

embassies: and distinction, 314; incidence of lawyers in, 315; short-term, 315. *See also* diplomacy; treaties

emergencies: and lawyers, 269; and state, 411; and immunities, 435-36

Emilia, 350

Emperor, 15, 255, 347, 374-75, 388, 414; rights of, 377; and Arezzo, 418

Empire, 56, 330, 457; and Florence, 119ff, 191; rights of, 374-75; idea of, 375

Empoli, Francesco di Jacopo, profile, 484

England, 252, 269, 291, 371

Epiphanius, 93n
Ercole II, Duke of Ferrara, 183
Ercole, Francesco, 415
Eremitani friars, 98
Estensi, marquises, 229; Azzo, 350-51; Niccolò, Marquis of Ferrara, 350-51
Eugene IV, Pope, 257, 284
executive power: and judicial competence, 124-27; and appeal, 138; and legal counsel, 171; nature and development, 397ff; and lawyers, 398ff; rotation of, 401; and *utilitas publica*, 401; *vs.* judiciary, 401-402, 471; and legislative power, 407; and *princeps*, 424-25, 446-48; and *plenitudo potestatis*, 426. *See also* Florence; state
Executor of the Ordinances of Justice, 14n, 92, 95, 138, 161n, 162, 398, 471; jurisdiction, 132, 133; and Eight on Public Safety, 136; eliminated, 137; and syndication, 144; and Moncione murder, 156, 159, 161
exile, right of, 467
*Extravagants*, 85. *See also* canon law

Fabbrica, Commune, 415n
Faenza, 312
Falconi, Tommaso di Messer Michele, lawyer, 189n; profile, 491
Fano, 475n
Farnese, Cardinal, 262, 263, 266
Fascism, 424n
Federighi, Carlo di Francesco, lawyer, 196n, 197, 206, 208, 211, 242, 296, 333n, 375, profile, 484; Laura di Carlo, 106
Felcari, Piero di Francesco, profile, 503
Felix V, anti-Pope, 366, 367
Feltre, 331
Ferrante of Naples, King, 381
Ferrara, 72, 109, 229, 323, 351, 357, 358, 457; University, 81, 83, 90, 183; Marquis of, 230, 323, 349, 375, 376; marquisate, 350-51
Ferrucci, family, 108
Feruffini, Giovanni, 463
Feudorum, Libri, 85
Fibindacci, family, 155, 233
Fiesole, 155

Fifth Lateran Council, 298
Filicaia, Piero di Berto, lawyer, 206, 269n; profile, 489
Firenzuola, Vicar, 177n
Firidolfi da Panzano, Rinaldo di Matteo, profile, 486
*fiscus*, defined, 430, 438
Fiumalbo, 229
Fiumi, Enrico, 388n, 403
Five on County, 398, 399
Flanders, 371
Flandrin, Guigon, 288
Florence, 79, 91, 107, 457; Archbishop, 18, 24, 131, 247, 275, 280; University, 67, 72, 73, 81, 83, 172, 186, 260-61, 285, 292, 436; and public finance, 76, 172ff, 234, 237, 242, 268, 468; schools, 78; territorial relations, 83, 92, 220ff, 418-19, 473-74; College of Doctors, 88; under Roman law, 92n; courts and justice, 94, 124, 126-27, 130ff; and Empire, 119ff, 191, 374-75, 414, 425; and problem of sovereignty, 119ff, 275; *vs.* papacy, 122, 176, 258-66, 286-87, 293-94, 298-301, 303-307, 334-36, 343-44, 367; and *imperium*, 123; and *populus liber*, 123, 423-25; *vs.* feudal rights, 157-58, 163; and taxation of clergy, 252ff, 267-68, 269-70; and Roman lawsuits, 266-67, 271ff, 281ff; and extraordinary measures, 270; and Pisa, 275, 324-25, 329, 330; and Church councils, 288ff; and diplomatic practice, 316ff, 326-28; and Lucca, 316, 344-47; *vs.* Milan, 317ff; and Bologna, 321, 331, 343, 377-79; and Siena, 325, 334ff, 349-50; and France, 328-30; and treaty violations, 333-34; and Ladislaus, 334-42; and Urbino, 342-43; and Cortona, 349-50; as arbitrator, 350ff; and Boucicaut, 355-58; and Genoa, 355-58, 369-73; *vs.* Pavia, 359; *vs.* Parma, 359-60; and Livorno, 362-63; and Savoy, 365-69; population of, 388; and concept of state, 390-91, 400-401; and executive powers, 397ff, 472-73; and chief offices, 402; as *princeps*, 414n, 415ff; and *plenitudo potestatis*, 426; as new state, 431; and Paolo

Vitelli, 433-35; and Bartolist formulas, 437; and mineral deposits, 437; and centralization, 457, 468-70; and separation of powers, 471

florin, value, 100n

Foiano, 231

Folchi, Jacopo di Simone, lawyer, 150, 161n; on Republic, 430; profile, 491

Foraboschi, Bartolommeo di Baldassare, lawyer, profile, 485

Foreign Office, British, 5

Forlì, 284, 365

Fornari, Jacopo de', 364

Fortini, Benedetto, notary, 164; Paolo, chancellor, 156-57, 160, 164-65, 166, 343n, 382

Fourteen, *balìa* of, 109

Fourth Lateran Council, 252, 257

France, 252, 272, 288, 289, 355, 361, 381, 471, 328-30

Francesco di Ser Benedetto di Marco, lawyer, 196-97, 361-62; profile, 493

Francesco Novello II da Carrara, Lord of Padua, 323, 326-28, 331, 332-33

Franchi da Sambuco, family, 69

Frederick III, Emperor, 376

"French league," 326

French Revolution, 470

Fucecchio, 286n, 419-20; and public law case, 422

furriers' guild, 14

Gabelle Commission, 397

Gabelle on Contracts, Officials of, 398, 399

Gaddi, Francesco di Agnolo, lawyer, 90, 236, 403n; profile, 495

Gaetani, Francesco di Benedetto, profile, 494; Piero, case of, 415-16

Galeata, Commune, 98-99, 222, 224, 225

Galen, 72

Galletti, Arrigo, Paduan lawyer, 327, 328, 331, 332n

Gallilei, Galileo, 297

Gallina, Gian Francesco, 463

Gambacorti, Piero, Lord of Pisa, 324

Gambassi, Bartolommeo, cleric, 98

Gamberelli, Giovan Battista di Bernardo, 71; profile, 495

Gargonza, 231

Gattaja, 382

Genoa, 130, 290, 314, 317, 320, 322, 323, 324, 329, 333, 359, 360, 457; and Florence, 355-58, 362-65, 369-73; Podestà of, 363-65; and College of Judges, 369n

Gentili da Tortona, Antonio, 463

German princes, 291

Germany, Nazi, 470

Gerson, Jean, 302

Ghibellines, 40, 45

Ghibellinism, 44

Ghini, Girolamo, 231

Gianfigliazzi, family, 66; Rinaldo, 47, 106, 180n, 320, 326, 327, 331, 332, 350, 353-55

Giovanni, Count, 98

Giovanni da Barbiano, Count of Cunio, 350-51

Giovanni da Fossa, 177n

Giovanni da Montevarchi, 278

Giovanni dalla Castellina, notary, 79

Giovanni del Maestro Ambrogio, 151

Giovanni del Maestro Neri da Poggibonsi, lawyer, 188n, 189n, 227; profile, 498

Giovanni di Messer Scolaio di Ser Berto, profile, 491

Giovanni di Ser Fruosino, lawyer, 43-44, 189; profile, 491

Girolami, Raffaello, 314

Giugni, family, 66; Bernardo, 230n, 242; Galeazzo di Luigi, profile, 490-91; Ugolino di Filippo, profile, 506

glossators, 29

Gonfalonier of Justice, 49, 109, 190-91, 194; and justice, 125; and criminal proceedings, 142; drawing for, 180-81; and *accoppiatori*, 194-95

government lawyers, *see sapientes communis*

governorships, number of, 221

Grain officials (commission), 392, 397

grammar, study of, 78-79

Grand Council (Florentine), *see under* Councils

Grascia Officials, 398, 399, 411

Gratian, 81

Graziani, Paolo, 156
Great Schism, 267, 281, 287, 288
Gregory XI, Pope, 287
Gregory XII, Pope, 290-91; and Florence, 289-95; denounced, 294
Grifo (Grifi) di Ser Guidone di Ser Grifo, 69; profile, 492
groups, study of, 4
Guadagni, family, 66; Veri (Vieri), 323, 370
Gualbert, St. John, 203
Gualterotti, family, 75, 392; Bartolommeo di Messer Francesco, profile, 490; Francesco di Lorenzo, lawyer, 74, 98-99, 107, 108, 167n, 201, 202, 206, 213, 215, 235, 258, 260, 265, 268, 284n, 373n, 381n, 443n, 444, embassy to Rome, 260-62, on fisc, 438, profile, 487
Guasconi, Biagio, 318; Francesco, profile, 507; Zanobi di Jacopo, lawyer, 284, 343, 375n, 376, profile, 484
Guatemala, 122
Gubbio, 63, 176
Guelf Society, 44, 45-46, 150, 187-88, 198, 290, 474; Captains, 241, 318, 332
Guelfs, 40
Guicciardini, family, 62, 65, 66, 75, 79; Francesco di Piero, lawyer, 63, 66, 68, 71, 74, 77, 78, 79, 89, 90, 167, 234, 390n, 392, 405n, 441, his social outlook, 64-65, studies, 80-81, career, 110-12, on public law cases, 226, 420-21, on Eight on Public Safety, 410-11, 432, profile, 489; Luigi, 317-18, 390n; Niccolò di Luigi, lawyer, 393n, 405n, profile, 490; Piero, 213n, 234
Guidetti, Guidetto, 156
Guidi, counts, 155; Count Marcovaldo, 155; Count of Poppi, 157, 158n, 163
Guidi, family, 69; in Signory, 69; Bartolommeo di Ser Giovanni, lawyer, 69, profile, 496; Giovanni, notary, 69
Guidi da Volterra, Jacopo, 475n
guild of lawyers and notaries, 11ff, 103, 146; as corporation, 12; powers of, 12; proconsul, 13, 14, 17-18, 22, 27, 39, 44, 274n; high rank, 14, 15-16;

membership and matriculation, 15, 24-25, 27-29, 31; consuls, 18-20, 22, 39, 43; petitions to, 18-20; advisors (twelve and fifteen), 20-21, 39; arbiters, 21, 52; *correctores*, 21, 52; examiners, 21, 22; defenders of guild laws, 22, 24, 52; provisor, 22-23; treasurer, 22-23; and magnates, 25-26, 41; and particularism, 25; as fraternity, 26-27; and heretics, 27, 95; and professional distinctions, 29ff; and favoritism, 32; schisms within, 40-46; and new men, 45; benefactors of, 46-47; and scrutiny commissions, 51; and parallels with Commune, 52; changes in, 54-57; and oligarchy, 57; lawyers in, 73-75; and charity, 95
guilds, seven major, 14
Guinigi, Paolo, Lord of Lucca, 352; *vs.* Florence, 344-47

Henry VII, Emperor, 457-58
heresy, 93
Hospitallers of St. John of Jerusalem, 264-65
Hungary, King of, 255

immunity, *vs.* public need, 435-36
*imperium*, and *princeps*, 456
Impruneta, 227
incest, 224-25
individuals, in history, 4
Inghirami, Baldo di Francesco, lawyer, 215; profile, 496-97
Innocent III, Pope, 247
Innocent VII, Pope, 247
Innocent VIII, Pope, 279n
*Institutes*, 68, 69. *See also* Roman law
Isolano, Jacopo, 463
Italian League, 230
Italy, 3, 456; and particularism, 25; and two laws, 91; and executive power, 139; and modern diplomacy, 311-12; rivalries in, 316-17
*iudices idiotae*, 34, 222, 398
*iura fiscalia*, and prescription, 417, 418n

Jacopo di Ser Antonio da Romena, 18
Jacopo di Vanni da Pisa, profile, 508

John XXII, Pope, 247, 270

John XXIII, Pope, 247, 283n, 340; and Florence, 337; and Ladislaus, 338-39. *See also* Cossa, Baldassare

judiciary, Florentine, 130ff; crisis of, 134ff, 234, 401-402; changes, 136-37; reforms, 138ff; and criminal cases, 142; weakened, 162; and executive power, 397ff. *See also* courts

Julius II, Pope, 268, 271, 298, 360; clash with Florence, 298-301

jurisdiction, conflicts of, 145ff; of Podestà and Signory, 154n

justice, and executive powers, 124-26. *See also* courts; judiciary

Justice, Florentine Council of, 39, 98, 107, 126, 131, 166-67, 227n; composition and jurisdiction, 141-42, 420, 421, 438; compared, 469

Justinian, 93n, 328

Juvenal, 79

Knight, William, 270

Lacedaemon, 328

Ladislaus, King of Naples, 291, 316, 317, 323, 325, 358, 377, 437; relations with Florence, 334-42; with John XXIII, 338-39; with Rome, 338

*laesa majestas*, crime of, 233, 428n, 445

Lambertelli, Vincenzo, profile, 508

Lampugnano, Oldrado di Uberto, Milanese lawyer, 459, 463; Uberto, lawyer, 318n, 459, 463

Lana guild, 14, 15, 465; in litigation, 98; 169

Landino, Cristoforo, profile, 504

Lanfredini, Lanfredino, 111

Lapi, Niccola, lawyer, 188n

law: in territory, 237-38; international, 374-75; and diplomatic maneuvering, 380-81; statutory law and oligarchy, 395; instrumentality of, 407-409, 428-29; and statecraft, 410-12; and flexibility, 411-12; customary, 413, 472; and *populus*, 413; positive, 413; Roman *vs.* municipal, 419; and coercion, 428-29; treatises on, 449-50; *vs.* political fact, 457

lawyers: pre-eminence of, 4, 5; number of, 5, 206; as representative figures, 6; and state, 6; and territorial government, 14, 220ff; defined, 31, 33-34; representation in guild, 40-41; their outlook, 41, 42; in Signory, 51; and social class, 62ff, 68-71, 481ff; and outsiders, 72-74, 176; "dynasties" of, 75; their education, 78ff, 90; canonists, 91; and judicial counsel, 94-95; their patron saint, 95, 96n; income and fees, 100ff; most prominent, 107-108; and judicial reform, 142-43; and syndication, 144-45; and jurisdictional conflicts, 145ff; and Bastari case, 150ff; and oligarchy, 163, 205-206, 209-11, 387ff, 395-96; and administrative problems, 171ff; and legislation, 183-84, 187-91; and municipal code, 184-87; on tax procedure, 192-94; and the constitution, 195ff; and scrutinies, 208-209; and Ten on War, 211-14; unity among, 214-15; and border disputes, 229-32; and executive power, 232, 398ff; and Church-state relations, 247ff, 283-84, 286ff; in diplomacy, 312ff; and "success," 392-94; and politics, 394; and political-legal views, 405, 407-409; and *civitas sibi princeps*, 414ff; on the *res publica*, 428; and one-man rule, 456-57

Lazari, Filippo di Sinibaldo, profile, 506

legislation, and new state, 472

legislative councils, 130; and tax fraud, 174. *See also* Councils

Lenzi, family, feud with Strozzi, 406-407; Piero, 406

Leo X, Pope, 111, 283n

Leonardo di Cesano da Pisa, profile, 508

Leoni, Leo di Francesco, profile, 502

Leoni, Leone di Giuliano, profile, 498

*lex regia*, ambiguity of, 446, 456

*licentia docendi*, 83, 86

litigation, varieties of, 94ff; between clerics, 97-98

Lionardo di Ser Giovanni di Ser Taddeo da Colle, profile, 494

Livorno, 220, 290, 324, 329, 355, 362-63, 369; Castle of, 239; Captain of, 372

Lodi, 380

Lombardy, 317, 475; and feudatories, 467

Louis II of Anjou, 334, 335, 336, 337, 357, 358

Louis XII, King of France, 298

Lucca, 72, 281, 312, 331, 349, 357, 358; war, 215; *vs.* Florence, 316

Lucignano, 231; disputed, 349-50

Ludovico I, Duke of Savoy, *vs.* Florence, 365-69

Lustignano, 231

Lycurgus, 328

Machiavelli, family, 66; Antonio, 188; Bernardo di Niccolò, 56, 79, 84, 102, 393, profile, 506; Francesco di Lorenzo, lawyer, 91, 208, 296, 297, 333n, 339, 340, 342n, 343, profile, 484; Girolamo di Agnolo, lawyer, 169n, 209, 210n, 211n, 396, banished, 67, profile, 485; Niccolò, 29, 79, 166, 314, 390

Magalotti, Filippo, 320, 322n

Magnates, 42; in guild, 25-26; law on, 189

*majestas*, in Roman law, 445

Malatesta, lords, 104, 341; Carlo, 325, 326

Malavolti, Sienese family, 396

Malchiostri, Francesco, profile, 507

Malegonnelli, family, 75, 272n; Alessandro di Messer Antonio, lawyer, 231, 269n, 349, 419n, profile, 489-90; Antonio di Piero, lawyer, 23, 67, 74, 98, 99, 100, 107, 108, 138, 190n, 201, 202, 206, 213, 235, 248, 250-51, 258, 268, 276-80, 281, 283, 284n, 377, 381n, 415n, embassy to Rome, 261-67, on papal power, 304-306, on public law case, 418, on mineral deposits, 437, profile, 486

Malespini, marquises, 160

Maletica, Calisto da, protonotary, 340

Maletta, Albèrico, 463

Manfredi, family: Astorre I, Lord of Faenza, 350-51; Guidantonio, Lord of Faenza, 382

Mangioni, Antonio, 136n

Mantua, 352-55; Lord of (Gianfrancesco I Gonzaga), 322, 326, 352-54

Marches, the, 72, 317

Marchi, Francesco, *see* Francesco di Ser Benedetto

Marchi, Tommaso di Messer Marco, lawyer, 75, 91, 106, 150, 153, 154n, 161n, 396; profile, 483

Marco di Cenno, lawyer, 71; profile, 491

Marseilles, 358

Marsuppini, Carlo di Messer Gregorio, profile, 503

Martelli, family, 63, 104, 210, 403n; Domenico di Niccolò, lawyer, 23, 187, 195, 196, 206, 210, 211, 243, 247, 351, 362, 417, 432, on public law case, 225, on Eight, 433, profile, 485

Martin V, Pope, 247, 283n, 303, 343, 378

Martini, Martino, notary on legislation, 156-57, 160, 166

Marzi, Demetrio, 55

Masi, G., 144n

Mass, 269, 286

Masseritia, Ufficiali della, 164-65

Matteo, tutor, 79

Matteo di Neroccio da San Gimignano, profile, 507

Maximilian I, Emperor, 111, 298

Mazzei, Lapo, notary, 101

Mazzinghi, Paradiso del Maestro Ugolino, profile, 505

Medici, family, 49, 54, 65, 67, 79, 104, 135, 165, 234, 254, 440, 465n, 481; bank profits, 77, 105; properties, 178-79; anti-Medici sect, 207; Averardo, 105, 187n, 363n; Cosimo, 19-20, 57, 178n, 380n; Duke Cosimo I, 93n, 475n; Giovanni di Bicci, 239n; Giovanni di Lorenzo, 80; Lorenzo di Giovanni di Bicci, 19-20, 284n; Lorenzo the Magnificent, 50, 63, 69, 71, 138, 425n, 440n; Lorenzo di Piero di Lorenzo, 111, 138, 141n, 178, 198, 440n, 442, 445; Veri di Tanai, 231, profile, 488

Mercanzia, court, 13, 107, 131, 132, 137, 138, 140, 141, 168, 198, 241, 242, 291, 361, 402, 465, 466n, 471; composition,

133; jurisdiction, 133; reformed, 134-35

Messer, use of title, 29

Meuillon, Guillaume de, 288

Michele da Rabutta, 327

Migliana, 227n

Migliorati, Giovanni di Messer Michele di Messer Lapo, profile, 503

Mignanelli, Giovanni, profile, 506

Milan, 3, 7, 72, 91, 252, 256, 267n, 299, 303, 314, 358, 359, 375, 376, 380, 456, 457, 460, 468, 471, 472; notaries in, 38; and appeal to Rome, 272; and Secret Council (Consiglio Segreto), 319, 458, 460, 461, 462-63, 468-69; and imperial vicariate, 457; Council of Provisions (Consiglio delle Provvisioni), 458, 460, 472n; Council of Twelve Hundred, 458, 459; and lawyers, 458, 459ff; chancellery, 459; College of Jurists, 459; Six of Treasury (Sei della Camera del Comune), 459; *sindaci*, 459n; Council of Justice (Consiglio di Giustizia), 460-61, 469; Captain of Justice, 460; executive and judiciary, 460; Six Consoli, court, 460; Podestà, 460; syndication, 461; lawyers in diplomacy, 461-62; Vicars General, 461, 469; territorial governors, 467; fisc, 468; *referendario*, 468; taxation in territories, 468; guild courts, 471n-472n; executive powers, 472-73; and territorial autonomy, 473-74

Millio, Filippo, 463

Mincio River, 331n, 352-55

Minerbetti, Andrea, 332

Mint Officials, 216, 397

Mirandola, 475n

Modena, 318, 319; lawyers in, 32-33

Modesti, Jacopo di Ser Michele, profile, 505

Moncione murder case, 120, 155ff; and conflicting jurisdictions, 162; defense in, 163n, 233, 402; Count Guido da Moncione, 425

Monte (funded public debt), 76, 128, 172, 176, 211, 253, 282, 356, 360, 365-68, 391; officials (commission), 13, 95, 165-66, 198, 211, 282, 361, 397-98,

399, 402; syndics, 179; and municipal statutes, 186

Monte Rotondo, 231

Montecarlo, 286n

Montecchio, Commune, 415n

Montegranelli, Count of, 104

Montemagno, Buonaccorso da, lawyer, 73, 352, 445, embassy to Lucca, 344-46, profile, 501; Giovanni di Messer Buonaccorso, profile, 498-99

Montepulciano, and Florence, 349-50

Montevarchi, 155

Morals Office (Commission) (Honestatis Officiales), 128, 392, 398

Muscini, Bernardo di Arrigo di Ser Piero, profile, 492

Naples, 256, 269, 316, 320, 329, 436; Kingdom of, 255

Nardi, Jacopo, historian, 191

Nardi, Lazzaro, 18

Narni, Bernardo di Francesco, profile, 506

Negusanto da Fano, Antonio, 227n

Nelli, Francesco di Giovanni, lawyer, 206, 269n, 270; on extraordinary measures, 436; profile, 488

Nello da San Gimignano, *see* Cetti

Nerli, family, 235; Benedetto, 213n

Neroni, Archbishop Giovanni, 248

new men, 44, 62; and guilds, 45, 57; rise arrested, 65

new state, *see* state

New Testament, 255

Niccoli, Jacopo di Bartolommeo, lawyer, 338, profile, 492; Niccolò di Bartolommeo, humanist, 338

Niccolini, family, 63, 65, 66, 75, 79; Agnolo di Messer Matteo di Messer Agnolo, profile, 497-98; Agnolo di Messer Otto, lawyer, 63, 64, 68, 75, 98, 102, 138, 190n, 201, 203, 204, 206, profile, 494; Biagio di Lapo, lawyer, 165, 206, profile, 493; Carlo di Messer Agnolo, profile, 497; Giovanni di Messer Otto, 80, 90; Girolamo di Messer Otto, 79; Jacopo di Messer Otto, 79; Matteo di Messer Agnolo, lawyer, 167n, 234, 236, 269, 284n, profile, 497; Otto di Lapo, lawyer, 23, 79n, 169n, 177, 196, 206, 209, 211, 243, 247, 283n, 351, 362, 379, 396, 423n, 441, on *iura fiscalia*, 417, defends Eight, 433, profile, 493

Niccolò da Prato, lawyer, 189n

Niccolò di Antonio da Rabatta, profile, 498

Nicholas V, Pope, 254; and Florence, 255-58

Nine of the Militia, *vs.* Eight, 166

Nobili, Cesare de', 231

Nobili, Guccio de', 150

nobility, 465; emergence of, 65-66, 76, 112, 205, 390; major and minor families of, 440

Nocturnal Officials, 53, 398; judicial powers of, 131

*notaio delle riformagioni, see* notary on legislation

*notaio delle tratte*, 48, 180-81

notaries, 5n, 6, 23; as functionaries, 13; and territory, 14; craft requirements, 34; and examinations, 34-36; in North Italian communes, 36n; defined, 37; types of, 38; number matriculated, 41; outlook of, 41; opportunism of, 42; and new men, 44; and opponents, 47-48; and pluralism, 47-48; statute against, 47-48; and fraud, 48; and administration, 49, 170-71, 400; in Signory, 49-51; and public office, 54-55; their social status, 55-56; their financial strain, 142; in territorial government, 221ff; and embassies, 312

notary on legislation, 13, 38, 156, 168n

Ogni Santi, friars, 103

Old Digest, 33; *see* Roman law

Old Testament, 255

oligarchy, 62, 231; "inner," 5, 395, 432, 440; and judicial crisis, 137-38; and techniques of control, 195-97; "wide" and "close," 204-205; consolidated, 205; and support of lawyers, 209-11; divisions within, 215, 341-42; defined, 387; size and nature of, 388-90; and legal careers, 393-94; and university appointments, 394; contraction of, 401

*operarios*, commission on cathedral, 103, 169

Ordinances of Justice, 25, 42, 150, 151, 163n

Orlandi, Rosso di Andreozzo degli, 101, 107, 159, 161n, 227; profile, 483

Orlandi, Tommaso di Michele, profile, 498

Orphans, Officials over, 398, 399

Orsini, family, 282; Alfonsina nei Medici, 273; Paolo, 261, 263, 266, 337

Otto di Guardia, *see* Eight on Public Safety

Otto di Pratica, *see* Eight on Foreign Affairs

Ovid, 79

Oxford, 292

Padua, 293, 317, 357, 358, 457, 461, 462; University, 81, 89, 90; doctorate in, 82n; College of Doctors (Lawyers), 101, 346, 368

Pagni, Cristiano, 475n

palace notaries, *see* chancellor; notary on legislation

Palarcioni, Jacopo di Angelo, profile, 491

Panciatichi, family, 234

Pandolfini, family, 63, 65, 66; Agnolo, 238, 241, 340, 343n, 378n; Carlo, 242; Filippo, 319; Francesco di Bartolommeo di Messer Carlo, profile, 497; Pier Filippo, 63, 64

Paniche, Lorenzo di Angelo, lawyer, 188n

Pantaleoni, family, 94; Piera, nun, 94

Paolo di Ser Angelo di Castro, lawyer, 87, 186; profile, 499-500

papacy, 188, 334-35, 360; and Florentine lawyer-diplomats, 283-84. *See also* Church; pope; individual popes

Paradiso ((Alberti villa), 96

Parente di Corrado da Prato, lawyer, 189n; profile, 498

Parenti, family, 390n; Piero, chronicler, 199n, 212, 214, 442

Paris, 292, 296

*parlamento*, of 1393, 164

Parma, *vs.* Florence, 359-60

Parte Guelfa, *see* Guelf Society

Passaggeri, Rolandino, 31

Passetti, Cosimo di Ludovico, profile, 504-505

Paul III, Pope, 266

Pavia, 292, 462, 463; University, 81; *vs.* Florence, 359

Pazzi, family, 63; conspiracy, 410; Alessandro, 390n; Andrea, 175; Guglielmo, 235

Pecci, Messer Piero di Bartolommeo, Sienese lawyer, 229n

penance, 286

people, Florentine, *see populus liber*

Pepi, Francesco di Chirico, lawyer, 56, 67, 77, 78, 98, 107-108, 110, 178, 206, 213, 236, 268, 273-75, 281, 283, 284n, 390, 396; and Ten on War, 198, 199, 200; characterized, 272; profile, 486

Perugia, 30, 72, 83, 109, 293, 302, 331, 334; University, 80, 90; claim on Lucignano, 349

Peruzzi, family, 63, 157; bankruptcy, 109; and Moncione murder, 163; Leonardo, 153; Ridolfo, 284n

Pescia, 286n, 414n, 420n, 475n

Philip the Fair, 257

physicians and spicers, guild of, 14, 30

Piazza de' Signori, and fire ordeal, 201-202

Piccinino, Niccolò, 194n

Picotti, G. B., 424n

Piedmont, notoriate in, 38

Piero da San Miniato, notary, 327, 328

Pietrasanta, 349

piracy, 280

Pisa, 109, 141n, 220, 221, 223, 239, 242, 249, 260, 290, 292, 295, 298, 322, 324, 329, 330, 331, 355, 358, 369, 415, 418, 481; notaries in, 35-36, 38; archdiocese of, 76; University, 77, 81, 250, 272, 307, 434, 481; Captain of, 92; Podestà of, 220n, 222; Five Provisors of, 238, 239, 240, 241; Porto Pisano, 239, 355, 370; Five on (another), 242-43; *contado* of, 242; and disorder, 242; and depopulation, 242; *conciliabolo* of, 268, 299; Council of, 288, 291-95, 296,

301, 302; and Florence, 324-25, 377; revolt, 433-34

Pistoia, 72, 92, 102, 220, 222, 225, 228, 279, 414n, 419; Podestà of, 92; Captain of, 164; civil strife in, 214, 234-36; County of, 226; statutes of, 238n

Pitti, family, 155, 272; and Moncione murder, 163; Buonaccorso, 164, 220n; Giannozzo, 175; Luca, 57

plot, Medicean (of 1497), 442-43

Po River, 352

Podestà (of Florence), 14n, 17, 43, 91, 95, 130, 131-33, 138, 142, 162, 168, 181, 464, 469, 471; court of, 96, 102; jurisdiction of, 132, 420; and Eight, 136; reforms, 140; and syndication, 144; *vs.* Signory, 154n; and Moncione murder, 156, 159, 161

Poggibonsi, 349

Poland, King of, 255

Poliziano, Angelo, profile, 507

Polverini, Jacopo, 475n

Pomerance, 249

Pontenano, 223

pope, 320, 375; power of, 303-307. *See also* Church

Popoleschi, family, 66; Bartolommeo di Tommaso, lawyer, 23, 66, 101, 106, 107, 206, 290, 291, 294, 295, 319, 321, 322, 323n, 335, 336, 369, profile, 483

Poppi, Count of, *see* Guidi counts

*populus*, and customary law, 413

*populus liber*, 415n, 437, 438; in public law, 423-25; *vs. princeps*, 447-48

Por Santa Maria guild, 14

Porciano, Count Piero da, 160

Porro, Antonio, 463

Post, Gaines, 405, 411

pouches for office, *see borse*

*praelectiones*, 86

Prato, 77, 102, 176, 220, 419, 475n; Del Dolce Hospital of, 101; Misericordia Hospital of, 102; Pisan Studio at, 275

prince, see *princeps*

*princeps*, in Roman law, 121, 123, 412-13; and Signory, 125-26, 127, 439; as city-state, 413ff; and *plenitudo polestatis*, 420; as *populus liber*, 423-25; and executive power, 424-25, 446-48;

and contracts, 425-26, 439; and privileges, 435, 439-40; and mineral deposits, 437; and salt gabelle, 437; and judicial power, 439; *vs. populus*, 446-48; and Grand Council, 447; and *imperium*, 456
Priorate, establishment of, 41-42
Priscianus, 79
*privilegium competentiae*, 93
proconsul, *see under* guild
*procurator*, 17, 54; defined, 30; functions of, 38-40; changing status, 39
Procurators, Twelve, 234
profession, legal: and corruption, 23-24; and social mobility, 68-71; and family fortunes, 70-71; attitudes toward, 71; and economic security, 76-77; and educational costs, 90; fees and income, 100-106; and recruitment for, 403-404
profits, banking, 77; commercial, 78
property, confiscation, 178
public good, *see* public utility; *utilitas publica*
public instruments, nature and importance, 37, 347-48
public office: and eligibility, 49; and notaries, 54-55; rotation through, 168; *tratte* for, 179-81; and citizens, 388-89, 392; and instrumentality, 410-11
Public Rights, Office on, 397
public utility, argument from, 422, 427; as political device, 441
Pucetti, Francesco di Ser Piero, lawyer, 19, profile, 493; Piero, notary, 19
Pucci, family, 403n; Antonio di Puccio, 63, 64; Giannozzo, 442; Puccio di Antonio, lawyer, 69, 102, 190n, 351, profile, 495
Pugi, Antonio, 273, 276
Pusterla, Milanese family, 468n

Quarantìa, defined, 142
Quistelli, Alfonso, 475n

Rabatta, Niccolò di Antonio, lawyer, 189n
Raffacani, Antonio, 156
"Ratio iuris," bull, 270

"reason of State," *see Staatsräson*
Rebel officials, 178, 392, 397
rebellion, theme of, 232ff
*rectores forenses, see* Podestà; Captain; Executor; Appellate Judge
Redditi, Bartolommeo di Andrea, profile, 495
*reggimento*, defined, 205
Regulators, 95, 276, 277, 397, 411n
Renaissance, and lawyers, 4
Renaissance state, *see* state
*repetitiones*, 86
reprisals, in international law, 359ff; reasons for, 359-60; trend in, 373
"retorsion," 358, 360-61
Rhodes, Knights of, 264-65
Ricasoli, family, 104
Ricci, family, 43, 187, 189; Giovanni di Ruggero, lawyer, 23, 43-44, 66, 88, 106, 150, 154n, 161n, 188n, 189, 317-19, 322, 331, 332, 333, 350, 396, 414n, 417, on treaty, 319, profile, 482; Uguccione, 43-44, 188
Ricciardo di Piero, notary, 148
*richiesti*, defined, 209; function of, 210-11
Ridolfi, family, 62, 66, 71; Antonio di Messer Lorenzo, 190n, 282; Giovan Battista, 213n, 214, 235; Lorenzo di Antonio, lawyer, 23, 66, 67, 74, 88, 91, 101, 106, 107, 181n, 182, 206, 241, 283n, 284, 289, 290, 291, 292, 293, 295, 303n, 318, 319, 320, 322n, 325, 326, 332, 337, 339, 340, 341, 342n, 343, 369, 370n, 375n, 380n, 382, 392, 393n, 399n, 428, on Pisan office, 240, on Signory, 425, *De usuris*, 427, profile, 483; Lorenzo di Giovanni, lawyer, 269n, profile, 490; Niccolò, 442
Ridolfi, Roberto, 202
Rimini, 295, 325
Rinuccini, Alamanno, 135
Ripoli, 227
Roberto of Meleto, Count, 231
Romagna, 231, 269, 317, 350, 382
Roman law, 4, 14, 29n, 80, 84-86, 87, 120n, 121, 126, 163, 175, 220, 293, 302, 326n, 374, 376, 397, 408, 421, 427n, 428, 434, 437, 474; revival of, 12,

347; doctorate, 81ff; courses in, 84-85; *vs.* canon law, 91; and common law, 92, 472; and *sacra*, 93, 191; cited, 93n, 94n, 125, 339n, 355, 367n, 368n, 410n, 413n, 417n, 418, 419n, 420n, 446, 456n; *princeps* in, 412-13; *vs.* municipal law, 419; *majestas* in, 445; and local rights, 456

"Romanesca" forest, 229

Rome, 72, 122, 262, 268, 269, 272, 276, 277, 278, 284, 304, 320, 334, 337, 360, 377, 378; appeal to, 266; cases pending in, 274; and Ladislaus, 338; College of Doctors (Lawyers) in, 368; Florentine merchants in, 373

Romolini, Francesco, profile, 508

Rondinelli, Giuliano, 201

Roselli, Antonio di Messer Rosello, profile, 500; Giovan Battista, profile, 506; Rosello di Ser Fino, lawyer, 150, 161n, 322n, profile, 498

Rossi, family, 104

Rota Romana, Sacra, 122, 247, 248, 267, 270, 278, 284, 285, 298, 357, 358; jurisdiction, 271; auditors at, 272

*Roviera*, Genoese boat, 364

Rucellai, family, 65, 66, 104; Bernardo, 213n, 214, 235; Francesco, 153; Luigi di Piero, profile, 490; Niccolò di Pancrazio, lawyer, 167n, profile, 488; Paolo, 264

Sacchetti, Tommaso, 320, 325, 326

*sacra*, and government buildings, 93; and Roman law, 191

safe-conducts, question of, 362

St. Antonino, 248

St. Ivo of Chartres, and lawyers, 95

St. Luke, and lawyers, 96n

St. Zenobius, chapel of, 96

salaries, professorial, 77, 104

Saliceto, Bartolommeo da, Bolognese lawyer, 414n

Salimbeni, Sienese family, 396

Sallust, 79

salt gabelle, officials of, 228

Salutati, 29

Salvemini, Gaetano, 41-42, 55

Salvetti, Tommaso di Ser Jacopo, law-yer, 177n, 178n, 196, 209, 211, 242, 243, 349, 379, 396n; on public law case, 225; and border dispute, 229-30; *Commentaria*, 467n; profile, 501

Salviati, family, 65, 66, 77, 272; Alamanno, 110, 111, 213n, 234; Jacopo, 291; Jacopo (another), 110, 111, 234; Maria di Alamanno, 110

San Bernabò, church of, 98

San Felice, church of, 276

San Gimignano, 72, 221, 222, 249

San Giovanni quarter, 270, 300; courts in, 133

San Martino at Pilli, church of, 98

San Miniato, 103

San Miniato Fiorentino, Castle of, 148

Santa Croce quarter, 269, 291, 396; courts in, 133

Santa Felicità, church of, 276

Santa Maria in Impruneta, 227

Santa Maria Novella quarter, 290, 291, 300; courts in, 133

Santa Maria Nuova, Hospital of, 103, 110

Santa Sophia, Commune, 231

Santa Trinità bridge, 79

Santo Spirito quarter, 240, 291, 300; courts in, 133

*sapientes communis*, 165, 166, 171, 180n; functions, 146-47; and Bastari case, 150, 154

Saracini, Giovanni di Cristoforo, 18-19; profile, 503-504

Saracini da Fano, Piero, clash with Signory, 167

Sarsina, Bishop of, 284

Savonarola, 48, 108, 201-203, 215, 259, 260, 297, 303, 304, 305-306, 307, 426, 442

Savoy, and Florence, 365-69

Scala, Bartolommeo di Giovanni, 71; profile, 504

Scarfi, Piero, 299-300

Schignano, 227n

Schnitzer, J., 202

schools, Florentine, 78

Scolao, Michi, lawyer, 189n

scrutinies, 180; problems of, 181-82, 195n, 196-97; and illegality, 208-209

Secchia River, 317

Secret Council, *see under* Milan
secretary, first, *see* chancellor
Segoloni, D., 415n
Sei di Mercanzia, *see* Mercanzia
Sentio of Spoleto, Count of Campello, 153, 163
Ser, use of title, 29
Sermini, Domenico di Ser Mino, lawyer, 69; profile, 491
Serragli, Niccolò de', notary, 45; Vannozzo, 290
Serristori, family, 69; Giovanni di Ser Ristoro, lawyer, 69, 96, 295, 323n, 335, 336, 338, 340, 341, 357-58, profile, 492; Ristoro, notary, 69
Settignano, 227
*Sextus, Liber*, 82, 85. *See also* canon law
Sforza, family, 460, 462, 467; Francesco, 194; Ludovico, Duke of Milan, 433
Siena, 30, 105, 109, 130, 229, 230, 249, 283n, 293, 312, 314, 320, 324, 325, 334, 335, 348, 349, 357, 358, 362, 445, 457; University, 81; Cardinal of, 273, 381; and Florence, 334ff, 349-50, 381; claims on Lucignano, 349-50
Sigismund, Emperor, 340, 341, 375-76
Signory (Florentine), 13, 57, 95, 110, 129, 137, 138, 183, 194, 233, 275, 336-37, 399, 411, 431-32, 469; and notaries, 37, 48, 49-51; and lawyers, 42, 51; and guild, 47; and new men, 65; and judicial powers, 97-98, 100, 124, 127, 130; and legislation, 124; its nature and authority, 125, 126-27, 149, 164, 170, 199-200, 201-204, 420, 425-26, 438-39, 439n; and *princeps*, 125-26, 127, 439; and appeal, 126, 132n, 133, 140, 142; relation to other offices, 127-29, 166, 179, 154n, 164, 166-67; and statutory controls, 128; and judicial crisis, 136; and syndics, 144; and *sapientes*, 146; and Bastari case, 147ff; and judicial immunity, 148-49, 152; and Moncione case, 155ff; and taxation, 174, 192; and *accoppiatori*, 194-95; *vs.* Church, 203-204, 266-67; and Ten on War, 211-14; and territory, 225ff; and rebellion, 237; and Roman lawsuits, 275-76; rebukes diplomats, 318, 319n;

and reprisals, 361; changes in, 398, 402; and imperial vicariate, 425; and trial of Paolo Vitelli, 433-34; and Medicean plotters, 442-45; and *majestas*, 445; *vs.* Grand Council, 447-48
Sixteen (Gonfaloniers), 181, 290, 299, 333; and guild, 47; and Bastari case, 151ff
Sixtus IV, Pope, 285n, 381
society, Florentine: changes in, 55-56; and upper-class families, 64-65; rising nobility, 76; and politics, 204-205; groups in 1490s, 440n. *See also* nobility
Society of St. Michael, 102, 103
Soderini, family, 62, 65, 66, 71, 75, 104; Bernardo di Messer Niccolò, lawyer, 393, profile, 486; Francesco di Messer Tommaso, prelate, 75, 268, 284n, *vs.* Florentine governor, 248-51, profile, 506-507; Giovan Vettorio di Messer Tommaso, lawyer, 110, 167, 202, 284n, 300, profile, 487; Giovanni, 239n; Niccolò di Tommaso di Messer Lorenzo, profile, 489; Ormannozzo di Messer Tommaso, profile, 490; Piero, Gonfalonier, 168, 185, 234, 298, 301
sovereignty, problem of, 119ff, 377-78, 405-406, 412ff
Sozzini, Bartolommeo, lawyer, 419n, 481, profile, 504; Mariano, lawyer, 409n
Spain, 330, 471
*specchio*, 190
Spinelli, Niccolò, Viscontean lawyer, 318, 461-62, 463
Spini, Cristofano, 291, 293
*Squarciafico*, Genoese vessel, 356-58
*Staatsräson*, 194n, 411, 427
state: Florentine idea of, 390-91; modern conception of, 412ff, 470; absolute, 476
state, Renaissance or new, 7, 435, 464ff, 470n, 471-77; in transition, 402-403; and sovereignty, 405-406; and emergencies, 411; as public good, 428, 431; as end and means, 429-31; and *plenitudo potestatis*, 429, 431; doctrine of, 434-35; and conspiracy, 465n; and lawyers, 466; and centralization, 466, 469-70; and judiciary, 469; and

custom, 472; and legislation, 472, 474; and administration of justice, 473

State Department, American, 5

state system, Florentine, 167, 169

statecraft, defined, 3; expert *vs.* layman in, 145, 170; and flexibility, 168; and law, 410-11

statutes, Florentine, lawyers and reform of, 184-87

*Statuti dei Comuni Soggetti*, described, 244, 466-67

Stelling-Michaud, S., 80

Strozzi, family, 65, 66, 71, 75, 79, 104, 274, 408; feud with Lenzi, 406-407; Antonio di Vanni, lawyer, 23, 67, 107, 110, 167n, 168n, 201, 202, 206, 213, 236, 268, 280-81, 284n, 301, 302n, 381n, 393n, 399n, 423n, 436, 443n, 444, 467n, on fugitives, 409-10, on statutory authority, 411, on public law cases, 418-20, 438-39, on utility of law, 428-29, on immunity, 435, on appeal, 438, notebooks of, 440, profile, 486-87; Benedetto, 106; Marcello di Strozza, lawyer, 192, 240, 241, 358, profile, 483; Matteo, 111; Michele di Piero, lawyer, profile, 486; Nofri, 406; Pagnozzino, 406, 407; Palla di Nofri, 239n, 284n; Pazzino, 149; Roberto di Carlo, vicar general, 76, 507

Studio Fiorentino, *see* Florence, University

Studio Pisano, *see* Pisa, University

Sumptuary Laws, Official on, 397

Surveyors, Communal, 397

syndication, 21, 23, 138, 152-53, 154n; procedure, 143-45; in Bastari case, 161n

Syndics on Rebels, powers, 183

*tamburazione*, 53

Tanagli, Guglielmo di Francesco, lawyer, 23, 67, 94, 169n, 193, 194, 195, 196, 206, 209, 242, 297, 363n, 375n, 376, 379, 380n, 396; profile, 484

Taverna, Alberto, Milanese lawyer, 458

taxation: and civil status, 158n; problems of, 172ff, 192-94; and fraud, 173ff; *balzello*, 178, 179; and Church, 269, 299, 304; in territory, 416-17, 422; and immunities, 474

Ten on Liberty, 398; judicial powers, 131

Ten on War, 13, 55, 95, 138, 198, 204, 275, 318, 324, 325, 327, 336-37, 338, 341, 365, 389, 397, 399, 402, 411, 415, 444; and Signory, 128; and statutory controls, 128; controversy over, 129, 211-14; competence of, 131, 438-39; and judicial crisis, 136; variability of, 168; constitutional status of, 198-201

territorial state, *see* state, Renaissance

territory: jurisdiction in, 222-23; justice in, 223-24; and requests for counsel, 224; and taxation, 234, 242-43; and administrative problems, 237ff

Third Lateran Council, 252, 257

Tici, Ticie di Ser Giovanni, notary, 326n

Tifernati, Lelio, profile, 506

Tolomei, Sienese family, 396

Tommaso di Garofalo da Sicilia, profile, 508

Tommaso di Ser Puccio, lawyer, 186n

Torelli, Buonaccorso di Messer Niccolò, profile, 499; Torello di Messer Niccolò, 73, 107, 338, 340, 351, 370n, on public law case, 415-16, profile, 499

Torelli, Lelio, 93n, 475n

Tornabuoni, Francesco, 370-72; Lorenzo, 373, 442

Torre, Luigi de, lawyer, 188n

Torriani, Milanese family, 468n

Tower Officials, 84, 95, 96, 97, 170, 183, 397, 422n; judicial competence of, 131; dispute with Pistoia, 228; provisor of, 228

Trani, Bishop of, 274

treasurers, communal, 165-66

treasury, 13; notaries of, 146-47; exitus accounts, 164-65

treaties, 317ff; drafts of, 319-20; language of, 321, 325-26; problems of, 323, 325, 330; interpretation of, 330ff

Tribunal of Six, *see* Mercanzia

Tuscany, 317, 334, 475; and Empire, 15; dukes, 142, 435, 475

tutors, use of, 78-79

Twelve (Good Men), 181, 294, 299, 333n; and guild, 46-47; and Bastari case, 151ff

Ubaldi, Angelo di Messer Alessandro degli, lawyer, 97, 161n, profile, 502; Angelo del Maestro Francesco, profile, 499; Baldo, *see* Baldus
Ubaldini, Benedetto di Bartolommeo di Antonio, profile, 485
Ubaldino da San Stefano, lawyer, 189n
Ufficiali della Torre, *see* Tower Officials
Ugolino da Correggio, 359-60
Uguccioni, Simone di Bernardo, lawyer, 206, 213, 396; profile, 486
Umbria, 334
universities, law courses, 84-85; lectures, 85-86; teaching methods, 86-87
Urban VI, Pope, 150, 289
Urbino, Count of, 342-43
*utilitas publica*, 125, 196, 292, 440; and executive power, 401
Uzzano, Niccolò da, 238, 241, 292, 293, 294, 295, 296, 320, 322

Val di Cecina, 250; vicariate of, 248; *vs.* Volterra, 418
Valdarno, Lower, 148n; Upper, 155, 162
Valleggio, dam, 354
Vallombrosa, 222
Vallombrosans, 111
Valori, family, 66; Bartolommeo, 158, 291; Filippo, 329; Francesco, Gonfalonier, 442
Vanni di Stefano, notary, 149
Varchi, Benedetto, historian, 183, 190, 191, 207-208; *Storia fiorentina*, 404
Velluti, family, in Signory, 108; Donato di Lamberto, lawyer, 80, 89, 112, 312, career, 108-10; Luigi di Piero, profile, 489
vendetta, 406
Venice, 53n, 91, 130, 139, 142n, 247, 252, 255, 256, 272, 284n, 291, 303, 314, 317, 320, 343, 354, 359, 362, 375, 376, 377; and mainland ambitions, 316; and contractual law, 321, 322; *vs.*

Catalonians, 351-52; Council of Ten, 431
*ventina*, tax, 192, 194
Verme, Jacopo dal, 463
Verona, 317
Verrucola, 160n
Vespucci, family, 65; Guidantonio di Giovanni, lawyer, 23, 74, 99-100, 107, 108, 134, 190n, 201, 203, 204, 206, 207, 213, 260, 298, 329, 330, 381, 382n, 401n, 426, 444, 445, Roman embassy of, 207, unpopularity, 214, on Pistoian disorders, 235-36, on papal power, 304-305, on public law case, 418, on appeal, 443, 446-48, on *princeps*, 446-47, on Grand Council, 447, profile, 494
Vettori, family, 66; Andrea di Neri, 321, 322, 350
vicariate, imperial, duration, 457-58
Vicomercate, Giovanni da, 463; Taddeolo (Taddiolo), 380n, 462, 463
Vietnam, 122
Villani, Filippo di Matteo, profile, 483; Giovanni, chronicler, 42, 78
Villani, Riccardo, 463
Villari, P., 202
Vinta, Francesco, 93n, 475n
Violi, Lorenzo, notary, 179, 231
Virgil, 79
Visconti, lords of Milan, 267n, 325, 458, 460, 461, 462, 467, 468, 473, 475; Bernabò, 272; Filippo Maria, Duke, 194n, 284, 316, 323, 342, 343, 344, 362, 376, 377, 379, 380, 461, 462; Gabriele Maria, 355-58; Giangaleazzo, 253, 272, 316, 317, 326, 331, 332, 333-34, 351, 361, 377, 437, 461, 462, 463, expansionist policies, 316-23, and Mincio River, 352-55; Luchino, 458; Matteo, and imperial vicariate, 457-58
Vitelleschi, Giovanni, Bishop of Recanato, 365-68
Vitelli, Paolo, trial, 433-35
Viviani, family, in Signory, 69; Francesco di Ser Viviano, lawyer, 69, 333n, profile, 492
Volterra, 72, 236, 438, 475n; diocese, 98; Bishop of, 248; Church of and

Florence, 248-49; and feudal rights, 249; *vs.* Val di Cecina, 418

*Volumen*, parts of, 85

Vulpi da Soncino, Bartolommeo, lawyer, 186, 416n, 417; profile, 501

wages, workers' and servants', 89

War Commission, *see* Ten on War

Zacci, Marco di Rosso, profile, 505

Zambeccari, Carlo, Bolognese lawyer, 353

Zecca, *see* Mint Officials